Bonds of Alliance

Bonds of Alliance

Indigenous and Atlantic Slaveries in New France

BRETT RUSHFORTH

Published for the
Omohundro Institute of Early American History and Culture,
Williamsburg, Virginia, by the
University of North Carolina Press, Chapel Hill

The Omohundro Institute of Early American History and Culture is sponsored jointly by the College of William and Mary and the Colonial Williamsburg Foundation. On November 15, 1996, the Institute adopted the present name in honor of a bequest from Malvern H. Omohundro, Jr.

Designed by Kimberly Bryant and set in Miller by Tseng Information Systems, Inc.
Manufactured in the United States of America

Library of Congress Cataloging-in-Publication Data
Rushforth, Brett.
Bonds of alliance : indigenous and Atlantic slaveries in New France / Brett Rushforth.
p. cm.
Includes bibliographical references and index.
ISBN 978-0-8078-3558-6 (cloth : alk. paper)
ISBN 978-1-4696-1386-4 (pbk. : alk. paper)
1. Slavery—New France—History. 2. Slave trade—New France—History. 3. Indian slaves—New France—History. 4. Indians, Treatment of—New France—History. 5. Indians of North America—History—Colonial period, ca. 1600-1775. 6. Canada—History—To 1763 (New France) I. Omohundro Institute of Early American History & Culture. II. Title.
HT1051.R87 2012
306.3'6209710162—dc23
2011050215

The paper in this book meets the guidelines for permanence and durability of the Committee on Production Guidelines of the Council on Library Resources. The University of North Carolina Press has been a member of the Green Press Initiative since 2003.

cloth 16 15 14 13 12   5 4 3 2 1
paper 17 16 15 14 13   5 4 3 2 1
THIS BOOK WAS DIGITALLY PRINTED.

for Rebecca

ACKNOWLEDGMENTS

It is a pleasure to acknowledge the many people whose time, insight, and support made this book more than I could have made it on my own. But I do so with some apprehension, knowing that my debts are too numerous to name and that no acknowledgment is equal to any of the obligations I have accumulated.

This book began more than a decade ago as a doctoral dissertation under the direction of Alan Taylor at the University of California, Davis. Obviously a model scholar, Alan was also the ideal mentor, balancing his pointed interpretive critiques with frequent encouragement. I have no idea where he finds the time and energy, but his deep intellectual engagement and unfailing support have made all the difference. Also at Davis, Clarence Walker shared his vast knowledge of the literature on comparative slavery and his unlimited capacity for interesting conversation over lunches at "the club." Steve Deyle's seminars were models of form and execution. His seminar on antebellum U.S. slavery offered my first introduction to many of the themes I explore in this book. Chuck Walker and Arnie Bauer introduced me to the history of Latin America and encouraged me to pursue comparative colonialism. Sally McKee helped me to think more carefully about late medieval and early modern French slavery. Among my fellow students at Davis, I'd like especially to thank Kyle Bulthuis, Robert Chester, Jeff Davis, Kim Davis, Kathleen DuVal, Steve Fountain, Scott Miltenberger, and Andy Young. Ken Miller deserves special mention. He patiently listened as I worked through every idea in this book, offering brilliant suggestions and sharp critiques. In this and many other ways, his friendship has been invaluable.

Beyond Davis, James Brooks generously agreed to be on my dissertation committee. His feedback was highly valuable, perhaps especially when our disagreements forced me to rethink facile conclusions. Kate Desbarats also graciously joined my committee, becoming a mentor on all things French Canadian. In addition to lending her unparalleled knowledge of New France, she invited me to McGill to teach and introduced me to a remarkable group of early Canadian historians: Pierre Boulle, Sylvie Dépatie, Tom Wien, Dominique Deslandres, Peter Cook, Denys Delâge, Laurier Turgeon, François Furstenberg, Léon Robichaud, and many others. I thank all of them for engaging my work and welcoming me into their intellectual community.

Having two years as a National Endowment for the Humanities postdoctoral fellow at the Omohundro Institute of Early American History and Culture was essential to the development of this book. The Institute is a scholar's paradise. I thank the indefatigable Ron Hoffman for creating such a rich intellectual life at the Institute, and Sally Mason and Beverly Smith for keeping it all going. For daily conversations and careful readings of my manuscript-in-progress, I thank my fellow fellows Wendy Bellion and Patrick Erben. Chris Grasso's comments—first on two *William and Mary Quarterly* articles, then as he read the whole manuscript near the end— were more helpful and influential than he knows. Fredrika J. Teute has been an amazing editor: smart and uncompromising but always willing to hear my voice rather than project her own. Gil Kelly provided copy editing that was, somehow, as insightful as it was careful. (After eight short years, *L'affaire du "gauntlet"* is officially forgotten.) Reading the entire manuscript at various stages for the Institute, Allan Greer, Greg Dowd, and Laurent Dubois offered learned and perceptive suggestions, allowing me to see things I had missed and saving me from many errors.

William and Mary has been a wonderful place to work on early modern North American and Atlantic history, both as a fellow and since my return in 2008. I thank all of my excellent colleagues, particularly Paul Mapp, Karin Wulf, Kris Lane, and Andy Fisher, all of whom read portions of the manuscript in its later stages. I'm also grateful to colleagues in Anthropology, especially Katie Bragdon and Martin Gallivan, who offered helpful feedback on Chapter 1, and Richard Price who had good suggestions on Martinique. I thank my former colleagues Rebecca DeSchweinitz, Spencer Fluhman, Chris Hodson, Andy Johns, Matt Mason, Jenny Pulsipher, and Neil York, as much for their friendship as for reading drafts of several chapters in our writing group. Andy applied just the right amount of pressure when my writing stalled, not least by beating me to the finish line. Chris read the whole manuscript as it neared completion, offering important feedback and encouragement. It has been my great good fortune to work with him on our coauthored book-in-progress, a massive undertaking that would be impossible to imagine without his intelligence, energy, and humor.

I thank Eric Hinderaker, a generous colleague and friend who took the time as he was finishing his own book to comment on my manuscript. Sue Peabody also helped a great deal, especially with her detailed suggestions on Chapter 2. Mike McDonnell helped me to trace the complicated lines of genealogy for several Detroit and Michilimackinac families and provided helpful feedback on Ottawa and métis connections across these communities. Alan Gallay and Susan Sleeper-Smith also provided valuable feedback on several of my articles and conference papers exploring the themes in this book. Bryan Moll provided critical research assistance on some of the Sioux material. I am also grateful to the linguists David Costa, Michael McCafferty, Daryl Baldwin, and Carl Masthay for generous and perceptive feedback as I worked through the Algonquian language material in Chapter 1 and Appendix A. They have shared their passion for the Miami-Illinois language, offered alternate translations and glosses, pointed to additional words and phrases, and clarified many points of grammar, but all linguistic and interpretive errors remain my own. I also appreciate Linda Baumgarten and Emily Williams for their help with the Native slave halter held by the Colonial Williamsburg Foundation.

My work has benefited from the thoughtful engagement of participants at many conferences and seminars, especially the Champlain–Saint Lawrence Seminar in Early American Studies, the *William and Mary Quarterly* / USC-Huntington Early Modern Studies Institute workshop, the Omohundro Institute's colloquium, Princeton's Colonial and Imperial Histories Colloquium, the McNeil Center's Summer Seminar, and the Triangle Early American History Seminar at the National Humanities Center. Portions of Chapters 1, 3, and 4 appeared previously in the *William and Mary Quarterly*. A portion of Chapter 6 appears in Adam Arenson, Barbara Berglund, and Jay Gitlin, eds., *Frontier Cities: Encounters at the Crossroads of Empire* (Philadelphia, 2012).

Conducting research in archives across Canada, France, the United States, and the Caribbean would have been impossible without financial support from many institutions. I am grateful for the support of the National Endowment for the Humanities, the Omohundro Institute, the American Philosophical Society, BYU's Kennedy Center and FHSS research funds, William and Mary's College of Arts and Sciences and Lyon Gardiner Tyler endowment, and Phi Beta Kappa's Northern California Association.

No one has given more than my family. My parents, Craig and Martha Rushforth, inspired me with a love of books from a very young age. Across decades, they have provided much-needed moral and material support as well as genuine friendship. My wonderful daughters—Kaelyn, Amy, Breanna, and Emily—gave purpose to my work and strengthened my hope in humanity, which occasionally faltered under the weight of my subject. My largest debt is to my best friend and partner, Rebecca Sorensen Rushforth. She married me when I was an industrial supply salesman with an unfinished master's thesis and an unrealized dream of becoming a historian. That I achieved anything is due in large measure to her unfailing support as I embarked on the long road toward a career I love and value. A woman of remarkable talent, she has inspired me to reach beyond what I thought was possible. And we've had a lot of fun along the way. Rebecca, I owe you more than I can ever repay, so this book—as everything else—is for you.

CONTENTS

Acknowledgments vii   List of Illustrations and Tables xii

List of Abbreviations and Short Titles xiv

PROLOGUE: Halter and Shackles 3

CHAPTER 1: I Make Him My Dog / My Slave 15

CHAPTER 2: The Most Ignoble and Scandalous Kind of Subjection 73

CHAPTER 3: Like Negroes in the Islands 135

CHAPTER 4: Most of Them Were Sold to the French 193

CHAPTER 5: The Custom of the Country 253

CHAPTER 6: The Indian Is Not like the Negro 299

EPILOGUE: Of the Indian Race 369

APPENDIX A: Algonquian Language Sources:
Summary and Sample Word List 383

APPENDIX B: "Ordinance Rendered on the Subject of the Negroes
and the Indians Called Panis" 393

APPENDIX C: Notes on the Demography of Enslaved Indians 397

Index 399

ILLUSTRATIONS AND TABLES

Maps

MAP 1: The Native Peoples of the Pays d'en Haut, ca. 1670 21

MAP 2: French and Neighboring Settlements in North America and the Caribbean 97

MAP 3: Key French Posts and Native Neighbors in the Pays d'en Haut 257

MAP 4: French and Native Settlements on the Island of Montreal 303

Figures

FIGURE 1: American Indian Slave Halter 5

FIGURE 2: French Slave Shackles 5

FIGURE 3: Iron Slave Collar 8

FIGURE 4: Man Holding a Calumet 31

FIGURE 5: Native Captives in the Mississippi Valley 41

FIGURE 6: "Woman Who Condemns to Death the Prisoner Given to Her" and "Woman Who Gives Life to the Prisoner Given to Her" 45

FIGURE 7: "Dog Dragging a Fish Called *Namé* or Sturgeon" 54

FIGURE 8: Missionaries Paying a Ransom to Release French Slaves 85

FIGURE 9: Nigritie and the Niger River 105

FIGURE 10: "Country of the Negroes" 105

FIGURE 11: Slave Torture and Bodily Preservation 129

FIGURE 12: Devices for Slave Torture and Restraint 131

FIGURE 13: "They Came and Killed Seven Dakotas Winter" 159

FIGURE 14: "Conjectures on the Existence of a Sea in the Western Region of Canada and Mississippi" 172

FIGURE 15: Coulipa, Enslaved Fox Indian Warrior 219

FIGURE 16: King of the Great Sioux Nation 225

FIGURE 17: Sioux Winter Counts 228

FIGURE 18: *Plan of Fort d'Orleans on the Missouri River* 240

FIGURE 19: *The Detroit River from Lake Saint Clair to Lake Erie* 277

FIGURE 20: *Villemarie on the Island of Montreal* 307

FIGURE 21: Interrogation of Joseph 313

FIGURE 22: "Dictionnaire illinois-français" 386

Tables

TABLE 1: Average Agricultural Production per Household in Detroit, 1750 278

TABLE 2: Individually Identifiable Indian Slaves by Date of First Appearance 292

TABLE 3: Age at Death of Indian Slaves in New France's Parish and Hospital Records, 1700–1760 335

ABBREVIATIONS AND SHORT TITLES

ADM: Archives Departementales de la Martinique. Fort-de-France, Martinique

AN: Archives Nationales de France. Paris

ANOM: Archives Nationales d'Outre-Mer (formerly Centre des Archives d'Outre-Mer). Aix-en-Provence

ASQ: Archives du Séminaire de Québec, Le Centre de Référence de l'Amérique Française, Musée de l'Amérique Française. Quebec

BANQ-M: Bibliothèque et Archives Nationales de Québec, Centre d'Archives de Montréal. Montreal

BANQ-Q: Bibliothèque et Archives Nationales de Québec, Centre d'Archives de Québec. Quebec

BN: Bibliothèque Nationale de France. Paris

DCB: Dictionary of Canadian Biography. Toronto, 1959–

FHL: Family History Library. Salt Lake City, Utah

Handbook: William C. Sturtevant, gen. ed., *Handbook of North American Indians.* Washington, D.C., 1978–

Jesuit Relations: Reuben Gold Thwaites, ed., *The Jesuit Relations and Allied Documents.* 73 vols. Cleveland, 1896–1901

LAC: Library and Archives of Canada (formerly National Archives of Canada). Ottawa

Languages: Ives Goddard, ed., *Languages,* vol. XVII of William C. Sturtevant, *Handbook of North American Indians.* Washington, D.C., 1978–

LC: Library of Congress, Washington, D.C.

Northeast: Bruce G. Trigger, ed., *Northeast,* vol. XV of William C. Sturtevant, *Handbook of North American Indians.* Washington, D.C., 1978–

Plains: Raymond DeMallie, ed., *Plains,* vol. XIII of William C. Sturtevant, *Handbook of North American Indians.* Washington, D.C., 1978–

RAB du PRDH: Gaëtan Morin, ed., *R.A.B. du P.R.D.H.* Chenlière Éducation. CD-Rom comprising more than 700,000 entries from Catholic Church and civic records of New France and early Canada before 1800; improved and expanded from earlier printed collection, Programme de Recherché en Démographie Historique, *Répertoire des actes de baptême, mariage, sépulture, et des recensements du Québec ancien, 1621–1799.* 47 vols. Montreal, 1980–1990

SHD: Archives de la Marine, Service Historique de la Défense. Rochefort, France

Wis. Hist. Coll.: Collections of the State Historical Society of Wisconsin

WJP: James Sullivan, ed. *The Papers of Sir William Johnson.* 14 vols. Albany, N.Y., 1921–1965

Bonds of Alliance

"I think it will end with questions not answers. . . .
It sets up the hypotheses and tests them in various ways,
and it gives answers, but these are not definitive. However,
they need not be definitive; they sing about the human
situation. It is a kind of truth these answers give, the truth of
sorrow and celebration, the truth that we are stamped with
immortality and the truth that we live meanly."
—Saul Bellow to Melvin Tumin, 1942

"If we have only to say 'humanity stinks in our
nostrils' then silence is better, because we have heard that news."
—Saul Bellow to Richard Stern, 1959

prologue

HALTER AND SHACKLES

In the collections of the Colonial Williamsburg Foundation rests an unusual relic of early modern slavery: a hand-crafted American Indian slave halter. It was fashioned in the mid-eighteenth century by a Native woman living near the Great Lakes, destined for a warrior in her village. The artisan began her task by gathering the stalks of a local hemp plant called dogbane, scraping away the outer bark, cracking the exterior shell to expose the fibers inside, and then rolling the hairlike tangle into a thin string. When she had repeated this process long enough to produce more than sixty feet of cord, she braided the strands together, forming two ten-foot ropes that would serve as the halter's reins. Between the reins she fastened a flat strap, about two inches wide and a foot long, woven from elm bark and dogbane fiber and embroidered with geometric shapes of red, black, and white moose hair. By looping an end so one rein could pass through it, she created a human choke collar that would fit across the throat and tighten if the slave tried to pull away. Along both sides of the collar she attached two rows of white trade beads to prevent fraying as the collar rubbed on the victim's skin. She carefully wrapped the reins with dyed and flattened porcupine quills that punctuated the halter's length and formed a smooth handgrip near its end to allow the captor to follow his charge and control the captive's movements. At one end of each rope she fastened five leather strings and attached metal tinkling cones to announce the slave's movements and minimize the risk of escape. It was a specimen of terrific beauty, simultaneously a work of fine art and a tool of human cruelty. Beneath its elegant embroidery was a restraint strong enough to bind a grown man, an experience one French colonist described as "more painful than one can imagine."[1]

1. On Native slave halters, see R. S. Stephenson, "The Decorative Art of Securing Captives in the Eastern Woodlands," in J. C. H. King and Christian F. Feest, eds., *Three Centuries of*

Because they were made almost entirely of organic materials, few Native slave halters survive intact. But they were common in the seventeenth and eighteenth centuries, used in every quarter of North America. Algonquians near Lake Michigan called them "sacant ꝡtagane,"[2] a term translated by the seventeenth-century Jesuit Jacques Gravier as "bridle" or "harness." His Algonquian dictionary and phrase book listed at least seven common expressions describing the use of slave halters, including "I pull him along by the neck" and "I tie him by the throat." When colonists brought horses into the Upper Mississippi Valley, Algonquian-speakers applied their words for slave halter—without alteration—to horses' reins, bridles, harnesses, and even saddles: a linguistic adaptation that drew upon Native metaphors describing enslavement as animal domestication. The creation and exchange of these halters was intensely personal, from the artisanal care taken by those who made them to the bonds of reciprocal obligation established when a warrior accepted them. Receiving a halter compelled the warrior to enslave enemies who would augment the village by their productive and reproductive labors.[3]

No honor was more important to a young man than capturing slaves. His success was celebrated in public ceremonies, etched into his war clubs, and displayed on his body with tattoos representing each enemy he had captured. Although the enslaved probably found little beauty in the halters that bound them, they would have understood that the physical and cultural work that produced their restraints also created a network of interest in their subordination. Their capture and domestication had been the shared purpose of the women who crafted their halters, the warriors who led them home like pets, and the community celebrating their capture. As an object revealing both the intent of the slavers and the earliest experiences of

<hr />

Woodlands Indian Art (Vienna, 2007), 55–66; [Pierre Boucher], *Histoire veritable et naturelle des moeurs et productions du pays de la Nouvelle-France vulgairement dite le Canada* (Paris, 1664), 123–124.

2. The letter combination here resembling the number 8 is the typographic ligature of the Greek *ou*, which places the letter *u* on top of the letter *o* in a single symbol. Jesuits used this symbol, borrowed from the common practice of rendering the Latin *ou* with ꝡ, when recording many Algonquian and Iroquoian words. Like *ou* in French, ꝡ can be pronounced *oo*, as in *nous*, or *w* as in *oui*. See Michael McCafferty, *Native American Place-Names of Indiana* (Urbana, Ill., 2008), 24–26.

3. Jacques Gravier and Jacques Largillier, "Dictionnaire illinois-français," MS, ca. 1690s, Watkinson Library Special Collections, Trinity College, Hartford, Conn., 184, 495, 518; Stephenson, "Decorative Art of Securing Captives," in King and Feest, eds., *Three Centuries of Woodlands Indian Art*, 55–66.

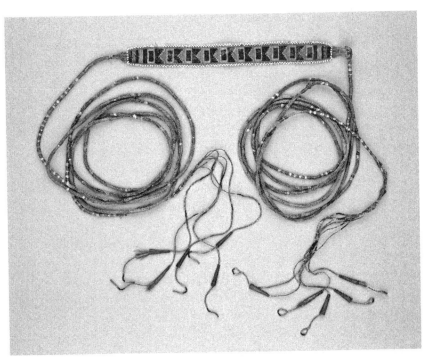

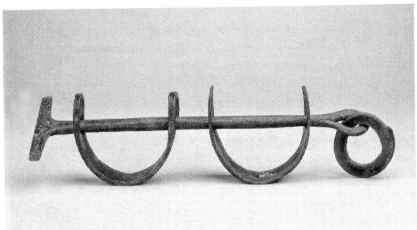

(above) FIGURE 1. American Indian Slave Halter. *Eighteenth Century, Great Lakes Region. Colonial Williamsburg Collection, 1996–816. Courtesy The Colonial Williamsburg Foundation*

(below) FIGURE 2. French Slave Shackles. *Eighteenth Century, Martinique or Guadeloupe. Musée de Quai Branly, 71.1881.45.25/Scala/Art Resource, N.Y. Permission Musée du Quai Branly, Paris*

the enslaved, the halter is a fitting emblem of indigenous North American slavery.

A more familiar artifact sits in Paris's Musée du Quai Branly: a pair of shackles that belonged to the French abolitionist Victor Schoelcher, who kept them as a token of the brutal plantation slavery he devoted his life to ending. The French called them *fers*, or irons. Adapted from the fetters placed on criminals and galley slaves during the Middle Ages, French slave shackles took two main forms, one joining the legs by a one-inch-thick bar, the other by a chain. By the eighteenth century, French manufacturers were mass-producing straight-bar shackles (called "long irons" by the English) for an expansive Atlantic market, supplying them by the thousands to the proliferating number of ships outfitting for African slaving voyages. Threading the bar through horseshoe-shaped ankle clamps, an eye at the bar's end was hammered or bolted closed to keep the clamps from sliding off. The irons could then be tethered by a chain should the master wish to fix the slaves in place. Slave traders often bound two captives with a single set of shackles, one by the right leg and the other by the left: a cost-cutting strategy that also limited slaves' mobility and inhibited them from committing suicide by jumping overboard. Quickly and cheaply cast and corroded by humidity, salt water, and all manner of bodily fluids, leg irons rusted and weakened, becoming less secure than they seemed. Ships' crews checked often to ensure that the shackles remained in place, sometimes taking the opportunity to release compliant captives from their fetters as a reward for model behavior. Effective to a point, the forced physical intimacy of being bound together could also spark conflict between slaves, and their awkward movements only aggravated the chafing, bruising, and blistering caused by months of skin-to-metal contact. As slavery expanded to staggering levels in the eighteenth century, leg irons became so widely recognized in French culture that they came to symbolize the essence of slavery in literary and colloquial expressions. To be in irons was to be a slave.[4]

---

4. Robert Harms, *The Diligent: A Voyage through the Worlds of the Slave Trade* (New York, 2002), 83, 295–297, 315; Robert Louis Stein, *The French Slave Trade in the Eighteenth Century: An Old Regime Business* (Madison, Wis., 1979), 101–105; Stephanie E. Smallwood, *Saltwater Slavery: A Middle Passage from Africa to American Diaspora* (Cambridge, Mass., 2007), 39–42, 120, 132, 162; Marcus Rediker, *The Slave Ship: A Human History* (New York, 2007), 234, 267–268; *Dictionnaire de l'Académie française*, 4th ed. (Paris, 1762), s.v. "fers" ("Il se prend aussi figurément et poëtiquement pour L'état de l'esclavage"). Some ship captains removed the irons from all of their slaves while in open waters, securing them again when they neared the port of debarkation. For Schoelcher's career, see Victor Schoelcher,

After crossing the Atlantic and arriving at an American port, slaves' shackles were removed when the slaves were sold to French planters seeking laborers for commercial farming operations. In France's tropical colonies, a brutal work regimen both defined slaves' lives and explained why they had been transported such great distances. Enslaved laborers produced a range of export staples in the French Caribbean, including sugar, tobacco, indigo, and coffee. They also worked subsistence farms, tended livestock, maintained buildings, provided domestic service, and carried cargoes to and from Atlantic vessels. The material culture of slavery in these colonies reveals the extent to which lifelong, coerced labor defined slaves' experience. In addition to shackles, Victor Schoelcher kept two other tokens of slaveholder brutality. The first is a whip made of a simple wooden shaft and a braded rope, knotted in several places near the end to reduce fraying and maximize pain. Whips were tools of public terror, wielded most often by slave drivers (whose fitting French title was *commandeur*) to encourage hard work and conformity to the master's wishes. Schoelcher also collected an iron collar featuring a matching pair of forked hooks protruding on either side. Clamped tightly around a slave's throat, the collar marked him as a danger to society and made him readily identifiable should he run away again. The hooks interfered with sleep and made swift movements dangerous, reportedly tearing ears, cheeks, and shoulders when slaves bent the wrong way. These objects, like the shackles that delivered slaves to the Caribbean, were produced en masse for an enslaved population that, by the late-eighteenth century, reached several hundred thousand, vastly outnumbering their French masters. The islands' cultural, legal, and economic life came to revolve around the dual objectives of maximizing slaves' production while minimizing their threat to French mastery.[5]

Abolition de l'esclavage: examen critique du préjugé contre la couleur des Africains et des sang-mêlés (Paris, 1840); Scheolcher, *Des colonies françaises, abolition immédiate de l'esclavage* (Paris, 1842); Nelly Schmidt, *Victor Schoelcher et l'abolition de l'esclavage* (Paris, 1994); Lawrence C. Jennings, *French Anti-Slavery: The Movement for the Abolition of Slavery in France, 1802–1848* (Cambridge, 2000).

5. "Carcan," 71.1881.45.81; and "Fouet de commandeur," 71.1881.45.32, Musée du quai Branly, Paris. Still the best general treatment of slavery, and especially slave labor and plantation management, in the French Caribbean is Gabriel Debien, *Les esclaves aux Antilles françaises, XVIIe–XVIIIe siècles* (Basse-Terre, 1974; rpt., Gourbeyre, Guadeloupe, 2000). See also Bernard Moitt, *Women and Slavery in the French Antilles, 1635–1848* (Bloomington, Ind., 2001), esp. 34–79; Caroline E. Fick, *The Making of Haiti: The Saint Domingue Revolution from Below* (Knoxville, Tenn., 1990), esp. 15–117; David P. Geggus, "Sugar and Coffee Cultivation in Saint Domingue and the Shaping of the Slave Labor Force," in Ira Berlin and

FIGURE 3. Iron Slave Collar. *Late-Eighteenth Century, French Caribbean. Musée du Quai Branly, 71.1881.45.81/Scala/Art Resource, N.Y. Permission Musée de Quai Branly, Paris*

Both the Native halter and French shackles were designed to humiliate and control people considered less than fully human by their captors. Both inflicted pain, restrained movement, and delivered slaves to their destinations. And both carried potent symbolism of the captive's subordination within larger systems of violent coercion. As products of the eighteenth century, the objects recall a period in which slavery became the driving force behind a globalizing economy rooted in plantation agriculture. In that century alone more than six million Africans were shackled and transported across the Atlantic to produce export staples for European markets. Yet the Native halter reminds us that slavery took many forms in the early modern Americas, and this variety persisted in both indigenous and colonial settings long after the African slave trade overshadowed other slaving cultures. Before their encounter with Europeans, many Native peoples throughout the Americas practiced forms of slavery, establishing patterns that would be exploited by European newcomers and adapted by Natives themselves to meet the challenges of colonialism.[6]

Philip D. Morgan, eds., *Cultivation and Culture: Labor and the Shaping of Slave Life in the Americas* (Charlottesville, Va., 1993), 73–98.

6. For the African slave trade, see David Eltis and David Richardson, *Atlas of the Transatlantic Slave Trade* (New Haven, Conn., 2010); David Geggus, "The French Slave Trade: An Overview," *William and Mary Quarterly,* 3d Ser., LVIII (2001), 119–138; Harms, *The Diligent;* Stein, *The French Slave Slave Trade.* For indigenous slavery, see, in addition to Chapter 1, Leland Donald, "Slavery in Indigenous North America," in David Eltis and Stanley L. Engerman, eds., *The Cambridge World History of Slavery,* III, *AD 1420–AD 1804* (Cambridge, 2011), 217–247; Donald, *Aboriginal Slavery on the Northwest Coast of North America* (Berke-

Although they were produced at nearly the same time and for similar purposes, these slave restraints, like the cultures that made them, can seem worlds apart. Slavery in Native villages and European colonies operated on vastly different scales and to very different ends. But European and Native practices were more closely entwined than their differences suggest. Colonizers traded between two and four million Indian slaves from the late-fifteenth to the mid-nineteenth century, most of whom were initially enslaved by other Native peoples. Adapting indigenous slaving practices to the new realities of the colonial world, Indians responded both to Europeans' demand for slaves and to the broader economic transformations wrought by colonial trade. Doing so led some Natives to redirect their energies toward slaving for Europeans, becoming long-term slave suppliers while reducing other subsistence activities. Others traded on European demand for slaves to gain weapons and military support in wars against their own enemies. In nearly all American colonies, the first generations of slaves included more Indians than Africans. From the sugar estates of Brazil to the rice plantations of South Carolina, enslaved Indians provided the initial labor and, through their sale, the preliminary capital that made plantation agriculture possible. Then, too, many of the earliest debates about the moral and legal underpinnings of plantation slavery took place in the context of enslaving Indians rather than Africans. Controversies over who could be enslaved and under what circumstances made comparisons between Indians and Africans central to early modern racial discourse, requiring any serious treatment of the racial dimensions of colonial slavery to take account of Indian as well as African enslavement. Indeed, the contours of New World slavery were formed in the dynamic interplay between indigenous and Atlantic cultures, a dialogue that persisted throughout the Americas for more than three centuries.[7]

ley, Calif., 1997); Christina Snyder, *Slavery in Indian Country: The Changing Face of Captivity in Early America* (Cambridge, Mass., 2010), esp. 1–45; Theda Perdue, *Slavery and the Evolution of Cherokee Society, 1540–1866* (Knoxville, Tenn., 1979), 3–18.

7. For Brazil, see Stuart B. Schwartz, "Indian Labor and New World Plantations: European Demands and Indian Responses in Northeastern Brazil," *American Historical Review*, LXXXIII (1978), 43–79; Schwartz, *Sugar Plantations in the Formation of Brazilian Society: Bahia, 1550–1835* (Cambridge, 1985); John M. Monteiro, *Negros da terra: índios e bandeirantes nas origens de São Paulo* (São Paulo, 1994); David Graham Sweet, "A Rich Realm of Nature Destroyed: The Middle Amazon Valley, 1640–1750" (Ph.D. diss., University of Wisconsin, 1974); Sweet, "Francisca: Indian Slave," in Sweet and Gary B. Nash, eds., *Struggle and Survival in Colonial America* (Berkeley, Calif., 1981), 274–291; John Hemming, *Red Gold: The Conquest of the Brazilian Indians* (Cambridge, Mass., 1978); A. J. R. Russell-

❖ This study explores the relationship between indigenous and Atlantic slaveries in New France, a colony centered on the Saint Lawrence River and stretching westward to a region the French called the *Pays d'en Haut*, or Upper Country (roughly the Western Great Lakes and Upper Mississippi Valley). Between about 1660 and 1760, French colonists and their Native allies enslaved thousands of Indians, keeping them in the towns and villages of New France or shipping them to the French Caribbean. Over time, a vast network of slave raiders, traders, and owners emerged, ensnaring both colonists and Indians in the violence that generated slaves and kept them under French control. Unlike many American colonies, where Indian slaves were replaced by Africans in the early stages of settlement, Native slavery predominated in New France throughout the colony's final century. Driven by the dual demands of alliance politics and economic profits, slavery in New France bridged the geographic and conceptual divides separating the worlds that produced the Great Lakes halter and the Caribbean shackles, forcing creative cultural adaptations that would transform both worlds. From the strategic violence that reduced Indians to bondage, through a slave trade that spanned half a continent, to the cultural norms and structures of restraint that shaped the daily lives of enslaved individuals, Indian slavery in New France profoundly affected both Native and French colonial societies.

Wood, "New Directions in *Bandeirismo* Studies in Colonial Brazil," *The Americas*, LXI (2005), 353–371, and Barbara A. Sommer, "Colony of the Sertão: Amazonian Expeditions and the Indian Slave Trade," 401–428.

For Central America and Mexico, see William L. Sherman, *Forced Native Labor in Sixteenth-Century Central America* (Lincoln, Nebr., 1979); David R. Radell, "The Indian Slave Trade and Population of Nicaragua during the Sixteenth Century," in William M. Denevan, ed., *The Native Population of the Americas in 1492*, 2d ed. (Madison, Wis., 1992), 67–76; Linda Newson, "The Depopulation of Nicaragua in the Sixteenth Century," *Journal of Latin American Studies*, XIV (1982), 253–286.

For South Carolina and the broader Southeast, see Alan Gallay, *The Indian Slave Trade: The Rise of the English Empire in the American South, 1670–1717* (New Haven, Conn., 2002); Gallay, ed., *Indian Slavery in Colonial America* (Lincoln, Nebr., 2009); Robbie Ethridge and Sheri M. Shuck-Hall, eds., *Mapping the Mississippian Shatter Zone: The Colonial Indian Slave Trade and Regional Instability in the American South* (Lincoln, Nebr., 2009); Joseph M. Hall, Jr., *Zamumo's Gifts: Indian-European Exchange in the Colonial Southeast* (Philadelphia, 2009); Paul Kelton, *Epidemics and Enslavement: Biological Catastrophe in the Native Southeast, 1492–1715* (Lincoln, Nebr., 2007). For the Southwest, see Juliana Barr, *Peace Came in the Form of a Woman: Indians and Spaniards in the Texas Borderlands* (Chapel Hill, N.C., 2007); Ned Blackhawk, *Violence over the Land: Indians and Empires in the Early American West* (Cambridge, Mass., 2006); James F. Brooks, *Captives and Cousins: Slavery, Kinship, and Community in the Southwest Borderlands* (Chapel Hill, N.C., 2002).

That French colonists enslaved large numbers of Indians might seem incompatible with the prevailing view of intercultural relations in New France and its hinterlands. French-Native interactions are widely known for the cultural adaptations and creative innovations that facilitated trade, diplomacy, and kinship across large portions of North America. Because they colonized New France in relatively small numbers, the French had no choice but to embed themselves within indigenous political economies, adapting to (if hoping to manipulate) Native interests to gain the economic and geopolitical advantages of American colonialism. Indians adapted, too. Eager to acquire French manufactured goods—especially cloth and metal tools but also guns and other weapons—Indians tolerated and sometimes even embraced the French interlopers to gain the material benefits of European commodities and to secure French military support against their enemies. Over time hundreds of small acts of cultural negotiation combined to create a regional culture that was neither French nor Indian, but rather a new creation of the colonial world.[8]

The slave trade grew from, and indeed offers a strong example of, these intercultural negotiations in the Pays d'en Haut. As the region's Natives encountered French traders and eventually settlers in the second half of the seventeenth century, they greeted them with rituals and gifts to signal their friendship and to invite the newcomers into an alliance. Among the most significant of these gifts were enslaved enemies, offered as a sign of trust and evidence of Native power. From these beginnings, Natives and the French developed a sustained slave trade built upon decades of small-scale exchanges of bodies, goods, and ideas. Slavery reveals a somber dimension to cultural accommodation in the Pays d'en Haut, showing that its success was often founded on a shared commitment to violence. Yet even this violence was a product of mutual adaptation and produced new cultural forms that persisted for generations.

If slavery fits comfortably within this broad understanding of French-Native cultural relations, it also forces reorientation. Among the Indians of

8. Richard White, *The Middle Ground: Indians, Empires, and Republics in the Great Lakes Region, 1650–1815* (Cambridge, 1991); Gilles Havard, *Empire et métissages: Indiens et Français dans le Pays d'en Haut, 1660–1715* (Paris, 2003); Catherine M. Desbarats, Avant-propos, in White, *Le middle ground: Indiens, empires, et républiques dans la région des Grands Lacs, 1650–1815* (Paris, 2009) 5–22; Desbarats, "Following *The Middle Ground*," *WMQ*, 3d Ser., LXIII (2006), 81–96; Christopher Hodson and Brett Rushforth, "Absolutely Atlantic: Colonialism and the Early Modern French State in Recent Historiography," *History Compass*, VIII (2010), 101–117.

the Pays d'en Haut, slaving was not only a means of bolstering population and production; it was, perhaps primarily, a performance of ethnic identity. Slave raids helped to maintain alliances by enforcing their boundaries, defining who was included or excluded and demonizing those on the outside. When the French arrived in the Pays d'en Haut, early observers thought they had found a world so ruined by Iroquois wars that ethnic markers of language, kinship, and regional settlement had broken apart, leaving, in the words of one historian, "a world made of fragments." This initial impression turned into a French fantasy, which willed the region's Indians into a single category, overlooking the ethnic boundaries that Indians themselves insisted still mattered. Adapted to this new colonial reality, the slave trade provided Natives with a powerful restraint to the French ambition of creating a regionwide alliance against the will of their allies. If French traders or diplomats insisted on befriending their allies' enemies, slaving became the preferred strategy for the offended ally to express discontent. In the contours of the Indian slave trade, then, we can read an indigenous counternarrative to the French story of ethnic shattering in the Pays d'en Haut. From this new perspective, the French insistence on mediating, rather than taking sides in, disputes between Native groups registers as a cynical attempt to exert authority rather than an example of French accommodation to Native cultural demands.[9]

Native slaving practices resonated well beyond the Pays d'en Haut, intersecting with and influencing slavery in the broader French Atlantic world. The supply of Indian slaves was rooted in the distant West, but the motives behind French demand and the models of slavery they sought to replicate in New France originated in the Caribbean. Over the seventeenth century, colonists in the Caribbean islands of Martinique, Guadeloupe, Saint Christophe, and eventually Saint Domingue developed a successful plantation economy dependent upon slave labor. The success of these plantations made the Caribbean an ideal colonial model, particularly when it came to slavery. New France's legal system continually cited justifications of slavery developed in the Caribbean to defend Native enslavement, protecting slaveholders' right to hold Indians as slaves. The export of enslaved Indians to the Caribbean ensured that this influence would run in both directions.

9. White, *Middle Ground*, 1–49; Havard, *Empire et métissages,* 113–203; Heidi Bohaker, "*Nindoodemag:* The Significance of Algonquian Kinship Networks in the Eastern Great Lakes Region, 1600–1701," *WMQ,* 3d Ser., LXIII (2006), 23–52. For a fuller discussion of Native ethnicities and regional alliances in the Pays d'en Haut, see Chapter 1.

Individual Native slaves contributed to the cultural diversity of places like Martinique and Guadeloupe, and the Indian slave trade forced renewed Caribbean debates about the moral and legal foundations of slavery.

Envious of Caribbean success, French colonists in the Saint Lawrence Valley spent the better part of a century trying to fit New France's Native slavery into a Caribbean mold. They largely failed. Instead, there emerged a set of complex, localized cultures of slavery that differed widely between the French settlements of the Pays d'en Haut and the Saint Lawrence Valley, all of them influenced by the free and enslaved Natives on whom the French depended for colonial success. For the enslaved, this local variation often meant that they lived their lives in a succession of very different places, forced to adapt to a wide range of regional norms. They could become enslaved wives of métis traders in Detroit, cooks in a Montreal hospital, plantation workers in the sugar fields of Martinique, or all of these in sequence.

In addition to outlining the cultural, economic, and legal structures of Native slavery in New France, then, I have aimed, wherever possible, to recover the details of enslaved individuals' lives: their names, ages, friends, lovers, occupations, and, occasionally, even their aspirations and fears. I believe that these portraits add an important dimension to my analysis, demonstrating the wide range of slaves' experiences and showing the limits of their opportunities. But telling their many stories is more than a narrative device. It reflects an ethical commitment to recognize the humanity of the enslaved, something their masters sought to deny. If their lives are useful because they illuminate the systems through which they passed, their value is intrinsic.

methodology

chapter one

I MAKE HIM MY DOG / MY SLAVE

On April 12, 1680, a Belgian monk-turned-missionary named Louis Hennepin tinkered with a canoe on the banks of the Mississippi River. As two French servants boiled a wild turkey for his lunch, Hennepin surveyed the strange and beautiful country before him. His party had traveled the Mississippi for eleven days without incident, but, as he awaited his meal, Hennepin "suddenly perceived . . . fifty bark canoes, conducted by 120 Indians, entirely nude, who descended this river with great speed." Hennepin called out to them, twisting his tongue around rudimentary Algonquian to assure the Indians of his good intentions. "Mistigouche," he cried, using the Algonquians' name for his people to identify himself and his servants as their friends. As Siouan speakers, the approaching war party did not understand his words. But, unfortunately for Hennepin, they got the message: these bearded foreigners were allies of the Algonquian-speaking peoples of the Mississippi Valley, the very peoples the Sioux had come to attack.[1]

---

1. "J'apperçus tout d'un coup . . . cinquante Canots d'ecorce conduits par six vingt Sauvages tous nuds, qui décendoient d'une fort grande vitesse sur ce Fleuve." Louis Hennepin, *Nouvelle découverte d'un très grand pays situé dans l'Amérique, entre le Nouveau Mexique et la mer glaciale* (Utrecht, 1697), 314–315. Catherine Broué discusses problems with Hennepin's credibility, concluding that the 1697 edition is largely reliable and highly valuable. Broué, "En filigrane des récits du Père Louis Hennepin: 'trous noirs' de l'exploration louisianaise, 1679–1681," *Revue d'histoire de l'Amérique française*, LIII (1999–2000), 339–366. For the negative view, see Jean Delanglez, *Hennepin's Description of Louisiana: A Critical Essay* (Chicago, 1941). Perhaps the foremost authority on seventeenth- and eighteenth-century Sioux history and culture, Raymond J. DeMallie concludes that Hennepin's writings, if evaluated carefully, "present valuable ethnographic detail" about the eastern Sioux. DeMallie, "The Sioux at the Time of European Contact: An Ethnohistorical Problem," in Sergei A. Kan and Pauline Turner Strong, eds., *New Perspectives on Native North America: Cultures, Histories, and Representations* (Lincoln, Nebr., 2006), 243.

Throughout this study I use the term "Sioux" rather than the recently fashionable "Dakota" because the latter term excludes those Sioux who are Lakota or Nakota and be-

Hennepin and his party quickly realized the danger and scrambled to evade an impending assault. Ditching the turkey in the brush, the servants ran to the canoe, joining Hennepin in a hasty retreat. Within seconds, Sioux canoes surrounded them. Raising ceremonial war cries, the attackers boarded Hennepin's canoe and took him captive. "We offered no resistance," Hennepin later recalled, "because we were only three against so great a number." Now using signs because he "did not know a word of their language," Hennepin tried to urge the Sioux on to their original target, but to no avail. Next he offered bribes, first tobacco from Martinique, then two wild turkeys they had saved for dinner. This pleased his captors, and their demeanor seemed to soften, but by nightfall Hennepin and the Frenchmen still feared for their lives. The servants resolved to die fighting like men, but Hennepin was more resigned to his fate, whispering a vow that he would "allow them to kill me without resistance in order to imitate the Savior, who gave himself voluntarily into the hands of his executioners."[2]

Rather than dying a martyr, Hennepin lived the next eight months as a captive among the Sioux. For nineteen days he and his companions were forced to row their overburdened canoe against the Mississippi's strong current. Reaching the northern edges of navigable waters, the Sioux destroyed Hennepin's canoe to prevent his escape and then marched the prisoners over half-frozen marshlands toward their villages. The prisoners faced daily threats to their lives, enduring "hunger, thirst, and a thousand outrages . . . marching day and night without pause." When Hennepin's hunger and fatigue caused him to lag, his captors set fire to the meadows behind him, forcing him to push ahead. In short, according to Hennepin, "The insults that these barbarians committed against us during our journey are beyond all imagining."[3]

---

cause "Sioux" is a much more widely recognized term among Anglophone readers. French sources from the seventeenth and eighteenth centuries do not allow a clear distinction between various Sioux bands, so the broader term also better reflects the historical record. Several modern tribal organizations in the United States use "Sioux" in their official names, but none uses "Dakota" except to designate their location. See Raymond J. DeMallie, "Sioux until 1850," in *Handbook*, XIII, *Plains*, part 2, 718; and, for a different perspective, Gary Clayton Anderson, *Kinsmen of Another Kind: Dakota-White Relations in the Upper Mississippi Valley, 1650–1862* (Lincoln, Nebr., 1984).

2. "Nous ne faisons aucune resistance, parce que nous n'êtions que trois contre un si grand nombre," 316; "Je ne savois pas un mot de leur langue," 320; "J'avois resolu de me laisser tuer sans resistance afin d'imiter le Sauveur, qui s'étoit remis volontairement entre les mains de ses bourreaux," 319: Hennepin, *Nouvelle découverte*.

3. "Le faim, la soif, et mille outrages . . . marché jour et nuit sans delai," 342; "Les Insultes,

When they reached the Sioux villages, the prisoners faced another wave of humiliating assaults. They were stripped naked, their bodies were painted, and they were forced to sing and dance as they drummed a rattling gourd. The warriors stood the prisoners in front of tall stakes, set in the ground and surrounded by straw and wood, erected to burn incoming captives. Then they began to negotiate Hennepin's fate. A few urged good treatment to curry favor with the French, but their voices were overwhelmed by those arguing for his execution. They began to torture him but were cut short when an influential war chief named Aquipaguetin stepped forward and claimed the priest as a replacement for his son, who had fallen at the hands of Hennepin's allies. In Aquipaguetin's charge Hennepin entered the chief's village, injured and demoralized but glad to be alive.[4]

As he made the transition to life in captivity, Hennepin found it difficult to make sense of his position in Sioux society or even to find the right word to define it. His captors themselves said that "they considered [him] a slave that their warriors had captured in their enemies' territory." Yet, because of his ceremonial adoption as Aquipaguetin's son, he expected a level of independence and respect he never achieved. He was beaten. He faced repeated death threats. He performed forced labor, farming with Aquipaguetin's wives and children on a nearby island. And he was under almost constant surveillance: "The more I hid myself, the more I had Indians after me . . . for they never stopped watching me." But it was hunger that troubled him the most. To keep him weak and dependent, Hennepin's newly adopted kin fed him only five or six meals a week, giving him just enough wild oats and fish eggs to keep him alive. "I would have been very content had they given me something to eat, as they did their children," he remembered. "But they hid [their food] from me . . . conserving what little fish they had to feed their children." Despite the metaphorical kinship conferred by his adoption, he and his captors understood the difference between real and fictive sons. "They thus preferred the lives of their children to mine," a distinction that even Hennepin admitted was only reasonable. If the priest could not fully grasp his experience as a Mississippi Valley captive, he was eager for it to end: "It must be said that it is a sweet and pleasant thing to come out of slavery."[5]

---

que ces Barbares nous firent pendant nôtre route, sont au dessus de toute imagination," 322: Hennepin, *Nouvelle découverte*.

4. Ibid., 355.

5. "Elles me consideroient comme un Esclave, que leurs Guerriers avoient fait dans le pays

Looking back from the twenty-first century, historians share Hennepin's dilemma, finding no easy shorthand to encapsulate so complex and unfamiliar an experience. Not only did Indians leave no written records of their own, but slaves' marginalization also made them less visible to outside observers, especially in societies like these that did not rely on slavery as a dominant mode of social or economic production. Even those who, like Hennepin, survived the ordeal of enslavement had only a fragmentary understanding of its meaning to their captors. Full of silences, their narratives often raise as many questions as they answer. This is particularly true of published accounts, like the Jesuits' insightful but carefully scripted *Relations,* which functioned as public performances for a particular French audience and thereby obscured many insights that modern scholars wish to glean from them. Reconstructing the practice of indigenous slavery requires a wider reconnaissance, gathering scattered shards of surviving evidence and relying on context to fill in the gaps that remain.

Using archaeology, ritual, and linguistics to supplement the observations of captives and other colonists, it is possible to trace the contours of indigenous slavery among the central Algonquian and Siouan peoples of the Pays d'en Haut. These sources take us beyond sketchy European impressions of Indian captivity and adoption to see the patterns of enslavement, domestication, and forced integration by which enemy outsiders were made into subordinate domestics. A rich body of linguistic records, in particular, reveals how Indians explained the place of slavery in their own societies. In the late-seventeenth century, Jesuits compiled and translated thousands of pages of Algonquian phrases, recorded from conversations with Native men and women and corrected over several years by Native informants. As transcriptions of Indians' own speech in their own language, these manu-

de leurs Ennemis," 362; "plus je me cachois, plus j'avois de Sauvages à ma suite . . . car ils ne me quittoient point de veuë," 320–321; "J'aurois esté fort content, s'ils m'eussent donné à manger, comme à leurs enfans. Mais ils se cachoient de moy . . . conservoient le peu de poisson, qu'elles avoient, pour en nourrir leurs enfans. . . . Elles préféroient donc la vie de leurs enfans à la mienne. En quoy il est certain, qu'elles avoient raison," 362; "Il Faut avoüer, qu'il est bien doux et bien agreeable de sortir de l'Esclavage," 463: Hennepin, *Nouvelle découverte.* For mistreatment and labor, see Louis Hennepin, *Description de la Louisiane, nouvellement découverte au Sud'Ouest de la Nouvelle France* (Paris, 1683), 246; Hennepin, *A New Discovery of a Vast Country in America, Extending above Four Thousand Miles, between New France and New Mexico* (London, 1698) (Wing H1451), I, 109. William Henry Foster similarly argues that the power of Native women to control slaves "came not from physicality but from the hearth." Foster, *The Captor's Narrative: Catholic Women and Their Puritan Men on the Early American Frontier* (Ithaca, N.Y., 2003), 9.

scripts are the nearest thing to contemporary Algonquian sources available, providing far greater clarity than the French observations that have to this point guided our understanding of captivity in the Pays d'en Haut. Because the words and phrases have a linguistic integrity and logic of their own—and because there are hundreds of examples of their connotations and contextualized meanings—they provide unprecedented depth to our understanding of indigenous slavery.[6]

The Indians who would engage in a century-long slave trade with French colonists brought their own complex and evolving practice of slavery to the colonial encounter. The act of enslavement dominated and defined Natives' thinking about slavery far more than the long-term status of those they enslaved. Indigenous slaves lived under a wide range of conditions, some dehumanizing and others nearly familial, and a particular slave's place in the community could change over time. But all of them had to pass through the ritualized system of enslavement designed to strip them of former identities and forcibly integrate them into the capturing village. In war dances and diplomatic ceremonies, through the binding and marking of bodies, and with a sophisticated language of dominion and ridicule, the Native peoples of the Pays d'en Haut articulated an elaborate idiom of slavery as a form of human domestication that reduced enemy captives to the status of dogs and other domesticated animals. Simultaneously expressing and seeking power, enslavement involved a series of scripted acts of physical and psychological dominion designed, in the words of several Algonquian and Siouan languages, to tame and domesticate captured enemies. In so doing, captors harnessed the enemy's power to serve the needs of their own people.

Although slaves were defined by their place in Native war culture, they also labored in agriculture and performed other useful tasks. For men, this work often violated gender norms, as they were compelled to perform traditionally female tasks like hoeing in the fields or carrying baggage on hunting expeditions. Female slaves often became subordinate wives, adding their reproductive and domestic labor to the households that incorporated them. Full of possibilities for social integration, enslaved women's work also carried many dangers, including the potential for sexual violence that seems to have been a hazard unique to their slave status. Some of enslaved individuals' most important labor was performed in the area of diplomacy. As both agents and objects of intercultural relations, indigenous slaves medi-

6. For a fuller discussion of the origin and nature of these dictionaries as well as a list of translated Algonquian terms relating to slavery and captivity, see Appendix A.

ated between the violent impulses that led to their enslavement and the alliance building that their bodies facilitated as symbols of generosity. As a regionally and temporally specific system of human bondage, Algonquian and Siouan slavery differed in important ways not only from European chattel slavery but also from other forms of Indian captivity in North America.

THE GENERAL CUSTOM OF THE COUNTRY

"Our Outagami are fully resolved not to treat The Nadouessi more humanely than they are treated by them."—Claude Allouez, Jesuit, 1672

The Pays d'en Haut was a biologically and climatically diverse region loosely bordered by Lake Huron on the east, the Minnesota River on the west, and the confluence of the Missouri and Mississippi Rivers on the south, comprising roughly the modern states of Minnesota, Wisconsin, Michigan, Indiana, and Illinois as well as parts of eastern Iowa and Missouri and western Ontario (see Map 1). Linked by a network of rivers and lakes—especially the Mississippi River and Lakes Michigan and Superior—the Native peoples in this region had a long history of interaction through trade, intermarriage, and warfare that bound their villages in a regional political economy that balanced the imperatives of trade with the harsh realities of intergroup competition and warfare.

Slavery and slave raiding had a deep history in the Pays d'en Haut, expressed most fully and brutally by the people of Cahokia, who dominated the mid-Mississippi from the tenth to fourteenth centuries. Centered on the eastern bank of the Mississippi River across from modern Saint Louis, Missouri, Cahokia had a population estimated between twenty and forty thousand, managing a system of subordinate alliances that drew goods and peoples from all across the midcontinent. Intensely hierarchical, Cahokia practiced slavery on a large scale. The presence of massive public earthworks demanding an ample supply of manual laborers, combined with evidence of ritual human sacrifice, indicates a tradition of slavery that supported the ruling elite and sustained the hierarchies that ordered this world and the next. Many slaves were killed for burial with their masters, interred with other prestige goods to honor and comfort the dead. In one dramatic example (discovered by archaeologists in the late-1960s), an elite man was buried with more than twenty thousand shell beads, flanked by a burial pit containing fifty-three murdered women and four men with severed heads and hands. The confluence of monumental public works with "theatrical" human sacrifice points, in the words of one archaeologist, to "the

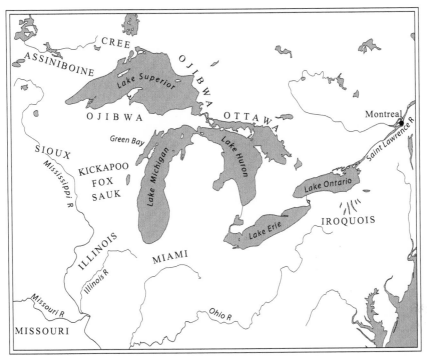

MAP 1. The Native Peoples of the Pays d'en Haut.
Drawn by Jim DeGrand

paramount importance of human labor and the ability to coordinate, control, and sacrifice it." A long-standing tradition of slave raiding and trading permeated Mississippian cultures well beyond Cahokia too, running the length of the Mississippi Valley and into the mound-building chiefdoms of the Southeast.[7]

Echoes of Cahokian slave raiding reverberated long after the city's collapse in the early fourteenth century. Archaeological remains suggest that, from the decline of Cahokia to the mid-seventeenth century, the Native villages of the Pays d'en Haut both suffered and conducted a nearly unbroken succession of raids and counterraids, what anthropologists flatly describe as low-level endemic warfare punctuated by periods of heightened violence.

7. Timothy R. Pauketat, *Ancient Cahokia and the Mississippians* (Cambridge, 2004), 92–93 ("paramount importance"); Pauketat and Thomas E. Emerson, eds., *Cahokia: Domination and Ideology in the Mississippian World* (Lincoln, Nebr., 1997); Jon Muller, *Mississippian Political Economy* (New York, 1997); Emerson, *Cahokia and the Archaeology of Power* (Tuscaloosa, Ala., 1997); Christina Snyder, *Slavery in Indian Country: The Changing Face of Captivity in Early America* (Cambridge, Mass., 2010), 13–45.

Of all burials uncovered from the late-precolonial period, for example, a significant proportion of all deaths were caused by war instruments like clubs, stone daggers, and arrowheads. Skeletal remains show signs of torture that correspond with later descriptions of Native captive rituals: scalping, finger mutilation, multiple blows from clubs, and live burning. Most of these torture victims were also adults and more often male than female, following later patterns of women's and especially children's being kept alive while men were killed. Skulls from several sites in the Pays d'en Haut exhibit healed cranial fractures consistent with nonfatal blows from war clubs. In some samples females with these injuries outnumbered males as many as four to one, whereas males had far more fatal injuries. Relatively few child remains exhibit any signs of torture or violent death. Evidence of warfare beyond the Pays d'en Haut confirms what later sources describe as a long history of raiding into bordering regions, especially the eastern Great Plains. Villages in the Missouri River valley, which would be the target of Illinois, Fox, and Sioux raids in the seventeenth and eighteenth centuries, suffered frequent raids in preceding generations, especially during periodic resource shortages traced to climate change. Summarizing a regionwide review of archaeological data from the fourteenth through sixteenth centuries, one team of researchers concluded that "outbreaks of violence occurred regularly, and each attack resulted in only a few deaths. . . . Internecine conflict . . . was a pervasive element in everyday life." Bones are poor guides to the cultural meanings of this violence, but some form of slavery evidently played an important role.[8]

Because these traumatized bones lay beside a diverse collection of trade goods, it is also clear that the region's endemic violence coexisted with

8. For forensic markers of slavery, see Richard D. Wilkinson and Karen M. Van Wagenen, "Violence against Women: Prehistoric Skeletal Evidence from Michigan," *Midcontinental Journal of Archaeology*, XVIII (1993), 190–216; Debra L. Martin, "Ripped Flesh and Torn Souls: Skeletal Evidence for Captivity and Slavery from the La Plata Valley, New Mexico, AD 1100–1300," in Catherine M. Cameron, ed., *Invisible Citizens: Captives and Their Consequences* (Salt Lake City, Utah, 2008), 159–180; Douglas B. Bamforth, "Climate, Chronology, and the Course of War in the Middle Missouri Region of the North American Great Plains," in Elizabeth N. Arkush and Mark W. Allen, eds., *The Archaeology of Warfare: Prehistories of Raiding and Conquest* (Gainesville, Fla., 2006), 66–100. The quality and range of the archaeological evidence from the mid-Missouri River sites represent, according to Bamforth, "some of the clearest evidence in the world for the existence of tribal warfare prior to Western contact" (66). For widespread, low-level violence, see George R. Milner, Eve Anderson, and Virginia G. Smith, "Warfare in Late Prehistoric West-Central Illinois," *American Antiquity*, LVI (1991), 581–603, esp. 589 ("outbreaks"), 594 ("Internecine conflict").

peaceful exchange relationships that facilitated broader alliances, trade, and cultural mixing. Violence and slavery, in other words, did not define the region's political economy. The peoples of the Pays d'en Haut responded to the region's ecological and climatic diversity with a creative range of subsistence practices, spanning the spectrum from intense reliance on hunting and fishing in the north to a much greater dependence on agriculture in the south. Allies traded grain for meat and leather to diversify their diets and to demonstrate friendship. Tools and decorative items often drew upon external resources, with goods like obsidian, turquoise, pipestone, porcupine quills, shell beads, and animal hides circulating broadly within the region and linking it to areas far beyond. Given the historical association between trade and kin-based alliances, this commerce represents a counternarrative to violence and slavery that simultaneously highlights the restraints on warfare and the imperatives of military alliance that drove slave raids and the captive trade.[9]

Although we know very few particulars, in the fifteenth and sixteenth centuries the search for security drew many peoples together into several fluid but relatively stable alliances. Broadly defined by linguistic affinity, five core ethnic clusters coalesced in the Pays d'en Haut: Miaimi-Illinois, Fox-Sauk-Kickapoo, Sioux, Cree-Monsoni-Assiniboine, and Ojibwa-Ottawa-Potawatomi. Linked by geographic proximity, intermarriage, language, and culture more than by political unity, these broad groupings remained more or less stable through the seventeenth century, negotiating familial, commercial, and diplomatic alliances with neighboring villages. These coalitions have been mistaken for "tribes" or "confederacies" when nothing so politically structured held them together. Instead, they were collections of closely allied villages speaking dialects of a shared language, intermarrying, and cooperating in trade and diplomacy.[10]

9. As Milner, Anderson, and Smith argue: "It is not surprising that evidence for both cooperative and antagonistic intergroup relationships occurs in the same archaeological context because these contradictory forms of behavior coexist among the inhabitants of hostile social environments. . . . The establishment and maintenance of contacts among members of different communities presumably were motivated in part by a desire to stabilize some aspects of a volatile social setting, thereby diminishing the hazards of everyday life." "Warfare in Late Prehistoric West-Central Illinois," *American Antiquity*, LVI (1991), 592. See also Helen Hornbeck Tanner et al., eds., *Atlas of Great Lakes Indian History* (Norman, Okla., 1987), 18–23; Gilles Havard, *Empire et métissages: Indiens et Français dans le Pays d'en Haut, 1660–1715* (Paris, 2003), 124–126.

10. Neal Salisbury, "The Indians' Old World: Native Americans and the Coming of Europeans," *William and Mary Quarterly*, 3d Ser., LIII (1996), 435–458. For Illinois social orga-

The Indians of the Pays d'en Haut have often been depicted as "refugees" whose societies were "shattered" and scattered by a combination of warfare and disease in the mid-seventeenth century, particularly the aggressive Iroquois expansion of the 1640s and 1650s. Yet, aside from the Hurons, a tiny population of true refugees who fled to the heart of the Pays d'en Haut after the Iroquois routed their villages in the late-1640s, all of the region's other peoples maintained ethnic and regional divisions broadly similar to those of the early seventeenth century. The Hurons' dislocation was more of a geographic than a cultural reorientation, as their villages had a long history of trade and cultural interaction with the Anishinaabes and other Algonquian-speakers around Lake Huron. Although villages did move to ensure proximity to resources and allies—as they had always done—Indians' sense of territoriality was rooted much more deeply than European colonizers first understood (or were willing to acknowledge). Far from "irrelevant," as one scholar described their territorial attachments in the late-seventeenth-century Pays d'en Haut, Natives forcefully explained the boundaries of their territory to French observers and fought to maintain control of hunting, fishing, and agricultural sites against their neighbors' pretensions. As Jonathan Carver observed long after Iroquois violence had passed:

> The most uncultivated among them are well acquainted with the rights of their community to the domains they possess, and oppose with vigour every encroachment on them. Notwithstanding it is generally supposed that from their territories being so extensive, the boundaries of them cannot be ascertained, yet I am well assured that the limits of each nation in the interior parts are laid down in their rude plans with great precision.

Rather than scattering in defeat, these peoples responded to Iroquois and other warfare—as well as to new trade opportunities—by moving villages to more secure locations nearby or by forming new defensive alliances. In this atmosphere, conflict over new territorial claims and over access to limited resources produced a new wave of warfare and slave raiding.[11]

nization, see Eric Hinderaker, *Elusive Empires: Constructing Colonialism in the Ohio Valley, 1673-1800* (Cambridge, 1997), 9–13; Charles Callender, "Illinois," in *Handbook*, XV, *Northeast*, 673–680; Callender, *Social Organization of the Central Algonkian Indians* (Milwaukee, Wis., 1962).

11. Jonathan Carver, *Three Years Travels through the Interior Parts of North-America . . .* (Philadelphia, 1789), 213–214. For Natives unmoored by Iroquois violence, see Richard White,

When they arrived in the Pays d'en Haut, French observers themselves misread Indians' annual subsistence cycles as evidence that they had been unmoored by Iroquois warfare. Routine seasonal movement left agricultural settlements all but empty several months a year as residents left summer towns for smaller winter villages that might house only a handful of extended family groups. Generally more difficult to see in the historical and archaeological records, winter villages were essential to Native territoriality, despite being dismissed by the French as mere campgrounds. The presence of multiple ethnic and linguistic groups at strategic trading centers like Green Bay, Michilimackinac, and Sault Sainte Marie also led French writers to overestimate ethnic fluidity in the Pays d'en Haut. Similar to other multiethnic trading centers around the continent—like The Dalles on the Columbia River or the Mandan villages on the Plains—these sites succeeded as trade centers precisely because they drew from a wide array of places and peoples in the region. Stumbling upon these villages and carrying an inflated sense of Iroquois power, French authors interpreted Indians' long-standing cross-cultural relations as Iroquois-induced chaos, even when the intermarriage and village sharing followed established linguistic and geographic patterns. What is more, the French exploited and exaggerated anti-Iroquois sentiments to bolster their own alliance-building efforts. To be sure, western Indians feared the Iroquois, and these fears were only heightened by the arrival of Huron refugees fleeing Iroquois raids. But, far from fundamentally reconfiguring their identities and political economies in response to the Iroquois threat, the peoples of the Pays d'en Haut drew on the strength of long-standing alliances and trade partnerships to protect

---

The Middle Ground: Indians, Empires, and Republics in the Great Lakes Region, 1650–1815 (Cambridge, 1991), 1–49, esp. 1 ("refugees," "shattered"), 17 ("irrelevant"). For earlier expressions of the "refugee" interpretation, see Louise Phelps Kellogg, *The French Régime in Wisconsin and the Northwest* (Madison, Wis., 1925), 103; George T. Hunt, *The Wars of the Iroquois: A Study in Intertribal Relations* (Madison, Wis., 1940), 101; R. David Edmunds, *The Potawatomis: Keepers of the Fire* (Norman, Okla., 1978), 5. For late-seventeenth-century Native territoriality in the Pays d'en Haut, see Havard, *Empire et métissages*, 113–203; Heidi Rosemary Bohaker, "*Nindoodemag:* The Significance of Algonquian Kinship Networks in the Eastern Great Lakes Region, 1600–1701," *WMQ*, 3d Ser., LXIII (2006), 23–52; Bohaker, "*Nindoodemag:* Anishinaabe Identities in the Eastern Great Lakes Region, 1600 to 1900" (Ph.D. diss., University of Toronto, 2006), esp. 12–16; William James Newbigging, "The History of the French-Ottawa Alliance, 1613–1763" (Ph.D. diss., University of Toronto, 1995), esp. 26–82; Andrew K. Sturtevant, "'Inseparable Companions' and Irreconcilable Enemies: The Huron-Wendats and Odawas of French Detroit," *Ethnohistory* (forthcoming). For a similar discussion of the Southwest, see Juliana Barr, "Geographies of Power: Mapping Indian Borders in the 'Borderlands' of the Early Southwest," *WMQ*, 3d Ser., LXVIII (2011), 5–46.

them from this distant but formidable enemy. Slavery played a central role in this strategy, weakening outsiders and strengthening relationships with allied neighbors.[12]

From the confluence of the Missouri and Mississippi Rivers through the Illinois River valley to the southern shores of Lake Michigan, Illinois and Miami villages occupied the most fertile and temperate territory in the Pays d'en Haut. Speaking mutually intelligible dialects of Miami-Illinois (Algonquian), these peoples lived in relatively large agricultural settlements that also controlled key trade routes linking the Great Lakes with the Mississippi and the eastern Plains. People in Miami and Illinois towns traded with and married one another but had no formal political ties beyond the extended kinship cemented by marriage. Generally friendly with the Anishinaabes to the northeast and the Missouris to the west, they had long-standing quarrels with the Foxes and their allies as well as the Sioux to the northwest. Although they would encounter the Iroquois on several occasions as military enemies, Illinois peoples did not flee in terror, moving their villages westward in response to Iroquois warfare. On the contrary, modern archaeological evidence suggests that, if anything, Illinois settlements moved farther up the Illinois River valley, edging closer to the Iroquois in the mid-seventeenth century during the peak of the Iroquois wars in the eastern Great Lakes. Given the growing presence of European goods in the remains of these villages, archaeologists speculate that the Illinois might have repositioned themselves to gain access to European commodities. Whatever the reason, there is no evidence of a shattered political economy or of a widespread westward flight from the Iroquois.[13]

12. Duane Esarey, "Seasonal Occupation Patterns in Illinois History: A Case Study in the Lower Illinois River Valley," *Illinois Archaeology,* IX (1997), 164–219; Bohaker, *"Ninddode-mag:* Anishinaabe Identities," 12–16. For an excellent discussion of Native seasonal movement in the Pays d'en Haut, see Michael J. Witgen, "An Infinity of Nations: How Indians, Empires, and Western Migration Shaped National Identity in North America" (Ph.D. diss., University of Washington, 2004), esp. 23–34, although Witgen draws different conclusions than I do here about the implications of ethnic fluidity.

13. Tanner et al., eds., *Atlas of Great Lakes Indian History,* map 6; J. Joseph Bauxar, "History of the Illinois Area," in *Handbook,* XV, *Northeast,* 594–601; Thomas Emerson and James A. Brown, "The Late Prehistory and Protohistory of Illinois," in John A. Walthall and Thomas E. Emerson, eds., *Calumet and Fleur-de-Lys: Archaeology of Indian and French Contact in the Midcontinent* (Washington, D.C., 1992), 77–128. For Illinois movement in the mid-seventeenth century, see Robert Mazrim and Duane Esarey, "Rethinking the Dawn of History: The Schedule, Signature, Agency of European Goods in Protohistoric Illinois," *Mid-continental Journal of Archaeology,* XXXII (2007), 145–200; Esarey, "Seasonal Occupation Patterns," *Illinois Archaeology,* IX (1997), 164–219.

Villages of the Foxes, Sauks, and Kickapoos, who spoke mutually intelligible Algonquian dialects, dotted the Wisconsin and Fox Rivers north of the Illinois country and west of Lake Michigan. Twentieth-century oral histories recall a period when these peoples lived much farther east, moving westward into the Great Lakes region before Europeans arrived. If these stories are read literally, placing them east of Lake Michigan, Fox westward movement occurred at least a century before the arrival of the French, as both the written and archaeological record places them in Wisconsin by the first half of the seventeenth century. Like the Illinois, these peoples practiced seasonal movement from agricultural to winter hunting villages throughout modern Wisconsin. Pressed between Sioux and Illinois enemies, the Foxes and their cousins compensated by gaining privileged access to Green Bay through an alliance with a collection of Potawatomi villages situated between the bay and the main body of Lake Michigan. Some evidence suggests that Sioux raids from the northwest had compressed the territory of the Fox-led alliance in the mid-seventeenth century, explaining lingering friction between the two groups at the time of French contact.[14]

The Sioux occupied a relatively large territory from the Minnesota River to the lake country in north-central Minnesota. Not yet the horse-mounted bison hunters of the nineteenth century, the eastern Sioux survived on a mixture of hunting, fishing, maple sugaring, and wild rice and oat gathering. They cultivated great quantities of tobacco for their own use and for trade.

14. Based on an overly literal reading of twentieth-century–origin stories, some scholars have argued the Fox-Sauk-Kickapoo grouping moved from modern Michigan to Wisconsin around the mid-seventeenth century, but it conflicts with other evidence showing a longer occupation of the Fox and Wisconsin River valleys. Oral history recalling life on the shores of great waters could also suggest a much shorter move, from the western shores of Lake Michigan to Lake Winnebago and the Fox and Wisconsin River valleys. No identifiable Fox sites have been found east of Lake Michigan, suggesting that the Iroquois wars had little to do with Fox village placement in Wisconsin. See Havard, *Empire et métissages*, 117; Tanner et al., eds., *Atlas of Great Lakes Indian History*, map 6; R. David Edmunds and Joseph L. Peyser, *The Fox Wars: The Mesquakie Challenge to New France* (Norman, Okla., 1993), 3–14; Charles Callender, "Fox," in *Handbook*, XV, *Northeast*, 636–647, and "Sauk," 648–655, and Callender, Richard K. Pope, and Susan M. Pope, "Kickapoo," 656–667. Callender, "Fox," 636, argues that the Foxes' eastern placement relies on "vague traditions and early cartographic data," which were notoriously unreliable. Edmunds and Peyser, *Fox Wars*, 9–10, esp. nn. 11–13, conclude that, at least for the Foxes, the evidence for seventeenth-century residence east of Lake Michigan is unpersuasive. Archaeologist Jeffrey A. Behm recently repeated the "refugee" interpretation of Fox village sites, dating Fox villages based as much on secondary historical accounts as on archaeological markers, in "The Meskwaki in Eastern Wisconsin: Ethnohistory and Archaeology," *Wisconsin Archaeologist*, LXXXIX (2008), 7–85.

Sioux settlements could be quite large at certain times of the year, generally organized as a cluster of smaller hamlets containing fifty or sixty extended family groups. In these more or less permanent residences the Sioux lived in framed bark lodges, but, because regular movement was essential to their subsistence strategy, they traveled with deerskin lodges for easier mobility. "This nation, which is very numerous," wrote an early French trader, "is always wandering, living only by hunting." Although he later qualified this claim by noting the presence of semipermanent villages where the Sioux would gather in spring and summer, he understandably compared the Sioux to more southerly peoples and found them less settled. Thriving on plentiful deer, elk, bison, fish, and wild grains, Sioux villages traded for corn with neighbors who occupied regions more suited to agriculture.[15]

Their Cree (Algonquian) neighbors, in alliance with the Assiniboines (Siouan), competed for control of the northern lakes and access to the northwestern shores of Lake Superior. Settled north and east of the Sioux, in modern northwestern Ontario, the Crees and Assiniboines lived well north of the best agricultural territories and thus relied exclusively on hunting, fishing, gathering, and trade for their subsistence. With access to excellent moose and beaver hunting grounds, however, they also played an important role in trade, linking Lake Superior to Hudson Bay, which sat within relatively easy reach to the northeast. Long-standing conflict plagued their southwestern borderlands, where Cree and Assiniboine territory abutted Sioux hunting lands and fisheries. At some point in the distant past this had, for the Assiniboines, been a fight among Siouan-speaking cousins.[16]

South of the Crees, arcing along the northern shores of Lake Superior and throughout much of modern northern Michigan, a wide array of Anishinaabe peoples lived in semipermanent villages and controlled key portage and trade centers. Speaking closely related dialects of Anishinaabemowin (Algonquian), the Ojibwa and Ottawa communities in this area lived on the Great Lakes' abundant fish, game, wild rice, and maple sugar, cultivat-

15. André Pénicaut, *Relation of M. Penicaut*, ed. Edward D. Neill, trans. A. J. Hill (Minneapolis, Minn., n.d.), 8 ("always wandering"); DeMallie, "The Sioux at the Time of European Contact," in Kan and Strong, eds., *New Perspectives*, 239–260; DeMallie, "Sioux until 1850," in *Handbook*, XIII, *Plains*, part 2, 718–760; Anderson, *Kinsmen of Another Kind*, 1–13; Douglas A. Birk and Elden Johnson, "The Mdewakanton Dakota and Initial French Contact," in Walthall and Emerson, eds., *Calumet and Fleur-de-Lys*, 203–240.

16. Tanner et al.,, eds., *Atlas of Great Lakes Indian History*, map 6; David Meyer, "Time-depth of the Western Woods Cree Occupation of Northern Ontario, Manitoba, and Saskatchewan," in *Papers of the Eighteenth Algonquian Conference* (1987), 187–200.

ing small fields of corn and legumes only rarely because of a short northern growing season. The Ottawa stronghold at Bawating (modern Sault Sainte Marie) provided access to Lakes Huron, Michigan, and Superior and thus had long been a site of trade involving most of the region's peoples, but it remained under Ottawa control both before and after midcentury warfare quickened the usual pace of village movement. Like the Illinois, the Ottawas were, not a single, politically-unified tribe, but rather a collection of closely allied villages with a shared history and clan structure that bound them together over generations. Even in times of disruption and dislocation, these bonds of kin and clan allowed the Anishinaabes to maintain both a persistent sense of community and a remarkable degree of cultural integrity.[17]

Overlaying the cultural and linguistic particularities that separated Ottawas from Sioux, Illinois from Crees, Miamis from Ojibwas, a regional diplomatic culture provided mechanisms for cooperative trade and methods of controlled warfare with enslavement at its center. Reciprocal diplomacy was balanced by reciprocal violence, and over time the form of that violence developed into a widely shared set of practices that one seventeenth-century Jesuit described as the "general custom of the country." According to Antoine Laumet de Lamothe Cadillac, all the region's Indians conducted warfare according to "the same maxim, the same practice, the same mode, and the same manner of fighting." Far from the irrational bloodlust that Europeans would see in these practices, they were, in fact, designed to discourage warfare because war councils knew that they risked their own people's enslavement each time they authorized a raid. Slavery in the Pays d'en Haut was thus indigenous not only because it was practiced by native peoples but because the peoples that practiced it were indigenous to the slave system; they resided in the region where reciprocal slave raiding, trading, and negotiating took place. Living within reach of potential slaves and slavers placed powerful limits on whatever social impulses would argue for violence. Indigenous slavery was thus driven, not by a high demand for slaves, but by the political and cultural imperatives of enslavement.[18]

17. Tanner et al., eds., *Atlas of Great Lakes Indian History*, map 6; Johanna E. Feest and Christian F. Feest, "Ottawa," in *Handbook*, XV, *Northeast*, 772–786, and E. S. Rogers, "Southeastern Ojibwa," 760–771; Bohaker, "*Nindoodemag*: The Significance of Algonquian Kinship Networks," *WMQ*, 3d Ser., LXIII (2006), 23–52; Newbigging, "History of the French-Ottawa Alliance," 25–41.

18. "La meme maxime, meme pratique, meme mode, et meme façon de combattre." Antoine Laumet de Lamothe Cadillac, "Relation du Sieur de la Motte Cadillac," MS, ca. 1693–1697, Newberry Library, Ayer MS 130; *Jesuit Relations*, LVIII, 67.

This regional war culture was most fully articulated in the rituals of the calumet, which balanced the competing impulses of war and peace through slavery. "There is nothing among them either more mysterious or more revered," wrote Jacques Marquette and Louis Joliet in 1681. "One does not give as much respect to the scepters of kings as they give to it; it seems to be the God of peace and war, the arbiter of life and death." Widely recognized as the central diplomatic ritual performed in the seventeenth-century Pays d'en Haut, the calumet was believed to originate among the Pawnees in the Missouri River valley, having been "communicated from village to village as far as the Outaoüas [Ottawas]" by the time the French arrived. Practiced by all the peoples of the region, the ceremonies associated with the calumet facilitated trade and diplomacy among friends by expressing a commitment to violence against common enemies. At every stage of what often became a multiday ceremony, the calumet drew upon enslavement as the earthly expression of otherworldly powers harnessed to protect and unite the ceremony's hosts and their guests.[19]

"This *calumet*," explained Louis Hennepin, "is a type of large smoking pipe, with a head of beautiful, well-polished, red stone, with a shaft two-and-a-half feet long made from a very strong reed, decorated with feathers of all types and colors, mingled and arranged with great care, with several locks of women's hair arranged in different ways with two wings." The pipe embodied the mystical and practical impulses that converged to produce the ritual's power. Its otherworldly symbolism was difficult for Europeans to read: according to one late-seventeenth-century writer, it was "the most mysterious Thing in the World." However limited their understanding, all French observers agreed that Indians believed it carried sacred powers. The Jesuit Pierre Le Sueur, who lived among the Sioux at the end of the seventeenth century, judged the calumet "a true religious cult," and trader and colonial official Claude-Charles de La Potherie wrote that the calumet was held "very sacred among these peoples."[20]

---

19. "Il n'est rien parmy eux ni de plus mysterieux ni de plus recommendable, on ne rend pas tant d'honneur aux sceptres des Rois qu'ils luy en rendent, il semble estre le Dieu de la paix et de la guerre, l'arbitre de la vie et de la mort." Jacques Marquette and Louis Joliet, *Voyage et découverte de quelques pays et nations de l'Amérique Septentrionale* (Paris, 1681), 23; Nicolas Perrot, *Memoir on the Manners, Customs, and Religion of the Savages of North America*, in Emma Helen Blair, ed. and trans., *The Indian Tribes of the Upper Mississippi Valley and Region of the Great Lakes* (Cleveland, 1911–1912), I, 186 ("communicated").

20. "Ce Calumet est une espece de grande pipe à fumer, dont la teste est d'une belle pierre rouge bien polie, dont le tuyau long de deux pieds et demy, est une Canne assé forte, ornée de

FIGURE 4. Man Holding a Calumet. *Louis Hennepin, Nouvelle découverte d'un très grande pays situé dans l'Amériques. Utrecht, 1697. Courtesy Special Collections Research Center, Swem Library, College of William and Mary*

Miami-Illinois–speakers called the calumet "ap8agana," and its shaft "ap8acanti," referring to the feathers with which the shaft was wrapped, drawing manit, or spiritual power, from these beings that lived between heaven and earth and therefore bridged the two worlds. The smoke, too, linked the sky world with land, drawing upon the power of the sun, which had grown the tobacco, by ingesting and then offering back the smoke from the plant. Indians sometimes made calumets in pairs, one painted

---

plumes de toute sorte de couleurs, meslées et ranges fort proprement, avec plusieurs nattes de cheveux de femmes, lassées de diverses manieres avec deux aisles": Hennepin, *Description de la Louisiane,* 80; Hennepin, *New Discovery,* I, 74 ("most mysterious"). For Le Sueur, see William A. Turnbaugh, "Calumet Ceremonialism as a Nativistic Response," *American Antiquity,* XLIV (1979), 688. "C'est un lien si Sacré parmi ces peoples": [Claude-Charles] Bacqueville de La Potherie, *Histoire de l'Amérique Septentrionale* (Paris, 1722), II, 15 [13] ("very sacred).

green and the other blue to represent the earth and sky, emblematic of the calumet's power to bring otherworldly power to bear on worldly matters. Alliances confirmed in a calumet ceremony thus represented far more than practical political agreements. They were sacred bonds, and those who violated them risked disaster. "They are persuaded," according to Hennepin, "that great misfortune would befall them were they to violate the faith of the calumet." La Potherie went even further, claiming that they believed that "whoever violates a Calumet shall perish, and incur the indignation of the Gods who have allowed the power of the Sun to give light to the earth."[21]

If the mystical power of the calumet came from another world, it derived much of its social authority from its physical creation. Because producing the pipe and the ceremonies that accompanied it demanded complex labor and coordination within the hosting village, calumet ceremonialism ensured broad participation—of both men and women—in diplomacy and broad support for the agreements reached. As each calumet took great effort to craft, only a limited number of calumets circulated. From killing ducks, birds of prey, porcupines, and sometimes rabbits to cutting cane reeds, quarrying, polishing, and boring out the pipe bowl without the advantage of metal tools, calumet production was a serious effort that drew upon—and drew in—all segments of society. Female artists decorated each calumet with distinctive marks to allow others to know its origins. According to one early account, "Every Nation adorns the *Calumet* as they think fit according to their own Genius and the Birds they have in their Country." Pierre-François-Xavier de Charlevoix agreed: "They say that according to the Manner in which the Feathers are disposed, they immediately know what Nation it is that presents it." Jacques Marquette experienced this aspect of calumet ceremonialism when he approached a Michigamea (Illinois) village downriver from the Peoria village that had given him a calumet. Sighting the French from a distance, the Michigameas readied for

21. Jacques Gravier and Jacques Largillier, "Dictionnaire illinois-français," MS, ca. 1690s, Watkinson Library Special Collections, Trinity College, Hartford, Conn., 46 ("ap8agana," "ap8acanti"); Perrot, *Memoir*, in Blair, ed. and trans., *Indian Tribes*, I, 186. "Tous ces Barbares sont généralement qu'il leur arriveroit de grands malheurs, s'ils avoient violé la foy du Calumet": Hennepin, *Nouvelle découverte*, 151. "Quicon'que viole un Calumet doit perir, et il s'attire en même tems l'indignation des Dieux qui ont laissé le pouvoir au Soleil d'éclairer la terre, et ne peuvent soufrir qu'un perfide fasse rien de contraire au Calumet qui est le gage de la Paix": Bacqueville de La Potherie, *Histoire de l'Amérique Septentrionale*, II, 14–15. For paired calumets, see Robert L. Hall, *An Archaeology of the Soul: North American Indian Belief and Ritual* (Urbana, Ill., 1997), 50–52.

attack despite Marquette's theatrical presentation of a calumet held above his head. Only when Marquette drew close enough for the Michigameas to recognize the pipe as a product of their Peoria allies did they stand down and welcome Marquette into their village. The labor of the Peorias who had produced Marquette's pipe fixed their commitment to its recipient and provided a visual endorsement of the foreigner to others within their alliance.[22]

The calumet was also embedded in a ceremonial complex that transcended the pipe's physical creation. Generally understood as an instrument of peace, the calumet's power was expressed through the violent imagery of enslavement. The ceremony occurred in four stages, sometimes lasting as long as two or three days. In the first stage, the chief offering the calumet gathered his people to welcome the guest to whom the pipe was being offered, and some of them formed either a circle or square within which the ceremonies would take place. The chief held the calumet to the sun, took several deep draughts, and blew the smoke toward the sky. The guests were then invited to smoke the pipe as a sign of their unity and shared power. In the third—and by far the longest—stage of the calumet ceremony, individual warriors entered the circle or square and began to "dance the calumet." After calling on his guardian spirits, the performer mimed the act of killing and capturing his enemies, using the pipe shaft as a simulated weapon against other dancers. This was done so gracefully, according to Jacques Marquette, that it "might pass for a very fine opening of a Ballet in France."[23]

Each warrior then retold, one by one, the story of every slave he had taken since becoming a warrior. "The third Scene," Marquette explained, "consists of a lofty Discourse, delivered by him who holds the Calumet . . . he recounts the battles at which he has been present, the victories that he has won, and the names of the Nations, the places, and the Captives whom he has made." The message was clear: his manitous, whose feathers adorned the pipe, gave him power over his enemies and would continue to do so. Accept our friendship, he implied, or suffer the fate of those whose stories I have told. He then offered slaves as a gift to ratify the alliance, bodies of

22. Hennepin, *New Discovery*, I, 74 ("every nation adorns"); "Chaque Nation l'embellissant selon son usage . . . particulier": Hennepin, *Nouvelle découverte*, 150; and [Pierre François-Xavier de] Charlevoix, *Letters to the Dutchess of Lesdiguieres; Giving an Account of a Voyage to Canada, and Travels through That Vast Country, and Louisiana, to the Gulf of Mexico* (London, 1763), 134 ("immediately know"). For the Michigameas, see Hall, *Archaeology of the Soul*, 7.

23. *Jesuit Relations*, LIX, 135–137.

evidence that his people would be a powerful ally or, if necessary, a dreaded enemy.[24]

Produced by the hosting village, bearing symbols of otherworldly power, and accompanied by slaves and other gifts, the calumet generated its symbolic meaning face-to-face, limited to the relatively small region where it was recognized and practiced. The farther one moved from the village where the pipe was created, the less likely one would be to find others who would recognize its marks and therefore be able to know the lines of alliance it represented. Louis-Armand de Lom d'Arce, baron de Lahontan, experienced these regional limits firsthand. Having been given a calumet as a token of friendship, probably by an Illinois village, he headed up the Missouri River. Upon reaching the village of a people he identified as "Gnacsitares," he produced the pipe, hoping it would signify his peaceful intentions and demonstrate his desire for alliance. His hosts did not react as he had anticipated. "Here ended the Credit and Authority of the Calumet of Peace," he wrote, "for the *Gnacsitares* are not acquainted with that Symbol of Concord." Underscoring the regional limits of this war culture, Lahontan's experience provides a valuable reminder that, in the seventeenth century, calumet ceremonialism was practiced only in the western Great Lakes and Mississippi Valley.[25]

Simultaneously symbolizing war and peace, performing violence to cement friendship, the calumet was an apt shorthand for the larger forces that Great Lakes war culture worked to balance. Those who quarried its stone, decorated its shaft, or provided and prepared food for the accompanying feasts joined in both the collective expression of friendship and the collective memory of war. These significant investments in time and resources gave everyone a stake in the maintenance of the peace that the ceremonies established or in the support of the warfare they celebrated. As the narrative center of the calumet dance and the punctuation at its conclusion, slaves

24. *Jesuit Relations*, LIX, 137.
25. [Louis-Armand de Lom d'Arce], Baron de Lahontan, *New Voyages to North-America* (London, 1703), I, 121 ("Gnacsitares"). For a new interpretation of Lahontan's journey up the Missouri, see Peter Wood, "Lahontan's Letter XVI: Frenchmen on the Missouri River in 1688," paper, Annual Conference of the Omohundro Institute of Early American History and Culture, Quebec, 2006. For the geographic limits of calumet ceremonialism, see Ian W. Brown, "The Calumet Ceremony in the Southeast and Its Archaeological Manifestations," *American Antiquity*, LIV (1989), 311–331; Louis André, "Preceptes, phrases, et mots de la langue algonquine outaouaise pour un missionnaire nouveau," ca. 1688, MS, John Wesley Powell Library of Anthropology, Smithsonian Institution, Washington, D.C. (the original is located in the Archives des Jésuites au Canada, Montreal).

stood at the heart of both Natives' regional war culture and the diplomacy that kept warfare from overtaking the region.

NIT'AOUAKARA — I MAKE HIM MY DOG / MY SLAVE

"This reception is very cruel; some tear out the prisoners' nails, others cut off their fingers or ears; still others load them with blows from clubs."
—Sébastien Rale, Jesuit, 1723

Indians of the Pays d'en Haut expressed their relationship to slaves through metaphors of domestication and mastery, comparing captives to dogs and other domesticated animals. More than a simple insult, the metaphorical domestication of enemy captives represented an elaborate cultural idiom that shaped the practice and defined the meaning of indigenous slavery. To shame and intimidate their enemies, Algonquians and Siouans treated their prisoners with great disrespect through symbolic acts of humiliation designed to strip them of their former identities and incorporate them as subordinate domestics. Beginning with demeaning abuse on the journey home, continuing through acts of torture as captives were received into the village, and culminating in ceremonial killing or forced incorporation, Indians designed their rituals of enslavement to demonstrate their mastery over weaker enemies and to secure the allegiance and passivity of those they would keep alive as slaves.

Anishinaabe-speakers called their slaves *awakaan,* which meant "captive," "dog," or "animals kept as pets." The earliest French lexicon of central Algonquian languages, recorded between 1672 and 1674 by Jesuit Father Louis Nicolas, included *aouakan,* meaning "slave or prisoner of war," as one of eight essential nouns for missionaries to know to effectively teach western Indians. After living among the Anishinaabes of Michilimackinac and Sault Sainte Marie, Lahontan composed his own dictionary of essential Anishinaabe terms, listing *Ouackan* for "slave."[26]

26. John D. Nichols and Earl Nyholm, *A Concise Dictionary of Minnesota Ojibwe* (Minneapolis, Minn., 1995), 14; Frederic Baraga, *A Dictionary of the Otchipwe Language, Explained in English* (Cincinnati, Ohio, 1853), 49–50, 453; C. Douglas Ellis, *Âtalôhkâna nêsta tipâcimôwina: Cree Legends and Narratives from the West Coast of James Bay* (Winnipeg, 1995), 55, 85, 159, 449. Although there are many variant spellings of *awakaan,* I use Nichols and Nyholm's version as the most recent standardization of the orthography. For Nicolas, see Diane Daviault, ed., *L'algonquin au XVIIe siécle: une édition critique, analysée et commentée de la grammaire algonquine du Père Louis Nicolas* (Sainte-Foy, Que., 1994), 5, 34, 106–107; [Louis-Armand de Lom d'Arce], Baron de Lahontan, *Voyages du Bon de Lahontan dans*

The most-advanced French linguist of Anishinaabemowin in the seventeenth century was Louis André, a Jesuit trained in Latin linguistics and later a linguistics professor at Quebec's Jesuit college. Living in several Native villages and working closely with Ottawa informants, he conducted a fourteen-year study of their language and produced an eight-hundred-page manuscript dictionary and phrase book designed to teach other missionaries the language. André recorded dozens of Anishinaabe terms and phrases relating to slavery, most of which expressed the metaphor of slaves as domestic animals. André wrote that the verb to enslave *(nit'aouakara),* for example, literally meant to make someone a dog. Often rendered in the first person possessive, it described enslavement as an act of animal domestication: to say "I make him my slave" was to say "I make him my dog." One of the most intriguing variations of this verb was translated by another Jesuit among the Ottawas as "I make him my plaything, my slave." Rendered in the diminutive form, it could be translated more literally as "I make him my little dog / puppy."[27]

Miami-Illinois–speakers also equated slaves with dogs, their most common domesticated animal. One Miami-Illinois word for slave was *arem8a,* meaning, in the words of the Jesuit Jacques Gravier, "dog, all domestic animals, and, as a term of contempt, slave." Gravier defined a female equivalent of this word, *ac8essem8a,* as "heifer, bitch, female animal." If dogs or slaves

---

l'Amérique Septentrionale (Amsterdam, 1705), II, 321. Jonathan Carver echoed Lahontan's spelling in his own word list more than sixty years later: "Esclave. Ouackan." See Carver, *Voyage dans les parties intérieures de l'Amérique Septentrionale pendant les années 1766, 1767, et 1768* (Yverdon, Switzerland, 1784), 312.

Linguists tend to distinguish between words' historically recorded forms and their standardized spellings by placing those words quoted from historical sources in quotation marks and placing standardized non-English words in italics. I break from that convention here—by generally italicizing all Algonquian words—for two reasons. First, because the Miami-Illinois language lost most of its native speakers quite early, it has relatively few standardized words, and none of the Algonquian languages has standardized forms for much of the seventeenth-century vocabularies I discuss here. Second, the large number of Algonquian words in the text would make the use of quotation marks cumbersome, interfering with the narrative rather than clarifying its meaning. Algonquian words quoted from historical sources are spelled as they were recorded in the original manuscript or printed text.

27. "Je le fais esclave": André, "Preceptes, phrases, et mots de la langue algonquine outaouaise," s.v. "esclave." "J'en fais mon joüet, mon esclave": Pierre Du Jaunay, "Dictionarium gallico-outaouakum," MS, 1748, copy in Smithsonian Institution Anthropology Library, s.v. "esclave." Du Jaunay also confirms André's translation of *nit'aouakara:* "nit'a8akan. mon [esclave] nit'a8akara. Je le fais esclave."

ran free, Miami-Illinois–speakers would say *acha8e nitaïa:* "my dog, animal, slave runs around." The word *nitaïa*—literally "my possession"—had one meaning that Gravier translated as "my domestic animal, my dog, my cat, also my slave."[28]

The act of domestication—turning enemies into dogs—began even before the warriors left their village for the raid. Raids originated in communal, and quite often contested, discussions of issues ranging from the need for retaliation to preemptive raids designed to weaken a threatening enemy. Among the Illinois, elder male relatives of anyone killed by an outsider could call a council and demand revenge. "If my strength and my courage equalled yours, I believe that I would go to avenge a relative as brave and as good as he was," one Illinois elder said in a late-seventeenth-century war council. "But being as feeble as I am, I cannot do better than address myself to you," the young warriors. He persuaded them to fight by appealing to their sense of collective revenge and individual masculine honor.[29]

Louis Hennepin witnessed similar negotiations among the eastern Sioux, seeing for himself the beginning of a process that had led to his own enslavement. The warrior or family initiating the raid sent invitations around the village, and sometimes to neighboring villages, to join in a war feast. Accepting this invitation meant accepting the call to war. Those who wished to join the war party gathered at the home of the one who invited them, singing their warrior songs as they arrived. In these songs, Sioux men recounted their deeds of bravery and recalled the captives they had taken, vowing similar success on this raid: "I am going to War, I will revenge the Death of such a Kinsman, I will slay, I will burn, I will bring away Slaves, I will eat Men." A feast and dance followed, called by the Sioux *šunkahlowanpi*—literally

28. "Chien, tte beste domestique et par mepris esclave"; "genisse, chienne, femelle de beste": Gravier and Largillier, "Dictionnaire illinois-français," 10. Anishinaabemowin also occasionally employed the term "alemwa" for dog, suggesting a proto-Algonquian origin. See, for example, André, "Preceptes, phrases, et mots de la langue algonquine outaouaise," s.v. "chien." For "Acha8e nitaïa," see Gravier and Largillier, "Dictionnaire illinois-français," 1. Carl Masthay, *Kaskaskia Illinois-to-French Dictionary* (Saint Louis, Mo., 2002), 47, translates the phrase as "my dog, animal, servant runs here and there," inexplicably substituting the English "servant" for the original French "esclave," or "slave." For *nitaïa*, see Gravier and Largillier, "Dictionnaire illinois-français," 14.

29. Pierre Deliette, "Memoir of De Gannes [Deliette] concerning the Illinois Country," in Theodore Calvin Pease and Raymond C. Werner, ed. and trans., *The French Foundations, 1680-1693*, Collections of the Illinois State Historical Library, XXIII (Springfield, Ill., 1934), 377 (hereafter cited as Deliette, "Memoir").

"ceremonial song of the dog"—described by later Sioux informants as "a parade with singing made by those who are on the point of going to war."[30]

Eating men and taking slaves expressed the central theme of the *šunkahlowanpi* and other war feasts in the Pays d'en Haut. As Pierre-François-Xavier de Charlevoix explained, warriors "say also in direct Words, that they are going to *eat a Nation;* to signify, that they will make a cruel War against it; and it seldom happens otherwise." The metaphorical equation of eating men and taking slaves found its physical expression in the ritual consumption of dog meat, which was the centerpiece of the warriors' feast that preceded the raid. "This feast is one of dog's flesh," explained Nicolas Perrot of the rite among the Anishinaabes, "which [among them] is ranked as the principal and most esteemed of all viands. . . . Feasts of this sort are usually made only on the occasion of a war, or of other enterprises in which they engage when on expeditions against their enemies." The practice was so entrenched in the Pays d'en Haut that one colonial official concluded, "The feast of dogs is the true war feast among all the savages." Dog feasts sometimes continued into the journey toward an enemy's territory, and evidence suggests that war parties sometimes killed and ate enemy dogs as a sign of power over them.[31]

Illinois warriors followed a similar logic in the ceremonial songs, dances, and feasts preceding slave raids. "When they wish to go to war," Pierre Deliette explained, a chief "offers them a feast, usually of dog." Then, "when the women see that they are preparing for this dance, they lead away all their dogs to a distance, for any of them that they find they kill and feast on." The ritual consumption of dogs takes on new meaning in light of Illinois and other Algonquian terminology for slaves as dogs. Because enemies, once conquered and domesticated, assumed the social position of dogs, they were considered *awakaan, arem8a, nitaïa,* just as the animals were. The departing warriors thus performed their intention to both destroy and consume their enemies—the dogs, the slaves—in the coming raid.[32]

30. Hennepin, *New Discovery*, II, 72; Eugene Buechel and Paul Manhart, *Lakota Dictionary: Lakota-English / English-Lakota* (Lincoln, Nebr., 2002), 191, 291.

31. Charlevoix, *Letters to the Dutchess of Lesdiguieres*, 131 ("eat a nation"); Perrot, *Memoir*, in Blair, ed. and trans., *Indian Tribes*, 53–54 ("most esteemed"); Antoine Denis Raudot, "Memoir concerning the Different Indian Nations of North America," in W. Vernon Kinietz, ed., *The Indians of the Western Great Lakes, 1615–1760* (Ann Arbor, Mich., 1940), 403 ("true war feast"); Henri Joutel, *The La Salle Expedition to Texas: The Journal of Henri Joutel, 1684–1687*, ed. William C. Foster, trans. Johanna S. Warren (Austin, Tex., 1998), 119.

32. Deliette, "Memoir," 376–377, 387. This tradition is also summarized in John A. Walt-

When captured, slave raiders could find their own logic turned disastrously against them. An Ottawa war chief named Sinagos, who had a reputation as a brutal slaver, conducted a raid in Sioux territory in the early 1670s, "putting the men to flight and carrying away the women and children whom they found there." Those who escaped the raid gathered reinforcements who pursued and captured Sinagos and the surviving captives. Recognizing his prominence, the Sioux decided to make an example of him rather than kill or enslave him. "They made him go to a repast," wrote Nicolas Perrot, "and, cutting pieces of flesh from his thighs and all other parts of his body, broiled these and gave them to him to eat—informing Sinagos that, as he had eaten so much human flesh and shown himself so greedy for it, he might now satiate himself upon it by eating his own."[33]

Because Indians imagined enslavement as the violent consumption of flesh, they compared freeing captives to vomiting: a violent release of the flesh they had eaten. When a Fox war chief entertained a French delegation in the 1680s, he offered his French guest some venison. When the Frenchman refused on the grounds that he was unhappy with Fox slave raids against French-allied Indians, the Fox man called for four captives, whom he released to his French guest. "Here is how reasonable the Fox can be . . . he vomits up the meat that he had intended to eat . . . even as it is between his teeth he spits it out, he asks you to return it to where he captured it." Jacques Gravier recorded an expression for releasing captives among the Illinois: "nisicarintamaꙕa ac8i8ssemahi. je done la vie a cinq prisoniers," I give life to five prisoners. The Algonquian verb means "to vomit."[34]

Carrying mental images drawn from this rich verbal and ceremonial milieu, warriors began their journey to enemy territory seeking slaves to domesticate. In the indigenous war culture of the Pays d'en Haut, taking captives took precedence over killing enemies and especially over territorial conquest, which was extremely rare. "When a Savage returns to his own country laden with many scalps, he is received with great honor," wrote Sé-

---

hall, F. Terry Norris, and Barbara D. Stafford, "Woman Chief's Village: An Illini Winter Hunting Camp," in Walthall and Emerson, eds., *Calumet and Fleur de Lys*, 149. The authors found the charred remains of dogs in ceremonial fire pits, providing additional evidence of this practice.

33. Perrot, *Memoir*, in Blair, ed. and trans., *Indian Tribes*, 189, 190.

34. "Le Chef prenant la parole dit, voici en quoi l'Outagamis peut être raisonnable . . . il vomit la viande qu'il a eû dessein de manger . . . et l'ayant entre ses dents il la crache, il te prie de la remettre où il l'a prise." Bacqueville de La Potherie, *Histoire de l'Amérique Septentrionale*, II, 214; Gravier and Largillier, "Dictionnaire illinois-français," 527 ("to vomit").

bastien Rale, "but he is at the height of his glory when he takes prisoners and brings them home alive." Such feats of bravery, Rale explained, allowed a warrior to be considered "truly a man." "They are so eager for this glory that we see them undertake journeys of four hundred leagues through the midst of forests in order to capture a slave."[35]

Once warriors carried captives a safe distance away from a raided village, they bound them tightly by the hands and neck with a halter. Keeping the captives' legs free except when they slept, the captors "immediately tie their hands and compel them to run on before at full speed, fearing that they may be pursued . . . by the companions of those whom they are taking away." Louis Hennepin explained the danger of slowing the captors down. "When they have taken a slave, they garrote him and make him run," he wrote shortly after his own release from slavery among the Sioux. "If he cannot keep up they strike him on the head . . . and scalp him." This was a second wave of sorting strong captives from those who might become an immediate liability or a long-term drain on local resources. The old and infirm were rarely taken from the village, and the necessity of running, bound, for long stretches with little food ensured another level of fitness for surviving slaves.[36]

When the retreating party stopped for the night, captors staked their prisoners to the ground. Pierre Boucher, who traded extensively with Great Lakes Algonquians and spoke several of their dialects, described the restraints in 1664:

When [the Indians of New France] capture prisoners . . . they bind them by the arms and by the legs with cords; except when they are marching, they leave the legs free.

In the evening, when they camp, they lay the prisoners with their backs against the ground, and they plant some small stakes in the earth next to the feet, the hands, the neck, and the head; then they bind the prisoner to these stakes so tightly that he cannot move, which is more painful than one can imagine.

---

35. Raudot, "Memoir," in Kinietz, ed., *Indians of the Western Great Lakes*, 355–356. For the Rale quote, see *Jesuit Relations*, LXVII, 171–173.

36. "Quand ils ont pris un esclave, ils le garotttent *[sic]* et le font courir; s'il ne peut les suivre, ils luy donnent un coup de hache à la teste et le laissent après luy avoir enlevé la peruque ou cheveleure": Hennepin, *Déscription de la Louisiane*, 63; *Jesuit Relations*, LXVI, 275 ("tie their hands").

FIGURE 5. Native Captives in the Mississippi Valley. *Vincenzo Coronelli, Partie occidentale du Canada ou de la Nouvelle France. Paris, 1688. Courtesy Library and Archives of Canada, Ottawa*

Binding served the obvious practical purpose of preventing escape, but it also symbolized the victim's powerlessness and inferiority. These were tamed creatures, captured in the wild and brought home to domesticate.[37]

In one illustration, drawn on a 1688 map drafted from several travel accounts and personal interviews, a captive is shown kneeling, tethered to a stake by the neck like a dog, being beaten from behind with a stick. Another captive is kneeling with her hands bound in front, attached to a tumpline in her captor's hands. In the emerging sign language of the eastern Plains, which included Sioux, Missouri, and even some Illinois territory, the word "slave" was signed by wrapping the thumb and middle finger of one hand around the wrist of the other and pulling the arm away from the body, implying physical control of the body and domination of the will. Supporting the interpretation of captive restraints as leashes, the Anishinaabes described releasing captives as "cut[ting] the cords on the dogs."[38]

Led along by a leash, captives faced physical and verbal abuse during their long march to the captors' village. An Illinois warrior might refer to a slave he had captured as *ninessacanta*, "my slave, the one whom I bring,"

37. [Pierre Boucher], *Histoire veritable et naturelle des moeurs et productions du pays de la Nouvelle France, vulgairement dite le Canada* (Paris, 1664), 123–124. For Boucher's familiarity with Native cultures, see Raymond Douville, "Boucher, Pierre," *DCB*, II. See also *Jesuit Relations*, XLVIII, 101–103. For the Illinois, see *Jesuit Relations*, LXVI, 273–275; Deliette, "Memoir," 381. For the Sioux, Ojibwas, and Ottawas, see Hennepin, *Description de la Louisiane*, 64.

38. Vincenzo Coronelli, "Partie occidentale du Canada ou de la Nouvelle France" (Paris, 1688), NMC-6411, LAC; Claude Charles Le Roy, Bacqueville de La Potherie, *History of the Savage Peoples Who Are Allies of France*, in Blair, ed. and trans., *Indian Tribes*, II, 39–41 ("cut the cords"). For sign language, see Garrick Mallery, *A Collection of Gesture-Signs and Signals of the North American Indians, with Some Comparisons* (Washington, D.C., 1880), 205–206, 236.

a phrase drawn from the root word "to beat, batter, bludgeon" and, occasionally, "to beat to death." Louis Hennepin found his repeated beatings more terrifying than debilitating, enhancing his captors' arbitrary power by making him fear constantly for his life. Indeed, the march northward to the Sioux villages was so disorienting for Hennepin that he lost all sense of place and distance, sketching on his return to Europe a map of the Upper Mississippi Valley that stretched it hundreds of miles north of its headwaters. Copied by several subsequent cartographers, Hennepin's bewilderment registered in European cartography long after his release from captivity.[39]

As the returning warriors neared their village, the war chief signaled their arrival with a series of high-pitched cries, one for each captive in the party. In some accounts, individual warriors also cried out once for each of the captives they had taken. "As soon as he arrives, all the people of the village meet together, and range themselves on both sides of the way where the prisoners must pass," wrote Sébastien Rale. "This reception is very cruel; some tear out the prisoners' nails, others cut off their fingers or ears; still others load them with blows from clubs." Among the most degrading of the gauntlet's many torments was the participation of women and children, whose taunts fell with special poignancy on captured male warriors. Like the ceremonies that initiated the slave raid, the logic of subordination required that captives' incorporation into village society be a public affair involving all segments of Native society.[40]

39. Gravier and Largillier, "Dictionnaire illinois-français," 28, 340. The first map influenced by Hennepin's information was a 1681 Paris map titled *Carte de la Nouvelle France,* which could have been drawn only from Hennepin because of its placement of the "Issati," or Sioux villages. Derek Hayes, *America Discovered: A Historical Atlas of North American Exploration* (Vancouver, 2004), map 92. Hennepin's own map, first published in his 1683 *Déscription de la Louisiane,* was reprinted several times into the early eighteenth century, including in his *Nouvelle découverte* (1697 and subsequent editions).

40. *Jesuit Relations,* LXVII, 173. Rale speculated that the Illinois adopted these cruelties only after their similar treatment as captives of the Iroquois: "It was the Iroquois who invented this frightful manner of death, and it is only by the law of retaliation that the Illinois, in their turn, treat these Iroquois prisoners with an equal cruelty." See *Jesuit Relations,* LXVII, 173–175. This statement should be assessed cautiously, however, as the French frequently minimized the violence of their allies and exaggerated that of the Iroquois. See, for example, a report from 1660 that describes French-allied Indians' tearing out fingernails, cutting off fingers, and burning hands and feet at Quebec, dismissed by another Jesuit as "merely the game and diversion of children" (*Jesuit Relations,* XLVI, 85–101, esp. 93). "Tout le Village assiste à cette derniere Ceremonie" (Bacqueville de La Potherie, *Histoire de l'Amérique Septentrionale,* II, 26). For a description of the gauntlet among eastern Algonquians,

Those disfigured by the gauntlet bore permanent marks of their status as a captive enemy, especially when such wounds occurred in conspicuous locations like the face or hands. Maiming the hands also served another purpose: preventing escape or rebellion. Describing a similar strategy used by the Iroquois, one Jesuit observed, "They began by cutting off a thumb of each [captive], to make them unable to unbind themselves." According to one account, Algonquians adopted this practice to avenge those captured by their Iroquois enemies. The resulting scarring and disfiguration were considered "the marks of their captivity," which remained with living captives long after the trauma of initiation had passed.[41]

Strategic slave marking registered in the Algonquian languages of the Pays d'en Haut. The Anishinaabes used a phrase that Louis André translated as "I cut a young slave to mark him." The Illinois had a whole family of expressions dealing with personal marking of slave bodies, all derived from the root word *isc8*, meaning "mark of imperfection / defect." These included *isc8chita*, "someone who has a cropped ear"; *isc8chipag8ta*, "bitten on the ear, ear removed with the teeth"; *nitisc8ic8rep8a*, "I crop his nose with my teeth." Other Indians of the Pays d'en Haut marked men in an especially painful way, using "red-hot javelins, with which they pierced the most sensitive parts of his body." Even these physical markers of slavery narrated the act of enslavement as domestication, emphasizing the very personal power exercised over these enemies by capturing warriors. Like enslavement itself, biting the tip from a captive's nose or ear was at once an alienating and terribly intimate act of dominion.[42]

Nose cropping might have survived from a Mississippian rite of incorporation that turned dangerous outsiders into domesticated insiders, claim-

---

see James Axtell, "The White Indians of Colonial America," *WMQ*, 3d Ser., XXXII (1975), 70–71. For the Iroquois, see Daniel K. Richter, "War and Culture: The Iroquois Experience," *WMQ*, 3d Ser., XL (1983), 557.

41. *Jesuit Relations*, L, 39 ("cutting off a thumb"), XLV, 257 ("marks"). For the best description of Iroquoian disfiguration, see Roland Viau, *Enfants du néant et mangeurs d'âmes: guerre, culture, et société en Iroquoisie ancienne* (Montreal, 1997), 172–186; William A. Starna and Ralph Watkins, "Northern Iroquoian Slavery," *Ethnohistory*, XXXVIII (1991), 43–45. For additional examples from the Pays d'en Haut, see *Jesuit Relations*, XLVIII, 85–101, LXVIII, 171–175. For hand mutilation, see also Gravier and Largillier, "Dictionnaire illinois-français," 176.

42. "Je coupe un jeu[n] esclave pour marquer": André, "Preceptes, phrases, et mots de la langue algonquine outaouaise," s.v. "marquer." "Qui a l'oreille coupée"; "mordu a l'oreille, oreille emportee avec les dents"; "je luy coupe le nés avec les dents": Gravier and Largillier, "Dictionnaire illinois-français," 111, 176. *Jesuit Relations*, XLVIII, 99 ("red-hot javelins").

ing warriors' spiritual power for the capturing village. Ancient Cahokian iconography includes prominent examples of a figure known as the "long-nosed god" that adorned amulets and earrings, many of which had bent or cropped noses. Archaeologists link this imagery to traditions in the Pays d'en Haut of potent spirit beings called "thunderers," who were sometimes twins, one domesticated and the other wild and threatening. Cropping the nose of the wild thunderer tamed him and transferred his significant power to the dominating village. Consistent with the intent of enslavement generally, this rite expressed the prowess of the captor while appropriating the power of the captive. Perhaps this is why enemy warriors perceived as especially threatening were made to "suffer according to their Merits." Those who cried out during torture were considered less potent and thus less worthy of an honorable death. "When a victim does not die like a brave man," according to Charlevoix, "he receives his death's wound from a woman or from children; he is unworthy, say they, to die by the hands of men." Even in death male captives faced the prospect of emasculation from their enemies.[43]

After being beaten and marked, slaves were undressed and forced to sing (in some cases the singing began before entering the village). This was the final metaphorical act of stripping slaves' former identities from them, preparing them for death or the forced integration that would follow. At least one Algonquian language made explicit the connection between the humiliation of stripping and slavery: Illinois-speakers used the phrase *niki8i-nakiha arena,* which meant both "I lift up his loin cloth" and "I treat him like a slave."[44]

Once the initial tortures subsided, another round of sorting divided captives marked for death from those who would stay alive as slaves. Among the Illinois, male heads of household "assemble and decide what they will do with the prisoner who has been given to them, and whether they wish to give him his life." Hennepin came to understand that his fate had been decided in the same way among the Sioux. "When the warriors have entered their lodges, all the elders assemble to hear the account of all that has happened in the war, then they dispose of the slaves. If the father of an Indian

43. For the long-nosed god and thunderers, see James R. Duncan, "Of Masks and Myths," *Midcontinental Journal of Archaeology,* XXV (2000), 1–26. Hennepin, *New Discovery,* I, 186 ("according to their Merits"). P. de Charlevoix, *Journal of a Voyage to North-America* (London, 1761), II, 107.

44. "Je luy oste son brayet, la traite en esclave": Gravier and Largillier, "Dictionnaire illinois-français," 209.

FIGURE 6. "Woman Who Condemns to Death the Prisoner Given to Her" and "Woman Who Gives Life to the Prisoner Given to Her." *[Louis-Armand de Lom d'Arce], baron de Lahontan, Nouveaux voyages . . . dans l'Amérique Septentrionale. The Hague, 1703. Courtesy Special Collections Research Center, Swem Library, College of William and Mary*

woman was killed by their enemies, they give [her] a slave in his place, and the woman is free to give him life or have him killed." The Anishinaabes did much the same, granting life to some and subjecting others to a slow and painful death. Although the particular reasons for sparing individual captives varied from family to family and village to village, captives could be kept alive to augment population growth, to replace a dead relative, or to facilitate alliances through trade. Once the captive had been granted life, he or she was washed, clothed, and given a new name, often that of the deceased he or she was intended to replace. One Illinois word describing the decision to grant life to a captive derives from the word meaning "to cure or heal."[45]

Captives marked to die were forced to sing what the French described as

45. Deliette, "Memoir," 384 ("assemble and decide"). "Quand les guerriers sont entrés dans leurs cabannes, tous les anciens s'assemblent pour entendre la relation de tout ce qui s'est passé en guerre, ensuitte ils disposent des Esclaves. Si le pere d'une femme Sauvage a esté tué par leurs ennemis, ils luy donnent un Esclave à la place, et il est libre à cette femme de luy donner la vie ou de le faire mourir." Hennepin, *Description de la Louisiane*, 65–66. For post-torture healing and naming, see Bacqueville de La Potherie, "History of the Savage Peoples Who Are Allies of New France," in Blair, ed. and trans., *Indian Tribes*, II, 36–43; Daniel K. Richter, *Ordeal of the Longhouse: The Peoples of the Iroquois League in the Era of European Colonization* (Chapel Hill, N.C., 1992), 50–74; Viau, *Enfants du néant*, 137–160. For "nimpelakiihaa," see Antoine-Robert Le Boullenger, "Dictionnaire français-illinois," MS, ca. 1720s, John Carter Brown Library, Brown University, Providence, R.I.; Daryl Baldwin, personal communication.

"chansons de mort," or death songs, according to Pierre Deliette, "to afford entertainment to their executioners." François de Montigny witnessed the spectacle when a Winnebago war party passed by an Illinois village "in triumph" with two Missouri slaves, "who were forced to sing their death songs, which is a custom among all the Indians." Called *kikit8inaki8a*, meaning "slave songs," by the Illinois, captives were forced to sing at the entrance of each household that had lost a family member to the captive's people, allowing grieving kin a chance at violent (or at least verbal) catharsis. Condemned slaves were handed a special staff and forced to march from cabin to cabin as they sang. At ten to twelve feet long, the staff was wrapped in feathers to signify the captors' otherworldly power over the slave. It must have also become a physical burden to captives who had to carry it around the village for hours. The staff was eventually planted in the ground to become a torture stake, where condemned slaves spent their final hours enduring a slow, smoldering death.[46]

Captors spared women and children more often than men. In addition to targeting the male warriors for revenge killings, this strategy maximized the demographic benefits of slavery, as increasing the number of adult males in a village would do little to change its reproductive capacity. During times of high mortality due to disease or warfare, female captives often represented the best hope for rapidly restoring lost population. Especially in the frequently polygynous societies of the Pays d'en Haut, female captives integrated smoothly into present social structures as second or third wives of prominent men. Children were especially prized because of the relative ease with which they assimilated into the capturing society, learning new languages and customs much more quickly than older captives. This selection process left a surplus of male captives, who were often traded outside the village. Welcomed communally, slaves were controlled individually. The warrior who captured each slave exercised mastery over the person as a private possession, and any family wishing to kill or adopt a slave would have to negotiate terms with the original master. This process could lead to con-

46. Deliette, "Memoir," 383 ("chansons de mort"); *Jesuit Relations*, XLV, 183 ("entertainment"). "En triomphe . . . ces pauvres prisonnieres qu'on obligeoit de chanter leur chanson de mort, qui est une maniere qu'ont tous les sauvages": the Illinois demanded the slaves' release because they were Missouris, "comme ayant toujours esté amis" ("as they had always been friends"): François de Montigny, "Lettre de M. de Montigny sur les missions du Mississippi," Aug. 25, 1699, 1–2, ASQ, SME 12.1/001/041. For the torture staff, see Deliette, "Memoir," 383–384; Gravier and Largillier, "Dictionnaire illinois-français," 573.

flict among the captors as the ultimate future of each slave became a matter of group deliberation.[47]

Of the many possible fates facing a captive who survived the rituals of domestication, the most familiar to modern readers is a captive's adoption into a household to take the place of the dead. If it was not the most common outcome, it was certainly the status that French observers recognized most readily. "When there is any dead man to be resuscitated, that is to say, if any one of their warriors has been killed, and they think it a duty to replace him in his cabin," wrote Sébastien Rale, "they give to this cabin one of their prisoners, who takes the place of the deceased; and this is what they call 'resuscitating the dead.'" In times of peace this role was played by other members of the same village, who took the place of prominent villagers who had died, thereby assuming their full identity and status. Nicolas Perrot insisted that among the Ottawas a dead person of high status was sometimes replaced by another resident of the village, "and they regard themselves as united to this family, as much as if they were actually kindred." But because the adoptee "must be of the same rank" as the dead, captives were rarely chosen to replace influential men and women.[48]

What captive adoption meant in Native societies is elusive at best. French law and culture granted an adopted father an essentially proprietary authority over the adopted child, and this shaped what French observers meant to convey with the notion of captive "adoption," never intended by French authors to indicate the creation of true kinship. Even captives themselves, like Louis Hennepin, found their relationship with adopted relatives hard to comprehend, not familial in any sense that they recognized yet still expressed as kinship. When it came to difficult choices, as it did with Sioux food supplies, Hennepin acknowledged that his adopted kin favored their actual relatives over the fictive kinship created by his ceremonial adoption. Transcending the limits of European observations and filling in their

47. Richter, *Ordeal of the Longhouse*, esp. 67–68; Gordon M. Sayre, *Les Sauvages Américains: Representations of Native Americans in French and English Colonial Literature* (Chapel Hill, N.C., 1997), 248–304. For Illinois social structure, see Susan Sleeper-Smith, *Indian Women and French Men: Rethinking Cultural Encounter in the Western Great Lakes* (Amherst, Mass., 2001), esp. 1–37, where she indicates the importance of women to integrating outsiders into Illinois kin structures. For a similar captive selection process among the Indians of the Southwest, see James F. Brooks, *Captives and Cousins: Slavery, Kinship, and Community in the Southwest Borderlands* (Chapel Hill, N.C., 2002), esp. 1–40.

48. *Jesuit Relations*, LXVII, 173 ("resuscitating"); Perrot, *Memoir*, in Blair, ed. and trans., *Indian Tribes*, I, 84 ("same rank"), 85 ("actually kindred").

silences, indigenous languages provide a glimpse of how Indians themselves understood the category of kinship created by captive adoption. Their own metaphors suggest meanings much more complex than colonists understood.[49]

When describing captive adoption, speakers of Miami-Illinois used the word _nirapakerima_, translated by Jacques Gravier as "I adopt him in place of the dead." The key stem of this word is _rapa_, which means "in the place of another." Forms of this word were used in many other settings that clarify the importance of place to its meaning. _Rapah8te8i_, for example, meant "attached / tied to a place," suggesting that the captive was more connected to the place of the dead than to his or her persona. The idea of the captive as a placeholder was implied by many other uses of the stem _rapa_. Stepping into a hole or putting a foot into stockings or boots, for example, were both expressed by a verb form of _rapa_ to express the placement of an item into a gap, an idea that Jacques Gravier recorded as "entredeux," or between two things. The death of a relative left a gap, an open space, that was occupied by the adopted captive, who served as a replacement.[50]

Understanding captive adoption as a link to place as much as to the people in it helps to explain the Illinois and Anishinaabe word for master: _entachita_. This word literally translates as "I stay at his place for a long time," which is related, not to kinship, but to domain. What the French saw as incorporation into a family Algonquians expressed as incorporation into a household, tying captives to the place of the master. Other forms of this word, also used by the Anishinaabes, mean "where he dwells," "at a certain place," "at his house," or "to stay in a certain place for a period of time." Jacques Gravier, who first translated this term from Miami-Illinois, rendered it "he who has me as a slave," or my master.[51]

Kinship terminology was conspicuously absent from Algonquian idioms

49. Kristin Elizabeth Gager, _Blood Ties and Fictive Ties: Adoption and Family Life in Early Modern France_ (Princeton, N.J., 1996); Hennepin, _Nouvelle découverte_, 362. Compare this to Perrot's report that Anishinaabe wives could turn to their extended kin when they needed protection or redress. Perrot, _Memoir_, in Blair, ed. and trans., _Indian Tribes_, I, 64–65.

50. Gravier and Largillier, "Dictionnaire illinois-français," 493.

51. Ibid., 168. C.f. Richard A. Rhodes, _Eastern Ojibwa-Chippewa-Ottawa Dictionary_ (New York, 1993), 94: "daad _vai_ live in a certain place, endaad 'where he dwells, at his house . . . daadaad _vai_ live in a certain place for a period of time, Ot; pres ndaadaa; cc e-ndaadaad, endaadaad"; Nichols and Nyholm, _Dictionary of Minnesota Ojibwe_, 42: "dazhi- pv3 in a certain place, of a certain place, there" and "dazhitaa _vai_ spend time in a certain place, play in a certain place; 1sg indazhitaa; prt endazhitaad," "endazhi- pv3 in a certain place," "endaad _vai_ his/her home."

describing adopted captives. Rather than using the common verb *nin-toohsimaa*, "I have him as a father," for example, Illinois captives identified their master by the household where they stayed. Only two recorded kinship terms applied to adopted captives or slaves. The first was an expression used by families who wanted to kill a slave from a returning war party. They would say to the warrior who captured the slave, *nitaꞷembima*, a unique word form meaning "that is my relative," which was said only "by the executioner to whoever brings a slave" to the village. Rather than indicating actual kinship, the term condemned the captive to death in memory of the dead relative. The Jesuit Thierry Beschefer recorded the presence of a second kinship term in 1683, specifically used to demean adoptees. Using a different form of the word *son*, captors signified "a submission of which They make use to command us, as They do the Slaves whom they have adopted." According to a French trader, among the Anishinaabes adopted captives "never lie in their Masters Huts," another mark of distinction from the household's actual kin similar to the exclusion experienced by Hennepin among the Sioux. The master was, in the words of Pierre Chaumonot, a "feigned parent," or fictive kin.[52]

Adopted slaves, then, were bound to a household of fictive kin, occupying the physical and metaphorical place of a child but constantly aware that they were not actual relatives. Slaves' history and the terminology used to describe them equated them more with the family's domestic animals than with their children. And because they had no actual kin but were attached to a household at the master's pleasure, they were bound to the family at a single point rather than through the multiple lines created by kinship. Like dogs, their linguistic equivalents, adopted slaves were thus part of the household but never really part of the family.

The presence of fictive kinship bonds created by slaves' ritual adoption followed a pattern of linking family and slavery in a wide range of historical slave systems. The expression of mastery in familial terms—what sociologists of slavery call "quasi-filial" kinship—pervaded slaveries from ancient Rome to the antebellum southern United States. Indeed, the English word

52. "Cest mon parent, dit le boureau a qui conque amene un esclave": Gravier and Largillier, "Dictionnaire illinois-français," 36. For Illinois kinship terms, see David J. Costa, "The Kinship Terminology of the Miami-Illinois Language," *Anthropological Linguistics*, XLI (1999), 28–53; *Jesuit Relations*, LXII, 213 ("to command us"). Pierre Deliette confirmed Beschefer's sense that calling adoptees "son" was a mark of disrespect. See Deliette, "Memoir," 363. For "never lie in their Masters Huts," see Lahontan, *New Voyages*, II, 37. For "feigned parent," see *Jesuit Relations*, XVIII, 29.

family derives from the Latin *famulus,* meaning household slave. Across vast cultural differences, masters have imagined themselves fathers, but they have always understood the difference between their slaves and their biological family. This was especially evident in the particular language of kinship used by those adopting slaves in the Pays d'en Haut, where they made careful distinctions between real and fictive sons, between actual kin and those forced to take their place in the household.[53]

Slaves' ritual subordination worked together with the language of fictive kinship in the context of diplomacy, as encapsulated in a 1674 French-Illinois encounter. When Jacques Marquette and Louis Jolliet completed their journey down the Mississippi River, they returned with a young male slave who had been given to them by a Peoria chief. As they arrived at the chief's village, he offered them a warm welcome, expressing his hope that the French and his people could form a new alliance. The past twenty years had not been kind to his people. Threatened by the Iroquois from the east and the Foxes and Sioux from the northwest, the Peorias hoped that the French visit signaled better times to come. Since rumors and goods traveled faster than the French themselves, the chief already knew of these strange and powerful foreigners, and indeed Marquette noted the presence of European cloth in the village. A few Peoria men had traded with the French and their Ottawa allies over the past few years, and he eagerly offered them his friendship. Inviting the travelers to stop and rest, he assured them of his good intentions. "How beautiful the sun is, O Frenchman, when thou comest to visit us! All our village awaits thee, and thou shalt enter all our Cabins in peace."[54]

Wasting no time, the chief presented his French guests to the "great Captain of all the Illinois," who lived nearby. This chief offered the French three gifts as a pledge of alliance. "The Captain arose," according to the French account, "and, resting His hand upon the head of a little Slave whom he

53. Orlando Patterson, *Slavery and Social Death: A Comparative Study* (Cambridge, 1982), 62–65; *Oxford English Dictionary,* s.v. "family." In 1576, the French political philosopher Jean Bodin wrote, "For the very name of a Familie, came of *Famulus* and *Famulatio,* for that it had in it a great number of Slaves: and so of the greatest part of them that are in subjection in the Familie, men call all the whole household a Familie; or els for that there was no greater means to gather wealth than by slaves and servants, which the Latines call *Famuli,* the auntients not without cause have called this multitude of Slaves and servants a Familie." Bodin, *The Six Bookes of a Commonweale,* ed. Kenneth Douglas McRae (Cambridge, Mass., 1962), 32.

54. *Jesuit Relations,* LIX, 117.

wished to give us," promised his friendship. "Here is my son," the chief said, "whom I give thee to Show thee my heart." After placing the slave in front of the French, the chief then offered "a second present, consisting of an altogether mysterious Calumet," a pipe attached to a reed shaft adorned with colorful feathers. A feast followed at which several Illinois Indians fed the Frenchmen, "as one would give food to a bird." These three tokens of friendship—a slave, a feathered pipe, and a meal—converged in a symbolic expression of Illinois strength and generosity to convince the French of their good intentions.[55]

When Marquette's new slave arrived in the village as a recent captive, he would have faced a terrible inversion of these symbolic offerings. Rather than giving him food, he and his people had become the food, consumed as dog's flesh in the flames and by their enemies in acts of violent dominion. Rather than receiving a calumet, the feathered staff he carried would have been a slave stick as he and his kin were forced to face their potential executioners. Rather than receiving a slave, he received a master, who expressed his relationship to the boy in terms of dominion rather than mutual friendship. His defeat was now replayed for Marquette as evidence of Illinois power—his submission reinforced as his fictive father gave him to a stranger as a diplomatic object. This young slave embodied the dual imperatives of indigenous slavery in the Pays d'en Haut, balancing the impulse for war with the drive for diplomacy and trade.

NITAÏA—MY POSSESSION / MY SLAVE

"I mark my slave to make him known [as mine]."
—*Algonquian Phrase Book, ca. 1690s*

If adoption emphasized slaves' status as their captors' fictive kin, Algonquian and Siouan sources make clear that even adopted slaves were owned and controlled by a master, dishonored by all within the village and living under constant threat of violence even long after their incorporation. In short, they became a form of property, described with the same words used to identify other personally owned objects like tools, food, clothing, or weapons. Language and ritual reduced slaves to the status of animals, and like dogs they became the personal possession of their masters. Understanding the status of dogs can clarify what Indians meant when they compared

---

55. *Jesuit Relations*, LIX, 119, 121 ("a little Slave"), 123 ("food to a bird").

slaves to their only truly domesticated animal. Dogs played many important roles in the households and villages of the Pays d'en Haut, ranging from the sacred to the mundane. Indians first domesticated dogs from wolves several thousand years ago, creating the only domesticated animal in most of North America. Biologists consider wolves "preselected" for domestication because they are social animals that recognize and respect a dominant alpha as their master. This social and submissive behavior is an essential characteristic for domesticated animals because it allows them to function as subordinates within human society. The domestication of dogs was a striking exception to the standard Native relationship with nonhuman animals as independent creatures demanding reciprocity rather than yielding to dominion and mastery. Dogs' cousins, wolves and foxes, were seen as powerful and independent spirit beings who demanded respect. Dogs, on the other hand, could be owned, trained, abused, and harnessed for human labor. They served their masters faithfully, but Indians studiously avoided spoiling them with food and affection to keep them dependent and eager to please.[56]

Dogs also figured prominently in Native rituals, both those enacting success in war and others seeking spiritual power for hunting, fishing, or healing. The Ottawas used dogs in the feast of the dead, as an item of food and an object of sacrifice. "Before eating," wrote Antoine Lamothe de Cadillac, "they set up two great poles and fasten a dog to the top of them, which they sacrifice to the sun and the moon, praying to them to have pity and to take care of the souls of their relations, to light them on their journeys, and to guide them to the dwelling place of their ancestors." The Ottawas also drowned dogs as a sacrifice to a powerful manitou that lived in Lake Huron, hoping the spirit would reciprocate with a plentiful harvest of sturgeon. According to Antoine-Denis Raudot, "They threw dogs, with their jaws and legs tied, into the water as a gift for him." Alexander Henry confirms the persistence of this ceremony in the Great Lakes a full century after European settlement. "On our passage" through the Pays d'en Haut, he wrote, "we encountered a gale of wind, and there were some appearances of dan-

56. Virginia DeJohn Anderson, *Creatures of Empire: How Domestic Animals Transformed Early America* (New York, 2004), 7–8, 17–18; Marion Schwartz, *A History of Dogs in the Early Americas* (New Haven, Conn., 1997), 1–28. See also Gravier and Largillier, "Dictionnaire illinois-français," 400, which suggests private ownership of domesticated animals, translating "ᴎissᴎerimᴎeᴎa, ᴎissᴎerimᴎeta" as "qui a plusieures chiens, bestes privees," or "someone who has several dogs, privately owned animals." For more on dogs and hunting, see Raudot, "Memoir," in Kinietz, ed., *Indians of the Western Great Lakes*, 364.

ger. To avert it, a dog, of which the legs were previously tied together, was thrown into the lake; an offering designed to soothe the angry passions of some offended Manito."[57]

The Sioux made dog sacrifices at a specific falls in the Mississippi, evoking language that linked the dog with slavery. "Thou art a Spirit," they would say, "grant that Those of my Nation may pass here without any Disaster; That we may meet with a great many wild Bulls; and that we may be so happy as to vanquish our Enemy, and take a great many Slaves." Later, captured slaves were returned to the falls to acknowledge that success was tied to the sacrifice. Like slaves marked for sacrifice, dogs destined to die were singled out for special ritual attention.[58]

But for most dogs, as for most slaves, daily life in the village was driven more by practical than ritual concerns. Dogs' main function in Indian society was hunting. "The Indians always bring a large number of dogs on their hunts," wrote Pierre-François-Xavier de Charlevoix. "These are the only domestic animals that they raise, and they only raise them for hunting . . . they are very faithful and very attached to their masters, who nevertheless feed them very little and never pet them." When Henri Joutel traveled down the Mississippi with the La Salle expedition, he found Indians' dogs so hungry that they chewed the leather straps on the Frenchmen's horses. "The dogs were always hungry because the Indians did not feed them too well," explained Joutel, "particularly in this season when they were in the height of corn production (unless they were hunting)." One Mississippi Valley people "tied up the mouths of the dogs and fastened a forepaw under the throat so they could not get to the stalks of corn" during harvest. Archaeological remains reveal that some Indians even filed down their dogs' teeth with stones to make them less dangerous to their masters or other handlers.[59]

---

57. Raudot, "Memoir," in Kinietz, ed., *Indians of the Western Great Lakes*, 283–284 ("two great poles"), 286 ("jaws and legs tied"). For Alexander Henry, see Schwartz, *History of Dogs*, 99.

58. Hennepin, *New Discovery*, 278 ("Thou art a Spirit"). For special treatment for sacrificial dogs, see Schwartz, *History of Dogs*, 85.

59. "Les Sauvages menent toujours à leurs chasses un grand nombre de Chiens; ce sont les seuls Animaux domestiques, qu'ils élevent; et ils ne les élevent, que pour la chasse . . . ils sont fort fidéles, et fort attaché à leurs Maîtres, qui les nourissent pourtant assez mal, et ne les caressent jamais": Charlevoix, *Journal d'un voyage*, V, 176; Joutel, *Journal*, ed. Foster, trans. Warren, 236 ("always hungry"), 241 ("tied up the mouths"). For filing teeth, see Schwartz, *History of Dogs*, 53. See also Lahontan, *New Voyages*, II, 44. Summarizing the distinctive role of dogs in Native American cultures, Schwartz writes, "Our own concept of the

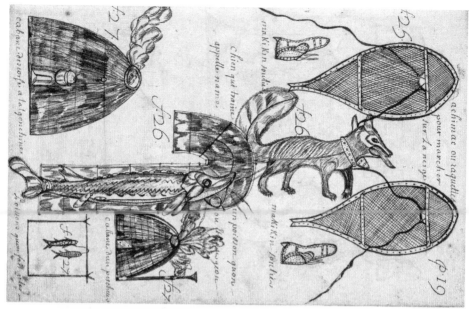

FIGURE 7. "Dog Dragging a Fish Called *Namé* or Sturgeon." *Louis Nicolas,*
"Codex canadiensis." MS, ca. 1670. Permission Gilcrease Museum, Tulsa, Ok.

In the Mississippi Valley and the Great Plains, dogs packed heavy loads
of meat, fish, and other supplies "on a travois": a sled or a woven tarp attached to the dog by two long poles or straps. The poles were twelve feet
long and "the thickness of a man's arm," connected to a leather "saddle" tied
around the dog's torso. In 1724, Étienne de Bourgmont encountered a large
group of Kansa Indians in the Missouri River valley who loaded their dogs
with a pile of bison hides that he estimated to weigh three hundred pounds.
For lighter loads, especially when snow made the dragging easier, leather
collars were placed around dogs' necks and attached to sleds with far more
flexible leather straps.[60]

In the 1680s a traveler highlighted the skill and discipline of Indians'
dogs by contrasting them to a French dog from La Rochelle who joined
them on a bison hunt. Frenzied by the thunderous stampede, the French

---

pet dog must be discarded . . . [or] we will lose sight of the complexity and richness of the lives
of those who inhabited a world far different from our own" (3).

60. Étienne de Véniard, sieur de Bourgmont, "Journal of the Voyage . . . to the Padoucas,"
in Frank Norall, ed., *Bourgmont: Explorer of the Missouri, 1698-1725* (Lincoln, Nebr., 1988),
136–137.

dog had no sense of how to behave, running wildly after the animals and chasing off the whole herd. Through intensive training and strategic starvation, Mississippi Valley dogs were taught to chase individual animals away from the pack, steering them toward the hunters. Male hunters controlled hunting dogs, but women controlled those used as pack animals, relying on them to share what was throughout the Pays d'en Haut the exclusively female burden of carrying loads on hunting and fishing expeditions. Other animals were also tamed and brought into the village to serve human purposes but never actually domesticated. La Salle commented on the similarity of the Illinois practice of capturing and rearing young bison with their treatment of slaves. "The buffalo calves are easy to tame and can be of great use," he wrote in 1680, "as well as the slaves in which these people are accustomed to traffic and whom they compel to labor for them."[61]

If the beginning and end of captive raids were collective affairs, the act of taking slaves was intensely individualistic, as was the right to their bodies, which was one of the most personal forms of property among the Indians of the Pays d'en Haut. Lahontan's claim that Indians were "utter Strangers to distinctions of Property, for what belongs to one is equally anothers," was an exaggeration that overlooked several categories of private property ownership and exclusive control, including domesticated animals and captives, both of which were controlled by individuals and families rather than villages or clans. Although the accumulation of private property did not translate into higher status, it did pay practical dividends to control both animals and people who could produce for the master's household. Speakers of Anishinaabemowin put the possessive to the term for dog to represent slave ownership. Pierre du Jaunay recorded that the Ottawa term *nit'aouakan* meant both "my dog" and "my slave." One family of Illinois terms derived from *nitaïa*, which was used to denote "my domestic animal, my dog, my cat, also my slave." Literally, the word meant "my possession." Gravier rendered another form of the word, *nitataïma*, as "I have him/her as a slave, as a domestic animal. That is my slave." When slaves were distributed throughout the village, those receiving slaves would say *nitintarehig8a*, "he

[handwritten margin note: another revision of narrative]

61. For strategic starving, see Joutel, *Journal*, ed. Foster, trans. Warren, 115, 181. For carrying, see Bourgmont, "Journal of the Voyage to the Padoucas," in Norall, ed., *Bourgmont*, 136–137; Lawrence J. Burpee, ed., *Journals and Letters of Pierre Gaultier de Varenne de La Vérendrye and His Sons* . . . (Toronto, 1927), 317–318. "Les petits beufs sauvages sont aisez a apprivoiser et peuvent etre d'un grand secours aussi bien que les esclaves dont ces gens ont coutume de faire commerce et qu'ils obligent de travailler": "La Salle on the Illinois Country, 1680," in Pease, ed., *The French Foundations*, 10.

gave him to me, or he made him my property." Whether a dog or a slave, to make someone the master of something or someone was *nitintareta8a*. Another variant, *nitaïag8a*, meant both "I am his slave, he is my master," and "he wagered me in a bet." Although apparently used sparingly, the expression speaks to masters' ability to dispose of slaves as they saw fit. Another Illinois word describing physical detention, *kiki8naki8i*, meant "slave" in the seventeenth century, but in modern usage the root has softened into a meaning that suggests being detained, held up, or merely running late. As used in the seventeenth century, the word rendered the slave in an inanimate intransitive form, the only of its kind referring to a person. The slave was thus grammatically as well as socially dead.[62]

Other words expressed the presence of verbal or physical markers designed to set a particular captive apart as belonging to a particular master. According to a seventeenth-century Jesuit, the Illinois used the term *nikikipenara*, meaning "I mark my slave to make him known [as mine]." The Ottawas had a similar term that Louis André recorded with the meaning "I cut a young slave to mark him." A French trader greeted an Ottawa war party returning from a raid in the 1690s. As their canoes approached, he heard "the songs of the slaves, who stood upright, each having a wand in his hand. There were special marks on each, to indicate those who had captured him." Warriors also used specific marks to signify their own success in slaving. Some made notches on their war clubs to indicate the number of prisoners captured or killed, as emblems of masculine honor. Others tattooed themselves with simple lines or images of war clubs, battle scenes, or the totemic symbols of their defeated enemies. And both within and beyond the calumet ceremony, all Indian warriors in the Pays d'en Haut affirmed their masculinity by performing complex dance rituals, during which they recounted their killing and capturing of enemies. As a check against the in-

62. Lahontan, *New Voyages*, II, 7 ("utter Strangers"). Yet the Algonquian and Siouan languages spoken by the peoples of the Pays d'en Haut are full of references to items controlled as private property. See, for example, Gravier and Largillier, "Dictionnaire illinois-français," 168–169 (and "nit'aouakan"); Du Jaunay, "Dictionarium gallico-outaouakum," s.v. "esclave." For the literal translation, see Masthay, *Kaskaskia Illinois-to-French Dictionary*, 122 (for original, see Gravier and Largillier, "Dictionnaire illinois-français," 14, 19). For "kiki8naki8i," see Pierre Pinet, "Dictionnaire" (commonly referred to as the "St-Jérôme Dictionary"), 210. The author thanks Michael McCafferty for bringing this word to his attention. Thanks, also, to Daryl Baldwin for the modern usage. For details about Pinet's dictionary, see McCafferty, "The Latest Miami-Illinois Dictionary and Its Author," *Papers of the Thirty-sixth Algonquian Conference* (2005), 271–286, and David Costa, "The St-Jérôme Dictionary of Miami-Illinois," 107–133; Appendix A.

evitable temptation to exaggerate, those who falsely boasted were publicly shamed by having ashes rubbed on their heads by other warriors.[63]

Warriors' claim on slaves' bodies began as an exclusive form of ownership. Although village politics demanded that slaves be distributed upon their arrival, the captor was never compelled to release a slave he preferred to keep, and those wishing to claim slaves for themselves had to compensate him for their release. Although this was not a sale in the sense that the human body had been assigned a price, it was nevertheless a recognition of the captor's right to possess the captive, and, as in all redistributive gift-giving, generosity brought additional prestige to the successful warrior.[64]

Subdued and controlled by male warriors, in the long run most indigenous slaves spent much of their time supervised by women, who in the cultures of the Pays d'en Haut generally managed the domestic resources and spaces on which slaves depended. Hennepin experienced this gendered control, constantly reminded by the women who supervised him that he was a slave and that he competed with their natural children for resources. Households, even the male-dominated cultures of the Pays d'en Haut, were run by women, making them what anthropologists call "matrifocal" (in contrast to "matriarchal," which implies a much broader reach for women's power in the society). Men were absent from the village for extended periods during hunting and raiding expeditions, leaving women as the primary guardians of slaves of all sexes and ages. Male agricultural laborers not only had to do women's work; they also labored under the supervision of women, a doubly demeaning fate that further differentiated male slaves from their fictive male kin.[65]

Female slaves who became secondary wives also had to negotiate a com-

63. For "nikikipenara," see Gravier and Largillier, "Dictionnaire illinois-français," 199; Masthay, *Kaskaskia Illinois-to-French Dictionary*, 138. "Je coupe un jeu[n] esclave pour marquer": André, "Preceptes, phrases, et mots de la langue algonquine outaouaise," s.v. "marquer." For "songs of the slaves," see Bacqueville de La Potherie, *History*, in Blair, ed. and trans., *Indian Tribes*, II, 37–38. For marking, see Raudot, "Memoir," in Kinietz, ed., *Indians of the Western Great Lakes*, 351. For tattooing, see Arnaud Balvay, "Tattooing and Its Role in French–Native American Relations in the Eighteenth Century," *French Colonial History*, IX (2008), 2–3. For the calumet dance and the shaming of liars, see Raudot, "Memoir," 347–348; and Perrot, *Memoir*, in Blair, ed. and trans., *Indian Tribes*, I, 54–59.

64. Deliette, "Memoir," 384.

65. For "matrifocal" households, see Richard R. Randolph, "The 'Matrifocal Family' as a Comparative Category," *American Anthropologist*, LXVI (1964), 628–631; Raymond T. Smith, "The Matrifocal Family," in Jack Goody, ed., *The Character of Kinship* (New York, 1973), 121–144; Sleeper-Smith, *Indian Women and French Men*, 30.

plicated relationship with the woman who managed the household: the senior wife. Blending into the gendered hierarchies of a household headed by a man but practically controlled by another woman, captive women faced the usual challenges of authority and power inherent to polygamy complicated by their status as a degraded outsider. One term for a subordinate wife, n8ki8i8agana, suggests the low status of this role. Meaning "the other wife, as in the second wife," it was a "term of contempt" that contrasted with kitcahi8eta, meaning "the most loved of his wives who is the mistress of all." If the master was a successful hunter or, especially, a prominent chief, a female captive's painful path into his household could result in significant social mobility, especially for their children. The Illinois used what Jacques Gravier considered a fairly common phrase, kiki8na8iba n8nghi 8ir8nig8tchi anapemari tchiraki8e8a, roughly translatable as "slave woman who is now better accommodated [because] her husband is rich."[66]

Demonstrating that slaves functioned as a kind of privately possessed property, the Illinois and Miamis offered slaves as both bride price and dowry. The suitor's "father, if he has one, or his uncle in lieu of him, takes five or six kettles, two or three guns, some skins of stags, bucks, or beavers, some flat sides of buffalo, some cloth, and sometimes a slave, if he has one, in short something of all he has, according to his wealth and the esteem in which the girl is held." The practice also went the other direction, with a woman's giving a slave to her new husband, conceivably one who could serve as her minion, making the slave a gift that benefited both husband and wife. Paying a dowry with a slave was sufficiently standardized to develop into a common Algonquian phrase, 8chit8a kic8[na8a] 8chihe8a atinta8aganari, niarinta a8ira, awkwardly glossed by Jacques Gravier as "she carries something, brings a slave to her husband. [said] of a young bride to whom has been given a slave that she brings to her husband's home."[67]

Being given away as a gift must have reminded Native slaves of the tenuous protections they received from their adopted kin. This degradation was constantly reinscribed with threats of violence and insulting language. As

---

66. "L'autre femme, comme la seconde f. terme de mepris": Gravier and Largillier, "Dictionnaire illinois-français," 355, and "la plus aimée de ses femmes qui est maitresse de tout," 224. For "better accommodated," see 399. The translation is based on Masthay's gloss of the Algonquian term in Masthay, Kaskaskia Illinois-to-French Dictionary, 237.

67. Deliette, "Memoir," 331 (bride price). "Elle porte qq chose, mene une esclave a son mary. d'une jeune mariée a qui on a doné une esclave quon mene chez le mary": Gravier and Largillier, "Dictionnaire illinois-français," 377.

a consequence of low status, adopted outsiders lived under the perpetual threat of violence and murder. Even after years of successfully participating in the capturing society, as one historian noted of the Iroquois, "a recalcitrant captive could expect a quick and unceremonious death." Illinois and Ottawa slaves could face violence as a consequence of their master's actions. In the 1690s, when an Illinois woman angered her brother, his rage fell upon "one of her slaves—whom he cruelly killed, out of revenge." The Illinois phrase meaning "kill my wife when I am dead" most likely referred to enslaved, subordinate wives, rather than to those who could turn to their kin for protection.[68]

NITAR8RIE8O—HE MAKES ME WORK

"Aquipaguetin also sent me to a neighboring island with his children and some women to work the land."—Louis Hennepin, Sioux captive, 1683

Dishonored and brought to heel by their captors, slaves were also domesticated in another sense: they performed valuable tasks for the *domus*, or household, to which they were bound. Although Indians did not demand that slaves produce valuable export commodities, indigenous slaves did contribute to the overall productivity of the master's family and village, and they had very little control over the nature or the fruits of their labors. All adoptees were expected to do the work of the person they replaced, thereby mitigating the social costs of that person's death. As in any preindustrial economy, Indians spent most of their labor on subsistence activities, which they divided along fairly rigid gender lines. Whether male or female, slaves generally played the roles assigned to women and children, enhancing the burden of shame born by male slaves, who would have understood the emasculating symbolism of hoeing in the cornfields or carrying baggage on a hunting expedition. The reproductive labor of female slaves provided additional strength to the master's household, countering population decline brought by the wars that originally prompted the slave raid.[69]

"The Women Slaves," wrote Lahontan of the Pays d'en Haut, "are employed to Sow and Reap the *Indian-Corn*," drawing on skills they would

68. Richter, *Ordeal of the Longhouse*, 69 ("recalcitrant captive"); Gravier and Largillier, "Dictionnaire illinois-français," 404. For the protection of kin, see Perrot, *Memoir*, in Blair, ed. and trans., *Indian Tribes*, I, 64–65.

69. Richter, "War and Culture," *WMQ*, 3d Ser., XL (1983), 531.

have learned from a very young age in their home village. Female slaves were also required to perform routine household chores, like drawing water and gathering wood. Nicolas Perrot noted that Anishinaabe women went for their own water only "if they have no servants in the house." Many Indian peoples had terms for these "chore wives" that distinguished them from insiders who married under their own will and who had extended families to protect them against a husband's violence or neglect.[70]

In the 1680s, Lahontan noted that, among the nations of the western Great Lakes, male captives assisted in the hunt by carrying their masters' baggage, tending to sled dogs, and preparing animal skins by picking fleas from them and stretching the skins to dry. Especially for the region's northern inhabitants, hunting was the most demanding and time-consuming form of work, making slaves especially desirable for these tasks. Sometimes slaves hunted, but they were not trusted to do so alone. Lahontan also recorded that captives among the Sauks, Potawatomis, and Menominees served food at ceremonial feasts for visitors. Masters sick with disease were "carried about by their Slaves" on a litter, an unpleasant and perilous task. If the master did not survive, slaves sometimes carried his body to the burial place (where family presumably attended). Slaves could also serve as messengers of death, carrying the news throughout the village.[71]

Many of the tasks assigned to male captives violated expected gender roles, as when they served food, prepared skins, carried packs on hunting expeditions, or performed farm labor, exacerbating the already negative experience of captivity. Louis Hennepin experienced this sort of labor-as-humiliation among the Sioux when he was forced to work alongside women and children in the fields. According to Hennepin, his master, Aquipaguetin, "sent me into a Neighbouring Isle, with his Wives, Children, and Servants, where I was to hough and dig with a Pick-axe and Shovel." Whether Hennepin even recognized this work as emasculating within Sioux culture is unclear. But his humiliation would have been obvious to everyone around

70. Lahontan, *New Voyages*, II, 18 ("women slaves"); Perrot, *Memoir,* in Blair, ed. and trans., *Indian Tribes,* I, 75 ("no servants"). For "chore wives," see Brooks, *Captives and Cousins,* 191; Pekka Hämäläinen, *The Comanche Empire* (New Haven, Conn., 2008), 257.

71. Lahontan, *New Voyages,* I, 53, 58, 62, 105, II, 2, 18, 24, 37, 46 ("carried about"), 48, 50–53, 62; *Jesuit Relations,* LIV, 93–95, LXVI, 263. Given Lahontan's intent to use Indians' egalitarianism as a foil to criticize European hierarchy, his description of slavery among western Algonquians is especially telling. If anything, such an admission subverted his ideological agenda. For Lahontan's motivations, see Paola Basile, "Lahontan et l'évolution moderne du mythe du 'bon sauvage'" (master's thesis, McGill University, 1997).

him, and enslaved Indian men would have no trouble recognizing the symbolic degradation of doing women's work.[72]

Some of slaves' most important work occurred beyond the bounds of the village as they acted as both agents and objects of diplomacy. In a general sense, slaves often served as translators and intercultural brokers in the tense but always fluid relationships that produced their captivity in the first place. In rare cases, this work opened avenues of opportunity for slaves to rise in stature as important intermediaries between their people and their master's. As in other North American regions, the violence that produced captives could also be a means of "cultural interpenetration," as everything from languages to pottery styles meshed in a violent web of connections that stretched all across North America.[73]

Slaves could facilitate language acquisition and serve as translators, although their ability to speak the captor's language could vary widely. For older captives, in particular, the inability to master a new language sometimes limited their effectiveness as diplomatic actors. In 1695, the Jesuit Gabriel Marest "resolved to learn the language of the Savages" in the Lower Mississippi Valley to facilitate relations with a new village. He tried to hire a tutor, but he struggled to learn much, because the man he hired "was a slave from another Tribe, who knew only imperfectly their Tongue." Yet slaves' linguistic knowledge was helpful in many contexts, making them important actors in rebuilding relationships among former enemies. At times, their third language was the most helpful. In 1669, one slave, who had been captured by the Illinois and given to the Ottawas as a token of friendship, finally became the slave of Jacques Marquette at Michilimackinac. Having learned to speak Illinois while enslaved among them, then Anishinaabemowin among the Ottawas, he provided Marquette with important geographic and cultural information about the Illinois. He also served as the first translator between the French and the Illinois. Acting as an agent of diplomacy did not free him from his enslavement—in fact, it led to his realienation to a new master—but it did give him a measure of independence as he shaped the understanding and influenced the actions of both his Illinois and French masters.[74]

---

72. Hennepin, *New Discovery*, II, 171. The original French version reads, "Aquipaguetin me menoit encore dans une Isle voisinne, avec ses enfans et des femmes pour labourer la terre" (Hennepin, *Description de la Louisiane*, 246).

73. Brooks, *Captives and Cousins*, 31.

74. *Jesuit Relations*, LIV, 177, LXVI, 105 ("slave from another Tribe").

All peoples in the Pays d'en Haut released enemy captives as a gesture of diplomatic goodwill when they hoped to bring an end to the cycles of revenge that had brought the slave into their village. Secure in their large numbers and never in need of slave labor for agriculture like many of their neighbors, the Sioux in particular were "often content with the glory of winning a victory, and sending back free and uninjured the prisoners taken by them in battle." They might have adopted this strategy more often than others because they lived on the western margins of this diplomatic world and had no direct access to Great Lakes trade networks except through potentially dangerous territory. Over time, however, reciprocal violence persuaded them that their interests were best served by treating captives as they could expect their own people to be treated. Claude Allouez witnessed the convergence of Fox and Sioux war culture, noting that the Foxes were "fully resolved not to treat The Nadouessi (Sioux) more humanely than they are treated by them," a reciprocity that would facilitate violence, to be sure, but also one that established protocols of war that could restrain potential attackers.[75]

Acting as an agent of diplomacy could be perilous work. In one example from the 1660s, a slave among the Potawatomis was released and sent to the Miamis with an invitation to join them against the French. When the slave arrived, he "said many unkind things about the French; he said that the Pouteouatemis held them in the utmost contempt, and regarded them as dogs." Unfortunately for the slave, there were French traders among the Miamis who heard his speech, and those "who had heard these abusive remarks, put him into a condition where he could say no more outrageous things." Slaves often carried unwelcome messages back to their own people, as when a group of Anishinaabes sent slaves back to their own nation with a war club painted black to declare war against the slaves' people.[76]

75. *Jesuit Relations*, LV, 171 ("often content"). More than anyone else, the Sioux seem to have released captives as a strategy of ingratiating themselves with potential allies. According to Raudot, "They generally send back any prisoners they make, in hope of obtaining peace; and it is only after they have lost a great many of their men and are tired of sending back prisoners without obtaining the result hoped for, that they burn them. They never torture them" ("Memoir," in Kinietz, *Indians of the Western Great Lakes*, 378). *Jesuit Relations*, LVIII, 67 ("fully resolved"). For the tendency of regional war cultures to develop through reciprocal violence, see Wayne E. Lee, "Peace Chiefs and Blood Revenge: Patterns of Restraint in Native American Warfare, 1500–1800," *Journal of Military History*, LXXI (2007), 703.

76. "Perrot Visits the Wisconsin Tribes, and Induces Them to Become Allies of the French," *Wis. Hist. Coll.*, XVI (1902), 47 ("many unkind things . . . could say no more"); Lahontan, *New Voyages*, II, 82.

Full of ambiguities, captives' ability to link former enemies could also be complicated by uncertainty about the captive's intentions, or even identity. Captives taken while very young were hard to distinguish from the captors' people, given that they learned the captors' language as children and adopted their style of dress and tattooing. French soldiers witnessed this confusion when a Fox enslaved by the Illinois claimed that he was actually an Illinois. "This unhappy person maintained to his last breath that he was an Illinois, and had been taken when a child by the Outagamies, who had adopted him." They did not believe him, but his assertion of Illinois identity implies both the possibility of such discoveries and the difficulty of assessing their accuracy. Had he provided a credible Illinois genealogy, he probably would have been freed; but, the younger he was when he had been captured, the less likely he would be to remember his Illinois family.[77]

Despite the possibilities available to slaves as agents of diplomacy, their most important diplomatic role came as they were made objects of trade, symbolic gifts that signified peace between peoples. Because of their symbolic power to mitigate the effects of warfare or murder, captives became an important medium of exchange in the gift-giving that characterized Indian diplomacy. Captives accompanied peace delegations as gifts ceremonially offered to allies or erstwhile enemies. "Usually, they are used to replace the dead," wrote Antoine-Denis Raudot of captives in the western Great Lakes, "but often some of them are also given to other nations to oblige these nations to become their allies." Employing the language of kinship, those offering slaves introduced them by saying, "Here is my flesh," to represent the physical blending of familial interest between two previously disconnected groups. Throughout the Mississippi Valley, ceremonial giving of slaves was described alongside the calumet by members of La Salle's expedition as one of the "ceremonies with which these tribes customarily confirm their alliances."[78]

In one of these exchanges a Fox chief received two Iroquois captives from his Algonquian "neighbors [who] took them prisoners and made me a present of them." Rather than keeping the slaves, he released them back to the Iroquois in an effort to initiate an alliance with them. This act high-

---

77. Charlevoix, *Journal of a Voyage to North-America*, II, 206.
78. Raudot, "Memoir," in Kinietz, ed., *Indians of the Western Great Lakes*, 341–410, 360 ("given to other nations"); *Jesuit Relations*, LIX, 121 ("here is my son"); Dubuisson, Official Report, 1712, *Wis. Hist. Coll.*, XVI (1902), 282 ("here is my flesh"); Joutel, *Journal*, ed. Foster, trans. Warren, 128 ("ceremonies").

lights the perils that slaves could pose as a diplomatic gift. Recipients had the option of releasing their newly acquired slaves and thereby forging a new alliance. But such risks were rarely taken, especially when slaves were given as part of the calumet ceremony. A gift of captives, even more powerfully than wampum or the calumet, signified the opposite of warfare, the giving rather than the taking of life. As living witnesses to the power and ferocity of their captors, captives also offered a subtle warning of the dangers one could face as the captor's enemy. In many cases this gift proved sufficient to erase long periods of violence between two peoples, satisfying the demands of customary justice and symbolizing the possibility of true friendship, as when the Potawatomis "made satisfaction of an old quarrel, by presents of slaves and pipes." Especially when coupled with the ceremonies of the calumet, slaves symbolized new friendships by demeaning a common enemy.[79]

At other times, a gift of captives could persuade an ally to action against a third party. In 1665, for example, while Nicolas Perrot negotiated an alliance with the tribes around Green Bay, he noted that the Potawatomis offered a captive to the Miamis to persuade them not to enter into an alliance with the French. When attacked by a Sioux war party in 1672, Perrot observed, the Ottawa chief Sinagos fell into captivity. After torturing Sinagos, the Sioux discovered a "Panys who belonged to [this] great chief," then released the captive "back to his own country that he might faithfully report what he had seen and the justice that had been administered." The Sioux chief hoped that, by freeing a captive of another western nation, he could persuade the captive's people to join him against Sinagos.[80]

Both practically valuable and symbolically potent, captives often passed from village to village through overlapping systems of captive exchange, journeying hundreds or even thousands of miles from their birthplace. The Illinois took captives from the central and southern Plains and traded them into the Lake Superior region. The Ottawas joined Upper Mississippi Valley allies to raid deep into the Southwest, then traded the captives as far east as Lake Nipissing. In 1669 Sulpician missionary François Dollier de Casson described meeting a Nipissing chief who "had a slave the Ottawas had presented to him in the preceding year, from a very remote nation in the south-

79. *Jesuit Relations*, LIV, 227 ("made me a present"); Dubuisson, Official Report, *Wis. Hist. Coll.*, XVI (1902), 284 ("presents of slaves and pipes"). For a discussion of "covering the grave" see White, *Middle Ground*, 75–82.

80. Perrot, *Mémoire*, in *Wis. Hist. Coll.* (1902), XVI, 30–31 ("faithfully report"), 46.

west." The next year, Dollier received from the Senecas a gift of two captives, one taken from the Ottawas near Michilimackinac and one from the Shawnees. They were to serve as guides and translators as Dollier and La Salle traveled through the Ohio River valley. Although the Ohio expedition never materialized, the captives remained in Dollier's possession as slaves. These diplomatic exchanges placed all enslaved captives at risk, reinforcing their own dependence on their hosts' goodwill for whatever social position they attained. The acts of violence that structured these raid-and-trade networks, producing the captives who passed through them, created barriers more often than they forged connections. Slaves' potential as intercultural brokers was also inhibited by the memory of their enslavement. Indigenous slaves thus became a symbol of peace only through a double act of violence: their initial capture and their forced subordination to an allied people.[81]

Slave labor was obviously not central to the economic or social organization of the Pays d'en Haut. Once slaves had been dominated and domesticated, they had fulfilled their most important purpose and thereafter filled roles more similar to the rest of the village. Policing the boundaries of slave status was thus less important than it would be in Atlantic societies that demanded slaves primarily for their productive and perpetual labor. Despite the persistent stigma attached to slaves and their constant vulnerability, the journey from degradation to integration was built into a system designed to produce the most fully assimilated and domesticated slaves possible. This goal ensured that indigenous slaves generally did not pass their status to the next generation. Not only was social rank rarely inheritable in most cultures of the Pays d'en Haut, but enslaving children did not meet the cultural demands that made slavery desirable. Neither the honor brought to warriors through the subordination of enemies nor the domestication of their power in the interest of the village was accomplished in this way. "Those who are allowed to live are like Slaves and valets among them," Louis Hennepin remembered. "But in time they lose their Slave status and are as if they were from their [captors'] Nation." Hennepin clearly overstated the universality of slaves' assimilation and honor, as his and many others' experiences dem-

---

81. *Jesuit Relations*, LIX, 127, LXVII, 171; "The Journey of Dollier and Galinée, 1669–1670," in Louise Phelps Kellogg, ed., *Early Narratives of the Northwest, 1634–1699* (New York, 1917), 167 ("had a slave"), 181–182, 190. Kellogg uses the word "tribe" instead of "nation" in her translation, but I have retained "nation" from the French original ("d'une nation fort esloignée du Sud-Ouest"). See "Récit de ce qui s'est passé de plus remarquable dans le voyage de MM. Dolleir et Galinée (1669–1670)," in Pierre Margry, comp., *Découvertes et établissements dans l'ouest et dans le sud . . .* (Paris, 1876–1886), I, 112.

onstrate, but other French observers generally agreed. As Lahontan wrote in the late-seventeenth century:

> Upon the Death of a Savage his Slaves marry the other Women Slaves, and live by themselves in a distinct Hut, as being then free, or such as have no Master to serve. The Children that spring from this sort of Marriages, are adopted and reputed the Children of the Nation, by reason of their being born in the Village and in the Country. *There's no reason,* say they, *that such Children should bear the Misfortunes of their Parents, or come into the World in Slavery, since they contributed nothing towards their Creation.*[82]

If Lahontan's tone suggests that his comment was as much a critique of hereditary status in Europe as a description of Indians' logic of ownership, his observation accurately explained one of the central differences between indigenous slavery and the labor-based chattel slavery developing simultaneously in the Atlantic world. Rather than a closed slave system designed to move slaves "up and out"—excluding slaves and their descendants from full participation in their masters' society, even when freed—indigenous slavery moved captives "up and in" toward full, if forced, assimilation. Slavery therefore maximized the productive and reproductive capacities of the capturing village as it robbed enemies of the same sources of strength.[83]

 Emphasizing this aspect of captivity to the exclusion of all others, however, both flattens and romanticizes the experience of indigenous slaves. Not only does it understate the persistent stigma and vulnerability associated with being a defeated outsider, but it also ignores the very real possibility that any captive could be traded to a third party and reenslaved in another unfamiliar environment. In a culture so conscious of kinship, the natal alienation of enslavement was its greatest burden, and the stain of slaves' identity never quite left them. Indeed, even years after a slave was "adopted and married," wrote Alexander Henry of the Ojibwas, "I never knew her to lose the degrading appellation of *wa'kan', a slave.*" Indicative

---

82. "Ceux à qui on donne la vie, sont parmy eux comme des Esclaves et des valets, mais à la longueur du temps ils perdent leurs Esclavages, et sont comme s'ils estoient de leur Nation." Hennepin, *Description de la Louisiane*, 68; Lahontan, *New Voyages*, II, 53 (block quote). See also William Christie MacLeod, "Debtor and Chattel Slavery in Aboriginal North America," *American Anthropologist*, XXVII (1925), 370–380.

83. For "up and in" versus "up and out" slave systems, see James L. Watson, "Slavery as an Institution, Open and Closed Systems," in Watson, ed., *Asian and African Systems of Slavery* (Berkeley, Calif., 1980), 10.

of slaves' persistent marginalization, Algonquian-speakers often drew upon slaves' degradation in their insults. According to Louis André, when "Missipissi," a powerful manitou who controlled the waters, failed to deliver sturgeon, they said that he "was worth nothing; that he was a slave." When Claude Allouez searched for a term to describe the devil to the Ottawas, he chose to call him a "vile slave" to show that he was powerless before God and "has no control over men's lives." The Jesuit's understanding of *awakaan* as an odious term was confirmed by a group of Anishinaabes of Green Bay, who feared that branding the devil a slave risked reprisals from the insulted manitou: "Thou hast no sense," they chided the Jesuits; "thou angerest the Devil too much." Jacques Gravier modified the metaphor, making Satan a master and threatening his Illinois listeners that they "will be the slaves of the devil, if they die without baptism." Gravier's description stuck, and a generation later Illinois Christians still called nonbelievers *tareg8a matchimanet8are*, slaves of the evil spirit, slaves of a slave.[84]

Simply calling someone a slave in any of the Algonquian or Siouan languages was considered a great offense, a universal "term of contempt," according to Gravier. The Illinois insult *matchirinisse* was a vocative diminutive meaning, roughly, "[you] pathetic little bad man," said to and about slaves. To avoid any ambiguity, Gravier wrote beside another form of the term, "It is an insult." One could abuse an Illinois man by calling him a woman: *kimitem8sserimere*, "I consider you a woman. You are a coward." For a much more serious insult, an antagonist could call him *kiki8na8arakiagana*, or "slave woman's vile / cheap vagina." Although difficult to translate, Jesuits rendered the term in Latin (to protect the innocent) as "vile membrum servae, viris sensu metaphor," literally "slave woman's worthless penis, said metaphorically about men."[85]

This cross-gendered and highly sexualized insult underscores the low status of slaves in the villages of the Pays d'en Haut. It also evokes the centrality of enslaved women's sexuality to their identity and purpose as

84. Alexander Henry, *Travels and Journals*, 307 ("degrading appellation"); *Jesuit Relations*, LVII, 289 ("worth nothing"), 281 ("vile slave" and "no control"), 269 ("no sense," "angerest"), 279, 283, 289, LXIV, 191 ("slaves to the devil"), 219. For eighteenth-century uses of Gravier's metaphor, see Le Boullenger, "Dictionnaire français-illinois," s.v. "esclave."

85. "Gueux, esclave. cest une injure. *it[em]* mechant homme." Gravier and Largillier, "Dictionnaire illinois-français," 259. The author thanks Michael McCafferty for pointing out the meaning of the vocative diminutive in this case. "Je te regarde comme une femme. tu es un lache": Gravier and Largillier, "Dictionnaire illinois-français," 199 ("kiki8na8arakiagana"), 298.

slaves. The value of enslaved women as kin-makers for capturing house-holds, while affording opportunities not available in closed slave systems, also made their bodies, and especially their reproductive capacities, a pri-mary object of enslavement. The question of slaves' assimilation was there-fore not a simple matter of softer slavery allowing assimilation and harsher slavery excluding outsiders permanently. Structuring slavery around forced assimilation gave a hard edge to the experience of enslaved women, whose loyalty and sexuality were policed with special vigor and violence.[86]

Because they had no actual kin within the village, slaves were extremely vulnerable to insult and injury. The Algonquian term *kichecam8tehaga-nec8e* meant "orphaned woman or girl without kin" and was described by a French writer as a "great insult." Were enslaved women to offend their master, their husband, or another of their husband's wives, they would have no extended kinship networks to rely upon for protection. One common word for a severe thrashing—*s8pikipacaminta*—meant "badly beaten like a slave." Serious mistreatment or abuse was described by the phrase *kiki8-nanga nintepinaric8o:* "He treats me like his slave."[87]

This familial isolation may, in part, explain the gendered violence re-ported by French men in the villages of the Pays d'en Haut. Because the Illi-nois, like most Algonquian and Siouan peoples, spared the lives of captured women more often than of men, there was a surplus of females living in their households. In a polygynous society, this posed little problem, provid-ing additional wives to prestigious men who could benefit from both their production and their reproduction. But French observers recoiled at the way some husbands treated their wives. According to Jacques Marquette, "They have several wives, of whom they are Extremely jealous; they watch them very closely, and Cut off Their noses or ears when they misbehave. I

86. There is a vast literature on the gendered implications of slavery, but, for an intro-duction among Native American women, see James F. Brooks, "'This Evil Extends Espe-cially . . . to the Feminine Sex': Negotiating Captivity in the New Mexico Borderlands," *Femi-nist Studies,* XXII (1996), 279–309; Brooks, *Captives and Cousins,* esp. 1–40. For gendered slavery in other contexts, see Gwyn Campbell, Suzanne Miers, and Joseph C. Miller, eds., *Women and Slavery,* I, *Africa, the Indian Ocean World, and the Medieval North Atlantic,* and II, *The Modern Atlantic* (Athens, Ohio, 2007); Jennifer Morgan, *Laboring Women: Re-production and Gender in New World Slavery* (Philadelphia, 2004); Kathleen M. Brown, *Good Wives, Nasty Wenches, and Anxious Patriarchs: Gender, Race, and Power in Colonial Virginia* (Chapel Hill, N.C., 1996).

87. Gravier and Largillier, "Dictionnaire illinois-français," 188 ("fille orpheline sans par-ents. grosse injure"), 533 ("badly beaten"). "Il me traite comme son esclave": Le Boullenger, "Dictionnaire français-illinois," s.v. "esclave."

saw several women who bore the marks of their misconduct." As mutilation (including nose cropping) carried specific symbolic meaning for slaves, and as an enslaved woman would have no father, uncles, or brothers to protect her from her husband's wrath, enslavement may help to explain how such violent acts could be tolerated by the Illinois. Rather than a pervasive feature of all Illinois gender relations, then, this violence may be what they called *tchekikic8 kiki8na8iki epinatonghi*: "that which one does to a slave."[88]

An enslaved wife's infidelity was the ultimate rejection of her master's authority and the most basic threat to his control over her reproductive labor. Infidelity also challenged the authority of senior wives who could find their coercive power over an enslaved sister wife challenged by her lover and his kin. It was punished brutally. Pierre Deliette described in gruesome detail the ritual gang rape of adulterous Illinois wives, who the evidence suggests were enslaved outsiders rather than Illinois women. Surrounded by her husband's male relatives, the adulteress was told that, because she was so hungry for men's flesh, she would get her fill of them now. They then raped her in turns, berating her for the act of disloyalty. Reminiscent of the language comparing slavery to consuming human flesh and mirroring the tortures enacted on slaving warriors who were forced to eat their own flesh, the ritual language suggests the victim's status as a slave. It also seems unlikely that this level of violence would be tolerated against an Illinois woman, whose kin could have come to her aid. Following a double standard, adultery brought lesser punishments to Indian men, but revenge occasionally drew slaves into the dynamic. Slaves could be given as a gift to mend internal disputes or violence within a village. When a man was killed by a jealous husband for seducing one of his wives, the murder could be covered by a generous gift, including a gift of slaves. Although an unlikely scenario, these customs would mean that, if an enslaved woman and her master / husband were both unfaithful, the slave could be raped for her punishment and then forced into another man's bed as a gift to cover her master's / husband's infidelity.[89]

88. *Jesuit Relations*, LIX, 127 ("cut off their noses"). For nose clipping as a mark of captivity, see James R. Duncan and Carol Diaz-Granados, "Of Masks and Myths," *Midcontinental Journal of Archaeology*, XXV (2000), 1–26. For the subordination of captive wives, see Judith A. Habicht-Mauche, "Captive Wives? The Role and Status of Nonlocal Women on the Protohistoric Southern High Plains," in Cameron, ed., *Invisible Citizens*, 181–204. "*Ce quon fait a ce qui est esclave*": Le Boullenger, "Dictionnaire français-illinois," s.v. "esclave."

89. Deliette, "Memoir," 334–337.

Such violence was rare because most of the enslaved understood the benefits of assimilation and sought to integrate themselves fully into their new households. Having seen a similar process in their own villages as they came of age and probably having participated in ritual violence as captives entered their home village, indigenous captives understood how successful slaves behaved. For those willing to adapt, there were relatively few constraints on moving up and into the captors' society. Those who resisted assimilation, if they survived at all, found themselves vulnerable to alienation, violence, and trade.

❖ The French did not find in the Pays d'en Haut a benign system of captivity that they would transform into slavery. The Siouan and Algonquian peoples there had an elaborate and often brutal war culture centered on a form of slavery, built on different assumptions and employed for different reasons than the plantation slavery developing in the contemporary Atlantic. Focused on the act of enslavement rather than the production of commodities, indigenous slavery was at its heart a system of symbolic dominion, appropriating the power and productivity of enemies and facilitating the creation of friendships built on shared animosity toward the captive's people. The intensely personal violence experienced during the first few months could be brutal and often deadly, but those who survived and weathered the storm of insults that followed found themselves in a system with many well-worn pathways out of slavery. These paths were often difficult to take, they were not available to everyone, and the prevalence of diplomatic slave trading served as a constant reminder of slaves' marginal and precarious position. And it goes without saying that, given the choice, no one would have sought enslavement, no matter what the outcome. But, if only in the next generation, slaves could at least hope to rise to full acceptance by the society that enslaved them, becoming identified with a people they once considered less than fully human.

Slavery in the Pays d'en Haut simultaneously disrupted and facilitated the broader political economy of trade and intermarriage that linked peoples and places throughout the region and beyond. Among allies, the sharing of enslaved enemies cemented alliances and created the bonds of fictive kinship that linked the region's peoples to one another across ethnic and linguistic lines. Among enemies, enslavement provided outlets for violent expressions of enmity that stopped short of total destruction and provided mechanisms of repopulation and enhanced productivity. As in all historical contexts, enslaved individuals in the Pays d'en Haut were agents as well as objects, responding to the trauma and alienation of slavery with creative adaptation to their new surroundings. French colonizers would bring their own evolving notions of slavery to the colonial encounter, which began a century-long conversation that would transform the vocabularies and structures of slavery in both the Pays d'en Haut and the French Atlantic world.

chapter two

THE MOST IGNOBLE AND SCANDALOUS KIND OF SUBJECTION

About 1690 a slave trader known only as Captain Bernard sailed to the French Caribbean with a cargo of African captives. He sold nearly all of them to colonial buyers, but kept one, named Louis, to serve him on his return to France. Louis attended Bernard for a year or two before he was sold to Antoine Benoist, one of Louis XIV's personal portrait artists, famous as the foremost wax sculptor in France. Louis served the artist as a domestic slave for eight years in Paris until, in 1703, Benoist arranged for Louis to be shipped to his son in Martinique. Sometime during Louis's Atlantic crossing—the third in his young life—he heard a rumor that slavery was illegal in France and that merely setting foot on French soil should have freed him. Although his own experience must have made him doubt the claim, shortly after arriving in Martinique in 1703 Louis petitioned the island's Superior Council, "claiming to be free by the privilege of the Kingdom of France."[1]

Louis built his appeal on a solid foundation. From the thirteenth to the sixteenth century, slavery, serfdom, and other forms of lifelong servitude in France slowly declined, replaced by a landed and relatively free peasantry. Although there were important exceptions, including Mediterranean galley slaves and a handful of domestic slaves in Atlantic port cities, French

---

1. "Prétendant estre Libre par le privilege du Royaume de France." Mithon to Pontchartrain, Nov. 20, 1704, ANOM, Colonies, C8A, XV, 348v. The document does not name the elder Benoist but identifies him as a Parisian and his son as an artist, both details that suggest Antoine Benoist. For Benoist, see Stanislas Lami, *Dictionnaire des sculpteurs de l'école française sous le règne de Louis XIV* (Paris, 1906), 27–30. See also Léo Elisabeth, *La société martiniquaise aux XVIIe et XVIIIe siècles, 1664-1789* (Paris, 2003), 268–270; Sue Peabody, *"There Are No Slaves in France": The Political Culture of Race and Slavery in the Ancien Régime* (New York, 1996), 13–15.

slavery reached its nadir in the sixteenth century as France's Iberian neighbors began to exploit large numbers of Africans and American Indians at home and abroad. France's regional courts took pride in claiming that France was too free for slavery, repeating the notion so often that it became something of a mantra in French legal circles: "There are no slaves in France." Some even claimed that the name of France, which derived from the word *franc*, or free, signified the kingdom's special commitment to liberty. In the first edition of its dictionary of the French language, published in 1694, the Académie Française followed the definition of *franc* with one of the term's common uses: "Every slave who sets foot in France becomes free and independent." A decade later, Louis hoped to capitalize on this sentiment, claiming that, having lived in France, he was no longer a slave but a free Frenchman.[2]

Learning of Louis's claim, his new master, the young Benoist, rushed his slave to the harbor and attempted to board a vessel bound for a Spanish port, hoping to sell Louis before colonial authorities could set him free. Refusing to be circumvented, the council intervened "to obviate the evil designs of the said Sieur Benoist," ordering Louis's immediate emancipation. Furious with the decision, Benoist bludgeoned Louis for initiating the suit and publicly rebuked the Superior Council for depriving him of his human property. Benoist appealed the case, threatening, "in not very respectful terms," to write directly to the royal court, where it seems he thought he could trade on his family connections. But in the end Benoist not only lost his slave but also earned a verbal thrashing "for speaking too freely" against his superiors.[3]

Louis's freedom suit launched a transatlantic inquiry into the place of slavery in France and its American colonies. None of the commentary was as informed as that of Michel Bégon, who wrote a memorandum on the case from La Rochelle in early 1704. Two decades earlier Bégon had been appointed intendant of the growing Caribbean colonies of Martinique, Guade-

2. Sue Peabody, *"There Are No Slaves in France"*; Peabody and Keila Grinberg, "Introduction: Slavery, Freedom, and the Law," in Peabody and Grinberg, eds., *Slavery, Freedom, and the Law in the Atlantic World: A Brief History with Documents* (Boston, 2007), 1–28. "Tout esclave qui met le pied en France devient franc et libre": *Dictionnaire de l'Académie française* (Paris, 1694), s.v. "franc." Mithon to the minister, Nov. 20, 1704, ANOM, Colonies, C8A, XV, 348v.

3. "Je le declaré Libre pour obvier aux mauvais desseins du dit Sr Benoist"; "des termes peu respectueux": Mithon to Pontchartrain, Nov. 20, 1704, ANOM, Colonies, C8A, XV, 348v–349.

loupe, and Saint Christophe (modern Saint Kitts), a post that included oversight of all commercial production and legal affairs. His first task, outlined in a royal commission, was to complete the drafting of a comprehensive slave ordinance, which, when issued in 1685, became the foundation for French slave law well into the nineteenth century. Following his service in the Caribbean, Bégon accepted a post in the Mediterranean managing the early modern world's largest fleet of galleys, manned by thousands of North African slaves and aimed at freeing enslaved Frenchmen. Since 1688, he had administered Rochefort, a growing port on France's Atlantic coast whose shipbuilding industry depended on overseas commerce, including the African slave trade. Having seen—and overseen—the development of French Atlantic slavery, Bégon found the notion that there were no slaves in France absurd: "a complete illusion."[4]

From the establishment of Caribbean colonies in 1626, Bégon wrote, French settlers had owned slaves. "Either blacks, Indians, or mulattos, they have brought these three sorts into every French territory, and they have taken them back without their claiming to be free." Slavery had become so central to the economic and social structure of the French Caribbean, he argued, that even freeing one or two slaves was regarded by the colonists as "destructive of their privileges, their commerce, and the establishment of their colonies." Not only was there "neither law nor ordinance to authorize the freeing of slaves who came to France," but long custom and formal law both supported the rights of French citizens to own slaves "and their posterity forever" as personal property. In short, Bégon described a vibrant French slave system that was economically necessary, legally protected, and socially demanded.[5]

4. "Une pure chimere": Michel Bégon, "Mémoire sur les esclaves des habitants des Isles françoises de l'Amérique qui prétendent être libres lorsqu'ils ont touché à la terre de France," 1704, ANOM, C8B, LXXIV. For Bégon's career, see Georges Duplessis, *Un curieux du XVIIe siècle: Michel Bégon, intendant de La Rochelle* (Paris, 1874); Yvonne Bezard, *Fonctionnaires maritimes et coloniaux sous Louis XIV: Les Bégon* (Paris, 1932).

5. "Il y a soisante dix huit ans que les habitans des Isles ont commencé a avoir des Esclaves qui sont ou noirs, ou sauvages, ou Mulatres, ils en ont amené de ces trois especes dans tous les forts de france, et les ont ramenés avec eux sans qu'ils ayent prétendu être libres"; "contraire à leurs privilèges, à leur commerce, et à l'etablissement de leurs Colonies"; "leurs enfans et leur posterité à l'infini"; "il ne paroist ny Loy ne ordonnance pour authoriser la liberté des Esclaves qui sont venus en france": all in Bégon, "Mémoire sur les esclaves," ANOM, C8B, LXXIV. Bégon was aware of the many local rulings and the general legal support for French free soil, but he distinguished this from a universal royal policy that applied equally throughout the kingdom and its overseas possessions. His reference to 1626 (seventy-eight years earlier) recalled the establishment of the first two companies concerned with the slave

Bégon wrote to defend the legal foundation of French Atlantic slavery precisely because he understood that it had a brief and contested history. When he was born in 1638, only a few hundred French colonists lived in Atlantic colonies, and they owned a mere handful of slaves. Numerically, the French were far more likely to become slaves than slaveholders. But, by the time Bégon died in 1710, French colonists commanded more than sixty thousand slaves, whose labor provided a significant proportion of France's overseas wealth. Elaborate legal codes—the most important of which Bégon had drafted himself—attempted to manage slaves' lives and direct their labor to the benefit of French masters. But Bégon recognized that the expansion of French slavery had occasioned intense debate and that, in many respects, his arguments were out of step with trends that had come to define the institution by the end of the seventeenth century.[6]

Both Louis and Bégon drew from a shared legal and historical tradition to make opposite claims about the nature of slavery and freedom within the French kingdom. From the late-medieval period, strong impulses within France and across Europe fostered a widespread aversion to slavery as a legal and social practice, providing Louis with ample legal precedent to support his claim of freedom. Provincial and royal authorities had ordered similar emancipations many times in the century and a half preceding Louis's appeal. But these acts of emancipation existed alongside an equally

---

trade, the Compagnie Normande charged with exploration and trade in Senegal, and the Compagnie de Saint-Christophe charged with colonization of the Caribbean. Abdoulaye Ly, *La Compagnie du Sénégal* (Paris, 1958), 32–36.

6. Historians have tended to ignore the first century of French colonial development in the Caribbean, focusing much more heavily on Canada than the Caribbean during the seventeenth century. See Philip P. Boucher, "The 'Frontier Era' of the French Caribbean, 1620s–1690s," in Christine Daniels and Michael W. Kennedy, eds., *Negotiated Empires: Centers and Peripheries in the Americas, 1500–1820* (New York, 2002), 207–234; Boucher, *France and the American Tropics to 1700: Tropics of Discontent?* (Baltimore, 2008), 144–167, which, despite an excellent overview of forced French labor, is unfortunately thin on the question of slavery. For brief overviews of the origins of French Atlantic slavery, see Robin Blackburn, *The Making of New World Slavery: From the Baroque to the Modern, 1492–1800* (London, 1997), 277–306; Peabody, *"There Are No Slaves in France,"* 11–13; Elisabeth, *La société martiniquaise,* 237–257; Jacques Petit-Jean Roget, *La société d'habitation à la Martinique: un demi-siècle de formation, 1635–1685* (Paris, 1980); Lucien Peytraud, *L'esclavage aux Antilles françaises avant 1789* (Paris, 1897), 1–52; Ly, *La Compagnie du Sénégal,* 21–64; Clarence J. Munford, *The Black Ordeal of Slavery and Slave Trading in the French West Indies, 1625–1715* (Lewiston, N.Y., 1991). For slave populations in the late-seventeenth and early eighteenth centuries, see James Pritchard, *In Search of Empire: The French in the Americas, 1670–1730* (Cambridge, 2004), 428–429; David Geggus, "The French Slave Trade: An Overview," *William and Mary Quarterly,* 3d Ser., LVIII (2001), 119–138.

significant tradition of human trafficking in France that, for Bégon, belied the claim that French soil was too free for slavery. Particularly in the sixteenth and seventeenth centuries, French privateers and royal galleys captured and enslaved vast numbers of North African Muslims, and French ports from Normandy to Provence supplied and hosted slave traders from France, the Netherlands, and Iberia. With American colonization in the seventeenth century, the demand for forced laborers grew exponentially.

The tension between antislavery sentiment in France and an expanding demand for enslaved laborers in its colonies profoundly shaped the culture and practice of slavery in the seventeenth-century French Atlantic. Bégon insisted on a uniform resolution to this tension, arguing, "The American colonies are so united and integrated into the body of the kingdom that they cannot be separated" and must be "governed by the same laws without distinction or difference." Not only did the local Caribbean elite disagree with Bégon on this point—freeing Louis and rebuking his master—but royal officials in France also rejected his claims. In 1707, responding to this and at least two similar cases involving enslaved women in France, Louis XIV's minister clarified his position: "The intention of his majesty is that the Negroes who have been brought into the kingdom by the inhabitants of the islands, who refuse to return there, may not be constrained to do so." Should slaves return to the Americas without invoking "the privilege of the soil of France," however, they renounced their freedom "by their voluntary return to the place of slavery." Bégon's notion of a unified French kingdom living under uniform laws, however much it served the needs of a centralizing state, did not apply to slavery. Replicating the legal pluralism of provincial France, where a baroque patchwork of distinct jurisdictions fragmented French legal practice, the law and practice of slavery divided the kingdom into zones of freedom and slavery, ensuring that those who held slaves were not the ones who enslaved them and that France could still protest its own unjust enslavement by North Africans while purchasing a spiraling number of slaves for the Americas.[7]

7. "Les Colonies de L'Amerique sont tellement unies et incorporées au Corps du Royaume qu'elles n'en peuvent être separées, et qu'elles sont regies et gouvernées par les mêmes Loix sans distinction ny difference": Bégon, "Mémoire sur les esclaves," ANOM, C8B, LXXIV. "L'intention de Sa Majesté est que les Negres qui auront été amenés dans le Royaume par les Habitans des Isles qui refuseront d'y retourner, ne pourront y être contrains . . . par leur retour volontaire dans le lieu de l'Eclavage": "Lettre du Ministre sur les Negres amenés en France," June 10, 1707, in M. Moreau de Saint-Méry, *Loix et constitutions des colonies françoises de l'Amérique sous le vent* (Paris, 1785–1790), II, 99.

Unlike the Indians they would encounter in the Pays d'en Haut, the French drew a sharp distinction between the practice of slavery and the act of enslavement. By placing all of the moral and legal burden on enslavement, the French distanced themselves from both the moral dilemmas and the practical problems associated with slaving violence. This maneuver allowed them to concentrate on the construction of an elaborate system of local power designed to maintain the enslaved population in perpetual bondage to extract maximum labor, operating on a scale and with a level of brutality unthinkable a century earlier. It also established the legal and cultural systems in which a variety of slaveries could flourish in different colonies within a single overseas empire. French colonists thus brought to the Pays d'en Haut a historically and culturally specific but still evolving form of slavery that would shape—and be shaped by—its North American counterpart.[8]

THERE ARE NO SLAVES IN FRANCE

"In Fraunce, although there be some remembrance of old servitude, yet is it not lawfull there to make any slave, or to buy any of others."
—Jean Bodin, Paris, 1576

The specific legal and cultural precedents that resulted in Louis's freedom date to the sixteenth century, when slavery was at historic lows in France. As in much of western Europe, slavery declined and all but disappeared in France during the late-medieval period, persisting mainly in Mediterranean coastal communities that hosted galley fleets manned by enslaved North Africans. At this time, the most common manifestation of slavery

---

For Louis XIV's agenda to centralize the state, see James B. Collins, *The State in Early Modern France* (Cambridge, 1995), esp. 79–124. For legal complexity in provincial France, see William Beik, *Absolutism and Society in Seventeenth-Century France: State Power and Provincial Aristocracy in Languedoc* (Cambridge, 1985); Zoë A. Schneider, *The King's Bench: Bailiwick Magistrates and Local Governance in Normandy, 1670–1740* (Rochester, N.Y., 2008); Michael P. Breen, *Law, City, and King: Legal Culture, Municipal Politics, and State Formation in Early Modern Dijon* (Rochester, N.Y., 2007). For notions of legal pluralism in the eighteenth-century French Atlantic, see Miranda Frances Spieler, "The Legal Structure of Colonial Rule during the French Revolution," *WMQ*, 3d Ser., LXVI (2009), 365–408; Malick Walid Ghachem, "Sovereignty and Slavery in the Age of Revolution: Haitian Variations on a Metropolitan Theme" (Ph.D. diss., Stanford University, 2001).

8. For an exploration of these questions in the English imperial context, see George Van Cleve, "Somerset's Case and Its Antecedents in Imperial Perspective," *Law and History Review*, XXIV (2006), 601–645.

in France was the threat of Muslim slave raids around the Mediterranean and its coastline as French ships, and even a handful of French villages, were targeted by Barbary pirates and slave raiders. By the mid-sixteenth century the rarity of slaves in France, the widespread sense that Frenchmen had become the target of unjust enslavement, and a desire to discredit France's international competitors combined to produce a culture—both popular and legal—that resisted slavery and placed a high burden of proof on those claiming its legitimacy. But in the half century between the 1570s and 1620s, the question of slavery confronted French society in new ways, forcing a range of responses from outright rejection of the practice to its acceptance under restricted circumstances. These debates were synthesized in one of the most influential works of political and legal theory in the early modern world: Hugo Grotius's *Rights of War and Peace*. Published only one year before the French crown authorized the first permanent settlements in the Caribbean, Grotius's work both distilled and shaped the specific context within which French Atlantic slavery developed in the seventeenth century.[9]

Two legal cases from Toulouse in the 1550s reveal the profound French skepticism toward slavery that framed these debates. The first involved a group of Gascon peasants who, in 1558, brought a complaint against their seigneur, the lord of La Roche-Blanche. Appearing before Toulouse's *parlement*, the city's chief judicial body, they acknowledged their willingness to show proper deference to their lord, "to trimme his vines, to till his grounds, to mow his meddows, to reape and thresh his corne," and to perform a host of other tasks that he required of them. But they found one of his demands intolerable. To ensure that the peasants remained under his control and continued to provide rents and labor, he warned anyone leaving his lands without permission that he would hunt them down and "lead them home againe in an halter [chevestre]." Reminiscent of controlling domestic animals, the threatened harnessing of peasants intentionally evoked slavery to a degree that the parlement found unacceptable. Declaring the treatment "prejudiciall unto the right of libertie," they forbade the lord to use it.[10]

9. For the decline of slavery in France from the fourteenth to the sixteenth centuries, see Charles Verlinden, *L'esclavage dans l'Europe medieval*, I, *Péninsule ibérique—France* (Brugge, 1955); Blackburn, *The Making of New World Slavery*, esp. 33–83; Gillian Lee Weiss, "Back from Barbary: Captivity, Redemption and French Identity in the Seventeenth- and Eighteenth-Century Mediterranean" (Ph.D. diss., Stanford University), esp. 20–122. Blackburn asserts that slavery was "extinct" in France by the sixteenth century (34), which overstates the totality of slavery's decline.

10. Jean Bodin, *The Six Bookes of a Commonweale*, ed. Kenneth Douglas McRae (Cam-

A few years later, a Genoese merchant traveled to Toulouse on business with his personal slave, an African he had bought during a visit to Spain. Recognizing the region's aversion to slavery, the "hoast of the house" where the merchant stayed "persuaded the slave to appeale unto his libertie." When he appeared before the attorney general of Toulouse to answer the appeal, the merchant argued that "he had truly bought his slave in Spaine, and so was afterward come to Tholouze, from thence to goe home to Genua, and so not to be bound to the laws of Fraunce." In response, the attorney general cited ancient law and modern precedent to prove "that slaves so soone as they came into Tholouze should be free." Finding the court unsympathetic to his claim of ownership, the merchant argued that, should they "deale so hardly with him, as to set at libertie another mans slave, yet they should at least restore unto him the money hee cost him." As the parlement discussed the possibility of compensation, the merchant—convinced that he would lose "both his dutifull slave and his money also"—emancipated the African on the condition that he serve the merchant until his death.[11]

These cases had a profound effect on Jean Bodin, a former Carmelite monk who was studying law in Toulouse when they were heard. Although Bodin was on his way to becoming Europe's most influential apologist for absolutist monarchy—by no means a champion of civil equality—he found slavery problematic, questioning the wisdom of allowing an institution "so dreadfull unto states and cities" to return to Europe after its four-century decline. The Toulouse cases grounded Bodin's antislavery sentiments and prompted him to write a brief history of slavery in Europe and the Mediter-

bridge, Mass., 1962), 42. Bodin's work, first published in French as *Les six livres de la république* (Paris, 1576), went through dozens of French editions and several translations, appearing in Latin, Italian, Spanish, and German before the end of the sixteenth century. The two most important translations are the 1586 Latin text translated by Bodin himself and the 1606 English translation by Richard Knolles. The only critical edition of Bodin is a heavily annotated reissue of the Knolles English edition, based on a minute comparison between the best French and Latin editions of the 1580s. Because it takes fullest account of both editions authored by Bodin, I have used the McRae edition here as it is more complete and reliable than any single French or Latin edition. I have noted discrepancies among the texts wherever I was aware of them. For Bodin and his publications, see Mario Turchetti, "Jean Bodin," in *The Stanford Encyclopedia of Philosophy* (Summer 2010 edition), ed. Edward N. Zalta, http://plato.stanford.edu/archives/sum2010/entries/bodin/. Bodin's work became a staple in French debates over slavery through the eighteenth century. See Peabody, *"There Are No Slaves in France,"* esp. 26–30. For Bodin as an antislavery thinker, see David Brion Davis, *The Problem of Slavery in Western Culture* (Oxford, 1966), 111–114; Ghachem, "Sovereignty and Slavery," 1–17.

11. Bodin, *Six Bookes of a Commonweale*, ed. McRae, 42.

ranean, which he later inserted into his most famous work, *Les six livres de la République,* first published in Paris in 1576.[12]

Bodin argued that slavery—"a thing most pernitious and daungerous"—had been all but eradicated in medieval France and ought to remain a distant memory despite recent pressures to reintroduce it. "In Fraunce," he wrote, "although there be some remembrance of old servitude, yet is it not lawfull there to make any slave, or to buy any of others." Claiming that it had been "more than 400 yeares agoe, since that Fraunce suffered in it any true slaves," he narrated an upward trajectory for French liberty flowing from a steady stream of decrees and court decisions that made slavery in France socially and legally unacceptable. Rooted in the tacit agreement of Christians not to enslave one another—a practice they adopted in imitation of Mohammed, "who set at libertie all them of his religion"—European suspicion of slavery grew as Christianity spread throughout the continent and as the threat of Islamic expansion forced Christian kingdoms into closer alliance with one another. Whether for religious, diplomatic, or economic reasons, then, beginning as early as the eighth century and picking up pace in the eleventh and twelfth centuries, "Christian princes by little and little released their servitude, and enfranchised their slaves." The decline of slavery in medieval France occurred fitfully over many centuries, but by Bodin's time there were few jurisdictions that did not have some local precedent favoring liberty over slavery and similar forms of involuntary servitude.[13]

The most famous of these precedents, decided in Bordeaux in 1571, would be cited for more than two centuries to support French free soil doctrine. Human trafficking had been a long-standing practice for Norman seafarers, who began selling enslaved Guanches from the Canary Islands as early as 1402. By the mid-sixteenth century, French—particularly Norman—traders had established several strongholds along the West African coast, concentrating on gold and ivory but dealing in small numbers of slaves, including many seized illegally from Portuguese or Spanish ships. English, Dutch, French, and Iberian ships involved in the African trade had stopped at Bordeaux since at least the 1550s, and the city's vibrant Iberian merchant community was growing in importance, clearly involved in the slave trade abroad. Most of these slaves never reached France but were delivered to the more developed slave markets of Spain and Portugal. Some

12. Ibid., 45.

13. Ibid., 44 ("pernitious and daungerous"), 42 ("In Fraunce . . . not lawfull"), 41 ("true slaves"), 40 ("set at libertie"), 39 ("Christian princes").

slaves, particularly those taken by pirates, were sold as far away as Brazil or the Spanish Caribbean. So in February 1571, when a cargo of enslaved "negroes and moors" arrived on a Norman vessel stopping at Bordeaux, it was not the novelty of French slave trading that caught people's attention. It was the merchant's attempt to sell them in French territory.[14]

Bordeaux's parlement had prominent members who viewed their role as protectors of French liberties. Among the most influential, the good friends and fellow scholars Michel de Montaigne and Étienne de La Boétie argued that by the law of nature all were born free. If people were to live by the principles of natural law, La Boétie wrote, "we would be naturally obedient to parents, subjects to reason, and slaves to no one." Neither of them was still in the parlement by 1571—La Boétie had died, and Montaigne had resigned—but their influence lingered. Invoking the free soil doctrine articulated in Toulouse just over a decade earlier, the parlement declared that all of the Norman's slaves "shall be set free," proclaiming that "France, mother of liberty, allows no slaves." Having both judicial and legislative powers, the court's decree became binding law.[15]

Decisions like these resonated with Bodin and throughout France at least in part because in the mid-sixteenth century the French were more liable to become slaves than slaveholders. Muslim corsairs in the Mediterranean went on a slaving spree in the sixteenth century, putting French sailors and coastal communities at risk. In 1579, it was estimated that Algiers alone

14. For early Norman slave trading, see Jean de Béthencourt, *The Canarian; or, The Book of the Conquest and Conversion of the Canarians in the Year 1402*, ed. and trans. Richard Henry Major (London, 1872). In the mid-1550s, an English captain named William Towrson identified two English ships bound for "Guinea" on the West African coast. They had come from Bordeaux and were laden with French wine and other goods. See Towrson's account of three separate journeys in Richard Hakluyt, *The Principal Navigations, Voyages, Traffiques, and Discoveries of the English Nation* ... (Glasgow, 1903–1905), VI, 231–232 (177–252 for a full account of Towrson's engagement with French trade in West Africa). For early Norman trade with West Africa and the Spanish Caribbean, see Charles de La Roncière, *Histoire de la marine française*, 2d ed. (Paris, 1909–1932), IV, 76–77.

15. "Si nous vivions avec les droits que la nature nous a donnés et avec les enseignements qu'elle nous apprend, nous serions naturellement obéissants aux parents, sujets à la raison, et serfs de personne." Quoted in Linton C. Stevens, "A Re-Evaluation of Hellenism in the French Renaissance," in Werner L. Gundersheimer, ed., *French Humanism: 1470–1600* (New York, 1969), 196.

"Au mesme mois et an, il y a Arrest donné par ladite Cour, par lequel est ordonné, que tous les negres et mores qu'un Marchand Normand avoit conduit en cette Ville pour vendre, seroient mis en liberté: la France mere de liberté ne permet aucuns esclaves": Gabriel de Lurbe, *Chronique bourdeloise* (Bordeaux, 1594; rpt. Paris, 1703), 33. For giving the ordinance the force of law, see La Roncière, *Histoire de la marine française*, IV, 80.

hosted a population of 25,000 European slaves, in addition to smaller but significant populations in Tunis, Morocco, and Tripoli. During Bodin's lifetime (ca. 1530–1596), North African states enslaved well more than 300,000 Europeans, tens of thousands of whom were French despite the crown's best diplomatic efforts with the Ottomans and their allies (known to defensive Christians as "the unholy alliance").[16]

Sailors felt the fear of Barbary enslavement more than anyone else, as capture at sea was the most likely path into slavery. In a 1637 account of a voyage to the Cape Verde Islands, the Capuchin priest Alexis de Saint-Lo conveyed the urgency with which seafarers met the threat of possible attack by Barbary corsairs. As they approached the African coast before heading south, they saw another ship in the distance that seemed to be commanded by a Turk (a generic term for a Mediterranean Muslim). As they braced for attack, Saint-Lo catechized a group of young people as he urged everyone to fight to the death rather than be taken alive and forcibly converted to Islam. Several on board, including three officers, "had experienced the barbarity of the Turks and had often spoken to the rest of the crew about the cruelties that this fierce nation commits against the Christians." The worst fate, according to the experienced crew, was to become a sex slave bound to "service" these men with "infamous, detestable acts against nature." Eventually, when the ship approached close enough to see the men on board, they were relieved to discover that the other ship was commanded by fellow Christians. Although they had been in no immediate danger, their reaction illustrates the depth of French fear of Barbary enslavement and its many horrors.[17]

In the early seventeenth century, the French priest Pierre Dan described the Barbary Coast as "a bloody theater, where many tragedies are enacted," calling upon the French king and French people everywhere to respond with compassion to "the cruelties and barbarities suffered by Christian slaves under the tyranny of Muslims, mortal enemies of our faith." By

16. Robert C. Davis, *Christian Slaves, Muslim Masters: White Slavery in the Mediterranean, the Barbary Coast, and Italy, 1500–1800* (New York, 2003), 23, 47–48. For the fullest account specific to the French, see Weiss, "Back from Barbary." For the "unholy alliance," see Edith Garnier, *L'alliance impie: François Ier et Soliman le Magnifique contre Charles Quint, 1529–1547* (Paris, 2008).

17. "Avoient experimenté la barbarie des Turcs, et souvent avoyent entretenu le reste de l'Equipage des cruautez que ceste farouche Nation exerce contre les Chrestiens"; "servissent à leur infame action destable contre la Nature": Alexis [de] S[aint]-Lo, *Relation du voyage du Cap-Verd* (Paris, 1637), 4–6.

the 1630s he could claim, "It would not be stretching the truth to say that they have put a million [Christians] in chains" (a number shown by modern scholarship to be basically accurate). One among hundreds of clerics to devote themselves to the redemption of French slaves, Dan raised money from grieving families and affronted Catholics that he took to Muslim states to purchase French men and women. His account of Muslim slaveholders' depravity, published in Paris in 1637, ran more than five hundred pages and included lavish illustrations depicting snarling slaveholders terrorizing French Christians, verbal and visual images that garnered further support for his efforts. In defense of French victims, Dan's account insisted on "the violence and misery of slavery," condemning the "continual labor" extracted from enslaved Christians by lazy Muslim masters who "forced them to [work] with blows from sticks, and gave them less rest than their horses."[18]

Beyond print, Dan and his fellow redemptioners celebrated their victories in highly public processions, parading redeemed slaves through towns and cities to publicize their success and raise funds for more redemptions. As part of their obligation to their redeemers, former slaves were required to participate in the processions for up to three months. Beginning with a parade in the streets of Marseille, the party then walked as many as five hundred miles through the French countryside to Paris. All along the way, townspeople turned out to celebrate the end of their compatriots' slavery. For a majority of people throughout France, then, the primary—if not the only—face of slavery was French, making antislavery sentiment more a matter of self-preservation than about the high ideals of protecting others.[19]

The threat of French enslavement, whipped into what one historian termed "corsair hysteria," contributed to the already widespread skepticism about slavery in sixteenth- and early-seventeenth-century France. As early as 1538, when a court in southern France freed a Greek slave belonging to an Italian master, the court claimed to do so "by the common law of France."

18. "La Barbarie est un theatre sanglant, où il s'est joüé quantité de Tragedies"; "les cruautez et les barbaries que souffrent les esclaves Chrestiens, sous la tyrannie des Mahometans, ennemis mortels de notre Foy"; "les violences et les miseres de l'esclavage"; "le continüel travail des leurs Esclaves. A quoy ils les forcét à coups de batons, et leur donnent moins de repos qu'à leurs chevaux": Pierre Dan, *Histoire de Barbarie et de ses corsaires* (Paris, 1637), 1 ("bloody theater"), 282 ("violence and misery"), preface ("continual labor"). For "a million [Christians]," see Davis, *Christian Slaves, Muslim Masters*, 8, and, for a detailed discussion of the probable numbers of European slaves, 3–26.

19. Weiss, "Back from Barbary," chap. 5 ("Processions of Redemption"), 213–269.

FIGURE 8. Missionaries Paying a Ransom to Release French Slaves. *Pierre Dan, Histoire de la Barbarie et de ses corsairs. Paris, 1649. Courtesy Library of Congress, Washington, D.C.*

It might have overstated the clarity of the law on the matter, but by 1607 the renowned legal philosopher Antoine Loisel could synthesize the general legal climate in similarly hopeful terms: "Everyone is free in this kingdom: as soon as a slave reaches its borders, being baptized, he is freed." His dictum would be repeated, almost verbatim, all over France in the seventeenth century, including in an oft-cited legal guide published by Hiérome Mercier, a counselor in the parlement of Paris. "By the general law of this kingdom all persons are free and independent," wrote Mercier. "That is why, when a serf or a slave takes refuge in France, as soon as he reaches its borders and is baptized, he is freed."[20]

20. "Selon le droit commun de France": Verlinden, *L'esclavage dans l'Europe medieval*, I, 851. "Toutes personnes sont franches en ce royaume: si tost qu'un esclave a attaint les

But saying there were no slaves in France did not make it so. Loisel, Bodin, and their contemporaries recognized that the freedom principle was more prescriptive than descriptive and that it was only one side of a contentious debate over slavery within France and throughout Europe. Although individual cases of legal emancipation gained widespread attention, like the Norman who brought a slave ship to Bordeaux in 1571, they also indicated a competing vision of French involvement in slavery. If the French were victims of enslavement in the Mediterranean, they also took thousands of North Africans as galley slaves, and as a result places like Marseille could never pretend to disallow slavery within their borders. So, even as Bodin saw all around him evidence of declining support for slavery, still the practice thrived. "If the Muslims have freed all the slaves of their religion . . . and the Christians have done the same," he wondered, "how is it possible that the whole world is still full of slaves?"[21]

The piecemeal solidification of French free soil doctrine, then, occurred in the context of a vigorous debate in France and throughout Europe over the relationship between natural law and slavery, disputed most forcefully among Iberians who by the 1570s had become heavily involved in slavery in West Africa, Brazil, Mexico, and the Caribbean. The trade of the Portuguese in West Africa began in the mid-fifteenth century, and by 1482 they had established São George da Mina in modern Ghana. As the name of the fort implies, the primary target was gold rather than slaves, but by the time Bodin wrote his history between eight and nine thousand enslaved Africans were traded each year on European vessels. France's role in the slave trade was small but not insignificant, as both French and Iberian ships sailing from French ports frequented the West African coast in the second half of the sixteenth century. Operating from a stronghold on the Cape Verde Islands, by the mid-1550s Norman gold and slave traders were

marches d'icelui, se faisant baptizer, il est affranchi": Antoine Loisel, *Institutes coutumières de la France* . . . (Paris, 1607), 24, quoted in La Roncière, *Histoire de la marine française*, IV, 80. "Par la Loy générale de ce Royaume toutes personnes sont libres et franches. . . . C'est pourquoy quand un serf et un esclave se refugie en France, aussitost qu'il en a attaint les marches et qu'il s'est fait baptizer, il est affrancy": H[iérome] M[ercier], *Remarques du droit françois* (Paris, 1657), 11. (For "corsair hysteria," see Davis, *Christian Slaves, Muslim Masters*, 5.)

21. "S'il est ainsi que les Mehemetistes ont afranchy touts les esclaves de leur religion, qui a cours en tout l'Asie, et Presque en toute l'afrique, voire en une bonne partie de l'Europe, et que les Chrestiens ayent fait le semblable, comme nous avons monstré, comment est-il possible que tout le monde soit encores plein d'esclaves": Bodin, *Les six livres de la république*, 45.

raiding Portuguese ships and trading on their own account with coastal peoples near modern Senegal. By 1604, the Portuguese would complain that French interlopers arrived "every year," ruining Portuguese commerce because the coast was "infested with French pirates who rob ships as they arrive or leave." Most of these ships did not return to France, though, so their impact on debates over French slavery was relatively modest, the 1571 case being a prominent exception.[22]

By the mid-sixteenth century a considerable community of Portuguese and Spanish merchants had grown up in the French port cities of Bordeaux, Nantes, Rouen, and La Rochelle, meaning that some of what passed as Iberian trade with West Africa began in French ports with French goods on ships manned by at least some French sailors. In 1574 the French king acknowledged the importance of these communities when he issued a special order for their protection that seems to have covered their right to continue the slave trade despite local rulings to the contrary. The New Christian communities at Bordeaux presented a joint petition to the king's council, likely responding to the 1571 ruling in that city forbidding slaves from entering French ports. Citing the communities' importance to French commerce, the king offered them "special protection" from all local efforts to interfere with their families, their property, or their "servants," ordering that "the said Spanish and Portuguese who have resided and do reside in our city of Bordeaux may freely and securely remain and continue the trade." The protection seems to have bolstered the communities' confidence, and by 1602 one report identified as many as one thousand Iberian merchant families along the western coast of France.[23]

Because of Spanish and Portuguese reliance on forced labor, Iberian legal scholars explored the nature and law of slavery with unique urgency,

---

22. Baltasar Barreira to Antonio Colaco, Jul. 22, 1604, and Baltazar [sic] Barreira to Manoel de Barros, Jan. 28, 1605, in A. Teixeira da Mota and P. E. H. Hair, eds. and trans., *Jesuit Documents on the Guinea of Cape Verde and the Cape Verde Islands, 1585–1617: In English Translation* (Liverpool, 1989), 3–4 ("every year"), 2 ("infested").

23. "Sauveguard special"; "serviteurs"; "lesdits Espagnols et Portugais qui ont ci-devant reside et resident en notre ville de Bordeaux, puissant librement et sùrement demurer et continuer le traffic et commerce": Moreau de Saint-Méry, *Loix et constitutions*, I, 9. The violence of the French civil wars, particularly shortly after Saint Bartholomew's Day, likely played a role in anti-Iberian violence, but it is suggestive that the only enumerated commodity protected in the king's order was the Iberians' "serviteurs." Whatever its cause, the effect of the decree would have been to shield Iberian slave traders from the 1571 ordinance. See also R[oland] Francisque-Michel, *Les portugais en France, les français en Portugal* (Paris, 1882), 173.

and their sixteenth-century writings informed French practice in the seventeenth century. Not only did French jurists and philosophers engage Iberian ideas, but they also used Spanish and Portuguese actions as negative examples that demonstrated the depravity of slavery. These Spanish debates took place during the sixteenth-century Renaissance when French humanists encountered slavery as a philosophical and legal problem in classical texts. Following the French invasions of Italy at the end of the fifteenth century and the subsequent arrival in Paris of classical scholars like Desiderius Erasmus and Jacques Lefevre d'Étaples, French readers took a profound interest in Italy's humanistic revival, drawn particularly to texts from ancient Greece and Rome. Generously patronized by François I, French intellectuals—especially in Paris, Lyon, and Toulouse—began translating classical texts into French; vernacular editions of Aristotle, Plato, Seneca, Justinian, and other classics appeared during the first half of the sixteenth century. Because slavery was so pervasive in the classical world, discussions of the institution appeared in nearly every text. Engaging these writings, French thinkers began to discuss the justice and merits of slavery despite the marginalization of the institution in France itself. What is more, the holding of galley and domestic slaves around Marseille, the growing involvement of French merchants in the Atlantic slave trade, and international competition with Iberian powers meant that, despite being a relative outsider to the Atlantic slave trade, France was deeply invested in international discussions about the legality and morality of slavery.[24]

Among the most influential French humanists discussing the issue was Louis Le Roy, a Norman intellectual with a classical education from Paris and legal training from Toulouse. His most influential work, a French translation of and commentary on Aristotle's *Politics*, became the definitive edition, such that another French translation did not appear for two centuries. Introducing Aristotle's view that some people were natural slaves, born with qualities that made them more fit to serve than to rule, Le Roy recognized that the point had become highly contentious. "Here," he wrote, "the Phi-

24. On French Renaissance humanism, see Gundersheimer, ed., *French Humanism*. On classical slavery, see Moses I. Finley, *Ancient Slavery and Modern Ideology* (New York, 1983); Keith Bradley, *Slavery and Society at Rome* (Cambridge, 1994); Alan Watson, *Roman Slave Law* (Baltimore, 1987). David Brion Davis writes, "The revival of classical learning, which may have helped to liberate the mind of Europe from bondage to ignorance and superstition, only reinforced the traditional justifications for human slavery" (*The Problem of Slavery in Western Culture*, 107). More accurately, the Renaissance revived two competing justifications of slavery, one based in natural law and the other in the law of nations.

losopher enters into a very serious dispute." But, in the end, Le Roy agreed with Aristotle and his Spanish followers that some "are born to obey, others to command." "Natural slaves," he concluded with Aristotle, were stupid and strong, "having slow, feeble minds but powerful bodies to do necessary work."[25]

Despite his acclaim, Le Roy met overwhelming resistance for his support of Aristotelian natural slavery. French legal scholars followed the Spanish debates closely, distinguishing themselves from their Spanish counterparts by rejecting natural slavery, justifying slavery by the law of nations rather than the law of nature. Bodin and his contemporaries rejected natural slavery in part to distance France from its Spanish competitors and lay moral claim to French presence in West Africa and the Americas. Bodin followed the debates about Spanish slavery with great interest, contrasting what he saw as his kingdom's superior approach to the issue. Praising Charles V for outlawing the enslavement of Indians, he still took satisfaction that in France "the slaves of strangers so soone as they set their foot within Fraunce become franke and free." He had seen this happen in the case of the Genoa merchant in Toulouse, and Iberians in Bordeaux had to seek royal protection to avoid a similar fate. If slavery were natural, and therefore divinely designed, no human law interfering would be defensible.[26]

According to Bodin, the history of the institution proved that masters often ruled over their intellectual and moral superiors, and owning slaves brought out the very worst in slaveholders, inspiring them to tyranny and violence. To accept Aristotle's logic—that the enslaved were inferior by nature and thus fit for slavery—would also have been an indictment of enslaved Christian compatriots and an acceptance of the superiority of their Muslim masters. Implying as much, Bodin asked, "For wise men to serve fools, men of understanding to serve the ignorant, and the good to serve the bad; what can bee more contrarie unto nature?"[27]

Rather than expressing innate inequality, then, Bodin argued that slavery arose from human rather than natural law, specifically the doctrine of just war, which he described as "the first beginning of slaves": the origin of slavery itself. Bodin accepted the captor's right to enslave his captives

25. Werner L. Gundersheimer, *The Life and Works of Louis Le Roy* (Geneva, 1966), 56. "Le Philosophe entre icy en une tres grave dispute"; "qui sont Tardifs et grossiers d'entendement, mais puissans de corps pour faire les oeuvres necessaires": Louis Le Roy, trans., *Les politiques d'Aristote* (Paris, 1599), 26, 27.

26. Bodin, *Six Bookes of a Commonweale*, ed. McRae, 42.

27. Ibid., 32–46, 34 ("wise men to serve fools").

rather than kill them, even if he doubted the purity of the captor's motives. "For who is hee that would spare the life of his vanquished enemie," he asked, "if he could get a greater profit by his death than by sparing his life?" Yet, despite his personal antislavery sentiments, Bodin acknowledged what he saw as a clear consensus on the matter of enslavement, which nations from ancient times to the present seemed to embrace. "The consent of all nations will that that which is gotten by just warre should bee the conquerours owne, and that the vanquished should be slaves unto the victorious." Unjust wars, including slave raids undertaken by a sovereign "to make of freemen his slaves," were tyrannical and indefensible under either natural or international law.[28]

Bodin's *Republic* garnered immediate attention in France and by 1600 was already in its fourteenth French edition. Only three years after its publication, one Englishman noted, "You can not steppe into a schollars studye but (ten to one) you shall likely finde open either Bodin de Republica or Le Royes Exposition uppon Aristoteles Politiques." On the issue of slavery, however, Bodin's position became by far the more influential. Impressed by Bodin's work, Henry III called upon Bodin as a political consultant, a role he played well into the 1580s. Although primarily concerned with the politics of kingdoms rather than international relations, Bodin profoundly influenced French thinking about slavery as a function of international law. Subsequent French thinkers followed his lead, justifying slavery abroad, even as domestically the institution eroded under a stream of decisions affirming French free soil doctrine. Bodin's contemporary, Estienne Pasquier, for example, argued that Aristotle's notion of natural slavery could neither explain nor justify human bondage. Yet, like Bodin, he found in international law ample support for the the institution. "When a man has been made a prisoner of war," he wrote in a discussion of Roman law, "it was found more expedient to keep him than to kill him."[29]

Hugo Grotius agreed. Having escaped imprisonment in the Netherlands, Grotius fled to Paris in 1621, where he published *The Rights of War and Peace (De jure belli et pacis)* in 1625. Like Bodin, Grotius rejected Aristotle's

28. Ibid., 34 ("first beginning"), 35 ("who . . . would spare the life"), 203 ("consent of all nations").

29. H.-J. Martin, "What Parisians Read in the Sixteenth Century," in Gundersheimer, ed., *French Humanism*, 138; Richard Tuck, *Natural Rights Theories: Their Origin and Development* (Cambridge, 1979), 44 ("schollars studye"); Weiss, "Back from Barbary," 30.

notion of natural slavery: servitude derived, not from the law of nature, but from the law of nations.

> There is no Man by Nature Slave to another, that is, in his primitive State considered, independently of any human Fact . . . but it is not repugnant to natural Justice, that Men should become Slaves by a human Fact, that is, by Vertue of some Agreement, or in Consequence of some Crime.

No one, in other words, was made for slavery, however base or backward one's culture. Only human law, "introduced by Custom and tacit Consent," could create slaves. The original and universal enjoyment of natural liberty was, in fact, central to the justice of slavery for Grotius. The tacit consent that allowed states to rule individuals and nations to deal with one another in the name of their people originated in human agency exercised in liberty. That same liberty allowed a prisoner to yield his or her life to a captor in exchange for lifelong slavery.[30]

For Grotius, as for Bodin and many others stretching back to the Roman laws compiled by Justinian, the law of nations provided that captives taken in a just war could be enslaved rather than killed. "Life is far preferable to Liberty," he explained. "Therefore GOD himself imputes it as an Act of his Favour, that he did not cut off his People with the Sword, but made them Captives." Where Bodin disparaged the greed that motivated captors to protect prisoners only to make them slaves, Grotius argued that captors' self-interest was the very reason the law was successful: aligning the state's desire to spare captives' lives with individual captors' desire for the spoils of war. Nothing could induce captors to spare their slaves' lives "but a Motive drawn from Interest." The prisoner could choose to die or to accept lifelong slavery. "The most ignoble and scandalous Kind of Subjection," Grotius

30. Hugo Grotius, *The Rights of War and Peace*, ed. Richard Tuck (Indianapolis, Ind., 2005), I, 75, III, 1360. Tuck's is the most complete and best-annotated critical edition. His introductory essay (I, ix–xxxiii) is also among the best short introductions to Grotius's life and work. Hugo Grotius, [*Déclaration en français de H. de Groot, expliquant les raisons de son arrivée en France* . . . (Paris, [1622])]. For Grotius's intellectual influence in Paris and broader France, see H. J. M. Nellen, "Grotius et le monde intellectuel parisien," *Nederlands Archief voor Kerkgeschiedenis*, LXXX (2000), 282–295. For his influence on subsequent application of international law, see Dan Edelstein, "War and Terror: The Law of Nations from Grotius to the French Revolution," *French Historical Studies*, XXXI (2008), 229–262; Tuck, *Natural Rights Theories*, 58–81, which characterizes Grotius as the most important figure in the history of early modern political philosophy.

wrote, "is that by which a Man offers himself to perfect and utter Slavery," "which obliges a Man to serve his Master all his Life long." Even if the only alternative was death, the law of nations treated the prisoner's choice as voluntary and permanent.[31]

Because prisoners could have been killed rather than kept alive, the captor granting a prisoner's life now possessed it, making slavery both perpetual and inheritable. "Neither do only they themselves become Slaves," Grotius reasoned, "but their Posterity for ever; for whosoever is born of a Woman after she is a Slave, is born a Slave." Explaining the perpetuity of servitude that originated in just war, Grotius argued that slavery granted life not only to the mother but also to the child, since her death in war would have prevented any future offspring: "If the Captor had been pleased to have used his utmost Power, he might have prevented their being born." Then, too, given the uncertainty of paternity in this pre-DNA age, Grotius accepted the Roman practice that a child's status would follow the mother's, "as the young ones of Beasts, so the Children of Slaves follow the Condition and Circumstances of the Mother." A child with a free father and an enslaved mother would be born a slave: as Tacitus had written, "she had *Servitio subjectum uterum, a Womb subjected to Bondage,* that is, her Child would be a Bondslave."[32]

The law of nations required that captives be taken in a justifiable war, leaving the burden of proof on the enslavers to demonstrate that they had undertaken the attack for generally acceptable reasons, fighting in defense of one's own sovereignty or an ally's safety. Because, in the eyes of Bodin, Pasquier, and Grotius, no humans were natural slaves, only the process of enslavement could determine the legality of anyone's slave status. By general agreement, according to Grotius, Christians exempted one another from bondage, even when it resulted from a just war. But it did not follow that all non-Christians were automatically lawful targets of enslavement. The circumstances of their capture still determined their legal position among their captors, even if one could argue that slavery would be the best thing for them: "For I must not compel a Man even to what is advantageous to him. For the Choice of what is profitable or not profitable, where People enjoy their Senses and their Reason, is to be left to themselves, unless some

---

31. Grotius, *Rights of War and Peace*, ed. Tuck, II, 556–557 ("perfect and utter Slavery"), II, 1143 ("Life . . . preferable to Liberty"), III, 1364 ("Motive drawn from Interest").

32. Ibid., II, 559 ("follow the Condition . . . of the Mother"), III, 1362 ("Posterity for ever"), III, 1364 ("prevented their being born").

other Person has gained any Right over them." These rights could be gained only in just wars, properly declared and executed.[33]

But international law applied only to the act of enslavement, not to the practice of slavery. Once persons were determined to be justly enslaved, they became the property of the person or nation that captured them. Significantly, this stripped the moral freight from buying slaves once they had been enslaved by another. "The Law of Nations," Grotius explained, "has in this Case put Men in the same Rank with Goods." The circumstances of enslavement were governed by the law of nations, but slavery—including the master-slave relationship—was governed only by the society in which the slaves lived. As a matter of human law, those relationships could be regulated, but states were under no obligation to do so, as "the Effects of this Right are infinite, so that there is nothing that the Lord may not do to his Slave . . . no Torment but what may be inflicted on him with Impunity, nothing commanded him but what may be exacted with the utmost Rigour and Severity; so that all manner of Cruelty may be exercised by the Lords upon their Slaves; unless this License is somewhat restrained by the civil Law." Regulating the practice of slavery thus became a separate category of legal and moral activity, governed by the slaveholding society rather than the law of nations.[34]

Grotius recognized that he did not write his treatise in a legal or political vacuum. He published in early-seventeenth-century Paris, where he interacted with many who had embraced France's drift away from slavery in the previous decades. Like Bodin, though, Grotius characterized France's free soil principle as a royal privilege specific to that kingdom rather than a legal or moral imperative governing European, or even French, actions abroad. From ancient times, he wrote, there had always been kingdoms that chose to exempt people within them from the burdens of slavery. These kingdoms enacted "peculiar Laws" which made them a "Place of Refuge for Slaves." This was the foundation, Grotius learned during his time in Paris, "on which that Privilege seems grounded among the *French*, given to Slaves to enter

33. Ibid., II, 1106 ("I must not compel"). On the agreement between Christian kingdoms to exempt one another's subjects from slavery, Grotius wrote, "But among Christians it is generally agreed, that being engaged in War, they that are taken Prisoners, are not made Slaves, so as to sell them or force them to hard Labours, or to such Miseries as are common to Slaves" (III, 1372). Yet being outside that agreement did not automatically make others subject to war and enslavement, and Grotius argued at length, "War cannot be justly made upon those who refuse to embrace the Christian Religion" (II, 1041).

34. Ibid., III, 1362–1363 ("Effects of this Right are infinite"), 1365 ("same Rank with Goods").

again on Possession of their Liberty, the Moment they come into the Dominions of that Kingdom, which is also now allowed, not only to those taken in War, but to all others whatever." Rather than a universal privilege granted by natural law, French free soil was a privilege particular to the kingdom of France that could exist alongside the kingdom's acknowledgment of the legality of slavery abroad. By the law of nature no one was a slave. By the law of nations some could be enslaved. By the laws of France even those justly enslaved elsewhere would regain their original liberty in France.[35]

Despite being a newcomer to the French intellectual scene, it would be difficult to overstate Grotius's influence on French thinking about slavery and its place in international law. Pierre Bayle, author of the monumental *Dictionnaire historique et critique,* characterized him as "one of the greatest men of Europe," noting that *The Rights of War and Peace* "received exceptional honor from the public." As one intellectual historian has written, because Grotius "was universally read, everyone working in any of the fields which he touched had to go through him before they could progress to their own ideas." The publication of this treatise, according to another, "launched the modern era of international law."[36]

As much as anything, the timing of Grotius's work ensured that it would shape the legal and political conversations that informed French colonialism in the seventeenth century. In the summer of 1626, less than a year after the publication of *The Rights of War and Peace,* Cardinal Richelieu—France's architect of overseas policy—offered to hire the author to help him craft charters for overseas colonization. For various personal reasons Grotius resisted, limiting his role to the translation of key documents from the Dutch East and West India Companies and some personal consulting with the cardinal on matters of international law. Despite Grotius's demurral, Richelieu made it clear that he read and followed Grotius as he crafted overseas policy. In fall 1626, when Richelieu commissioned the first French companies to colonize the Caribbean, they reflected Grotius's Dutch-to-French translations and embraced many of his central ideas. With *The Rights of War and Peace* Grotius punctuated a conversation that had developed over

35. Ibid., III, 1371.
36. "L'un des plus grands hommes de l'Europe" and "reçu du publique un honneur très-particulier": Pierre Bayle, *Dictionnaire historique et critique,* 5th ed. (Amsterdam, 1740), II, 614, 618; Edelstein, "War and Terror," *French Historical Studies,* XXXI (2008), 233; Jon Miller, "Hugo Grotius," *Stanford Encyclopedia of Philosophy* (Summer 2009 Edition), ed. Zalta, http://plato.stanford.edu/archives/sum2009/entries/grotius/.

the better part of a century in French legal and political culture. His synthesis also provided a model that would allow for the simultaneous rejection of slavery within the geographic bounds of the French kingdom and the expansion of French involvement in slavery overseas.[37]

The widespread rejection of Aristotelian natural slavery meant that French ethnic and religious chauvinism would not suffice to justify enslavement, particularly considering the depth of legal precedent that would challenge anyone claiming slave property on that basis. Slavery existed in France, particularly galley slavery in Marseille, and the slave trade operated from that and other port cities. But before the 1620s those activities occurred either in such a specific context (like the galleys) or among specific populations (like the Iberian New Christians in Bordeaux) that clashes were rare. As Caribbean colonial expansion began in the second quarter of the seventeenth century, French colonists, merchants, jurists, and royal officials were forced into a sustained discussion about the legality and morality of slavery that shaped not only where slavery would be practiced and under what conditions but also which peoples would—and would not—be targeted as slaves.

SLAVES TO THE KING

"In their own country most of them are slaves to the king or to others; they are sold to the Europeans at quite a good price."—Jacques Bouton, Martinique, 1640

Although Michel Bégon was right that slavery existed from the beginning of French colonization in the Americas, in the early seventeenth century it would have been difficult to predict a French colonial world dependent on enslaved labor, and not only because of France's ambivalence toward the practice. From the very early stages of French colonization in the Atlantic world, slavery was only one among many labor strategies available to investors and colonists, and exactly the role it would play was far from certain. Not only was slavery still rather poorly defined as an institution, but the social and political models that would allow it to flourish had yet to be developed. By the end of the century, the enslavement of Africans, in particular,

---

37. Erik Thomson, "France's Grotian Moment? Hugo Grotius and Cardinal Richelieu's Commercial Statecraft," *French History*, XXI (2007), 377–394; "Acte d'association des Seigneurs de la Compagnie des Isles de l'Amérique," Oct. 31, 1626, in Moreau de Saint-Méry, *Loix et constitutions*, I, 18, and "Commission donnée par le Cardinal de Richelieu aux Sieurs d'Enambuc et de Rossey, pour établir une Colonie dans les Antilles de l'Amérique," I, 20.

would come to dominate Caribbean economies, and the particular process by which that happened would shape slavery in the Caribbean and profoundly influence the law and culture of slavery in France's North American colonies. It would also guide decisions about who would be enslaved, ensuring a preference for African over Indian laborers.

For all the discussions on the law of slavery in France, at the beginning of the seventeenth century it was still not entirely clear what slavery was, so clarifying slaves' legal status included developing a clearer definition of who they were and what function they were bound to serve. The vast majority of French people had such a limited experience with slavery during the sixteenth century that they hardly knew how to define the term, which, according to period dictionaries, vaguely comprised servants, prisoners of war, serfs, galley oarsmen, and convict laborers. There were many possible pathways a slave's life could follow, including many that ended in freedom. This was nowhere more true than in the Caribbean, where French involvement in slavery predated officially sanctioned settlement by at least seventy years. Since the mid-sixteenth century, French pirates had seized and sold Iberian cargoes that included slaves, both Indian and African. Yet many of these captives became free members of buccaneer communities scattered around the islands, none of which depended on the kinds of labor that would favor slavery.[38]

French ships began plying the Caribbean basin shortly after its discovery by the Spanish, but colonizing efforts did not begin in earnest until the mid-1620s, when the first permanent and officially sanctioned colonies were established. With Brazilian and, more recently, Virginian models of profitable staple production, French investors hoped to cash in on the growing European demand for sugar and tobacco as well as other crops like cotton and indigo. But the development of these commodities began slowly, with most French farms yielding a variety of subsistence grains, vegetables, and a small staple surplus. By 1640 there were about one thousand French colonists on Martinique, living on terraced farms along the island's western and southwestern shores to avoid constant friction with the Caribs, who inhabited the remainder of the island. On Hispaniola and nearby Tortuga a few

---

38. For definitions of slavery, see Jean Nicot, *Thresor de la langue française, tant ancienne que moderne* (Paris, 1606), s.v. "esclave." For the Caribbean, see Jean-Pierre Moreau, *Les petites Antilles de Christophe Colomb à Richelieu: 1493-1635* (Paris, 1992), esp. 143–182; Alexander O. Exquemelin, *The Buccaneers of America*, trans. Alexis Brown (Mineola, N.Y., 1969) 53–66.

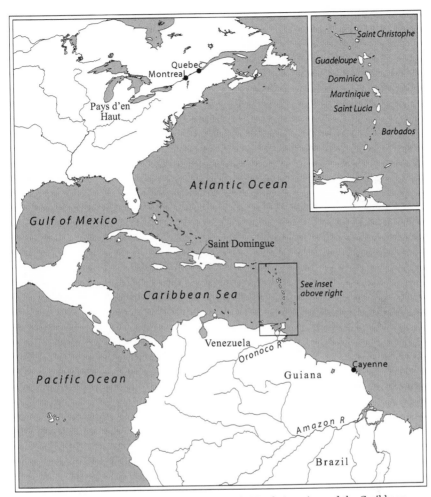

MAP 2. French and Neighboring Settlements in North America and the Caribbean.
Drawn by Jim DeGrand

hundred French buccaneers scratched out a living, and, beginning in the 1590s, many of them began to farm, employing indentured servants and seasonal wage laborers but as yet few slaves. As colonists began to rely on slaves in growing numbers in the 1630s and 1640s, they drew on the legal and philosophical discussions of the previous decades to formulate a remarkably consistent rationale for enslavement that reconciled a widespread French commitment to pursuing free soil at home and slavery abroad.[39]

39. Jacques Bouton, *Relation de l'establissement des françois depuis l'an 1635: en l'isle de la Martinique, l'une des Antilles de l'Amerique* (Paris, 1640); [Jean-Baptiste] Du Tertre, *His-*

The widespread French understanding of African societies as law-bound kingdoms combined with the French understanding of the law of nations to produce the dominant rationale for the enslavement of Africans in the Americas. These ideas, far more than abstract if pervasive notions of Africans' ethnic inferiority, justified African slavery to most French colonists in the early seventeenth century on both sides of the Atlantic. It is obviously difficult to gauge how widely these ideas were shared, especially given the scarcity of sources. But among those who commented on the early French colonies, the law of war dominated discussions of Africans' enslavement, even among many whose primary relationship with slavery would have made them sympathetic to other explanations.

As early as the fourteenth century, French writers began to describe African polities as kingdoms, in which powerful—sometimes despotic—kings ruled over violent subjects who lived to "glut themselves with revenge." The resulting wars produced great numbers of slaves, presumed legitimate because they originated under the sovereignty of an African state. Explanations of African kingdoms' relationship to slavery varied in their particulars—some noting the absence of private land ownership, others stressing the importance of arbitrary law—but they all shared the theme that sovereign polities, rather than individual slave raiders, controlled enslavement and thus possessed the right to sell those slaves to foreign merchants. In the sixteenth century, André Thévet emphasized that sub-Saharan Africa was a land of kings and that their warring kingdoms captured so many prisoners that "their greatest wealth" and "the greater part of their traffic" consisted of "men whom they sell."[40]

French travel writers in the early seventeenth century reinforced this vision of African kingship, explaining the production of slaves by appealing to a combination of African and international law. In 1637, for example, Alexis de Saint-Lo described African society as a series of competing

toire générale des Antilles . . . (Paris, 1667–1671), I; Pierre Pelleprat, *Relation des missions des P. P. de la Compagnie de Jesus dans les isles, et dans la terre ferme de l'Amérique meridionale* (Paris, 1655), esp. part 1; Boucher, "The 'Frontier Era' of the French Caribbean, 1620s–1690s," in Daniels and Kennedy, eds., *Negotiated Empires*, esp. 211–216.

40. Bodin, *Six Bookes of a Commonweale*, ed. McRae, 556 ("glut themselves"). "Sa plus grande richesse gist en esclaves"; "d'autant que le plus grand de leur trafic, ce sont les hommes qu'ils vendent": André Thevet, *La cosmographie universelle d'Andre Thevet, cosmographe du Roy* (Paris, 1575), I, 70. For the earliest European accounts of African kingship, see John K. Thornton, *Africa and Africans in the Making of the Atlantic World, 1400–1800*, 2d ed. (Cambridge, 1998), 77–84.

monarchies governed by elaborate systems of law and protected by well-established militaries. He called African headmen "kings," who ruled over "subjects," rightly subduing those who denied their authority. Strongly influenced by his familiarity with the more centralized Islamic states to the north, Saint-Lo characterized all African polities as kingdoms. His contemporary Claude Jannequin went to Africa in 1637 to seek the riches of the Niger River, which he had heard could rival those of Mexico. There he found coastal kings jealous of their territory and suspicious of French motives. Trading animal skins, ivory, gum arabic, and a little gold, Jannequin related reports of a vast profusion of kingdoms along the Niger River, including some that had long since crumbled like the "Kingdom of Senega" and the "Kingdom of Tombuto [Timbuktu]." Reinforcing the French understanding of African polities as centralized—even idealized—kingdoms, Jannequin emphasized the great authority and respect commanded by African kings. "These people have such great respect for their Kings," he wrote, "that they never pass by them without kneeling on the ground and throwing sand on their backs as a sign of humility."[41]

Although Jannequin did not acknowledge his own involvement in the slave trade, he saw it all around him in these local kingdoms. Rather than pursuing war for territorial gain, he explained, African customs dictated that they fight "in a completely different manner from that which is practiced in Europe." Finding their greatest prestige in cattle and captives, Jannequin wrote, "they only make incursions, ravage the enemy territory, take captives, whoever they can catch, carrying off cattle and goats, which are their only riches." André Brüe, director of France's commercial operations in Senegal at the end of the seventeenth century, offered a similar assessment. "This is the way negro kings ordinarily make war," he wrote. "Decisive battles between opponents rarely occur; the campaigns consist of incursions and pillages. Each side seizes from the other a large number of their subjects, which they then sell as slaves to the merchants who visit their coasts." Enslavement, then, was a recognized aspect of the law of war in this part of the world, practiced by sovereigns against the subjects of competing kingdoms with recognizable patterns and predictable reciprocity.[42]

41. S[aint]-Lo, *Relation du voyage du Cap-Verd*, 149. "Royaume de Senega" and "Royaume de Tombuto"; "Ces hommes portent un si grand respect à leurs Roys, qu'ils ne passent jamais, pardevant eux, qu'ils ne mettent les deux genoux en terre, jetans du sable sur leur dos en signe d'humilité": Claude Jannequin, *Voyage de Lybie au Royaume de Senega, le long de Niger* . . . (Paris, 1643), 66–67, 77, 80 (kingdoms), 93 ("such great respect").

42. "D'une façon toute diferente, de celle que l'on pratique en Europe" and "ils font seule-

Later French accounts of West Africa perpetuated this tradition. "They live under the dominion of a king," reported another French traveler in 1671, "who has governors in the places that are far from him, and when they go to war, these governors have orders to bring him the soldiers that he demands of them." When Nicolas Villault de Bellefond described the Africans he encountered in Senegambia a few years later, he found them mostly contemptible: "They are naturally great lyers, and not to be believed," prone to theft and other crimes. Yet he never associated these qualities with Africans' enslavement. Instead, he placed the responsibility for slavery on the shoulders of sovereign African polities that traded along the coast with the French and other Europeans. Villault's description of West African trade partners as kings meant that, whatever their negative qualities, he acknowledged their sovereignty, if only for self-serving purposes. For example, Villault depicted the "King of *Boure*," or Sierra Leone, as heading a mediocre court and living in a palace that "would not make a good residence for a justice of the peace." Despite these shortcomings, he was still identified as a king, and his brother as a "prince" who was "grave, and intelligent enough in his affairs."[43]

Farther south, on the coast of modern Liberia, Villault narrated his encounter with another West African king who made a much greater impression. As they traded with his subjects, without warning a sudden panic struck the villagers, and they scattered. Fearing attack, Villault armed himself, only to find out that the commotion had come from word that the king was approaching. The pomp of the king's entrance underscored his importance, reinforcing the image of African kings' authority over their people. "Before him marched his Drum, and his Trumpet," Villault wrote, as well as "eight or ten of his kindred and friends, and the rest were his Officers: his Wives, and his Daughters, marched on his side, behind him his slaves fol-

---

ment des incursions, ravagent les pays ennemis, prennent captifs, ceux qu'ils peuvent attraper, emmenent boefus, et capris, qui sont toutes leurs richesses": Jannequin, *Voyage de Lybie au Royaume de Senega*, 93 ("different manner," "only make incursions"); André Brüe, quoted in James F. Searing, *West African Slavery and Atlantic Commerce: The Senegal River Valley, 1700–1860* (Cambridge, 1993), 29.

43. "Ils vivent sous la domination d'un Roy, qui met des Gouverneurs dans les lieux qui sont esloignez de luy, et lors qu'il a guerre, ses Governeurs ont ordre de luy envoyer les soldats qu'il leur demande": *Relation du voyage fait sur les costes d'Afrique*, in Henri Joustel, *Recueil de divers voyages faits en Afrique et en l'Amérique* (Paris, 1674), 5; [Nicolas] Villault, *A Relation of the Coasts of Africk Called Guinee* (London, 1670), 27, 36, 43 (the original French is Villault, *Relation des costes d'Afrique, appellées Guinée* [Paris, 1669]).

lowed. . . . By him he had four Slaves marching, two of them covering him with two large Bucklers, and the other carrying his bow and arrows, and javelin." His appearance awed his subjects, who lined the road "singing, and dancing, and leaping up and down, and testifying their joy in a thousand different postures." The king himself was "a grave and venerable old man . . . very sensible and majestick." Villault conducted negotiations in Portuguese with the king, who assured him that "the French should be always welcome to him."[44]

This king and his personal slaves epitomize French description of enslavement in West Africa throughout the seventeenth century. Sensitive to French critiques of slavery and eager to ensure the legal protection of purchased captives, everyone with an interest in the trade made a point of appealing to centralized West African states as the legal provider of slaves. When the African slave trade was first sanctioned by French law in trade company charters, the right to this trade rested on a relationship between European and African sovereigns, who sold slaves to the French in conformity with the law of nations. In 1681 Louis XIV issued letters patent for the Compagnie de Sénégal, charged with delivering slaves to the Americas, citing the "treaties made with the Negro kings" from Cape Verde to the Gambia River as the basis for trade. Four years later, when the Senegal Company failed to deliver enough slaves to the Caribbean, the crown created the Compagnie de Guinée, granting it full authority to make independent treaties with "les Rois Negres," or "Negro Kings," who controlled the West African coast to obtain a regular supply of captives. The 1696 charter reorganizing the Senegal Company used similar language, citing "treaties made with Negro kings" as the key to French trade in Africa.[45]

When the French wrote about the kings of "les Negres," they meant to suggest something more specific than the fact that these kings had dark skin. The language of the slave trade charters reflected a specific French

---

44. Villault, *Relation of the Coasts of Africk*, 58–62.

45. "En vertu des traitez faites avec les Roys noirs": MS copy of lettres-patentes, July 1681, ANOM, Colonies, C6A, I. "Lettres-patentes du Roy en forme d'Edit, portant confirmation de la nouvelle Compagnie du Sénégal et Côtes d'Afrique et de ses Privileges," July 1681, in Moreau de Saint-Méry, *Loix et constitutions*, I, 357, and "Lettres-patentes sur l'Etablissement d'une Compagnie pour le Commerce exclusive aux Côtes d'Afrique, depuis la riviere de Serre-Lyonne, jusqu'au Cap de Bonne-Espérance, sous le nom de Compagnie de Guinée," Jan. 22, 1685, I, 411, and "traités faites avec les Rois Noirs," I, 547, and "Lettres-patentes, portant établissement d'une nouvelle Compagnie Royale du Sénégal, Cap Vert et Côte d'Affrique," March 1696, I, 547.

understanding of the nature of West African states that reinforced the notion that Africans were enslaved according to the law of nations. Since the fourteenth century, notions of powerful and wealthy kingdoms dominated French understanding of sub-Saharan Africa. In 1375, for example, the French king received an elaborate map of the known world as a gift. Just south of the Sahara Desert, the map depicted an African king seated on a throne and boasting a crown and scepter of pure gold. In his hand he held a giant nugget of gold toward the trans-Saharan trade routes. Along those routes, even the tents of the Saharan traders were capped with golden orbs. Dozens of cities littered the region, represented by turreted castles flying welcoming white flags. The map identified the king as the "Senyor dels Negres," or Lord of the Negroes, and the accompanying text identified him as Musa I, the great Mansa—or emperor—of the Mali Empire. The empire was at the time likely the world's greatest producer of precious metals, an essential source of salt for North Africa and Egypt, and one of the world's most important centers of Islamic learning. Unencumbered by competing nobles and shielded by a protective ring of fortified towns, the Malian ruler must have seemed powerful indeed, underscoring Ibn Battuta's description of Mali just a few years before. "There is complete security in their country," Battuta wrote in 1359. "Neither travellers nor inhabitants in it have anything to fear from robbers or men of violence."[46]

References to a large and powerful kingdom in "distant lands" along the Niger River, dubbed the Kingdom of the Negroes, thus drew from deep tradition. Echoes of that tradition are recognizable in French narrative accounts of the region of Nigritie throughout the seventeenth century. The most developed treatment, simply titled *Relation de la Nigritie*, appeared in 1689. Authored by the missionary Jean-Baptiste Gaby, the book combined firsthand observations from Gaby's 1687 voyage to Senegal with plagiarized selections from another French explorer's manuscript account. Even as he criticized Europeans' limited understanding of the Niger River valley, Gaby himself inaccurately conflated the Senegal and Niger Rivers, mapping a massive, imaginary waterway stretching eastward from the Atlantic across much of the African Sahel. All along the banks of the Niger—"so named,"

46. For the Catalan Atlas, see Abraham Cresques, *Mapamundi: The Catalan Atlas of the Year 1375*, ed. Georges Grosjean, Bibliothèque nationale de France (New York, 1978), which reproduces the image and provides English translations of the Catlan text. For Ibn Battuta, see George E. Brooks, *Landlords and Strangers: Ecology, Society, and Trade in Western Africa, 1000–1630* (Boulder, Colo., 1993), 49.

he thought, "because it watered the Country of the Negroes"—he described the existence of kingdoms that, several generations before, had formed a single, unified kingdom. Oppressed by an unjust king, a group of princes fomented a revolution. The resulting warfare splintered the original kingdom into several smaller states, collectively known as the Negro kingdoms, whose territory constituted Nigritie. The lingering wars between these kingdoms, fought mostly on defensive terms by the coastal peoples, generated large quantities of captives, who were "then sold and delivered to foreign merchants as slaves."[47]

Although Gaby criticized the slave trade, he nevertheless framed enslavement in terms of the law of nations and its demand for formal state declarations in a just war. The Negro kings pursued war according to the law of nations, he insisted, taking care to make a formal declaration according to solemn ceremonies recognized by both parties to the conflict. Tales of the original despotism that led to the kingdom's fragmentation also reinforced the notion that French allies fought a defensive war, the one unambiguous category of just war under the law of nations. When a king allied to the French was successful in these wars, the king sorted the captives, keeping the best for himself. Then "the high officers are to sell to the French, or to the Portuguese, the prisoners they have made, and keep the rest of the spoils for their own use."[48]

Seventeenth-century French maps registered this understanding of Nigritie, which formed a distinct region south of the Sahara and north of the coastal area they labeled "Guinea." In a 1650 map of Africa by Nicholas Sanson, straddling a poorly plotted Niger River were the words "Pays des Negres," or in one English copy of the map: "Negroland." Just five years later Pierre DuVal drew a very similar map clearly identifying the "partie," or region, of Nigritie. Although the cartographer claimed to list "kingdoms that are known to Europeans, within their territory, according to the latest information," his depiction of the Niger River flowing due west into the

47. "Les Païs éloignez"; "Il est appellé de ce nom, parce qu'il arose le Païs des Negres"; "encore vendus et livrez aux Marchands étrangers en qualité d'esclaves": Jean-Baptiste Gaby, *Relation de la Nigritie* (Paris, 1689), 3 ("distant lands"), 22 ("so named"), 48–53, 53 ("sold and delivered"). For Gaby's plagiarism, see Charles Becker, "À propos d'un plagiaire: le père Gaby," *Notes africaines*, CXXXIII (1972), 17–21. For a brief discussion of the later, eighteenth-century French understanding of "nigritie," see Robert Harms, *The Diligent: A Voyage through the Worlds of the Slave Trade* (New York, 2002), 16–20.

48. "Les hauts Officiers sont vendre aux François, ou aux Portugais, les prisonniers qu'ils ont faits, et gardent le reste du butin pour leur usage": Gaby, *Relation de la Nigritie*, 63.

Atlantic from East Africa suggests how little this latest information had to offer about the Sahel. Thirty years later Louis XIV's Italian cartographer, Vincenzo Coronelli, drew a map of Africa that better reflected what Europeans knew, or rather did not know, about the continental interior. Telling as a measure of French geographic knowledge, it also vividly illustrates the way that Nigritie named a vast unknown. Beyond the plotted limits (called "costes" or borders) of familiar coastal regions lay the "Pays des Negres," or "Country of the Negroes."[49]

The placement of Nigritie in the French geographic imagination made it uniquely suitable as the presumptive source of slaves. Whether slaving raids headed north from Guinea or east from Senegambia, the vast interior of Nigritie would have been the presumed target. Indeed, Nigritie functioned best in the fiction of the just slave trade when it remained distant and dimly understood, pliable enough to cover a wide range of circumstances and geographies. Actual knowledge of the peoples and politics governing the interior kingdoms would threaten the categorical acceptance of all Africans captured from this region as legitimate slaves. As one Englishman noted when he visited Gorée off the coast of Senegal, Frenchmen carefully maintained the fiction of just enslavement through willful ignorance: "It is well known no questions are asked concerning the means by which they gain possession of them." As French knowledge of Senegambia pressed deeper into the continent, the imagined boundaries of Nigritie receded in direct proportion to their new understanding.[50]

In the Caribbean, too, the French narrated African enslavement as a product of the law of nations rather than the law of nature, with captives bought from sovereign African allies rather than enslaved by the French. Among the earliest observers of the French Caribbean was Jacques Bouton, a petulant Jesuit who levied insults at nearly everyone he met. Although the islands as yet boasted no large plantations when Bouton visited in the late-1630s, he already recognized the benefits of African slave labor to the development of France's Caribbean economy. "Among the French there is

49. Maps: Nicholas Sanson, *Afrique* (Paris, 1650); Herman Moll, *Negroland and Guinea: With the European Settlements, Explaining What Belongs to England, Holland, Denmark, Etc.* (London, 1727); Pierre DuVal, *Costes de Guinée avec les royaumes qui y sont connus des européens, au dedans des terres, selon les relations les plus nouvelles* (Paris, 1677); Vincenzo Coronelli, *Route Maritime de Brest à Siam* (Paris, 1687).

50. See, for example, the shifting boundaries between Sanson, *Afrique* (1650), and Coronelli, *Route maritime de Brest à Siam* (1687). For the quote, see Searing, *West African Slavery*, 35.

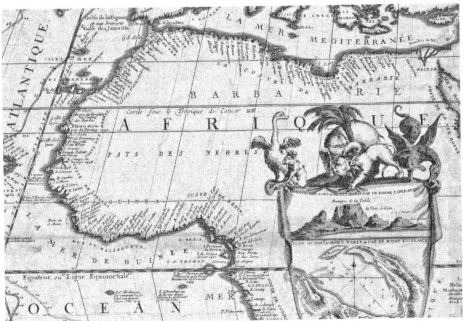

(above) FIGURE 9. Nigritie and the Niger River. *Pierre DuVal,*
Costes de Guinée. Paris, 1677. Courtesy Bibliothèque Nationale de France, Paris

(below) FIGURE 10. "Country of the Negroes."
Vincenzo Coronelli, Route maritime de Brest à Siam, et de Siam à Brest.
Paris, 1687. Courtesy Bibiothèque Nationale de France, Paris

a good number of blacks, or Moors of Cape Verde and elsewhere," he reported, "[but] not so many that one would not want more of them." Because they served for life, demanded no wages, adapted well to the tropical climate, and subsisted on leaner rations, Bouton concluded that "a black slave is much more useful than a French servant."[51]

Bouton had no shortage of contemptible things to say about the Africans he encountered. He described them as "rude and stupid," "impertinent," suffering from "an intolerable ignorance" of European religion and manners. They were "extremely lazy," and unless driven to work "they would pass their time sleeping or chatting." Bouton concluded that Africans were overly fond of alcohol and, of course, not fond enough of clothing: "They need only a little linen to cover their shame." Despite his negative reading of African conduct and culture, however, Bouton did not use these characterizations to justify their enslavement by the French. In fact, Bouton seemed to feel no need to *justify* French slaveholding at all, but he did *explain* slavery in terms that people in metropolitan France could accept. "This miserable nation seems destined for nothing but servitude and slavery," he wrote, "and in their own country most of them are slaves to the king or to others; they are sold to the Europeans at quite a good price." Although recognizing slaves' misfortune, Bouton invoked the two key factors that indemnified the French from their enslavement under the law of nations: African sovereignty (slaves to the king) and their purchase, rather than capture, by Europeans.[52]

51. "Parmy les François il y a des noirs, ou mores du cap-vert, et ailleurs assez bon nombre, non pas si grand toutesfois qu'on n'en desirast davantage"; "un esclave noir est bien plus utile qu'un serviteur françois": Bouton, *Relation*, 98–99. For the larger context of missionary activity among enslaved Africans in the Caribbean, see Sue Peabody, "'A Dangerous Zeal': Catholic Missions to Slaves in the French Antilles, 1635–1800," *French Historical Studies*, XXV (2002), 53–90.

52. "Grossier et hebeté"; "impertinent"; "une insupportable ignorance"; "ils sont fainéants grandement"; "passeront le temps à dormir ou causer"; "n'ont besoin que de quelque linge pour couvrir leur honte"; "Cette miserable nation semble n'estre au monde que pour la servitude et esclavage, et dans leur pays mesme ils sont la plus-part esclaves du Roy ou d'autres; on les vend aux europeans à assez bon marché": Bouton, *Relation*, 99–102. For a brilliant but somewhat different reading of Bouton and his contemporaries, see Sue Peabody, "'A Nation Born to Slavery': Missionaries and Racial Discourse in Seventeenth-Century French Antilles," *Journal of Social History*, XXXVIII (2004–2005), 113–126. See also Pierre H. Boulle, *Race et esclavage dans la France de l'Ancien Régime* (Paris, 2007), 21–80, which surveys the history of racial thinking in early modern France; Guillaume Aubert, "'The Blood of France': Race and Purity of Blood in the French Atlantic World," *WMQ*, 3d Ser., LXI (2004), 439–478, which explores the interplay between metropolitan and colonial ideas about race.

Later visitors to the French Caribbean made the link between African sovereignty, the law of nations, and African enslavement even more explicit. Writing in 1655 another Jesuit, Pierre Pelleprat, discussed the role of slavery in the burgeoning, if still modest, agricultural economies of Martinique and Guadeloupe. "The French use neither oxen nor horses in cultivating their lands," he reported, "but only slaves who were brought to them from Africa, or from the coasts of America farthest from the islands." Explaining the source of African slaves, Pelleprat wrote:

> The continual wars made by the kings and lords of the Negroes are the principal cause of the slavery of so many people, because the conqueror sells as slaves the prisoners of war he takes among his enemy, and takes for the same purpose the women and children who live in these places and in villages that he attacks. Moreover, the Lords have the right, by the laws of the country, to enslave their subjects whenever they see fit. . . . Fathers and mothers have the same power over their children and frequently make use of it to discharge their family or to punish their disobedience. The kings sometimes even sell their own wives, who in their captivity always retain some mark of their original dignity.[53]

For Pelleprat, the "principal cause" of Africans' enslavement was neither racial inferiority nor heathenism. Instead, even this Jesuit, who might be expected to favor a religious explanation, appealed to sovereignty and the law of war. African polities, specifically the kingdoms of Nigritie, were headed by powerful kings who exercised their arbitrary authority according to their own systems of law. As leaders of recognizable polities, these kings had the right, according to the law of nations, to enslave the prisoners they captured among their enemies. The sovereignty of African "lords" allowed

---

53. "Les François ne se servent ny de boeufs, ny de chevaux dans la culture de leurs terres; mais seulement des Esclaves qui leur viennent d'Afrique, ou des costes de l'Amerique les plus éloignées des Isles." Pelleprat, *Relation*, part 1, 50.

"Les guerres continuelles que se font les Rois, et les Seigneurs des Negres sont la principale cause de l'esclavage de tant de persónes, parce que le vainqueur vend comme esclaves les prisonniers de guerre qu'il fait sur son ennemy, et enleve, pour la mesme fin, les femmes, et les enfans qu'il recontre dans les lieux, et dans les bourgades qu'il fource: d'ailleurs les Seigneurs ont droit, par les loix du pays; de faire esclaves leurs sujets quand bon leur semble. . . . Les peres, et les meres ont le mesme pouvoir sur leurs enfans, et s'en servent souvent ou pour en décharger leur famille, ou pour punir leur desobeissance. Il arrive quelquefois que les Rois vendent leurs propres femmes, qui dans leur captivité conservent tousjours quelque marque de leur premiere dignité": ibid., 51–52.

them to operate according to the laws of their country, which condoned the enslavement of criminals or family members at the sovereign's discretion. As if to underscore his readers' appreciation for Africans' monarchical political structure, Pelleprat claimed that, even as slaves, African queens received deferential treatment from their captors and fellow slaves, "as if they were still their queens. Such is the veneration these peoples have for royalty!"[54]

It is worth noting that neither Pelleprat nor Bouton, both deeply committed to their Christianizing mission, appealed directly to Africans' heathenism to justify their enslavement. But both men hoped to turn slavery into salvation. "It is their good fortune to be among the French," Bouton claimed, "who treat them quite gently, and among whom they learn that which is [necessary] for their salvation." Bouton doubted Africans' ability to comprehend Christianity, but Pelleprat was more sanguine. To make the point that slavery could be profitable to slaves as well as to French investors, Pelleprat told the story of "a young Negro," who looked on the bright side of his servitude. He "once told us . . . that had he remained free he would be a slave to Satan," Pelleprat remembered. "Instead by being made a slave to the French he was made a child of God." A realist, Pelleprat acknowledged, "They are not all so spiritual or so perceptive." Such self-serving tales justified the Jesuits' access to slaves and their demands that masters attend to slaves' religious instruction. But neither Bouton nor Pelleprat ever used them to explain enslavement itself.[55]

Jean-Baptiste Du Tertre, a Dominican missionary who became one of the first to chronicle the French Caribbean, spoke out against slavery after a four-year stint in the islands in the 1640s. Having seen the suffering of slaves—people he insisted were fellow "children of God"—he lamented, "Our inhabitants treat these poor wretches exactly as we treat horses in France." In addition to his unflinching assertion that Christianity "rejects and abhors all slavery," he also called upon key aspects of French slavery

54. "Tous les Esclaves qui ont esté sujets des Rois leurs maris les respectent autant, et leur obeissent aussi ponctuellement, que si elles estoient encore leurs Reines. Tant ces peuples ont de veneration pour la Royauté!": ibid., 52.

55. "Ce leur est un bonheur d'estre avec les François, qui les traittent assez doucement, et parmy lesquels ils apprendront ce qui est de leur salut": Bouton, *Relation*, 102. "Un jeune Negre nous disoit une fois à ce propos dans l'Isle de la Martinique, *qu'il auroit euë en son pays, parce que s'il fust demeuré libre il seroit esclave de Sathan, au lieu qu'estant esclave des François il avoit esté fait enfant de Dieu*. Ils ne sont pas tous si spirituals ny si clairvoyans": Pelleprat, *Relation*, part 1, 56.

discourse to discredit the practice. Where Bouton, Pelleprat, and dozens of West African chroniclers maintained that slaves were taken in just wars according to the law of nations, Du Tertre claimed otherwise. "The strangest thing," he wrote, "is that they are not content making slaves of their enemies taken in war; but for the smallest theft one is enslaved and subject to being sold to foreigners with his whole family." Some even sold their own children, or themselves, in exchange for brandy: "committing to a lifetime of harsh servitude to get drunk once." Invoking an image with which nearly all French readers would sympathize, he compared African slaves' suffering to that of European slaves in Muslim control, writing that French colonists beat their slaves with switches and bull pizzles "just as the Turks beat their slaves with batons."[56]

Not that Du Tertre liked Africans. He found their culture, their bodies, and even their odors offensive and difficult to explain to a European audience. He regarded them as stupid, undisciplined, and lacking even the basic human emotion of familial attachment. But he did hope for their conversion to Christianity, which he believed would, in time, improve their manners and elevate their culture. Despite their "ignorance and stupidity," he took comfort in the belief that "most among them, after having been instructed and baptized, are very constant in the faith, very good Christians, and often serve as an example of piety to the French." His disdain for Africans could not be considered racial in any modern sense. Not only did he insist that African deficiencies were religious and cultural, and thus malleable, but he also drew sharp distinctions among various African peoples. Nor did his ethnic chauvinism translate into justification of enslavement or support for slavery. Although many have explained the origins of African enslavement by citing Europeans' negative ethnic images of Africa and its peoples, for

<hr/>

56. "Enfans de Dieu"; "le Christianisme . . . qui rejette et abhorre tout esclavage"; "ce qui est de plus estrange, c'est qu'eux mesmes ne se contentment pas de faire esclaves leurs ennemis pris en guerre; mais au moindre larcin qu commet un d'entr'eux, il est rendu esclave et sujet à ester vendu aux estrangers, luy et tous ses parens"; "s'engagent pour toute leur vie à une dure servitude, pour avoir de quoy s'enyvrer une fois"; "ne plus ne moins que les Turcs donnent des bastonnades à leurs esclaves": Jean-Baptiste Du Tertre, *Histoire générale, des isles de S. Christophe, de la Guadeloupe, de la Martinique, et autres dans l'Amerique . . .* (Paris, 1654), 473, 476, 480. Du Tertre published a much-revised and expanded edition of this work between 1667 and 1671 (*Histoire générale des Antilles*), which reflects important changes in the history of slavery in the period. For a detailed discussion of those changes, see Peabody, "Nation Born to Slavery," *Journal of Social History*, XXXVIII (2004–2005), esp. 115–120.

Du Tertre—as for his proslavery contemporaries—there was no direct re-lationship between the two.[57]

Du Tertre's antislavery sentiments, like opposition to slavery in metro-politan France, made the fiction of just enslavement all the more important, not least because he implicitly accepted its logic. Offered over a century in Europe, Africa, and the Americas, these justifications amounted to much more than an abstract set of ideas. Because French free soil was rooted in dozens of local and royal precedents, slavers ran up against powerful forces that they could meet only with evidence, however contrived, that their par-ticipation in slavery met the requirements of the law of nations even if it ran counter to the royal privilege that guaranteed higher liberties in France itself. These stories might have been little more than a cynical rationaliza-tion of a practice that people wanted in any case, but these rationalizations shaped the system of slavery in important ways, determining who could be enslaved and how.

THEY ALSO USE INDIANS

"The French not only use Negroes as slaves; they also use Indians, taken from various American nations."—Pierre Pelleprat, Martinique, 1655

By the time the Caribbean became a serious object of French interest, Euro-peans had used West African slaves for two hundred years, creating trade networks and narratives of justification that made French adoption of Afri-can slavery an immediately viable option for supplying labor to their new colonies. But, like all Europeans, the French also enslaved Indians in their Caribbean settlements, relying on hundreds (and probably thousands) of slaves who came from nearby islands or the South American mainland. Where Iberian models clearly supported the adoption of African slavery, the case was more complicated for Indians. During the first century of Euro-pean colonization, Iberians had enslaved several hundred thousand Indians in Mexico, Central America, the Caribbean, and South America, and in the 1630s Brazil still acquired thousands of enslaved Indians each year. The sugar estates of northeastern Brazil, which inspired such envy in the minds of French colonists, had been cleared and constructed by far more Indians than Africans, and the transition to predominantly African labor there had

57. "La pluspart d'entr'eux, après avoir esté instruits et baptisez, sont tres-constans en la foy, tres-bons Chrestiens, et qui bien souvent servent d'exemple de pieté à nos François." Du Tertre, *Histoire générale, des isles,* 475.

occurred only a few decades before. In Brazil as a whole during the 1630s there was likely a rough balance between the number of Indian and African slaves. Indians had successfully cleared and planted land, constructed estates, and set up the semi-industrial operations that would become iconic in the late-sixteenth century when Africans took them over.[58]

Yet the Iberian experience also provided many reasons to avoid Indian slavery. In the century before settling in the Caribbean, the French had followed the debates about Spanish cruelties in the New World, turning their rivals' mistreatment of Indians—including enslavement—into an argument to support French colonization. As early as the 1570s, long before French plans for Caribbean colonization took shape, Jean Bodin condemned Spain's enslavement of Indians and praised Charles V for attempting (however unsuccessfully) to eradicate the practice from his New World colonies. Bartolomé de Las Casas is only the best known of a whole chorus of Catholic voices raised against the Indian slave trade, not because Indians were somehow less suited to slavery than Africans, but because American colonization created a distinctive relationship between Europeans and Indians. The papal land donations that undergirded Iberian geopolitical claims to the New World required them to Christianize and care for the Native peoples of the Western Hemisphere, and it was difficult to support territorial claims with a papal decree when its provisions were openly flouted.[59]

French colonists responded to these mixed messages in ways that were equally divided, some embracing Indian slavery as a necessary and useful

58. John M. Monteiro, *Negros da Terra: índios e bandeirantes nas origens de São Paulo* (São Paulo, 1994); Stuart B. Schwartz, *Sugar Plantations in the Formation of Brazilian Society: Bahia, 1550–1835* (Cambridge, 1985), esp. 1–72; Barbara A. Sommer, "Colony of the Sertão: Amazonian Expeditions and the Indian Slave Trade," *The Americas*, LXI (2005), 401–428; David Graham Sweet, "A Rich Realm of Nature Destroyed: The Middle Amazon Valley, 1640–1750" (Ph.D. diss., University of Wisconsin, 1974); Alida C. Metcalf, "The *Entradas* of Bahia of the Sixteenth Century," *The Americas*, LXI (2005), 373–400; Muriel Nazzari, "Transition toward Slavery: Changing Legal Practice regarding Indians in Seventeenth-Century São Paulo," *The Americas*, XLIX (1992), 131–155. For a broad overview of Indian slavery in the Americas, including population estimates vis-à-vis African slavery, see Brett Rushforth, "American Indians and Slavery," in Edward Baptist, ed., *Slavery in the Americas* (ABC-Clio, forthcoming).

59. Bodin, *Six Bookes of a Commonweale*, ed. McRae, 42; William L. Sherman, *Forced Native Labor in Sixteenth-Century Central America* (Lincoln, Nebr., 1979); D. A. Brading, *The First America: The Spanish Monarchy, Creole Patriots, and the Liberal State, 1492–1876* (Cambridge, 1991), 58–101. For the legal and moral distinctions between Indians and Africans in early Iberian discussions of slavery, see José Eisenberg, "António Vieira and the Justification of Indian Slavery," *Luso-Brazilian Review*, XL (2003), 89–95.

source of labor, others wishing to trade French benevolence as a kind of international currency to weaken Iberian land claims and to open new doors for trade and exploration. Indian slavery was initially justified in terms very similar to African slavery, but the proximity of Indian populations and the shifting demands of French commerce and diplomacy eventually discredited Indian slavery in the Caribbean, and it rapidly declined. Like African slavery, colonists discussed Indian slavery in terms of the law of nations. No one in seventeenth-century France argued for Indians' enslavement based on Aristotelian principles of natural slavery. But maintaining the fiction of just enslavement became impossible in the Caribbean as the French squeezed into the islands' tight quarters. It was one thing to appear on the African coast prepared to believe in the just enslavement of a distant enemy kingdom. It was quite another to settle and trade among a wide variety of peoples who could become targets of enslavement. The characteristics that made Nigritie work as a model for just enslavement were the very things hardest to replicate in France's Caribbean colonies. And often they found that they could gain more by protecting Native allies from Iberian slavers than they could by enslaving Indians themselves.

For the first half century of colonization, settlers used Indian slaves in many different capacities. Pierre Pelleprat lived in the Caribbean basin (first at Martinique and then in Guiana on the northeast coast of South America) a full generation before African slavery would become the default form of labor on French plantations. Mid-seventeenth-century Martinique, for example, still had many mixed-use farms through much of the seventeenth century, before sugar monoculture choked out the many alternatives that had characterized the early generations of farming in the islands. Mixed agriculture was produced by a diverse labor pool of Indians, Africans, and French laboring side by side. "The French not only use Negroes as slaves," Pelleprat noted upon his arrival; "they also use Indians, taken from diverse nations of America." Although he noted that Indian slaves were not as numerous as Africans, he hopefully assessed their potential as enslaved agricultural workers. "They are better formed, more intelligent, more agreeable, and more tractable" than the African slaves he had encountered, a judgment leading him to compare them favorably to France's largest and most successful body of productive farmers: "They are no less intelligent than our peasants in France."[60]

60. "Les François ne se servent pas seulement de Negres pour Esclaues; ils en ont encore de Sauvages, tirez de diverses nations de l'Amerique . . . ils sont mieux faits de corps, ont

For his part, Bouton had little good to say about the moral or intellectual character of Indian slaves, but he did acknowledge their usefulness as laborers. Like the Africans he described earlier, they were "libertines, idlers, idiots." But they were also excellent fishermen and skilled hunters, which were indispensable skills in the early days of colonization when food supplies were still insecure. French colonists drew upon enslaved Indians' knowledge of the region. "Indian slaves . . . are very adept at fishing and hunting," wrote Du Tertre, "for these tasks just one is worth as much as and often more than two Negroes." Many French colonists relied on Indian slaves for their food supply because, as Du Tertre explained, "it takes only one to feed quite a large family." Although Du Tertre reported that Indians were rarely used as agricultural workers, the assertion likely resulted less from their inability to farm (as later colonists would assert) than from the high demand for their knowledge and skills. Significantly, no writer in the seventeenth century mentioned enslaved Indians' getting sick or dying of disease, a story that would come to dominate later discussions of why colonists shifted to a nearly exclusive reliance on Africans.[61]

If Caribbean colonists found Indian slaves useful, they also found it difficult to support their enslavement over time. Having vilified their Iberian predecessors in the Americas for enslaving the Natives, the French established legal and moral imperatives to protect, rather than enslave, American Indians. Colonists also struggled to maintain the fiction of Indians' just enslavement in the same way that they could for Africans. Assertions of African sovereignty effectively supported European domination of enslaved Africans. But to argue for the sovereignty—and thus territorial control—of Indians in the Americas would invalidate European colonization. If Indians lived in sovereign kingdoms, their enslavement could easily be attributed to the wars and laws of those kingdoms. But the same argument would brand European settlements as violations of the law of nations: illegal invasions of sovereign territory. What is more, because French settlers

[handwritten margin note: Indian/African difference; moral precedents]

l'esprit meilleur, sont plus doux, et plus traitables, et n'ont pas moins d'esprit que nos païsans de France." Pelleprat, *Relation*, part 1, 58. For mixed economy and various sources of labor in the first decades of Caribbean settlement, see Boucher, *France and the American Tropics*, 112–167.

61. "Libertins, faineants, stupides": Bouton, *Relation*, 103, 104 (quote). "Sauvages esclaves . . . sont fort adroits à la pesche et à la chasse; en ce cas un seul vaut bien souvent mieux que deux Negres, car il n'en faut qu'un pour nourrir une assez ample famille": Du Tertre, *Histoire générale, des isles*, 480–481. See also Richard Price, "Caribbean Fishing and Fishermen: A Historical Sketch," *American Anthropologist*, LXVIII (1966), 1363–1383.

lived and traded among Indians on a much broader scale, they continually faced claims by competing colonists that Indians had been enslaved illegally: in slave raids rather than just wars. The situation was clearly the same in Africa, but there were no French interests vested in the African interior to raise credible objections.[62]

Living within a world of enslavement also generated a set of practical concerns that made Indian slavery less desirable than African slavery. The closer French colonies were to the source of slaves, the more they risked falling victim to violent reprisals for slave raids. These problems arose very quickly on the smaller islands of the Lesser Antilles, but, as French interests spread onto the South American mainland, the violence of raids and counterraids associated with slavery forced colonists to rethink their reliance on enslaved Indians. Small in numbers but with great ambitions, French colonists chose, instead, to ally themselves with Indians facing slave raids by other Europeans, positioning themselves as protectors rather than predators. Practically useful as an argument for Indian alliance, these claims were also politically and legally useful in arguments against European competitors in South America.[63]

From the earliest stages of French colonization in the Caribbean, metropolitan planners and colonial officials went to great lengths to contrast their activities with those of the Spanish. Reflecting the language of his Spanish predecessor Bartolomé de Las Casas, the Dominican priest Pierre Pelican expressed his hope that the French could "gain by gentleness the naturals of this island," using friendship rather than force to establish themselves in the islands. Thirty years later Charles de Rochefort believed that Pelican's ideals had been realized, claiming that French settlement succeeded by alliance rather than domination. "When the French established themselves at Martinique, Guadeloupe, and Grenada, they did so by agreement with the Caciques and chiefs among the Caribs," he wrote. "We are not guilty of the same violence as the Spaniards; . . . the establishment of our colonies in the Islands had no resemblance to theirs." Avoiding Indian slavery allowed France to claim more than the moral high ground: it supported France's

---

62. For a similar dynamic in English discussions of the issue, see Michael Guasco, "To 'Doe Some Good upon their Countrymen': The Paradox of Indian Slavery in Early Anglo-America," *Journal of Social History*, XLI (2007–2008), 389–411.

63. For an excellent discussion of shifting French perceptions of Indians as kingdoms, see Peter Cook, "Kings, Captains, and Kin: French Views of Native American Political Cultures in the Sixteenth and Early Seventeenth Centuries," in Peter C. Mancall, ed., *The Atlantic World and Virginia, 1550–1624* (Chapel Hill, N.C., 2007), 307–341.

contention that Spain's legal claim to the Americas, if it had ever been just, was invalidated by its mistreatment of Indians.[64]

These ideals—genuine for some, anti-Spanish posturing for others—influenced the founding legal texts of French colonialism. In the 1626 act of association establishing the first Caribbean trade company, the islands' proximity to Spanish claims ("situated at the entrance of Peru") was among the document's primary concerns. The charter justified French presence in the Caribbean only on those islands "not possessed by Christian princes," and only to the extent that they settled there "in order to instruct the inhabitants of the said islands in the Catholic, Apostolic, and Roman religion." The explicit goal was trade rather than conquest, but, unlike seventeenth-century charters for African trade companies, the American charters made no mention of kings and no pretentions to Indians' territorial sovereignty. Instead, the only islands off limits were those occupied by other Europeans. Still, trading with and converting Indians provided the legal rationale for French presence in territory that was already claimed by Spain. By 1642 the French crown dictated that Catholic Indians become full French subjects, possessing all the rights of the French. In a royal edict concerning the islands, the king decreed, "The descendants of the French living in the said Islands, as well as the Indians who convert to and follow the Christian faith, shall be counted and considered natural-born Frenchmen."[65]

Added to the already-challenging burdens posed by French skepticism

64. "Lors que les François se sont établis à la Martinique, à la Gardeloupe, et à la Grenade, ils l'ont fait par l'agréement des Caciques, et des principaus d'entre les Caraibes . . . nous ne sommes pas coupables des memes violences que les Espagnols . . . nôtre procedé en l'établissement de nos Colonies aus Iles, n'a pas esté semblable au leur": Charles Rochefort, *Histoire naturelle et morale des isles Antilles de l'Amérique* . . . (Rotterdam, 1665), 283. For "gain by gentleness," see Philip B. Boucher, *Cannibal Encounters: Europeans and Island Caribs, 1492–1763* (Baltimore, 1992), 43. For a broader discussion of French challenges to Spanish sovereignty in the Americas, see Boucher, *France and the American Tropics*, 40–61.

65. "Situées à l'entrée de Pérou": "qui ne sont point possédées par des Princes Chrétiennes"; "et ce tant afin de faire instruire les habitans desdites Isles en la Religion Catholique, Apostolique et Romaine." Subsequent charters repeated essentially the same rationale. See, for example, "Contrat de Rétablissement de la Compagnie des Isles de l'Amérique, avec les articles accordés par Sa Majesté aux Associés," Feb. 12, 1635, in Moreau de Saint-Méry, *Loix et constitutions*, I, 29–33.

"Les descendans des François habitués esdites Isles, et meme les Sauvages qui seront convertis à la Foi Chrétienne et en feront profession, seront censes et réputés naturels François, capable de toutes charges, honneurs, successions et donations, ainsi que les originaires et regnicoles, sans être tenus de prendre lettre de declaration ou neutralité [naturalité]": "Édit concernant la Compagnie des Isles de l'Amérique," March 1642, ibid., I, 54.

toward slavery, these provisions made the justification of Indian enslavement all the more tenuous. Drawing on the law of nations, which allowed the purchase of those already enslaved, French descriptions of Indians' enslavement were nevertheless far weaker than their arguments for Africa. Indian slaves, Pelleprat noted, were taken from nations, like the Arawaks, who were "enemies of those who are allied to us." Yet, unlike the sovereign kingdoms of Africa, French writers argued that the societies producing Indian slaves had no standing as nations and were virtually bereft of law. According to Pelleprat, Indians "have neither laws nor Magistrates, and only recognize their Captains, whom they respect and obey, but more by inclination than duty. . . . The children obey their parents only when they want to, because they do not punish them, and do not even admonish them." When Indians, who ran in "bands" rather than resided in kingdoms, went to war, they did so by surprise, intending to kill the men and capture women and children. They "take the girls and the women to make them slaves," Pelleprat claimed, "who, to tell the truth, have nothing but the name [of slaves], because they treat them as if they were from their own nation." These slaves, through rituals of alliance, came into French hands in large enough numbers to constitute a significant proportion of the Caribbean labor force.[66]

Other French observers likewise compared African polities (which they had never visited) with those of the Americas. In 1655, for example, Charles de Rochefort assessed the Indians of the Caribbean and Guiana to be driven, not by law, but by "inhumanity, barbarity, and rage." In a chapter entitled "That which Passes for Government among the Caribs," Rochefort noted that Caribbean Indians had neither kings nor lords, unlike the Africans. "None of these chiefs command all of the nation, and they have no influence on the other captains," he wrote. The resulting lawlessness and instability forced him to "dip [his] plume in blood and create a horrifying tableau" to adequately describe Native Caribbean slave taking.[67]

66. "Ils n'ont ny loix, ny Magistrats, et ne reconnoissent que leurs Capitaines, qu'ils respectent, et ausquels ils obeïssent, mais par inclination plûtost que par devoir. . . . Les enfans n'obeïssent à leurs parens qu'autant qu'il leur plaist; car ils n'exercent aucun châtiment sur eux, et ne les menacent pas meme de parolle"; "Ils . . . enlevent les filles, et les femmes pour en faire des esclaves; qui, à vray dire, n'en ont que le nom, puis qu'ils les traittent comme si elles estoient de leur propre nation": Pelleprat, *Relation*, part 2, 55–58. Compare one of his Jesuit contemporaries, Giacinto Brugiotti da Vetralla, who described African slaves in essentially the same way ("slaves in name only"), cited in Thornton, *Africa and Africans*, 87–88.

67. "L'inhumanité, de la barbarie et de la rage"; "De ce qui tient lieu de Police chez les

In contrast, Rochefort applauded Africans for embracing an idealized royal authority that even absolutist France would never achieve. "In the Kingdom of Congo in Africa," Rochefort declared with no personal knowledge, "all the subjects speak kneeling to the king, having in their hands a vase filled with sand that they pour on their heads. The Negroes in the country of Angola also cover themselves with earth when they face their prince, to testify that they are but dust and ashes before him." Although he made no explicit references linking this to African slavery, his work illustrates how widely the French idea of African kingship had spread by the middle of the seventeenth century.[68]

Because of their successful employment of Indian slaves, French authorities continued to support their acquisition through allied Indians. But the use of Indian slaves posed special practical risks to the colonists, who stood in danger of becoming party to the destabilizing violence that produced captives in the first place. The most direct threat to stability and peace arose as a result of French colonists' attempts to capture Indian slaves directly. As early as 1636, only a few years after French settlement, a French colonist attempted to acquire a few Indian slaves by kidnapping some Carib Indians on the island of Dominica, which lies between Martinique and Guadeloupe. In reprisal, the Caribs attacked several French settlements on Dominica, threatening to spread the violence to the larger villages on the other islands. The French counsel harshly disciplined the offender and forbade anyone to participate in slave raiding.[69]

As a matter of colonial security, settlers preferred to obtain their Indian captives from the mainland, keeping the French population a safe distance from their allies' raids and their enemies' revenge. Writing just four years after the kidnapping incident, Bouton implied as much when he noted that Indian slaves came from "the mainland," not from the island Natives who surrounded them. Pelleprat's description of Indian slaves' origins incorporated this idea also, writing that they arrived from the American mainland "farthest from the Islands." Du Tertre emphasized the distinction as well. "The slaves that ordinarily serve our settlers are of two kinds, namely

---

Caraibes"; "Nous allons tremper nôtre plume dans le sang et faire un Tableau qui donnera de l'horreur": Rochefort, *Histoire naturelle*, 518, 536.

68. "Au Royaume de Gago en Afrique, tous les sujets parlent à genous au Roy, ayant en leurs mains un vase plein de sable, qu'ils se jettent sure la teste. Le Négres du païs d'Angole se couvrent aussi de terre, quand ils recontrent leur Prince, comme pour témoigner qu'ils ne sont devant luy qu'poudre et cendre": ibid., 521.

69. Boucher, *Cannibal Encounters*, 43.

Negroes, whom we call in France Moors or Ethiopians; and Indians from the mainland, and not those of the islands." The idea of a distant slave supply was to become a recurring theme in French discussions of American slavery, shaping the construction of the plantation labor system during the second half of the seventeenth century.[70]

Nothing reinforced the need for insulation from Indian warfare more than a series of battles between the French and the Caribs from 1654 to 1660, which dramatically transformed the physical and diplomatic landscape of the Caribbean. Following the 1636 violence sparked by a French slave raid, colonists reestablished a working, if often tense, relationship with the Caribs, based largely on the barter of French goods (especially guns) for Caribbean pearls, fish, birds, and crocodiles. Caribs utilized French weapons to fight their Taino enemies, trading captives to the French as slaves.

In 1654, a ship's captain named Parquet blurred the line between alliance and slavery, enraging the Caribs by capturing one of their people and beating him in public. Parquet came to believe that the Carib, taken from the island of Saint Vincent, had killed his brother. So, according to Du Tertre, "he had him attached to the mast of his boat, and had him whipped by his sailors with such cruelty that they cut up his whole body." The sailors then released the Carib, apparently to send a warning message to his people. Rather than cowering, however, "this outrage done to one of their Nation" persuaded the Caribs to "destroy the new French Establishments," first on Saint Christophe and then throughout the neighboring islands.[71]

Facing reprisals, Parquet rounded up a small group of Caribs and sentenced them to be executed "by a hatchet blow, in the same manner that they have killed several Frenchmen." Predictably, another public display of French violence against the Caribs did little to ameliorate their anger, "serving only to foment war." During the following year, as Caribs and French clashed in Saint Vincent, the war slowly spread to Martinique and Guadeloupe, where Caribs raided French settlements throughout 1655 and 1656.[72]

---

70. "De la terre ferme": Bouton, *Relation*, 104. "Les plus éloignées des Isles": Pelleprat, *Relation*, part 1, 50. Du Tertre, *Histoire générale, des isles*, 473.

71. "Il le fit attacher au mast de son basteau, et le fit fouïeter par ses matelots avec tant de cruauté, qu'ils luy déchirerent tout le corps"; "cét outrage fait à un de leur Nation"; "ruïner les nouveaux Establissemens des François qui leur faisoient ombrage": Du Tertre, *Histoire générale des Antilles*, I, 465–466.

72. "À coups de hache, de la mesme maniere qu'ils avoient tuez plusieurs François"; "ne servit pourtant qu'à fomenter la guerre": ibid., 467.

As alarming as Carib raids were to the French settlers, Native violence inspired an even more terrifying development. In 1656, a large number of slaves in Guadeloupe, presumably both African and Indian, took advantage of the instability to rise against their French masters. Having been armed by their masters for defense against the Caribs, these slaves "fought for their liberty" using French arms against the colonists. Two of the ringleaders secretly planned to overthrow the French and establish "two Kings of their Nations" to rule over the island. For two weeks, the slaves ranged freely around Guadeloupe, pillaging and destroying French property and "threatening to cover the whole Island in fire and blood." Martinique slaves' participation in Carib violence was less direct, but many refused orders, stole or destroyed their master's property, or went to live in Native villages from which they would raid French plantations. This low-level violence lasted nearly two full years on Martinique before the colonists could suppress it.[73]

The destruction of these years reminded colonists of the danger they faced when capturing local Indians whose people were in a position to retaliate. Parquet's whipping of the Carib captive, a particularly symbolic form of cruelty, sparked massive reprisals and inspired a multi-island slave rebellion. The collusion between warring Caribs and the slaves also suggested the need to divide slaves and free Indians, who together greatly outnumbered French settlers. French colonists also came to recognize that supplying slaves through capricious local alliances could be frustrating, especially when alliances shifted and thus cut off access to Indian slave imports. It could also be dangerous. Having armed local Indians to provide slaves, the French found their own weapons turned against them.

Of course, similar dangers attended the African slave trade, but French planters were insulated from its effects. Living an ocean away, Caribbean societies never had to experience the instability of West African slaving, which increased dramatically during the second half of the seventeenth century as European demand for slaves rewarded African warfare with valuable manufactured goods. Moreover, because they bought nearly all of their African slaves from Dutch or Spanish ships, the French were doubly removed from the instability and insecurities of enslavement. This distance allowed them to utilize slaves without participating in—or even thinking much about—their capture, reinforcing their tendency to rationalize Afri-

73. "Combattoient pour leur liberté"; "deux Roys de leur Nations"; "menaçant de mettre toute l'Isle à feu et à sang": ibid., 465–469.

can slavery in terms of international law, categorically distinct from the slaving violence they witnessed in the Americas.

In this context, African slavery expanded steadily throughout the Americas in the second half of the seventeenth century. In addition to the general expansion of slaves' availability, two specific developments in the 1660s and 1670s created a significant rise in the French demand for slaves. The first was the growth of sugar cultivation. Following the Portuguese expulsion of the Dutch from Brazil in 1654, many Dutch planters and their slaves fled to French islands for refuge, bringing with them knowledge and experience in producing sugar on a large scale. French planters learned quickly, and by the mid-1660s they had established several estates after the Brazilian model. The second was a sharp drop in French immigration to the islands, which produced a serious labor shortage in all the French islands, prompting a surge in African slave imports. By the 1680s, the enslaved population on France's Caribbean islands had exploded to nearly twenty-five thousand, surpassing the colonies' European populations and transforming colonial society.[74]

As African slavery expanded, French enslavement of Indians receded. Embedded in the indigenous world of slaving that produced American captives, Indian slavery became hotly contested and was thus a less secure prospect for colonists' investment. Colonists did not much care where their slaves came from, particularly during times of international war when France's outsourced African slave trade became insecure. The porous world of the seventeenth-century Caribbean ensured that ships from all around the Americas passed through French colonies frequently, engaging in all manner of smuggling, including the trafficking of enslaved Indians. But, by the early eighteenth century, Caribbean officials had formally outlawed the enslavement of Indians, hoping to deter smugglers by making slave raiding a capital offense. A case before Martinique's Superior Council in 1704 confronted the issue of Indian slave raiding and confirmed the colonies' pro-

74. For the Dutch expulsion from Brazil, see Schwartz, *Sugar Plantations in the Formation of Brazilian Society*, 173–195. For its effects on the French Caribbean, see Robert Louis Stein, *The French Slave Trade in the Eighteenth Century: An Old Regime Business* (Madison, Wis., 1988), 7–10; Stein, *The French Sugar Business in the Eighteenth Century* (Baton Rouge, La., 1988), 40–43. Philip Boucher cautions against reading the transition to large-scale sugar production as a rapid and total transformation (*France and the American Tropics*, 127–138). For the drop in French laborers, see Gabriel Debien, "Les engagés pour les Antilles, 1634–1715," *Revue de l'histoire des colonies*, XXXVII (1951), 1–280. For slave populations, see Pritchard, *In Search of Empire*, 428.

hibition. In the summer of 1703, two petty traders from Martinique were imprisoned by French officials as they returned from a slave-raiding expedition along the Oyapock River, which separated French Guiana from neighboring Brazil. Ascending to a remote village beyond the river's impassable rapids, the men and their Native partners had attacked an unsuspecting community, capturing ten women and eight children and killing four others "as they defended themselves." Before leaving with their slaves, the raiders set fire to the victims' homes and crops. As they returned with their prey, the traders' hopes must have been high. Sold at several hundred livres apiece, eighteen slaves would yield a profit that would have taken years to accumulate in legitimate trade. And by raiding Native villages near their Portuguese rivals in a time of war, they might have rationalized they were doing the colonies a favor.[75]

Colonial leaders disagreed. Concluding that the slave raiders had targeted Natives who were longtime allies of the French, Martinique's Superior Council "condemned them to death and confiscated their goods," setting aside some of the profits from the seizure to provide "presents for reconciliation with this nation." The council acted quickly and publicly, believing it was essential to "make an example of such violence" before it set a precedent that could be "detrimental to commerce" with the South American mainland. When news of the execution reached Paris, French officials offered terse but clear approval: "Bon," they wrote in the margin. "Good."[76]

Their endorsement of the executions reflected not only the legal and moral weight attached to enslavement but also serious geopolitical concerns about France's territorial ambitions in South America. From a meager base in Guiana, French colonists hoped to make incursions into territories claimed by the Portuguese by protecting Indians from Portuguese slave raids. As François Froger observed when he visited Brazil in 1695, Portuguese colonists were importing into São Paulo alone as many as three hundred enslaved Indians each year "whom they drive as herds of oxen; and having tamed a little, they dispose of them in the country to till the ground, or employ them in fishing for gold." When he arrived in Guiana he noted that France's Indian allies offered a similar trade in slaves to the French, but the governor, Pierre Eléonore de Férolles, had prohibited it because he

75. "Quatre de ces indiens ont esté tuez en se defendant": ANOM, Colonies, C8A, XV, 304v–305.

76. "Les a cond[am]né a mort, et confisqué leur biens"; "des presents pour la reconciliation avec cette nation"; "si on ne faisoit point d'examples de semblables violences": ibid.

wanted to pursue commerce in the continental interior. The only way to do so would be to forbid slaving and offer protections to potential victims of Brazilian raids. Despite this stance, and Férolles's role in the French slavers' execution, he was accused of supporting a slaving expedition of his own in 1704, targeting the Portuguese-allied Arrouas Indians. This about-face so angered the Jesuits that they refused to grant absolution to anyone who bought slaves from this raid, including the governor's wife. Enraged that the missionaries questioned the virtue of a woman who "lived as if she were in a convent," Férolles defended his support for raids against the Arrouas, "who would destroy the colony if I let them." That Férolles defended his wife's honor and his own policy by portraying the raid as a defensive and, therefore, just war only reinforced the logic that had made justifying Indian slavery so difficult to begin with.[77]

PERFECT AND UTTER SLAVERY

"The most ignoble and scandalous Kind of Subjection is that by which a Man offers himself to perfect and utter Slavery . . . which obliges a Man to serve his Master all his Life long."—Hugo Grotius, Paris, 1625

In 1682 Michel Bégon received notice that his first cousin, Jean-Baptiste Colbert, had arranged to have him appointed as intendant, or chief civil and legal official, of France's Caribbean colonies. His family connections and strong legal credentials were not all that set him apart for the position. The previous year he might have been involved in the rechartering of the Sene-gal Company, familiarizing him with at least the African side of the slave trade. Colbert charged Bégon with an enormous but rather straightforward task: the writing of a comprehensive ordinance to regulate slavery in all of France's Caribbean colonies. Bégon's predecessor had begun the synthesis, sketching a rough outline containing general principles of slave governance.

---

77. "Qu'ils touchent comme des troupeaux de Boeufs; et lorsqu'ils les ont un peu assu-jettis, ils les envoyent à la compagne cultiver la terre, ou les employent à pescher de l'Or": [François] Froger, *Relation d'un voyage . . .* (Paris, 1698), 81, 127. It was the governor of Guiana, Pierre Eléonore de Férolles, who first imprisoned the French slavers who were exe-cuted. In 1704 he was himself implicated in an Indian slaving scheme. For Férolles's impris-onment of the French slavers, see Jan. 23, 1704, ANOM, C8A, XV, 304v. For his involvement in slave raiding, see Boucher, *France and the American Tropics*, 216. "Elle vit comme sy elle estoit encore dans le couvent"; "qui auroit detruit La Colonie sy je me fait laissé": Férolles to the minister, Apr. 17, 1705, ANOM, Colonies, C14A, IV, 64.

But, working with the islands' governor, Charles de Courbon de Blénac, Bégon would have to complete it. Eager for this opportunity to advance in the royal administration, he sailed for the Caribbean that fall.[78]

When Bégon arrived in Martinique, Blénac presented him with the meager efforts of the previous two years. Bégon spent the next three months poring over every surviving slave ordinance issued on all of the French islands except Saint Domingue, which was at the time France's only Caribbean colony without a majority-slave population. Bégon then met with the local governors and superior councils of the three most-populated island colonies (Martinique, Guadeloupe, and Saint Christophe), and discussed slave management with the islands' "principal inhabitants": all of whom would have been wealthy planters with slaves. Informed by these conversations, he synthesized existing law and practice into a sixteen-page memorandum containing dozens of provisions for slave management. Sent to Versailles in February 1683, Bégon's memoir became—with only a few minor adjustments—the first comprehensive slave code in the French Caribbean and one of the most influential bodies of slave law in the early modern world.[79]

When Louis XIV issued the edict declaring royal policy on the matter in March 1685, he included a cover letter asserting the royal authority behind the law:

78. Bégon signed an official copy of the charter for the reorganized Compagnie du Sénégal. MS copy of lettres-patentes, July 1681, ANOM, Colonies, C6A, I; Charles de Courbon de Blénac to the minister, Mar. 12, 1683, C8A, III, 212–212v. Blénac, enjoined by the king to take part in the drafting of the slave code, made a minimal effort to be involved, writing that Bégon had constructed the law "in his presence" but not even claiming in self-justification a significant role for himself. Bégon was the only one to sign the memorandum and, given his legal background and acquaintance with the operations of the Senegal Company, he was by far the more qualified. For a fuller account of the origins of the slave code, see Vernon Valentine Palmer, "The Origins and Authors of the Code Noir," *Louisiana Law Review,* LVI (1995), 363–407, although Palmer overestimates the contribution of Blénac and Jean-Baptiste Patoulet, Bégon's predecessor. See also Alan Watson, "The Origins of the *Code Noir* Revisited," *Tulane Law Review,* LXXII (1997), 1041; Ghachem, "Sovereignty and Slavery," 17–40; Bernard Vonglis, "La double origine du Code Noir," in Liliane Chauleau, ed., *Les abolitions dans les Amériques* (Fort-de-France, Martinique, 2001), 101–107; Louis Sala-Molins, *Le Code Noir, ou le calvaire de Canaan* (Paris, 1987). For Patoulet's brief memoir, see "Memoire de M. Patoulet sur la conservation, la police, le jugement, et le chastiment des esclaves," May 20, 1682, ANOM, Collection Moreau de Saint-Méry, F3, CCXLVIII.

79. Blénac to minister, Mar. 12, 1683, ANOM, C8A, III, 212–212v; Michel Bégon, "Projet de Reglement de M[onsieu]rs de Blenac et Begon sur la police et autres matieres concernant les Esclaves des isles de l'Amerique concerté avec les principaux habitans et les off[icie]rs des con[sei]ls Souverains," Feb. 13, 1683, ANOM, Collection Moreau de Saint-Méry, F3, CX.

Our beloved and faithful, having considered it fitting to establish in our French American islands the law that must be observed regarding the slaves who are there, we have dispatched our letters patent in the form of an edict, which you will find attached, which we mandate and order you to implement without any restriction, modification, or difficulty, nor finding fault, for such is our pleasure.[80]

The king wished to give the impression that this slave code (dubbed the Code Noir in the eighteenth century) reflected the imposition of his unalterable will. Yet, read carefully, the code provides an ethnographic lens onto the daily operation of French slavery in the late-seventeenth-century Caribbean, not because colonists and slaves precisely observed the law, but because the law grew out of a series of power struggles between the enslaved and their would-be masters. These struggles, first registered in local acts designed to solve immediate human problems, expressed masters' and slaves' opposing interpretations of slavery and competing aspirations for life in the colonies. They thus reveal not only the ideals of French masters but also the actions of enslaved Africans and Indians whose daily assertions of their own humanity challenged the fiction of their status as property.[81]

80. "Nos amez et feaux ayant estime a propos d'establir en nos isles Françoises de l'Amerique la jurisprudence qui doit ester observe a l'esgard des Esclaves qui y sont, Nous avons fait expedies nos letters patentes en forme d'Edit, que vous trouverez cy jointes, a l'enregistranant desquelles, nous vous mandons et ordonnons de proceder sans aucune restriction, modification, ny difficultie y ny faites faute Car tel est n're plaisir." The only surviving copy of this letter was registered by the sovereign council of Guadeloupe in 1685, preserved by Moreau de Saint-Méry in his vast collection of Caribbeana. See ANOM, Collection Moreau de Saint-Méry, F3, CCXLVIII.

81. The first references I have found to the 1685 ordinance as the "Code Noir" were two letters written in Martinique in April and May of 1713. It seems that this became a convenient shorthand for the law, which was generally referred to as "the edict of March 1685," or "the ordinance of March 1685" before the 1710s. The later document used these designations intermittently, alongside "Code Noir." Not until the 1720s would it assume the legal status of a "code," rather than an "ordinance" or "edict." See Phélypeaux to Minister, Apr. 6, 1713, ANOM, C8A, XIX, 80–85v, in Peabody and Grinberg, eds., *Slavery, Freedom, and the Law,* 39–41; unaddressed letter of May 20, 1713, ANOM, Collection Moreau de Saint-Méry, F3, XC. As Richard S. Dunn argued for the contemporary English Caribbean, "The slave laws enacted by the island legislatures in the seventeenth century tell us a good deal about the treatment of Negroes and the character of slavery in the Caribbean colonies. These laws set formal standards, to be sure, which were not necessarily enforced. But it was the big planters on the islands who sat in the assemblies and composed these laws, which is to say that in the statute books the chief slaveholders articulated their views on how to handle Negroes." *Sugar and Slaves: The Rise of the Planter Class in the English West Indies, 1624–1713* (Chapel Hill, N.C., 1972), 238.

Perhaps the most-telling aspect of the 1685 slave ordinance was a topic that it omitted. Neither Bégon's memoir nor the king's edict included any statement about who could be enslaved and under what conditions. In part this reflected the nature of the document as a set of laws governing local practice, but similar slave codes often made at least some statement on the conditions of enslavement or particular populations that could be enslaved. The ability of the French to so clearly separate the process of enslavement from the practice of slavery proved essential to the system of controls that masters erected around their slaves. Taking the justice of enslavement for granted, the ordinance focused only on making the system of slavery work to produce maximum rewards for individual French slaveholders and for French colonial society. Following Grotius, who declared that the law of nations placed slaves "in the same Rank with Goods," the code clarified slaves' status as movable, inheritable property. Slave status was also passed from mother to child, meaning that a child of an enslaved mother would be a slave irrespective of the father's legal standing.[82]

If the law considered slaves to be property, it also reluctantly acknowledged their humanity. Indeed, most of the provisions of the 1685 slave ordinance reflected slaves' unwillingness to cooperate with a system so manifestly against their interests. If there is a single story of the first half century of slavery in the Caribbean, it is the story of colonists' daily struggle to structure systems of punishments and rewards that would keep enslaved people—Africans and Indians—under control and working productively. In many cases slaves acted to meet their most basic human needs (food, shelter, safety, and community), forcing slaveholders into compromises that shaped French society even as the French struggled to control the lives of the enslaved. Yet alongside those compromises French slaveholders found the means to develop a remarkably brutal regime of control that, although designed to keep slaves alive and working productively, willingly sacrificed slaves' bodies and lives whenever it served broader French interests.

When Patoulet first sketched the contours of Caribbean slave law, he identified four categories that he felt made sense of the chaos of particu-

---

82. See, for example, the Virginia slave code of 1705, a similar effort to synthesize English slave law, which contained three provisions about who could be enslaved and where they could be held as slaves. William Waller Hening, ed., *The Statutes at Large, Being a Collection of All the Laws of Virginia, from the First Session of the Legislature, in the Year 1619* (Philadelphia, 1823), III, 447–462, articles 4–6; Bégon, "Projet concernant les Esclaves," ANOM, Collection Moreau de Saint-Méry, F3 CX; and Slave Ordinance of March 1685, articles 44–46.

lar issues facing slaves and slaveholders: "maintenance," "policing," "justice," and "punishments." In his much-expanded memoir, Bégon added two more: religion and manumission. The first category dealt with slaves' basic requirements for food, clothing, medical care, and shelter. So long as slaves could remain strong enough to work, masters had every incentive to avoid providing such necessities. They skimped on rations. They allowed slaves to hunt or forage for their own food, or even to tend subsistence gardens on weekends to supplement the master's provisions for them. Some gave their slaves a cheap, sugar-based liquor called "guildive" to mask hunger. Others failed to give them adequate clothing. Not surprisingly, in the face of these deprivations slaves found creative ways to provide for themselves and their families. They stole pigs, goats, chickens, and garden vegetables from neighboring plantations, creating friction among planters and encouraging slaves to wander beyond their masters' surveillance. They engaged in hunting, which required them to carry weapons and travel away from French settlements toward Indian and maroon communities. The more these methods moved slaves toward full subsistence, the less masters could control them by withholding necessities. So slaveholders agreed, as a matter of public order and a mechanism of control, to ensure slaves' reliable and complete dependence on their masters for daily needs. In the final version of the 1685 slave ordinance, masters agreed to mandatory minimum subsistence requirements for their slaves and forbade one another to encourage slaves' independence by requiring their self-sufficiency. To prevent slaves from becoming independent, they also declared that anything belonging to a slave would become the master's property.[83]

Seeking other forms of independence and craving the community of family and friends, even the best-fed slaves still tried to move independently around the island. They gathered for weddings, funerals, religious ceremonies, trade, and communal subsistence activities like fishing and hunting. They met for sex and conversation, to fight an enemy or to visit a friend. A whole string of colonial ordinances between the 1660s and 1680s attests to slaves' desired mobility and the threat it posed to masters' authority. In 1664, for example, colonists had to ensure, by law, that slaves did

83. "La conservation," "la police," "le jugement," "les chastiments": Jean-Baptiste Patoulet to the king, May 20, 1682, ANOM, Collection Moreau de Saint-Méry, F3, XC; Patoulet, "Memoire au Roy," and Bégon, "Project concernant les Esclaves," F3, XC; Slave Ordinance of March 1685, articles 22–29. The French term "police" has no good English equivalent, but in this case "policing" seemed to capture the dual meaning of management and surveillance that is implied in Patoulet's and Bégon's use of the term.

not sneak around at night, sell goods without a pass from their masters, or go to other plantations to steal sugar. Noting slaves' tendency to escape to maroon communities, in 1672 Martinique's council ordered the death penalty for all maroons, offering reimbursement to masters for the price of the slave. According to the governor, this ordinance "did not have the success" they desired, with widespread desertion still very common throughout the island. To curb the problem, he issued an ordinance ordering the militia to sweep the island in search of maroons and to require all slaves encountered outside their master's plantation to produce a pass giving them permission to be abroad. Endorsing limitations on unregulated slave travel, Martinique's officials wrote, "Nothing is more necessary for the security of the inhabitants of the islands and for preventing slave revolts." Unregulated movement continued to be a problem for the next several years, but colonial authorities addressed it repeatedly until slaves without passes found it much more difficult to travel the main roads and mill about town and were forced into the backcountry. Martinique's officials ordered a one-thousand-livre penalty for anyone allowing slaves to gather on his property, even for dances, or "calindas," a fine twenty times higher than for buying stolen goods from a slave. The severity of the punishment registered the height of their obsession with perpetual control and the depth of their fear that such control was impossible.[84]

Over time colonists recognized that one way to allay the dangers of slaves' inevitable mobility was to police their use of potential weapons. Beginning in the 1660s and culminating in the 1685 ordinance, French slaveholders forbade slaves to carry large sticks, guns, knives, or other menacing objects, and they punished French merchants who sold these implements to the enslaved. Masters could allow their slaves to hunt and fish for them, but they had to provide the slave with papers or some other pass recognizable to neighboring colonists. But it was almost impossible to completely restrict

---

84. "Réglement de M. de Tracy, Lieutenant Général de l'Amérique, touchant les Blasphémateurs et la Police des Isles," June 19, 1664, and "Arrêt du Conseil de la Martinique, touchant les Negres fugitives, et le Remboursement de ceux suppliciés," June 20, 1672, in Moreau de Saint-Méry, *Loix et constitutions*, I, 117–122, 264, and "Ordonnance du Gouverneur-Général des Isles, touchant les Negres Marons," Aug. 28, 1673, I, 268–269. "Rien n'est plus necessaire pour la sécurité des habitans des isles et pour empescher la revolte des negres": [Patoulet] to Blénac, April, 1681, ANOM, Colonies, C8A, III, 6. "Extrait des arrets et ordonnances Rendus pour la Police des negres au Conseil Souverain de l'Isle Martinique," July 3, 1684, ANOM, Collection Moreau de Saint-Méry, F3, CCXLIX, f. 101. The original ordinance was issued on Aug. 16, 1678.

slaves' acquisition of weapons, particularly knives and machetes that were used in cutting cane. This was doubly true of Indian slaves, whose work hunting and fishing required that they carry weapons and work somewhat independently.[85]

Because they could not legislate slaves' submission, planters relied on violence to coerce them. Determining the most effective forms of this violence occupied a great deal of slaveholders' attention during the early generations of slavery. Given the legal precedent granting masters complete control over slaves' bodies, even to the point of death, these discussions centered on practical rather than moral concerns. The first had to do with masters' interest in slaves' bodies as instruments of labor. Killing or destroying a slave undermined the master's reason for having the slave in the first place. Slaveholders also feared that overly severe punishments would lead slaves to risk flight or, worse, armed rebellion. Over time, these collective fears were registered in a series of laws stipulating uniform punishments for slaves' crimes. When slaves ran away the first time, for example, they would have their ears cropped and be branded on the face with a fleur-de-lis. Their second offense would lead to the severing of a leg (moderated to a severed hamstring in the 1685 ordinance). The third offense brought death. When slaves stole pigs, canoes, sugar, horses, cattle, indigo, ginger, and tools—for subsistence or sale—they could be punished by having a leg cut off. Stealing cattle or horses brought execution. By 1677 a slave's attacking a French person also became a capital offense. In his 1682 memoir, Patoulet's solution to the menace of unauthorized slave gatherings was that any French colonist discovering slaves engaged in such activity could "kill them without scruple." This was moderated by Bégon to encourage free colonists to take offending slaves to prison, though it did provide that a colonist could justify killing slaves in self-defense, defined as vaguely and broadly as possible. The final ordinance removed the license to kill, but stopped short of stipulating the lengths to which colonists could go to enforce the provision.[86]

The tension between punishments that destroyed slaves' bodies and masters' desire to extract from them a lifetime of labor fueled a sadistic creativity among slaveholders. Cutting off someone's leg, assuming one sur-

---

85. Slave Ordinance of March 1685, article 15.

86. "Réglemens du Conseil de la Martinique, touchant la Police des Esclaves," Oct. 4, 1677, and "Arrêt du Conseil de la Martinique, touchant les Canots et Chaloupes, et l'enlevement d'iceux par les Esclaves," July 17, 1679, in Moreau de Saint-Méry, *Loix et constitutions*, I, 306–307, 327; Patoulet, "Memoire au Roy," and Bégon, "Projet concernant les Esclaves," ANOM, Collection Moreau de Saint-Méry, F3,XC.

FIGURE 11. Slave Torture and Bodily Preservation. *François Froger,* A Relation of a Voyage Made in the Years 1695, 1696, and 1697. *London, 1698. Permission The Mariners' Museum, Newport News, VA*

vived the trauma and blood loss, seriously limited the person's working capacity. Severing a hamstring was little better. In the interest of preserving productivity, one French planter devised an alternative: chaining the slave's ankle to a metal band around his throat. Whenever the slave relaxed the leg he would choke, but, when he held the leg up, his muscles would fatigue, cramp, and spasm. There is no question that this was a torturous experience, but in the end the master preserved the slave's body for labor. Other devices, adapted from the tools of medieval torture, kept slaves from eating, secured them to trees for whipping, and, of course, chained them in place.[87]

Masters' punishments were rarely regulated by law, but public interest

87. Froger, *Relation d'un voyage*, between 150 and 151.

demanded some limits. In 1671 the state punished one cruel owner with a light fine for beating his slave nearly to death and burning her genitals with a firebrand. The state's intervention came during the height of tensions between maroon communities and French colonists, which had amplified some colonists' fears that slaveholders' violent punishments could spark widespread reprisals. This fear, apparently expressed to Bégon during his interviews, led him to stipulate that masters themselves could only chain, whip, or beat their slaves with sticks or rods—but not torture them. Poorly defined, the only guidance the law gave on the meaning of torture was the prohibition of dismemberment and mutilation by private parties. These penalties, as well as branding and execution, could be carried out only by the island's Superior Council. If a master or overseer killed a slave during punishment, he could face criminal charges, but enforcement was structured to protect masters rather than slaves. Not only would the master's fellow slaveholders have to choose to pursue a case against him, but the Superior Council was empowered to grant a pardon to masters or overseers should they determine that the death was accidental or justified.[88]

Masters sometimes overlooked slaves' misdeeds either because the crime did no harm to the master or because the declared punishment for the slave's crime risked the loss of the slave. Afraid of losing their slaves to public execution, for example, colonists concealed their slaves' acts of defiance, prompting the council at Martinique to offer payment to masters who "brought their criminal slaves to justice." Punishments that would maim or kill a slave eventually fell under public authority, ensuring that masters, to save their property, would not allow dangerous or rebellious slaves to live. By 1685 planters had worked out an elaborate system of reimbursement. When a master delivered a slave for execution, provided that the master was not an accomplice to the capital crime, two other planters would assess the monetary value of the slave, and the state would pay the master that amount to compensate for his loss. As a further inducement to bring dan-

88. "Arrêt du Conseil de la Martinique, contre un Maître cruel," May 10, 1671, in Moreau de Saint-Méry, *Loix et constitutions*, I, 224–225; Bégon, "Projet concernant les Esclaves," ANOM, Collection Moreau de Saint-Méry, F3, CX; Slave Ordinance of March 1685, articles 42–43. Malick Ghachem follows Jean Bodin in emphasizing the inherent conflict between the sovereignty of states over subjects on the one hand and of masters over slaves on the other. Given that most limits on masters' authority arose locally and were thus largely self-imposed by planters, it is not clear how that theoretical tension manifested itself in legal codes or actual social practice. See Ghachem, "Sovereignty and Slavery," esp. 1–170.

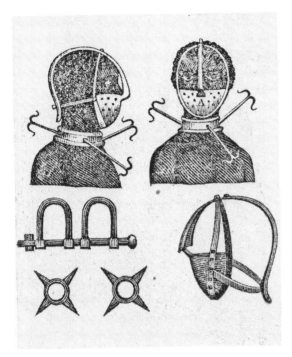

FIGURE 12. Devices for Slave Torture and Restraint. *Thomas Branigan,* The Penitential Tyrant; or, Slave Trade Reformed: A Pathetic Poem. *Courtesy Library of Congress, Washington, D.C.*

gerous slaves to justice, courts were forbidden to collect legal fees for criminal proceedings against slaves.[89]

As another means of preventing slaves' independence, the 1685 ordinance also created a uniform system for forcibly integrating slaves into French culture through the rituals and daily regimens of Roman Catholicism. Probably at the behest of the islands' Catholic missionaries, the ordinance required masters to instruct and baptize slaves within two weeks of their arrival, to avoid working them or having them conduct trade on Catholic holy days, and to sanctify their marriages in the church. The law also granted special burials to Christian slaves in ritually sanctified cemeteries, with non-Christian slaves to be buried in a field near where they died. European tradition forbade Christians to hold other Christians as slaves, but, because that custom arose from a common agreement to prevent Christian enslavement, making a slave into a Christian had no bearing

89. "Livrer à la Justice leurs Esclaves criminels": "Arrêt du Conseil de la Martinique, touchant le payment des Negres suppliciés," July 16, 1665, in Moreau de Saint-Méry, *Loix et constitutions,* I, 148; Slave Ordinance of March 1685, articles 40–41.

on his or her slave status. In their view, reducing a Christian to slavery was forbidden; elevating a slave to Christianity was not.[90]

As one of the few areas of the 1685 ordinance imposed from above, the religious provisions sparked immediate controversy. Slaveholders seem to have supported slaves' cultural indoctrination and ritual submission to Catholic authority required by the ordinance. To the extent that they were successful, these requirements would only reinforce hierarchy, encourage faithful service, and discourage independent religious gatherings. But planters resisted restrictions on when slaves could work, a command they simply seem to have ignored. They also appealed to Martinique's Superior Council—which in turn appealed to the crown—to reinstate slaves' ability to conduct trade on Sundays and other holy days, a long tradition in the islands on which both sellers and buyers had come to depend. Martinique's ruling elite likewise pushed back against a provision in the ordinance that would revolutionize the way the court system conducted trials. Traditionally, slaves could not testify against their masters, even if they had been the only witness to a crime, to prevent giving slaves the ability to exact revenge through false testimony. In the 1685 ordinance, however, slaves were forbidden to testify against any whites, a restriction that threatened to destroy the court's ability to prosecute most crimes, as more than half the potential witnesses would be excluded. Responding to pressure from the islands, the crown revised both parts of the ordinance to restore Sunday markets and allow slaves to testify against anyone but their masters. That the crown so quickly, and with so little actual pressure, yielded to planters' call to restore "the way things had been done before the said ordinance" underscores the nature of French slave law as a product of local responses to actual colonial conditions. Local practice generated most of the March 1685 ordinance, and the rare contradiction to precedent met with swift resistance by Caribbean elites.[91]

90. Slave Ordinance of March 1685, articles 2–8; Peabody, "'Dangerous Zeal,'" *French Historical Studies*, XXV (2002), 70–71. For Jesuits' use of Catholicism to encourage slaves' obedience and cultural integration in their eighteenth-century Latin American estates, see Arnold J. Bauer, "Christian Servitude: Slave Management in Colonial Spanish America," in Mats Lundahl and Thommy Svensson, eds., *Agrarian Society in History: Essays in Honour of Magnus Mörner* (London, 1990), 89–107.

91. For the general dynamics of religion and slavery in the islands, see Peabody, "'Dangerous Zeal,'" *French Historical Studies*, XXV (2002), 53–90; Debien, *Les esclaves aux Antilles françaises, XVIIe–XVIIIe siècles* (Basse-Terre, 1974), 249–295. For arguments over slaves' market activities and court testimony, see King's Council to Superior Council of Martinique, Oct. 13, 1686, AN, Fonds du Conseil du Roi, Série E, MDCCCXXXV.

Legal pluralism provided the mechanism to smooth over most conflicts between Caribbean planters and their metropolitan counterparts. As Louis's 1704 freedom suit demonstrated, however, human movement (forced and free) occasionally brought distinct legal zones into contact, demanding resolution to questions that had been avoided by geographic isolation. The crown's response to Louis's and similar cases asserted the primacy of France's free soil principle, even as it encouraged planters to maintain the geographic isolation that made the system work. The crown issued an official edict to that effect in 1707, ordering that any "Negro" who set foot on French soil would be freed, but only if invoking the free soil privilege before returning to the islands. "At the moment that, of their own free will, they have departed," the king wrote, "they can no longer claim the privilege of the soil of France, which they have seemingly renounced by their voluntary return to the place of slavery." Had Louis sued for his freedom under this regulation, he would have been denied, because he had already returned to Martinique. This ruling simultaneously discouraged planters from bringing slaves to France and prevented the return of freed slaves to the islands, drawing clear regional lines around opposing legal practices. Demonstrating that French antislavery sentiment was pervasive enough to trump local concerns, the 1707 decree also reinforced the principle that—at least within their own territories—colonies could develop whatever approach to slavery best met local needs.[92]

❖ Despite Michel Bégon's assertion that the laws of slavery in the French kingdom should uniformly support the enslavement of Indians, Africans, and mulattoes, French Atlantic slavery had come to depend, by the early eighteenth century, on nearly the opposite. Legal pluralism, rather than legal uniformity, defined slavery in the French Atlantic world. In France, nearly a century of political and legal pressures produced the profound commitment to free soil principles that allowed Louis to be emancipated. Colonial slaveholders resented any restriction on their slaveholding, complaining to their superiors that French law ought to support their interests.

92. "L'intention de Sa Majesté est que les Negres qui auront été amenés dans le Royaume par les Habitans des Isles qui refuseront d'y retourner, ne pourront y être contrains; mais que du moment que de leur pleine volonté, ils auront pris le parti de les suivre et de se rendre avec eux dans l'Amérique, ils ne puissant plus alléguer le Privilege de la Terre de France, auquel ils semblent avoir renoncé par leur retour volontaire dans le lieu de l'Eclavage": "Lettre du Ministre sur les Negres amenés en France," June 10, 1707, in Moreau de Saint-Méry, *Loix et constitutions*, II, 99.

rather than bend to such arcane distinctions. What these slaveholders did not acknowledge was the degree to which they depended on France's legal pluralism—and the fictions it made possible—for both the global expansion of slavery and the nearly total control they enjoyed over its local practice.[93]

In sharp contrast to the cultural imperatives of indigenous slavery in the Pays d'en Haut, then, the French insisted upon the separation of enslavement from slavery. This created distinct legal geographies in Europe, Africa, and the Americas, influencing not only where slavery would be practiced but which peoples would be enslaved. Morally, too, the French came to separate the act of enslavement from the domination of human chattel, placing the entire ethical burden of slavery on enslavement and presuming the moral neutrality of perpetually controlling purchased slaves and their offspring. It was considered far worse to reduce persons to slavery than to terrorize them into remaining slaves for life. Pursued vigorously during the second half of the seventeenth century, slavery in the French Caribbean brought great success—and often fabulous wealth—to colonists willing to accept the shaky moral arithmetic of Atlantic slavery. This success made France's Caribbean economy and its brutal labor system the envy of less-profitable colonies like New France, where settlers would attempt to replicate its success by embracing a system of colonial slavery that drew on both indigenous and Atlantic influences.

93. For colonists' complaints about French free soil, see Mithon to minister, Nov. 20, 1704, ANOM, C8A, XV, 349–351; Bégon, "Memoire sur les esclaves," ANOM, C8B, LXXIV. For a sustained discussion of the tensions between Caribbean slaveholders and the French state in Saint-Domingue, see Ghachem, "Sovereignty and Slavery."

*• Evolution of
New French
trade system
that was defined by legal
pluralism & regional
differences*

chapter three

LIKE NEGROES IN THE ISLANDS

Rumor spread quickly in the French Atlantic. Hundreds of people circulated regularly between the Caribbean and the Saint Lawrence in the early eighteenth century, and sharing news was among the first things merchants, officers, and sailors did when they arrived at port. No document survives to show the route the information took, but by 1708 word reached Canada that Caribbean officials had both freed an African slave and executed French traders for selling enslaved Indians. Canadians seem also to have learned of the king's 1707 declaration making free soil the French kingdom's official policy. These reports prompted considerable disagreement over the legality of slavery in Canada and its hinterlands, where a small but growing number of colonists had begun investing in slave labor over the previous generation. Unlike the Caribbean, where Indian slavery had been declared illegal and slave raiding made a capital offense, most of the slaves in New France were Indians. According to the colony's intendant, Jacques Raudot, many began to wonder whether Indians—or anyone—could be legally held as slaves in greater France. Some went so far as to encourage slaves to leave their masters "under the pretext that there are no slaves in France." Others harbored fugitives. This legal ambiguity had a chilling effect on the value of colonists' investment in slaves, as it rendered their claim to ownership insecure and frustrated plans to expand the slave trade.[1]

1. "Soub pretexte quen france il ny a point desclaves": Jacques Raudot, "Ord[onan]ce rendüe au sujet des neigres et des Sauvages nommez Panis," Apr. 13, 1709, BANQ-Q, E1, S1, P509. For a full transcription and translation of this ordinance, see Appendix B. For the fullest discussion of intercolonial communications in the French Atlantic, see Kenneth J. Banks, *Chasing Empire across the Sea: Communications and the State in the French Atlantic, 1713–1763* (Montreal, 2002). For oral or informal news and information networks, see Laurent Dubois, "An Enslaved Enlightenment: Rethinking the Intellectual History of the French Atlantic," *Social History*, XXXI (2006), 1–14. For the modest trade between Martinique and

The nervous chatter of New France's slaveholders reached Raudot and other colonial officials with added force because many of the colony's elite, including the governor and members of the Superior Council, had recently bought Indian slaves themselves. Merchants in Quebec's and Montreal's commercial districts had also entered the market, buying and selling a small number of Indian slaves in the first decade of the eighteenth century. But those who bought slaves complained that they were continually "cheated out of the considerable sums paid for them because of the notions of liberty inspired in them by those who have not bought them, which means that they almost always desert their masters." Whether informally or by petition, slaveholders' concerns forced Raudot and the Superior Council to address the standing of slavery in New France. On April 13, 1709, Raudot issued an ordinance confirming slavery's legality in the colony, declaring, "All the Panis [Indians] and Negroes who have been bought, and who shall be bought hereafter, shall be fully owned as property by those who have purchased them as their slaves."[2]

There is no record that Raudot himself owned a slave, but he had a stake in slavery's protection. Charged with managing New France's legal and economic affairs, Raudot would have felt doubly frustrated by the colony's ambivalent approach to the subject. Not only did it undermine what he considered a legal form of commerce, challenging the authority of local law, but it also foreclosed a potential avenue for economic diversification and development. In economic terms, Raudot had inherited his post at the worst possible time. A spectacular collapse in the European market for North American furs had eviscerated the colony's primary export, leaving colonial officials scrambling for new prospects. He obsessed over ways to develop new enterprises, looking to the Caribbean as both a model of economic success and a potential consumer of Canadian goods. In a series of memo-

---

Quebec in the first decade of the eighteenth century, see Jacques Mathieu, *Le commerce entre la Nouvelle-France et les Antilles au XVIIIe siècle* (Montreal, 1981), 22–31; and Jacques Raudot to the minister, Nov. 1, 1709, ANOM, Colonies, C11A, XXX, 229–258v. For the 1707 royal decree on French free soil, see "Lettre du Ministre sur les Negres amenés en France," June 10, 1707, M. Moreau de Saint-Méry, *Loix et constitutions des colonies françoises de l'Amérique sous le vent* (Paris, 1785–1790), II, 99.

2. "Lesquels se trouvent souvent frustrez des sommes considerables quils en donnent par une idée de liberté que leur inspirent ceux qui ne les ont pas achetez, ce qui fait quils quittent quasi toujours leurs maitres"; "tous les Panis et Negres qui ont Eté achetez et qui le seront dans la suite appartiendront en plaine proprieté a Ceux qui les ont achetez": Raudot, "Ord[onan]ce rendüe au sujet des neigres et des Sauvages nommez Panis," BANQ-Q, E1, S1, P509.

randums following his arrival in Canada in 1705, Raudot and his son (who served under him as co-intendant) outlined a vision of development designed to emulate the Caribbean's successful export system and profit from its need for foodstuffs and other items that New France could provide. In his hopeful plans, slavery would play a prominent role.[3]

Raudot insisted that New France, for all its differences, must be established "on the same footing" as the Caribbean and, to make that possible, that Canada's enslaved Indians should be considered the equivalent of enslaved Africans. "The people of the Panis nation are needed by the inhabitants of this country for agriculture and other enterprises that might be undertaken," he wrote, "like Negroes in the Islands." Knowing that African slavery was well established by the early eighteenth century, Raudot drew upon the legal fictions that had allowed that system to thrive in the face of French antislavery sentiments. No fewer than nine times Raudot noted that Indian slaves were purchased, rather than enslaved, by the French. Echoing the language of Grotius and the many African and Caribbean chroniclers who followed, the intendant indemnified French slaveholders from any involvement in the act of enslavement. These slaves "can only be obtained from Indians who capture them in their territory," he insisted, coming into French hands only when their captors "sold them to the people of this country." What was more, the particular nation he identified as the victims of slavery—"the Indians called Panis"—lived in a land "far distant from this one," suggesting the essential divide between territories of enslavement and those of slavery. Raudot also explained to colonists that the free soil principle did not apply to Canada, reminding them that slavery thrived in France's American colonies despite its questionable standing in France.[4]

Although Raudot compared New France to the Caribbean, he realized

3. Jacques Raudot to minister, Nov. 1, 1709, ANOM, Colonies, C11A, XXX, 229–258v; Antoine-Denis Raudot, "Mémoire de Raudot, fils, sur les affaires presents du Canada," Aug. 7, 1706, ANOM, Colonies, C11A, VIII, 40–52, and Raudot to minister, Nov. 13, 1707, XXVI, 238–241. For the collapse of the fur trade, which began in the 1690s and lasted until around 1714, see W. J. Eccles, *The Canadian Frontier, 1534–1760* (Albuquerque, N.Mex., 1969), 124–125, 145; Louise Dechêne, *Habitants and Merchants in Seventeenth-Century Montreal*, trans. Liana Vardi (Montreal, 1992), 67–76; James Pritchard, *In Search of Empire: The French in the Americas, 1670–1730* (Cambridge, 2004), 156–162.

4. "Toutes les colonies doivent etre regardées sur le meme pied"; "les peuples de la nation Panis sont aussy necessaires aux habitans de ce pais pour la Culture des terres et autres ouvrages qu'on pouroit entreprendre, comme les Negres le sont aux isles"; "sauvages quon nommee panis dont la nation est tres Eloignée de ce païs": Raudot, "Ord[onan]ce rendüe au sujet des neigres et des Sauvages nommez Panis," BANQ-Q, E1, S1, P509.

that slavery in his colony had arisen from developments that were particular to North America.[5] Over the previous generation, New France and its Indian allies had constructed an elaborate and far-flung system of commercial and military alliances on which the colony depended for its security. Embedding themselves within systems of indigenous diplomacy involved engagement with indigenous forms of slavery, particularly when Indians offered slaves as gifts signifying friendship and shared diplomatic purpose. Beginning in about 1660, cultural, diplomatic, and economic forces within the growing French-Indian alliance network converged to draw the French and their Native allies into the Indian slave trade. Allied Indians offered slaves to French colonists as culturally powerful symbols of their emerging partnership. Although French bureaucrats initially rejected slaves as legitimate tokens of friendship, many western traders experimented with Indian slavery as a means of strengthening trade relations while securing valuable laborers. Following the Great Peace of Montreal in 1701, New France struggled to prevent warfare among its Indian neighbors and to keep its Native allies from defecting to the English. French officials found that the slave trade offered one of the most effective means of stabilizing the precarious alliance created by the new treaty, embracing French involvement in the trade for diplomatic as well as economic reasons. Indian slaves therefore became increasingly available as their exchange grew more central to the maintenance of the alliance.

As Indian slaves passed into New France, especially after 1701, a growing number of French families bought them as laborers. Frustrated by a sagging fur trade and eager to mimic the success of their Caribbean counterparts, colonists embraced this source of slaves as a possible way to transform New France into an agricultural and raw materials exporter supplying the Caribbean and greater France. Others used slaves to supplement the colony's chronically short labor supply, buying slaves to work as domestics, farm workers, or semiskilled shop hands. To protect these investments and to put an end to disputes over slaves' legal status, Raudot issued his 1709 ordinance, which attempted to shape the nature of slavery and its place in French colonial society. Raudot and his successor, Michel Bégon (son

---

5. Raudot acknowledged one year later that his authority to legalize Indian slavery was a response to specific local circumstances and thus was restricted to New France. Jacques Raudot, "Ordonnance qui permet au sieur Mounier de reprendre son Panis," Mar. 23, 1710, LAC, Fonds des Ordonnances des Intendants de la Nouvelle France, MG8-A6, III, 319–321. For a full discussion of Caribbean exports and their implications for the law and practice of slavery in Canada, see Chapter 6.

of the Caribbean administrator who drafted the 1685 slave code), worked to recreate the dynamics that had made African slavery such a brutal success in the islands. Not only did they wish to turn Indian slaves into units of property serving colonists' lifelong labor needs, but they also tried to separate French slaveholding from the enslavement that enabled it. By trying to make Indian slaves "like Negroes in the Islands," Raudot, and the thousands of French colonists who would follow his lead, linked indigenous and French Atlantic slaveries, creating opportunities for the adaptation and innovation that would yield a wide range of regional approaches to slavery in the Pays d'en Haut and throughout the French colonial world.

THEY ASSURED ME OF THEIR FRIENDSHIP

"They assured me of their friendship, and as proof gave me three slaves."
—*Daniel Greysolon Dulhut, Quebec, 1678*

New France had been settled for a full century by the time Raudot issued his ordinance in 1709, but the slave trade had only slowly developed over the previous four decades. Although colonists built strong relationships with Algonquians, Montagnais, and Hurons, they received few captives from these besieged allies, whose regional war culture did not value slaves as symbolic gifts as in the Pays d'en Haut. When the French occasionally received captives, they generally executed or evangelized them. The settler population was too small and too focused on trade to demand slave labor, and religious idealists often intervened to claim captives for the faith. Beginning in the 1660s, French colonists began spreading westward, entering the Pays d'en Haut in large numbers to engage in trade and alliance building. Adapting to the region's diplomatic culture, French colonists began receiving slaves in larger numbers.

Until the mid-1660s, low levels of migration, conflict with the Iroquois, and weak colonial administration stunted New France's development. Although Samuel de Champlain established Quebec in 1608, the settlement grew very slowly, amounting to little more than a commercial entrepôt with only a few dozen settlers when a company of English-backed privateers claimed possession of it in 1629. Although a treaty agreement returned the Saint Lawrence to French control almost immediately, the privateers had siphoned away fur trade revenues and captured French supply ships, worsening an already desperate situation. When Champlain returned to Quebec in 1633, he was essentially starting over. During the previous four years the fur trade had declined, Iroquois raids had increased, and many of the colony's rough wooden structures were burned or falling apart. Champlain and his successors slowly revived the colony, restoring the network of relationships established between French colonists and Native peoples through the fur trade, shared military ventures, and newly formed kin relations.[6]

In the Saint Lawrence Valley, nothing shaped early colonial development more than conflict with the Iroquois, which simultaneously energized religious zeal and discouraged migration. From the beginning of settlement the French naturally aligned with the Montagnais, Algonquians, and Hurons against the more distant Iroquois. Linking trade and alliance (which, according to one Iroquois observer, Indians "take to be one thing"), the French became both commercially and militarily involved with their Native hosts, making them the enemies of the Iroquois who threatened the colony far more than its English competitors in the seventeenth century. In the late-1640s, Iroquois warriors spread out across the Great Lakes to attack their enemies, striking with special force against their Huron antagonists. Village after village fell under the onslaught, scattering survivors in all directions. They then turned to the Hurons' French allies, nearly destroying the tiny village of Three Rivers, which stood as the last bastion of defense between Iroquoia and the rest of the colony. Fully half a century after settlement, then, in 1661 the Ursuline nun Marie de l'Incarnation could write that "the persecution of the Iroquois . . . keeps the entire country in continual apprehension." If God did not blind them to French weaknesses, she believed, "they would already have exterminated us." If the Ursuline mystic overstated Iroquois intent to obliterate the French, she captured the sense of vulnerability that pervaded the colony in the mid-seventeenth century. The alliances that had drawn French colonists into war with the Iroquois, however, also protected them. Although under threat themselves, Algonquians, Montagnais, and surviving Hurons fought alongside French militia to defend the fledgling colony.[7]

6. David Hackett Fischer, *Champlain's Dream: The European Founding of North America* (New York, 2008), 406–441; Peter E. Pope, *Fish into Wine: The Newfoundland Plantation in the Seventeenth Century* (Chapel Hill, N.C., 2004), 80–82; Bruce G. Trigger, *Natives and Newcomers: Canada's "Heroic Age" Reconsidered* (Montreal, 1985), 164–229; Marcel Trudel, *The Beginnings of New France, 1524–1663* (Toronto, 1973), 161–180.

7. Daniel K. Richter, *The Ordeal of the Longhouse: The Peoples of the Iroquois League in the Era of European Colonization* (Chapel Hill, N.C., 1992), 29; Marie de l'Incarnation, *Word from New France: The Selected Letters of Marie de l'Incarnation*, ed. and trans. Joyce Marshall (Toronto, 1967), 265. For the Iroquois assaults on New France and its allies, see Richter, *Ordeal of the Longhouse*, 50–74; Trigger, *Natives and Newcomers*, 259–289. For perceptions

Pierre Boucher was one of the minor French officers who fought along-side these Indians. He had gained the trust of the Hurons after living for years among them as a lay servant to the Jesuits, eventually marrying and fathering a child with a Huron woman. Iroquois depredations were thus deeply personal to him, and he shared these anti-Iroquois sentiments with Louis XIV and Jean-Baptiste Colbert when they invited him to France in 1662 to report on the colony's progress. "We have an enemy who pens us into a little corner and prevents us from venturing out and making discoveries," he wrote of the Iroquois, "so he will have to be destroyed." The Iroquois were never destroyed, but an infusion of French troops allowed the colony to send raiding parties throughout Iroquoia, forcing the Iroquois to sue for peace. Concluded in 1666, the treaty between New France and the Iroquois would more or less hold for two decades, breaking down in the mid-1680s with new implications for the slave trade.[8]

Through the 1660s, warfare with the Iroquois produced almost no slaves for New France. The colony's Native allies in the Saint Lawrence Valley occasionally gave captives to the French, but these gifts were exceptional and almost never translated into perpetual slavery. In the late-1650s, for example, a group of Algonquians gave three Iroquois to the French at Quebec, where priests promptly ushered them to the seminary for religious instruction. "Reasons of State condemned them to death," read a Jesuit's report of their arrival, "but Christian piety exempted them from the stake—two being dispatched with the musket; while the third proved to be the son of one of our good Hurons here." The Huron was freed, and no slaves remained. What the "reasons of state" might have been remains obscure, but keeping Iroquois captives in the Saint Lawrence would have been dangerous, and those who remained would have been most easily monitored and controlled by missionaries. Most often, French writers reported that allied Indians kept Iroquois prisoners for themselves, torturing or killing them as "the custom of the nation regulates." Nor did the Iroquois offer slaves to the French as diplomatic gifts. Even in peacetime their relations were strained,

---

of the Iroquois threat to New France, see Peter N. Moogk, "Reluctant Exiles: Emigrants from France in Canada before 1760," *William and Mary Quarterly*, 3d Ser., XLVI (1989), 463–505.

8. [Pierre Boucher], *Histoire veritable et naturelle des moeurs et productions du pays de la Nouvelle France, vulgairement dite le Canada* (Paris, 1664), 143–144. For Boucher's life, see Raymond Douville, "Boucher, Pierre," *DCB*, II, 82–87; Montarville Boucher de La Bruère, "Pierre Boucher," *Cahiers des Dix*, II (1937), 237–260. For French-Iroquois warfare in the 1660s, see José António Brandão, *"Your Fyre Shall Burn No More": Iroquois Policy toward New France and Its Native Allies to 1701* (Lincoln, Nebr., 1997), 105–116.

and, at least in the mid-seventeenth century, Iroquois war culture placed a much higher value on incorporating than on trading enemy prisoners. Disease and warfare had sharply reduced Iroquois population, placing a premium on the demographic and economic benefits of absorbing outsiders.[9]

During the 1660s, French colonizers and their Indian allies began to construct an elaborate system of commercial and cultural ties that drew the French into the continental interior. Although mostly private and often illegal, this western trade owed much of its force to the assumption of royal control over New France in 1663, which initiated, in the words of one scholar, "a total reorganization in all domains: ecclesiastical, economic, civil, and military." The most profound transformation lay in the colony's relationship with Amerindians, who had always been important actors in the fur trade, but who came to occupy a larger role in the imperial contest for North America between France, Britain, and Spain. Battered by the well-armed Iroquois, Indians of the western Great Lakes and Upper Mississippi Valley sought French alliance. Threatened by the English and their Iroquois supporters, Louis XIV also needed allies in North America. During the late-1680s and early 1690s, the French crown began to express a willingness to subsidize the fur trade—essentially paying traders to sell at a loss—to secure Native alliances. Cheaper than raising an army to defend France's North American holdings, this strategy fostered a remarkable expansion of French imperial influence to regions as far as Lake Superior and the Missouri River valley.[10]

As they expanded their alliances with western nations, many French traders and diplomats accepted slaves as symbolic gifts from the Indian peoples they encountered. In 1670, for example, Jacques Marquette received

9. *Jesuit Relations*, XLVI, 85–101, XLVIII, 107–111, 111 ("Reasons of state"), LXVI, 169 ("custom of the nation"). For the most complete discussion of Iroquoian captivity as well as a discussion of whether it should be considered adoption or slavery, see Daniel K. Richter, "War and Culture: The Iroquois Experience," *WMQ*, 3d Ser., XL (1983), 528–559; William A. Starna and Ralph Watkins, "Northern Iroquoian Slavery," *Ethnohistory*, XXXVIII (1991), 34–57; Roland Viau, *Enfants du néant et mangeurs d'âmes: guerre, culture, et société en Iroquoisie ancienne* (Montreal, 1997), esp. 137–199; Leland Donald, *Aboriginal Slavery on the Northwest Coast of North America* (Berkeley, Calif., 1997), 260–268.

10. Marcel Trudel, "New France, 1524–1713," *DCB*, I, 33 ("total reorganization"); W. J. Eccles, "The Fur Trade and Eighteenth-Century Imperialism," *WMQ*, 3d Ser., XL (1983), 341–362; Catherine M. Desbarats, "The Cost of Early Canada's Native Alliances: Reality and Scarcity's Rhetoric," *WMQ*, 3d Ser., LII (1995), 609–630; Gilles Havard, *Empire et métissages: Indiens et Français dans le Pays d'en Haut* (Paris, 2003), esp. chap. 6: "Onontio et ses enfants: alliance et logique d'empire."

an Indian captive as a token of friendship after caring for an ailing Kiskakon Ottawa man. "Saying that I had given him his life," wrote Marquette, "he gave me a present of a slave that had been brought to him from the Illinois, two or three months before." Explaining the captive's origin, Marquette wrote, "The Illinois are warriors and take a great many Slaves, whom they trade with the Outaouaks [Ottawas] for Muskets, Powder, Kettles, Hatchets, and Knives." Four years later Marquette described the position of the Illinois in the regional slave trade: "They are warlike, and make themselves dreaded by the Distant tribes to the south and west, whither they go to procure Slaves; these they barter, selling them at a high price to other Nations, in exchange for other Wares." Marquette's experience indicates the dual nature of trading slaves in Illinois and Ottawa society. Neither wholly economic nor exclusively symbolic, captives could signify friendship and secure valuable trade goods.[11]

Farther west, the Sioux also offered captives to French visitors as signs of friendship. In 1700, a Sioux chief held a feast to honor French trader Pierre Charles Le Sueur, offering him as gifts two powerful symbols of alliance: food and slaves. Invoking the ceremonial language of kinship associated with indigenous slavery, the Sioux chief pointed to his people and said to the French visitors, "No longer regard us as Scioux, but as Frenchmen." Le Sueur gratefully received the gift and invited the Sioux to abandon their seasonal migrations and settle permanently near the French.[12]

During the 1670s, as the fur trade strengthened ties between the Saint Lawrence Valley and the Pays d'en Haut, the captive trade formerly confined to the West began to take place between Indians and French merchants at Montreal. In 1678, for example, Ottawa traders approached Daniel Greysolon Dulhut as part of the ritual gift exchanges routinely accompanying the fur trade. "They assured me of their friendship," wrote Dulhut, "and as proof gave me three slaves." We have no record what Dulhut gave in exchange for the captives, but they proved to be invaluable assets on his journey west to initiate friendships with the Assiniboines and the Sioux.[13]

11. *Jesuit Relations*, LIV, 177 ("present of a slave"), 191 ("great many slaves"), LIX, 127 ("They are warlike"). For the French original, see Jacques Marquette and Louis Jolliet, *Voyage et découverte de quelques pays et nations de l'Amérique Septentrionale* (Paris, 1681), 21.

12. "Le Sueur's Voyage up the Mississippi [1700]," *Wis. Hist. Coll.*, XVI (1902), 192.

13. "Mémoire du sieur Greyselon Du Lhut adressé à Monsieur le Marquis de Seignelay" (ca. 1682), and "Lettre du sieur Du Lhut à M. le Comte de Frontenac," Apr. 5, 1679, in Pierre Margry, comp., *Découvertes et établissements des Français dans l'ouest et dans le sud*

Like many French colonists who would receive slaves from their Native allies, despite accepting the Ottawas' gift, Dulhut rejected the cultural assumptions that motivated it. Rather than valuing these people for their expression of power over an enemy or of the symbolic unification of French and Ottawa interests, Dulhut simply viewed them as subordinate laborers who would reduce the burdens of his pending journey to Lake Superior. The clearest example that Dulhut rejected the logic of indigenous slavery came in 1684 following the murder of two Frenchmen at Lake Superior. Upon learning of the death of his countrymen, Dulhut seized a group of Indian suspects and brought them to Michilimackinac for trial. According to custom, Dulhut wrote of the incident, the offending party offered a gift of "some slaves, which was only meant to patch up the assassination committed upon the French." Dulhut's emissary "perceived their intention, and therefore would not allow it, telling them that a hundred slaves . . . could not make him traffic in the blood of his brothers." When the party met with Dulhut himself, he echoed the emissary's statement: "I said the same thing here in the councils, so that they [the Ottawas] might not in future believe that they could save by presents those who might commit similar acts."[14]

Rather than allowing the gift of slaves to cover the offense, Dulhut demanded and carried out the execution of two Indians for the murder. Not that Dulhut objected to the slave trade: he had already shown his willingness to use enslaved Indians as laborers. Instead, he rejected the logic of indigenous slavery that turned domesticated bodies into such powerful symbols of friendship that they compensated for murder. By ignoring the links between indigenous slavery and alliance building, Dulhut jeopardized the already-precarious coalition in the western Great Lakes at a dangerous moment. In 1684, rumors of Iroquois preparations for a massive assault on New France spread throughout the colony and across the Atlantic. The French began to mobilize a large army and sought to induce their Native allies to join them against the Iroquois. Dulhut's actions alienated key western allies essential to New France's ability to survive another war with the

---

de l'Amérique (Paris, 1876–1886), VI, 21 ("three slaves"), 29; Yves F. Zoltvany, "Dulhut, Daniel Greysolon," DCB, II.

14. Dulhut to the minister, Apr. 12, 1684, Wis. Hist. Coll., XVI (1902), 114–125, quotation on 123. For a complete discussion of the origins and outcome of this controversy, see Richard White, The Middle Ground: Indians, Empires, and Republics in the Great Lakes Region, 1670–1815 (Cambridge, 1991), 77–80, although White underestimates the breach Dulhut's actions created within the alliance, treating the episode as an example of successful compromise on the middle ground.

more powerful Iroquois. When the French asked the Indians at Michili-mackinac to arm themselves for impending battle, the Ottawas demurred, secretly warning other tribes against participation. "The French invite us to go to war against the Iroquois," one of them said. "They wish to use us in order to make us their slaves. After we have aided in destroying the enemy, the French will do with us what they do with their cattle, which they put to the plow and make them cultivate the land. Let us leave them to act alone." By killing the accused murderers in violation of Native conceptions of jus-tice, the French underscored for the Indians their unwillingness to play by the rules of alliance. Ironically, Dulhut's refusal to accept a gift of slaves to raise the dead instilled the fear of enslavement in New France's Indian allies, expressed in the familiar idiom of slaves as domesticated animals.[15]

Talk of a new wave of Iroquois warfare in New France, particularly with such ambivalent allies, struck panic in the colony. Nothing had shaped the first half century of New France's development more than fear of the Iro-quois, even when the fear was exaggerated. The relative calm between the French-Iroquois peace agreement of 1666 and the renewal of tensions in 1684 had allowed the French to spread westward and dramatically expand the fur trade, but all of that seemed threatened by a new surge of anti-French sentiment in Iroquoia. Canadians braced for the worst. In France royal officials tried to formulate a broader strategy to eliminate the Iroquois threat from North America while dealing with a host of other concerns. As the Iroquois conducted an unjust offensive war, argued an official dispatch from Louis XIV in 1684, their enslavement could be considered just under the law of nations. And their labor could certainly be useful. "As it tends to the good of my service to diminish, as much as possible, the number of the Iroquois," the king instructed, "and moreover, as these savages, who are very strong and robust, will serve usefully in my galleys, I will that you do every-thing in your power to make a great number of them prisoners of war and have them embarked by every opportunity that will offer, in order that they be conveyed to France." A similar plan had been discussed and abandoned more than twenty years earlier, but the 1684 letter offered the first official sanction of Iroquois enslavement.[16]

15. Claude Charles Le Roy, Bacqueville de La Potherie, *History of the Savage Peoples Who Are Allies of France*, in Emma Helen Blair, ed. and trans., *The Indian Tribes of the Upper Mis-sissippi Valley and Region of the Great Lakes* (Cleveland, 1911–1912), II, 24.

16. For the period of French-Iroquois peace, see Brandão, *"Your Fyre Shall Burn No More,"* 117–129. For plans to enslave the Iroquois in the galleys, see Louis XIV to M. de La Barre, July 31, 1684, in E. B. O'Callaghan, ed., *Documents relative to the Colonial History of*

For the next three years, the Iroquois and the French maintained an unstable peace, initiated by a 1684 treaty and upheld despite sporadic bursts of violence. In 1686, as growing tensions indicated the probability of war, the French crown reiterated its intent to seek Iroquois slaves for the galleys. As the French "possibly may take several Iroquois prisoners in the course of this war," suggested a letter from Versailles that year, "his Majesty desires him to keep them in confinement until an opportunity will offer to send them to France, as his Majesty thinks he can employ them in the Galleys." As the French would be engaged in their capture, calling them prisoners rather than slaves served a double purpose. It encouraged colonial military officers to participate in their capture and justified their later designation as slaves taken in a just war.[17]

When warfare resumed in 1687, Jacques-René de Brisay, marquis de Denonville, the governor of New France, intended to fulfill the king's orders to send the Iroquois to the galleys. Emphasizing that this was a defensive, and therefore just, war, New France's military and colonial leadership embraced the crown's plan of Iroquois enslavement. Meeting little success in the early stages of the conflict, Denonville orchestrated a plan to capture a large number of Iroquois while minimizing the risk to his troops. Initially keeping the plans to himself, Denonville requested that the Jesuit Jean de Lamberville of the Onondaga mission persuade the Iroquois to come to Fort Frontenac for a peace conference, where he would seize them and send them to

---

the State of New-York (Albany, N.Y., 1853–1887), IX, 233 (hereafter cited as *NYCD*). In 1663, an unsigned letter suggested that, because the Iroquois inhibited both trade and colonization, they should be attacked and either killed or sent to France as galley slaves. See "Memoire de ce qui est à faire en Canada," Jan. 22, 1663, ANOM, Colonies, C11A, II, 36–39.

17. "Abstract of M. de Denonville's Letters and of the Minister's Answers Thereto," 1686, *NYCD*, IX, 315. For French-Iroquois conflicts between 1684 and 1687, see Brandão, "*Your Fyre Shall Burn No More*," table D1. For a rich discussion of France's struggle to find sources of galley slaves, see Paul Walden Bamford, "The Procurement of Oarsmen for French Galleys, 1660–1748," *American Historical Review*, LXV (1959–1960), 31–48. Bamford divides galley oarsmen into two categories, slaves and *forçats*. The slaves, usually procured from northern Africa, constituted only about a third of the galley labor force during the 1680s, but the French considered them the most valuable and vigorous oarsmen, describing them as "tall, extremely vigorous, very resistant to fatigue," much like Louis XIV's description of the Iroquois. The *forçats*, or French convict laborers, served alongside the enslaved oarsmen for terms ranging from a few months to life. Thus, although Louis XIV initially described the Iroquois as "prisoners of war," they most likely fell into the category of "slave" once they arrived at the Mediterranean. For the most complete treatment of the forçats, see André Zysberg, *Les galériens: vies et destins de 60 000 forçats sur les galères de France, 1680–1748* (Paris, 1987).

France. Had Lamberville known of Denonville's plans, he would never have agreed to arrange the conference. He understood that taking slaves by perfidy would not only enrage the Iroquois but would also dishonor the French among their allies. As planned, Denonville and the intendant, Jean Bochart de Champigny, successfully captured and sent to France fifty-one Iroquois men, thirty-six of whom were Oneida and Onondaga chiefs come to negotiate peace. These captives combined with an unknown but relatively large number of Iroquois prisoners taken in dozens of campaigns in the small-scale raids that characterized warfare in the borderlands between Canada and Iroquoia.[18]

Denonville, recognizing the value of these prisoners in future negotiations with the Iroquois, requested that French officials ensure their availability for return should diplomacy prevail. "Since we may be able to arrange a general peace settlement sometime in the future," he wrote to his superiors, "I believe that it would be very useful for the colony if you were to keep them in a place where they can be recalled if need be." Denonville had earned his reputation fighting Algerian pirates in the Mediterranean in the 1660s, so the plan to bolster French galleys might have resonated with him. But he also had a healthy respect for Iroquois military power, so he needed to maintain access to Iroquois prisoners for bargaining power. Unsure whether the crown would grant a request to keep the prisoners available, Denonville sent the Iroquois prisoners to Marseille, where they arrived in late-1687.[19]

18. See Louis Henri, Chevalier de Baugy, *Journal d'une expédition contre les Iroquois en 1687, rédigé par Le Chevalier de Baugy, aide de camp de M. le marquis de Denonville* (Paris, 1883), 45; *Jesuit Relations*, LXIII, 23, 267, 304, LXIV, 255–257. Pointing to a 1687 edict ordering Denonville to send the Iroquois to the galleys, William Eccles and Jean Leclerc argue that Denonville had yet to receive orders to enslave the Iroquois before inviting them to Fort Frontenac, clearing him of the charge of intentional deception. This argument ignores the two earlier edicts, however, especially the one dated 1686 and addressed to Denonville himself. See Eccles, "Denonville et les galériens Iroquois," *Revue d'histoire de l'Amérique française*, XIV (1960), 408–429, and Jean Leclerc, "Denonville et ses captifs Iroquois," 545–558. For Lamberville's experience with Iroquoian captive customs, see *Jesuit Relations*, LXII, 55–107.

The number of Iroquois shipped to France has been a matter of dispute since the 1680s, when the Iroquois and the French claimed higher and lower numbers, respectively. For the most-detailed analysis of the question, and the source of my numbers, see Leclerc, "Denonville et ses captifs Iroquois," 549–553.

19. William J. Eccles, *Frontenac: The Courtier Governor* (Toronto, 1959), 186 ("recalled if need be"). For the arrival of the first Iroquois slaves in the Mediterranean, see "Table du

The governor's position reflected the contemporary ambiguities of French Atlantic slavery, blurring the lines between defining the Iroquois as temporary war captives and reducing them to lifelong slavery. The French typically divided galley oarsmen into two categories, Christians (including, particularly after 1685, Protestants) and non-Christians, mostly "Turks" and, by the 1680s, a growing number of sub-Saharan African slaves bought in Cape Verde or Senegal. Galley captains kept separate records for each group, labeling Christians "forçats," or forced laborers, and the rest "galeriens," or galley slaves. Initially, administrators in Marseille were unsure how to categorize the new Iroquois arrivals, noting that some of them even "have a tincture of our religion, and that they show signs of being baptized." A group of priests who used the galleys as fertile grounds for converting Muslims and Protestants sought to protect the Iroquois from overly harsh treatment, concerned that they might be unjustly enslaved Catholic converts.[20]

Fearful that this uncertainty would undermine the Iroquois's usefulness as galley slaves, in early 1688 Jean-Baptiste Colbert, marquis de Seignelay, offered a clarification to Michel Bégon, who had since left the Caribbean to oversee the king's Mediterranean galleys. Dismissing Denonville's notion that the Iroquois should receive any special consideration, he told Bégon, "His majesty wishes that you treat them the same as the Negroes from Senegal." Seignelay would have known that Bégon, in particular, would understand the analogy. When Bégon's draft of the Caribbean slave code arrived in France five years earlier, it had been Seignelay who edited and reissued it under the king's authority as the royal edict of 1685.[21]

Designated as slaves, the Iroquois labored alongside enslaved Africans and a growing number of eastern European Muslims who had been captured in the Holy Roman Empire's recent invasion of Ottoman Hungary

---

registre des ordres du roy et depeches concernant les galeres pendant l'année 1687," Dec. 18, 1687, AN, Fonds de la Marine, B6, XIX, 249v–250.

20. "Les Iroquois ont quelque teinture de n[ot]re Religion, et qu'ils donnent des marques qu'ils ont esté baptisez": "Table du registre des ordres du roy et depeches concernant les galeres pendant l'année 1687," Dec. 18, 1687, AN, Fonds de la Marine, B6, XIX, 249v–250. For distinctions among galley oarsmen, see Paul W. Bamford, *Fighting Ships and Prisons: The Mediterranean Galleys of France in the Age of Louis XIV* (Minneapolis, Minn., 1973), 139.

21. "Lettre du minister a Mons. L'intendant des galeres, a Versailles, 1688," in *Collection de manuscrits contenant lettres, memoires, et autres documents historiques relatifs a la Nouvelle-France* (Quebec, 1883), I, 426. Seignelay sent the 1684 call for Iroquois enslavement to Bégon's brother-in-law, Jacques de Meulles, who was intendant of New France at the time.

and bought by French agents in Trieste. Jean Bion, a French chaplain on the galleys who converted to Protestantism because of the terrors he witnessed there, wrote that galley slaves rejected Christianity because they would "rather be transformed into a Dog, than be of a Religion that countenances so much barbarity, and suffers so many Crimes." When they did not row fast enough, the oarsmen were beaten with a long rod that fell across the arms or backs of the slacker and anyone unfortunate enough to be nearby. As Jean-Baptiste Colbert wrote of galley slave discipline, "Nothing less than the rod and chain will do." Disease, too, added to the brutal labor conditions. Quarantined and observed before being put to sea, galley slaves were parceled out one and two at a time, a side benefit that also kept large groups of compatriots from rowing together and supporting one another. This was the case for the Iroquois, who were penned in Marseille awaiting the call to the oar, which began to come for them in January 1688.[22]

Had the Iroquois galley experiment proven successful, it might have paved the way for a different kind of Atlantic slave trade, clearing France's Native enemies from North America while populating the Mediterranean with North American slaves. By all reports, Iroquois labor matched, if it did not exceed, that of other slaves, inspiring enthusiasm in both Versailles and Marseille. With so many other demands for slave labor, French galleys were forced to rely on a growing proportion of forçats to man the oars. Then, too, Muslim slaves were dangerous cargo: sought for redemption by fellow Mediterranean Muslims, they could invite fierce reprisals on French ships transporting them to Marseille. Iroquois and other North American slaves could have mitigated these challenges that continually plagued the galleys.[23]

22. For discussions of buying Muslim slaves from around the Mediterranean, see "Table du registre des ordres du roy et depeches concernant les galeres pendant l'année 1687," Aug. 28, 1687, AN, Fonds de la Marine, B6, XIX, 180v, and "Table du registre des ordres du roy et depeches concernant les galeres pendant l'année 1688," Jan. 15, 1688, B6, XX, 7–8v. For "so much barbarity," see John Bion, *An Account of the Torments the French Protestants Endure aboard the Galleys* (London, 1708), 7, 14, 16. For "rod and chain," see Bamford, *Fighting Ships and Prisons*, 127. For quarantine, see "Table du registre des ordres du roy et depeches concernant les galeres pendant l'année 1688," Jan. 21, 1688, AN, Fonds de la Marine, B6, XX, 16v; for disease, see Feb. 3, 1688, XX, 26–28.

23. For the difficulty of recruiting slaves for the galleys, see "Table du registre des ordres du roy et depeches concernant les galeres pendant l'année 1687," Aug. 28, 1687, AN, Fonds de la Marine, B6, XIX, 180v, Oct. 28, 1687, XIX, 221, Oct. 31, 1687, XIX, 222v–223; Bamford, "The Procurement of Oarsmen for French Galleys, 1660–1748," *AHR*, LXV (1959–1960), 31–48.

But the Iroquois ensured the plan's failure. Iroquois diplomats predictably resented their compatriots' enslavement in the galleys, not least because of its egregious violation of North American laws of war. Rather than confronting an enemy, the French had invited the Iroquois to Fort Frontenac under the pretext of friendship. Instead of seeking captives to incorporate into local French households, the French sought slaves for brutal labor on distant seas. One sympathetic French observer recorded the reaction of an Iroquois captive, bound and awaiting transport. The prisoner said that his people had been "betray'd without any ground" and that they had been "tied to Posts, and whip'd in such a manner, that [we] could neither sleep, nor guard off the Flies." In response to Iroquois willingness to pursue trade and peace, he complained, "[We were] doom'd to Slavery, and to see [our] Fathers, and the ancient Men of [our] Country, murder'd before [our] eyes." Then he uttered a warning: "Assuredly, the five Villages will revenge our Quarrel, and entertain an everlasting and just Resentment of the tyrannical Usage we now meet with."[24]

The Iroquois carried out the threat. Over the next decade, they killed twice as many French colonists as they had killed in the eighty years since the French established Quebec. In 1688, when a large Iroquois force threatened to destroy Montreal, Father Lamberville negotiated a meeting between Denonville and the Iroquois, who desired "to get back their compatriots, who had been treacherously put into irons and taken to the galleys in france." Denouncing French duplicity, Lamberville recalled, the Iroquois threatened heavy reprisals if the slaves did not return. Should the French betray them again, they warned, "their people would know very well how to avenge it." Colonists began to blame Denonville's galley scheme for perpetuating the war, which, in the eyes of his critics, was waged "with no just pretext." Fearful of an overwhelming assault on Montreal and fearing for his political life, Denonville urged his French superiors to return the slaves. In 1689, when Governor Louis de Bouade de Frontenac sailed from France to replace Denonville as governor-general, he brought with him twenty-one Iroquois slaves.[25]

24. [Louis-Armand de Lom d'Arce], Baron de Lahontan, *New Voyages to North-America . . .* (London, 1703), I, 71–72.

25. Brandão, *"Your Fyre Shall Burn No More,"* 93–94, table D1; *Jesuit Relations,* LXIV, 255–257 ("get back their compatriots . . . avenge it"; "d'avoir fait la guerre sans aucuns juste pretexte"); unsigned memorandum, Oct. 30, 1688, ANOM, Colonies, C11A, X, 91 ("no just pretext"); Lahontan, *New Voyages,* II, 154; *Jesuit Relations,* LXIII, 23, 267, 304, LXIV, 255–257; Eccles, "Denonville et les galériens Iroquois," *Revue d'histoire de l'Amérique française,*

The return of the enslaved Iroquois not only failed to end the war but also jeopardized the western alliance. For one thing, most of the slaves never came back. Some had clearly not survived the perilous world of galley warfare, and French officials reported that in mid-1689 many still remained on the Mediterranean, out of communication until their galleys returned to port. French failure to return the slaves angered the Iroquois, but the fact that they returned any at all concerned French allies. After witnessing New France's submission to Iroquois demands for the return of the galley slaves, the Ottawas and others at Michilimackinac feared that they had cast their lot with the weaker party. "After seeing the cowardly manner in which he had allowed himself to be defeated on this last occasion at Montréal," wrote Jesuit Father Étienne de Carheil in 1689, "it was evident to them that they could no longer expect anything from his protection." In a statement attributed to an Ottawa chief, Carheil explained the significance of the galley slave incident in shaping the Indians' opinions of the French. "Far from compelling the foe to surrender his prisoners," noted the Ottawa, "he had himself, on the Contrary, been compelled to surrender those whom he had seized solely through treachery; and even to bring back from france those who had been sent thither." Why should they sacrifice trade with the English and risk their lives in war for such a weak and unpredictable nation? As a result of French actions, the Ottawas, Miamis, and Foxes all made overtures to the Iroquois during 1689, exploring the possibility of establishing a separate peace that would leave the French abandoned by its allies to face the Iroquois alone.[26]

That Bégon—a Caribbean administrator and perhaps the French world's foremost expert on slave law—could move to the Mediterranean and oversee American Indian galley slaves suggests both the fluidity of seventeenth-century slavery and the unexpected ways that its many expressions could be linked in French minds and institutions. The failure of Iroquois enslavement had nothing to do with the performance of Iroquois slaves, who by

XIV, 408–429, and Leclerc, "Denonville et ses captifs Iroquois," 545–558. Many other factors contributed to the increase in Iroquois attacks on the French, the most important of which was the encouragement of the English, who declared war on New France in 1689. The willingness of the Iroquois to fight alongside the English, however, is at least partly tied to the galley slave incident.

26. For Iroquois slaves remaining on the Mediterranean, see "Mémoire du roi à MM. de Denonville et de Champigny," May 1, 1689, ANOM, Colonies, B, XV, 54–62. For "cowardly manner" and "compelled to surrender," see *Jesuit Relations*, LXIV, 31–33. For allies' courting the Iroquois, see Bacqueville de La Potherie, *History, Wis. Hist. Coll.*, XVI (1902), 134–142, 147.

all accounts were among the strongest oarsmen in the galleys. After supervising Iroquois slaves at Marseille and comparing them to Africans in the Caribbean and Mediterranean, Michel Bégon remained an advocate of using enslaved Indians on plantations. But, in New France, Indian slavery embedded the French in a morally and militarily dangerous world in a way that purchasing slaves from distant suppliers never would have. The Iroquois galley experiment yielded such a negative outcome that it reinforced already-widespread doubts about the wisdom of enslaving Indians, particularly when the victims lived in reasonable striking distance of colonial settlements. What is more, French colonists found it hard to defend the morality of enslaving enemies, some of whom might have been fellow Catholics, by subterfuge. Although a wide variety of slaves rowed side-by-side in the galleys, the French were beginning to articulate legal and ethical distinctions between prisoners of war from Ottoman Hungary, purchased slaves from sub-Saharan Africa, and enslaved American Indians.[27]

If New France's officials shied away from enslaving Indians after 1688, they continued to want slaves, riding a wave of enthusiasm for the benefits of forced labor in the Caribbean. French settlers in the Saint Lawrence Valley heard a constant refrain, through both official channels and maritime gossip, that slaves made colonies rich. Well aware that the Canadian climate could not produce the tropical staples that thrived in the Caribbean, New France's colonists hatched inventive, if occasionally absurd, plans to use slave labor to diversify the colony's economy. The attorney general of the colony's Sovereign Council, François Ruette d'Auteuil, visited Paris in 1688, and talk of slavery was everywhere. The royal ordinance on slavery had been issued only three years earlier, and the Royal African Company—then called the Compagnie de Guinée—was expanding rapidly. Ruette d'Auteuil used his time at court to lobby the crown for permission to import slaves from the Caribbean to Canada. "Laborers and domestics are so scarce and so extraordinarily expensive in Canada," agreed intendant Jean-Baptiste de Lagny, "that it ruins everyone who attempts any enterprise." The best remedy, he argued, was to import "Negro slaves," who would find ready buyers in the colony's "principal inhabitants," including Ruette d'Auteuil himself.[28]

27. Michel Bégon, "Mémoire sur les esclaves des habitants des Isles françoises de l'Amérique qui prétendent être libres lorsqu'ils ont touché à la terre de France," 1704, ANOM, Colonies, C8B, LXXIV.

28. "Les gens de travail et les Domestiques sont d'une rareté et d'une cherté si extraord. re en Canda qu'ils ruine tous ceux qui font quelque entreprise . . . le meilleur moyen pour y remedier seroit d'avoir des Esclaves Negres . . . si sa Ma.té agrée cette propo'on quelques uns

Ruette d'Auteuil's political enemies, including Governor Frontenac, who was also in Paris in 1688, ridiculed the proposal, arguing that Africans would freeze to death in Canada's climate. The king sympathized with this concern, saying that colonists who bought slaves might find them useless in the cold, but in the end he conceded the benefits that slaves could offer the colony. The king thus authorized African slaves' importation in 1688 as the failures of the Iroquois galley experiment became clear. Ruette d'Auteuil returned to Canada in 1689 to face more opposition to his slave scheme, which his detractors dismissed mostly on grounds of the Canadian climate. Ruette d'Auteuil responded by citing the benefits of owning slaves: they were "well suited to all kinds of labor" and one had to pay for them only once. As for climate, he argued, large numbers of enslaved Africans thrived in nearby New England and New York. Those who were cold could wear beaver robes, which (he might have said tongue in cheek) would produce great quantities of the "greasy" pelts that European hatters preferred.[29]

Ruette d'Auteuil's arguments prevailed but made little difference. Despite the crown's authorization of African slave imports into New France, only eleven African slaves appear on colonial records between 1689 and 1709. During the same period, the plantations of the French Caribbean absorbed more than fifty thousand slaves from across the Atlantic. Given the demand for laborers, both real and perceived, a handful of Africans did nothing to satisfy either Ruette d'Auteuil's "principal inhabitants" or the urban merchant elite who hoped to emulate them. Unlike officials in Quebec and Paris who emphasized the risks of enslaving Indians, western traders saw Indian slavery as a potential solution to the colony's labor shortage. Instead of danger, they saw opportunity. Throughout the 1690s, French colonists involved in the fur trade continued to buy Indian captives from the Pays d'en Haut, trading them extralegally as slaves into the Saint Lawrence Valley. Because they were unauthorized, these private exchanges left few traces in historical documents. But, during the 1690s, Indian slaves began appearing in the public records of Montreal and Quebec, indicating a small but growing acceptance of Indian slavery among New France's western

des principaux ha'ns en feront achepter des Negres aux Isles . . . et il est luy mesme dans cette resolution": "Résumé de diverses lettres ou demandes avec commentaires," 1688, ANOM, Colonies, C11A, X, 190. For Ruette d'Auteuil's political battles, see Marine Leland, "Ruette d'Auteuil de Monceaux, François-Madeleine-Fortuné," *DCB*, II. See also Robin W. Winks, *The Blacks in Canada: A History* (Montreal, 1997), 4–5.

29. "Propres a toutes sortes de travaux": Mémoire de Ruette d'Auteuil, April 1689, ANOM, Colonies, C11A, X, 345–345v.

merchants and, by the early eighteenth century, colonial officials. In 1691, for example, Pierre Moreau dit Lataupine brought a young Indian slave to Quebec's Hôtel-Dieu, the local hospital, because of an illness. The hospital register says nothing of the young man's origins, but Moreau's background provides a likely explanation. In 1672, Moreau entered a partnership with Louis Jolliet and several others to create a fur-trading company that would help fund Jolliet's exploration of the West. Through this company, and often illegally on his own, Moreau traded among the Ottawas at Michilimackinac. Moreau certainly had witnessed slave exchanges in the West, including Jolliet's receiving a slave as a gift in 1674. As they had so many times before, the Ottawas must have offered a slave to Moreau either in exchange for minor trade goods or as a gift accompanying their trade in furs.[30]

In 1700, Jean-Baptiste Bissot de Vinsenne brought an Indian slave to Montreal, where he baptized him Jean-René. The baptismal record indicates that Vinsenne bought his slave "from the Iowa near the Arkansas [Quapaw]." Vinsenne, Jolliet's brother-in-law, spent the latter half of his life in the West as a military officer and trader. Considered the colony's foremost authority on the Miamis, he earned a post among them in 1696. While there, Vinsenne likely received his slave in negotiations with the Mascoutens or Illinois, both of whom frequently raided the Iowas. In the same year, René-Claude Fézeret baptized a young female slave who had served as a domestic in his home for several years as Marie-Joseph. Fézeret, Montreal's first gunsmith and a lifelong western merchant, traded firearms with the Ottawas for this slave while staying at Michilimackinac. And in September 1700 the "panis" slave Jacques appeared in Montreal's baptismal register, "brought from Illinois by the Sieur Charles Lemaitre dit Auger." These examples provide a faint but clear documentary outline of the early Indian slave trade. The colony's Indian allies, especially the Ottawas, Ojibwas, and Illinois, enslaved their western enemies and then offered them as symbolic gifts to French merchants associated with the fur trade. Once in French hands, slaves were generally taken to the colony's two principal towns, Montreal and Quebec.[31]

30. For number of African slaves, see Marcel Trudel, *Dictionnaire des esclaves et de la propriétaires au Canada français* (La Salle, Que.,1990), 7–263, esp. 127 for Moreau; Raymond Douville, "Provost, François," *DCB*, II. For French slave trade numbers, see David Geggus, "The French Slave Trade: An Overview," *WMQ*, 3d Ser., LVIII (2001), 119–138, esp. table 1.

31. For baptism, see Trudel, *Dictionnaire des esclaves*, 65. For Vinsenne, see Yves F. Zoltvany, "Jean-Baptiste Bissot de Vinsenne, Jean-Baptiste," *DCB*, II; *Jesuit Relations*, LXX, 316; "Letter of Count de Pontchartrain to Governor de Vaudreuil," June 9, 1706, *Wis. Hist. Coll.*,

As French colonists grew more interested in owning slaves, significant changes in the French-Indian alliance system increased the importance of the captive trade and made Indian slaves more readily available to potential French buyers. In the summer of 1701, the French negotiated what has come to be known as the Great Peace of Montreal, a treaty by which the Iroquois promised to cease warfare against the French and their allies and to remain neutral in all conflicts between the French and the English. Responding to the violence surrounding the Iroquois galley incident, a series of brutal reprisals by the French and their western allies pressured the Iroquois to negotiate peace in the late-1690s. Following the Treaty of Rijswijk in 1697, which for the moment ended French-English imperial warfare in North America, French officials made a strategic decision to shift their policy in North America, remaking their colonies in the Saint Lawrence and Mississippi Valleys into geographic barriers to English expansion. This would require the cooperation of a vast number of Indian villages throughout the eastern woodlands. To facilitate the task, Louis XIV appointed a new governor of New France, Louis-Hector de Callière, the younger brother of one of his most-trusted European diplomats. In Callière's letter of commission, written in 1699, the king urged the new governor to implement the provisions of the Treaty of Rijswijk, specifically enjoining the governor to make peace with the Iroquois and to strengthen New France's alliance with western Indian nations. Coveting the royal favor that followed his brother's success in European diplomacy, the Canadian governor began sending envoys to the Pays d'en Haut and Iroquoia almost immediately. Having personally led armies against the Iroquois only three years before, Governor Callière became the chief proponent of renewed diplomacy. Throughout 1699 and 1700, Callière sent French envoys to dozens of villages in the Pays d'en Haut. Kondioronk, Ononguicé, Misouensa, and many other Native diplomats worked across village lines to overcome differences and to encourage broad support for the peace agreement. After a series of negotiations at the village and regional levels, Callière and his Native counterparts secured

XVI (1902), 228; Edmond Mallet, *Le Sieur de Vincennes: fondateur de l'Indiana* (Levis, Que., 1897), 4–6. For consistency, I have used the spelling of the *DCB*, "Vinsenne," rather than the more widely recognized "Vincennes." On the Mascoutens' raiding the Iowas, see Bacqueville de La Potherie, *History*, in Blair, ed. and trans., *Indian Tribes*, II, 89.

For Fézeret's trade with the Ottawa, see "Transport à René Fezeret . . . d'un congé . . . portant permission d'aller traiter aux Sauvages outaouais et autres nations," Sept. 10, 1694, LAC, MG8, C8, Congés et permis enregistrés à Montréal; Trudel, *Dictionnaire des esclaves*, 79; Baptism of Sept. 19, 1700, *RAB du PRDH*, record 42253.

commitments for a formal meeting to ratify a Great Peace settlement. In August 1701, about thirteen hundred Indians from thirty-eight separate nations gathered at Montreal. Coming from the Upper Mississippi and Lower Missouri, from the western shores of Lake Michigan and the eastern shores of Lake Superior, these Native diplomats—all male—were accompanied by women who acted as counselors, companions, and provisioners. With their arrival, the Indian population of Montreal Island, normally about equal to that of the French, temporarily overwhelmed it by a ratio of nearly two to one.[32]

The Indian delegates, along with their French hosts, met to find a solution to decades of violence that had, in one way or another, touched almost every village from the Finger Lakes in modern New York to the Fox River valley in modern Wisconsin. The big picture involved orchestrating a peace with the Iroquois, who had battered, and been battered by, the French and their western Indian allies since midcentury. But there were plenty of other concerns. Factions in every camp opposed the peace: Ottawas doubted the sincerity of Onondagas, Potawatomis mistrusted Foxes, Hurons felt threatened by Ojibwas. There had, for some, been too many deaths, too many captives taken, and too many former agreements violated. And there was much still at stake. For at least five seasons the French fur trade had been spiraling downward because of oversupply, and western nations worried that peace with the Iroquois would introduce new competition at exactly the wrong time. Many of the Native delegates felt that this peace came at quite a high price, and they made a point of it, taking "great care to explain above all that they were sacrificing their private interests to a desire for peace."[33]

Attempting to reverse decades of French policy encouraging violence against the Iroquois proved challenging. The French strove, against barriers of their own making, to negotiate peace between their allies and the Iroquois, hoping to prevent small outbreaks of violence from erupting into general warfare. In so doing, officials at Quebec would finally come to ap-

32. Louis XIV to Louis-Hector de Callière, May 27, 1699, ANOM, Colonies, Nouvelle-France, Correspondance officielle, 1st Ser., I, 350–354 (François de Callières used the silent *s* at the end of his name, but Louis-Hector did not, so I have maintained the distinction here); Gilles Havard, *The Great Peace of Montreal of 1701: French-Native Diplomacy in the Seventeenth Century*, trans. Phyllis Aronoff and Howard Scott (Montreal, 2001), esp. 91–107; Bacqueville de La Potherie, *Histoire de l'Amérique Septentrionale*, IV; Lettre de Callière et Champigny au ministre, Oct. 5, 1701, ANOM, Colonies, C11A, XIX, fols. 3–22v.

33. P. F. X. de Charlevoix, *History and General Description of New France*, trans. John Gilmary Shea (New York, 1866–1872), V, 150.

preciate what most western traders and negotiators already understood: that trading slaves, if conducted according to Native customs, offered one of the most important available means of forging and maintaining alliances among Indian nations. This realization would inspire French colonial officials to rethink their policy on Indian slavery, not only allowing but eventually promoting the trade in Indian slaves.[34]

An early test of French willingness to adapt to diplomatic slavery came in the early stages of the treaty negotiations. For months, Governor-General Louis-Hector de Callière had been threatening the Sauks with retribution for killing a French trader among the Sioux. Speaking for his Sauk allies, the Potawatomi chief Ononguicé presented to Callière a "small slave," saying: "Here is a little flesh we offer you; we captured it in a country where people travel by horse. We wipe the mat stained with the blood of that Frenchman by consecrating it to you. Do with it as you please." Callière, eager to see the peace negotiations succeed, agreed to accept the slave, thereby pardoning the Sauks for the murder. He demanded only that the Sauks and their allies return to the Iroquois any prisoners taken from them in previous battles.[35]

Throughout the peace negotiations, no issue received more attention than the return of Iroquois slaves, which was, according to one French participant, "the most essential article of the peace." Although glossed in French sources as a European-style prisoner exchange, indigenous slaves played a far more complicated role in the negotiations during and after the treaty. The Iroquois had demanded that New France's allies return all living Iroquois prisoners, and many of the western allies had made reciprocal demands of the Iroquois. At the conference, then, each delegation made an accounting of the prisoners offered. Koutaoiliboe, chief of the Kiskakon Ottawas, spoke first. "I did not want to fail, my father," he assured Gover-

34. The most comprehensive treatment of the 1701 treaty is Havard, *The Great Peace of Montreal of 1701*, trans. Aronoff and Scott. This is a translated and substantially revised version of Havard's earlier book, *La Grande Paix de Montréal de 1701: les voies de la diplomatie franco-amérindienne* (Montreal, 1992). For other studies of the 1701 peace conference, see J. A. Brandão and William A. Starna, "The Treaties of 1701: A Triumph of Iroquois Diplomacy," *Ethnohistory*, XLIII (1996), 209–244; Daniel K. Richter, "Cultural Brokers and Intercultural Politics: New York–Iroquois Relations, 1664–1701," *Journal of American History*, LXXV (1988–1989), 40–67; Anthony F. C. Wallace, "Origins of Iroquois Neutrality: The Grand Settlement of 1701," *Pennsylvania History*, XXIV (1957), 223–235; and a special issue of *Recherches amérindiennes au Québec*, XXXI (Spring 2001), commemorating the tercentennial of the treaty. For the specific problems mentioned here, see also Richter, *Ordeal of the Longhouse*, 214–235; Brandão, *"Your Fyre Shall Burn No More,"* 126–129.

35. Bacqueville de La Potherie, *Histoire de l'Amérique Septentrionale*, IV, 209–210.

nor Callière, "having learned that you were asking me for Iroquois prisoners, to bring them to you. Here are four that I present to you to do with as you please." The other delegates spoke in similar terms, but several noted that the Iroquois gave few captives in return. In all, French allies returned thirty-one Iroquois prisoners, a small fraction of the Iroquois captured during the previous war.[36]

In order to assuage Iroquois anger over the disappointing number of captives returned, French officials pledged to facilitate prisoner exchanges until all parties were satisfied. Accordingly, Callière and Montreal's governor Philippe de Rigaud de Vaudreuil pressed the Ottawas, especially, to return Iroquois captives. In 1705, growing impatient with the continual demands of the French, Ottawa warriors attacked a party of Iroquois who had come to trade at Fort Frontenac. As soon as the violence subsided, the French, fearing that Iroquois retaliation could escalate into full-scale war, demanded that the Ottawas and Iroquois join them to negotiate peace. At the conference, the Iroquois berated the Ottawas for attacking them and destroying the "great tree of peace" planted by the French at Montreal. Promising reprisals if no satisfaction could be made, the Iroquois nevertheless left the door open for peace. They demanded that, in addition to returning all Iroquois prisoners, the Ottawas provide them with non-Iroquois captives to replace those killed in the attack. In the interest of peace, the Ottawas agreed to "search among the Sioux" for "slaves . . . to replace their [Iroquois] dead."[37]

This new demand, familiar enough to the Ottawas as a legitimate means of restoring peace, again tested the limits of French accommodation. Up to this point, French officials found it easy to encourage the return of an enemy's prisoners as a condition of peace. Now, however, the Iroquois were asking the French to facilitate the enslavement of an uninvolved third party to cover the Iroquois dead. However they felt about it, to maintain peace the French had to support the Iroquois request and oversee the acquisition of Sioux captives. Since war with England had resumed three years earlier,

36. Joseph Marest to La Mothe Cadillac, Oct. 8, 1701, *Wis. Hist. Coll.*, XVI (1902), 207 ("essential article"). For an English translation of the 1701 treaty text, see Havard, *The Great Peace of Montreal of 1701*, appendix 3, quotation on 211. For Callière's demanding Iroquois prisoners of his allies, see Bacqueville de La Potherie, *History*, in *Wis. Hist. Coll.*, XVI (1902), 201.

37. "Paroles des Outaouais de Michilimackinac," Aug. 23, 1705, ANOM, Colonies, C11A, XXII, 255–255v.

FIGURE 13. "They Came and Killed Seven Dakotas Winter." *Battiste Good, Sioux Winter Count, detail. National Anthropological Archives, Smithsonian Institution, MS2372, inv. 08746805. Courtesy Smithsonian Institution, Washington, D.C.*

New France needed Iroquois neutrality more than ever to avoid costly losses on its southern frontier.

The Ottawas, however, did not deliver the captives the following summer as they had promised. Angry at this betrayal, the Iroquois approached Vaudreuil, now governor-general of the colony. "Abandon the Ottawas to us, and hold us back no longer," the Iroquois demanded. "Our warriors are all ready." They were grateful that the French had secured the return of the Iroquois prisoners, but without the promised Sioux captives to resurrect their dead they would surely attack the Ottawas and seize their captives by force. Vaudreuil assured the Iroquois that he was doing all he could to ensure Ottawa compliance. The previous spring he had sent an envoy to Michilimackinac to bring back as many captives as he could for the Iroquois. There, the Ottawa chief Companissé had given the French four Sioux captives, promising "that he would bring me next year, without fail, the remainder of the slaves he had promised you." Vaudreuil then offered the captives to the Iroquois and vowed personally to deliver the balance owed them by the Ottawas. "I stay your axe as regards Michilimackinac," Vaudreuil concluded, "until they have had time to keep their word."[38]

38. "Talk of Marquis de Vaudreuil with the Sonnontouans," Sept. 4, 1706, Michigan Pioneer and Historical Society, *Historical Collections*, XXXIII (1904), 285–287 (spelling mod-

One reason the French went to such great lengths to participate in this diplomatic slave trade was their fear that a direct delivery from the Ottawas might draw them too close to the Iroquois. The French wanted peace between the two peoples, but they also wanted to prevent an Ottawa-Iroquois alliance. "It is not proper to have the Outaouas, Hurons, and other Indians friendly with the Iroquois," reads a margin note in Vaudreuil's 1703 report to France. "Some adroit effort must be made to prevent them becoming good friends." Understanding the symbolic bonds created through captive exchange, the French intervened to prevent Iroquois-Ottawa rapprochement and to benefit from Iroquois gratitude. That way, were the Iroquois to reestablish a military alliance with the English, at least they would not take the Ottawas with them to the detriment of New France.[39]

In addition to promoting the interests of the colony, Vaudreuil had personal incentives to deliver the slaves and ensure peace. He had served in an army that retreated from the Iroquois in 1687, and he held great respect for the strength of their warriors. Moreover, writing only three months before his meeting with the Iroquois, Vaudreuil's superior at Versailles reminded him, "You have nothing so important in the present state of affairs as the maintenance of peace with the Iroquois and other Indian nations." He then warned that, in the event of failure, "I shall not guarantee to you that his Majesty would be willing to allow you to occupy for any length of time your present post."[40]

During the next two years, Vaudreuil and other colonial officials worked persistently to ensure the transfer of captives from the Ottawas to the Iroquois. In 1706, Vaudreuil again pressured the Ottawas to provide "living slaves . . . to replace the Iroquois dead." In 1707, he sent strict orders to the French at Michilimackinac to ensure that the Ottawas deliver to the Iroquois "the remaining slaves that they promised to provide." He even arranged for a canoe to transport the slaves, a policy explicitly sanctioned by the crown, "it being of the utmost importance to the preservation of the Colony" to avert the pending war. By 1708, when the Ottawas finally

ernized); Battiste Good, winter count for 1705–1706, Smithsonian Institution, NAA MS 2372: http//wintercounts.si.edu/html_version/html/thewintercounts.html.

39. "Speeches of the Outaouaes of Misilimakinac," Sept. 27, 1703, *Wis. Hist. Coll.*, XVI (1902), 223.

40. Yves F. Zoltvany, "Rigaud de Vaudreuil, Philippe de," *DCB*, II, 565–574; "Letter of Count de Pontchartrain to Governor de Vaudreuil," June 9, 1706, *Wis. Hist. Coll.*, XVI (1902), 228–229 ("nothing more important").

delivered the promised slaves to the French, Vaudreuil and his intendant, Jacques Raudot, had come to learn the power of Indian slavery. They concluded, in a joint letter to their superiors, that captive exchanges were the sole means of maintaining peace between their two most important Indian neighbors, the Ottawas and the Iroquois. Informed with this new understanding, New France's officials grew increasingly reliant on symbolic slave trading in native diplomacy. When asked by Versailles in 1707 to buttress the French alliance with the Abenakis, for example, Vaudreuil sent orders to Jean-Paul Legardeur de Saint-Pierre to buy "a young panis slave to be given to the Abenakis" as a token of friendship.[41]

The Abenakis also received slaves from the French in exchange for English prisoners. During the frontier raids of Queen Anne's War, the Abenakis and other allied Indians captured hundreds of English settlers and attempted to integrate them into their village as adoptive kin or, occasionally, as slaves. Joseph Dudley, governor of Massachusetts, was outraged and wrote to Vaudreuil, "I cannot allow that Christians should be slaves of those wretches." Dudley threatened that, if the French did not secure the release of English captives among the Indians, he would turn over French prisoners at Boston to his Indian allies. This threat as well as the desire to exchange English for French prisoners encouraged Vaudreuil and many others to buy slaves from France's western allies to trade for English captives living among the Indians of the East, especially the Abenakis and the Kahnawake Iroquois.[42]

As colonial administrators increasingly relied on the slave trade to negotiate peace, strengthen friendships, and redeem English prisoners, they

41. "Lettre de Vaudreuil et Raudot au ministre," Apr. 28, 1706, ANOM, Colonies, C11A, XXIV, 3–6, and "Instructions de Vaudreuil à Jean-Paul Legardeur de Saint-Pierre," July 6, 1707, XXVI, 65–68. For quotation, "Réponse de Vaudreuil aux Onontagués," Aug. 17, 1707, XXVI, 87–93. "Louis XIV to M. de Vaudreuil," June 30, 1707, *NYCD*, IX, 808–809 ("utmost importance"); "Lettre de Vaudreuil et des intendants Raudot au ministre," Apr. 30, 1706, ANOM, Colonies, C11A, XXIV, 8–9, and for other efforts to obtain the promised slaves, see XXIV, 3–6 and XXVIII, 212–216. "Letter of Count de Pontchartrain to Governor de Vaudreuil," June 9, 1706, *Wis. Hist. Coll.*, XVI (1902), 229, for Versailles; "Instructions de Vaudreuil à Jean-Paul Legardeur de Saint-Pierre," July 6, 1707, ANOM, Colonies, C11A, XXVI, 65–68 ("to be given to the Abenakis").

42. For Dudley and Vaudreuil, see John Demos, *The Unredeemed Captive: A Family Story from Early America* (New York, 1994), 79–99. For the best explanation of "redeeming" in this period, see Emma Lewis Coleman, *New England Captives Carried to Canada between 1677 and 1760, during the French and Indian Wars* (Portland, Maine, 1925), I, 69–129. For efforts to exchange Indian for English captives, see Demos, *Unredeemed Captive*, 85–86.

also encountered western traders, prominent merchants, and minor colonial officials eager to buy slaves themselves. In 1702, at the death of François Provost, the king's lieutenant in Quebec and governor of Trois-Rivières, his Indian slave Louis passed to his widow, Geneviève. Provost likely had obtained Louis in connection with his fur-trading ventures, which began in 1697 when he established a company to export furs to France. In 1703, Marie-Françoise, an eighteen-year-old Indian slave of Pierre d'Ailleboust d'Argenteuil, died in Montreal. Argenteuil, a prominent military officer and seigneur, had kept her as a domestic slave in his Montreal home for several years.[43]

Three records from 1706 show the growing involvement of New France's administrative elite. That year the Superior Council member and close associate of the intendant, Jacques-Alexis Fleury d'Eschambault, baptized his Indian slave, Charles-Alexis, in Montreal. Jacques Barbel, a well-known Montreal judge who used his office to front an illegal fur trade operation, reclaimed a "panis" slave he had "loaned" to a friend. And the governor of New France, Philippe de Rigaud de Vaudreuil, paid to have one of his Indian slaves nursed back to health by the nuns of Quebec's Hôtel-Dieu. Given Vaudreuil's interest in the illegal fur and musket trades at Montreal, he likely had obtained Jacques there through his middleman, Pierre You de La Découverte, who got his own Indian slaves from the Illinois.[44]

La Découverte's association with the Upper Mississippi Valley began in the early 1680s and extended to the early eighteenth century. While in the Pays d'en Haut, La Découverte obtained an Indian slave he named Pascal. Born about 1690, Pascal had been captured, traded to the Miamis, and carried to Montreal with La Découverte by 1703. Pascal typified the slaves entering Montreal and Quebec during the first decade of the eighteenth century: 87 percent were male and, on average, age fourteen. These slaves

43. Trudel, *Dictionnaire des esclaves*, 78, 138, 267, 402; Douville, "Provost," *DCB*, II.

44. Trudel, *Dictionnaire des esclaves*, 56–57, 274, 327; "Liste apostillée des conseillers au Conseil supérieur de Québec," ANOM, Colonies, C11A, CXXV, 322–324; André Vachon, "Barbel, Jacques," *DCB*, II.

For Vaudreuil's slave, see Trudel, *Dictionnaire des esclaves*, 407; for Vaudreuil's interest in the illegal fur trade, see "Summary of an Inspection of the Posts of Detroit and Michilimackinac, by d'Aigremont," Nov. 14, 1708, *Wis. Hist. Coll.*, XVI (1902), 259. For La Découverte, see Albertine Ferland-Angers, "You de La Découverte, Pierre" *DCB*, II. The French minister of marine labeled La Découverte an "arrant trader," accusing him of trading illegally in the West and hinting that Vaudreuil had turned a blind eye to his dealings. See "Letter of Count de Pontchartrain to Governor de Vaudreuil," June 9, 1706, *Wis. Hist. Coll.*, XVI (1902), 231–232.

experienced traumatic childhoods before entering their permanent status as slaves in French settlements.[45]

From the Illinois country, however, Indian slaves did not always travel to the Saint Lawrence. Instead, French and Indian traders there often sold slaves to the much more developed markets of English Carolina, where thousands of Indian slaves either labored on plantations or embarked for the Caribbean. Between 1707 and 1708, the governors of New France and Louisiana learned that the French settlers "living among the Kaskaskia Illinois were inciting the savage nations in the environs of this settlement to make war upon one another and that the French-Canadians themselves were participating in order to get slaves that they afterward sold to the English." French coureurs de bois and their Miami and Illinois partners spent much of the first decade of the eighteenth century working with Carolina traders to bring slaves and furs from the western Ohio Valley to southeastern English ports.[46]

45. *RAB du PRDH*, 42745, May 10, 1704. Several Illinois, Miami, and Ottawa warriors banded together to raid the "Ozages and the Kanças" just before La Decouverte acquired Pascal, making his origin among one of those two peoples likely. See Bacqueville de La Potherie, *History, Wis. Hist. Coll.*, XVI (1902), 157. Youville's honorary title, "de La Découverte," signified his participation in La Salle's discovery of the mouth of the Mississippi River. For his continued relationship with Tonty and La Forest as well as his presence in the Illinois country, see "La Forest Sells Half-interest to Accault, April 19, 1693," in Theodore Calvin Pease and Raymond C. Werner, eds. and trans., *The French Foundations, 1680-1693*, Collections of the Illinois State Historical Library, XXIII (Springfield, Ill., 1934), 264–266. In 1694, Youville fathered a child by a Miami woman, moving sometime before the end of the decade to Montreal; Ferland-Angers, "You de La Découverte," *DCB*, II.

46. For the most complete treatment of the Carolina Indian slave trade, see Alan Gallay, *The Indian Slave Trade: The Rise of the English Empire in the American South, 1670-1717* (New Haven, Conn., 2002), esp. 288–314, table 2. Gallay estimates that from 1670 to 1715 as many as fifty-one thousand Indian slaves passed through South Carolina, although this number does not include those arriving from the Illinois country. See also James H. Merrell, *The Indians' New World: Catawbas and Their Neighbors from European Contact through the Era of Removal* (Chapel Hill, N.C., 1989), 36–37; J. Leitch Wright, Jr., *The Only Land They Knew: American Indians in the Old South* (1981; Lincoln, Nebr., 1999), esp. 126–150. Richebourg Gaillard McWilliams, ed. and trans., *Fleur de Lys and Calumet; Being the Pénicaut Narrative of French Adventure in Louisiana* (Baton Rouge, La., 1953), 122–123 (translation modernized). For similar charges a few years later, see "Letter of Ramezay and Bégon to French Minister," Nov. 7, 1715, *Wis. Hist. Coll.*, XVI (1902), 331–332. For the best treatments of French trade into Carolina between 1700 and 1710, see Eric Hinderaker, *Elusive Empires: Constructing Colonialism in the Ohio Valley, 1673-1800* (Cambridge, 1997), 35; Verner W. Crane, "The Tennessee River as the Road to Carolina: The Beginnings of Exploration and Trade," *Mississippi Valley Historical Review*, III (1916–1917), 3–18; Crane, "The Southern Frontier in Queen Anne's War," *AHR*, XXIV (1918–1919), 379–395.

To officials at Quebec, the Carolina trade threatened not only a loss of revenues but also a loss of military allies to a wartime enemy. One of the earliest lessons the French learned in native diplomacy was the inseparability of trade and alliance. They feared that, if the Illinois and Miamis developed strong trade relationships with Carolina, the English would easily win the military alliance of these peoples and threaten French survival. Thus, in 1708 Louisiana's governor, Jean-Baptiste Le Moyne de Bienville, sent an emissary to Kaskaskia with presents for the Indians and stern words for the French meant to halt the slave trade. Bienville had built his most important alliances in Louisiana by protecting the victims of Carolina's slave raids, and he did not want to risk these alliances by allowing his own people to extend the slave market into a new quarter. In the end, however, French officials in Louisiana and Quebec understood the limits of their coercive power in the distant Illinois country. The 1709 slave ordinance indicates a growing concern among Quebec officials about the potential of English slave sales to weaken Illinois and Miami commitments to the French alliance. Raudot implied that it would be better for the French to sell Indian slaves in Montreal than to "sell them to the English of Carolina."[47]

On this and many other occasions, French officials accepted Indian slavery as part of a larger effort to build Native alliances in the Pays d'en Haut against their Indian and European enemies. In the Caribbean, where French colonists did not depend on Native trade and alliance, French officials worked to limit and eventually to eliminate Indian slavery to keep the moral and military implications of enslavement safely distant from the practice of slavery. In New France, however, Indian slavery uniquely linked colonists' demand for slaves with the imperative of maintaining alliances against the English. If Indian slavery embedded the French within a system of indigenous enslavement and trade to a degree that was unmatched anywhere in the French Atlantic, slaveholders and officials wanted it to become something different, something more like what French colonists enjoyed in the Caribbean.

47. "Lettre de Callière et Beauharnois au ministre," Nov. 3, 1702, ANOM, Colonies, C11A, XX, 56–78. See also Crane, "Road to Carolina," *Mississippi Valley Historical Review*, III (1916–1917), 16–17. For broader French involvement in the Carolina trade at this time, see Gallay, *Indian Slave Trade*, 308–312. McWilliams, ed. and trans., *Fleur de Lys and Calumet*, 122–123. "Les traffiquent le plus souvent avec les anglois de la Caroline": Raudot, "Ord[onan] ce rendüe au sujet des neigres et des Sauvages nommez Panis," BANQ-Q, E1, S1, P509.

THE INDIANS CALLED PANIS

*"It is well known the advantage this colony would gain were its inhabitants
able to securely purchase the Indians called Panis, whose country is far
distant from this one."—Jacques Raudot, Quebec, 1709*

Although he must have known that enslaved Indians came from many different regions, Raudot studiously avoided painting with too broad a brush when he sanctioned Indian slavery in New France, possibly knowing that it could spark resistance from his superiors, who only five years earlier had supported the execution of Indian slavers in Martinique. By narrowing the target to a specific set of victims known as "the Panis nation," Raudot and his successors created a North American counterpart to the African kingdoms of Nigritie: a distant and populous nation at war with more proximate allies, poorly understood but clearly identified as legally and morally enslavable. Over the next half century French slaveholders would identify most of their slaves as Panis, despite the wide variety of nations from which their allies had captured them. This provided a degree of legal clarity intended to allow Indian slavery without the continual justification of each captive's enslavement under the law of nations. It also revealed, as it attempted to obscure, tensions between the diplomatic realities that produced indigenous slaves and the economic imperative that their status as legal property be guaranteed.

Nearly all historians who have acknowledged slavery in Canada have accepted the French designation of Panis as a more or less straightforward identification of the modern Indian tribe known as the Pawnees, who in the eighteenth century lived in the middle reaches of the Missouri River and its tributaries. Even without a close analysis of slaves' actual origins, this conclusion strains credibility. It would have been impossible for hundreds of Native villages allied to France—spanning Lakes Superior, Michigan, and Huron, stretching across modern Quebec, Ontario, Ohio, Indiana, Illinois, Wisconsin, and Minnesota—to converge, consistently and for an entire century, on precisely the same cluster of Pawnee villages from two hundred to more than a thousand miles away. Warriors would have to bypass enemy territory (or risk passing through it twice, on the way out and back) to reach a people who had little reason to deserve their attack. This is not to suggest that no Pawnees were enslaved. But during the eighteenth century the Indian slave trade in the Pays d'en Haut could never have targeted a single victim so exclusively. What is more, the Pawnees' population actually rose in the eighteenth century as their towns became the putative targets of intensified slaving.[48]

Rather than the primary victims of French slave raiding, the Pawnees and other Missouri River nations were initially among the most important suppliers of New France's Indian slaves. As early as the 1690s, strong evidence of a French-Pawnee alliance filtered into New Mexico. In 1697, a group of Navajos reported to their Spanish allies that a combined French and Pawnee force had defeated them in a slave-raiding expedition on the central Plains. In 1706, Spanish captain Juan de Ulibarri reported that combined parties of Panis and French slave raiders were routinely attacking the Spanish-allied Plains Apaches on the central Plains. These Panis would then "sell to the French the Apache women and children whom they take prisoners." Although Apache slaves do not appear in New France's records until the late-1710s, the slaves mentioned by Ulibarri might have been among the more than one hundred Panis that colonists acquired between 1696 and 1710.[49]

Far more than incidental by-products of the French-Pawnee alliance, Indian slaves stood at the center of the groups' trade relations. The nations of the lower Missouri, Platte, and Loup Rivers had little to offer the French besides corn, bison hides, and captives, and the former two items generated little interest among French traders. The Illinois nations produced

48. Marcel Trudel asserted that about two-thirds of all Indian slaves in New France were Pawnees (*Dictionnaire des esclaves*, xvi, and *L'esclavage au Canada français: histoire et conditions de l'esclavage* [Quebec, 1960], 57–98, esp. 83). Other than the label "Panis" itself, however, Trudel provides no evidence that these slaves originated among the Pawnees. Dozens of historians have followed Trudel's lead. See, for example, James Pritchard, who wrote that "so many of them came from just one tribe, the Panis or Pawnee in the Missouri River Valley, that *panis* became a synonym for *esclave* or slave" (*In Search of Empire*, 41). See also Allan Greer, *The People of New France* (Toronto, 1997), 56, 77, 87; Maureen G. Elgersman, *Unyielding Spirits: Black Women and Slavery in Early Canada and Jamaica* (London, 1999), 4–5; W. J. Eccles, *Canadian Frontier*, 149, and *The French in North America, 1500–1783* (East Lansing, Mich., 1998), 86. One notable exception was Richard White, whose detailed study of the eighteenth-century Pawnees suggested that the designation was inaccurate: "The very word 'Pani' came to mean a slave taken from the plains by tribes allied to the French, but the Pani slaves of the French were usually not Pawnees at all. Indeed, the Pawnees seem to have continued to prosper and expand during this period." White, *The Roots of Dependency: Subsistence, Environment, and Social Change among the Choctaws, Pawnees, and Navajos* (Lincoln, Nebr., 1983), 152.

49. Alfred Barnaby Thomas, ed. and trans., *After Coronado: Spanish Exploration Northeast of New Mexico, 1696–1727: Documents from the Archives of Spain, Mexico, and New Mexico* (Norman, Okla., 1935), 13–14, 74; James F. Brooks, *Captives and Cousins: Slavery, Kinship, and Community in the Southwest Borderlands* (Chapel Hill, N.C., 2002), 61.

more than enough food for their French allies, and by the 1730s French settlements in the region harvested a substantial annual surplus that they shipped to Louisiana. Bison hides, on the other hand, had a certain utility, but their value in colonial and Atlantic markets remained low compared to other skins and furs. Yet the Pawnees and their neighbors coveted French manufactured goods, especially firearms and metal tools, which they could use in conjunction with the horses they recently procured from the Southwest in warfare and bison hunting. Since the French sought captives more than their other available commodities, many Panis peoples exchanged slaves for French goods.[50]

With this information, Paul Lecuyer's 1704 claim to have purchased his young slave from the Pawnees seems credible. As an errant trader who kept no permanent residence along the Saint Lawrence, Lecuyer spent much of his time in the West bartering with Indian allies. It might have been his relationship with the Illinois that brought him into contact with the Pawnees. According to Pierre Deliette, who lived for decades among the Illinois, Missouri River nations including the Pawnees routinely visited the Illinois country for trade around the turn of the eighteenth century. "This Missouri River," he wrote sometime before 1710, "has many nations along its banks, and there are still more inland. . . . Several Indians of the nations that live there . . . often come to trade among the Illinois."[51]

The Missouri Indians maintained the most consistent presence among the Illinois and their French allies. As early as the 1680s, Missouri villages began trading furs and captives with members of the expedition of René-Robert, Cavalier de La Salle. During the 1710s, Étienne de Véniard, sieur de

50. For Illinois country agriculture, see Winstanley Briggs, "Le Pays des Illinois," *WMQ*, 3d Ser., XLVII (1990), 30–56; Carl J. Ekberg, *French Roots in the Illinois Country: The Mississippi Frontier in Colonial Times* (Urbana, Ill., 1998), esp. 213–238; Daniel H. Usner, Jr., *Indians, Settlers, and Slaves in a Frontier Exchange Economy: The Lower Mississippi Valley before 1783* (Chapel Hill, N.C., 1992), 165–192.

51. Pierre Deliette, "Memoir of De Gannes [Deliette] concerning the Illinois Country," in Pease and Werner, eds. and trans., *The French Foundations*, 387. The earliest surviving copy of the Deliette memoir dates from the 1720s, but other authors relied on the memoir for information as early as 1710. See, for example, Antoine Denis Raudot, "Memoir concerning the Different Indian Nations of North America," in W. Vernon Kinietz, ed., *The Indians of the Western Great Lakes, 1615–1670* (Ann Arbor, Mich., 1940), 341–410, which borrows heavily from Deliette.

In 1727, Paul Lecuyer was listed in Saint-Pierre as one of the "habitants qui ne tiennent pas feu et lieu," literally, "inhabitants who do not keep hearth and home," meaning that he maintained no permanent residence. See "Ordonnance de l'intendant Dupuy," May 8, 1727, BANQ-Q, E1, S1, P1842.

Bourgmont (who lived among the Missouris for several years and fathered a child by a Missouri woman), established a French-Missouri alliance that would last into the 1740s. As with most French-Indian trade in the Mississippi Valley, this alliance secured slaves for the French as well as furs. In 1717, for example, Michel Bisaillon returned from a western trade voyage to Laprairie, near Montreal. In addition to beaver pelts, Bisaillon had purchased an adult female slave, whom he described as a "Panis recently brought in from the distant Indian nations called Missouris." The slave was pregnant and soon gave birth to a girl whom Bisaillon baptized as "Marie-Catherine, *sauvagesse.*"[52]

Yet trade relations between the Illinois and the Missouri River peoples were not always peaceful. Deliette noted that some Illinois villages remained at war with the Pawnees as well as the more southerly Wichitas during the first decade of the eighteenth century. Writing in 1710, Antoine-Denis Raudot concurred, suggesting that Illinois raids on Missouri River peoples produced many captives. "As the people they go to attack are neither so brave nor so warlike as themselves," he related, "they carry off entire villages. They kill the men and scalp them and take only the women and the children, whom they grant life." Some of these captives, especially the young boys, became French slaves. Many of the captors adopted the women or traded them to individual traders, who kept them as wives. Moreover, French-allied Indians in other western regions continued to raid the Missouri River valley for captives as well. In 1718, Jean-Baptiste Robillard baptized an Indian slave in Lachine said to be of the "vicara," or Arikara, nation. At Green Bay, Winnebagos traded Panis captives to French traders, as did the Ottawas at Michilimackinac and Detroit.[53]

But Illinois conflicts with Missouri River villages proved the exception rather than the rule. As Antoine-Denis Raudot explained:

52. Baptism of Sept. 20, 1717, *RAB du PRDH*, 18388. For French-Missouri relations, see Frank Norall, ed., *Bourgmont: Explorer of the Missouri, 1698–1725* (Lincoln, Nebr., 1988), 15–27; Mildred Mott Wedel, "The Identity of La Salle's *Pana* Slave," *Plains Anthropologist*, XVIII (1973), 203–217; Wedel, "Claude-Charles Dutisné: A Review of His 1719 Journeys," Part I, *Great Plains Journal*, XII (1972–1973), 5–25, and Part II, 147–173. The Missouris backed their alliance with military action during the Fox Wars, when they joined French forces. See Dubuisson to Vaudreuil, 1712, *Wis. Hist. Coll.*, XVI (1902), 272.

53. Deliette, "Memoir of De Gannes," in Pease and Werner, eds. and trans., *The French Foundations*, 386; Raudot, "Memoir," in Kinietz, ed., *Indians of the Western Great Lakes*, 402–403; Trudel, *Dictionnaire des esclaves*, 25.

The war, of which I told you in my last letter, that the Illinois make on the Pawnee and on other savage nations who are on the banks of the Missouri is not of long duration; these people not being warlike like themselves and having need of their trade to get axes, knives, awls, and other objects, the Illinois buy these things from us to resell to them. The need that these nations have for peace makes them do all that is necessary to conserve it. They go every year to the Illinois to carry them the calumet, which is the symbol of peace among all the nations of the South.

Throughout the 1710s, French traders and their Illinois allies generally cooperated with Missouri River villages to exchange captives for French manufactured goods. Few, if any, of these would have been actual Pawnees.[54]

Rather than designating a specific Indian people known today as the Pawnees, then, the term applied to diverse array of western peoples. As Augustin Grignon recalled, later in the eighteenth century *Panis* was a general term used to designate a wide variety of peoples. Of all the Indians "consigned to servitude" in that western post, he wrote, "for convenience sake, I suppose, they are all denominated Pawnees." After establishing Fort Saint Louis on the Illinois River in 1682, La Salle received as tokens from the Illinois two "pana slaves," an adult woman and a boy about fifteen years old, who "had been taken by the Panimaha, then by the Osages, who had given him to the Missouris, and they to the nation from which I have had him." The elaborate route by which this unfortunate young man arrived in La Salle's hands indicates both the complexity and the ubiquity of captive exchanges on New France's western frontier. It also reveals the fallacy of assuming that Panis slaves were primarily taken from the Pawnees. In the seventeenth century, names similar to *Panis* actually referred to a great number of Plains nations, only some of which have clear modern equivalents. On a single map made in 1688, for example, French cartographer Jean-Baptiste Franquelin listed as separate nations the "Panimaha," "Panetoca," "Pana," "Paneake," and "Paneassa," any or all of whom could have suffered at the hands of Illinois raiders. Of these groups, none can be said with any certainty to be ancestors to the modern Pawnees.[55]

54. Raudot, "Memoir," in Kinietz, ed., *Indians of the Western Great Lakes*, 404.

55. Augustin Grignon, "Seventy-two Years' Recollections of Wisconsin," *Wis. Hist. Coll.*, III (1857; 1904), 256 ("for convenience sake"); Wedel, "The Identity of La Salle's *Pana* Slave," *Plains Anthropologist*, XVIII (1973), 204 ("taken by the Panimaha"); Jean-Baptiste Louis

When seventeenth-century French observers noted the source of Illinois slaves, for example, they always suggested diverse victims. Claude-Charles Le Roy, Bacqueville de La Potherie, for example, recounted a captive-raiding expedition undertaken by the Illinois against "the Ozages and the Accances [Quapaws]." Pierre Deliette noted that Missouri River nations "often come to trade among the Illinois," indicating that these captives might have come in trade from the various "Panis" villages rather than by Illinois raids upon those groups. And by analyzing the available documentation on La Salle's "pana slave," anthropologist Mildred Wedel concluded that the boy was most likely a Wichita, captured by the Skiri Pawnees, stolen by Osages, and traded to the Illinois via Missouri middlemen.[56]

In the French records of the seventeenth and eighteenth centuries, the term *Panis* referred not only to the Skiri Pawnees but also to the South Band Pawnees, the Arikaras, and the Wichitas. Period travel reports and the maps they generated indicate that groups designated by some form of Panis resided along most of the Mississippi's major western tributaries. In his 1718 map, for example, French cartographer Guillaume Delisle identified sixty-six villages of "Panis" peoples spread from northern Texas to the Dakotas. These included four villages of "Paniassa" (Wichitas), ten of the "Panis" (South Band Pawnees), twelve of the "Panimaha" (Skiri Pawnees) as well as forty additional villages of "Panis" (Arikaras and Skiri Pawnees) to the northwest.[57]

Even as late as the 1730s, French colonists had achieved little clarity on the location or population of the peoples they called "Panis." In a lengthy "enumeration" of Indians with whom the French interacted, "les Panis" ap-

Franquelin, *Carte de l'Amérique du nord* (Paris, 1688). The authoritative discussion of the etymology and historical usage of the term "Pawnee" is Douglas R. Parks, "Pawnee," in *Handbook*, XIII, *Plains*, part 1, 515–547; and William W. Newcomb, Jr., "Wichita," in *Plains*, part 1, 548–566.

56. Bacqueville de La Potherie, *History*, in Blair, ed. and trans., *Indian Tribes*, II, 36 ("Ozages and the Accances"); Deliette, "Memoir of De Gannes," in Pease and Werner, eds. and trans., *The French Foundations*, 387 ("often come to trade"); Wedel, "Identity of La Salle's *Pana* Slave," *Plains Anthropologist*, XVIII (1973), 204–205.

57. Wedel, "Identity of La Salle's *Pana* Slave," *Plains Anthropologist*, XVIII (1973), 203–217; Douglas R. Parks, "Pawnee," in *Handbook*, XIII, *Plains*, part 1, 543–545, and Newcomb, "Wichita," part 1, 563–566; Guillaume de L'Isle, *Carte de la Louisiane et du cours du Mississippi* (Paris, 1718); Parks, "Bands and Villages of the Arikara and Pawnee," *Nebraska History*, LX (1979), 229–230. The Panis information in the Delisle map was largely drawn from a few travel narratives, especially Bourgmont's 1714 journeys up the Mississippi River. See Norall, ed., *Bourgmont*, 21–25.

peared near the bottom of the list with other Missouri River peoples, with the explanation that the French "know nothing of these nations but their name." Indeed, there were African parallels to French conceptions of Panis country, which, like Nigritie, they believed to flank an interior river flowing away from known territories toward a large sea. Like the misplaced Niger River in contemporary African maps, early North American maps mistook accounts of the Missouri River's western origins for reports of a great River of the West, which they hoped would lead to a vast western sea. One influential cartographer sketched an admittedly conjectural image of the waterway, placing the Panis as the lone people on its banks. The river met the western sea at the fabled city of Quivira, which was represented on the map by an impressive castle. This murkiness was, in fact, the ideal situation for New France's slave system, as it allowed the colony to mimic the fictions that supported African slavery in the French Atlantic world: to make North American Indians "like Negroes in the Islands."[58]

If French travelers and cartographers left an ambiguous record of the people known as Panis, parish priests, notaries, and court recorders more than a thousand miles away obscured the issue still further. In 1704, for example, Father Pierre Remy baptized an enslaved boy at Lachine, near Montreal. The priest clearly struggled to grasp the child's ethnic identity. In the marginal annotation, which served as a quick guide for finding individual records, he wrote "B[aptism]. Joseph panis," and then began to write "Algonquian" before stopping halfway to cross it out. In the record's body, Remy identified the slave as "Paul, Indian of the panis nation, about ten years old." Had the priest stopped there, only recording the details relevant to the ritual, this record, like hundreds of others, could lead to the mistaken conclusion that the slave was a Pawnee Indian. But Remy continued, noting that the child's master, Paul Lecuyer, "said that he first bought the said Indian from the said panis," but that he was later captured by the Fox Indians and sold to Lecuyer a second time. Considering the boy "redeemed" from the hands of the Foxes, the priest extracted a promise from his mistress, who acted as his godmother, "to raise and instruct him in the Catholic faith," a double erasure of his origins.[59]

58. "Ne sachant de ces nations que le nom": "Dénombrement des nations sauvages qui ont rapport au gouvernement du Canada," 1736, ANOM, Colonies, C11A, LXVI, 255. "Conjectures Sur l'Existence d'une Mer dans la partie Occidentale du Canada Et du Mississipi Par G. Delisle de l'Academie royale des sciences," memoranda on French colonies in America, including Canada, Louisiana, and the Carribean, Newberry Library, Ayer MS 293, I, 133.

59. Baptism of Aug. 17, 1704, Saints-Anges de Lachine, FHL. The best assessment of the

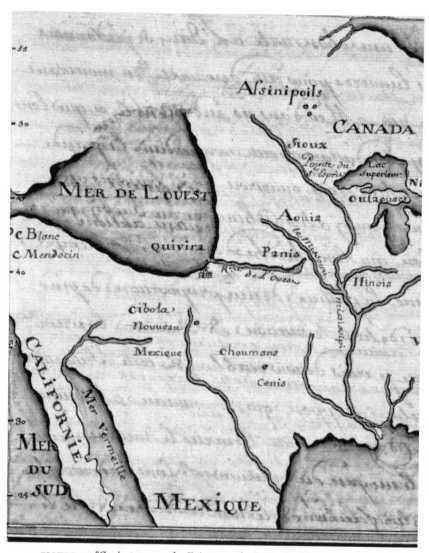

FIGURE 14. "Conjectures on the Existence of a Sea in the Western Region of
Canada and Mississippi." *Guillaume Delisle, Royal Academy of Sciences, ca. 1718–1723.*
Newberry Library, Ayer MS 293. Photo courtesy the Newberry Library, Chicago

By the turn of the eighteenth century, "Panis" had become the presumptive ethnicity of any Indian held as a slave in New France; it thus became a generic term meaning Indian slave. When the Fox slave Jacob was murdered in 1728, for example, legal records identified him as "Jacob, of the Panis nation," despite the court's knowledge that he was a Fox Indian. Catholic records often combined "panis" with other identifiers, as when the priest at Verchères buried a Sioux slave woman, describing her as a "panis of the Sioux nation." At Quebec's Hôtel-Dieu, hospital nuns similarly recorded Indian slaves with ambiguous origins, like the slave Dorothee, listed as a "panisse Illinoise." In Dorothee's case, as in many others, a more precise identifier did not always clarify a slave's origins. As strong and consistent allies to the French, the Illinois were never targets of French slavery. Rather, the recorder was likely referring either to the Illinois peoples who sold the slave to the French or to the Illinois country where she was acquired.[60]

Even when French slaveholders knew the exact origin of their slaves, Raudot's 1709 ordinance provided strong incentives to withhold that information and claim the legal protection guaranteed to enslaved "Panis." Intendants and governors consistently held that "Panis" Indians could legally be enslaved, but they never fully determined the legal standing of other Native captives. Moreover, if colonists obtained slaves as a by-product of unlicensed trading, their slave property would be subject to confiscation. Thus, to ensure the legal protection of their slaves as property, slave owners might have intentionally deceived religious and civil record keepers. This practice could account for the growing tendency of slaveholders to identify their slaves as "Panis" as the century progressed. By the 1750s, fully two-thirds of all Indian slaves were identified in French records as "Panis."[61]

---

location of Pawnee village sites in the eighteenth century is Parks, "Bands and Villages of the Arikara and Pawnee," *Nebraska History*, LX (1979), 214–239.

60. "Jacob pany du nation": "Procès contre Lapalme, factionnaire, soldat de la compagnie Contrecoeur, accusé du meurtre de Jacob, panis, esclave de Julien Trottier, sieur Des Rivières," June 13, 1728, BANQ-M, TL4, S1, D3433; burial of Apr. 12, 1735, *RAB du PRDH*, 184885, and burial of Feb. 8, 1719, 73580.

61. During the 1750s, 315 of the 481 new slaves appearing in extant records are identified only as "Panis" or some variant. An additional 119 are identified only as "sauvage." Compared to the 15 Sioux and 7 Plains Apaches, the most numerous exceptions, the "Panis" seem even more significant. See Appendix C.

FOR AGRICULTURE AND OTHER ENTERPRISES

"The people of the Panis nation are needed by the inhabitants of this
country for agriculture and other enterprises that might be undertaken,
like Negroes in the Islands."—Jacques Raudot, Quebec, 1709

When Raudot compared "Panis" slaves to "Negroes in the Islands," he was, in part, just being hopeful. In the early-eighteenth-century French Atlantic, the most successful colonies thrived on the production of agricultural staples with African slaves, generating massive wealth for many private investors and starting to yield a significant revenue base for greater France. But Raudot's analogy also asserted a particular vision of Indian slaves' economic potential and their legal place within French colonial society that drew on African and Caribbean models. For Raudot, Indian slaves were "like Negroes" in two important ways: in the work they would do (agriculture and a broad category of "other enterprises") and in their identity as a specific nation, subject to the laws of war and legally enslaved by France's Native allies.

From its inception, New France struggled to find a sufficient number of workers to meet even its basic needs. Migration to New France, never high to begin with, dropped precipitously in the 1670s, stunting the colony's population growth. Among those who did come to Canada, more than two-thirds returned to France, and the result was a deficiency of free workers. Despite tireless efforts to recruit unfree labor, the importation of indentured servants (*engagés*) virtually ended in 1666, and French colonists and administrators were left chronically anxious about labor shortages. In 1688, intendant Jean-Baptiste Lagny complained, "Laborers and servants are scarce and extraordinarily expensive in Canada, which ruins everyone whose enterprise depends on them."[62] Lagny sent a formal request to Louis XIV, noting that he and other colonial leaders "think that the best way to remedy the situation would be to have Negro slaves." He assured the king that, should imports be allowed, several of the colony's "principal inhabitants" stood ready to buy them when they arrived in the Caribbean and ship

---

62. "Résumé des rapports du Canada avec les notes du ministre," 1689, in *Collection de manuscrits*, I, 476. Peter N. Moogk, "Reluctant Exiles," *WMQ*, 3d Ser., XLVI (1989), 463–505; Moogk, *La Nouvelle France: The Making of French Canada—A Cultural History* (East Lansing, Mich., 2000), 87–120; Gabriel Debien, "Engagés pour le Canada ou XVIIe siècle vus de La Rochelle," *Revue d'histoire de l'Amérique française*, VI (1952–1953), 177–220.

them north to New France. The king agreed to Canadians' importation of African slaves "to do their farming," but only a handful arrived.[63]

So the labor problem persisted, leading the governor and intendant to despair in 1716, "The small number of inhabitants in Canada causes all enterprise to fail because of the difficulty of finding workers." Labor shortages also constrained colonial agriculture. According to Gédéon de Catalogne, who surveyed the seigneuries of the Saint Lawrence Valley in 1712, "Compared to the vast extent of the settlement, there is not one-quarter of the laborers needed to clear and cultivate the land." As a result, French farmers were forced to clear their land piecemeal, often hiring themselves out for part of the year to provide for their family's needs before the land could produce a viable harvest. Much of their land simply remained uncleared and unplanted.[64]

The first decade of the eighteenth century also witnessed New France's worst economic crisis since its founding, thus adding to the colony's inability to invest in African slave labor. Between 1700 and 1710, the glut of beaver pelts on the French market depressed prices by 75 percent, sinking to an all-time low around 1708. With public finances strained beyond capacity by the war with England, official outlays to diversify the economy were out of the question. Yet precisely because of wartime expenses, colonial officials felt growing pressure from Versailles to increase self-sufficiency and to generate revenue. In 1707, Governor Vaudreuil complained of the "deplorable state" of New France's economy but despaired of any solution.[65]

Raudot and his son were more optimistic, perhaps because they had less experience (and less personal stake in the fur trade) than the governor. They recognized the importance of the fur trade in maintaining diplomatic rela-

63. "Les gens de travail et les Domestiques sont d'une rareté et d'une cherté si extraord[inai]re en Canada qu'ils ruine tous ceux qui font quelque entreprise"; "On croit que le meilleur moyen pour y remedier seroit d'avoir des Esclaves Negres"; "quelques des principaux ha[bita]ns"; "pour faire leur culture": "Résumé de diverses lettres ou demandes avec commentaires," 1688, ANOM, Colonies, C11A, X, 190; and Geggus, "The French Slave Trade: An Overview," *WMQ*, 3d Ser., LVIII (2001), 119–38, esp. 135, table 1.

64. "Mémoire de Messieurs Vaudreuil et Bégon au Ministre," Oct. 14, 1716, in *Collection de manuscrits*, III, 21 ("causes all enterprise to fail"); "Mémoire de Gédéon de Catalogne sur le Canada," Nov. 7, 1712, ANOM, Colonies, C11A, XXXIII, 233v ("not one quarter of the laborers needed"); Dechêne, *Habitants and Merchants*, trans. Vardi, 152–154.

65. "Lettre des sieurs Vaudreuil et Raudot au ministre," Nov. 15, 1707, ANOM, Colonies, C11A, XXVI, 9–49. For the fur collapse, see Dechêne, *Habitants and Merchants*, trans. Vardi, 67–76, table 15.

tions with their western allies, admitting that it was "the only way to pacify upper-country Indians," but they insisted that the time had come to diversify and develop the Canadian economy. Their proposals reflected a new emphasis on colonial development that was at once more geographically narrow and economically broad. Since the 1690s the crown had emphasized a policy of colonial contraction, abandoning some posts in the West in favor of a more intensively colonized Saint Lawrence Valley. For the Raudots, this intensification could work only with a greater labor supply. In 1706 Antoine-Denis Raudot outlined a plan by which New France could provide salt beef, grain, pork, wood, pine tar, and many other commodities to the islands, allowing them to concentrate on producing sugar and other staples. Without a dramatic expansion in laborers, however, he acknowledged that the plan would fail. His father, too, became a strong advocate for economic diversification in New France. Only months after issuing the ordinance on slavery in 1709, he wrote a report to his superiors underscoring the importance of moving beyond the fur trade. Arguing that the colony should only consider the fur trade a mere "accessory" to the trade in agricultural staples, he pointed to the colony's export of wheat, peas, biscuits, tallow, butter, eggs, cheese, wooden planks and shingles, oil, cod, salmon, and eels. These commodities, he argued, could supply other French colonies were there sufficient labor to develop them.[66]

Raudot's replacement, Michel Bégon, agreed with the need to develop the economy with slave labor. The son of the Caribbean intendant of the same name, Bégon came of age with the sugar and plantation regimes that his father had helped secure. The elder Bégon made the case for greater slave imports in the Caribbean during the 1680s, when there were already several thousand working French fields. "Without Negroes," he argued, "virtually nothing can be accomplished in the islands." Naturally, the younger Bégon echoed his father's sentiments for his own colony. Knowing Canada's climate would not support tropical agriculture, he hoped to follow the English example and have northern mainland colonies provide food and supplies to the Caribbean. "The majority of Englishmen and Flemings of the government of New York, adjacent to that of Montreal, never labor in agriculture," Bégon wrote in a 1716 appeal for a shipment of slaves. "It is their Negroes that do all their work," he continued, "and that colony provides the

66. Antoine-Denis Raudot to minister, Nov. 1, 1709, ANOM, Colonies, C11A, XXX, 240v, Aug. 7, 1706, C11C, VIII, 40–52, Nov. 13, 1707, C11A, XXVI, 238–241; Jacques Raudot to minister, Nov. 1, 1709, ANOM, Colonies, C11A, XXX, 256v–257.

grain necessary for the subsistence of the English islands." Since slaves in the colony would not produce the most lucrative export goods, New France's colonists could not afford the rising prices for African slaves traded on the Atlantic market. Nor did trade routes favor African slavery as a solution to New France's labor shortage, since ships traveling to the Caribbean from Africa had little reason to venture north to the Saint Lawrence.[67]

Although the crown ignored Bégon's request for intervention, his appeal expressed the dual nature of New France's demand for slaves. The intendant began by noting the demonstrable lack of available labor within the colony and the resulting high cost of hiring workers. Since the 1670s, such concerns had repeatedly surfaced to explain the colony's disappointing economic progress. Yet the crux of Bégon's argument rested on the colony's potential, rather than actual, labor needs. During the 1710s the colony exported very little grain to the Caribbean, and iron smelting would not begin for nearly a generation. The cultivation of flax and hemp, both potentially lucrative export crops, was only beginning to capture either the interest of landholders or the support of colonial bureaucrats. But as late as 1720 Bégon still expressed his hope that the availability of slave labor for New France's colonists would "cost the king nothing and contribute to the expansion of agriculture." Like Lagny a generation before, Bégon assured naysayers that there was plenty of demand for slaves in Canada and that slave traders could demand a comparable price to the Caribbean. He might have been wrong about the potential of commercial agriculture—there were climatic limits and shipping constraints that made Canada a difficult place to produce staple crops—but his hopeful espousal of slavery was shared by many of the New France elite.[68]

67. "Sans negres on ne vient a bout de Rien dans les isles": Michel Bégon to minister, June 18, 1684, ANOM, Colonies, C8A, III, 317; "Vaudreuil et Bégon au Ministre," Oct. 14, 1716, in *Collection de manuscrits*, III, 21–22. For slave prices, see Robert Louis Stein, *The French Slave Trade in the Eighteenth Century: An Old Regime Business* (Madison, Wis., 1979), 137–150.

68. "Ne couste rien au Roy et qu'elle contribuera à l'augmentation de la culture des terres": Michel Bégon (fils) to François Vachon de Belmont, Nov. 15, 1720, Archives du Seminaire de Saint-Sulpice, Montreal, S21, 3.11.2.

For grain exports, see Richard C. Harris *The Seigneurial System in Early Canada: A Geographical Study* (Madison, Wis., 1966). For ironworks, see Joseph-Noël Fauteux, *Essai sur l'industrie au Canada sous le régime français* (Quebec, 1927); Réal Boissonnault, *Les forges du Saint-Maurice, 1729–1883: 150 Years of Occupation and Operation* (Ottawa, 1983), 9–36.

For flax and hemp (discussed at length below), see William Bennett Munro, ed., *Documents Relating to the Seigniorial Tenure in Canada, 1598–1854* (Toronto, 1908), esp. 146;

Despite enthusiastic support from colonial leaders, most colonists' embrace of Indian slavery was slow, in part because of the very economic crisis that argued for slaves' importation. Merchants and farmers in the Saint Lawrence Valley experienced financial strain. Fur trade engagements dropped precipitously, with a corresponding decline in the quantity of trade goods merchants could profitably send west. A general monetary crisis decreased the availability of reliable currency and limited merchants' ability to extend credit. As French merchants began charging the colonists higher prices for essential textiles and manufactured goods, colonial wheat prices continued to fall, widening the gap between the income farmers earned and the expenses they incurred. Because of Montreal's dependence on the fur trade and the relative immaturity of its agricultural development, its residents suffered more than most. Still, slaves did trickle in, and by 1709 about 13 or 14 percent of Montreal's households owned at least one Indian slave.[69]

Merchants' participation in the Indian slave trade might have been fueled, rather than hindered, by the economic crisis. Unable to profit from western trade with conventional cargoes, many merchants seem to have reduced their losses by selling Indian slaves acquired in the West during trade expeditions. Maurice Blondeau, for example, who specialized in the western trade, partnered with Alphonse Tonty at Michilimackinac. Beginning in 1696, when all but a few merchants were banned from the western fur trade, Blondeau's business began to falter. He continued to trade illegally until, in 1698, the intendant Jean Bochart de Champigny ordered his goods and effects seized. The reopening of legal trade at Detroit in 1701 promised renewed profits, but, if Blondeau's fortunes mirrored those of most merchants, little materialized. Possibly as a result, in 1703 he began to carry a few Indian slaves on his return journeys to Montreal. In addition to the two slaves he acquired for himself during this period, he appears to have sold at least one to his friend and business partner François Lamoureux dit Saint-Germain. This experiment proved to be the beginning of a long connection to the slave trade

Colin Coates, *The Metamorphoses of Landscape and Community in Early Quebec* (Montreal, 2000), chap. 3.

69. Dechêne, *Habitants and Merchants*, trans. Vardi, 67–89, 296. I obtained the figure on Montreal's households by comparing the number of Indian slaveholders in Montreal with the number of known households in 1704, drawn from the Adhemar database at the Centre Canadien d'Architecture, Montreal. The database documents between 248 and 261 households in the town in 1704. With 35 slaveholding households, this equals a range of 13.4%–14.1%.

for the Blondeau family, which owned twenty-four Indian slaves during the eighteenth century and traded many more to other French colonists.[70]

Thus, the changing conditions of French-Indian diplomacy made captives readily available and relatively inexpensive at a time when French labor was scarce and costly. These slaves worked in many different capacities, contributing substantially to the wealth of slave owners and to the productivity of the colony in general. Surviving documents yield few details about slaves' work before 1709, but a few telling examples show slaves working in the fur trade, agriculture, and domestic service. Because Indian slavery originated in western trade, exploration, and diplomacy, the slaves' first tasks were often associated with these activities. Trader and explorer Louis Jolliet, for example, used "a young slave, ten years old" to aid him on a journey from the upper country to Quebec. When their canoe capsized near Montreal, the slave drowned, causing Jolliet "much regret . . . [because] he was blessed with natural goodness, quick-wittedness, diligence, and obedience." Characteristic of many similar documents, Jolliet's letter gives no details about the specific tasks assigned to his slave. Jolliet wrote to encourage Bishop François de Laval-Montigny's commitment to western missions, knowing that strong church support would help his own ambitions in the region. Jolliet therefore emphasized the tractability of western Indians and their responsiveness to Catholic teachings. "He spoke French," Jolliet concluded, and was "beginning to read and write."[71]

At Michilimackinac, Pierre Hubert dit Lacroix purchased in 1696 an Indian slave, also named Pierre, from the voyageur Ignace Durand. After using Pierre as a slave for five years, Hubert released him from slavery and hired him as an indentured servant, promising him fifty livres, a gun, and some wheat at the completion of a two-year contract. For less than three hundred livres, then, Hubert had compelled Pierre's services for seven years. Comparable French labor could have cost up to eight times as much. One

---

70. François Béland, "Blondeau, Maurice-Régis," *DCB*, V; "Liste de ceux qui sont montés à Michilimackinac avec Tonty," Oct. 23, 1697, ANOM, Colonies, C11A, XV, 143, and "Lettre de Champigny au ministre," Oct. 27, 1698, XVI, 130–138. For the Blondeau slaves, see Trudel, *Dictionnaire des esclaves*, 282–283. There is no surviving documentation of a slave sale from Blondeau to Lamoureux, but Blondeau seems the most likely supplier of Lamoureux's slave, based on their business connections and Blondeau's other slave sales. For Lamoureux's slaves, see Trudel, *Dictionnaire des esclaves*, 358, and Chapter 6, below.

71. "Lettre de Jolliet à Monseigneur de Laval," Oct. 10, 1674, in Jean Delanglez, *Louis Jolliet: vie et voyages, 1645–1700* (Montreal, 1950), 403.

of the reasons Hubert could purchase a slave for such a bargain was that Durand, the original proprietor, had received Pierre as a gift from Ottawa traders at Michilimackinac. As a result, Durand could part with his slave for much less than the value of his labor and still earn a substantial profit.[72]

When slaves passed from the West to the rural settlements of the Saint Lawrence, they primarily worked as domestic and farm laborers. Especially before 1700, these slaves' activities come to us only in fragments. René Chartier, for example, owned an Indian slave in Lachine, a developing farming village near Montreal. When the Iroquois attacked and leveled the settlement in 1689, Chartier, most of his family, and his slave were killed. The mass burial record belatedly created in 1694 contains the only evidence remaining about Chartier's slave: "pani-slave of Rene Char[t]ier, killed by the Iroquois." Chartier, like most of the seventy or so families settled in Lachine, worked hard to clear enough land to subsist. His young slave likely performed routine farming chores, freeing Chartier to clear additional land and improve the family's home. Unlike the domestic servants bound to other Lachine families, however, Chartier's slave could claim no contractual protection and would be at his master's mercy for release from servitude.[73]

Among the newcomers who moved to Lachine following the Iroquois raid was Guillaume de Lorimier de La Rivière, a captain in the colonial troops, who settled there sometime before 1696. Like many of his contemporaries, Lorimier used his position as a military officer to procure Indian slaves, by 1708 acquiring an adolescent he called Joseph. Because Joseph was several years older than the average Indian slave, he worked alongside Lorimier and his sons clearing, planting, and harvesting. Given Lorimier's frequent absences during Queen Anne's War, Joseph often worked the farm alone, and by 1708 he had developed sufficient skill to farm a separate plot of land. In addition to Joseph's agricultural work, Lorimier benefited from the domestic labor of Marie-Anne dit L'Anglais, an English captive taken

72. For Pierre's life, see sale dated Mar. 6, 1701, Greffe Adhémar, BANQ-M; Trudel, *Dictionnaire des esclaves*, 84. In the 1690s, securing the services of a French laborer in the West cost voyageurs about 350 livres per year, plus provisions. See, for example, "Engagement of Simon to Tonti and La Forest, September 13, 1693," in Pease and Werner, eds. and trans., *The French Foundations*, 283–285.

73. Death of Aug. 5, 1689, *RAB du PRDH*, 14543 ("extract from a note by Lachine's priest dated 28 Oct. 1694"); Trudel, *Dictionnaire des esclaves*, 23. For Lachine's population, see Eccles, *Canadian Frontier*, 120. For land clearing and servants, see Dechêne, *Habitants and Merchants*, trans. Vardi, 152–168.

in 1703 and held by Lorimier as a servant. Because there were no separate slave or servant quarters, Joseph and Marie-Anne lived in proximity, and in 1708, Marie-Anne became pregnant with Joseph's child.[74]

Shortly after discovering the pregnancy, Lorimier granted them leave to marry and settle on an adjacent plot of land. Following the marriage, Marie-Anne continued to work as a servant, but Joseph's status is more difficult to determine. He appears in the records between 1708 and his death in 1720 as many things—"habitant," "pany," "serviteur," "fermier" (tenant farmer), and "sauvage"—but never "esclave." In 1716, Marie-Anne left Joseph to live a "scandalous life" with a neighboring Frenchman. When Joseph discovered them together, he unsuccessfully attacked them with a hatchet, landing both himself and Marie-Anne in a Montreal prison. Trying to justify her actions before the court, Marie-Anne suggested that she deserved better than a "sauvage" for a husband. Were Joseph still a slave, she almost certainly would have pointed to that status as another reason she could not stay with him. Thus, Joseph likely received his freedom from Lorimier at the time of his marriage, but he never fully recovered from his degraded status.[75]

Among the witnesses to Joseph and Marie-Anne's wedding was André Rapin dit Skaianis, another freed Indian slave who lived nearby. As with Joseph, Skaianis's childhood status survives clearly enough—he was a slave, captured by allied Indians and traded in 1686 at Montreal to André Rapin dit Lamusette. But in 1699, the year Skaianis turned eighteen, his master died, willing to Skaianis a bull and a heifer "for the services he had rendered to the family he had joined at the age of five." Skaianis immediately began to cultivate his own land, and in 1706 he married a poor French widow, Anne Gourdon, a neighbor and longtime friend of his former master's family. Lachine's parish priest recorded Skaianis as the "adoptive son" of his former owner, André Rapin, an indicator of just how far Skaianis had traveled since his capture twenty years earlier. In 1723, after the death of his first wife, he contracted with Charles Nolan, a fur and slave trader, to run canoes

---

74. For Lorimier, see Moogk, "Lorimier de La Rivière, Guillaume de," *DCB*, II. The most complete record of Joseph's and Marie-Anne's lives is a Montreal court case from 1716. See "Procès contre Marie-Anne Winder dite l'anglaise, servante, épouse de Joseph Riberville, panis, accusée de débauche," Apr. 9, 1716, BANQ-M, TL4, S1, D1893. For the pregnancy and subsequent marriage, see marriage of July 31, 1708, *RAB du PRDH*, 14373; Trudel, *Dictionnaire des esclaves*, 25.

75. "Procès contre Marie-Anne Winder dite l'anglaise," Apr. 9, 1716, BANQ-M, TL4,S1, D1893; Trudel, *Dictionnaire des esclaves*, 25.

loaded with trade goods to Michilimackinac and return with furs. After his contract expired, Skaianis returned to Lachine and settled on his farm, remarrying at the age of sixty-three to a well-established French widow.[76]

As these stories indicate, Indian slavery in New France before 1709 mirrored the fluidity and ambiguity found in the "charter generations" of many slaveholding societies. Skaianis successfully integrated into French life, for example, owning livestock and a farm, taking a French wife, and freely contracting his labor. Joseph did not fare quite as well, but he still attained a measure of autonomy that slave status would have denied him. Although we do not know how typical these experiences were, the uncertain legal status of all Indian slaves mitigated the severity of their servitude and created paths to freedom. Their presence as free members of society could also be destabilizing, and it is possible that friendships like the one between the former slave André Rapin dit Skaianis and his enslaved neighbor Joseph contributed to anxiety about the legal status of Indian slaves in the colony. By formalizing the legal status of Indian slaves in 1709, New France's civil officials sought to make Indian slavery in the colony more like the chattel slavery of the French Caribbean. Colonists would buy and sell slaves with enforceable contracts, and the weight of the colony's police power would fall on those seeking to interfere with slaveholders' property rights.[77]

On June 15, 1709, Montreal notary Antoine Adhémar recorded the first Indian slave sale to occur since the legal recognition of Indian slavery two months earlier. Seigneur and military officer Pierre-Thomas Tarieu de La Pérade purchased Pascal, a nineteen-year-old Indian male, from Madeleine Just de La Découverte (the wife of Pascal's original owner) for 120 livres. The notarial record itself signified the new structures Raudot had erected

76. Marriage of July 31, 1708, *RAB du PRDH*, 14373, of Apr. 18, 1706, Lachine, 14366, of Aug. 17, 1744, Lachine, 115977; Dechêne, *Habitants and Merchants*, trans. Vardi, 327 n. 28 ("services he had rendered"); Trudel, *Dictionnaire des esclaves*, 24. The name "Skaianis" appears with several variant spellings, including Kaianis, Scaianis, Scaiennis, Skaiennais, Skaiennis, Skayanis, and Skianis. I have chosen the spelling that appears most frequently.

77. For "charter generations," see Ira Berlin, *Many Thousands Gone: The First Two Centuries of Slavery in North America* (Cambridge, Mass., 1998), 15–92. Skaianis and Joseph appear together on at least one Catholic record, demonstrating that they at least knew each other and were likely friends. See baptism of Mar. 11, 1721, Lachine, *RAB du PRDH*, 14066. For another example of the destabilizing fears caused by freed Indian slaves, see the murder trial of Nicolas, a "panis" accused of murdering New France's executioner and one of his children: "Procès de Nicolas, sauvage (amérindien) de la nation Panis, accusé d'avoir blessé (Marie-Josèphete) Maréchal, demanderesse, et son petit enfant âgé de 14 mois, d'avoir assassiné (Jacques) Élie, son mari, et un de ses enfants âgé de 5 ans," May 25, 1710, BANQ-M, Fonds Conseil souverain, TP1, S777, D133.

to protect Indian slave property, carefully outlining the amount and method of payment and declaring the sale legally enforceable. Similar documents would be cited in court records throughout the eighteenth century to confirm the enslaved status of individual Panis and to settle disputes over slaveholders' property.[78]

Pascal's life, too, represents both the origins of New France's Indian slave system and the transformation effected by its legalization. When he first entered the colony as the slave of Pierre You de La Découverte, Pascal had passed through a raid-and-trade network more dominated by Indian than French cultural norms. This captive exchange carried Pascal from his home on the Great Plains to a mixed French and Miami settlement in the Pays d'en Haut, where La Découverte lived with his Miami wife and métis child. As a slave of La Découverte, Pascal likely performed a combination of domestic chores and tasks associated with La Découverte's illegal fur and liquor trade on Montreal's Isle-aux-Tourtres. La Pérade's motives for acquiring Pascal, however, marked an important point of departure for Pascal and many other French-owned Indian slaves. Pascal was the first of thirteen Indian slaves that La Pérade purchased between 1709 and 1751, and their labor on his seigneurial estate largely removed them from the world of French-Indian exchange that characterized much of the early slave experience. La Pérade, described by one of his subordinates as "a furious man who is out of his mind," treated free laborers so harshly that he could not find anyone willing to work for him. His reliance on slaves reflected his desire to develop his seigneury into a respectable and lucrative enterprise, much more akin to his Caribbean counterparts than to La Découverte's ambitions related to Indian trade.[79]

Seemingly encouraged by the new legal clarity and buoyed by officials' encouragement of slavery, colonists experimented with a number of uses for slave labor in the 1710s and 1720s. In all areas of New France's economy, colonists began using Indian slaves to lighten existing labor loads and to develop new enterprises previously restricted by labor shortages. In the economy of the household, where a majority of Indian slaves labored as domestics, French colonists of sufficient means sought to free themselves from work they felt was beneath them by purchasing slaves as a substitute for scarce French servants. Slaves also labored in the agricultural economy,

78. Sale of June 15, 1709, Greffe Adhémar, BANQ-M.
79. Trudel, *Dictionnaire des esclaves*, 419–420; André Vachon, "Jarret de Verchères, Maire-Madeleine," *DCB*, III ("furious man").

where they performed the drudgeries of land clearing, harvesting, milling, and tending animals. Although most Indian slaves supplemented family labor and produced primarily for local consumption, in time some would also cultivate export crops and develop much-needed infrastructure on the colony's seigneuries. Especially in Montreal and Quebec, merchants and craftsmen utilized Indian slaves as shopworkers, semiskilled laborers, and dock loaders, often hiring them out to third parties and claiming the salaries for themselves. In the West, a few Indian slaves were hired out to work in the fur trade, but the majority worked on farms to supply corn and wheat to the garrisons and traders at the forts.

French colonists most often used Indian slaves as lifelong domestic servants. The demand for domestic slaves did not come from an absolute shortage of available household labor, however. New France's families at all social levels were large, and children began doing domestic work at a young age. Yet, because early modern Europeans equated high social status with freedom from work, most well-stationed French colonists refused to require menial labor of their children. Instead, they sought to acquire as many domestic servants as their finances would allow. During the seventeenth and eighteenth centuries, French authors wrote extensively about the need for wealthy men and women to obtain a large number of servants to signify, and to solidify, their high social status. In France, the elite took such prescriptions to heart, hiring so many domestics that by the 1750s servants constituted about 10 percent of France's urban population. French and creole elites in New France sought to replicate this social world, hiring servants as much for their value as status symbols as for their productive labor. Given the shortage of available French servants, however, many of New France's families turned to Indian slaves as an alternative source of unfree laborers.[80]

Between 1714 and 1719, for example, Montreal's governor Claude de Ramezay secured four male and two female Indian slaves to serve at his château and sawmill. Ramezay had thirteen children who, in theory, could have performed all of the family's necessary household labor. In this status-conscious world, however, he could not maintain his rank and authority with his children's tending gardens, cleaning stables, stocking the icehouse,

---

80. Although Danielle Gauvreau suggests that Quebec's merchant class had somewhat lower fertility rates, it still had enough children to accomplish a household's basic upkeep. See Gauvreau, *Québec: une ville et sa population au temps de la Nouvelle-France* (Quebec, 1991). For French notions of work and status, see Sarah C. Maza, *Servants and Masters in Eighteenth-Century France: The Uses of Loyalty* (Princeton, N.J., 1983); Cissie Fairchilds, *Domestic Enemies: Servants and Their Masters in Old Regime France* (Baltimore, 1984).

or serving at the château's many social functions. His Indian slaves, ranging from eight to sixteen years old, performed these chores in addition to caring for Ramezay's younger children. Although occasionally joined by French servants, Ramezay's Indian slaves proved to be the most enduring source of domestic labor for the governor.[81]

More than one hundred of Ramezay's Montreal neighbors also acquired Indian slaves during the 1710s and 1720s. Most of these slaves were young, more demographically comparable to French household servants than to slaves in other American colonies. With a median age of thirteen, the female slaves could perform most domestic tasks immediately upon arrival, including cleaning, laundry, and some child care. The slightly younger male slaves, with a median age of twelve, could clean, carry wood, tend to domestic animals, and run errands in town. The presence of Indian slaves on such errands was so common that it rarely evoked comment. Yet, when court cases required an explanation of slaves' whereabouts, colonists acknowledged slaves' presence and described their activities to the court.[82]

Montreal merchant Pierre Lestage illustrates the more common Montreal slaveholders who purchased a few young Indian slaves as domestics during the early years of the trade. In 1712 Lestage married a freed New England captive named Esther Sayward and immediately began building a respectable residence in town. Within a year, the couple purchased three Indian slaves, two males and a female, between seven and ten years old. When one of the male slaves, Ignace, died in 1714, Lestage acquired a French domestic servant, Théophile Barté. Because he was eighteen years old, however, Barté did not remain in the Lestage household for more than three years. The Indian slaves proved more permanent, remaining with the family for more than a decade. In 1725 Madame Lestage, going by her Catholic name, Marie-Joseph, returned to New England to "see her family and to arrange her domestic affairs." She took with her one of her Indian slaves, a Fox woman named Marie-Madeleine, whom she called her "femme de chambre," or chambermaid.[83]

81. For Ramezay's slaves, see Trudel, *Dictionnaire des esclaves*, 404. For Ramezay and his family, see Yves F. Zoltvany, "Ramezay, Claude de," *DCB*, II. For Ramezay's French domestic servants, see engagement of Sept. 4, 1704, Greffe Antoine Adhémar (Montreal), BANQ-M, and engagement of May 13, 1707, Greffe Antoine Adhémar (Montreal).

82. Trudel, *Dictionnaire des esclaves*, 267–430. During the 1710s, the median age for both male and female slaves at first appearance was 12 years. During the 1720s, the median rose to 15 for females and 12.5 for males. See Appendix C.

83. For slaves, see baptisms of Sept. 21, 1713, *RAB du PRDH*, 44142, 44147. For Théophile

In Quebec, too, colonists bought Indian slaves as domestics, although not nearly on the scale of Montreal. Less directly connected to the Indian trade that brought slaves into the colony, Quebec never rivaled Montreal as a center of Indian slavery. Despite having a population nearly double Montreal's, Quebec had fewer than one-third as many Indian slaves during the 1710s, and fewer than half as many during the rest of the French regime. The most notable exception to this trend was Governor-General Charles de Beauharnois, who owned at least twenty-five Indian slaves by the early 1730s, at the time nearly a quarter of the city's Indian slave population. As governor, Beauharnois stood at the symbolic center of the Indian alliance system and thus acquired more slaves than any other colonist under French rule. Like Claude de Ramezay in Montreal, Governor Beauharnois acquired these slaves to indicate his social and political power and to serve his family and the many dignitaries who visited the governor's residence. When traveling or appearing in public, Beauharnois had several Indian slaves that attended him as personal "lackeys," or valets: one Fox, two Apaches, and two Inuits, all males in their early teens.[84]

As in Montreal, most slaveholders in Quebec owned only a few Indian slaves. Like Superior Council member and prominent merchant Guillaume Gaillard, many of the city's slaveholders held powerful positions in colonial government, commerce, or both. Gaillard purchased three or four Fox slaves during the 1710s, who served in his home as domestics. Gaillard twice hired a French servant, once in 1699 and again in 1724, but he desired the prominence implied by slave ownership and the permanence of their labor. Having begun the eighteenth century managing the estates of prominent French colonists, Gaillard sought to secure his reputation as a man of standing in his own right, and owning slaves symbolized his rise to the top of Quebec society. At least fifteen other members of the Superior

---

Barté, see contract dated Aug. 12, 1715, Greffe Chambalon (Quebec), BANQ-M. For the journey to New England, see "Permission accordée par M. le gouverneur général à mademoiselle de Lestage," May 1, 1725, LAC, MG8, C8, transcript, II, 532–537. There is no clear identification of the "femme de chambre" as the Indian slave, but there is no record of any other servant or slave in the Lestage household who could fit that description.

84. Trudel, *Dictionnaire des esclaves*, 276–277. The records describe the slaves as "laquais," or "laquais du château," "apartenant à" Beauharnois. The Apaches were designated "Patoca" in the baptismal records, which many have interpreted as identifying the Comanches. For a discussion of the Patocas, or Padoucas, as Apaches, see Frank R. Secoy, "The Identity of the 'Paduca': An Ethnohistorical Analysis," *American Anthropologist*, LIII (1951), 525–542.

Council joined Gaillard in slave ownership between 1710 and 1760. Many, like Superior Council member Charles Guillimin, struggled to find suitable French domestic labor. In 1727, Guillimin hired fifteen-year-old Antoine Fortier at eighty livres per year to be his domestic servant. When Fortier abandoned his service, the intendant, who was Guillimin's close associate, ordered him to return. No future record of the boy exists, but, whether or not he returned, Guillimin never again contracted for a French servant. Instead, he continued to rely on his enslaved Indian domestic, Simon, who had worked in his household for a decade.[85]

In the many seigneuries of the Saint Lawrence Valley between Quebec and Montreal, French colonists also bought Indian slaves as visible symbols of wealth and status and with the hope of developing their seigneuries into profitable enterprises. Like their urban counterparts, prominent French seigneurs disdained household chores and manual labor as marks of low social status. In a widely read contemporary French volume describing the well-ordered seigneurial home, the grand seigneur ideally possessed no fewer than thirty domestic servants. Yet New France's seigneurs found a shortage of willing domestic servants, which, when combined with the colony's general lack of day laborers and other low-wage help, frustrated seigneurs' efforts to craft for themselves the life of leisure they hoped to achieve.[86]

Like many of his counterparts, Pierre-Thomas Tarieu de La Pérade, seigneur of Sainte-Anne, turned to Indian slave labor. Upon receiving a seigneurial grant in 1704, La Pérade began searching for laborers to clear and improve his land, construct a house and outbuildings, and meet his family's domestic needs. To supplement free labor, La Pérade began buying Indian slaves in 1709. Over the next two decades, he and his wife, Madeleine

85. Hervé Biron, "Gaillard, Guillaume" *DCB*, II. For Gaillard's French domestics, see engagement of July 27, 1699, Greffe Gageot de Beaurivage (Quebec), BANQ-M, and engagement of Feb. 22, 1724. For conflict with Beauharnois and Dupuy, see S. Dale Standen, "Beauharnois de la Boische, Charles de, Marquis de Beauharnois," *DCB*, III. For Superior Council members, see Trudel, *L'esclavage*, 140. The precise number of Gaillard's slaves is uncertain because some records refer to his slaves without noting their names, possibly referring to his three named slaves or to additional unknown individuals. For Fortier, see "Ordonnance qui condamne Antoine Fortier . . . à retourner sans délai chez le sieur Guillimin," June 4, 1727, LAC, MG8-A6 9A, 299–303. For slaves, see Trudel, *Dictionnaire des esclaves*, 341.

86. For the ideal seigneurial household, see Maza, *Servants and Masters*, esp. 7–10. For the seigneurial system, see Allan Greer, *Peasant, Lord, and Merchant: Rural Society in Three Quebec Parishes, 1740–1840* (Toronto, 1985).

de Verchères, acquired twelve additional Indian slaves—five males and seven females—who cleared land, worked on the family's farm, and labored in their home as cooks, laundresses, seamstresses, and table servers.[87]

Although few other seigneurs acquired as many slaves as La Pérade, as many as 150 of the colony's seigneurs owned at least one Indian slave. As in seventeenth-century Virginia or eighteenth-century New England, most slaves in New France's agricultural regions worked alongside their masters, supplementing rather than supplanting French family labor. Many seigneurs and their widows, however, kept their slaves with them in Montreal or Quebec, living as absentee lords of poorly developed seigneuries. In some regions along the Saint Lawrence, however, colonists bought slaves to produce profitable cash crops, especially flax and hemp. By 1720, New France annually produced nearly seventy thousand pounds of flax, which colonists sold locally to weavers in Montreal and exported to France or other French colonies. Hemp production rose sharply in the 1720s as colonists responded to the incentives of intendant Bégon, who encouraged cultivation by artificially elevating its price. Yet production of these crops was uneven, with yields concentrated in two or three settlements. The seigneury most committed to hemp production, for example, was Batiscan, a tiny village between Trois-Rivières and Quebec. During the 1720s, at least twenty-six slaves labored in Batiscan, many of them working the flax and hemp fields belonging to various members of the Rivard family. Batiscan's Indian slave population reflected the unique focus of the area's slave economy. Unlike the colony as a whole, where 53 percent of slaves were female in the 1720s, Batiscan's slaves were 73 percent male. Averaging twenty years old, these slaves were also older than the average slave in other parts of the colony. Although women and children participated in preparing hemp for shipment, the cultivation was done almost entirely by adolescent or adult males, possibly explaining the settlement's preference for older male slaves.[88]

87. For La Pérade, see Coates, *Metamorphoses;* Pierre-Georges Roy, *La Famille Tarieu de Lanaudière* (Quebec, 1922). For La Pérade's slaves, see Trudel, *Dictionnaire des esclaves,* 419–420.

88. Trudel, *Dictionnaire des esclaves,* xxviii, indicates that 178 seigneurs owned slaves, but he did not differentiate between Indian and African slaves or between the French and British periods. For the occupational diversity of seigneurs and their frequent residence away from the seigneury, see Harris, *Seigneurial System,* esp. 41–87; see also Trudel, *Dictionnaire des esclaves,* 267–430, for seigneurs with slaves in other locations. For flax, see Munro, *Documents Relating to the Seigniorial Tenure,* 146 n. 2; for hemp, Coates, *Metamorphoses,* 43. For uneven flax and hemp production, see Harris, *Seigneurial System;* Coates, *Metamorphoses,* chap. 3. For Batiscan's slaves, see Trudel, *Dictionnaire des esclaves,* 7.

The success of Batiscan's hemp cultivation would have encouraged intendant Bégon, who persistently tried to convince the crown that New France could produce cash crops with slave labor. In 1721, Bégon again requested the authorization of more slave imports, repeating his earlier assertion that slaves were essential to the colony's prosperity. In what had become the standard formula followed by intendants seeking to justify New France's faltering economy, Bégon wrote that "the lack of servants and laborers is hampering the colony's development" and recommended as a solution a "massive influx of slaves . . . for the cultivation of hemp" and other cash crops, including flax. Likely because of the recent financial collapse of the Compagnie des Indes, from whom he requested the shipment of slaves, Bégon never saw the 101 "Negroes" he requested. Yet an even higher number of Indian slaves arrived before he returned to France in 1726. Hemp cultivation consequently rose to impressive levels. But his successor, Claude Thomas Dupuy, did not share his enthusiasm for the crop. Claiming that essential grain production suffered as colonists shifted their attention to cash crops, Dupuy slashed hemp prices in 1727, a policy supported by the next intendant, Gilles Hocquart, who reduced prices even further in 1729. A few years later, the experiment ended entirely.[89]

Although only a handful of French colonists worked their Indian slaves in flax and hemp fields, many purchased them as moneymaking investments, employing them as skilled or semiskilled servants in their own professions and hiring them out as day laborers to others. Jean Chiasson, a Montreal carpenter, seems to have worked his teenaged male slave in both ways. In 1714, Chiasson hired out his slave, who sometimes worked in his shop, to the Congrégation Notre-Dame for a term of three months. The sisters of the Congrégation agreed to pay forty-five livres to Chiasson for the slave's services. Although the agreement seemed mutually beneficial, giving cash to Chiasson and a cheap worker to the church, the nuns refused to pay, perhaps counting on the lack of a signed contract to protect them from liability. Chiasson took the matter to Montreal's royal court, which ordered the Congrégation to pay Chiasson his slave's salary. Had the church freely paid Chiasson, we would know neither of the slave's existence nor of the hiring agreement, a case indicating the likelihood that many others owned or hired slaves beyond our view. Enough other evidence survives, as well, to

89. "Résumé d'une lettre et de mémoires de Bégon," Jan. 13, 1721, ANOM, Colonies, C11A, XLIII, 74–87, "Lettre de Dupuy au ministre," Oct. 20, 1727, XLIX, 274–302v, and "Lettre de Hocquart au ministre," Oct. 25, 1729, LI, 276–285.

suggest that Chiasson was not alone in the practice. In 1716, for example, Montreal tanner Jean-Louis Plessy dit Bélair bought an Indian slave named Étienne and apprenticed him to a nearby shoemaker, gaining a small fee in the short term and the possibility of much higher returns in the future. François, a fourteen-year-old Indian slave who likely worked in his master's butcher shop and tannery, appeared in a Quebec baptismal register in 1720.[90]

Indian slaves also contributed their labor to the textile industry, which generated essential goods for local consumption and for western trade. Although the crown initially discouraged clothmaking in New France, arguing that all value-added manufacturing ought to be done in the mother country, by 1705 the governor and intendant praised Agathe Legardeur de Repentigny for establishing a weaving shop at Montreal. They suggested that she purchase Indian servants to work as weavers, possibly thinking that the Natives would contribute insight into the Indian cloth market. After the legalization of Indian slavery, Madame Legardeur de Repentigny acquired a female Indian slave, named Marie-Angélique-Mathurine, who worked by her side for more than two decades. Indian slaves also helped to create finished clothing and blankets as menials to tailors and seamstresses. In 1716, Montreal tailor Pierre Billeron dit Lafatigue baptized Louis, a fifteen-year-old Indian slave who worked as a servant in his shop. In 1720 at Quebec, another tailor, Louis-Claude-Solomon Liard, owned a female slave, who might have worked in the same capacity. That nine other tailors owned slaves as well indicates their apparent usefulness to the craft.[91]

Many other crafts also commanded a small share of Indian slaves' labor. Among the seven bakers to use slave labor were a father and son, both

90. For the nuns' hiring out their slave, see "Procès entre Jean Chiasson, maître menuisier, demandeur, et les religieuses de la Congrégation Notre-Dame, défenderesses, pour le payement du salaire d'un panis," Mar. 14, 1714, BANQ-M, TL4, S1, D1557. For Du Plessy, see Peter N. Moogk, "Plessy (Plessis), dit Bélair, Jean-Louis," DCB, III. For Étienne, see baptism of July 29, 1731, RAB du PRDH, 145381. For François, see baptism of Apr. 5, 1720, RAB du PRDH, 64454; Trudel, Dictionnaire des esclaves, 134. François's master, Jean-Baptiste Larchevêque dit Grandpré, was one of a few who combined the butchering and tanning trades, a dual career that was officially forbidden to discourage vertical monopolies. See Moogk, La Nouvelle France, 77–79.

91. Trudel, L'esclavage, 168; Trudel, Dictionnaire des esclaves, xxviii, 68, 144; Fauteux, Essai sur l'industrie; Moogk, La Nouvelle France, 82; "Pontchartrain à Raudot," June 30, 1707, ANOM, Colonies, série B, LXXIX, 66v–71v; baptism of Sept. 21, 1713, RAB du PRDH, 18276, and burial of Apr. 2, 1738, 169275.

named Antoine Poudret, who acquired three Indian slaves named Marie, Cécile, and Louise. Another father and son, Montreal surgeons Joseph and Claude Benoist, bought two Indian slaves, one male and one female. The surgeons' skills did not help their slaves, however, both of whom appear only in parish burial records. The boy died at only eight years old. In virtually every craft practiced in the colony, Indian slaves played a role, although usually very small. Blacksmiths, masons, roofers, gunsmiths, and cobblers all supplemented the meager supply of servants and apprentices with the labor of Indian slaves.[92]

Merchants and officers participating in the fur trade also purchased or hired enslaved Indians to mitigate their own labor difficulties, offering another avenue for masters wishing to rent their slaves to others. Although the fur trade never experienced an absolute shortage of available manpower, French workers often failed to fulfill their obligations—trading merchants' goods for their own profit, leaving before the contract expired, demanding higher pay than originally agreed, or simply not showing up at an expedition's appointed time. In 1714, Governor Vaudreuil also complained to his superiors of the high wages demanded by day laborers in the Pays d'en Haut, which greatly increased the cost of financing the western posts. Merchants and officers therefore occasionally relied on Indian slaves to assist them in their journeys when French workers failed to appear or demanded too much from them.[93]

During the first two decades following Raudot's ordinance, hundreds of French colonists used Indian slaves "for agriculture and other enterprises": in their homes, on their farms, and in the local exchange economy. Bégon's hopes to develop colonial industry on the backs of slaves never fully materialized, but colonists nevertheless bought thousands of Indian slaves either to answer immediate demand for menial laborers or in hopeful anticipation of future profits. To meet the needs of these colonists, dozens of merchants and military officers began to buy and sell Native men, women, and children

92. Burial of Feb. 25, 1735, *RAB du PRDH*, 151481; Trudel, *Dictionnaire des esclaves*, 48, 278, 400.

93. For problems with engagés, see, for example, "Lettre adressée à Lemoine dit Monière, négociant, par Marin, de Lachine, lui disant que son engagé Francoeur l'a abandonné," Aug. 16, 1739, BANQ-M, TL4, S1, D4656, and "Procès entre un nommé Marin, demandeur, représenté par Alexis Lemoine Monière, négociant, pour avoir été abandonné au départ de Lachine par un nommé Francoeur, engagé," Aug. 19, 1739, S1, D4519.41. Vaudreuil au ministre, Sept. 16, 1714, ANOM, Colonies, C11A, XXXIV, 279–296v.

as a modest supplement to their revenues from the fur trade. This trickle would swell into a steady stream of human trafficking that would flow into the Saint Lawrence Valley for the next half century.

❖ Jacques Raudot and his successors hoped to use enslaved Indian labor to eclipse the fur trade economy, imagining a distant and poorly understood nation as the "Negroes" of North America. Yet the more slaves the colony demanded, the more implicated it became in western trade and diplomacy. New France's Indian slave system never fully escaped its origins in the alliances that first brought Indian captives into French hands as slaves. The colony's native allies in the Pays d'en Haut remained the suppliers of Indian slaves, and they continually demanded French accommodation to their customs. Moreover, shifts in the western alliance complicated New France's slave policies, especially when the colony wished to befriend nations, such as the Foxes or Sioux, whose people they held as slaves. Often, slaveholders' claims on Indians as property clashed with the demands of an alliance that required a more fluid exchange of captives and slaves than French property law would allow. By accepting "a little flesh" to stabilize their alliance with western Indians, the colonists of New France acknowledged the symbolic power of captive exchanges to build union and foster peace. Yet, rather than willingly embracing their allies' captive customs, French officials assented only when natives demanded their participation. Ironically, then, Indian slavery originated as a partial defeat of New France's power over its Indian neighbors. From that defeat, however, the French built an exploitative labor system that redirected their impulse for control and domination onto distant Indian nations.

The legal pluralism and regional distinctiveness that characterized French Atlantic colonialism ensured that New France's slave system would evolve on its own terms as a dialogue between the indigenous and the Atlantic slaveries that had produced it. Embracing the legal and cultural diversity that defined the broader French Atlantic, colonists and their Native allies responded to these new forces to create new expressions of slavery, captor and captive alike bound by the alliances that drew French and Native peoples together in eighteenth-century North America.

chapter four

MOST OF THEM WERE SOLD
TO THE FRENCH

In 1742 a small group of Sioux leaders accepted the invitation of Paul Marin, a French trader and minor colonial official, to negotiate an alliance with his governor in Montreal. French-Sioux relations had been turbulent over the previous half century, cycling rapidly from friendship to antipathy and back again. Having sent representatives to Montreal in each of the past two years to little effect, the Sioux were leery of French promises. But recent years had been hard on the Sioux, and an especially devastating raid the year before convinced them they had no choice but to seek French alliance. At the end of a two-month journey from their Upper Mississippi River villages to Montreal, they were introduced by Marin to the governor, Charles de Beauharnois. To underscore the distance they had traveled, the Sioux chiefs announced themselves as the "people from halfway across the world," explaining that they were prepared to form an alliance if they could be assured protection from their enemies, particularly Crees, Assiniboines, and Monsonis, who had attacked them the previous spring. "More than 160 of our men were killed," they complained, "not counting the women and children." As the offending nations were allied to the French, the Sioux leaders hoped the governor could restrain them and arrange some kind of compensation for the grieving families.[1]

Negotiations began well. Expressing their good fortune to be received by the French governor, the Sioux chiefs offered him a calumet, which he

---

1. "Nous autres gens de l'autre côté de la moitié de la terre"; "plus de 160 hommes, sans compter les femmes et les enfans": "Paroles des Sioux, Sakis, Renards, Puants de la pointe de Chagouamigon et Folles Avoines à Monsieur le marquis de Beauharnois," July 1742, ANOM, Colonies, C11A, LXXXVII, 213–213v.

smoked, "to show you how I wish peace and quiet to reign amongst the Nations of my Children." But sometime during the next six days a startling encounter changed the tone of the discussions, sending the Sioux emissaries back home in a rage. It might have been at the home of Paul Marin's brother-in-law, Jean-Baptiste Hervieux, a merchant whose residence on Rue Saint-Paul stood only a few blocks from the governor's château where the council took place. Three weeks earlier, Hervieux had baptized a new slave: a seven-year-old Sioux girl he called Charlotte after his wife, Charlotte Marin. Or it might have been at the nearby residence of Hervieux's brother, Louis, who presented his Sioux slave for baptism just a few months earlier. In either case, as the Sioux men interacted with their French hosts, they were shocked to come across Sioux children serving them as slaves. Charging back to the governor's residence, they demanded an audience. The Sioux reminded the governor that they had come to Montreal offering more than they asked and making no firm demands, a course they would have followed "had we not found two of our children, who started to weep as soon as they saw us."[2]

Having passed through a translator and through the selective disclosure of a colonial governor reporting to his superior, the surviving account provides little detail. But even through these filters the anger of the Sioux chiefs is palpable. "We hope, my father, that you will not keep them from us, and that we will be taking them back with us." For emphasis, their spokesman said again, "I will be satisfied if you would be kind enough to give us our two children, who wept when they saw us." He then threatened the governor by suggesting that he could not guarantee French safety from his young warriors. "Although I am a chief," one of the Sioux warned, "the young men do not always obey my will, so I ask you to have pity on me."[3]

2. "Mon Pere, nous n'aurions ôsé vous demander aucune grace, si nous n'avions pas trouvé deux de nos Enfans, qui se sont mis a pleurer lors qu'ils nous ont vûs": "Paroles des Sioux, Sakis, Renards, Puants de la pointe de Chagouamigon et Folles Avoines à Monsieur le marquis de Beauharnois," ibid. The first Sioux meeting with the governor occurred on July 18, the second on July 24, 1742. For the Sioux slaves, see baptism of Charlotte, "sauvagesse de la nation des Sioux," June 23, 1742, Notre-Dame-de-Montréal, FHL, and baptism of Antoine Sigefroid, "sauvage de la nation des Sioux," Nov. 20, 1741. For Hervieux's relationship with Paul Marin, see marriage of Pierre Jean-Baptiste Hervieux to Charlotte Marin, Sept. 14, 1739, *RAB du PRDH*, 150020. For Hervieux's home, see Adhemar database, Centre Canadien d'Architecture, Montreal (http//www.cca.qc.ca/adhemar/).

3. "Nous Esperons, Mon Pere, que vous ne nous les reffûserés pas, et que nous les Emmennerons avec nous. Mon Pere, je serois glorieux si vous aviés la bonté de nous accorder nos deux Enfans, qui ont pleuré en nous voyant. Mon Pere, quoique je sois chef, les jeunes gens

Beauharnois initially promised to allow the enslaved children to return with the chiefs, but not without announcing that he expected Sioux compliance in return. "You see that I refuse you nothing," he said, "in the hope that you will do my will." Answering the Sioux threat with one of his own, the governor warned, "You are to be pitied, if your young men listen not to your words." If the chiefs failed to restrain Sioux warriors against the French and their allies, he would "let loose all my Frenchmen and the Nations that ask no better than to swoop down on your villages, to revenge themselves for all you have done in the past." Beauharnois knew the devastation that his allies had visited upon the Sioux the previous year, and he realized that the Sioux would be keen to avoid another attack.[4]

To emphasize that the French held the power in this negotiation, the governor used the Sioux reaction over their enslaved children to his advantage. Shortly before the arrival of the Sioux chiefs, Beauharnois had received a report of the past year's raid, informing him that French allies had not only killed dozens of Sioux warriors but had also taken a large number of women and children captive. "The number of slaves was so great," the governor wrote in a separate letter, "that, according to the report and the expression of the savages, they occupied in their march more than four arpents." Stretching nearly eight hundred feet, this coffle of Sioux slaves could have included as many as 150 people. So, even as he negotiated peace with the Sioux chiefs, their kin were bound for Montreal to be sold to the French as slaves. "During your return journey you may meet some of your people coming from those Places," he told the emissaries. "Be not uneasy about them. You can come and get them next year." It is hard to imagine that the Sioux found his assurances comforting. He was asking them to pass by scores of their enslaved kin being dragged to the streets of Montreal for sale as French slaves, the very thing that soured negotiations to begin with. To make matters worse, the governor then hinted that he might not be able to persuade the two Sioux children to leave the comforts of French life. He might, in fact, have been powerless to return the children, but not for the reasons he gave: because the children were legally enslaved, he could not deny their masters' property right over them. The chiefs must have wondered why they had trusted the promise of a friendly reception, but for the

---

ne font pas toûjours ma volonté, c'est pourquoy je vous prie d'avoir pitié de moy": "Paroles des Sioux, Sakis, Renards, Puants de la pointe de Chagouamigon et Folles Avoines à Monsieur le marquis de Beauharnois," July 1742, ANOM, Colonies, C11A, LXXVII, 213–213v.

4. Ibid.

moment they could do little but agree to the governor's terms and go home. There is no evidence that they took the children with them. Returning to the Mississippi, their description of Sioux slaves in Montreal enraged their beleaguered community, and warriors gathered for revenge. Tensions with the French escalated, and talk of alliance all but disappeared.[5]

Variations of the Sioux experience played out repeatedly in the first half of the eighteenth century, serving as a constant reminder of the complex relationship between Indian slavery and Indian alliances in New France. As much as the French hoped to recreate the dynamics of Caribbean slavery, they found that their allies had different ideas. French administrators wanted their slaves to originate in far distant lands, allowing them to separate the practice of slavery from the messy realities of enslavement. "We do not see that this trade could ever have any effect on our Indians," Beauharnois's successor wrote a few years later, "the slaves only being purchased from . . . far distant nations who get them from others with whom they are at war, and it matters very little to them what becomes of those that they have sold." These officials echoed the hopeful pronouncements of Jacques Raudot, who had insisted forty years earlier that the violence of slave raiding would remain beyond the pale of French settlement and trade, in lands "far distant" from French interests. Like Nigritie, the vast interior of western North America would ideally serve as a safe and justifiable source of slaves.[6]

As French colonizers sought to enlarge their influence in the West, they embraced an ever-expanding number of Indians as commercial and military partners. Native peoples already secure in the French alliance wished to limit its scope, blocking their enemies' access to French goods and support. Asserting their prerogative to define the boundaries of alliance, Anishinaabes, Illinois, Crees, Assiniboines, and other allies demanded that the French honor their commitment to them by excluding their historical enemies, just as the French demanded that they exclude the English. In this

5. Governor to minister from Pierre Gaultier de Varennes de La Vérendrye, in Lawrence J. Burpee, ed., *Journals and Letters of Pierre Gaultier de Varennes de La Vérendrye and His Sons* . . . (Toronto, 1927), 381; "Réponse de Beauharnois aux paroles des Sioux . . . ," July 28, 1742, ANOM, Colonies, C11A, LXXVII, 235–236v.

6. "Nous ne voyons pas que cet Envoy pût Jamais faire aucune Impression sur nos sauvages, les Esclaves n'etant achettés que des . . . nations tres Eloignées qui les font sur d'autres avec lesquels ils sont en Guerre et Ils s'Embarrassent très peu de quoy deviennent Ceux qu'ils ont Vendu": Bigot et La Jonquière au ministre, Sept. 26, 1749, Collections Moreau de Saint-Méry, F3, XCV. "Très eloignée": Jacques Raudot, "Ord[onan]ce rendüe au sujet des neigres et des Sauvages nommez Panis," Apr. 13, 1709, BANQ-Q, E1, S1, P509 (for a full transcription and translation, see Appendix B).

battle of wills, the Indian slave trade emerged as the most valuable tool employed by New France's Native allies to limit French expansion and determine the makeup of the French-led alliance. By raiding enemy villages for captives and then giving or selling these captives to the French as slaves, these peoples drove a deep and often fatal wedge between the French and their erstwhile allies. Despite persistent French efforts to befriend Foxes, Sioux, and other western peoples, French colonists' demand for slaves allowed allied Indians to shape the contours of the alliance to their advantage against French wishes, effectively blocking French westward expansion at several key eighteenth-century moments. Rather than acting solely as a system of colonial domination, then, the Indian slave trade also provided allied Indians a way to oppose colonial power.

Although Indians employed long-standing practices in the slave trade to assert control over North American diplomacy, they found that engagement with the French transformed their own practice of slavery even as it limited French options. Ritual expressions of enslavement like the calumet or the marking of slaves' bodies were adapted to new dynamics of trade and diplomacy, transforming the cultural performance of slavery as they altered the war culture in which they were embedded. The colonial slave trade also eroded historical constraints on Native warfare by offering new incentives for violence while transforming local exchange economies. The incorporation of women and children as slaves in Native villages—historically a long-term benefit to the captors' community—declined sharply in the mid-eighteenth century as Natives sought the short-term rewards available for trading them away. Not only did this alter the social dynamics within slave-raiding villages, but it also hurt Indians' ability to rebound from the demographic disasters of warfare and disease. Bound by alliance, French and Native slaveries produced creative tensions that neither French nor Indian participants could fully control, and to which everyone would adapt with terrific creativity.

PEOPLE WHOSE CHILDREN WE ARE WITHHOLDING

*"To make peace, it is necessary to begin by restoring to the [Foxes] all
the slaves of their nation whom the French hold. It is [unnatural] to think
that peace can be made with people whose children we are withholding."*
—Philippe de Rigaud de Vaudreuil, Quebec, 1716

In a 1723 state-of-the-colony report to crown officials, Philippe de Rigaud de Vaudreuil congratulated himself on successfully concluding peace negotiations with the Fox Indians in a conflict historians call the Fox Wars. Pitting New France's Indian allies against a coalition of Foxes, Sauks, Kickapoos, and Winnebagos, this series of clashes claimed thousands of lives and destabilized the Pays d'en Haut for the better part of thirty years. Charged with maintaining the region's Indian alliances, Vaudreuil's self-satisfied letter announced that he had thwarted recent plans by his Native allies to attack Fox villages, sending a well-respected French officer to the region "to Persuade them to be Reconciled and to Live in Peace." As he had done many times before, Vaudreuil pressured western Indians to embrace the Foxes as allies rather than enemies, seeking greater regional stability to facilitate French commercial and territorial expansion.[7]

To avoid difficult questions, Governor Vaudreuil never mentioned to his French superiors that his household, like scores of others in New France, was served by Fox slaves who had been captured in the very attacks he claimed to oppose. Just two months later, the governor summoned Father Étienne Broullard to his residence to baptize two Indian women, age thirty-five and fourteen, who were given the Christian names Marguerite-Geneviève and Marie-Louise. They were slaves, "captured in Fox country" and now residing in the governor's palace. Vaudreuil's official duties required that he make peace with the Foxes, but like hundreds of other colonists he also participated in the slave trade that brought these women and their kin to New France in large numbers. For the previous ten years, enslaved Foxes had trickled into Canada as allied Indians attacked their villages, making Fox men, women, and children the dominant source of enslaved labor in the Saint Lawrence Valley during the 1710s and 1720s. Because these slaves do not appear in the official reports that have informed earlier studies, their lives have been seen, if acknowledged at all, as interesting but insignificant side notes to the story of French-Native diplomacy. But the records discussing these slaves, produced by parish priests, notaries, and court reporters a thousand miles from the violence, offer a valuable window onto the ways that French slaveholding shaped, and was shaped by, the vagaries of their western alliances, which drew them into the historically complex world of indigenous slavery—altering that world in the process.[8]

7. Vaudreuil au ministre, Oct. 2, 1723, ANOM, C11A, XLV, fols. 136–141v; *Wis. Hist. Coll.,* XVI (1902), 431 (quote).

8. Baptism of Dec. 13, 1723, *RAB du PRDH,* 65055; Registres Notre-Dame-de-Québec, Dec. 13, 1723, FHL; Marcel Trudel, *Dictionnaire des esclaves et de leur propriétaires au Canada français* (La Salle, Que., 1990), 141. Marguerite-Geneviève's 1725 burial record indicates that she was still Vaudreuil's slave two years later. Registre des mortuaires et malades,

From their first encounter in the 1660s to the end of the seventeenth century, the French and the Foxes shared a desire for alliance. With the Iroquois threat looming, each side profited from the other's assurances of protection, and both could benefit from the trade that accompanied such relationships. In 1679, a group of French and Foxes smoked the calumet together, signifying their peaceful intentions and inaugurating what each hoped would be a long and peaceful relationship. But it was clear from the beginning that France's allies had a competing vision for the alliance they were building. Allied Indians, including the Illinois, Ottawas, Ojibwas, Miamis, and Hurons, despised the Foxes and resented French overtures to their enemy. Even as they needed Fox cooperation during the Iroquois wars, they expressed disdain for this people, and they wanted them excluded from French protection and trade.[9]

During the 1670s and 1680s, Fox villages came under attack from all of these groups, sparking rounds of reprisals that placed the Foxes in a precarious position among powerful enemies. These conflicts ebbed and flowed with the currents of the Iroquois threat, but animosity remained the norm throughout the last quarter of the seventeenth century and into the eighteenth. When Foxes sought security in numbers, clustering with other Iroquois enemies in multiethnic trade centers, cramped proximity often sparked new violence among these historical enemies, creating a tense atmosphere in the Pays d'en Haut. Anti-Iroquois war parties occasionally united Fox warriors with enemy peoples, but for most of the seventeenth century the Foxes occupied the very margins of the French-Indian alliance system, never welcomed by their old enemies despite these expedient compromises. Illinois, Ottawa, Ojibwa, and Huron war parties clashed with Foxes throughout the 1680s and 1690s, even as they faced a common Iroquois enemy.[10]

Hôtel-Dieu-de-Québec, Oct. 1, 1725, FHL. Only one historian of the Fox Wars has even acknowledged the slave trade. In a brief but beautifully illustrated article, Joseph L. Peyser discussed the sale of a handful of high-profile Fox captives to Martinique in the early 1730s, but he treated the incident as an anomaly, a tragic but isolated human interest story with no connection to the wars themselves: "The Fate of the Fox Survivors: A Dark Chapter in the History of the French in the Upper Country, 1726–1737," *Wisconsin Magazine of History*, LXXIII (1989–1990), 83–110.

9. [Louis] Hennepin, *A New Discovery of a Vast Country in America, Extending above Four Thousand Miles between New France and New Mexico* (London, 1698), I, 132–137.

10. R. David Edmunds and Joseph L. Peyser, *The Fox Wars: The Mesquakie Challenge to New France* (Norman, Okla., 1993) 1–13; Hennepin, *New Discovery*, I, 134; Nicolas Perrot, *Memoir on the Manners, Customs, and Religion of the Savages of North America*, in Emma

By the time of the general peace conference in Montreal in 1701, the Foxes seemed closer to the Iroquois than to any of their neighboring Algonquian peoples. Still, the Fox delegate to the peace negotiations expressed his desire to have a French presence in their territory. "[If we] had a black robe, a blacksmith, and several Frenchmen among us," he pleaded with the governor, "the [Ojibwas] would not be bold enough to attack us." The Ojibwas were not the only ones who wanted to drive the Foxes from the French alliance. The Illinois had a long-standing feud with their Fox neighbors, maligning them to the French as "devils on earth." "They have nothing human but the shape. . . . One can say of them that they have all the bad qualities of the other nations without having a single one of their good ones." The Illinois never fully explained their reasons, but Claude de Ramezay, an interim governor of New France, agreed that the Illinois were the "irrevocable foes" of the Foxes. Governor Vaudreuil concurred: the Illinois and Miamis "have always been Enemies of the Renards," or Foxes. Still, the French wanted them within the alliance, so they invited them to the 1701 peace as full partners.[11]

The French decision to establish a new settlement at Detroit the same year only deepened these divisions. Although never exclusive middlemen

---

Helen Blair, ed. and trans., *The Indian Tribes of the Upper Mississippi Valley and Region of the Great Lakes* (Cleveland, 1911–1912), I, 356–372. For early Fox clashes with other French allies, see Claude-Charles, Bacqueville de La Potherie, *Voyage de l'Amérique: contenant ce qui c'est passé de plus remarquable dans l'Amérique septentrionale depuis 1534 jusqu'à present* (Amsterdam, 1723), II, 49; Perrot, *Memoir*, in Blair, ed. and trans., *Indian Tribes*, 356–363. For Iroquois raids, see José António Brandão, *"Your Fyre Shall Burn No More": Iroquois Policy toward New France and Its Native Allies to 1701* (Lincoln, Nebr., 1997), table D.1. Brandão's detailed summary of all known Iroquois raids suggests that White and other historians have overestimated the Iroquois threat to the Upper Country. To be sure, this follows the tone of French documents, but many of these accounts were written by people who only gained by exaggerating the Iroquois threat in the West to persuade western Indians to confront the Iroquois in the East. Gilles Havard, *Empire et métissages: Indiens et Français dans le Pays d'en Haut, 1660–1715* (Paris, 2003), 127, which argues that "les sources françaises ont généralement exagéré les consequences des guerres iroquoises," a conclusion shared by William James Newbigging, "The History of the French-Ottawa Alliance, 1613–1763" (Ph.D. diss., University of Toronto, 1995), 120–158.

11. Gilles Havard, *The Great Peace of Montreal of 1701: French-Native Diplomacy in the Seventeenth Century*, trans. Phyllis Aronoff and Howard Scott (Montreal, 2001), esp. chap. 5; Edmunds and Peyser, *Fox Wars*, 6 ("Frenchmen among us"), 29–30. The "devils on earth" sentiment was expressed by Antoine-Denis Raudot, New France's intendant, who reported what he learned from the Illinois in "Memoir concerning the Different Indian Nations of North America," in W. Vernon Kinietz, ed., *The Indians of the Western Great Lakes, 1615–1760* (Ann Arbor, Mich., 1965), 383. Claude de Ramezay to minister, Sept. 18, 1714, *Wis. Hist. Coll.*, XVI (1902), 303, and Vaudreuil and Bégon to minister, Sept. 20, 1714, 304.

in the Great Lakes fur trade, the Ottawas, Ojibwas, and Illinois lived much closer to the French and thus could command a larger proportion of their commerce. As the French moved westward, these peoples were faced with the dual threat of having the Foxes become better armed and of losing their position of strength within the region's fur trade networks. The French hoped that their presence there would allow them to intervene in these disputes more effectively, compelling mediation to enlarge and stabilize the western alliance.[12]

Meanwhile, the diminished Iroquois threat removed what little incentive Ottawas, Ojibwas, and Illinois felt to remain at peace with the Foxes. Skirmishes over the next few years renewed the deep hostilities that had been only thinly masked by the necessity of wartime cooperation. Illinois villages, which had been on the offensive against Fox, Sauk, and Kickapoo targets since at least the 1670s, suffered counterraids from these groups throughout the 1690s and early 1700s. In 1703 and 1708, Fox warriors attacked the Ojibwas near the southeastern corner of Lake Superior, killing several warriors and taking a large number of Ojibwa captives. As kin and close friends of the victims, the Ottawas agreed to come to their aid against the Foxes, and counterraids began later that year. Although the fighting directly involved only the northernmost Ottawa and Ojibwa villages, information passed quickly along trade networks, and soon the villages around Detroit were well aware of Fox aggression. Despite these conflicts, French officers persisted in their efforts to join these peoples "in feelings of peace and union," hoping to avoid taking sides in a dispute among peoples they regarded as allies.[13]

In this tense environment, the French naively invited the Foxes to live among the allied peoples whose villages surrounded Detroit. Articulating his vision of an expansive western alliance, Governor Vaudreuil ordered Jacques-Charles Renaud Dubuisson, Detroit's new post commander, to "give all his attention to preventing the Indian allies from making war on

---

12. "Lettre de Lamothe Cadillac au Ministre à propos de l'établissement du Détroit," Oct. 18, 1700, ANOM, Colonies, C11A, XIV, 56–59; W. J. Eccles, *The Canadian Frontier, 1534–1760*, rev. ed. (Albuquerque, N.Mex., 1983), 135–139; Susan Sleeper-Smith, *Indian Women and French Men: Rethinking Cultural Encounter in the Western Great Lakes* (Amherst, Mass., 2001), 19.

13. Réponse de Vaudreuil aux Indiens, July 29, 1709, ANOM, Colonies, C11A, XXX, 85–92v, 89 (quote); Newbigging, "History of the French-Ottawa Alliance," 309–313. Edmunds and Peyser refer to this continuing violence against the Foxes as an "intertribal cauldron" that simmered to a boil in the years before the Fox came to Detroit (*Fox Wars*, 59–61).

one another." But this was an impossible commission that represented the governor's wishful thinking more than his understanding. Repeatedly imploring his allies to forget their "old quarrels" and "live together in peace and unity" with their Fox enemies had little effect.[14]

Instead, the Foxes' move to Detroit in 1711 forced allied Indians to assert their own vision of a more limited alliance that would not only exclude the Foxes but aggressively attack them. Violence erupted almost immediately, beginning with a flurry of raids and counterraids in the villages near Detroit. During one skirmish, the Foxes struck two Huron and Ottawa villages, capturing the wife of a powerful Ottawa chief, who vowed revenge. Needing little encouragement, a group of Ottawas, Hurons, Ojibwas, Illinois, Potawatomis, and some Miamis surrounded the fortified Fox town near Detroit, threatening to kill all of them unless they released their prisoners and returned to their lands west of Green Bay. Rather than embracing the Foxes as kin as Vaudreuil had hoped, Native allies violently expressed their intention to define the Foxes as enemies. Their attack represented an assertion of control over the alliance that the French were in no position to deny.[15]

Besieged and badly outnumbered, the Foxes desperately appealed for French mediation, hoping that Vaudreuil's more inclusive vision of the alliance would prevail. At a hastily arranged meeting late in 1712, the Fox war chief Pemoussa begged French military officers for mercy. Following a long-established protocol for cementing alliances, Pemoussa offered several slaves to signify his friendly intentions, defining himself as a kinsman, rather than an enemy, to the French and their allies. "Remember that we are your brothers," he said to the assembly of Native leaders. "In shedding our blood, it is your own you shed. I beg you, therefore, to calm the mind of our Father, whom we have unfortunately angered. These two slaves are to replace a little blood that we have perhaps shed." Pemoussa said all the right words: they were brothers, children of the same father, and the blood spilled between them had been insignificant. He also gave the right presents. In this dangerous world of symbolic diplomacy, no gift carried greater weight than a human body, and Pemoussa wisely offered slaves as his best hope to save his people.[16]

14. Vaudreuil à Dubuisson, Sept. 13, 1710, ANOM, Colonies, C11A, XXXI, 79v, and Vaudreuil à ministre, 1710, 81–88v.

15. The best summary of these raids is Edmunds and Peyser, *Fox Wars*, 64–71, which distills the French official correspondence on the issue.

16. P. F. X. de Charlevoix, *History and General Description of New France*, trans. John Gilmary Shea (New York, 1866–1872), V, 260.

Speaking for a group of French-allied nations, an Illinois warrior rejected Pemoussa's claim to kinship, promising to protect their French father from Fox duplicity. "Better than [the French governor] does, we know your evil heart, and do not intend to abandon him to your mercies. Return at once to your fort; we merely await that to renew the action." Pemoussa fully understood what it meant for the Illinois to reject his symbolic gift of slaves: the Foxes were not kin; they were enemies, and so could no longer expect to participate in the alliance. Defined as enemies, the best they could hope for was to be spared alive as slaves. Making one final appeal to kinship, this time depicting the Foxes as the most beloved elders in a young man's life, Pemoussa begged again: "Remember that you are our grand-nephews; it is your own blood you seem so eagerly to thirst for; would it not be more honorable to spare it, and more profitable to hold us as slaves?"[17]

He then offered six wampum belts, tied to resemble shackles, saying: "Here are six belts, that we give you, which bind us to you like your true slaves. Untie them, we beg you, to show that you give us life." But the belts would remain tied. Rejecting Pemoussa's offer of peace, the Foxes' enemies surrounded and attacked them. One French observer reported that, after Pemoussa was allowed a safe retreat, "all the Foxes were cut in pieces before they could regain their weapons. The women and children were made slaves, and most of them were sold to the French."[18]

No words could express as clearly as these actions the Foxes' outsider status in the eyes of their attackers. Had the Foxes been kin, had they been allies, had they shared a common identity as Algonquian children of the French governor, the aggressors would have accepted their gifts of slaves and wampum as appropriate payment for their crimes. Their customs would have demanded it. Instead, the attackers' refusal to receive Fox gifts signaled their intention to prevent a Fox-French alliance. When the French joined them in the slaughter and took their own share of the captives, they were merely being good allies, supporting their fictive kin against a reviled enemy. In this role, they continued to arm their allies and to send soldiers from New France against the Foxes. French officials wanted to pursue a policy of mediation with the Foxes, feeling they needed as many commercial and military allies as possible. But, just as they demanded that their

17. Ibid., 261, 263.
18. Dubuisson to governor [1712], *Wis. Hist. Coll.*, XVI (1902), 282, and Gaspard Chaussegros de Léry, "Account of the Seige of Detroit [1712]," 294–295 ("Renards" transcribed as "Foxes" here and below).

Native allies help them defeat their European enemies, Native allies demanded that the French side with them against their Fox enemies. They could not abide an ally who embraced and lavished gifts upon their enemies—a deadly serious breach of the obligations of the fictive kinship that bound them. Fox violence demanded a commensurate response—the killing of warriors and the capture of enemy villagers—that answered the demands of justice and restored balance to grieving families.[19]

But, as violence around Detroit dragged on, French officials wearied of the fighting and longed to return to their dream of creating a unified alliance in the Pays d'en Haut. Between 1713 and 1716, French policy wavered between grudging support for the war against the Foxes and efforts to secure a peaceful resolution. After three years of intermittent warfare, in 1716 French and Native forces defeated a large group of Foxes, grinding the violence to a bloody halt. The French used the occasion to try again to expand the limits of the alliance in opposition to their allies' interests. That fall, under heavy pressure from the French, the Foxes and their enemies gathered in the Saint Lawrence Valley to negotiate peace. Once again led by Pemoussa, the Foxes arrived at Quebec hopeful of restoring their standing as French allies. Pemoussa performed willingly, even eagerly, several public displays of friendship. He gave gifts to French officers, returned prisoners to allied nations, and allowed himself to be baptized "after having performed acts of faith," taking the name of Louis in honor of the French king. Pemoussa agreed to even the most exacting French terms, which demanded:

That they [the Foxes] shall make peace with all the nations dependent on the king with whom the French trade.

That they shall by forcible or friendly means bring the Kikapous and Mascoutins, their allies and our enemies, to make Peace, as they do, with all the nations in general.

---

19. Daniel K. Richter, "War and Culture: The Iroquois Experience," *William and Mary Quarterly*, 3d Ser., XL (1983), 528–559. William Newbigging argues persuasively that the Ottawas resented French efforts to mediate a peace between them and the Foxes after a series of clashes in 1708. "This was not the response the Ottawas wanted. They did not expect Vaudreuil to act as a mediator, but rather they wished to see him act in the Ottawa interest. The role of a mediator resolving disputes was totally alien to their culture and they could not understand such a relationship within the terms of the Great Lakes world. They expected Vaudreuil. . . . to pledge his support and then to act immediately to prove his good intentions. . . . Blinded by his fear of the English and the Iroquois, Vaudreuil could not see the problem from the Ottawa perspective. His only concern was to eliminate the danger of an open confrontation in the west." Newbigging, "History of the French-Ottawa Alliance," 311.

That they shall restore or cause to be restored all the prisoners, of every Nation, whom they hold, which they have done.

That they shall go to war in distant regions to get slaves, to replace all the dead who had been slain during the course of the war.

That they shall hunt to pay the Expenses of the military preparations made for this war.

Although dressed in new, more European language, this agreement essentially reiterated the offer Pemoussa made to the French and their allies four years earlier at Detroit. The Foxes would return prisoners and give symbolic gifts, including slaves captured "in distant regions," to their fictive kin, both Native and French. Through this process, they would "replace the dead" who had fallen, restoring the bonds of kinship severed by the war. Whether expressed in Native terms as "gifts" or in French terms as reparations, the goods and bodies required of the Foxes signified the common interest that underlay the diplomatic agreement. As they had done for half a century, Fox and French leaders articulated a vision of the western alliance that would include all the nations in general.[20]

Obviously pleased by this turn of events, New France's governor, Philippe de Rigaud de Vaudreuil, praised the agreement, which restored French hopes for an expansive (but not expensive) western alliance. Although this had been "a brief war," he predicted to his French superiors, "the peace that it created shall not be of a short duration." A year later, Vaudreuil reported, with more hope than knowledge, that "the Outaois Indians and other Nations of the upper country who are allies of the French, Have since last year been very peaceably disposed, [and] that their relations with each other have been amicable, and that they have the sentiments which they ought to have toward the Foxes."[21]

The Ottawas and other allied Indians, however, resented the French governor's attempt to dictate how they should feel about their enemies, particularly when he would not brook their flirtations with the English. After all, the French signed the Fox peace, according to one candid French ob-

---

20. Vaudrueil au Conseil de Marine, ANOM, Colonies, C11A XXXVI, 59–60v; baptism of Dec. 1, 1716, Sainte-Famille de Boucherville, FHL; Délibération du Conseil de Marine sur des lettres de Vaudreuil et Louvigny, Dec. 28, 1716, ANOM, Colonies, C11A, XXXVI, 280v, and Vaudreuil to the Council of the Marine, Oct. 14, 1716, 71–74v; *Wis. Hist. Coll.*, XVI (1902), 343 (block quote), 341–344.

21. Vaudreuil au Conseil de Marine, Oct. 30, 1716, ANOM, Colonies, C11A, XXXVI, 59–59v; *Wis. Hist. Coll.*, XVI (1902), 345 ("Savages" transcribed as "Indians" here and below).

server, "even though our allies were not inclined to it." The military commander who first proposed the armistice claimed to have the support of New France's Native allies, but one Frenchman admitted that "he deceived himself, if he really thought so." "We are even assured that they did not conceal their dissatisfaction." Asserting their prerogative to define the limits of the French-Native alliance, these groups rejected French efforts to force mediation. Over the following decade, they would slowly draw the French into renewed and far more destructive war with the Foxes, limiting the expansive reach of French imperialism through strategic violence.[22]

The 1716 treaty acknowledged the symbolic power of slaves to end French-Fox bloodshed. But, if slaves offered the greatest hope for peace, they could also spark renewed warfare. The French had received scores of Fox slaves during the previous four years, placing them in a difficult diplomatic position between their allies and the Foxes. By accepting these slaves, French colonists had symbolically acknowledged their enmity against the Foxes, implicitly committing military support to their allies in future disputes. Governor Vaudreuil understood that, if he did not act to reverse that message, the treaty would fail. "To make peace," he wrote, "it is necessary to begin by restoring to the Foxes all the slaves of their nation whom the French hold . . . it is [unnatural] to think that peace can be made with people whose children we are withholding."[23]

The Foxes agreed. Visiting Montreal two years later, a Fox delegation assured the French "that they Are disposed to maintain peace with all the nations Who are allied with us." But, along with assurances of friendship, the Foxes also begged the French to "dissipate the fear which still Possessed them, by restoring to them some of their Children—that is, some of their people who were Slaves among the French." For the Fox delegation, the French holding of Fox slaves was more than merely symbolic. These were their children, and on their visits to Montreal and Quebec they must have seen some of them held in French custody. Beginning in 1718, every recorded complaint made by the Foxes against the French and their Native allies centered on the return of Fox captives, the most significant issue perpetuating the Fox Wars into subsequent decades.[24]

22. Claude Charles, Bacqueville de La Potherie, *History,* in Blair, ed. and trans., *Indian Tribes,* I, 268 ("allies . . . not inclined to it"); Charlevoix, *History of New France,* trans. Shea, V, 306 ("deceived himself").

23. "Proceedings in French Council of Marine," Mar. 28, 1716, *Wis. Hist. Coll.,* XVI (1902), 340.

24. *Wis. Hist. Coll.,* XVI (1902), 377–379.

Despite clear instructions to the contrary, issued repeatedly from Versailles and Quebec, French colonists retained and continued to acquire new Fox slaves following the 1716 peace accords, supporting anti-Fox violence by proxy. Emanating from every level of Canadian society, the French demand for slaves offered ample opportunity for Ottawa, Ojibwa, and Illinois warriors to capture Fox villagers and offer them to the French, thereby driving a wedge between these erstwhile allies. Anti-Fox slave raids were not primarily driven by market demands. But the ready acceptance of Fox captives by French colonists allowed allied nations to define the limits of French diplomatic, territorial, and commercial expansion in the West. Over time, the French enslavement of Foxes would erode whatever hope for peace existed in 1716, sparking the second, and far more destructive, phase of the Fox Wars.

New France's appetite for Fox slaves originated with the bloody battles of 1712, when the French and their allies captured large numbers of Fox women and children. Just three years earlier, New France's intendant, Jacques Raudot, had declared official support for the Indian slave trade by guaranteeing the protection of Native slaves as property. Many French officers and merchants therefore returned from the Fox campaigns with young captives who could legally serve their households as slaves. Between 1713 and 1716, about eighty Fox slaves appear in the colony's parish and court records, belonging to as many as sixty different French families. The actual number of slaves and slaveholders was certainly much higher, given the improbability that every slave and every master appear in surviving records.[25]

These Fox slaves served families in Montreal and Quebec as well as in smaller seigneurial villages like Batiscan and La Prairie with strong connections to the West. Fox slaves initially entered the colony in one of two ways. Either French military officers returned with them as spoils of war, or merchants provisioning the army at Detroit or Michilimackinac brought slaves to the Saint Lawrence to trade or sell. In either case, neighbors, family, and friends seem to have acquired these slaves directly from men involved in the western campaigns. In 1714, for example, a Sulpician priest baptized a young Fox slave, named François-Michel, who belonged to Jean-Baptiste Bissot de Vinsenne. Vinsenne had fought at Detroit during the 1712 siege of the Foxes. During the final stages of the standoff, a Fox emissary addressed him: "I will surrender myself; answer me at once, my Father, and tell me

25. *RAB du PRDH*, records for "renard," "renarde," "renards," "outagami," and "outagamis," supplemented by Trudel, *Dictionnaire des esclaves*.

if there is quarter for our families. Answer me." Vinsenne responded with a promise that he knew he could not keep. According to the French report, "Sieur de Vincennes called out to them that he granted their lives and safety." When the Foxes surrendered and slaughter ensued, Vinsenne gave his own sort of quarter to this young boy, who became his slave in Montreal. Constant Marchand de Lignery, whose son was the boy's godfather, would lead a failed expedition against the Foxes the following year, in 1715, and a much more successful one in the late-1720s.[26]

In another example, Pierre Legardeur de Repentigny baptized his Fox slave, Mathurine, in 1713. Repentigny, a captain in the colonial troops, participated in several western campaigns, and his brother and cousin both commanded war parties against the Foxes. The potential to return home with slaves gave French military officers a personal stake in supporting violence against the Foxes, but lower-ranking soldiers also benefited by obtaining Fox slaves. In Batiscan, for example, Marie Catherine Rivard-Loranger appears either as the owner or godmother of several slaves, some of whom were Fox captives brought by her son, a voyageur among the Illinois who fought in the early battles of the Fox Wars.[27]

Occasionally, voyageurs and merchants connected to the war also acquired Fox slaves. The incentive for these men to enslave and sell Fox prisoners was high. At western posts, the colony's military leadership banned voyageurs from undertaking fur trade journeys during the height of the conflict, drafting all of them to fight the Foxes "without pay." Although many subverted the law and continued their fur trading, for those who could not escape military service the slave trade promised profits that could offset the loss of fur revenues. Because Fox prisoners were taken in large numbers during the campaign, voyageurs could contribute to the war effort and then sell Fox captives to make up the money they lost by skipping a trade season.[28]

26. Baptism of Feb. 2, 1714, *RAB du PRDH*, 44212. For Vinsenne at the Fox siege, see "Another Account of the Siege of Detroit [1712]," *Wis. Hist. Coll.*, XVI (1902), 294. For Lignery, see Edmunds and Peyser, *Fox Wars*, 79–81, 111–117.

27. Baptism of Sept. 21, 1713, *RAB du PRDH*, 44145, of Feb. 17, 1714, 7941, of Jan. 13, 1715, 7962; Registres Notre-Dame-de-Montréal, BANQ-M, film 111; Trudel, *Dictionnaire des esclaves*, 7.

28. For the ban on voyageurs' trade activities, including quote, see "Déclaration de Laporte de Louvigny dans le cadre de la guerre contre les Renards," Nov. 7, 1716, BANQ-M, TL4, S1, D2057. For two voyageurs imprisoned for desertion because they ignored the edict and continued trading, see "Procès contre Pierre Leboeuf, voyageur, Jean Verger dit Desjardins, voyageur, Jean Gauthier, engagé, habitant de Cap-Saint-Michel, et Pierre Mongeau,

Michel Bisaillon exemplifies this type of trader. With his loyalty to France in question because of his suspected ties to English merchants, Bisaillon hoped to clear his name through valiant service in the Fox Wars. He used his long-standing trade relationships with Illinois Indians to mobilize their support for French attacks during the first phase of the war. As a result, he obtained several Fox captives that he later sold as slaves to Montreal merchants. In 1717, for example, he sold a young female slave to René Bourassa dit La Ronde for four hundred livres.[29]

The brothers Louis and Jean-Baptiste Gastineau supplied wheat and other provisions to the western troops during the Fox Wars, returning to their homes near Trois-Rivières with two slaves, one of whom was baptized in 1714 as "Jean Baptiste, Indian of the Fox nation, belonging to Sieur Gatinau." Their commercial support for the Fox Wars rewarded them with slaves to add to their list of profitable commodities. Many other merchants active at Detroit also acquired slaves during the early Fox campaigns, including the well-positioned Pierre Lestage, who garnered at least two young Fox slaves, Ignace and Marie-Madeleine. The children's godfather, Ignace Gamelin, also traded Indian slaves in both Montreal and Detroit, acquiring one for his own household by early 1714. Pierre Biron, who supplied goods to the military during the Fox Wars, baptized a young Fox girl as his slave the same year. Called Marie-Joachim, she would serve as a house slave to Biron, then to his widow, and finally to their neighbor for nearly twenty years until her death in 1733.[30]

Presumably through their connections with merchants and military officers, many well-placed French officials also received their share of Fox slaves during the first four years of the conflict. François-Marie Bouat, an

---

engagé, habitant de Cap-Saint-Michel, accusés de désertion," July 17, 1716, BANQ-M, TL4, S1, D1840.

29. Francis Jennings, "Bisaillon, Michel," *DCB*, III; sale dated Nov. 28, 1717, Greffe Barrette (Montreal), BANQ-M.

30. For Jean-Baptiste, see baptism of Feb. 17, 1714, *RAB du PRDH*, 7942. For Gastineau's provisioning trade, see "Account of de Lignery for Expenses Incurred by Him," Feb. 17, 1720, *Wis. Hist. Coll.*, XVI (1902), 384. For Ignace and Marie-Madeleine, see baptisms of Sept. 21, 1713, Registres Notre-Dame-de-Montréal, BANQ-M, film 111. For Gamelin's slave trading, see Chapter 3. For his own slave, see baptism of Feb. 11, 1714, *RAB du PRDH*, 44219. For Biron's slaves, see baptism of May 19, 1714, and burial of Feb. 14, 1733, Notre-Dame-de-Montréal, FHL; "Procès entre Julien Trottier DesRivières, marchand, plaignant, et Marie-Joachim, panise, esclave de la veuve Biron, et Jean-Baptiste Gouriou dit Guignolet, soldat de Blainville, fils du sergent Jean-Baptiste Gouriou dit Guignolet, accusés respectivement de vol et de recel," Jul. 17, 1725, BANQ-M, TL4, S1, D3159.

influential Montreal judge, baptized his Fox slave, Marguerite, in 1713. The seigneur and well-known naval lieutenant Charles-Joseph Amiot de Vince-lotte also had a young Fox slave girl, baptized in 1714 as Marie-Madeleine-Charlotte. In 1713, François, a Fox boy, was baptized as the slave of Augustin Lemoyne, with highly visible and powerful godparents: Charles Lemoyne de Longueuil and Catherine de Ramezay, the daughter of Montreal's gover-nor and future interim governor of the colony. Even more visible was Guil-laume Gaillard, a member of New France's Superior Council and Governor Vaudreuil's close associate, who had purchased at least three Fox slaves by 1716 to serve in his home as domestics.[31]

With such a numerous, widespread, and visible collection of Fox slaves in the colony, Vaudreuil's statement about the importance of returning Fox captives becomes all the more understandable. Yet, because Indian slavery was guaranteed in Raudot's 1709 ordinance and served the interests of the colony's most powerful families, the governor's pledge to return Fox pris-oners proved untenable. Not only did the French retain most of the Fox prisoners-made-slaves, but they also continued to purchase Fox slaves over the next several years from their Indian allies in the Pays d'en Haut. Still, Vaudreuil had orders from Paris to make peace with the Foxes, so his official reports omit any mention of the steady stream of Fox slaves entering French households. When the Foxes came to Montreal in 1718 to demand the re-lease of these slaves, Vaudreuil's actions only made matters worse. Knowing what he did about his neighbors' slaves, his response to the delegation was nothing short of insulting. Responding to their request, Vaudreuil smugly noted, "As it was extremely important to dismiss the Foxes well satisfied, I believed . . . I ought to grant them twelve." Although the governor under-stood that this step left nearly all of the disputed Fox captives in French slavery, he also recognized the limits of his authority. He could not force colonists to give up their legally protected slave property. But, to the Foxes, the French retention of so many captives served only to deepen their dis-trust of the French and their allies.[32]

This growing wedge between the French and the Foxes weakened French claims on the Foxes as allies, subtly but steadily edging them out of the

31. Baptism of Sept. 21, 1713, *RAB du PRDH*, 44146 (Marguerite), of Oct., 1, 1714, 63624 (Marie-Madeleine-Charlotte), of June 3, 1713, 44087 (François), of Nov. 26, 1713, 63501 (Marie-Louise-Geneviève), of July 9, 1719, 64333 (Louise-Catherine-Angélique); Trudel, *Dictionnaire des esclaves*, 331.

32. Vaudreuil to Council, Oct. 30, 1718, *Wis. Hist. Coll.*, XVI (1902), 379.

alliance just as the other Native allies had hoped. To deepen the divide, allied Indians continued to attack Fox villages in violation of the 1716 peace agreement, trading or giving these slaves to French officers as tokens of alliance. The Illinois, especially, raided the Foxes for captives and sold them as slaves to their French allies. "In various encounters," Governor Vaudreuil admitted, "[the Illinois] had killed or taken prisoners many Fox Indians . . . notwithstanding the fact that on eight different occasions the Foxes had Sent back to them several slaves of their nation."[33]

Fox men, women, and children captured in these raids continued to stream into Montreal even after the French-brokered peace. In 1717, for example, Jean-Baptiste Poudret baptized a teenage male slave in Montreal, identified by the priest as an "Indian of the Fox nation." He likely obtained the slave from the military officer who acted as his slave's godfather, Joseph-Hippolyte Leber de Senneville, who had recently returned from the west. Many colonists buying these slaves either hid their purchases or identified their slaves as Panis, rather than Fox, Indians. For instance, when Joseph-Laurent Lefebvre bought a Fox slave in 1722, the notary initially recorded that she was a "Renard," or Fox Indian. In an apparent attempt to conceal the slave's origins, the notary then struck out "Renard" and replaced it with "panise." With diplomats demanding the return of Fox prisoners, a notarized acknowledgment of a Fox slave's origins could undermine the slave owner's claim to legal possession. Despite obvious French efforts to obscure the identity of Fox slaves, nearly one hundred more of them appear in New France's colonial records following the 1716 treaty. The distribution of these slaves, like those captured before the peace negotiations, suggests a pervasive acceptance of and demand for the enslavement of Fox Indians.[34]

These slaves performed many tasks, including domestic service, urban skilled labor, and some field work. During the 1710s, for example, the tiny village of Batiscan received a disproportionate number of Fox slaves, employing them in Michel Bégon's hemp-growing scheme. Although the experiment eventually failed, the area showed a strong, if brief, demand for Fox teenagers to cultivate this cash crop for export to the French navy. Other Fox slaves, like Jacob, who belonged to Julien Trottier Desrivières, worked on Montreal's riverfront loading and unloading canoes for western trade.

33. Vaudreuil to minister, Oct. 2, 1723, ibid., 428–429.
34. Baptism of Mar. 27, 1717, *RAB du PRDH*, 44776; sale of Oct. 7, 1722, Greffe Barrette (Montreal), BANQ-M.

Most were house servants. But even domestic slaves proved highly valuable, many of them selling for as much as four hundred livres: a third of a French officer's annual salary.[35]

Because Fox slaves were, according to Governor Beauharnois, "sold, traded, or given to the French by allied Indians," their presence in French colonial records provides a meter to gauge allies' activities unrecorded in the documentary record. For every captive appearing in French records, other captives lived undetected among the French, and still others remained with their Native captors. Combined with those who died during slave raids, those who suffered ritual killing, and those who died in transit, the number of anti-Fox raids and the number of Fox casualties must have been remarkably high. Given the unrelenting persistence of these raids and the string of broken promises by the French and their allies, the Foxes predictably grew weary of diplomacy.[36]

During the early 1720s, the Foxes four times requested French intervention to prevent the Illinois and other allied Indians from attacking their villages for captives. Finally, their patience grew thin, and they retaliated with great force. Vaudreuil conceded that "the Foxes were less in the wrong than the Illinois for the war they have had together . . . it is not Surprising that, after having been attacked four successive times without making any reprisals, [the Foxes] Should have been aroused the Fifth time they were attacked." Yet Vaudreuil deceptively suggested to his superiors that he was doing all in his power to prevent Illinois raids. The Foxes, he explained to the commandant of Illinois country,

> claim to have Grievances against the Illinois, because the latter detain their prisoners. I am convinced that, if they were to give satisfaction to the Foxes on this point, it would not be difficult to induce The latter to make peace. I employ every means to attain this end, by ordering all the Commandants of the posts to work Efficaciously for that object.

35. "Résumé d'une lettre et de mémoires de Bégon," Jan. 13, 1721, ANOM, Colonies, C11A, XLIII, 74–87; "Procès contre Lapalme, factionnaire, soldat de la compagnie Contrecoeur, accusé du meurtre de Jacob, panis, esclave de Julien Trottier, sieur DesRivières," June 13, 1728, BANQ-M, TL4, S1, D3433; Trudel, *Dictionnaire des esclaves*, 7. See, for example of slaves' value, Sale of Oct. 7, 1722, Greffe Barrette (Montreal), BANQ-M; "Vente d'une Sauvagesse nommée Angélique, de la nation des Renards," Oct. 5, 1733, Greffe Dubreuil, FHL; "Vente d'une Renarde de nation nommée Thérèse," Sept. 14, 1737, Greffe Boisseau, FHL; "Vente d'une femme âgée de 36 ans, Sauvagesse de nation renarde, esclave," Oct. 31, 1740, Greffe Pinguet de Vaucour, FHL.

36. Beauharnois et Hocquart à Maurepas, Oct. 4, 1733, ANOM, Colonies, C11A, LIX, 110v.

Although Vaudreuil owned at least two Fox slaves from these very attacks and saw many others serving his neighbors, he blamed the Illinois rather than the French colonists who made slave raiding so advantageous.[37]

By 1724, the Foxes made it clear to the French that they would resume open war with the Illinois and their French defenders unless Fox captives were returned. "They are indignant," wrote Constant Marchand de Lignery, "because, when peace was made in 1716, they sent the Illinois back their prisoners while the Illinois did not return theirs, as had been agreed upon in the treaty. Thus ... I consider that it is necessary, if we wish to secure this peace between them, to commence by accomplishing that." Despite his clear understanding of this problem, Lignery did not write as an innocent or impartial bystander. Many of his friends and family in Montreal owned Fox slaves, and at least one of these slaves was his godson.[38]

The Jesuit missionary Charles Mesaiger similarly recorded Fox demands that had gone unanswered by the Illinois and the French:

> The facts in question Are: Whether there Are any Fox Slaves among The ilinois; Whether it is True that, when the peace was made in 1716, the Fox Slaves Were not given up According to Agreement; Whether any slaves have been captured in the last war; Whether those who were made Slaves at either time Are still Alive, or are dead; finally, Whether the French have burned The Slaves whom the ilinois captured on the last occasion—for The Fox clamors loudly On These points.

For the Foxes, the origins—and the potential solution—to this conflict lay in the slave trade. After hearing this complaint so many times, Mesaiger concluded that there was "no prospect of securing peace . . . Unless you help [the Foxes] to get back those Slaves whom they miss so much."[39]

37. Vaudreuil to minister, Oct. 2, 1723, *Wis. Hist. Coll.*, XVI (1902), 430. Unaware of the many Fox slaves flowing into New France during this time, Edmunds and Peyser dismissed Vaudreuil's claim that Illinois captive raids stood at the root of the conflict. Instead, they offer the improbable explanation that Vaudreuil was venting his bitterness that the Illinois country was removed from his jurisdiction in 1717 (*Fox Wars*, 100–101). Vaudreuil to Boisbriant, Aug. 17, 1724, *Wis. Hist. Coll.*, XVI (1902), 442–443 (quote); baptism of Dec. 13, 1723, Notre-Dame-de-Québec, FHL; Trudel, *Dictionnaire des esclaves*, 407.

38. Lignery to Boisbriant, Aug. 23, 1724, *Wis. Hist. Coll.*, XVI (1902), 445; baptism of Sept. 21, 1713, *RAB du PRDH*, 44145.

39. Messager to commandant, Oct. 2, 1724, *Wis. Hist. Coll.*, XVI (1902), 447. "Des esclaves tant regrettée": Mesaiger à Du Tisné, Oct. 15, 1724, ANOM, Colonies, C11A, LVI, 268–269. *Wis. Hist. Coll.*, XVI (1902), 449, translates the phrase more literally, but I believe less accurately, as "slaves who are so much regretted."

To placate the Foxes and their allies, Vaudreuil proposed an inspection of Illinois villages to determine whether they held any Fox prisoners. Reporting the results of the inspection, conducted in 1725, a French officer flatly declared, "Our Illinois have no slaves belonging to the Foxes." An Illinois chief, Anakipita, offered a similarly calculated denial: "[The Fox chief] says that his Slaves have not been given back to him. Where are they? Is there a single one in our villages?" Anakipita and his French counterpart spoke a literal truth to conceal Illinois guilt in the Fox attacks. As Vaudreuil knew, the disputed Fox slaves were already in French hands, far from the Illinois communities that had initially seized them.[40]

Even at this late date, the Foxes still seemed willing to return to the French alliance if they could secure the return of their captives. They wanted to be considered as allies and kin rather than enemies of this powerful coalition. But, to accomplish that, French officers realized that it would require their own Indian allies, especially the Illinois and Ottawas, to reverse their policy and treat the Foxes as such. "No untoward consequences will result from this affair," French officers concluded regarding captive raids, "if the [Illinois] send back to the Foxes' village the captives they have taken, with presents to cover the dead, according to custom; and by that means they will disarm the Foxes and prevent the formation of other bands [of warriors]." Although their own attempts at establishing friendship had been rejected, the Foxes apparently stood ready to accept their enemies as kin to facilitate their relationship with the French.[41]

In 1726, the Foxes again approached the French, this time at Green Bay, begging for the governor to mediate in these disputes. French authorities, wishing to expand trade in the area, were only too happy to oblige. Again, the Foxes, Sauks, and their Winnebago allies gave presents to French post commanders and traders, asking them to "pity us, our children, and our

40. Du Tisné to Vaudreuil, Jan. 14, 1725, *Wis. Hist. Coll.*, XVI (1902), 451. Du Tisné actually received a report four days earlier that the Illinois had only one Fox slave, a young woman, who was held pending exchange. See Thaumur, Kereben, et Le Boullenger à Du Tisné, Jan. 10, 1725, ANOM, Colonies, C11A, LVI, 267–267v. In an unrelated memoir, Louisiana's governor, Jean-Baptiste Le Moyne de Bienville, remarked in 1725 that the Illinois "are actively getting their revenge" for earlier Fox attacks, supporting Vaudreuil's and others' conclusion about the culpability of the Illinois in the conflict. As Louisiana absorbed some Fox slaves as well, Bienville likewise wrote with firsthand knowledge. See his "Memoir on Louisiana [1725]," in Dunbar Rowland and Albert Godfrey Sanders, eds. and trans., *Mississippi Provincial Archives, 1704–1743: French Dominion*, III (Jackson, Miss., 1929), 533.

41. "Resumé of French relations with the Foxes [1727]," *Wis. Hist. Coll.*, XVII (1906), 4.

women" by supporting a "general peace" in the region. It was at this meeting that the Winnebago chief, Ouenigueri, gave French traders Marie-Marguerite "as a gift" to signify his good intentions, saying, "I give you my word for myself and my young people," that he would maintain peace despite being attacked by French allies. The French governor, hearing reports of this meeting, wrote exultantly to his superiors in France: "I think you have already learned with great satisfaction . . . of the peace effected with the Foxes. It gives me infinite pleasure, Monseigneur, to confirm the news." Following a decade of precedent, the Foxes and the French again sought mediation and peace to accomplish their shared goal of widening the alliance to allow French expansion into Fox country.[42]

But, by this time, hundreds of French colonists had given a decade of support to anti-Fox slave raids, rewarding their allies' violence with valuable goods and often with direct military support. Many French post commanders had private interests in the slave trade, placing them in a poor position to negotiate a peace that would end their access to Fox slaves. And both of New France's governors who dealt with the Fox problem—Philippe de Rigaud de Vaudreuil and Charles de Beauharnois—owned a host of Indian slaves, including several Foxes. Despite their clear imperial designs on expanding into Fox territory, despite their very practical need to avoid warfare among potential allies, French officials supported the Illinois, Ottawas, Ojibwas, and Hurons against the Foxes. Finally, for the Foxes, these insults proved too much to endure. French assurances of mediation and alliance therefore did nothing to pacify them, and their reprisals against the Illinois and Ottawas erupted into all-out war.

As a result, the peace arranged in 1726 did not last even a year. By the summer of 1727, previously reluctant French colonial officials determined to side with their allies against the Foxes, pressured by a host of traders and post commanders who had direct ties with the Fox slave trade. From the

---

42. For 1726 meeting, see Lignery à Deliette, June 15, 1726, ANOM, Colonies, C11A, XLVIII, 415–418v. For Ouenigueri, see "Procès opposant Marc-Antoine Huard de Dormicourt, à Marguerite Duplessis Radisson, se disant la fille naturelle de feu sieur Duplessis Faber (Lefebvre), frère du sieur Duplessis Faber, résidant à Montréal, capitaine d'une compagnie dans les troupes de la Marine, qui conteste le fait qu'elle soit une esclave, et plus particulièrement celle du sieur Dormicourt," Oct. 1, 1740, BANQ-Q, TL5, D1230. This is a suit brought by the slave, Marie-Marguerite, in which her original master testifies of his presence at the 1726 meeting where he received her as a gift. For Marie-Marguerite's life, see Chapter 6. For the governor's quote, see Beauharnois to minister, Oct. 1, 1726, *Wis. Hist. Coll.*, III (1857; 1904), 159.

Illinois country, Pierre Deliette wrote adamantly that the French should exclude the Foxes from the alliance and support French allies against them. Deliette, like many of his counterparts in the West, was responding partly to pressure from his Native allies, who still resented French efforts at rapprochement with the Foxes. But Deliette also had a personal interest in maintaining the Fox slave trade. He, along with several family members and neighbors in Montreal, owned Fox and other Indian slaves, who served alongside nearly a hundred other Fox slaves in the area.[43]

Faced with these continuing raids in violation of French assurances and never receiving the promised return of their captives, Fox warriors finally abandoned their efforts to secure French alliance, declaring open war on New France and all its Indian allies. In the spring of 1727 they murdered a party of seven French soldiers, launching a series of attacks that was all too powerfully met by French retaliation. These new raids bred deep and mutual resentment among the French, their allies, and the Foxes, finally putting an end to French-Fox efforts to expand the western alliance. The warfare that followed brutalized the Foxes, as French soldiers and allied Indian warriors took concerted aim at their settlements west of Lake Michigan. Persuaded by western post commanders to pursue the war wholeheartedly, French authorities invested soldiers and money to crush a people they had once called children. For the next four years, French-Indian war parties descended on Fox villages with stunning force. In 1728 a combined French-Native war party of more than fourteen hundred traveled into Fox territory. Finding the villages empty because the Foxes had been warned of the attack, the army torched all of the homes and crops to force a Fox surrender. When Beauharnois considered extending mercy in 1729, allied Indians pressed their agenda, attacking Fox settlements, killing hundreds, and taking an unknown number of slaves, who were divided among their villages and sold to the French. By summer 1730 the Foxes had been thoroughly routed, and several hundred refugees wandered through dangerous territory in search of shelter. Rejected by the Sioux to the west, they hunkered down in a makeshift fort where they were soon surrounded by another massive French-Indian force, which starved them into submission.

43. Deliette both advocated French attacks on the Foxes and led many of these attacks himself, accompanied by Illinois warriors. In 1727 and 1728, Deliette attacked a Fox-Sauk encampment near the southern tip of Lake Michigan, prompting a new round of reprisals. See Edmunds and Peyser, *Fox Wars*, 108–111. For Deliette's actions, see Beauharnois au ministre, Oct. 1, 1726, ANOM, Colonies, C11A, XLVIII, 181–182, and Lignery à Liette [Deliette], 410–412v.

Rather than granting them quarter, the standoff ended in a bloodbath with at least four hundred Foxes killed and another four hundred "made Slaves and scattered among all the Nations," including a large number who ended up in French households.[44]

Many of the enslaved Foxes who survived this disaster were young children, like five-year-old Pierre-Denis, bought by Denis Duplessis and presented for baptism in Quebec just three months after the bloodletting ended in the West. Two weeks later Louis Parent brought another five-year-old Fox slave to be baptized in the same parish. The same year, the western military officer Paul Marin baptized his seven-year-old slave girl when she was about to die from an unnamed sickness. Named Marie, the record initially identified her as a "pany," probably reflecting Marin's description of her status as a slave. The priest later struck this out and replaced it with "Renard," or Fox, when he learned more about the enslaved girl's identity. These three children were joined by many others, including Joseph Frontis, Amable, Pierre, Charles, and Marie-Françoise: all between five and seven years old and all victims of the Fox slaving spree of 1728–1731. Appearing disproportionately in baptismal records, it is unclear whether children predominated in overall slave populations during these years or were just more likely to be baptized than older slaves.[45]

Enslaved Fox adults faced more unpredictable fates and appeared only sporadically in surviving records. The experience of Coulipa, an enslaved Fox war chief, suggests a path mostly followed by adult men. In 1730 Coulipa was brought to Quebec and given to French colonial officials "on behalf of the Miami nation," which had taken him in the recent campaigns. He was apparently a warrior of some renown and an important architect of the Foxes' anti-French alliances. Unlike Fox children, Coulipa was feared as a potential hazard to colonial safety, so he was shipped to France, where he was to work as a slave or be sent to the galleys. Shortly after leaving Quebec, the ship carrying Coulipa sank, although he and most of the ship's goods

44. Conseil de marine à Perriers, July 22, 1737, ANOM, B, L, 543; Beauharnois et Depuy au ministre, Oct. 25, 1727, ANOM, Colonies, C11A, XLIX, 48–49v, and Beauharnois à Liette, Aug. 20, 1737, 120–121; Peyser, "Fate of the Fox Suvivors," *Wisconsin Magazine of History*, LXXIII (1989–1990), 87–93.

45. Baptism of Dec. 28, 1730, Quebec, *RAB du PRDH*, 159089, of Jan. 11, 1731, 159097, of Apr. 15, 1732, Montreal, 145532; of Apr. 12, 1732, 185104 (Joseph Frontis, age seven), of June 22, 1732, 104208 (Amable, age five), of Oct. 17, 1732, 145656 (Pierre, age six), of Feb. 15, 1733 (Charles, age seven), of Apr. 6, 1733, 159718 (Marie Françoise, age six); of Apr. 15, 1732, Notre-Dame-de-Montréal, FHL.

were saved. Sent to France in 1731, the Fox chief worked as a slave in the naval town of Rochefort until his death there in 1732. Just three weeks after Coulipa's demise, another enslaved Indian, named Baptiste, entered the hospital in Rochefort, where he would die several weeks later. The latter was likely a different Fox chief, sent by New France's governor Charles de Beauharnois "to serve as a domestic to his brother, intendant of Rochefort."[46]

For a time slaves like Coulipa and the Fox children signaled French victory in the Fox Wars, prompting celebrations throughout the colony. But the 1730 triumph proved ephemeral and was soon followed by a Fox resurgence. Frustrated and facing pressure from his superiors, Governor Beauharnois issued an order for his soldiers and his allies to "kill [the Foxes] without thinking of making a single prisoner, so as not to leave one of the race alive in the upper Country." Beauharnois, however, hoped to maintain the supply of slaves that had been one of the Fox Wars' greatest benefits to his colony (and to his own household—he owned at least eight Fox slaves himself). "If [the Sieur de Villiers] is obliged to exterminate the men," he added, "the women and children who remain will be brought here, Especially the children." If they could not finesse a Fox alliance, the French could at least achieve two objectives that had proved dangerously incompatible over the past two decades: expanding into Fox territory and maintaining access to Fox slaves.[47]

Although the governor's enmity against the Foxes pleased allied Indians, this order went too far for their comfort. The French had insisted for more than twenty years that the Foxes were their allies and kin. Such a fierce and total reversal made some Native allies question their own status with the French, wondering whether "their turn may come" for such a betrayal. And,

46. Hocquart au ministre, Nov. 14, 1730, ANOM, Colonies, C11A, LIII, 207–208v. See Beauharnois et Hocquart au ministre, Jan. 15, 1731, ANOM, Colonies, C11A, LIV, 3–9v; "Registre Mortuaire," Archives de la Marine, Rochefort, France, Sept. 26, 1732 (Coulipa, spelled "Goulipare") and Oct. 22, 1732 (Baptiste). On Beauharnois's sending a slave to his brother, see Claude Le Beau, *Aventure du Sr. C. Lebeau, avocat en parlement ou voyage curieux et nouveau parmi les sauvages de l'Amérique Septentrionale . . .* (Amsterdam, 1738), II, 172–173, quoted in Havard, below. The records are vague and sometimes contradictory about which of these two men was Coulipa and whether it was Coulipa or another Fox chief sent by Beauharnois to his brother. Gilles Havard concludes that Beauharnois would not have sent a dangerous and feared warrior to serve his brother, which suggests that Le Beau was referring to the chief who became known as Baptiste after his baptism. See Gilles Havard, "Coulipa: le destin tragique d'un Indien renard," in Mickaël Augeron, ed., *Rochefort, La Rochelle: les Amériques en partage, XVIIe–XIXe siècle* (Paris, forthcoming). The author thanks Professor Havard for sharing this essay before publication.

47. Beauharnois to minister, July 1, 1733, *Wis. Hist. Coll.*, XVII (1906), 182–183. For Beauharnois's Fox slaves, see Trudel, *Dictionnaire des esclaves*, 276–277.

Guerrier Renard. Redouté Par Toutte Les Nations, Par Leur Valleur Et Vitesse, Faisant 25 a 30 Lieües

Par Jour Sans Autre Prouision Que Les Herbes Et les Feüilles Des Bois

jla Sont Enuiron 4 a 500 Homme Portant Les Armes.

Diuisés En 3 ou 4 Village, De Puis quilz ont La Gurre Auec Les François

Presque Touttes Les Nations Prennent La Maniere De Se Faire Les Cheueux A La

Renarde

Quand jl ont Vne Chemise, jl La Mette En Braguet. Quand jl Faut quil Se Batte

FIGURE 15. Coulipa, Enslaved Fox Indian Warrior. *1731. FR BNF 40492830.*
Courtesy Bibliothèque Nationale de France, Paris

even if these peoples wanted to exclude and weaken the Foxes, theirs was not a culture of total war. As a result, they participated in anti-Fox violence on their own terms, severely reducing, but never eliminating, the Fox population.[48]

Jesuit historian Pierre-François-Xavier de Charlevoix was firsthand witness to the devastation:

> A new enemy [has arisen], as brave as [the Iroquois], less politic, much fiercer, whom we have never been able to subdue or tame, and who, like those insects that seem to have as many lives as parts of their body, spring to life again, so to say, after their defeat, and, reduced almost to a handful of brigands, appear everywhere, have aroused the hatred of all the peoples on this continent, and for the last twenty-five years and more, interrupt commerce, and render the roads almost impracticable for more than five hundred leagues around. These are the Outagamis, commonly called the Foxes.[49]

This bloody contest exacted a costly toll from the Foxes, who dwindled from a population of several thousand in the 1710s to only a few hundred by the mid-1730s. But, as Charlevoix observed, this victory came at a high price for the French. Not only did thousands of men, women, and children die in the conflict, but the Foxes' retaliation limited French commercial and imperial expansion, blocking their westward reach just as their allies had hoped to do.[50]

From this conflict, hundreds of slaves entered New France as tokens of alliance between that colony and its Native allies. Although previously ignored, these slaves permeated—and powerfully influenced—the history

---

48. Beauharnois to minister, Oct. 17, 1736, *Wis. Hist. Coll.*, XVII (1906), 256; Edmunds and Peyser, *Fox Wars*, 170–201.

49. Charlevoix, *History of New France*, trans. Shea, V, 256–257. I have substituted "peoples" for the translator's "nations," since in the French original Charlevoix wrote "tous les Peuples de ce Continent" rather than "toutes les nations de ce continent." For original, see Pierre François de Charlevoix, *Histoire et description générale de la Nouvelle France* (Paris, 1744), IV, 94.

50. Résumés de lettres concernant les Renards, 1733, ANOM, Colonies, C11A, LX, 448–463. Edmunds and Peyser count the Fox population as 140 in 1732, in *Fox Wars*, 221. This figure does not account for the large number of Fox slaves in Indian and French settlements. For the effects of the Fox Wars on French-Indian alliances, see Richard White, *The Middle Ground: Indians, Empires, and Republics in the Great Lakes Region, 1650–1815* (Cambridge, 1991), 149–175. Like Edmunds and Peyser, however, White ignores the significance of Fox demands that the Illinois return their captives.

of the Fox Wars. When Foxes wanted to forge an alliance with their attackers in 1712, they offered slaves. They did the same when they made peace in 1716, promising to capture still more in distant lands to fulfill their diplomatic obligations. When Fox diplomats pressured the French for greater support, it was invariably to recover those of their nation captured by enemies: they missed their children. Perhaps most significantly, when Native allies perceived French desire to embrace the hated Foxes, they used slave raids to register their dissatisfaction with the French, defining the limits of alliance through strategic violence.

This violence allowed New France's Indian allies to exert their control over the alliance system, blocking French expansion whenever it threatened to strengthen their enemies. If the Fox Wars provided, as one historian has written, a "primer for alliance politics," then this was their most important lesson. When French officials sought, repeatedly and forcefully, to define the Foxes into the alliance, their allies fought what they perceived to be a betrayal of their friendship. By raiding the Foxes for slaves and then placing these slaves into French hands, Illinois, Ottawa, Ojibwa, and Huron warriors alienated their Fox enemies from their French allies, drawing the two sides into war. Anti-Fox violence both supported the alliance and restricted French ambitions for its expansion. New France's Indian allies would repeat this pattern up and down the Mississippi Valley during the first half of the eighteenth century, blocking French efforts to expand westward among the Plains Apaches in the 1720s and the Sioux in the 1730s and 1740s. The Fox Wars thus established a powerful precedent for Indians' use of intervillage violence to limit and direct France's commercial and territorial ambitions in North America.[51]

CARRYING AID TO THEIR ENEMIES

"They had a request to make to me . . . which is to prevent . . . Frenchmen from going any more to the Sioux . . . as they were carrying aid to their enemies."
—Antoine de Lamothe Cadillac, Detroit, 1703

Among the diplomatic functions of indigenous slavery in the Pays d'en Haut, perhaps the most important was the way that giving slaves to allies reinforced shared antagonism toward the slaves' people. The region's core rituals of diplomacy—greeting, feasting, and calumet ceremonies—all culminated in the giving of slaves. To accept a slave from an ally created in-

51. Ibid., 149.

centives for peaceful trade among friends but barred such activities with the slave's people. As the French learned in the Fox Wars, the symbolism of slavery and its attending commitments were deadly serious matters for their allies, and they ignored them at their peril. Indians, on the other hand, found that French demand for slaves could serve a comparable function, if for very different reasons. Giving slaves to the French, particularly when those slaves would not be returned to their Fox families, allowed Indians to limit French choices in the alliance even when colonial leaders wanted to open the alliance to the Foxes.

A similar pattern emerged as French traders tried to expand among the Sioux, whose northern location and large population made them the target of intense French interest as early as the 1660s. Like many people at the western edge of the Pays d'en Haut, the Sioux encountered French goods before they met the French. Seeing the utility of metal tools and the power of French firearms (to which they attributed a mystical power they called "wakan," similar to Algonquians' manitou), they sought French friendship by making an alliance in the 1660s with an Ojibwa group the French called Saulteurs, people of the rapids. The Sioux encountered immediate resistance from France's allies, however, and conflict soon erupted over access to French trade. Boasting a population of more than thirty thousand, with a territory open to the west, on their eastern borders the Sioux were flanked by a crescent of antagonistic peoples—Cree, Assiniboine, Ottawa, Fox, and Illinois—each of whom had a stake in excluding them from the French alliance. These conflicts ensured that the dominant theme of early French engagements with the Sioux was the need to establish peace between French allies and potential Sioux partners. As the Jesuit Claude Allouez summarized, "They are warlike, and have conducted hostilities against all their neighbors, by whom they are held in extreme fear."[52]

This fear magnified the Sioux in the minds of their enemies, whose

52. Claude Allouez, "Father Allouez's Journey to Lake Superior, 1665–1667," in Louise Phelps Kellogg, ed., *Early Narratives of the Northwest, 1634–1699* (New York, 1917), 132. For the best overview of the Sioux at the time of French contact, see Raymond J. DeMallie, "The Sioux at the Time of European Contact: An Ethnohistorical Problem," in Sergei A. Kan and Pauline Turner Strong, eds., *New Perspectives on Native North America: Cultures, Histories, and Representations* (Lincoln, Nebr., 2006), 239–260; Gary Clayton Anderson, *Kinsmen of Another Kind: Dakota-White Relations in the Upper Mississippi Valley, 1650–1862* (Lincoln, Nebr., 1984), 29–57; Colin G. Calloway, *One Vast Winter Count: The Native American West before Lewis and Clark* (Lincoln, Nebr., 2003), 240–243. For Sioux perceptions of French goods, see Bruce M. White, "Encounters with Spirits: Ojibwa and Dakota Theories about the French and Their Merchandise," *Ethnohistory*, XLI (1994), 369–405.

descriptions distorted early French perceptions of Sioux society. Louis Nicolas's sketch of a Sioux chief, the earliest surviving image of a Sioux individual, describes him as "King of the Great Nation of the Sioux. . . . He Reigns in a vast Country beyond Michilimackinac." Some felt that the Sioux were "too far off for [us] ever to obtain any service from them." But others traveled west to learn more. The first record of French encounter in Sioux country was written by Pierre-Esprit Radisson, who traveled west of Lake Superior in 1659–1660 to Sioux villages around Mille Lacs Lake. Radisson and his companions received a generous welcome that included a calumet ceremony. The Sioux "made us smoake in their pipes after they kindled them," Radisson wrote. "It was not in common pipes, but in pipes of peace and of the warrs, that they pull out but very seldom, when there is occasion for heaven and earth." Although the ceremonies began well, when Radisson ignited some gunpowder to impress them, the Sioux abandoned the conference "believing . . . that we weare the Devils of the earth." After a week of failed efforts to convince them otherwise, Radisson and his party left the village with nothing resolved. When he returned to the Saint Lawrence bearing western furs and intelligence on western nations, Radisson was arrested and fined for unauthorized trade. Incensed at this treatment, he defected to the English colonies, sailed for London, and returned to North America as an agent of the Hudson's Bay Company, using his knowledge of the distant West to aid English rather than French expansion.[53]

The archaeological record suggests that small-scale trade brought some French goods into Sioux households, but it was almost twenty years until another serious attempt to formalize a Sioux alliance occurred. From 1678

---

53. Antoine Laumet de Lamothe Cadillac, "Report of Detroit in 1703," Aug. 31, 1703, Michigan Pioneer and Historical Society, *Historical Collections*, XXXIII (1904), 177; Pierre Esprit Radisson, *Voyages of Peter Esprit Radisson*, ed. Gideon D. Scull (1885; rpt., New York, 1967), 207–209 (quotes on 207 and 209, respectively); Grace Lee Nute, "Radisson, Pierre-Esprit," *DCB*, II.

"Roy de la Grande Nation des Nadouessiouek . . . Il Regne dans un grand Pais au dessu de la Mesilimakina": [Louis Nicolas], "Les raretes des Indes," ca. 1670–1700, MS, Gilcrease Museum, Tulsa, Okla. Nicolas placed Sioux country "above" Michilimackinac, by which he seems to have meant farther into the Pays d'en Haut. If the description postdated Hennepin's account in 1683, he might have written "above" to suggest north, reflecting Hennepin's distortion of the Upper Mississippi discussed in Chapter 1. Nicolas's manuscript developed over two or three decades, with most of the sketches predating their captions by many years, so it is impossible to give an exact date for the Sioux portrait. Certainly from the seventeenth century, its placement in the manuscript and description of an unknown Sioux territory suggest the 1670s. See Germaine Warkentin, "Aristotle in New France: Louis Nicolas and the Making of the *Codex Canadensis*," *French Colonial History*, XI (2010), 71–107.

through 1680, Daniel Graysolon Dulhut made a series of journeys to Sioux country, hoping "to cause them to make peace with all the nations around Lake Superior who dwell in the dominion of our invincible monarch." Predictably, Dulhut found his king considerably less invincible in Sioux country. In an inversion of the 1742 Sioux experience in Montreal, Dulhut learned during his 1680 visit that Louis Hennepin and his servants had "been seized and taken away as slaves for more than three hundred leagues" to another group of Sioux villages. Because the Sioux were eager to establish a French alliance, they eventually agreed to release their French slaves, treating their new French guests to the rituals of alliance, including two separate calumet ceremonies. Angry at the treatment that Hennepin and his companions had received, Dulhut rejected the calumets and made preparations to leave, "letting them know of the just indignation I had against them, rather than remain after the violence they had done to the said Reverend Father and the two Frenchmen who were with him." To escape the tense atmosphere, and to make a statement that they would not abide their people's becoming slaves, Dulhut, Hennepin, and the captives made a hasty retreat in the early spring of 1681, dragging their canoes over the still-frozen river.[54]

Despite these tensions, Dulhut's journeys and Hennepin's published account of this vast, unexplored territory made Sioux country a popular destination for French traders looking to escape the regulation and competition of trade at official posts. During the early 1680s a large number of coureurs de bois were reputedly exploiting the Sioux's newfound interest in French goods. During the last two decades of the seventeenth century, French traders engaged informally but frequently with the Sioux, a practice that, like contemporary overtures to the Foxes, angered their Illinois, Ottawa, and Cree allies. Embedded within these communities and linked by ties of fictive and often marital kinship, French traders ended up on opposite sides of a series of conflicts because they "take the side of one nation against another"—from the perspective of French officials an unacceptable division of their people. From the Sioux perspective, though, French divisions were a boon that gave them access to the goods, particularly metal tools and firearms, that they wanted.[55]

54. Daniel Greysolon Dulhut, "Memoir of Duluth on the Sioux Country, 1678–1682," in Kellogg, ed., *Early Narratives of the Northwest*, 332–333.

55. "Prénent le party d'une nation contre une autre": Champigny to the minister, Oct. 13, 1697, ANOM, Colonies, C11A, XV, 130, and Duchesneau to the minister, Nov. 13, 1681, V, 296–296v.

FIGURE 16. King of the Great Sioux Nation. *Louis Nicolas, "Codex canadiensis."*
MS, late-seventeenth century. Permission Gilcrease Museum, Tulsa, Ok.

One of the illegal traders insinuating himself into Sioux society in the early 1680s was Pierre Le Sueur. As a servant of the Jesuits he learned dialects of Anishinaabe and Siouan languages, and like many before him he deserted the restrictions of Jesuit service for the rewards of Indian trade. He spent most of the 1680s and 1690s living among and trading with the Sioux, and by the 1690s his diplomatic activities made him their greatest advocate. In 1695 he brought a group of Sioux diplomats to Montreal, the first of their people to have made that journey. Three years later he went to France to recruit support for Sioux trade, forming a Compagnie des Sioux with investors interested in developing Mississippi Valley trade. In the run-up to the Great Peace in 1701, Le Sueur argued for Sioux participation, but, when other French allies threatened to withdraw, the Sioux were excluded from the conference. There seems to have been a fairly reliable cease-fire in preparation for the peace conference, but, when Le Sueur ordered trade goods for Sioux country, his request for guns was vetoed by colonial authorities so as to avoid shattering the temporary peace the peoples enjoyed.[56]

The cease-fire did not last long, and by 1703 allied Indians had persuaded colonial authorities to forbid trade in Sioux country altogether. Despite these prohibitions, Native allies continued to complain that French traders were continually "carrying aid to their enemies." As commandant of Detroit, Antoine Laumet de Cadillac was flooded with complaints from allied nations, which he summarized in 1703:

> As avarice and the desire to trade for beaverskins urged the French to go to the Sioux in search of them, our allies complained strongly of it, and pointed out to me that it was unjust that at the very time when they had arms in their hands in our own quarrel against the Iroquois, the French were going to the Sioux taking munitions of war to have them killed. And they begged me to set that right, the more because the French passed over their lands and in front of their villages, which was violating the people's rights.[57]

As with the Fox Wars, slavery became a central point of contention and a meaningful diplomatic motif in Sioux efforts to befriend the French over the consistent objections of French allies. The 1706 Ottawa raids on Sioux

---

56. A. P. Nasatir, "Le Sueur, Pierre," *DCB*, II; Havard, *Great Peace of Montreal of 1701*, trans. Aronoff and Scott, 123.

57. Cadillac, "Report of Detroit in 1703," in Michigan Pioneer and Historical Society, *Historical Collections*, XXXIII (1904), 174–175.

villages for slaves to appease the Iroquois in fact served a double purpose: satisfying the terms of the French-orchestrated peace and striking back at the Sioux for their encroachment on the alliance the peace secured. The series of slave raids between 1706 and 1708, combined with depressed prices for beaver pelts, temporarily diminished Sioux interest in French alliance, but both French and Sioux individuals continued to build on the relationships that had sustained support for the alliance over the past generation.

Passing through Fox territory to reach the Upper Mississippi Valley became nearly impossible during the Fox Wars, limiting French access to Sioux trade during the 1710s and early 1720s. But Sioux motivation for French alliance continued to mount. In addition to their desire for French manufactured goods, they also faced relentless pressure from their well-armed Cree, Assiniboine, Fox, and Illinois antagonists. A century later, Sioux winter counts and the stories that interpreted them still recalled these years as devastating ones for the eastern Sioux, filled with slave raids, disease epidemics, and seasonal hunger. The short descriptions given for many of these years convey at least part of the reason the Sioux persisted in courting the French. "The war parties met, or killed three on each side winter" (1711). "Came and attacked on horseback and stabbed a boy near the lodge winter" (1716). "Used them up with belly ache winter" (1735). "Attacked them while gathering turnips winter" (1742).[58]

Despite this instability, some French traders continued to trade with the Sioux, ignoring pressure from French authorities who intervened on behalf of their Cree and Assiniboine allies because they feared losing these northern peoples to British trade on Hudson Bay. The ideal solution from the imperial perspective would have been to trade equally with all Indians. As they articulated in the Fox case, French colonists dreamed of a world where they oversaw an alliance of Sioux, Cree, and Assiniboine villages, all cooperating in trade and fighting the British. But some of their policies created perverse incentives for French traders, who profited more from having fewer competitors in the West. Native traders might have recognized this as well, seeing that expanded French trade generally meant that goods spread more thinly rather than proliferated. During the 1720s and 1730s, trade licenses often allowed a degree of flexibility, authorizing trade among the

58. Battiste Good, Winter Count, in Candace S. Greene and Russell Thornton, eds., *The Year the Stars Fell: Lakota Winter Counts at the Smithsonian* (Washington, D.C., 2007), 74, 75, 77, 79–82; Smithsonian Institution, NAA Ms. 2372, http://wintercounts.si.edu/html_version/html/thewintercounts.html.

FIGURE 17. Sioux Winter Counts. *Detail. Battiste Good. National Anthropological Archives, Smithsonian Institution, MS 2372, inv. 08746806, 08746807. Smithsonian Institution, Washington, D.C.*

Sioux if there was peace, or among their neighbors if there was not. This flexibility removed merchants' stake in a particular outcome in Native diplomacy, allowing them to act more like the illegal traders who obviously had no specified trade partners.[59]

Hopeful that a lull in the Fox Wars would restore safe passage to Sioux territory, colonists formed a new Sioux Company in 1726. In exchange for exclusive license to Sioux furs, the investors agreed to build a fort and a chapel as well as housing for a post commander and Jesuit missionaries, which they did the next year. Had the Fox peace held, enthusiasm for Sioux trade would have certainly drawn large numbers of traders, who began to apply for licenses almost immediately. Only a few months later, Fox violence flared again, destabilizing the Sioux post and preventing investment in western trade. Fearing both violence and theft, by 1728 most of the Sioux Company's directors and investors had "renounced [the Sioux post] and no longer Wish to send there. The rupture that we have had with the Foxes, through whose country one must pass to go by Canoe to the Sioux, have Induced them to think of it no longer." Yet officials continued to support Sioux trade, "in order to Maintain the sioux in these happy dispositions, to keep the Foxes in check, and to frustrate the steps that they might take to win the hearts of the Sioux, who will always reject their proposals so long as they see the French among them." In 1731, when the Fox threat again subsided, Gov-

59. Vaudreuil and Bégon to minister, Mar. 12, 1720, ANOM, Colonies, C11A, XLI, 183v.–184v. See trade licenses at Montreal: "Permission," June 26, 1729, BANQ-M, TL4, S34, P278, and "Permission," July 12, 1735, P429.

ernor Beauharnois again pressed the case for expansion into Sioux country. "Tranquility, for so many years disturbed in the upper country, will now reign, and Enable us to continue our Establishments there," he wrote after the Fox surrender. "I thought first of all of that amongst the Sioux . . . and I sent back a party there this year." Reestablishing the post in 1732, the Sioux expressed "great satisfaction at receiving the French there."[60]

Pursuing the French dream of a regionwide alliance, however, again invited strategic slave raiding by France's disgruntled allies and constrained French efforts to expand westward. In 1731 Beauharnois also sent Pierre Gaultier de Varennes de La Vérendrye to the West in search of the Western Sea, a presumed water passage to the Pacific. La Vérendrye's enterprise depended upon the friendship of the Crees, Assiniboines, and Monsonis, who had spent the previous half century trying to keep the French and Sioux apart. But La Vérendrye had been charged with keeping the peace among all the peoples around Lake Superior and the Upper Mississippi. Balancing the interests of the Crees and Assiniboines on the one hand and the Sioux on the other proved difficult, but La Vérendrye enjoyed relative success for the first three years. In 1734, however, he made a series of decisions related to Indian slavery that would destroy Sioux trust in the French and ultimately lead them into an alliance with the resurgent Foxes, creating dangerous instability in the region during the late-1730s and early 1740s.[61]

Indian slavery had long been a part of La Vérendrye's experience in New France. Several of his family members held Indian slaves before his departure from Montreal, and at least one of his business partners, Ignace Gamelin, figured prominently in the Indian slave trade during the 1720s. Within months of his arrival in the West, La Vérendrye's nephew had purchased three Mandan slaves and taken them to Montreal for sale, and La Vérendrye himself had received at least two slaves from western Indians as gifts. Still, La Vérendrye did not travel west intending to obtain Sioux slaves. In his early negotiations he consistently discouraged anti-Sioux raids to protect French traders established among them. In 1732, Governor Beauharnois reported approvingly of La Vérendrye's diplomatic efforts: "He stopped several war

---

60. Beauharnois and Hocquart to the minister, Oct. 25, 1729, *Wis. Hist. Coll.*, XVII (1906), 78 ("happy dispositions"), 79 ("renounced it"), Beauharnois to minister, Oct. 1, 1731, 140 ("Tranquility"); Michigan Pioneer and Historical Society, *Historical Collections*, XXXIV (1905), 97 ("great satisfaction"). For Fox-Sioux relations in 1727–1728, see Edmunds and Peyser, *Fox Wars*, 90.

61. W. J. Eccles, "La Mer de l'Ouest: Outpost of Empire," in Eccles, *Essays on New France* (Oxford, 2007), 96–109.

parties, and prevented the Monsoni from going to attack the Sioux living at a distance on the prairies." The next year, La Vérendrye offered gifts to the Crees, Assiniboines, and the Sioux as symbols of peace, forbidding all of them to go to war. "I told the Savages," La Vérendrye wrote to the governor, "that I was barring the road to the Sioux among whom the French are; and I sent to the Sioux a collar and a pipe of peace on behalf of our savages." As they had since the early eighteenth century, however, the Cree and their allies resented La Vérendrye's overtures to their enemies. Telling La Vérendrye that their "hearts are bitter against the Sioux" for a recent attack, the Monsonis demanded in 1734 that the French provision them for a raid. In May of that year, La Vérendrye consented to the raid, sending his son with a well-supplied war party that attacked and devastated several Sioux hunting parties.[62]

There were many reasons that La Vérendrye shifted from discouraging to supporting violence against the Sioux. According to his own explanation, he simply had no choice. He needed Cree and Assiniboine friendship to fulfill his mission in the West, and he had to satisfy their demands for Sioux blood. French demand for Sioux and other Indian slaves, however, provided another incentive. La Vérendrye stood to profit from the attacks by selling Sioux slaves to traders heading east for Montreal. Given his preoccupation with his considerable debt (a daunting fifty thousand livres), he must have thought of the financial returns of turning Sioux war captives into French slaves. In February 1734, only three months before sanctioning warfare against the Sioux, La Vérendrye had purchased his first slave—probably a Sioux—from his Cree allies. Recording the transaction, he wrote, "I gave, in return for the slave, a cloak, a shirt, leggings and breeches, a knife and awl, powder and ball." The next month, the Crees brought another slave to La Vérendrye, who noted, "I paid for the slave as on the previous occasion." At the time, these two slaves alone would have sold in Montreal for around seven hundred livres, vastly more than the cost of goods to purchase them. Thus, in addition to satisfying the terms of alliance with the Crees, Assiniboines, and their neighbors, French support of anti-Sioux violence in 1734 brought personal profits to the French officer charged with maintaining peace in the region.[63]

62. Burpee, ed., *Journals and Letters of La Vérendrye*, 94, 96, 99, 108, 175. For family members and business partners with slaves, see Trudel, *Dictionnaire des esclaves*, 321, 331–334, 429–430.

63. Burpee, ed., *Journals and Letters of La Vérendrye*, 172 ("in return for the slave"), 173 ("paid for the slave"), 397, 404, 434–435, 451.

La Vérendrye sold at least one of the captives from the 1734 raid to his business partner, the merchant René Bourassa dit La Ronde. Bourassa had been trading slaves since at least 1717 at Montreal, Green Bay, and Michilimackinac. Bourassa returned to Montreal in 1735, and, given his history of slave trading, it is likely that many of the new Sioux slaves arriving there had been sold by him. Returning to the West, Bourassa was chastised by French authorities for his well-known illegal trade and required (as a check on his illegal activities?) to transport a new Jesuit, Jean-Pierre Aulneau, charged with preaching to the Sioux or, if possible, to the peoples of the Missouri River. Aulneau's new assignment made him uneasy, and Bourassa was just the kind of rogue he and most other Jesuits despised. After the long journey west, Bourassa and Aulneau spent the winter of 1735–1736 with La Vérendrye on the shores of Lake Superior. Aulneau found the post terrifying, full of violence and run by deceit, and he wondered whether he was up to the task. Writing to another Jesuit in Quebec, he expressed his hope that he might be able to report some success, but his first six months made him fear the worst. "What the issue of all these projects will be is known to God alone," he confided, "and, who can tell, perhaps instead of receiving the announcement of their realization you may hear the news of my death."[64]

A few weeks later, Bourassa left La Vérendrye's post for Michilimackinac, taking with him a female Sioux slave captured in the recent raid. Along the way, Bourassa encountered a Sioux war party intent on revenge for the French-sponsored attacks. His account of events was murky. He claimed that the Sioux captured and were about to kill him, when his slave saved him by telling his attackers he was not involved in the slave raid. "He has done me nothing but good," the Sioux slave supposedly told her people. "If you want to be avenged for the attack made on you, you have only to go further on and you will find twenty-four Frenchmen, amongst whom is the son of their chief [La Vérendrye], the one who slaughtered us."[65]

Following the slave's directions, but apparently leaving her with Bourassa, the Sioux surprised a combined party of French and Indians at Lake of the Woods, killing all twenty-one people there, including La Véren-

64. "Enregistrement d'une permission accordée par Charles de Beauharnois, gouverneur de la Nouvelle-France, du 9 juin, à Bourassa, conducteur du canot du Père Aulneau, missionnaire, d'un canot et six hommes, pour conduire le missionnaire et transporter les marchandises pour la traite au poste de La Vérendrye," June 9, 1735, BANQ-M, TL4, S34, P415; Jean-Pierre Aulneau to Jacques Bonin, Apr. 30, 1736, *Jesuit Relations*, LXVIII, 303–305.

65. Burpee, ed., *Journals and Letters of La Vérendrye*, 211–212.

drye's son, who had supported the earlier raids, and Father Aulneau, whose prescient letter predicting his death had yet to reach Quebec. To send a vivid message to the French of the dangers they would face as Sioux enemies, the Sioux warriors mutilated the young La Vérendrye's body and beheaded nearly all the victims. "The Sieur La Véranderie was stretched on the ground, face downwards, his back all hacked with a knife," wrote Joseph-François Lafitau, a close friend of the Jesuit killed in the raid. "There was a large opening in his loins, and his headless trunk was decked out with garters and bracelets of po[r]cupine quill."[66]

Calling the massacre a "sad accident," the elder La Vérendrye never acknowledged his own culpability. Nor would he stop selling Sioux slaves, despite an order from New France's governor to do so. Responding to the massacre, Governor Beauharnois rushed instructions to the commandant of Michilimackinac, where Bourassa and others presumably intended to sell their Sioux slaves:

> You will positively forbid, sir, all the Frenchmen of Your post to buy any Indian slave from the Assiniboins, it being of Infinite consequence for the colony to prevent this trade. Thus I order you to see to it consistently that that does not happen, and in case you learn that there might be several at your post, you will make the decision that you Deem the most appropriate for having them sent back to Their home.[67]

Beauharnois recognized that buying Sioux slaves from the Assiniboines and their allies would imperil the lives of French traders among the Sioux and prevent further French expansion. That outcome appealed to the Crees, Assiniboines, and Monsonis, who wanted to control the degree of French penetration into the West and thus occupy a favored position in the region's trade. They wished to block French alliances with the Sioux and thereby reduce the quantity of manufactured goods—especially guns and ammunition—that their enemies could use against them. Without alliance from the French, the Sioux would be vulnerable to raids by their better-armed foes. Slaving raids therefore offered the Crees, Assiniboines, and Monsonis

---

66. Lafitau to Father General, Apr. 4, 1738, in Arthur E. Jones, ed., *The Alneau Collection, 1734–1745* (Montreal, 1893), 94.

67. Burpee, ed., *Journals and Letters of La Vérendrye*, 267 ("sad accident"); Beauharnois to Saint-Pierre, Aug. 28, 1736, in Joseph L. Peyser, ed. and trans., *Jacques Legardeur de Saint-Pierre: Officer, Gentleman, Entrepreneur* (East Lansing, Mich., 1996), 34–35 (block quote).

the best available means of accomplishing these goals. Not only would their attacks sever the French and the Sioux, but the raids themselves would also secure them valuable goods.

For the Crees and their partners, the Lake of the Woods disaster could not have come at a better time. French-Sioux trade stood on the brink of a massive expansion in 1735–1736, which would have bolstered Sioux strength and aligned the French more completely with Sioux interests. In 1735 trade licenses were approved for a trade caravan to include sixty men and a vast quantity of goods for La Vérendrye's post. That year, the governor had cheered the massive infusion of furs from far western posts: of 178,000 beaver pelts in the entire colony, 100,000 had come from Sioux country and the Lake Superior posts. The first wave of slaves and pelts piqued the interest of several Montreal merchants, six of whom received licenses for Sioux trade within ten days of the 1736 disaster, before news of the killings had reached the Saint Lawrence. Added to the sixty men already authorized, the number of new traders heading for Sioux country would have been well more than one hundred and possibly closer to two hundred. Shutting down this pending flow of French trade to Sioux country was one of the central goals of the slave raids, and the disintegration of the Sioux trade that followed demonstrates the strategy's success.[68]

Some Sioux bands realized what they stood to lose and tried to make peace with the French, despite the latter's support for Sioux enemies. Following the Lake of the Woods killings, a group of Sioux diplomats came to the French post in their territory seeking reconciliation. Recognizing that the slave trade stood at the center of the conflict, they offered the French commander "two little girl slaves," begging him to "continue to give them what they needed for the subsistence of their families." Other Sioux were emboldened by the attack, sometimes to the point of recklessness. One overly confident chief visited Fort Beauharnois wearing an earring made from a silver seal taken at Lake of the Woods. When the French officer, Jacques Legardeur de Saint-Pierre, asked him where he had got it, "the chief did not reply, and began to laugh. The officer *tore off the seal with the ear*, telling him he was very bold to appear before him with such a thing."

68. "Enregistrement d'une permission accordée par Charles de Beauharnois, gouverneur de la Nouvelle-France, du 7 juin, au lieutenant De la Veranderie," June 7, 1735, BANQ-M, TL4, S34, P412; Beaharnois to minister, Oct. 26, 1735, ANOM, Colonies, C11A, LXIV, 159. The trade licenses, dated June 13 and 15, 1736, are in the files of the Conseil souverain, BANQ-Q: TP1, S35, D9, P44, P45, P54, P55, P56, P57.

Fearing for their safety and unwilling to restore good relations with the Sioux, Legardeur de Saint-Pierre abandoned and burned the fort in 1737. The French officer's violent reaction reverberated to the colonial capital, eliciting calls to annihilate the Sioux. After reading his report of the Sioux attacks, Governor Beauharnois concluded "that there is no likelihood of its ever being possible to have any Trade with that Nation and that he acted properly in abandoning his fort." Instead of trying to restore relations with the Sioux, the governor argued, "It would be a great boon if we could destroy them because they occupy the finest Hunting grounds."[69]

Taking advantage of the tensions, between 1735 and 1745 La Vérendrye and his business partner, Clément Lérigé de La Plante, sold to the colonists of the Saint Lawrence Valley dozens, perhaps hundreds, of slaves, many of whom originated in anti-Sioux raids by the Crees and Assiniboines. When the French governor chided an allied Indian war party for attacking the Sioux, they explained that they had French sponsors. "My Father, do not be angry with us. It was against our will that war parties were raised. It was [La Plante] who wanted it really, speaking in the name of our Father and handing out fine presents." La Plante predictably appeared in the Saint Lawrence records owning at least five Indian slaves in the 1730s and 1740s.[70]

In what must have been among the most spectacular of these slave raids, a Monsoni war chief named La Colle assembled a large party of Cree and Assiniboine warriors to conduct the 1741 attack on a Sioux encampment that produced a spectacular slave coffle headed for Montreal. So great was the success of the Crees and Assiniboines in these slave raids that in 1742 the governor complained that La Vérendrye and his partners traded "more slaves than packages [of beaver]." La Vérendrye and his associates had little trouble finding French buyers for so many slaves, in spite of the governor's prohibitions and the 1742 renewal of French-Sioux alliance. One of the more often-mentioned middlemen in this trade was René Bourassa, both La Vérendrye's business partner and La Plante's son-in-law. Between these three men and their various business associates, their family members, friends, and neighbors in Montreal found an ample supply of Sioux slaves.

69. Beauharnois to the French minister, Oct. 14, 1737, *Wis. Hist. Coll.*, XVII (1906), 270 ("little girl slaves"), 271 (*"tore off . . . the ear"*). For Sioux threat at French post, see Lafitau to Father General, Apr. 4, 1738, in Jones, ed., *Alneau Collection*, 94; Beauharnois to the French minister, Oct. 14, 1737, *Wis. Hist. Coll.*, XVII (1906), 267–269, and Legardeur de Saint Pierre to Beauharnois, 269–274.

70. Burpee, ed., *Journals and Letters of La Vérendrye*, 291 ("do not be angry"); Trudel, *Dictionnaire des esclaves*, 372.

Bourassa baptized his twelve-year-old Sioux slave, Antoine, in 1739 and attended as godfather or witness at many other enslaved Sioux baptisms and burials. Colonists had strong incentives to conceal the identity of their Sioux slaves, recognizing that attempts to restore a French-Sioux alliance might result in government pressure to release them. Therefore, despite dozens of accounts of widespread Sioux slaving, only forty-two slaves were identified as Sioux in parish and notarial records during this period.[71]

Despite its destabilizing effects, La Vérendrye considered his role in the Indian slave trade a service worthy of the king's favor. Seeking a promotion in the French military, he wrote to Paris in 1744, "I have sacrificed myself and my sons for the service of his Majesty and the good of the colony; what advantages shall result from my toils the future may tell." Citing the reasons he deserved the king's honor, he continued, "Do the great number of people my enterprise provides with a living, [and] the slaves it procures to the colony . . . count for nothing?" By alienating the Sioux, however, La Vérendrye had cost the colony much more than he realized. By 1736, most Sioux had not only severed their relationship with the French but also declared their intention to join the Foxes and their allies in raiding the French and their Indian allies throughout the western Great Lakes region. When French-Sioux relations warmed again in 1741–1742, French-supported slaving was again the key obstacle to establishing a long-term alliance and encouraging French settlement and trade farther west.[72]

Despite the heavy cost of French support for captive raids, French administrators did nothing to stem the flow of Sioux slaves. In addition to buying slaves for his own household, the governor continued to grant western posts to men involved in the slave trade. When La Vérendrye retired from his western post in 1744, Governor Beauharnois appointed for his replacement Nicolas-Joseph Noyelles de Fleurimont. Although Beauharnois claimed that Noyelles was "the most suitable person both for negotiating with the Savages of the place and for keeping them at peace with the Sioux," Noyelles expanded La Vérendrye's slave-trading enterprise. Indeed, following his appointment to the post he added four Indian slaves to the seven he already owned, and his associates continued to trade them to others. This is

---

71. Burpee, ed., *Journals and Letters of La Vérendrye*, 380–381 ("more slaves than packages [of beaver]"). For Bourassa's slave, see baptism of Oct. 9, 1739, *RAB du PRDH*, 123017. Bourassa married Marie-Catherine Lériger, one of La Plante's two daughters, in 1721. Louis Lavallée, *La prairie en Nouvelle-France, 1647–1760* (Montreal, 1992), 218.

72. Burpee, ed., *Journals and Letters of La Vérendrye*, 451–452.

not to suggest that Noyelles was not qualified for the job. On the contrary, his ability to negotiate with the colony's Indian allies was the very quality that made him such a successful slave trader. But embracing some allies by enslaving others made it impossible to fulfill his commission to facilitate New France's westward expansion by building broader western alliances.[73]

Indeed, the slave trade ensured that the French would never craft a coherent policy toward the Sioux. Despite serious failings during La Vérendrye's stay in the West, many French traders wanted another opportunity to bring the Sioux into the alliance. In 1749, Governor Jacques-Pierre de Taffanel de La Jonquière approved the establishment of a new post among the Sioux, hopeful that "by means of that establishment we might push our discoveries much farther Toward the West." Recalling the disaster at Lake of the Woods in 1736, his superior in Paris feared the worst, criticizing the governor for being "in haste to enter upon such an undertaking." But, since the post was already established by the time the French minister could weigh in, all he could do was hope "that they who are destined to form that post will have a happier fate than most of the French who have formerly been sent among those Indians."[74]

Throughout the 1750s, the minister's skepticism proved more accurate than La Jonquière's hopefulness. Throughout the decade, French merchants continued to buy Sioux captives for the slave market, supporting allied nations in their warfare against Sioux encampments. In 1751, Illinois and Cree raiders independently struck the Sioux, inviting a round of reprisals against the Crees in 1752 and the French-allied Peoria Illinois in 1753. The opening battles of the Seven Years' War quickly diverted French attention from Sioux country, and the French abandoned the Sioux post by 1756 with neither trade revenues nor western discoveries to show for their efforts.[75]

As they had with the Foxes, New France's Native allies used the slave

73. For Noyelles's appointment, see ibid., 400. For his slaves, see Trudel, *Dictionnaire des esclaves*, 391.

74. La Jonquière and Bigot to minister, Oct. 9, 1749, *Wis. Hist. Coll.*, XVIII (1908), 33 ("push our discoveries . . . west"), and minister to La Jonquière and Bigot, Apr. 15, 1750, 61 ("happier fate").

75. For Sioux slaves in the 1750s, see, for example, burial of Feb. 7, 1751, *RAB du PRDH*, 264948, baptism of Sept. 22, 1751, 25478, baptism of July 28, 1753, 311928, and baptism of Sept. 2, 1755, 241077. La Jonquière to minister, Sept. 16, 1751, *Wis. Hist. Coll.*, XVIII (1908), 76–80, and Jacques Legardeur de Saint-Pierre, "Memoir [1753]," 133–134. For abandoning the Sioux post, see *Wis. Hist. Coll.*, XVIII, 133 n. 69.

trade to limit the expansion of colonial settlement and trade into Sioux territory. Viewing the French embrace of their Sioux enemies as a violation of their own alliance, Cree, Assiniboine, Ottawa, Ojibwa, and Illinois Indians maneuvered the French into supporting anti-Sioux slave raids. Strategies of indigenous enslavement combined with the French understanding of slaves as personal property to amplify the power of slave raiding as a diplomatic tool. At key moments when the potential for French expansion was highest—just after the 1701 peace talks, in 1735–1736, and in 1741–1742—French demand for Sioux slaves undermined an alliance that would have drawn colonial settlement and trade deep onto the North American Plains.

Other French efforts to expand onto the Plains faced similar obstacles. The farther one strays from centers of colonial settlement, the thinner and more episodic the evidence becomes. But what documentation survives from early French efforts to expand into the Missouri River valley suggests that, as with the Foxes and the Sioux, the Plains Apaches became the victims of strategic slave raids by Indian rivals seeking to control French westward expansion. French traders spread into the Missouri River valley long before it was either legal or well documented. Bison hides and even Spanish trade goods passed through overlapping trade networks across the Plains and made their way to the Mississippi settlements by the early eighteenth century. So did slaves. Although there is little French evidence from the early years of the trade, Spanish sources registered slaving activities by the 1710s. In 1719, the viceroy of Mexico, the marqués de Valero, expressed his concern that French-supported slave raids against the Apaches were part of a larger French effort to launch a war against Spain's North American colonies. Valero therefore ordered New Mexican officials to support the Apaches, "as the Apache nation aided by ourselves could inflict considerable damage on the French and block their evil designs." In addition to curbing French expansion, Spanish authorities might have hoped to redirect Apache violence away from New Mexico, where they had been conducting raids for decades. Accordingly, Spanish authorities armed Apache warriors on the condition that they aim their raids at Pawnee and other French-allied villages along the eastern margins of the Plains.[76]

76. Order of Valero, Aug. 1, 1719, in Alfred Barnaby Thomas, ed. and trans., *After Coronado: Spanish Exploration Northeast of New Mexico, 1696–1727: Documents from the Archives of Spain, Mexico, and New Mexico* (Norman, Okla., 1935), 138–139. Within a year, the French would, indeed, declare war on Spain, although the European conflict had little influence in the nations' American colonies and certainly had little influence over voyageurs' purchase of Plains captives.

Spanish efforts to block French influence reached their peak in the summer of 1720, when a company of Spanish soldiers and armed Apache allies ventured to the Platte River to confront the Pawnees. Likely warned in advance of Spanish-Apache movements, the Pawnees—aided by French, Osage, and Oto warriors—routed the expedition. "A horde of men," one Spanish survivor recalled, "attacked both with guns and arrows and wrought the havoc that is known." That havoc included the death of thirty-five Spanish and eleven Indian men as well as an unknown number of Pawnees and French. The defeat became legendary in New Mexico and would discourage further Spanish ventures across the Plains for more than half a century.[77]

With the Spanish in retreat, many French authorities, especially those overseeing Louisiana, sought to quiet the violence of slaving raids and focus on peaceful trade. Having assumed the administration of the Illinois country in 1717, Louisiana officials inherited a region where the fur and slave trades went hand in hand. Hoping to expand trade westward, however, the Company of the Indies demanded an end to the Indian slave trade in 1720. Consistent with Louisiana's overall strategy, this policy acknowledged that slave raiding destabilized Indian communities and jeopardized French trading interests. "The Company has been notified," read the 1720 ordinance, "that the voyageurs who trade on the Missouri and Arkansas Rivers attempt to sow division among the Indian nations and to cause them to go to war to acquire slaves, which they buy. This is not only contrary to the laws of the king but also very detrimental to the commerce of the Company and to the establishments that it proposes to make in that country." To facilitate trade and to allow further French settlement along the Missouri and Arkansas Rivers, the Company ordered Louisiana's governor, Jean-Baptiste Lemoyne de Bienville, to arrest, imprison, and confiscate the goods of anyone caught carrying Indian slaves.[78]

In 1720 France's regent, the duc d'Orléans, commissioned Étienne de

---

77. Testimony of Aguilar, Santa Fé, 1 July 1726, in Thomas, ed. and trans., *After Coronado*, 227. Douglas Parks suggests of the Villasur expedition: "That military disaster caused the Spaniards to retreat beyond the Sangre de Cristo Mountains in 1720 and not return to the central Plains for more than 80 years." Douglas R. Parks, "Pawnee," in *Handbook*, XIII, *Plains*, part 1, 518. The best treatments of this well-known expedition are Thomas's introduction in *After Coronado*, 33–39; David J. Weber, *The Spanish Frontier in North America* (New Haven, Conn., 1992), 169–171. For Osage and Oto participation, see Étienne de Véniard, sieur de Bourgmont, "Journal of the Voyage . . . to the Padoucas [1724]," in Frank Norall, ed., *Bourgmont: Explorer of the Missouri, 1698–1725* (Lincoln, Nebr., 1988) 125, 135.

78. Ordinance of Oct. 25, 1720, in Pierre Margry, comp., *Découvertes et établissements des Français dans l'ouest et dans le sud de l'Amérique* (Paris, 1876–1886), VI, 316.

Bourgmont to establish a post on the Missouri River designed to foster peaceful trade with the many warring nations of the region, especially the previously victimized Plains Apaches. In a document bearing the regent's initials, Bourgmont was charged with "making peace among all the Indian nations between Louisiana and New Mexico in order to open a safe trade route and . . . establishing a post, which will shield the mines of the Illinois from the Spaniards and will open the bordering lands to very advantageous trade." In practice, Bourgmont's goal would prove elusive because of a persistent demand by French colonists to purchase Indian slaves and the eagerness with which villagers along the Missouri and Arkansas Rivers wished to meet that need. Anticipating the mission's failure and hopeful of personal profits from the slave trade, Governor Bienville wrote to the commander of the Illinois country urging him to prevent Bourgmont's departure altogether. Instead of fostering peace with the Apaches, Bienville suggested, "we should drop the idea and push our nations towards war with them and trade in slaves for the account of the Company." Bienville recognized that Indian slaves were more valuable to the colony than buffalo hides or worn Spanish trade goods, the main items available from the Apaches. Especially in New France, where the slave trade was legal and therefore more secure, slaves sold for much more than the cost of goods used to purchase them. But, in Louisiana, Bienville was in the minority, and his suggestion never became policy. The actions of French voyageurs, soldiers, and local officials demonstrated the pervasiveness of this preference.[79]

As a result, Apache slaves continued to flow into New France despite Bourgmont's promises of peace. Of the five Canadian participants in Bourgmont's expedition, at least two returned to New France with Indian slaves, possibly Apaches traded in Kansa or Missouri villages. And, although Bourgmont had forbidden any member of his expedition to buy slaves on the journey, he personally bought six slaves from the Kansas in a diplomatic exchange designed to secure their cooperation at the Apache peace conference. It was probably no accident that these slaves included at least one Apache, a woman called Marie-Angélique, whom Bourgmont kept until his death, returning with her to France, where she was baptized in 1728.[80]

79. Quoted in Norall, ed., *Bourgmont*, 34, and Bourgmont to Boisbriant, Aug. 20, 1723, 45. Norall uses the term "tribes" for the French "nations," which I retain here.

80. Bourgmont, "Journal of the Voyage to the Padoucas," in Norall, ed., *Bourgmont*, 125, 132. The two Canadians returning with slaves were Quesnel and Hamelin, the latter of whom was an active slave trader throughout the 1720s and 1730s. For Quesnel's slaves, see Trudel, *Dictionnaire des esclaves*, 343 (Hamelin), 403 (Quesnel); for Marie-Angélique,

FIGURE 18. *Plan of Fort d'Orleans on the Missouri River. Jean-François-Benjamin Dumont de Montigny. Ca. 1720s. ANOM, Aix-en-Provence, FR CAOM 04DFC63B. Permission Centre de Archives d'Outre-Mer*

In Louisiana, which would have been a more logical destination for Apache slaves than distant Canada, Indian slavery hovered between being officially discouraged and being illegal, ensuring that it would never thrive in New Orleans or other major slaveholding centers. Fearful of collusion between Indians and Africans, Louisiana officials hoped to keep the groups separate. In 1728, Louisiana's governor Étienne Périer wrote a memorandum about "the Indian slaves who are being trafficked in this province," concluding that the practice was "contrary to the welfare of this country." Not only did the slave trade sow divisions among the region's Indians, but Indians tended to run away from their masters, and "being mixed with our negroes may induce them to desert with them." Reiterating the logic expressed a generation before at the colony's founding, he argued that by out-

---

see 88. Dumont de Montigny traveled throughout Louisiana and up the Mississippi in 1721, producing a detailed account of his journey with dozens of similar sketches. Although this sketch must have been produced at the same time, it was not included in his larger manuscript, held at the Newberry Library and published as Dumont de Montigny, *Regards sur le monde atlantique, 1715-1747* (Sillery, Que., 2008).

lawing Indian slavery the French could convince Indians that the English wanted to destroy them whereas the French wanted to protect them. "When they see that we do not wish any slaves and that we forbid the trade in them," he explained, "they will be easily persuaded that we are better friends of theirs than the other European nations." Traders with enslaved Apaches, then, either sold them in Louisiana's outposts in modern Illinois and Texas or, most often, took them to Canada.[81]

In New France, where Apache slaves passed as legal property, the 1724 peace with the distant Apaches meant very little. Traders with connections to the Illinois country continued to trade Apache slaves with little concern for, or perhaps even knowledge of, France's attempt to court peace with their victims. Indeed, 80 percent of the colony's Apache slaves were acquired after 1725, and during the 1730s Plains Apaches constituted a quarter of all Indian slaves of known origin. That Governor Beauharnois owned at least three Apache slaves by the early 1730s demonstrates that, despite claims to the contrary, Apache enslavement received official sanction in the colony. In 1733, Beauharnois and the intendant explained that they approved the enslavement of "Apaches, who are sold to voyageurs by our Indian allies and are brought to Montreal, where they are considered as slaves . . . in the same manner as is practiced in the Americas for the Negroes." When the commandant of the Illinois country tried to outlaw "Panis" and Apache slave raiding, considering it to be "an unjust war made against nations who have never given any insult to the French," Beauharnois rebuked him, reminding him that he had no authority to contradict such a long-standing Canadian practice.[82]

Unlike the Apache slaves kept by French voyageurs at Natchitoches and other southern outposts, however, those in New France were more often young boys rather than women. Although in general colonists would have preferred young adult males, the slave raiders generally killed these captives. In addition to cultural prescriptions for the ceremonial torture and

81. "Perier to [the Abbe Raguet]," May 12, 1728, in Rowland and Sanders, eds. and trans., *Mississippi Provincial Archives, 1701–1729: French Dominion*, II (1929), 573–574.

82. "Lettre de Beauharnois et Hocquart," Oct. 4, 1733, ANOM, Colonies, C11A, LIX, 110 ("in the same manner as . . . for the Negroes"). During the 1730s, only 101 of the 290 new slaves individually named in extant records are clearly identified by nation of origin. Of these, 25 were Plains Apaches, and 32 were Foxes. See Appendix C. "Une guerre injuste que l'on faisoit aus deux Nations qui n'ont jamais fait aucune insulte aux françois": "Extrait d'une lettre du gouverneur Beauharnois à d'Artaguiette, commandant aux Illinois," 1735, ANOM, Colonies, C11A, XLIII, 259.

killing of enemy warriors, the Missouris, Pawnees, Kansas, and Wichitas used the slave trade to weaken the Apaches, a strategy that required killing those warriors who might strike back at them. The slave trade therefore not only allowed French voyageurs and colonists to profit from western violence, but it also supported the goals of allied Indians who wished to prevent a French-Apache alliance. By raiding the Apaches and selling their victims into French slavery, these nations frustrated France's imperial policy by alienating the Apaches from the French and by motivating French traders to support raids that generated this profitable commodity.[83]

For the Apaches, these slave raids came at a particularly bad time. During the 1720s Comanche raiders, emboldened by their recent acquisition of horses and guns, pushed southward into Plains Apache territory. Weakened and distracted by Pawnee, Kansa, Osage, and Wichita slave raiders—and deprived of the weapons that would have come from alliance with the French—the Apaches could not defend themselves against the Comanche threat. As a result, they suffered devastating losses during the 1720s and 1730s, and the survivors fled the region, seeking refuge among their Apache relations in the Southwest or in new settlements farther east. "The Pados were in former times the most numerous nation on the continent," wrote one eighteenth-century observer of the Plains Apaches, "but the wars which other nations have made against them have destroyed them to such an extent that at present they form only four small groups who go wandering from one side to the other continually, which saves them from the fury of the other nations." Squeezed by slave raids sponsored by two competing colonial powers, Plains Apaches ended the century with sharply reduced numbers moving through territory claimed by other, more powerful, peoples.[84]

The Apache victims of French-sponsored raids were not the only ones to suffer from the cycles of violence supported by the slave trade. Pawnees in-

83. For the predominance of female slaves at southeastern posts, see Juliana Barr, "From Captives to Slaves: Commodifying Indian Women in the Borderlands," *Journal of American History*, XCII (2005–2006), 19–46; Kathleen DuVal, "Indian Intermarriage and Métissage in Colonial Louisiana," *WMQ*, 3d Ser., LXV (2008), 267–304.

84. The most complete treatments of Comanche and Apache warfare in the 1720s are Thomas W. Kavanaugh, *Comanche Political History: An Ethnohistorical Perspective, 1706–1875* (Lincoln, Nebr., 1996), 63–79; Morris W. Foster and Martha McCollough, "Plains Apache," in *Handbook*, XV, *Plains*, part 2, 926–928 (quote 928). The best treatment of Comanche expansion and coordinated domination of large sections of the Great Plains is Pekka Hämäläinen, *The Comanche Empire* (New Haven, Conn., 2008).

creasingly faced attacks from Spanish-allied groups on the Plains, and many of them ended up enslaved in New Mexico. The Otos, who sold Apache slaves to French traders during the 1720s, themselves faced violence from both the Apaches and the invading Comanches in reprisal for captive raiding. They suffered significant population loss to counterraids, according to one of their chiefs, who complained to Bourgmont in 1724, "All the French in this land know that we are a nation destroyed by war." This perpetual violence compelled the French to abandon hopes of westward expansion onto the central Plains, forcing the closure of Bourgmont's Missouri River post before it was even completed and discouraging further settlement until the second half of the eighteenth century.[85]

The slave trade thus created a broad barrier to French expansion that arced from Green Bay northeast to the headwaters of the Mississippi and south to the Missouri. In this way, Indian slavery ironically functioned as a tool of anticolonial power. It also wedded the French practice of slavery to the local politics of the Pays d'en Haut, preventing metropolitan agendas from governing the course of colonial trade and settlement. As colonial administrators had hoped, French distance from this sector of the slave supply insulated them from some of the dangers inherent in forging alliances through the exchange of slaves. But the French could never claim, as they hoped in the 1740s, that the western slave trade made "little impression" on them or their nearby allies. The many diplomatic and material benefits of the captive trade by New France's Indian allies ensured that the slave trade would not be confined to the distant Plains but would affect the very nature and extent of French colonialism in North America.[86]

MOST OF THEM WERE SOLD TO THE FRENCH

"The women and children were made slaves, and most of them were sold to the French."—Gaspard Chaussegros de Léry, Detroit, 1712

Even as they used the slave trade to control French-led alliances, following diplomatic patterns that had emerged generations before the colonial encounter, Indians also innovated, adapting their practice of slavery to meet

---

85. Minutes of an Indian Council, Nov. 19, 1724, quoted in Norall, ed., *Bourgmont*, 82 ("a nation destroyed by war"). For Pawnee enslavement in New Mexico, see James F. Brooks, *Captives and Cousins: Slavery, Kinship, and Community in the Southwest Borderlands* (Chapel Hill, N.C., 2002), 14–16, 146.

86. Bigot et La Jonquière, July 26, 1749, ANOM, Colonies, C11A, CXIX.

new realities. Just as the French embedded themselves in a system of in-digenous slavery, Indians attached themselves, via a growing slave trade, to the emerging world of French slavery, which sought a large number of captive laborers taken in distant lands. Until the late seventeenth cen-tury, indigenous slavery in the Pays d'en Haut existed within a complex set of regional relationships designed to ensure that the impulse for warfare was balanced by the impulse for trade and alliance. When neighbors were simultaneously potential trade partners and potential enemies, conduct-ing a slave raid would necessarily come at the expense of trade and subsis-tence activities, providing a disincentive to slavery. Warriors on slave raids could miss an entire hunting season, and raids blocked, even if only tempo-rarily, avenues of trade. The ceremonies of the calumet embodied this dy-namic tension, expressing the desire for peace and alliance through a nar-rative of violence and enslavement. As the "general custom of the country," then, slaving violence punctuated, but never dominated, relations among the peoples of the Pays d'en Haut.

In the eighteenth century, French slave trading offered incentives that altered these calculations by allowing Native peoples to conduct warfare as a means, rather than an alternative, to trade and subsistence. There is no contemporary evidence that the Indians of the Pays d'en Haut changed their fundamental perceptions of captive enemies—shifting from seeing them as dominated and domesticated enemies to seeing them as dehuman-ized, salable commodities—but their decisions in relation to these people reflected new incentives that altered the function of slavery in the region. It thus made a profound difference that colonists' demand for captured Indians ensured that "most of them were sold to the French." Unlike Iro-quoia, where Jesuits and other French commentators living within Native communities wrote in detail about changing war culture, there is very little commentary on the issue from the eighteenth-century Pays d'en Haut. But the sheer level of violence offers one piece of evidence that something had changed. Early French explorers noted tensions and witnessed raids, but the scale of the Fox Wars and the anti-Sioux attacks could not have been sustained over the centuries that preceded French arrival. The low-level en-demic violence of the archaeological record and early descriptions of Native warfare existed alongside equally important evidence of regionwide (and extraregional) trade, suggesting that the chaos of the eighteenth century reached new levels.

To take only one example, consider the tense standoff in Montreal in 1742, when the discovery of Sioux slaves unraveled French and Sioux plans for reconciliation and trade. The 1741 raid that brought slaves to Montreal shows how the French slave trade allowed Native allies to blend previously competing spheres of activity: slaving and subsistence and trade. When the Monsoni chief La Colle approached La Vérendrye for support in a raid against the Sioux in the 1730s, La Vérendrye used the necessity of subsistence activities to dissuade him. La Colle "proposed to me to send several small parties against the Sioux," he reported, but La Vérendrye told him he could not support it, because "that would prevent the autumn hunting and the gathering of the wild oats for them as well as for us." Without the canoes full of supplies from Montreal, he explained, they would not have enough provisions or ammunition to sustain themselves. Yet, despite such persuasion, La Colle and his coalition of Cree, Assiniboine, and Monsoni warriors continued to raid the Sioux and sell their captives to the French, whose purchases more than compensated for the subsistence activities foregone during the slave raids. In 1741, La Colle organized two hundred warriors for the spectacular raid on Sioux villages that produced nearly as many captives. As the governor reported, these slaves were headed, not for La Colle's Monsoni village, but for Montreal, the homes of which presented immediate evidence of the slave trade, and the markets of which made it possible for La Colle to simultaneously expand both slaving raids and peaceful trade. French payment for slaves allowed their allies to underwrite attacks on neighboring Indians, both weakening their enemies and making it more difficult for the French to mediate between them. As Jonathan Carver noted after touring the Pays d'en Haut in the 1760s, the French demand for slaves "caused the dissensions between the Indian nations to be carried on with a greater degree of violence, and with unremitted ardor."[87]

If the image of an eight-hundred-foot slave coffle heading toward Montreal indicates the vastly expanded scale of slave raids in the Pays d'en Haut, it also signals another important transformation of indigenous slavery: the growing tendency to trade or sell, rather than domesticate and incorporate, most captured women and children. Through the end of the 1730s the Indian slave population in the Saint Lawrence Valley was more male than female (55 percent to 45 percent of identified slaves between 1700 and 1740). In the 1740s and 1750s, however, French demand for domestic servants and Natives' willingness to trade more women and girls shifted the

87. Burpee, ed., *Journals and Letters of La Vérendrye*, 223 ("prevent . . . hunting and . . . gathering"); Jonathan Carver, *Three Years Travels through the Interior Parts of North-America* . . . (Philadelphia, 1789), 177 ("greater degree of violence").

demographic profile dramatically. During the 1750s about two-thirds of all Indian slaves arriving in New France were female.[88]

The demographic significance of this shift is impossible to measure, or even to estimate. But sources describing slaves' incorporation into Native households, as subordinate wives, replacements for the dead, or additional children, all point to the role it played in demographic strength and recovery. Slave raids, according to one early source, "are most often conducted to repopulate when they have been attacked by an epidemic or by war." The continual decline of Native villages cannot be attributed solely to Natives' incorporating fewer captives, but it certainly played a role, particularly given the reproductive labor expected of enslaved women (and girls who survived to become women). Jonathan Carver might have been right that, because of French demand for slaves from the Pays d'en Haut, "fewer of the captives are tormented and put to death, since these expectations of receiving so valuable a consideration for them have been excited." But, because most women and children would not have been killed in the first place, the gender shift within the French slave population could have come only at the expense of slavery's repopulation function in Native societies. The only group for which reliable numbers survive is the Illinois, whose population declined sharply between the 1730s and the 1760s. Although partially explained by disease, Illinois villages had suffered repeated epidemics before the 1730s without major population loss. Beginning in the late-1720s, however, their decline was strongly influenced by two factors associated with the slave trade: a series of Fox and Sioux raids combined with fewer captives incorporated into polygynous Illinois households.[89]

The shift away from incorporation and toward trade also profoundly limited how slaves themselves could act as restraints on warfare. As potential translators, cultural go-betweens, or goodwill offerings at a time of peace negotiations, captives acted in ways that could overcome the effects of the

---

88. For the sources and statistics of slave demography, see Appendix C.

89. "Cette guerre se fait très souvent pour se repeupler lorsqu'ils ont été attaqués d'une maladie populaire, ou que par les guerres": Antoine Denis Raudot, *Relation par lettres de l'Amérique Septentrionale . . .*, ed. Camille de Rochemonteix (Paris, 1904), 94; Carver, *Three Years Travels,* 178 ("fewer of the captives are tormented"). The only sustained population study of any Indian group in the Pays d'en Haut during the eighteenth century is Emily J. Blasingham, "The Depopulation of the Illinois Indians," Part 1, *Ethnohistory,* III (1956), 193–224, and Part 2, 361–412. Blasingham notes the importance of Fox / Sioux raids as well as declining polygamy, without mentioning the slave trade, which strongly influenced both factors.

violence that had enslaved them. As one historian has suggested, captives also played an important role as "resident aliens," deterring warfare or at least mitigating its intensity because the attacking people knew they might encounter their kin during the raid. By trading away more slaves, Native villages had fewer avenues available for reconciliation, particularly if they were unable to return captives when peace negotiations demanded it. The Fox Wars provided many examples of the tensions that could arise when one nation knew its people had been taken by another but the offending nation could not produce the captives in order to make peace.[90]

Perhaps nothing reconfigured indigenous slavery more than colonists' expectation that it function as a permanent and inheritable system of labor. Because French law ordered that Indian slaves "shall be fully owned as property by those who have purchased them," masters had greater claim on the slaves they bought than did French diplomats, who sometimes needed to release slaves for diplomatic purposes. When the Sioux chiefs complained of their children's enslavement, Beauharnois could promise—but never guarantee—their release. Indeed, knowing the limits of his power to take another's slave property, the governor offered the promise only conditionally. "I allowed them to take [the slaves] with them," he said, "if they would like to go." He then told the Sioux chiefs that he could not persuade the slaves to return with them and that their desire to stay was evidence of "the gentleness with which the French had treated them." Seeing that they doubted his sincerity, accusing him of pressuring the slaves, he offered to allow the Sioux chiefs to pick any two slaves in the Monsoni-led coffle on its way to Montreal, believing that "the hope they had of getting back their slaves" was the best means of controlling them.[91]

Some of the factors altering regional war cultures in the Pays d'en Haut are best understood by looking at the evolution of the calumet ceremony. The rituals associated with the calumet expressed the central tension within indigenous slavery between war and peace, keeping the Pays d'en Haut in relative balance for at least two centuries prior to French arrival. By wedding

90. Wayne E. Lee, "Peace Chiefs and Blood Revenge: Patterns of Restraint in Native American Warfare, 1500–1800," *Journal of Military History*, LXXI (2007), 701–741, 725 ("resident aliens"); Brooks, *Captives and Cousins*, esp. 58–63; Juliana Barr, *Peace Came in the Form of a Woman: Indians and Spaniards in the Texas Borderlands* (Chapel Hill, N.C., 2007), esp. 69–108.

91. Raudot, "Ord[onn]ance rendüe au sujet des neigres et des Sauvages nommez Panis," Apr. 13, 1709, BANQ-Q, E1, S1, P509; Beauharnois to the minister, Sept. 24, 1742, ANOM, Colonies, C11A, LXXVII, 110v–111v.

slavery to diplomacy and by increasing the cost and difficulty of present-ing slaves to neighboring people, even the calumet's glorification of slave raiding was always tied to a community's aspirations for peace. But, as the practice of the calumet spread throughout the expanding French alliance, beginning in the 1690s, its specific use of slavery as a mode of diplomatic communication became increasingly rare. By the mid-eighteenth century, only those groups farthest west and least entangled in French-Native diplo-matic webs continued to express the peaceful hopes of calumet ceremoni-alism in the martial language of enslavement. This decoupling of enslave-ment from peacemaking likely contributed to the "unremitted ardor" with which Carver saw the peoples of the Pays d'en Haut pursue the slave trade.

The calumet's spread presented real problems of intercultural transla-tion, not only between Indians and French but between those Indians who practiced the calumet and those who did not. The events surrounding the Great Peace of 1701 brought these challenges into sharp relief. As Iroquois and Algonquian delegations converged on Montreal, tensions ran high. Yet, when the largest group from the Pays d'en Haut arrived, it was greeted cor-dially by the Saint Lawrence Iroquois at Kahnawake, who were also hosting some of the Iroquois diplomats from the south. As more than one thousand Indians prepared to sit down together for a feast, a group of Algonquians gathered to perform a spontaneous calumet ceremony. A dozen men formed a circle, and men and women surrounded them to observe. Taking the lead, an Ottawa chief named Outachia held a calumet above his head and began to sing. Entering the circle, he danced, accompanied by the thrumming of rattling gourds and shouts so loud that French observers compared them to gunshots. Acting out his former deeds of courage, he used the calumet as a mock war club, shouting, "I have . . . killed four Iroquois." Having come to the delegation with dozens of Iroquois captives in tow, Outachia and the warriors who followed him had ample evidence of their power. But none of the Iroquois complained. If they seemed unperturbed by the ritual, it was likely from ignorance of its meaning. In their own culture of hospitality, Iro-quoian peoples used tobacco as a sign of welcome and peace, so they likely read the calumet as an elaborate curiosity that had basically familiar mean-ing. A few Iroquois had received calumets in the past as diplomatic gifts sig-nifying peace, but they had no experience with the full ritual accompanying this display. Seemingly pleased with the spectacle, many Iroquois watched and then sat to eat with the French and their Algonquian allies.[92]

92. Bacqueville de La Potherie, *Histoire de l'Amérique Septentrionale*, IV, 197–198.

The French, too, read the calumet in a way that emphasized its peace-making over its signification of war. After the formal treaty ceremony, Montreal's governor, Louis Hector de Callière, brought out a calumet that had been given to him by the Miamis to symbolize that nation's alliance with France. According to Pierre-François-Xavier de Charlevoix, "The Chevalier de Callieres smoked it first, de Champigny after him, then de Vaudreuil, and all the chiefs and deputies, each in turn." But Callière presented a self-serving reconfiguration of the calumet's meaning aimed at shifting diplomatic power from local Indian communities to French colonial centers. "I invite you all to smoke this calumet which I will be the first to smoke, and to eat meat and broth that I have had prepared for you," he told the crowd, "so that I have like a good father the satisfaction of seeing all my children united. I shall keep this calumet that was presented to me by the Miamis so that I can have you smoke it when you come to see me." Although approximating some elements of the calumet ceremony like raising the pipe above his head, performing in a public space, and offering food, Callière's central demand ran counter to the ceremony's message that peace and war—giving and taking life—were bound together. Unlike Outachia's performance in the days leading up to the conference, Callière insisted, "I am determined that there be no more talk of the attacks made during the war." Instead of giving slaves to his new allies to demonstrate his power, Callière as host demanded that his guests release their captives to the Iroquois.[93]

As they offered captives to the Iroquois, many also gave them a calumet to keep as a symbol of their new alliance. "I am of one body with you my Father," said the Potawatomi chief Ounanguissé. "Here is an Iroquois prisoner whom I took in war, in presenting him to you, permit me to give him a calumet to take back to his people to smoke when we meet." One Ottawa chief claimed to have no Iroquois prisoners to return, so he gave them two slaves from another nation "with whom you will do as you please." He also offered "a calumet that I give to the Iroquois to smoke as brothers when we meet." Although both were intended as signs of peace, in the war culture of the Pays d'en Haut the act of freeing slaves and giving a calumet expressed the desire for peace in very different terms. Yet, for the Iroquois, this Algonquian innovation would have resonated, as their primary diplomatic symbol—the wampum belt—was often associated with releasing prisoners.

93. Charlevoix, *History of New France*, trans. Shea, V, 152 ("Calliere smoked it first"); "English Translation of the Montreal Treaty of 1701," in Havard, *Great Peace of Montreal of 1701*, trans. Aronoff and Scott, 211 ("I invite you all to smoke" and "no more talk").

Many accounts refer to strings or belts of wampum as metaphorical fetters, binding the parties in mutual agreement. Giving them away represented the freeing of captives and the giving of life. When releasing captives at the peace conference, the Iroquois delegates offered wampum rather than pipes. Symbolic of alliance and peace, both symbols depended upon the cultural grammar surrounding them in their more local and regional contexts. As they spread well beyond the bounds of those regional war cultures, however, the expectations surrounding their manufacture and giving as gifts changed as well.[94]

The physical creation of the calumet also changed over the course of the eighteenth century, altering the historically broad community investment in pipes' creation and thus limiting their involvement in the alliances they ratified. European manufacturing had a profound effect on the spread of calumets. With metal tools to bore holes in pipestone and metal knives to cut, hollow, and decorate shafts, calumets became far more common in the late-seventeenth century. With no European mediation, they spread into the Southeast from the Lower Mississippi Valley, where they were encountered and encouraged by French traders in the early eighteenth century. In the Northeast, it became more common to display calumets manufactured in Europe, which became one of the most-demanded luxury goods traded to Indians beginning in the 1730s. Eventually taking the form of a pipe-tomahawk, these metal-bowled pipes passed from nation to nation beyond European view. The renewed importance of pipes also prompted a new surge in indigenous pipe manufacturing. In Seneca burial sites, for example, pipes were the only indigenous item that increased in frequency following the adoption of European technologies.[95]

By the time the Sioux chiefs arrived in Montreal in 1742, they offered the governor a calumet but found that it had a very different meaning in the context of the French alliance network. As Callière had done in 1701, Beauharnois smoked the pipe with the Sioux, but in a way that undermined rather than reinforced its expression of balance between alliance and warfare. Rather than respecting Sioux power as they demonstrated their suc-

---

94. "English Translation of the Montreal Treaty of 1701," in Havard, *Great Peace of Montreal of 1701*, trans. Aronoff and Scott, 212–213. For wampum's association with freeing prisoners, see Dubuisson to governor, [1712], *Wis. Hist. Coll.*, XVI (1902), 282; *Jesuit Relations*, XXVII, 255, XLI, 71, LXII, 93.

95. Ian W. Brown, "The Calumet Ceremony in the Southeast and Its Archaeological Manifestations," *American Antiquity*, LIV (1989), 311–331; Timothy J. Shannon, "Queequeg's Tomahawk: A Cultural Biography, 1750–1900," *Ethnohistory*, LII (2005), 589–633.

cesses in war, Beauharnois smoked only "to show you how I wish peace and quiet to reign amongst the Nations of my Children," a list of nations that included those who had recently enslaved Sioux children. Far from providing a cathartic opportunity for Sioux warriors to demonstrate their prowess, remembering each slave they had taken, the governor urged them "to forget all that has been done on both sides, and, when you meet while hunting, to live like true brothers." In Montreal the calumet had become a bland symbol of a French-dominated peace that took little consideration of allies' interests and offered little respect for their power. Stripped of its locally produced social meaning and removed from its regional system of taboos and otherworldly sanctions, Beauharnois's calumet insulted rather than welcomed his Sioux guests.[96]

Calumets continued to have deep meaning for peoples of the Pays d'en Haut, but within the context of this expanded political economy they became less and less tied to the giving of slaves. Although accounts of elaborate calumet ceremonies punctuated by gifts of slaves abound in the seventeenth century, they almost entirely disappear by the 1730s. This loss did not cause increased slave raids, but the subtle evolution of calumet ceremonialism is a telling example of how reconfiguring the geographic and cultural protocols of a regional war culture could change the incentives that balanced the demands of war and peace. The Fox Wars as well as French conflicts with their would-be Sioux and Apache allies indicate that the slave trade weakened incentives to avoid war and eroded the mechanisms designed to stop a war once it began. If these conflicts demonstrate the ability of slaving to curtail the geographic and demographic spread of French colonialism in North America, then, they also represent the transformative power of New France's slave trade among the peoples of the Pays d'en Haut.

❖ Despite French insistence that the Algonquian and Siouan peoples of the Pays d'en Haut unify as children of a French father, living in harmony with one another and fighting French enemies, Indians themselves had other ideas. When Pemoussa expressed his concurrence with the French vision of inclusive Algonquian kinship, his would-be brothers denied his claims and violently enforced the divisions they wished to maintain. When Sioux chiefs traveled to Montreal seeking friendship, Cree and Assiniboine allies brought coffles of Sioux slaves to sell in the streets. By doing so these Indians ensured that they, rather than the French, would determine the

96. Beauharnois to minister, July 1742, *Wis. Hist. Coll.*, XVII (1906), 402–403.

limits of alliance in the Pays d'en Haut. They also defined its character. But if this alliance was "largely Algonquian in form and spirit," the reason is not that it reflected an Algonquian culture of mediation rather than a French culture of "force and obedience." Such false dichotomies obscure the intimate connections between warfare and alliance that placed the slave trade at the heart of the Fox Wars. Like Marguerite-Geneviève—a Fox slave serving a French governor who wanted peace with her people—all Fox captives embodied the tensions between mediation and violence that riddled both Algonquian and French societies. During the Fox Wars and beyond, the Indians of the Pays d'en Haut used these tensions to their advantage, compelling their French father to accept their enemies as his own.[97]

Native engagement in the French slave trade of the eighteenth century was thus a double-edged sword, allowing Indians to restrain French colonial ambitions but transforming their historical practice of slavery, often in destructive ways. From the symbolism of the calumet to the incentives balancing peace and warfare, selling slaves to New France had profound implications for Natives' ability to restrain the waves of violence that French slavery rewarded. The deep bonds between slavery and Native alliances that made the slave trade possible also shaped the French practice of slavery. Evolving out of an Atlantic system that ensured a regionally and legally diverse approach to the institution, French slavery developed in multiple directions, differing not only between the Caribbean and North America but also between the Saint Lawrence Valley and the colony's western settlements of Detroit and Michilimackinac. These varied French expressions of slavery owed a great deal to the indigenous slavery of the Pays d'en Haut, which provided them both with captives and with ideas about what role those captives could play in their society.

more than a dichotomy

97. White, *Middle Ground*, 143, 145.

chapter five

THE CUSTOM OF THE COUNTRY

In the rustic mission church at Michilimackinac, a small group gathered on July 11, 1745, as the Jesuit priest Pierre Du Jaunay baptized two Indians. The first was an Ojibwa woman whose late sister had been married to a voyageur named Charles Hamelin. The second was Hamelin's slave, a twenty-year-old woman "desiring holy Baptism and sufficiently instructed, who took the name of marie Athanase according to the desire of her deceased mistress." Since 1739, Hamelin had suffered great losses: the deaths of a fourteen-year-old daughter, a nine-year-old son, and his wife. At least one daughter was still living, born in 1743, although it is not clear to whom: whether to Hamelin's Ojibwa wife or to his slave, who was certainly his sexual companion after his wife's death and possibly before. Three years later, his slave also died at Michilimackinac and was buried beside his wife. With no one to care for his daughter, he took her back to Montreal, where she had been born, presumably to place her with relatives. But the five-year-old girl died shortly after they arrived. Four days later Hamelin signed a trade license for another journey to the Pays d'en Haut.[1]

Marie-Athanase was only one of many slaves appearing in the sparse records surviving from New France's western posts. At Michilimackinac, where she lived, fully a third of all entries in Catholic baptismal records involved an Indian slave, and another third involved free Indians like Hamelin's wife and sister-in-law. At Detroit, Fort Saint Joseph, and many other settlements slaves were interspersed among the small French popula-

---

1. Baptism of July 11, 1745, Mackinac Baptisms, *Wis. Hist. Coll.*, XIX (1910), 14–15 (hereafter cited as Mackinac Baptisms). For Hamelin's family, see baptism of July 3, 1738, Notre Dame de Montréal, FHL, burial of Apr. 25, 1739, burial of Mar. 10, 1743, baptism of Mar. 12, 1743, burial of Sept. 16, 1748, Lapérade, FHL. For Hamelin's trade license, see "Enregistrement d'une permission accordée . . . à Charles Hamelin, d'un canot et cinq hommes, pour se rendre au Poste de Michillimakinac," Sept. 20, 1748, BANQ-M, TL4, S34, P775.

tion, playing a wide variety of roles in French households. Like indigenous slaves in Indian villages, French-owned slaves in the Pays d'en Haut were predominantly women and children, and they performed both domestic and agricultural duties that were indispensible to the function of French society there. Enslaved Indian women used their skills to work cornfields, to dress skins, and to prepare food. In some ways, because it continued to rely on the demographic and agricultural productivity of forcibly integrated women and children, slavery in New France's western posts retained some indigenous slave practices longer than the Indian peoples who responded to French demand for their slaves.[2]

Occupying a transitional space between Native villages and the towns of the Saint Lawrence Valley, the colonial outposts of the Pays d'en Haut blended indigenous and Atlantic slaveries in interesting and innovative ways. The larger patterns of cultural negotiation, adaptation, and innovation that characterized French-Indian relations in the region included developing new ways of domesticating captives. Many, like Marie-Athanase, played roles that looked a great deal like the slavery that her mistress would have witnessed in her Ojibwa village as a child. Slaves were incorporated into households to serve their masters, and their position could shift into and out of subordination to look a lot like the kinship they theoretically enjoyed. Hamelin's first wife, Marie-Athanase, might well have acted as mistress and primary wife to her namesake, who played the role of an enslaved, subordinate wife. Her request that their slave take her name when she died offers a tantalizing suggestion of one way Hamelin's Ojibwa partner shaped their household. Following Anishinaabe custom, their slave became a placeholder for his wife when she departed. In ways both subtle and significant, Indian women shaped slavery on New France's western periphery, less because of their distance from French centers of power than because these women managed and controlled many of the French households where slaves lived.

Like indigenous slaves in Native communities, enslaved women and children in French control were extremely vulnerable. The line between a negotiated partnership and naked power could be thin, especially because so-

2. For an overview of New France's western posts and their populations, see Marthe F. Beauregard, *La population des forts françaises d'Amérique . . .* , 2 vols. (Montreal, 1984); R. Cole Harris, ed., *Historical Atlas of Canada: From the Beginning to 1800* (Toronto, 1987), plates 39–41; W. J. Eccles, *The Canadian Frontier, 1534–1760*, rev. ed. (Albuquerque, N.Mex., 1983).

cial norms and kinship structures afforded few protections to the enslaved. Whether a woman was a wife or a sex slave—or some combination of the two—is often impossible to tell from surviving records, but such a stark dichotomy likely oversimplifies the daily negotiations of power and practice that we have no way of seeing from this remove. Most surviving records reveal only the outcomes of these relationships rather than their dynamics: children born, names given, marriages performed, bodies laid to rest. Taken together these events resemble an incomplete pointillist painting, with the blank spaces offering room for multiple interpretations of individual situations but the whole providing a strong impression of the system's overall dynamics. As they were incorporated into French and métis households, enslaved Indians faced an array of perils and possibilities that ranged from sexual violence and forced labor to the formation of independent relationships that often led to their full acceptance into French colonial society.

If these dynamics are not always clear, one part of slaves' experience was unambiguous: most of them were only passing through the Pays d'en Haut on their way to another destination. Throughout the last decades of French involvement in North America, the diplomatic function of slaves as symbolic offerings continued to link French and Native communities, tightening the bonds that joined the diplomatic and commercial aspects of slave trading. As the staging grounds for the French slave trade, posts like Michilimackinac and Detroit therefore offered most slaves only a temporary experience. Slave traders used their connections with merchants in the Saint Lawrence Valley to profit from slaves' displacement, an important thing to remember when considering the nature and experience of slavery in the West. Part kin building, part flesh peddling, and part profit-driven trade, slavery in Michilimackinac, Detroit, and other western posts reflected the larger processes of creative reinvention that characterized the French-Native encounter in the Pays d'en Haut and that made slavery in French North America such a diverse and regionally specific experience.

À LA FAÇON DU PAYS

"I administered holy Baptism to a little bastard girl, born this morning of the panis slave of Constant Villeneuve, who accuses herself of having become enciente [pregnant] by her Master."
—*Marin-Louis Lefranc, Michilimackinac, 1759*

The richest accounts of slavery in the western posts survive in the terse entries of three baptismal registries from Michilimackinac, Detroit, and

Fort Saint Joseph, concentrated in the last two decades of French control of these settlements. Recording slaves' names, births, and deaths as well as masters' identities, ages, and sometimes lovers and spouses, these documents offer an intimate view of the relationships that developed in some of the households keeping Indians as slaves. At all three locations, slaves lived within tightly knit French and Indian kin networks created by the bonds of marriage and friendship and the fictive ties of the Catholic ritual community. Although slaves' position within these kinship networks is generally hard to discern, they did form sexual and marital relationships, both coerced and consensual, with French men involved in western trade and diplomacy and occasionally with one another. These relationships have important implications for how we understand intermarriage between French men and Indian women in the eighteenth century, as a significant proportion of marriages "à la façon du pays" ("in the custom of the country") rested on coercion rather than cooperation. A number of enslaved women and girls eventually carved out space for themselves as free women, mothers, and wives in these communities. But, as a common denominator in both French and indigenous slaveries, sexual violence permeated the slave experience in the Pays d'en Haut, so that negotiating a rise to social acceptance and freedom sometimes required prolonged submission to what could be defined as serial rape.[3]

Many enslaved Indian women in the posts of the Pays d'en Haut first appeared in Catholic records as they bore children to the French men who owned them. Most refused to identify their child's father, leaving the relationships that led to the pregnancy invisible in the historical record. It is also likely that priests knew the identity of more fathers than they recorded, facing pressure to cover the actions of influential Frenchmen who could make their jobs difficult if the priests identified them. But, when fathers were named, they were nearly always either the slave's master or a passing voyageur. Daniel Villeneuve, for example, was an interpreter and former

---

3. For intermarriage, see Jennifer S. H. Brown, *Strangers in Blood: Fur Trade Company Families in Indian Country* (Norman, Okla., 1980); Sylvia Van Kirk, *Many Tender Ties: Women in Fur-Trade Society, 1670–1870* (Norman, Okla., 1980), esp. 28–52; Susan Sleeper-Smith, *Indian Women and French Men: Rethinking Cultural Encounter in the Western Great Lakes* (Amherst, Mass., 2001); Kathleen DuVal, "Indian Intermarriage and Métissage in Colonial Louisiana," *William and Mary Quarterly*, 3d Ser., LXV (2008), 268–304; Ann M. Little, "Gender and Sexuality in the North American Borderlands, 1492–1848," *History Compass*, VII (2009), 1606–1615. See below for a sustained discussion of rape and enslaved women's sexuality.

MAP 3. Key French Posts and Native Neighbors in the Pays d'en Haut.
Drawn by Jim DeGrand

voyageur at Michilimackinac, married to an Ottawa woman named Domi-tilde Oukabe (sometimes spelled Ourapé or Ocapé). Constant and Daniel, his métis sons, found work moving back and forth among the posts of the West, including Constant's job as a rower on an expedition to La Véren-drye's Lake Superior post in 1747.[4]

Integrated into a world where domesticated captive women served a vital reproductive role and conditioned by French notions of slaves as property, the Villeneuves took advantage of slaves' sexual accessibility. In 1759 an en-slaved woman belonging to Constant Villeneuve reported that her master fathered her daughter, a "little bastard girl," who was baptized at Michili-mackinac and given the name Charlotte by her godmother, Charlotte Bou-rassa. His neighbor's slave had a child baptized three years later, "being the son of Constant Villeneuve according to what the slave said." Magdelaine, the slave of a Monsieur Chaboille (or Chaboillez) had three children, two of whom had an unknown father. That she was willing to identify the first father, Daniel Villeneuve, but not the others may suggest that the other two children belonged to her master and she was afraid to accuse him of sexual indiscretion. Some masters confessed to fathering children by their slaves, like Jean-Baptiste Sans Crainte, who in 1760 presented his own son for bap-tism, born to "a slave belonging to him." The slave was never identified by name and was likely not present at the ceremony, suggesting either that Sans Crainte chose to identify himself as the father or that his paternity was an open secret in the community. Indeed, the knowledge that masters took advantage of slaves' vulnerability—even when they were quite young—was widespread enough to be considered a basic element of female slaves' ex-perience in the French-settled Pays d'en Haut.[5]

Beyond their masters, enslaved Indian women in the western posts were also made sexually available to voyageurs passing through the Pays d'en Haut, a brutal colonial adaptation of the consensual sexual hospitality

4. Daniel Villeneuve was married to Domitille Oukabe, an Ottawa woman at Michili-mackinac, and he had a son named Jean-Baptiste, who was born in 1723, about three years before Constant. A 1739 apprenticeship contract for Constant as a blacksmith identifies "Domitille Ocapé" as Constant's mother. See marriage of Nov. 23, 1761, Notre Dame de Montréal, burial of Nov. 24, 1761, Laprairie, *RAB du PRDH*, 299083, 319347; "Brevet d'ap-prentissage en qualité de forgeron," Aug. 22, 1739, Greffe Porlier (Montreal), BANQ-M. The author thanks Michael McDonnell for clarifying the often-confusing snippets of information regarding this family.

5. Baptism of Apr. 25, 1762, Mackinac Baptisms, 65, of Apr. 30, 1759, 56, of Oct. 9, 1760, 61.

practiced in some Native communities. Western posts had small permanent populations but hosted an endless stream of merchants, laborers, and military personnel who stopped for trade or stayed during the region's punishing winters. Enslaved women bore children to many of these men. In a telling example from Detroit in 1727, a girl named Marie Anne was born to "a panisse belonging to the Sieur Pierre Mallet and a man that he did not know." At Michilimackinac René Bourassa's slave, the twenty-two-year-old Marianne, bore a child in 1750, "whom she declared to belong to Sieur Jasmine," her master's associate who passed through the post the previous year as a voyageur. The Jesuit Pierre Du Jaunay baptized the child of an enslaved Sioux woman, "Marie Françoise, born about two months ago of a Scioux female slave, whom she declares to belong to a Frenchman called chevreaux now in the north."[6]

Marie Françoise's story shows how slaves in the Pays d'en Haut continued to serve as symbols of alliance between French and Native peoples against common enemies. Chevreaux's northern trade meant that he had developed relationships with the Cree and Assiniboine traders who would have been the source of the Sioux slave. Another French trader with Cree ties, Charles Chevalier Tallier, fathered a son by a different Sioux slave at Rainy Lake, the village where the Monsoni chief La Colle lived and where he had gathered warriors for the massive 1741 raid on Sioux villages. The presence of the Sioux slave, the slave's sexual relationship with a French trader, and the move of that slave and her son to Michilimackinac underscore the intimate relationship between slavery, alliance, and trade in the French communities of the Pays d'en Haut. They also serve to highlight the many faces of violence that often undergirded the alliances that sustained the French presence in the region.[7]

Priests might have intervened to shield Indian women from the coer-

6. Baptism of Apr. 8, 1727, Sainte Anne de Détroit, FHL; baptism of Mar. 17, 1750, Mackinac Baptisms, 28, of May 26, 1750, 30. For the relationship between Indians' sexual hospitality and colonialism, see Kathleen M. Brown, "The Anglo-Algonquian Gender Frontier," in Nancy Shoemaker, ed., *Negotiators of Change: Historical Perspectives on Native American Women* (London, 1995), 26–48; Gordon Sayre, "Native American Sexuality in the Eyes of the Beholders, 1535–1710," in Merril D. Smith, ed., *Sex and Sexuality in Early America* (New York, 1998), 35–54; Kirsten Fischer, *Suspect Relations: Sex, Race, and Resistance in Colonial North Carolina* (Ithaca, N.Y., 2002), esp. 70–74; Richard Godbeer, "Eroticizing the Middle Ground: Anglo-Indian Sexual Relations along the Eighteenth-Century Frontier," in Martha Elizabeth Hodes, ed., *Sex, Love, Race: Crossing Boundaries in North American History* (New York, 1999), 91–111.

7. Baptism of August 1747, Mackinac Baptisms, 23.

cive sex that always attended slavery in some form, as some Jesuits did when Illinois women turned to them for leverage against abusive or coercive men. But there is no evidence of priests' sympathizing with or sheltering slaves, particularly when unmarried women bore children. The sexual double standard already prevalent in European society was doubled again by slavery, as enslaved women were considered useful commodities whose bodies could yield both pleasures and profits. French record keepers said little about these relationships, generally noting that the child's father was unknown with no further commentary. But, when slaves did identify their child's father, a step that could be risky when French men wanted to maintain the illusion of probity, priests tended to blame the slaves. This is what happened to Constant Villeneuve's unnamed slave, who, in the mind of the priest, "accuse[d] herself" of becoming pregnant by her master. When enslaved mothers withheld the identity of a child's father, it could provoke sarcasm from frustrated priests. Rather than using the standard language that a child had an "unknown father" ("père inconnu"), one Detroit priest emphasized the claim's absurdity when he baptized the child of a slave "whose father is totally unknown."[8]

There were, of course, consensual relationships between slaves and between enslaved women and French men. Liaisons between two slaves were rare, because there were only a few adult males held in the western posts, and, when these relationships did occur, they were unlikely to be recorded in Catholic registers. The few exceptions indicate that those who were free to marry often enjoyed other freedoms, sometimes including emancipation. At Michlimackinac in 1737, for example, a freed Indian slave named Jean Baptiste married a twenty-year-old Indian woman called Marianne.

8. "Dont on ne connait point le pere": the implication of this phrase is not transparent and could be translated simply as "whose father is unknown," but, because the language differs from the standard "père inconnu" phrasing and because the priest elsewhere generally used "pas" instead of "point" to express the negative, it has a different charge than a simple note that the father was unknown. Baptism of Feb. 29, 1752, Sainte Anne de Détroit, FHL; baptism of Apr. 30, 1759, Mackinac Baptisms, 56 ("accused herself"). The best discussion of protections offered to some Indian women by priests, and by Catholicism generally, is Susan Sleeper-Smith, "Women, Kin, and Catholicism: New Perspectives on the Fur Trade," *Ethnohistory*, XLVII (2000), 423–452. Most priests in the Pays d'en Haut supported French-Indian intermarriage as a way to prevent unsanctioned sexual relationships that they knew would continue with or without their intervention. See Eric Hinderaker, *Elusive Empires: Constructing Colonialism in the Ohio Valley, 1673–1800* (Cambridge, 1997), 114–116; Jennifer M. Spear, "Colonial Intimacies: Legislating Sex in French Louisiana," *WMQ*, 3d Ser., LX (2003), 75–98; Spear, *Race, Sex, and Social Order in Early New Orleans* (Baltimore, 2009), esp. 1–99.

The priest implied that the relationship had begun some time before but that, after Jean Baptiste was freed, she became his "lawful wife." At the Detroit home of Charles Chauvin two adult slaves, an unnamed "panise" and a man called Pierre, had a child that Chauvin named Bonaventure. At Michilimackinac, Charles and Marie were the only Indian slaves "lawfully married" before 1760, although other relationships certainly existed beyond the priest's view. Marie was at Fort Saint Joseph with her master, the elder René Bourassa, when she bore a child in 1758. Although the priest identified Charles as the child's father, he did not note Charles's presence at the baptism, making it possible that Bourassa—who had a reputation as a philanderer—had fathered his slave's child.[9]

The lines between consent and coercion are unclear in most French records and were surely unstable and contested in the eighteenth century. But enslaved women in the western posts occasionally managed to form long-term relationships, which, even if they began in the context of unequal power, developed into something more advantageous to both partners. A telling example is an enslaved woman in Detroit named Barbe, who bore five children between 1752 and 1759. No record preserves the name of the children's father(s), but the most likely candidates are the two men who owned her in the 1750s. Her first master, Guillaume Dagneau Douville de Lamothe, came from a well-connected merchant and military family with a home in Montreal and a tradition of circulating through New France's western posts. By 1750, Lamothe was supplying corn, brandy, and tobacco to western Indians at Detroit and Fort Saint Joseph, submitting his expenditures to the king for reimbursement as diplomatic expenses. In that year's census, he declared one slave in his household, presumably Barbe, first identified by name at the birth of her son in 1752. Although Lamothe traveled regularly between the Pays d'en Haut and Montreal, he seems to have been in Detroit when Barbe's children were conceived. He also came from a family with a history of using Indian women for labor and probably sex. His brother hired a free Montagnais woman as a domestic servant, paid her poorly, and then pressed to have her hanged in 1756 for petty theft. At trial she claimed to be pregnant, which could have been either a strategic move

9. Baptism of Oct. 13, 1737, Mackinac Baptisms, 5 ("lawful wife"); baptism of Mar. 5, 1752, Sainte Anne de Détroit, FHL; baptism of Jan. 14, 1756, Mackinac Baptisms, 43; baptism of May 26, 1758, in George M. Paré and M. M. Quaife, eds., "The St. Joseph Baptismal Register," *Mississippi Valley Historical Review*, XIII (1926–1927), 230 (hereafter cited as "St. Joseph Baptismal Register"); Trudel, *Dictionnaire des esclaves*, 227.

to delay the execution or the accusation that prompted her employer's rage in the first place. In either case, Lamothe's family history and his access to Barbe make it plausible that he fathered at least some of her children.[10]

The actions of Lamothe's wife heighten suspicion of her husband's involvement with their slave. After Barbe's fifth pregnancy in seven years, Madame Lamothe gave her away "as a free gift" to a Detroit trader, François Leduc dit Persil. Her willingness to sacrifice domestic labor in Detroit, where there were so few alternatives, may indicate how specifically Madame Lamothe wanted Barbe out of her home. There could be other explanations, including the possibility that Leduc was the children's father and made some arrangement with his neighbors to take possession of Barbe. Leduc did spend a great deal of time interacting with Indians and knew many men who had taken Native women as sexual or marital partners. Leduc first traveled to the Pays d'en Haut twenty-two years earlier as a voyageur, eventually settling in Detroit by the late-1740s, where he planted wheat and raised a handful of domestic animals. Barbe seems to have joined this household in 1759, where she would have helped with harvests and cared for the family's chickens and pigs.[11]

But soon after she became Leduc's "gift," she also became something other than a slave. Never again identified by that status, Barbe blended into a mixed French and Indian society that spent relatively little energy policing the exit routes from slavery. In this ethnically mixed environment, she did not bear the burden of race that would face other slaves in the Americas. She bore no stain of being an *affranchi*, or freed slave. With this goal in

10. For Barbe, see baptisms of Aug. 16, 1752, of Sept. 12, 1753, of Apr. 22, 1756, of Mar. 28, 1758, of Oct. 9, 1759, Sainte Anne de Détroit, FHL; Trudel, *Dictionnaire des esclaves*, 231–232. For Lamothe, see "état des fournitures faites à Détroit par Guillaume Dagneau Douville de Lamothe," June 6, 1750, ANOM, Colonies, C11A, CXIX, 232, "Certificat de Robert Navarre à propos d'une fourniture de tabac de Guillaume Dagneau Douville de Lamothe," July 11, 1750, CXIX, 231, "Dénombrement des habitants du Détroit," 1750, G1, CCLXI, 31. For Lamothe's brother, see "Procès entre Alexandre Dagneau Douville, capitaine d'infanterie, plaignant, et Marie-Anne, sauvagesse montagnaise, accusée de vol de linge," Sept. 9, 1756, BANQ-M, TL4, S1, D6117, and "Procès criminel contre Marie-Anne, sauvagesse montagnaise (Amérindienne), pour vol," Sept. 9, 1756, TL5, D1858.

11. "En pur don": baptism of Oct. 9, 1759, Sainte Anne de Détroit, FHL. For Leduc, see "Congé d'un canot par Charles de Boische, Marquis de Beauharnois, gouverneur de la Nouvelle-France, au sieur Monbrun de la Sondraye," June 21, 1737, BANQ-Q, TL1, S35, D9, P106; "Enregistrement d'une permission accordée par Charles de Beauharnois, gouverneur de la Nouvelle-France, le 22 avril, à Desrivières, de deux canots et douze hommes, pour se rendre au Poste de Nepigon," July 11, 1747, BANQ-M, TL4, S34, P736; "Dénombrement des habitants du Détroit," 1750, ANOM, Colonies, G1, CDLXI, 31.

mind, Barbe's sexuality might have been a strategic choice rather than prolonged abuse, or somehow a shifting negotiation of both. But whether she chose the path that led to her freedom or was forced to take it, the cost of social integration was high: three of her children died within days of their birth, and a fourth lived only three months. Only after seven years of sexual companionship with a French man (or men), five pregnancies, four deaths, and one final move did she maneuver her way into some form of social acceptance that included the right to her own body and her one surviving child.[12]

The experience of Marie-Marguerite-Caroline, an enslaved Sioux woman at Detroit, followed a similar course with better results. She first gave birth in 1753 to the son of a passing voyageur named Champagne, who probably enjoyed her companionship as part of Detroit's unspoken tradition of sexual hospitality. Whatever the nature of their encounter, it was fleeting: Champagne disappeared by the time of the child's birth. Starting in 1759, Marguerite-Caroline began a more meaningful and beneficial liaison with her master's neighbor and probable relative, Fermin Landry dit Charlot, bearing him five children by 1771. Their relationship became well known, not mentioned by the priest in the early baptismal records but later said to be public knowledge. Their partnership eventually created enough of a scandal that Marguerite-Caroline's master allowed her lover to buy her freedom on the condition that they marry. To ensure their good behavior, her master kept the couple's six-year-old daugher, Suzanne, as a slave until the couple could buy her. Like Barbe, Marguerite-Caroline formed a long-term relationship that helped her rise up and into French colonial society. She obviously would not have chosen to become a slave or an object of French sexual generosity, nor would she have relished the thought of seeking freedom while leaving her daughter behind. But intimacy with a French man eventually elevated her social standing and yielded full legal and social integration for all but one of her children.[13]

Sexual unions like these were common enough in New France's western posts that they must be considered part of what it meant to form marriages "à la façon du pays." That French men and Indian women forged sexual and

12. See burial of Aug. 26, 1752, Sainte Anne de Détroit, FHL, of Sept. 21, 1753, of June 8, 1758, of Oct. 15, 1759.

13. Baptism of Nov. 16, 1753, Sainte Anne de Détroit, FHL, of June 16, 1759; Trudel, *Dictionnaire des esclaves*, 245. Trudel asserts that there was no familial relationship between her master, Claude Landry dit Saint-André, and her future husband, Fermin Landry dit Charlot, but their familiarity and shared last name make some family tie likely.

marital bonds conjures a set of specific assumptions, almost always positive, that mark this world as "culturally flexible," a place where exercising power was less important than forging mutually beneficial alliances. Alongside these voluntary unions, which "transformed French traders into Indian husbands, fathers, and brothers," slaves' relationships also followed the customs of the country by providing mechanisms for captive outsiders to navigate not only the power relations of slavery but also those of kinship.[14]

Because enslaved women were vulnerable, masters in most slaveholding cultures tended to be sexually opportunistic if not outright predatory. But the meaning of sex between masters and slaves is complex and controversial, all the more so because surviving sources are largely silent on the nature of these relationships. From one viewpoint, any sex that occurred in the context of such unequal power—when the woman was never entirely free to refuse—should be considered a form of sexual extortion akin to, if not equal to, rape. What is more, the power relations of colonialism created dynamics between European men and indigenous women that have led some to characterize interracial sex in colonial borderlands as inherently violent and coercive. But enslaved women could also use sex strategically, reaping rewards for themselves and their children by seducing their masters or other French men. Slaves' actual experience in the French posts of the Pays d'en Haut must have spanned the range of these possibilities, even if there is no way to reconstruct the character of any given relationship from what little information we have. But, however unequally they began, some long-term, mutually affectionate, and fairly balanced relationships between masters and enslaved women clearly developed.[15]

14. Sleeper-Smith, *Indian Women and French Men*, 42. For enslaved Indian women as sexual partners in Louisiana's French settlements, see Juliana Barr, *Peace Came in the Form of a Woman: Indians and Spaniards in the Texas Borderlands* (Chapel Hill, N.C., 2007), 84–86; DuVal, "Indian Intermarriage and Métissage," *WMQ*, 3d Ser., LXV (2008), 271–273.

15. For discussions of rape, sexual consent, and slavery, see Karen Y. Morrison, "Slave Mothers and White Fathers: Defining Family and Status in Late Colonial Cuba," *Slavery and Abolition*, XXXI (2010), 29–55; Wendy Anne Warren, "'The Cause of Her Grief': The Rape of a Slave Woman in Early New England," *Journal of American History*, XCIII (2006–2007), 1031–1049; Edward E. Baptist, "'Cuffy,' 'Fancy Maids,' and 'One-Eyed Men': Rape, Commodification, and the Domestic Slave Trade in the United States," *American Historical Review*, CVI (2001), 1619–1650. For the sexual power dynamics of colonialism, see Richard C. Trexler, *Sex and Conquest: Gendered Violence, Political Order, and the European Conquest of the Americas* (Ithaca, N.Y., 1995); Gary B. Nash, "The Hidden History of Mestizo America," *JAH*, LXXXII (1995–1996), 941–964; Ann Laura Stoler, *Carnal Knowledge and Imperial Power: Race and the Intimate in Colonial Rule* (Berkeley, Calif., 2002); Little, "Gender and Sexuality in the North American Borderlands," *History Compass*, VII (2009), esp. 1609–1610.

Slavery at Detroit, Michilimackinac, and Fort Saint Joseph followed indigenous patterns of incorporation, allowing some slaves and most of their offspring a way to rise up and into the dominant society. But the overlay of French cultural practices also shaped these relationships, particularly through the influence of Catholicism. Aside from keeping slaves "well disposed" toward the power structures within their community, Catholic ideologies and rituals embedded slaves within a set of social relationships that transcended their legal status. Since the seventeenth century, French colonists had pushed Catholicism as a means of ensuring slaves' cultural and social integration and thus their acquiescence to their masters' authority. The 1685 ordinance governing slave law in the Caribbean demanded that slaves be taught the basic doctrines of Catholicism and baptized, with no consent or faith required. No similar law evolved in New France, and because of the French empire's practice of legal pluralism the 1685 Caribbean code had no legal standing in the colony. Still, New France's colonists believed that the rituals of Catholicism served interconnected religious and social functions aimed at integrating Indian slaves into French communities, albeit as unwilling and subordinate members. Taken seriously by some for their explicitly spiritual dimensions, Catholic indoctrination and ritual created real and imagined communities of practitioners that brought slaves into a mixed French and Indian world.[16]

These relationships were both expressed in and strengthened by the practice of godparenting. It is possible to make too much of the fictive kinship created by slaves' receiving godparents at baptism, particularly in these sparsely populated posts where that role was generally played by whoever happened to be present when the ritual occurred. But slaveholders' extended families did participate in the sacraments of one another's slaves, reinforcing their shared commitment to the social relations created by slavery and expressing a form of cultural power over their charges. These rituals of incorporation, together with the priests' program of cultural reeducation, were more than empty mechanisms of control. They expressed French social and metaphysical understandings of the world that their slaves were sometimes forced and sometimes enticed to embrace. It was not uncommon for slaves' religious and ritual lives, like their domestic world, to be overseen by other Indians. As wives of French slaveholders or neighbors involved as godmothers, Native women supervised and monitored much of the captive population in the West.

16. Baptism of Mar. 30, 1755, Mackinac Baptisms, 40.

At Fort Saint Joseph, the métis matriarch Marie Madeleine Réaume dominated the Catholic kinship networks that bound French men, Indian women, and their respective communities together, facilitating the fur and cloth trades that made the relationship mutually profitable. Raised by an Illinois mother and a French father, Marie Madeleine, according to one of her biographers, had a childhood that "blurred the boundaries of her French and Indian heritage and whose adult identity was defined by the ever-expanding Catholic kin network of the fur trade." She was also a slave-holder and a member of one of the West's most active slave trading families. Between 1740 and her death in the 1750s, she, her daughters, and her sons-in-law would act as masters, mistresses, and godparents to dozens of slaves. Although these slaves were incorporated into a social world that recognized few racial or ethnic boundaries, only a handful of these kinless outsiders would rise to become full participants in a world defined by and navigated through extended family relationships. In 1740, Marie Madeleine and her husband baptized their own "slave girl . . . of the panise nation . . . thirteen years old and named Marie Jeanne." Although they invited another trader to be the child's godfather, Marie Madeleine took the role of godmother herself, a role officially discouraged for masters and mistresses.[17]

A similar pattern was followed by Domitilde, the Ottawa wife of Daniel Villeneuve who became, after Villeneuve's death, the wife of Augustin Langlade. Both of her husbands traded slaves as well as furs, and she was thus the mistress of at least seven enslaved Indians over three decades. At Detroit and Michilimackinac, she also acted as godmother to several other slaves, who became her metaphorical children—a role that translated well in the cross-cultural negotiations of the Pays d'en Haut. At Michilimackinac in 1744, Domitilde became the godmother of Anne, a young enslaved girl at Michilimackinac. In 1750 she became godmother to Basile, whose mother had become pregnant from a passing voyageur associated with René Bourassa. She blended the roles of mistress and godmother with her own slave in 1752, overseeing her indoctrination "for a long time," naming her Marie at baptism, and then supervising the slave's first communion.[18]

Many other Native women played similar roles. In Detroit, a Miami woman named Marguerite Ouabankikoué became the godmother of

---

17. Sleeper-Smith, *Indian Women and French Men*, 45 ("blurred the boundaries"); baptism of Apr. 28, 1740, "St. Joseph Baptismal Register," 218 ("marie jeanne").

18. Baptism of Sept. 27, 1744, Mackinac Baptisms, 13, of March 17, 1750, 28, of Sept. 10, 1752, 33.

a handful of slaves, including Joseph in 1712 and Jean-Baptiste in 1714, among the earliest slaves to appear in that settlement's records. One of the founders of Detroit, along with her husband Pierre Roy, Ouabankikoué became a key figure in the social networks through which the fur trade operated. She pioneered these relationships for women like Catherine, an Illinois woman living in Michilimackinac whose French husband lived in the Illinois country. She became both mistress and godmother to a slave born in 1747. In the absence of her husband, the care and correction of this slave and her mother rested entirely on Catherine's shoulders, a role she would likely have learned to play in her Illinois village as a child.[19]

In their role as godmothers, both Native and French women chose names for slaves in their charge, extending fictive kinship to a broader set of cultural forbears. In theory, the ceremonial naming of slaves helped them to become more French and Catholic. According to a 1703 guide to the rites of Catholicism in New France, the purpose of ceremonial naming was to fashion character and to invoke otherworldly power: "The church prohibits priests from allowing the child to be given profane or ridiculous names, like Apollo or Diana, etc. But it commands that the child be given the name of a male or female saint, according to sex, to enable that child to imitate the saint's virtues and feel the effects of God's protection." Like other forms of ritual incorporation, renaming slaves resonated with Indians as much as with the French, as slaves were often renamed and groomed to take the metaphorical place of another. Nor was renaming uncommon among free Indians, who often took new names, according to a seventeenth-century Jesuit, "to revive the memory of a brave man, and to incite him who shall bear his name to imitate his courage." New names also marked important rites of passage, especially those associated with coming of age. "When he passes from childhood to adolescence, he changes his name as the Romans changed their robes. He takes another name when he attains manhood."[20]

19. Baptism of Apr. 11, 1712, Sainte Anne de Détroit, FHL, of June 2, 1714; baptism of Oct. 25, 1747, Mackinac Baptisms, 22. For Marguerite Ouabankikoué and Pierre Roy, see Karen Marrero, "Encountering Cadillac: Detroit before 1701," University of Windsor Humanities Research Group, *Working Papers*, XI (2003), 41–46.

20. Baptism of Jan. 6, 1753, Mackinac Baptisms, 34, of Sept. 17, 1752, 33. "L'Eglise défend aux Curez de permettre qu'on donne des noms profanes ou ridicules à l'enfant, comme d'Apollon, de Diane, etc. Mais elle commande qu'on lui donne le nom d'un Saint ou d'une Sainte, selon son sexe, afin qu'il enpuisse imiter les vertus et ressentir les effets de sa protection auprès de Dieu": *Rituel du Diocèse de Québec* (Paris, 1703), 23–24 ("profane or ridiculous names"); *Jesuit Relations*, XXII, 289 ("revive the memory of a dead man"), XXII, 287 ("as the Romans changed their robes"). For the best synopsis of the literature on Indian naming

Slave-naming patterns in the western posts thus reflected a blend of French and Native imperatives, making them quite different from the naming practices within French plantation slavery. Unlike many slaves in the French Caribbean or in neighboring English colonies, who were given comical or derogatory names, Indian slaves in New France answered to the same names as their free French counterparts. The three most common male slave names in the colony—Jean-Baptiste, Joseph, and Pierre—were also the three most common French names. The most common name for female slaves, as among the French, was Marie. Yet even in Catholic records there are faint traces of indigenous naming that survived efforts to replace slaves' Algonquian or Siouan names. Because this practice was most likely among those who remained aloof from Catholic rituals, it must have been far more common than Catholic records reveal. When Pierre Du Jaunay baptized a two-year-old child in 1755, he noted that the child's mother was "Misoumanitou, being a slave belonging to mr. de villebon." The name translates as "forest spirit," possibly a reference to an Algonquian spirit being who greeted the dying in a final, ecstatic vision as they passed into the afterworld. Like Misoumanitou, all slaves suffered a death and rebirth as they passed into the capturing society. Another Indian, baptized at Fort Saint Joseph, was identified as the child of "sip8assan and pi8alam8." Although the priest never mentioned the possibility, pi8alam8 is a form of the Miami-Illinois term "alem8a," meaning dog or slave. That Angélique L'Archeveque, an Illinois métisse, was the godmother and presumably the translator raises the possibility that she communicated the man's status as his name.[21]

Like their Native counterparts, French and métis households in the Pays d'en Haut sometimes blurred the boundaries between kinship and slavery by using the language of adoption. Many of these families bought young children from allied warriors or ransomed them from Indian communities following a war, owning them and forcing them to integrate as subordinate family members but calling them adoptees rather than slaves. In 1715

---

practices, see David French and Katherine S. French, "Personal Names," in *Handbook*, XVII, *Languages*, 200–221.

21. For Misoumanitou, see baptism of Aug. 24, 1755, Mackinac Baptisms, 42. For Pi8alam8, see baptism of Apr. 28, 1752, "St. Joseph Baptismal Register," 222. The frequency of slaves' French names was calculated using more than two thousand references in Catholic parish registers and various legal and administrative documents. For the most common French names in the colony, see Le Programme de recherche en démographie historique, "Noms et prénoms," http://www.genealogie.umontreal.ca/fr/nomsPrenoms.htm, accessed May 1, 2010.

a young boy who survived the early phase of the Fox Wars was baptized and named Jean-Baptiste. Although he was legally a slave, the priest wrote that he was "adopted by Jacques Hubert dit La Croix." The same year, another Detroit resident, Jacques Philis, presented his slave for baptism, "a boy of the Fox nation, whom Philis had adopted." Other very young Fox survivors occupied a liminal status between slave and adoptee. François, for example, was a two-year-old Fox child at Michilimackinac, captured following Governor Beauharnois's 1733 call to exterminate Fox men and sell their women and children. A neighbor's slave, the four-year-old Marie-Madeleine, was probably captured at about the same time. Both were called slaves but had no enslaved parents to care for them and thus spent their early years being cared for alongside their masters' and mistresses' children.[22]

As Native allies moved through these spaces, often bringing slaves with them, they also brought disease. The most-devastating example occurred in a well-known epidemic of 1757, spread widely by the movements of Indian and métis warriors fighting with the French during the Seven Years' War. The baptismal registries of Michilimackinac show that slaves, like all who resided in these tight quarters, were vulnerable to these diseases. As a proportion of deaths, slaves are likely overrepresented because of their availability to priests for baptism and burial: other Indians, and indeed French, who were more mobile were more likely than slaves to die beyond the view of the missionaries keeping records. Still, the toll on Michilimackinac's slaves was high. During 1757 a third of those buried at the post were Indian slaves who died of smallpox that fall. They often succumbed so quickly that their names were barely taken down. Records that normally ran a paragraph became short sentences: no godparents, no witnesses, just a priest afraid of losing souls as his mission lost so many lives. Incomplete entries from a single week in 1757 give a sense of how completely the epidemic had disrupted normal life. "On the 27th [of October] I privately baptized a female panis belonging to Mde. Blondeau." "On the 2nd of November I privately baptized a little boy, a panis belonging to Mde. Blondeau." "On the 4th I privately baptized ouabikeki, who died on the 5th and a girl panis of Mr. langlade, the younger." The young suffered most. As French residents fell to the epidemic, enslaved children were sometimes left with no supervision or provisions. A few weeks into the crisis, a "little boy" showed up at

---

22. "Adopté par Jacques Hubert dit La Croix": baptism of Nov. 26, 1715, Sainte Anne de Détroit, FHL; "un petit garçon de la nation des Renards, que Philis a adopté": baptism of [1715], Sainte Anne de Détroit, FHL; baptism of Jan. 1, 1734, Mackinac Baptisms, 4.

the home of the post's commandant: he had been "abandoned and is said to belong to Chambele (since dead)." The commandant's own slave Louise, ten or eleven years old, was nursed through a near-fatal encounter sometime the following year.[23]

This priest's desperate—and genuinely dangerous—ritual contact with dying slaves underscores that, for many, the rites of Catholicism were taken more seriously for their otherworldly power than for their social effects. Yet priests could also be hardheaded rationalists when it came to support for slavery. Despite some claims to the contrary, there is no evidence of western missionaries' opposing Indian slavery in New France.[24] By the eighteenth century, Catholicism already had a long history of supporting slavery in principle and practice, and the missionaries of New France were no different. One of the most important reasons for this support was that in some areas slaves represented a large proportion of Indian converts. During the 1750s in Michilimackinac, for example, Indian slaves accounted for more than one third of all baptisms (43 of 125), more than all free Indians and métis combined (38), and more than all French recipients (37). Since converting non-Christians was their sole purpose for residing in this distant country, Jesuits and Recollets accepted Indian slavery as a means to that end. And nearly all of them had slaves of their own. The Detroit Recollet Bonaventure Léonard, for example, owned at least two slaves, including Charles, whom he trained to become a sexton at Detroit's Sainte Anne Parish in the 1740s and 1750s. In this role, Charles attended hundreds of ceremonies that gathered most of Detroit's elite community, encountering many grieving families at their most vulnerable as he prepared bodies and graves for burial.[25]

---

23. Baptisms of Oct. 27, Nov. 2, Nov. 4, 1757, Mackinac Baptisms, 51. For the worst period of the epidemic, see Mackinac Baptisms, 47–51. For the 1757 epidemic and its connection to the Seven Years' War, see D. Peter MacLeod, "Microbes and Muskets: Smallpox and the Participation of the Amerindian Allies of New France in the Seven Years' War," *Ethnohistory*, XXXIX (1992), 42–64. For Louise, see baptism of Apr. 14, 1759, Mackinac Baptisms, 56.

24. Writing in the 1760s, Jonathan Carver claimed that the Jesuits had initially opposed Indian slavery and that they, in 1693, had obtained a ban on the trade from sympathetic officials in France. Neither the Jesuits' plea nor a royal ban exists. At least one historian has cited Carver to substantiate his claim that the Jesuits opposed Indian slavery. See Carver, *Three Years Travels*, 347; Almon Wheeler Lauber, *Indian Slavery in Colonial Times within the Present Limits of the United States* (New York, 1913), 79.

25. Proportions calculated from Michilimackinac baptisms, 1750–1759, in Mackinac Baptisms, 28–61. The division between French and métis should be considered approximate, since French names in the parish register could designate a métis child if the priest did not mention the child's Indian name or that of his Indian father or (more likely) mother. For

At the level of church policy, New France's bishop, parish priests, and Jesuit missionaries generally followed clearly stated guidelines relating to the region's Indian population, slave or free. In 1702, thirteen theologians gathered at the Sorbonne in Paris to establish the principles and procedures governing the baptism of New France's Indians. They discussed fifteen "problems concerning the Indians," ranging from the propriety of baptizing "the children of infidel Indians who have not yet attained the age of reason," to whom specific points of doctrine must be taught before an adult Indian convert could be considered "sufficiently instructed" to receive baptism. Two related principles governed church policy regarding potential Indian converts in the eighteenth century. First, to avoid making a mockery of the Sacrament, it was better to avoid baptizing anyone who was likely to reject the faith in the future. Consistent with this principle, Bishop Saint-Vallier ordered all missionary and parish priests "to use great caution only to baptize [Indian] adults after long instruction and a long probation, and children only in evident danger of death."[26]

To ensure that the convert willingly and knowingly accepted baptism and its commitments, the theologians explained:

> One is obliged to explain all the mysteries of our religion to an adult before baptizing him, that is to say all that he is required to believe . . . such as the unity of God in three persons, the mystery of our redemption, that there is an eternal afterlife to reward our good works, or similarly to punish our wickedness . . . that there are seven sacraments, especially baptism, penance, and the Eucharist; the Ten Com-

Bonaventure Leonard's slaves, see Trudel, *Dictionnaire des esclaves*, 233–234. Jesuits controlled thousands of slaves on plantations in Peru, Chile, Mexico, Louisiana, and Maryland by the mid-eighteenth century. Arnold J. Bauer summarized for Latin America: "Slavery was an integral feature of Jesuit enterprise in colonial Spanish America; not only in tropical agriculture, where everyone used slaves . . . but also in the mixed-economy estates at higher elevations or in temperate zones. Moreover, slavery not only endured on these Jesuit properties, it flourished. And it flourished at a time when private owners were rapidly making a transition to wage labor regimes." See Bauer, "Christian Servitude: Slave Management in Colonial Spanish America," in Mats Lundahl and Thommy Svensson, eds., *Agrarian Society in History: Essays in Honour of Magnus Mörner* (London, 1990), 89–107. The Jesuits in New France owned slaves, including those at Michilimackinac. See, for example, baptism of Apr. 17, 1756, Mackinac Baptisms, 43.

26. G. Fromageau, "Difficultés qui regardent les sauvages, dont on demande la solution," Aug. 10, 1702, *Mandements, lettres pastorales, et circulaires des évêques de Québec* (Quebec, 1887), I, 434–450 ("problems . . . children of infidel Indians"), and Jean de La Croix de Saint-Vallier, "Lettre pastorale touchant le baptême des sauvages," I, 188 ("use great caution").

mandments and the commandments of the church must also be taught.

The only exception to these rules was when a potential convert seemed mortally ill, in which case priests could accept the merest mention of faith as qualification for an adult's baptism. Sick children could receive the Sacrament regardless of their parents' position toward the church.[27]

Demanding adherence to these policies, New France's bishop circulated them to all of the colony's clergy, ordering subordinate priests "not merely to accept this instruction respectfully, but also to conform your behavior to it." Nevertheless, the interpretation of these principles as they applied to Indian slaves varied substantially across the colony. Enslaved Indians occupied a unique position regarding these requirements for baptism. Although almost all of them had non-Catholic parents, they lived under the proximate authority of Catholic masters who could ensure their proper exposure to Catholic doctrine, ritual, and culture. Thus, the threshold for slaves' "sufficient instruction" was far lower than for other Indian converts. Parish and missionary priests consistently baptized Indian children who "belonged to those who are already baptized," clearly a standard met by almost all of New France's Indian slaves.[28]

Still, the missionary priests of the Pays d'en Haut generally demanded that the slaves they baptized be "sufficiently instructed" before receiving the rite, and they often described the slaves they baptized as having been "catechumens" for some time. Jesuit priest Pierre Du Jaunay wrote this characteristic entry in 1744: "I solemnly administered holy baptism to a young Indian girl, aged about 10 or 12 years, a slave of Boiguilbert, sufficiently instructed and desiring holy baptism. She took the name of anne; her godfather and godmother were Sieur jean marie Blondeau, voyageur; and Domitille, wife of mr. langlade." If Du Jaunay followed protocol, this girl learned the Catholic doctrines of deity, sin, and salvation as well as the basic expectations placed on baptized church members. As godparents, Jean-Marie Blondeau and Domitille Langlade were bound to support the slave in the event that her master died, abandoned her, or fell into apostasy. The priest thus doubly guarded the slave against the fiery punishments of hell while offering hope of an eternal paradise. He also protected himself

27. Fromageau, "Difficultés qui regardent les sauvages," ibid., I, 441–442.

28. Jean de La Croix de Saint-Vallier, "Lettre pastorale touchant la résolution de plusieurs difficultés qui concernent les missions des sauvages," Oct. 6, 1703, ibid., I, 452 ("conform your behavior"); *Jesuit Relations,* LX, 269 ("belonged . . . already baptized").

from charges that he profaned the Sacrament by administering it indiscriminately, something most priests took fairly seriously in this period.[29]

The Recollet priests at Detroit also demanded slaves' instruction before baptism. In 1739, for example, Father Bonaventure Léonard explained the demands he made upon one of Detroit's slaveholders regarding the religious instruction of his slaves. "He [Louis Campeau, their master] promised to bring them up and instruct them as his own children and if he is obliged to sell them, only to sell them to a Roman Catholic, without which [assurance] I would not have baptized them." But, by demanding that Campeau rear his slaves in Catholicism, Léonard freed himself from the primary responsibility for their religious training. When he came into possession of his own slave, Léonard baptized her and the child she bore from an unknown father. Priests at Fort Saint Joseph followed the same guidelines and left similar records. When Marguerite, a thirty-five-year-old "panise," was baptized in 1752, the priest described her as "a convert sufficiently instructed and desiring it [baptism] for a long time." What signs of interest she might have offered or the priest might have accepted are unclear. But by the mid-eighteenth century, priests were widely committed to at least the appearance of moderation in their quest for Native converts, even among slaves, who were in no position to refuse.[30]

Even in their own records priests' assertions of a slave's interest in baptism often rang hollow. When Pierre Du Jaunay baptized Antoine, a fifteen-year-old slave who was about to die, he claimed that the boy "had been sufficiently instructed previously and desired baptism for a long while." Why the cleric waited for a mortal illness to fulfill that desire remains unclear. Yet, as a matter of course, the high bar set for Catholic indoctrination and demonstrable interest in the rite of baptism ensured that most Indian slaves would never appear in the baptismal and burial registries kept by the priests. Nor are surviving records nearly as complete at Indian missions as their counter-

29. For Michilimackinac, see baptism of June 24, 1743, Mackinac Baptisms, 10, of Feb. 13, 1754, 36, of Apr. 17, 1756, 43. For Fort Saint Joseph, see baptism of Mar. 24, 1742, "St. Joseph Baptismal Register," 219, of Apr. 15, 1752, 223; baptism of Sept. 27, 1744, Mackinac Baptisms, 13 (the translation there reads "Savage," which I changed to "Indian" for consistency with my other translations). For Du Jaunay, see *Jesuit Relations*, LXXI, 171, 251–253; David A. Armour, "Du Jaunay, Pierre (Pierre-Luc)," *DCB*, IV.

30. Baptism of Apr. 12, 1739, Sainte Anne de Détroit, FHL ("as his own children"); baptism of Apr. 15, 1752, "St. Joseph Baptismal Register," 223 ("desiring ... for a long time"). For another example of a priest's enjoining masters to ensure their slaves' Catholic upbringing, see baptism of Oct. 7, 1736, Sainte Anne de Détroit, FHL.

parts in French colonial parishes. As the Jesuit Jean-Baptiste de Lamorinie scribbled across one page in the Fort Saint Joseph baptismal registry, eight years after his arrival, "Since I am here I have failed to enter in the register all the indian children whom I have Baptized but all are dead as well as the other indians of more advanced age with the exception of the old maynard and the son of patchi paost which I shall forthwith enter." Lamorinie overstated the extent of his omissions, but the general sense he gave was correct. New France's western posts hosted vastly more Indians, enslaved and free, than we can see in surviving records. Priests' interest in claiming as many as possible for their faith generally led them to support slavery among otherwise independent populations and to see Catholicism as the best means of effecting slaves' cultural reeducation and domestication.[31]

For a range of spiritual, social, or sexual purposes, then, Native slaves in the Pays d'en Haut were forcibly incorporated into a large number of French and métis households. Slaves were vulnerable, sometimes abused, and often subject to disease, but the mixed French and Indian system there offered many pathways toward freedom. Although characterized by coercion and sexual violence, in no sense could this be considered a form of racial slavery, where the legal status—and the presumed characteristics justifying enslavement—applied to generations of slaves' descendants. But there were aspects of slavery in New France's western posts that more closely resembled its French Atlantic counterpart, which valued slaves for the productivity of their labor and the possibility that they and their offspring could become lifelong, inheritable property.

TO TEND THE CORN

"The said Sieur de Repentigny is so committed to cultivating his land that he has already begun looking to buy two slaves whom he will use to tend the corn that he will harvest."—Jacques Pierre de Taffanel de La Jonquière, governor of New France, 1751

Although always dominated by trade, New France's western posts also developed small settlements that provided merchants with storehouses, military security, and subsistence staples to keep French traders from becoming dependent on Native food sources. With the exception of the Illinois country, which had been annexed to Louisiana in 1717, Detroit had the greatest

---

31. Baptism of July 17, 1749, Mackinac Baptisms, 27 ("desired . . . for a long while"); "St. Joseph Baptismal Register," 232 ("failed to enter").

potential for developing a stable French community of farmers and merchants. One of the challenges to French agriculture in the West had always been that settlers could make more money in the fur trade, legally or illegally, than they could as farmers. Many traders picked up piecework as they passed through the posts, but most of them resisted regular interruptions in the time they dedicated to trade. As a result, during the first half century of settlement at Detroit, the fur trade expanded at the expense of agricultural development, as even many farmers left land uncleared or uncultivated to spend time gathering furs. "The inhabitants of Detroit," complained Joseph Gaspard Chaussegros de Léry in 1749, "at present do not like to work." Similar complaints became a regular refrain among colonial planners, who believed Detroit could grow to rival the Illinois settlements.[32]

To facilitate this growth, in 1749 the governor and intendant offered twenty-two French families generous inducements to leave the Saint Lawrence Valley and settle at Detroit. In addition to a modest plot of land, the government provided each family with tools, seed, and livestock, plus enough food to sustain the family until their farms could yield what they needed. A consensus had emerged that Detroit, still a tiny settlement of fewer than one hundred French families, held the key to realizing these aims. "This post," wrote the governor and intendant,

> has with much reason at all times been considered very interesting and important, not only from its position with reference to the savage Nations it controls, but Also as a barrier to the Encroachment of the English and because of the provisions it can supply to the Voyageurs of the Southern posts.

They concluded that only a large settled population would answer these ends, producing a sufficient surplus of grain and livestock to provision half of New France's western garrisons as well as providing a large enough male population to form a local militia.[33]

Chaussegros de Léry praised this project as the key to maintaining a French presence in the upper country. "There is no doubt that if this post

---

32. Gaspard-Joseph Chaussegros de Léry, "Léry's Report of His Journey to Detroit," Oct. 22, 1749, in Ernest J. Lajeunesse, ed., *The Windsor Border Region: Canada's Southernmost Frontier: A Collection of Documents* (Toronto, 1960), 47.

33. La Jonquière and Bigot to minister, Oct. 5, 1749, ANOM, Colonies, C11A, XCIII, 31, in *Wis. Hist. Coll.*, XVIII (1908), 30–32, 30 (block quote). On support for Detroit's expansion, see also minister to La Jonquière and Bigot, May 14, 1749, *Wis. Hist. Coll.*, XVIII (1908), 27–29.

falls into the hands of the English, the upper country will be lost to us," he wrote. But, should the current plan work, "we can be assured that no matter what attempts our enemies might make, they will not be able to succeed, even if the Indians should happen to give them a hand." As Louis-Antoine de Bougainville explained in 1757, this added production could significantly improve the French imperial position in the West by supplying France's western garrisons. "These provisions," he wrote, "will cost the king less than those sent from Montreal, the cost of transportation of which is immense, and the difficulty of the passage renders uncertain the subsistence of the garrisons." With a productive and populous Detroit, "nothing would be easier than to bring all the succor necessary in provision and beasts to furnish all the posts."[34]

Because of its ability to link Native trade and alliance with the growth of colonial settlements, Indian slavery became an important component of Detroit's expansion, boosting agricultural production while strengthening flagging alliances between the French and their Indian neighbors. According to Detroit's first census, conducted in 1750, more than a quarter of the ninety-six French families there owned Indian slaves, who constituted about 7 percent of the enumerated population. Not surprisingly, Detroit's slaveholders came from the wealthiest segment of French society and produced a disproportionate amount of the village's grain and livestock. Per household, slave owners cultivated almost three times as much land and produced more than twice as much wheat and oats as non-slaveholding families. Masters also owned twice as many horses, pigs, chickens, and oxen—and three times as many cows—as their non-slaveholding counterparts. Thus, although slaveholders constituted only one-fourth of Detroit's population, they produced about half of the town's wheat, oats, and beef, the three most important provisions for the military garrison.[35]

34. Léry, "Journey to Detroit," in Lajeunesse, ed., *Windsor Border Region*, 48 ("into the hands of the English"); Louis Antoine de Bougainville, "Memoir of Bougainville," [1757], *Wis. Hist. Coll.*, XVIII (1908), 173–174, 170 ("these provisions . . . nothing will be easier"). (This is not to be confused with Bougainville's journals, which are published in English as Edward P. Hamilton, ed. and trans., *Adventure in the Wilderness: The American Journals of Louis Antoine de Bougainville, 1756–1760* [Norman, Okla., 1990].)

35. Wheat: 46 percent; oats: 41 percent; beef: 55 percent. Calculated from "Census of the Inhabitants of Detroit on September 1st, 1750," in Lajeunesse, ed., *Windsor Border Region*, 54–56. A partial translation of the census is provided in Donna Valley Russell, ed., *Michigan Censuses, 1710–1830, under the French, British, and Americans* (Detroit, 1982), 15–17. A microfilm of the original is held at the National Archives of Canada in Ottawa: "Dénom-

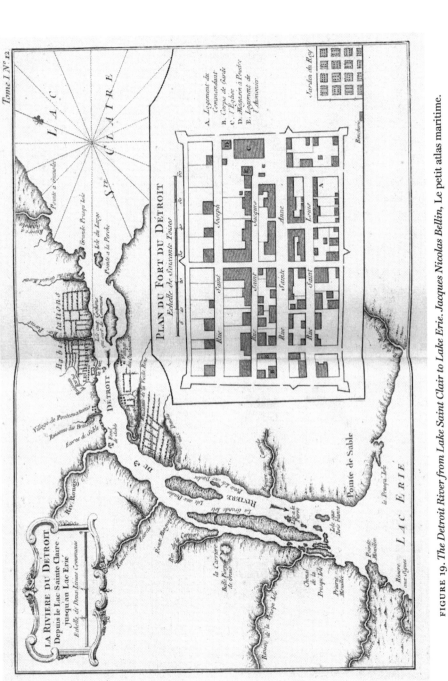

FIGURE 19. *The Detroit River from Lake Saint Clair to Lake Erie. Jacques Nicolas Bellin,* Le petit atlas maritime. *Paris, 1764. Permission The Mariners' Museum, Newport News, VA*

TABLE 1. Average Agricultural Production per Household in Detroit, 1750

Commodity	In Households with Slaves (N = 25)	In Households without Slaves (N = 71)
Wheat (sheaves)	1,100	500
Oats (sheaves)	200	100
Chickens	36	18
Cows	10	3
Oxen	4	2
Pigs	4	2
Horses	2	1
Corn planted (arpents)	2	1
Total land planted (arpents)	41	14

Even as it supported French plans for the productive expansion of Detroit, the Indian slave trade also strengthened French alliances with the Ottawa, Ojibwa, Potawatomi, Saulteur, and Huron villages surrounding the French settlement. During the War of the Austrian Succession, the tepid commitment of these peoples to the French threatened to dismantle the alliance system in the upper country, especially during 1747 when the Hurons led a large party of pro-English Indians against the French garrison. After the war, French traders and diplomats focused considerable energy on regaining the allegiance of their former allies around the region. Significantly, the two families who dominated the Indian slave trade during the 1750s—the Labuttes and Cuilleriers—also played key roles in restoring French alliances with the Ottawas, Potawatomis, and Ojibwas.[36]

No Detroit settler linked trade, alliance, and agricultural production more effectively than Pierre Chesne dit Labutte. By any measurement, Labutte was among the most successful of Detroit's farmers. In 1750, he, his two slaves, and three sons produced four thousand sheaves of wheat, four times the average of his fellow slaveholders and eight times more than the average non-slaveholder. He planted more than one hundred arpents (about eighty-five acres) of land, compared to an average of fourteen ar-

brement des habitants du Détroit, 1750," MG1-G1, CDLXI, fol. 31, hereafter cited as Detroit Census, 1750.

36. For a discussion of anti-French sentiments among the region's Indians during King George's War, see Richard White, *The Middle Ground: Indians, Empires, and Republics in the Great Lakes Region, 1650–1815* (Cambridge, 1991), 186–222.

pents planted by non-slaveholders. With more than two dozen cows, his farm also generated large quantities of milk, butter, and beef. Worth as much as one hundred livres apiece, these animals represented a substantial financial asset that, with his two bulls, produced annual profits through breeding.[37]

Labutte's wealth made him something of a patron in Detroit, facilitating trade and funding Catholic missionary efforts in the region. In 1755, the Recollet priest Simple Bocquet recorded one especially generous gift: "Pierre Labutte, Sr., moved by a holy and religious good will for the glory of God and the decoration of his temple, has resolved to give alms to our church in the sum of a thousand livres in merchandise, to be taken from his warehouse at our selection." The priest wrote that he was "touched by a just thankfulness for so signal a favor," a generosity that revealed Labutte's wealth and his position on the top rung of Detroit's social ladder. One thousand livres equaled about six years' salary for Detroit's laboring class and approached the 1,062 livres paid annually to French military captains in the Pays d'en Haut. During the 1750s and 1760s, Labutte used his wealth to buy at least eleven Indian slaves, who bolstered his productive capacity and elevated his status among Detroit's most influential families.[38]

Like most of Detroit's residents, slaveholder or not, Labutte built his career around forging and maintaining Indian alliances through kinship, trade, and warfare. Shortly after his initial arrival in Detroit during the 1720s, Labutte married Marie-Madeleine Roy, the métis daughter of Pierre Roy and his Miami wife, Marguerite Ouabankikoué, who themselves had been slaveholders from the 1710s. Four years after Marie-Madeleine's death in 1732, Labutte married another métis woman, Louise Barrois, the daugh-

---

37. Detroit Census, 1750. For the price of cows at Detroit, see "Account-Book of the Huron Mission of Detroit . . . ," *Jesuit Relations*, LXIX, 257, 269; "Certificat de Paul-Joseph Lemoyne de Longueuil," Apr. 25, 1746, ANOM, Colonies, C11A, CXVIII, 58, in which Labutte's business partner, Antoine Moison, furnished a cow valued at eighty livres to feast the Hurons, Potawatomis, and Ottawas. Donna Valley Russell identifies "Chêne, pére" as "Charles, father," but Charles was Labutte's brother, and other documents indicate that he had nowhere near enough land or animals to answer to this entry on the census. See Russell, ed., *Michigan Censuses*, 16.

38. George Paré, *The Catholic Church in Detroit, 1701–1888* (Detroit, 1951), 200 (alms quote). For laborers' salaries, see "Account Book of the Huron Mission," *Jesuit Relations*, LXIX, 247, LXX, 21. For captains' salaries, see Charles de Raymond, *Le dénombrement de tous les postes du Canada* [1754], in Joseph L. Peyser, ed. and trans., *On the Eve of Conquest: The Chevalier de Raymond's Critique of New France in 1754* (East Lansing, Mich., 1997), 133 n. 66. For Labutte's eleven slaves, see Trudel, *Dictionnaire des esclaves*, 303.

ter of François Lothmane dit Barrois and "Marianne sauvage," likely an Ottawa woman. Through marriage, Labutte entered into the kinship networks that structured trade and alliance in the upper country. With these connections, Labutte and his second wife, Louise, traded widely with the Indian villages surrounding the French settlement during the 1740s and 1750s. Labutte and his Indian kin exchanged shirts, tobacco, ammunition, and beads for furs, skins, meat, and slaves. These relationships, both personal and economic, exposed him to the diverse languages spoken by the Indian peoples of the Detroit and Saint Joseph River regions. By the 1750s, he had learned to speak Miami, Potawatomi, and Ottawa. These linguistic skills ensured that he would play a prominent role in diplomatic councils during the turbulent years between 1754 and 1764 as the region's Indians struggled to secure their interests during the French and British battle for North America. Well after the British takeover, Labutte would remain an official "Indian interpreter for the Potawatomis and Ottawas."[39]

Labutte's Indian slaves originated in and strengthened the alliances forged by intermarriage, trade, and joint warfare. His first recorded slave, a teenaged Plains Apache named Antoine, died in 1732 during the same epidemic that claimed his first wife, Marie-Madeleine. Because the Illinois country was the most important source for Apache slaves, Labutte probably bought Antoine through the well-established trade relationships that thrived between his Miami kin on the Saint Joseph River and the Illinois. Labutte's later slaves, all listed simply as "panis" in Catholic records, are harder to trace. But Labutte's close relationship with the Réaume family suggests that he maintained his connections with the Miami, Illinois, and Potawatomi families around Fort Saint Joseph, who likely captured the slaves from among their western enemies.[40]

39. For Labutte, Roy, and Barrois, see *Marriage Records, Ste. Anne Church, Detroit, 1701–1850* (Detroit, 2001), part 1, appendix A, 25. The main evidence of Louise's Ottawa origins is Labutte's unusually close relationship with Detroit's Ottawa community. He spoke other languages and interpreted for other nations, but his contemporaries linked him with the Ottawas more than another group. For Labutte's trade, see "Account Book of the Huron Mission," *Jesuit Relations*, LXX, 49–51. For Labutte's role as translator, see George Etherington to Henry Gladwin, Aug. 9, 1763, in Charles Moore, ed., *The Gladwin Manuscripts* (Lansing, Mich., 1897), 643 (quote, spelling, and capitalization modernized), 656. For more on Labutte as interpreter, see David Armour, "Pontiac," *DCB*, III.

40. Joseph Réaume signed as a witness to the burials of two of Labutte's slaves. Sainte Anne parish register, burials of Jan. 26, Feb. 9, 1759, FHL. His brother, Jean-Baptiste Réaume, would become Labutte's brother-in-law in 1763 when he married Agathe Barrois, the métis sister of Labutte's second wife, Marie-Madeleine Barrois. Marriage of Dec. 11, 1763,

Like Labutte himself, his slaves moved in and out of roles that reflected the blurring of Native and French cultural influences. It is tempting, for instance, to read his massive pledge of alms to the Detroit parish as a form of penance for a prolonged relationship with his slave, Charlotte. Although she never named the father(s) of the five children she bore between 1754 and 1769, Charlotte was Labutte's slave for all of those years, living in his home under the supervision of his métis wife, Louise Barrois. After fifteen years of sexual companionship and losing three of her five known children, she remained a slave on the last record where she appears. During these years, she would have played an important role in growing the roughly two acres of corn and caring for more than twenty-five cows and a handful of horses and hogs on the Labuttes' farm.[41]

Labutte's brother-in-law, Jean-Baptiste Cuillerier dit Beaubien, also melded French and Indian interests in agriculture, trade, and alliance. In 1742, Cuillerier married Marie-Anne Barrois, the métis sister of Labutte's wife, Louise Barrois, and thus was linked by kinship to Detroit's Ottawa village. Together with his brother, Antoine Cuillerier dit Beaubien, Jean-Baptiste developed impressive agricultural and commercial holdings that elevated Detroit's economic standing and strengthened French ties to key Ottawa, Potawatomi, and Miami villages. Like Labutte, the Cuilleriers also bought several Indian slaves. The two brothers, who are often indistinguishable in the records, owned at least sixteen Indian slaves between them.[42]

In 1739, for example, Jean-Baptiste Cuillerier baptized two of his slaves at Detroit, "Renez, of the Chickasaw nation, about 14 to 16 years old, and Josephte, of the Fox nation, between 14 and 16 years old, both belonging to the Sieur Cuillerier, who promised me that he would instruct them and give them a Christian education as if they were his own children." The slaves' Fox and Chickasaw origins reflect the contours of the Indian slave trade during the 1730s and early 1740s. Cuillerier's Ottawa ties allowed him to profit from their participation in these French-Indian wars while rewarding them for

---

Marriage Records, Ste. Anne Church, Detroit, 1701–1850, part 1, 17. Their father, Hyacinthe Réaume, was Labutte's neighbor (Detroit Census, 1750). For the best treatment of kinship and trade between Detroit and Fort Saint Joseph in the 1740s and 1750s, see Sleeper-Smith, *Indian Women and French Men*, 38–53.

41. For Charlotte, see Trudel, *Dictionnaire des esclaves*, 234. For Labutte's farm production, see Detroit Census, 1750.

42. For Cuillerier and Barrois, see *Marriage Records, Ste. Anne Church, Detroit, 1701–1850*, part 1, appendix A, 30. For production, see Detroit Census, 1750. For a list of their slaves, see Trudel, *Dictionnaire des esclaves*, 309–310.

fighting France's enemies. By the 1750s, when the Fox and Chickasaw conflicts had ground to a halt, the Ottawas did not fight such a clearly defined set of enemies, making it likely that the Cuilleriers' slaves came from farther west or from among Ohio Valley Indians who had become friendly with the English.[43]

The Cuillerier brothers traded with all of the Indian villages surrounding Detroit and throughout the Pays d'en Haut. Jesuit account books offer a glimpse of their trade, especially with the Hurons who were most closely associated with the Jesuit mission. In the credit column, the missionaries recorded that they provided the Cuilleriers with glass beads, wampum, powder, shot, vermilion, awls, and shirts, which they traded with Indians for furs, skins, meat, and slaves. The Cuilleriers paid the missionaries in beef, butter, pork, wine, chickens, and canoes. Although these transactions were recorded in a ledger with crude attempts to account for debits and credits, much of the Indian trade occurred off-book and often blurred the line between diplomatic gift-giving and commodity trade. But when French traders and diplomats claimed such gifts as their personal property, they violated the express demands of their superiors in Quebec and Paris. In 1742 the French crown demanded that all diplomatic gifts given by Indian allies to French traders, diplomats, or post commanders become the property of the state, to be traded or sold to defray the mounting costs of Indian diplomacy.[44]

Antoine Cuillerier, for example, submitted reports detailing the expenses he incurred as an official supplier of visiting Indians at Detroit: five cows slaughtered for a feast, a thousand wampum beads offered as a token of friendship, flour milled on the king's account for visiting delegations. Yet not once did he report receiving reciprocal gifts from the Indians. By reporting his accounts this way, Cuillerier could demand payment for items

43. For baptism of May 17, 1739, Sainte Anne de Détroit, FHL (Renez and Josephte). For a discussion of the Ottawas' enemies during the 1750s, see William J. Newbigging, "The History of the French-Ottawa Alliance, 1613–1763" (Ph.D. diss., University of Toronto, 1995).

44. For the Cuillerriers' trade, see "Account Book of the Huron Mission," *Jesuit Relations,* LXX, 21–39. For the state's efforts to recover the costs of Native diplomacy, see S. Dale Standen, "'Personnes sans caractère': Private Merchants, Post Commanders, and the Regulation of the Western Fur Trade, 1720–1745," in Hubert Watelet and Cornelius J. Jaenen, eds., *De France en Nouvelle-France: société fondatrice et société nouvelle* (Ottawa, 1994), 287. For the best discussion of the political economy of gift-giving and Native military alliance, see Catherine M. Desbarats, "The Cost of Early Canada's Native Alliances: Reality and Scarcity's Rhetoric," *WMQ,* 3d Ser., LII (1995), 609–630.

that he gave as "gifts," even when he received valuable commodities, including slaves, in return. Merchants like Cuillerier therefore had strong incentives to support warfare in the West, because they could profit both from the captives generated by the conflict and from the provisions they offered for its resolution, charged to the king at a profit. Thus, it was "a rather common thing in Canada," groaned the king's minister in 1755, "to make a great commotion, and even to start wars in connection with private incidents of trade of but little interest to the nation." In another sense, though, the slave trade served the interests of the state by allowing Detroit's settlers to pursue agricultural and commercial interests simultaneously. When Bougainville surveyed the region in 1757, he praised Detroit for its recent growth. Had another war with the British not consumed French attentions at the time, Detroit would have likely grown into a substantial agricultural and trading community similar to the French villages of the Illinois country.[45]

The Cuilleriers maximized this potential, developing an extensive agricultural enterprise that included rich harvests of grain, productive herds of cattle, and a busy gristmill and forge. Only slave labor could account for their ability to maintain so many economic activities at once. The two families had only one teenaged son between them in 1750, yet together—in addition to their trading endeavors—they planted nearly one hundred arpents (eighty-five acres) of land and kept almost three hundred chickens and thirty cows. Although there were many French and Indian day laborers in the Detroit area, no records indicate that the Cuilleriers hired out the work on their farm, in their mill, or at their forge. Their slaves therefore contributed substantially to the family's wealth and allowed the brothers to maintain their trade relationships with surrounding Natives. Because the Cuilleriers left no account books, estate inventories, or personal letters, we cannot know for certain what tasks their slaves performed, but their economic activities suggest a range of possibilities.[46]

45. For cows, see Certificat, Oct. 22, 1747, ANOM, Colonies, C11A, CXVII, 118; for wampum, 122; for flour ["*farines qui ont été blutées par moi Cuillerier pour le roi"*], see Mémoire, June 6, 1749, ANOM, Colonies, C11A, CXVIII, 370. For encouraging warfare, see "Memorandum from the King," Mar. 22, 1755, *Wis. Hist. Coll.*, XVIII (1908), 152 ("rather common . . . to make a great commotion"). For Detroit's growth, see Bougainville, "Memoir," *Wis. Hist. Coll.*, XVIII (1908), 173–175. The best overview of agriculture in the Illinois country is Carl J. Ekberg, *French Roots in the Illinois Country: The Mississippi Frontier in Colonial Times* (Urbana, Ill., 1998).

46. Detroit Census, 1750; "Account Book of the Huron Mission," *Jesuit Relations*, LXX, 21–39.

The Chickasaw slave René, for example, began working for Antoine Cuillerier in 1739 as a young teenager and remained his slave until he died in 1755. René probably cleared a good portion of Cuillerier's forty-three planted acres of land, harvested substantial crops of wheat and oats, and worked at the gristmill. Josephte, the Fox woman baptized with René in 1739, probably worked the family's two and a half acres of corn, cared for a large number of domestic animals, and helped with household chores such as cooking and child care. At the posts of the Pays d'en Haut, French families routinely purchased Indian women for their horticultural skills, relying on them to plant and harvest the corn that they sold to soldiers, traders, and visiting Indians. When Louis Legardeur, chevalier de Repentigny, wished to establish a farm at his new post of Sault Sainte Marie, he immediately bought two Indian slaves. "The Said Sieur de Repentigny is so desirous of cultivating the land," the governor explained in 1751, "that he has already taken steps to procure two slaves whom he will employ in taking care of the Indian corn he will harvest on such land." The Cuilleriers did the same, parlaying their close ties with Indian traders into agricultural surpluses that expanded their economic reach.[47]

The two principal Indian slaveholders at Michilimackinac, René Bourassa dit La Ronde and Charles-Michel Mouet de Langlade, also translated their close ties with the region's Native communities into complex economic ventures. Standing at the center of Michilimackinac's French-Indian alliance system, they also owned nearly a quarter of the post's known Indian slaves. René Bourassa, born in 1688 on the south shore of the Saint Lawrence at La Prairie, entered the fur trade in the 1710s, traveling as a merchant-voyageur to every major western post during the 1720s and 1730s. As we have seen, Bourassa joined many of New France's most prominent merchants and military officers in western business ventures, including the Sioux slave trade with La Vérendrye and La Plante. From 1736 to 1737, Bourassa lived among the Ojibwas in present-day Minnesota, apparently learning their language and establishing close personal ties with key Ojibwa traders. Thereafter, Bourassa returned to Michilimackinac, settling there permanently with his family by the mid-1740s. A 1749 map of Michilimackinac reveals that Bourassa owned one of the most desirable of

47. La Jonquière to minister, Oct. 5, 1751, *Wis. Hist. Coll.*, XVIII (1908), 103. "Le dit. S. de Repentigny soit si fort s'attacher à la culture de ces terres, qu'il est déjà entré en marché de deux Esclaves qu'il lemployera à soigner le Bled d'inde qu'il ceüillera": La Jonquière to minister, Oct. 5, 1751, ANOM, Colonies, C11A, XCVII, 107–107v.

the fort's forty homes, adjacent to the post commander at the center of the public square. He also owned a field outside the fort, but he left no record of how much, or even what, his farm produced. Michilimackinac's parish register reveals Bourassa as one of the best-connected and most reliable residents of the fort. During the 1750s, he, his wife, Marie-Catherine, or his daughter, Charlotte, acted as godparents in almost half of the mission's baptisms.[48]

Bourassa and his family had particularly strong ties to the métis communities at Michilimackinac and other western posts. Through his extensive travel and trade, Bourassa established friendships in many Native villages around the Pays d'en Haut, especially among Indians married to or living with other French voyageurs. Members of his family often acted as witnesses to marriages between French men and Indian women as well as to their children's baptisms. In 1752, for example, Marie-Catherine sponsored a métis convert at his baptism:

> Reverend father de la morinie, a missionary of the society of Jesus, solemnly administered the Sacrament of holy Baptism to a young man about thirteen or fourteen years old, natural son of Mr. la plante and of an Indian woman of Cammanettigouia, he being sufficiently instructed and desiring holy Baptism. He took the name of louis at the sacred font. The godfather was Mr. de Gonneville; and the godmother Mlle Bourassa who signed here.

Marie-Catherine had more than a passing interest in this young man. He was her half-brother, born to her father, Clément Lérigé de La Plante, and his Cree or Assiniboine partner. Two of Bourassa's children also married into métis families. In 1744, their eldest son, René, married Charlotte Chevalier, making him a brother-in-law to an Ottawa woman and tying him closely to the mixed French-Indian villages along the Saint Joseph River. Ten years later, their daughter, Charlotte, married Charles-Michel Mouet de Langlade, Michilimackinac's most prominent Ottawa métis.[49]

48. For Bourassa's and Langlade's slaves, see Trudel, *Dictionnaire des esclaves*, 286–287, 389. For Bourassa's life and career, see David A. Armour, "Bourassa (Bouracas, Bourasseau), dit La Ronde, René," *DCB*, IV; Louis Lavallée, *La Prairie en Nouvelle-France, 1647–1760* (Montreal, 1993), 217–218. For his home at Michilimackinac, see Michel Chartier de Lotbinière, Map of Michilimackinac [1749], reprinted in Peyser, ed. and trans., *On the Eve of the Conquest*, 94. For godparenting, see Mackinac Baptisms, 28–59.

49. Mackinac Baptisms, 32; "Register of Marriages in the Parish of Michilimackinac," *Wis. Hist. Coll.*, XVIII (1908), 471–472, 481, and marriage contract dated Aug. 11, 1754,

Because of Bourassa's linguistic skills, his friendship with Native and métis families, and his long experience with Indian trade, Michilimackinac's post commanders often relied on him to supply trade goods and diplomatic gifts to the many chiefs and warriors who visited the post or to provision departing French and Indian war parties. Marie-Catherine often took charge of these activities in her husband's absence, writing her own certificates to the intendant requesting payment for services rendered. At the end of the War of the Austrian Succession in 1748, for example, the French held a feast at Michilimackinac to celebrate what they perceived as their victory over the British. To show appreciation for allied Indians' support during the war, and to lure wavering villages back into the French camp, the commander at Michilimackinac ordered René Bourassa to supply more than one thousand livres worth of goods, which he gladly provided, "as much for the festivities as for the presents made to the Indians on the occasion of the peace." The items Bourassa offered at the celebration—meat and grain from his farm and trade goods from his warehouse—represented the complex relationship between alliance and slavery in New France. Bourassa's generosity strengthened the alliance by affirming French respect for Native customs and by responding to Indians' material demands. Yet Bourassa produced these goods with enslaved Indian labor. By 1748, Bourassa had owned at least six Indian slaves, four of whom remained alive, and their work allowed their master to engage in extensive trade and still produce ample agricultural goods used to provision allied Indians.[50]

Bourassa's provisioning trade highlighted the messy realities of slave trade diplomacy, as when his Sioux slave, Antoine, helped to produce the goods that Bourassa offered to the Saulteurs to encourage them to make peace with the slave's own people. For Bourassa, this arrangement offered the best possible combination of competing French objectives. He profited from the goods he gave to the Saulteurs, which he charged to the king's ac-

135–140. For the Chevaliers' connection with the St. Joseph settlements, see Sleeper-Smith, "Women, Kin, and Catholicism," *Ethnohistory*, XLVII (2000), 434, 448 n. 56.

50. For Bourassa's provisioning, see, for example, "État de ce que Bourassa a fourni, par ordre de Verchères, pour la subsistance des Sakis, Renards, Sioux et Pouants retournant à leurs villages," Nov. 9, 1742, ANOM, Colonies, C11A, LXXXI, 360, and "Mémoire de Bourassa qui a fourni cent livres de graisse, par ordre de Noyelles," Sept. 17, 1747, CXVII, 384. For Marie-Catherine's management of financial affairs, see "Mémoire de Marie Laplante Bourassa," June 13, 1747, CXVII, 363. "Certificat . . . au sujet de fournitures faites par le sieur Bourassa," Sept. 17, 1749, CXIX, 169 ("festivities . . . presents"). For a list of Bourassa's slaves, see Trudel, *Dictionnaire des esclaves*, 287.

count. In case the Saulteurs chose to defy French demands, which in this case they did, Bourassa could then profit from the slave trade. This was a dangerous game in the 1750s, when alliance was anything but certain even among those nations most closely tied to Michilimackinac, such as the Ottawas, Ojibwas, and Potawatomis. French officials, recoiling from the costs of the recently concluded war, grew stingy with gifts while French merchants, unable to obtain the quantity of trade goods they desired, raised their prices. Therefore, English efforts to lure French-allied nations into their Ohio Valley trade networks drew many influential chiefs away from the French during the first few years after King George's War. Nevertheless, mainly through the efforts of individual Ottawa families and headmen, the better part of these three nations remained at least loosely attached to French interests.[51]

From both French and Ottawa perspectives, the most important person holding the precarious alliance together was Charles-Michel Mouet de Langlade, a métis born at Michilimackinac to Augustin Mouet de Langlade, a successful French merchant, and his Ottawa wife, Domitilde. From his father, Charles inherited wealth, a French education, extensive trade connections, and political influence within New France. From his mother, Langlade inherited fluency in the Ottawa language, familiarity with Algonquian customs, and access to the commercial, military, and kinship networks that governed alliance and trade in the western Great Lakes. Langlade's maternal uncle, the influential Ottawa war chief Nissowaquet, trained Langlade to fight like an Ottawa. Langlade then proved those skills in the Chickasaw War, during which he secured his reputation as a potent Ottawa warrior. In 1750, Langlade fathered a child by an Ottawa woman, named Agathe. Although the relationship lasted only two years, it expanded Langlade's social and familial ties within the Ottawa community surrounding Michilimackinac.[52]

---

51. For Antoine, see Trudel, *Dictionnaire des esclaves*, 287. For provisioning Saulteurs, see White, *Middle Ground*, 182. For Bourassa's role in the Sioux slave trade, see Chapter 4.

52. Michael A. McDonnell, "Charles-Michel Mouet de Langlade: Warrior, Soldier, and Intercultural 'Window' on the Sixty Years' War for the Great Lakes," in David Curtis Skaggs and Larry L. Nelson, eds., *The Sixty Years' War for the Great Lakes, 1754–1814* (East Lansing, Mich., 2001), 79–105; Paul Trap, "Mouet de Langlade, Charles-Michel," *DCB*, IV, 563–564; Sandra J. Zipperer, "Sieur Charles Michel de Langlade: Lost Cause, Lost Culture," *Voyageur: Northeast Wisconsin's Historical Review*, XV (1999), 24–33; Newbigging, "History of the French-Ottawa Alliance," 373–375. According to Newbigging, 374: "More than any other person, Langlade had the ability to rejuvenate the alliance. . . . A person with a foot in both

Nothing demonstrates Langlade's importance within the French-Indian alliance system as much as his leadership in warfare during the early 1750s. During the first three years of peace following the War of the Austrian Succession, French officials reported a steady attrition among New France's Native allies, who increasingly sought independence from the French and access to British goods. At Pickawillany, a mixed Miami and Piankshaw village between the Wabash and Great Miami Rivers, British traders established permanent roots by 1749, threatening to expand trade into traditionally French territory and further destabilize the already shaky alliance system. French officials initially sought the assistance of their traditional Indian allies, but to no avail. The lucrative British trade had lured many previously loyal chiefs, and thus their villages, out of the French orbit.[53]

French authorities initially hoped to muster the support of many allied Indians in a show of force that would drive the English traders away from the Ohio and restore their erstwhile allies to French interests. This strategy failed spectacularly, not least because French officers had damaged their credibility by their recent miserliness. French officers reported that none of their traditionally loyal allies would join them in an attack on the Miamis. When the French governor struggled to gain allied support by appealing to their metaphorical kinship, he turned instead to Charles Langlade, whose actual kinship with the Ottawa proved more successful. In 1752, Langlade, the Ottawa chiefs Mikinak and Nissowaquet, and a party of 250 Anishinaabe warriors attacked Pickawillany, defeating the largely defenseless village when its young men were away hunting. Hoping to rid the Ohio of the traders' influence, Langlade exchanged his Indian prisoners for five British traders who hunkered within the palisades. With errant Indians soundly defeated, English traders in custody, and the French-Ottawa alliance at its

---

[French and Ottawa] worlds. . . . Langlade was not merely a symbolic presence signifying the rebirth of the alliance, he was also a product of the alliance itself and a man who would fight passionately in defence of the interests which had tied the French and the Ottawas together since Champlain arrived at Lake Huron."

53. Duquesne to Machault, Oct. 10, 1754, in Theodore Calvin Pease and Ernestine Jennison, ed., *Illinois on the Eve of the Seven Years' War, 1747-1755*, French Series, III, Collections of the Illinois State Historical Library, XXIX (Springfield, Ill., 1940), 904–905, and "The Administration of Kelerec and Duquesne, 1753-1754," 812. The best summaries of events at Pickawillany are Fred Anderson, *Crucible of War: The Seven Years' War and the Fate of Empire in British North America, 1754-1766* (New York, 2000), 24–32; Hinderaker *Elusive Empires*, 42–44; White, *Middle Ground*, 227–233. Newbigging, "History of the French-Ottawa Alliance," 368–374, gives a brief account that adds some important detail about particular Ottawa chiefs and their motives for participating.

strongest in years, Langlade returned to Michilimackinac a hero in both French and Ottawa eyes.[54]

That Langlade owned and traded Indian slaves suggests, even more dramatically than Bourassa's provisioning, the inseparability of slavery and alliance in this region. Langlade learned the benefits of Indian slavery at a young age, as he personally escaped many of life's drudgeries thanks to the labors of Marie-Madeleine, Charles, Marie, Jean-Baptiste, and two other unnamed slaves belonging to his parents. As he grew into his role as an Ottawa warrior and diplomat, Langlade also came to appreciate the symbolic power of captive exchanges within that culture as well as the material benefits his people could gain by selling their war captives to the French. Langlade's involvement with Indian slavery only strengthened with his marriage, in 1754, to Charlotte Bourassa, the daughter of René Bourassa and Marie-Catherine Lérigé de La Plante. Like her husband, Charlotte had been reared in a family that owned many Indian slaves, a tradition that, through her mother, extended back two generations. Both families' social circles, too, comprised several French and métis families that joined their interest in the fur trade with their acquisition of Indian chattel. Indicative of this pattern, of the twenty-one family members and friends witnessing the couple's marriage, sixteen—or more than three-fourths—were Indian slaveholders.[55]

Charles Langlade acquired his slaves from his Ottawa kin, who sold or gave them as tokens of their friendship. Throughout the French period, the Ottawas continued to offer captives as emblems of alliance with all of their allies, French and Indian alike. When the Potawatomis trespassed into Ottawa hunting territory in 1734, for example, tensions between the groups flared. To avert a crisis, the Potawatomis offered the Ottawas a gift of Fox slaves to appease them and to assure them of their goodwill. Gifts like this also signified the Ottawas' commitment to their French allies. Augustin Langlade, through his wife's influential kin network, built a long-term trade relationship with the Ottawas, which included receiving slaves captured among their enemies. Years later his son Charles Langlade "had two [slaves], given him by the Ottawas, who were of the Osage tribe." Al-

---

54. Anderson, *Crucible of War*, 24–32; Hinderaker, *Elusive Empires*, 42–44; White, *Middle Ground*, 227–233; Newbigging, "History of the French-Ottawa Alliance," 368–374.

55. Marriage of Aug. 12, 1754, "Register of Marriages in the Parish of Michilmackinac," *Wis. Hist. Coll.*, XVIII (1908), 481, and marriage contract, Aug. 11, 1754, 135–140. For a list of Augustin Mouet de Langlade's slaves, see Trudel, *Dictionnaire des esclaves*, 389.

though no other document reveals the precise origins of Langlade's slaves, they most likely came in the same way: following an Ottawa raid against an enemy, they offered their captives to Langlade in exchange for both his trade goods and his alliance. When New France's governor wanted to elevate French esteem among allied Indians, he called upon the services of Michilimackinac's two most prominent Indian slaveholders. On a larger scale Michilimackinac itself encapsulated the intimate ties between alliance, slavery, and commerce in the Pays d'en Haut. The post boasted the lion's share of western slave trade during the 1750s, and—not coincidentally—it also hosted the largest métis community in greater New France and served as the diplomatic center of the French-Indian alliance system.[56]

SOLD, CEDED, AND TRANSFERRED

"Jean-Baptiste Auger . . . by these presents has sold, ceded, quit, and transferred now and forever with the guarantee of these acts and promises . . . a panisse about twenty-two years old."—Jean-Claude Panet, notary, 1749

For all of the ways that slavery adapted to the particular cultural contexts of the Pays d'en Haut, most slaves were eventually sold away to a buyer in Montreal, which hosted the most Indian slaves of any French settlement and served as a hub for the Saint Lawrence Valley slave trade. Because there were no notaries in New France's western settlements and no royal courts to intervene in disputes, we have no records of slave sales in Detroit or Michilimackinac and thus no window onto the dynamics of that side of the trade. Montreal's records occasionally capture the grueling journey from the West, particularly for young slaves or those who had been tortured by their captors. Because most French traders could not read and write, we know almost nothing about the arrangements for transporting and feeding slaves during this time. Records do indicate that some of the slaves died in transit or soon after their arrival. In 1742, for example, a parish priest in Lachine recorded the death of a young girl who died shortly after completing the journey: "The sixth of October was buried in the cemetery of this parish the body of an Indian belonging to M. Maugras, merchant of Montreal and voyageur, who died yesterday aged about nine years, after being conditionally baptized two days ago coming from Michilimackinac." Such glimpses are extremely rare. To see how most slaves made their way from Detroit and

---

56. Grignon, "Recollections," *Wis. Hist. Coll.*, XVIII (1908), 179 ("given him by the Ottawas"); Newbigging, "History of French-Ottawa Alliance," 342–343.

Michilimackinac to Montreal and beyond, we have to look at the scattered records indicating sales and other arrangements that transferred slaves from western French owners to masters or mistresses in the heart of the colony.[57]

New France's merchants responded enthusiastically to a growing demand for Indian slaves that started in the 1710s and strengthened for half a century. Although merchants initially participated in the slave trade to supplement flagging returns from other commodities, the Indian slave trade eventually thrived in its own right, enriching many of the merchants and military officers who participated in it. Despite potential profits, however, the trade remained modest in scale for many reasons. Not only were slaves difficult and costly to transport from the West to the Saint Lawrence, but slaves tended to come into French possession one or two at a time in the face-to-face exchanges of the Pays d'en Haut. The surges of Fox and Sioux slaves at particular moments of conflict were the exceptions, inspiring so much commentary and producing such conflict because they were so unusual.

Although colonists were supposed to formalize all slave sales with a notarized contract to prevent disputes over slaves' legal status or ownership, such contracts remained rare. Despite nearly two thousand individually identifiable Indian slaves appearing in New France's church and court records, fewer than thirty notarized sales survive. Like much of the colony's small-scale trade, slave sales largely occurred as private transactions, beyond the view of notaries and thus absent from surviving documents. Furthermore, unlike the British colonies, New France had no newspapers, an absence depriving us of the rich details found in slave sale and runaway advertisements. As with slave demand, the surviving notarial deeds, sacramental records, and court documents allow a glimpse, however imperfect, of the Indian slave trade in the eighteenth century.[58]

The best gauge of slave trade volumes into the colony is Catholic parish

---

57. "Le sixieme doctobre a eté inhumé dans le cimetiere de cette paroisse le corps d'une sauvagesse appartenante a mr maugras marchand de montreal et voyageur laqu'elle est decedée dhier agée d'environ neuf ans apres avoir ete ondoyëe depuis deux jours en venant de missilimakinak." Burial of Oct. 6, 1742, Saints-Anges de Lachine, FHL.

58. For the best treatments of slave sale advertisements in colonial British America, see Steven Deyle, "'By Farr the Most Profitable Trade': Slave Trading in British Colonial North America," *Slavery and Abolition*, X (1989), 107–125; Robert E. Desrochers, Jr., "Slave-for-Sale Advertisements and Slavery in Massachusetts, 1704–1781," *WMQ*, 3d Ser., LIX (2002), 623–664.

TABLE 2. Individually Identifiable Indian Slaves
by Date of First Appearance

Decade	Male	Female	Total (N = 1,748)
1670–1679	6	2	8
1680–1689	9	1	10
1690–1699	18	1	19
1700–1709	57	10	67
1710–1719	171	118	289
1720–1729	108	120	228
1730–1739	150	141	291
1740–1749	140	214	354
1750–1759	183	299	482

registers, which recorded the baptisms, births, and burials of many slaves. Although they vastly undercount slaves, these documents provide the most consistent measure of the trade's volume over time, assuming that the level of slaves' presence in these records rose and fell with the colony's overall slave population. It is essential to remember that these can provide only a barometer rather than an actual accounting of slave population, which was much higher than these numbers suggest. According to this measure, the sharpest percentage increase in slave traffic occurred between 1709 and 1715, when the number of new Indian slaves appearing in Catholic registers rose from an average of five per year to more than twenty-five. This likely reflects the growing confidence colonists felt that their investments in slave property would be protected by Raudot's 1709 slave ordinance. Thereafter, annual additions rose slowly, to thirty in the 1730s, thirty-five in the 1740s, and nearly fifty in the 1750s. Before 1740, more than 90 percent of known Indian slaves lived in the Saint Lawrence settlements between Montreal and Quebec. With more slaves being kept in western posts during the 1740s and 1750s, Montreal's share of the total dropped as its overall numbers continued to rise.[59]

Even as the volume and composition of the slave trade shifted, the average price colonists paid for slaves remained fairly constant. By 1715, Indian

59. Of the 912 total known slaves through 1739, Detroit had a mere 54, and Michilimackinac only 13, for a combined total of 7.3 percent. For the sources of slave demography, see Appendix C.

slaves sold in Montreal and Quebec for just under 350 livres, an average that would not change for the rest of the French regime. Female slaves, because they tended to be older, sold for an average of 400 livres, 28 percent more than the male average of 312 livres. One adult woman commanded the impressive sum of 700 livres, nearly twice the average price, but such significant deviations were rare. The majority of colonists paid for these slaves with some form of cash, but, as in all sectors of New France's economy, payments in kind remained significant throughout the eighteenth century. Because of periodic shortages of available currency, many slave sales relied on creative combinations of payment methods. In 1711, for example, Pierre-Thomas Tarieu de La Pérade bought a sixteen-year-old male for 200 livres, a rare bargain. Despite the low price, La Pérade still could not produce the sum. He promised, instead, to pay "100 livres in four bills of 32 livres and one bill of 4 livres, the other 100 livres in a bill signed by monsieur the treasurer of the navy" to be paid out in goods five months later. Thus, La Pérade, a naval officer, relied on the promise of future government funds to purchase a personal slave, the contract granting power to "the said sieur de La Pérade to use the said panis and dispose [of the slave] to anyone for his profit as he sees fit."[60]

The only other slave to sell so cheaply after 1709 was a seventeen-year-old named Jacques Nichououe, bought for two hundred livres in 1724 by Louis-Hector Piot de Langloiserie. The bargain price reflected the unusual circumstances of the sale. In the buyer's contract, the notary wrote that Nichououe "is not at present in the power of the said seller, having deserted him about six months ago." Unless the buyer knew something the original owner did not, Langloiserie made quite a gamble by investing in a slave who had been missing for half a year. To ensure that Langloiserie bore the entire risk, the contract obliged him "to search for the said panis, and if he cannot recover him he has no guarantee against the seller." The original owner accepted the low price of the sale only because he literally had nothing to lose.[61]

In many cases, an owner assumed the risks of sale by offering slaves on

---

60. Prices calculated from twenty-six surviving notarized slave sales, LAC, MG8-A23, Greffes de notaires de la Nouvelle-France et du Québec; "La vente des esclaves par actes notariés sous les régimes français et anglais," *Rapport de l'archiviste de la province de Québec,* 1921–1922 (Quebec, 1922), 109–123. For seven hundred livres, see sale of Sept. 8, 1753, Greffe Du Laurent, reprinted in "La vente des esclaves," *Rapport,* 118. For La Pérade, see sale of Aug. 31, 1711, Greffe Chambalon (Québec), BANQ-M.

61. Sale of May 16, 1724, Greffe David (Montréal), BANQ-M.

credit, accepting monthly or annual installments from the buyer. In 1740, for example, Catherine Lemoyne bought a Fox slave woman for 350 livres, offering the owner 50 livres at the time of sale and 100 livres per year for the following three years. On another occasion, François de Gannes sold a male slave on credit to a sieur Lamy, a Montreal merchant. When Lamy failed to pay the final 100 livres, de Gannes appealed to the intendant, who ordered Lamy to pay the remainder immediately, "in cash."[62]

Yet cash payments were not always feasible for prospective buyers, especially farmers who had significantly less currency than urban residents or merchants who invested most of their assets in trade goods. In rural La Prairie, for example, Joseph-Laurent Lefebvre bought a female slave in 1722 for "forty bushels of peas and a lean, two-year-old pig." For that sum, plus a little grain to feed the pig when it first arrived, Lefebvre would own the slave "in full proprietorship," reflecting the language of Raudot's 1709 ordinance guaranteeing legal property protections for slave buyers. In 1740, Quebec merchant François Lambert purchased an adult Sioux woman. The language of the notarized bill of sale has a very different tone from earlier discussions of the Sioux slave trade, seemingly an effort to disentangle the trade from its murky origins in Indian diplomacy:

> Before the royal notary in the district of Quebec . . . was voluntarily sold and ceded by those present, now and forever . . . a girl, aged about eighteen or nineteen years, born of the Indian enemies of the French called Sioux of the Prairies, whom the seller said that he owned as a slave . . . and he delivered her now to the said buyer to make her his domestic servant in the same capacity as a slave.

In payment, Lambert offered two barrels of tafia (a low-grade rum), three barrels of molasses, and two bushels of rice, but only eighty livres in cash, which was all he could spare at the time. Lambert's cash shortage was not uncommon among colonial merchants, especially in Quebec, where French goods were most readily available.[63]

---

62. *"Comptant"*: "Ordonnance de l'intendant Dupuy qui condamne le sieur Lamy, marchand à Montréal, à payer comptant au sieur de Gannes (de Falaise) la somme de cent livres pour un des quatre termes d'un billet donné pour la vente d'un esclave panis," July 19, 1727, BANQ-Q, E1, S1, P1894. For Catherine Lemoyne, see sale of Oct. 31, 1740, Greffe Pinguet de Vaucour (Québec), BANQ-M.

63. "Pardevant le notaire royal en la prevoté de quebec . . . a volontairement vendu et cedé par ces presentes des maintenant et a toujours . . . une fille agée de dix huit a dix neuf ans ou environ née de sauvages ennemis des françois nommez Scioux des praries et qu le d. vendeur

Although a few slaves passed through the hands of French-based négo-ciants at Quebec, local merchants and military officers, nearly all of whom lived permanently in New France, dominated the trade. Together, mem-bers of these two groups constituted more than two-thirds of New France's slave owners; they controlled an even greater proportion of the slave trade. Like all economic activity in the colony, the slave trade operated through extended family networks. Maurice Blondeau, for example, one of the earli-est to trade Indian slaves in New France, married the sister of his busi-ness partner, François Lamoureux, who also traded slaves in Montreal. Blondeau later introduced the business to his nephews, Joseph, Thomas, and Jean-Baptiste Blondeau, who traded slaves at Montreal, Lachine, and Michilimackinac from the 1720s to the 1750s. Joseph, in turn, connected his uncle to other key slave traders through his own subsequent business partnerships, most significantly with Ignace Gamelin and Charles Nolan Lamarque.[64]

These family merchant networks, although mostly controlled by men, also included a small but significant group of women, nearly all of whom were the widows of former traders. Upon the death of her merchant hus-band, Gabriel Côté, Cécile Gosselin became what one contemporary called a "bourgeoise négociante," a middling merchant in her own right. By 1744, she had traded at least one Indian slave at Montreal, an adult woman named Marguerite. Marguerite Forestier, the widow of military officer Jean-Baptiste Bissot de Vinsenne, continued her husband's slave trading as the controller of his estate. After his death in 1710, Forestier purchased as many as three Indian slaves and resold at least one, a seven-year-old girl named Catherine, to another military family in Montreal. At the turn of the eighteenth century, Forestier's husband was among the first military officers to participate in the Indian slave trade. Over the next two genera-tions, however, receiving and trading Indian slaves became a major activity

---

a dit luy appartenir comme esclave . . . et la livrée presentement au d. sr. acqueureur pour en faire sa servante domestique en la d. qualité d'esclave." Sale of Oct. 20, 1740, Greffe Pinguet de Vaucour (Québec), BANQ-M. For peas and a pig, see sale of Oct. 7, 1722, Greffe Barrette (Montréal), BANQ-M.

64. Bégon to minister, Nov. 12, 1714, ANOM, Colonies, C11A, XXXIV, 303–320v; François Béland, "Blondeau, Maurice-Régis," DCB, V; Trudel, Dictionnaire des esclaves, xxviii, 282–283. For Joseph Blondeau's connections with these traders, see "Procès entre Marie Cardinal, veuve de Jacques Hubert dit Lacroix, demanderesse, et Joseph Blondeau, défendeur, pour la dissolution d'une société," June 27, 1729, BANQ-M, TL4, S1, D3612. For distinctions between French-based and local merchants in eighteenth-century New France, see J. F. Bosher, The Canada Merchants, 1713-1763 (Oxford, 1987).

for colonial officers. With unique access to the western posts that generated most of the colony's slaves, it is not surprising that post commanders and other prominent military personnel widely participated in the trade. Of the thirty-seven most important military families in New France, thirty-three, or nearly 90 percent, owned at least one Indian slave.[65]

As French-British rivalries led them into another colonial war in 1744, colonists again faced the difficult task of negotiating the release of British prisoners taken by their Indian allies. In 1747 the commandant at Michili-mackinac bought a young Indian slave for three hundred livres, "by the order of Monsieur de Beaucours, governor of Montreal, to give to the wife of the late Kancépas, Winnebago chief, to replace an Englishwoman that the said Indian released to the King at Montreal." Seeing the success of this strategy, the following year Governor Roland Michel de La Galissonière placed orders at Michilimackinac for several Indian slaves to be used for this purpose. "I had promised some slaves to several of our resident Indians," he wrote to the post's commander, Jacques Legardeur de Saint-Pierre, "in order to take some Englishmen out of their hands." La Galissonière had already ordered Saint-Pierre to buy one slave for this purpose in 1747 and requested again, "If any come in the spring and if they are not too expensive, you will be able to buy seven or eight more like this one who was charged to the king's account." The governor, who was new both to the colony and to the Indian slave trade, did not realize that Saint-Pierre had gouged him on his first request by claiming to have paid five hundred livres to the Indians at Michilimackinac for a single male slave. No other male ever sold for as much, not even in Quebec, where distance from the source of slaves increased prices substantially.[66]

65. For the thirty-seven military families, see Peter N. Moogk, *La Nouvelle France: The Making of French Canada—A Cultural History* (East Lansing, Mich., 2000), 187–188. Moogk identifies the colony's most prominent military families as those in which "two or more generations received the Cross of Saint Louis, a special award for long-serving officers." For Gosselein, see Trudel, *Dictionnaire des esclaves*, 281–282, 307 ("bourgeoise négociante").

66. "Par l'ordre de Monsieur de Beaucours Gouverneur de Montreal, pour donner a la femme de feu Kancépas, Chef Püant en Remplacement d'une Angloise qui le d. Sauvage avoit remise au Roy a Montreal": "Certificat de Charles-Joseph de Noyelles de Fleurimont," Sept. 5, 1747, ANOM, Colonies, C11A, CXVII, 410.

For La Galissonière quote, see La Galissonière to Saint-Pierre, Sept. 4, 1748, in Joseph L. Peyser, ed. and trans., *Jacques Legardeur de Saint-Pierre: Officer, Gentleman, Entrepreneur* (East Lansing, Mich., 1996), 108. For the price charged to the governor for the slave, see "Inventory of the possessions and belongings left after the death of M. le Gardeur de St. Pierre [1755–1756]," 305.

The practice of exchanging Indian slaves for English prisoners was not new. French colonists traded Indians for English captives forty years earlier during the War of the Spanish Succession. But these earlier transactions always occurred quietly, without official sanction or funding. La Galissonière, on the other hand, openly charged these slaves to the king's account, claiming that this human currency, unlike direct cash payments, "will serve to satisfy the most stubborn of our resident Indians." Had future governors pursued this policy, especially during the Seven Years' War, the slave trade would have expanded even more dramatically than it did in the final decade of French control.[67]

Despite the richness of these records, they capture only a small fraction of the slaves who passed from Native to French hands. Most of these slaves were taken to the Saint Lawrence with traders who either had no legal right to be in the West or who had very specific restrictions placed on the items they could trade and the peoples with whom they could do business. Of course, for most western traders, these restrictions existed to be broken, but they offered incentives for this legally flexible majority of merchants and speculators to keep their slaves off the books when they returned. Family relations, business partnerships, and other hints are all we have to reconstruct the routes taken by those slaves who are in the records, and of course there is no way of knowing how often slaves passed into or through the system undetected. That extraordinary circumstances often produced the documents attesting to slaves' existence indicates that many, and probably most, slaves in the colony will remain invisible.

❖ When, in the mid-1750s, a group of Indians inadvertently killed a young man at Fort Saint Joseph, they mourned with his family, and, to cover his death and hold his place, they gave his grieving mother a "panis" slave. The commander of the Miami post, Pierre-Roch Saint-Ours Deschaillons, declared the gift a diplomatic offering to the French, claiming the slave for himself as the king's representative. Exercising one of the perquisites of his office, Saint-Ours then sold the slave for his personal profit, pocketing the five hundred livres he received from the buyer: a substantial sum equal to nearly half his annual pay. The grieving mother, already destitute and thus doubly indignant at the wealthy commandant's greed, took him to court to demand the money from the slave's sale. She won the case and pocketed what must have seemed to her an enormous sum of money. The incident

67. Peyser, ed. and trans., *Jacques Legardeur de Saint-Pierre*, 108.

occurred at the very edge of French colonial reach but reveals the heart of a complex and contested slave system in the Pays d'en Haut.[68]

Slavery in New France's western outposts evolved organically and locally as part of the larger process of cultural invention that defined French-Native relations in North America. It generated new cultural norms that should be understood on their own terms rather than as weak or adulterated versions of the ideal type that evolved in the French Caribbean. The systems were linked, of course, but each had its particular history adapted to a specific constellation of demographic, economic, climatic, and cultural demands. Coming into French hands as diplomatic gifts or in trade for valuable goods, slaves occupied many positions in the western posts of New France. But they also became objects of a lucrative slave trade in Montreal and beyond, transforming their value and the way they experienced the condition of slavery. Those who remained found themselves embedded in a system of kin-based subordination, asked to perform a wide range of tasks from sexual hospitality to tending chickens. Supervised by Indian women, they also used their agricultural skills to expand French agriculture, particularly the corn that most of them would have learned to plant and tend in their home villages. Despite many avenues toward kinship and community integration, slaves belonging to French masters and mistresses in the Pays d'en Haut faced the very real possibility that, however well they navigated the pathways open to them, they would face another forced migration to Montreal—or beyond to the Caribbean.

68. Fonds des chambres des milices de Montreal, BANQ-M, TL12; Trudel, *Dictionnaire des esclaves*, 262.

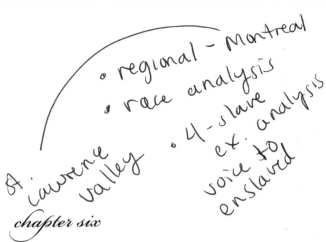

regional - Montreal
race analysis
St. Lawrence valley
4 - slave ex. analysis, voice to enslaved

chapter six

THE INDIAN IS NOT LIKE THE NEGRO

Louis-Antoine de Bougainville was not known for his keen understanding of Indians. Although often a brilliant synthesizer of colonial knowledge, which he avidly consumed during his two-year tour of North America, Bougainville had something of a tin ear when it came to the continent's Natives. He minimized their importance to New France's economy and utterly misunderstood their role in the colony's defenses. At one point he famously expressed frustration at Indians' independence, wishing the French military could have "on hand only a specified number of these mosquitoes," who seemed to swarm or flee unpredictably. So it was largely by accident that, in 1757, Bougainville expressed a bit of pithy wisdom about Indian slavery.[1]

It was an offhand comment in a long memorandum detailing New France's far-flung settlements during the Seven Years' War. Having never been to the Pays d'en Haut, he interviewed post commanders, merchants, and soldiers to learn what he could about New France's western borderlands. Tacked onto a list of commodities flowing eastward to the Saint Lawrence, Bougainville noted that merchants at the Lake Superior posts annually exported "more than fifty to sixty red slaves, or panis of *Jatihilinine*, a nation living on the Missouri who play in America the role of negroes in Europe." His note captured both the hopes of French slaveholders to replicate the dynamics of Atlantic slavery and the ways that engagement with distant Indian peoples shaped those efforts.[2]

1. Quoted in Stephen Brumwell, *Redcoats: The British Soldier and War in the Americas, 1755-1763* (Cambridge, 2002), 43. See, also, Ian K. Steele, *Betrayals: Fort William Henry and the "Massacre"* (Oxford, 1990), 73.

2. "Il faut compter de plus cinquante à soixante esclaves rouges ou panis de *Jatihilinine*, nation située sur le Missouri et qui joue, dans l'Amérique, le rôle des nègres en Europe": Louis-Antoine de Bougainville, in Pierre Margry, ed., "Mémoire de Bougainville sur l'état de la Nouvelle France à l'époque de la Guerre de Sept Ans, 1757," in *Relations et mémoires*

Like the enslaved Africans he and his readers would have seen in Europe, most of the Indian slaves Bougainville encountered in New France were urban domestics, supplementing rather than structuring the labor regime of the cities where they lived. As they had elsewhere in the French Atlantic, slaveholding practices in Montreal and surrounding settlements developed locally, responding to specific and immediate needs. Rather than an incomplete or failed version of French slavery in the Caribbean, then, Native slavery in New France was a thing of its own. By the 1750s, colonists in the Saint Lawrence Valley had used slaves for more than half a century to perform tasks ranging from household chores to skilled trades. They had also developed methods of supervision that allowed slaves to function in the mobile environment of urban slavery. For their part, enslaved people learned to negotiate the peculiar social and cultural labyrinths through which they moved, exercising what independence they could within the narrow channels constructed around them. They formed friendships, coped with enemies, and adapted to the constraints of living in proximity to their French, métis, and free Indian neighbors.

Although Bougainville's enslaved "panis" traveled a great distance from the Missouri to the Saint Lawrence, they never left Indian country. Montreal was deeply embedded in a Native political economy that placed unique demands on slaveholders and slaves alike. Surrounded by thousands of Indians living in independent villages, and supplemented by hundreds who lived in seasonal encampments near the colonial town, Montreal's free Indian population represented a significant proportion of its population. Although not to the degree of the Pays d'en Haut, many of Montreal's slaveholders and slave traders were either métis themselves or connected to mixed French and Native communities in the West. These alliances shaped slaves' daily experience and complicated their legal standing in the colony.

Then, too, Bougainville's use of the term "red slaves" recalls that, during the eighteenth century, notions of race became entangled with slavery in new and meaningful ways. In the sixteenth and seventeenth centuries, neither indigenous nor Atlantic slavery expressed a clear or causal relationship between race and slavery. But, between the 1680s and the 1750s, within the context of the French plantation economy both notions gradu-

---

inédits pour servir à l'histoire de la France dans les pays d'outre-mer (Paris, 1867), 54. The identity of the "Jatihilinine" remains unclear but likely refers to Blackfeet Indians, captured in the northern Plains by Cree and Assiniboine warriors. See "Memoir of Bougainville," *Wis. Hist. Coll.*, XVIII (1908), 187 n. 38.

ally hardened until they became much more rigid ideologies reinforced by law. Destabilizing alliances between free blacks and enslaved Africans in the Caribbean led to the growing racialization of both groups as natural subordinates, innately fit for slavery or, at best, a highly circumscribed freedom. The complex relationships between free and enslaved Indians in New France had almost the opposite effect. Whereas free blacks were marginal to the Caribbean economy, and to some degree a threat to its fundamental social order, free Indians were essential to New France's economic success and one of the colony's defining features. This basic distinction meant that the relationship between race and slavery was imagined very differently for Indians and Africans. As Indians were increasingly racialized in the first half of the eighteenth century, they were cast as too free for slavery rather than too servile for freedom.[3]

The forces shaping slavery in the Saint Lawrence Valley are especially visible in a single neighborhood along Montreal's Rue Saint-Paul, which housed the majority of the town's western merchants and an unusually high concentration of slaves. In the few blocks on either side of the *place du marché*, or public marketplace, fully half of all colonists who owned a home in 1725 also owned an Indian slave. Pressed into such proximity, colonists and slaves in this neighborhood engaged in daily negotiations of power and privilege. The lives of four enslaved Indians from this neighborhood provide an intimate glimpse into the social, legal, and cultural contours of this slave system in ways that would be impossible anywhere else in the colony. Taken together, their experiences reveal how Indian slavery adapted to the demands of trade and alliance in a colony that depended on Indians for its survival. In very personal ways, each of them lived within and helped create the defining dynamics of slavery in the eighteenth-century Saint Lawrence Valley. These dynamics were especially pronounced in Montreal but were more or less seen throughout the Saint Lawrence settlements. Many of the

3. For the seventeenth-century relationship between race and slavery in the French Atlantic, see Chapter 2. For the evolution of racial ideology in metropolitan France, see Pierre H. Boulle, *Race et esclavage dans la France de l'Ancien Régime* (Paris, 2007); Guillaume Aubert, "'The Blood of France': Race and Purity of Blood in the French Atlantic World," *William and Mary Quarterly*, 3d Ser., LXI (2004), 439–478; Sue Peabody, *"There Are No Slaves in France": The Political Culture of Race and Slavery in the Ancien Régime* (Oxford, 1996). For growing constraints on free blacks in the eighteenth-century French Caribbean, see Laurent Dubois, *A Colony of Citizens: Revolution and Slave Emancipation in the French Caribbean, 1787–1804* (Chapel Hill, N.C., 2004), esp. 249–276; John D. Garrigus, *Before Haiti: Race and Citizenship in French Saint-Domingue* (New York, 2006), esp. 195–225; Dominique Rogers, "De l'origine du préjugé de couleur en Haïti," *Outre-Mers*, XC (2003), 83–101.

practical arrangements, legal structures, and cultural assumptions that developed in Montreal to manage enslaved Indians came to shape the entire colony, reaching beyond New France to the Caribbean as growing engagement between the two regions intensified during the eighteenth century.[4]

JOSEPH

"Asked whether the said Sarrazin paid for his voyage and how much he gave him, he said yes, but it was [paid] to his master and not to him and he did not know how much."—Interrogation of Joseph, enslaved Indian, regarding a 1712 smuggling voyage

As the source of new captives and the heart of the colonial economy, free Indians played a central role in shaping slavery in New France. For Joseph, a young adult belonging to a métis master, this influence would be hard to overstate. Linked to the Native communities around Montreal by his master's kinship and commerce, Joseph spent much of his time living, trading, negotiating, and working with other Indians, most of whom were free. Yet the dominant presence of free Indians was less important for the ways it mitigated the rigors of slavery than for how it directed his labors and the economic activities of his master. Although his master's involvement in Indian trade gave him more mobility than most slaves, he was not free to come and go as he pleased. And Joseph certainly could not have run home. It has been widely assumed that enslaved Indians' proximity to Indian country would have made it easy for them to run away. But Joseph lived more than two months' journey from the land where he was captured, and the Ottawa and Nipissing traders he encountered daily were probably his captors and original masters. Instead of opening pathways to liberation, then, free Indians channeled Joseph's labors toward the shadowy and often

4. Of the 129 people with title to a lot on Rue Saint-Paul or Place du Marché in 1725, 64 (49.6 percent) owned at least one Indian slave. This figure includes those cases in which the property owner was married to the slaveholder, but not those cases in which other immediate family members owned slaves. It also excludes institutions, such as the Hôtel-Dieu and the Sulpician Seminary, both of which employed slaves at one time or another. For slaveholders and the number of slaves, see Marcel Trudel, *Dictionnaire des esclaves et de leurs propriétaires au Canada français* (LaSalle, Que., 1990), 267–430. Since Trudel counts only those slaves individually identifiable in surviving records, his estimates are highly conservative. For those owning property, I relied on the Adhémar database of the Centre Canadien d'Architecture in Montreal, which contains data for every known lot in Montreal proper in 1725. The database is available online at http://www.cca.qc.ca/adhemar/; physical copies of the documents are available at the Centre Canadien d'Architecture.

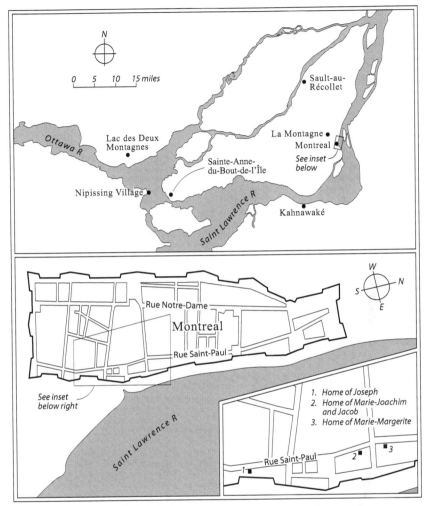

MAP 4. French and Native Settlements on the Island of Montreal.
Drawn by Jim DeGrand

dangerous world of fur, firearms, and liquor smuggling that were central to his master's wealth and Montreal's economic and diplomatic success.[5]

Montreal was a natural collection point for the free Indians who lived and visited there. Eight times the size of Manhattan, the island of Montreal cre-

5. "Interrogé si Le d. Sarrazin ne lui a pas païé son voïage et Combien il lui a donné. A dit quouy mais que Cest a son maistre et non pas a lui et ne scait point Combien": "Procès contre Nicolas Sarrazin, avironnier, Pierre Sarrazin et Joseph, esclave panis de François Lamoureux, accusés d'avoir préparé un voyage de traite dans l'Outaouais, sans permis," Feb. 18, 1712, BANQ-M, TL4, S1, D1328.

ates a choke point in the Saint Lawrence River that provides both environmental and commercial advantages to its human inhabitants. By narrowing the river channel, the island forms what is now known as the Lachine Rapids: "the most violent rapid it is possible to see," according to Jacques Cartier, who in 1535 became the first European to reach the island. Impossible to pass in a boat or canoe, the rapids made Montreal a strategic portage as Native and, later, French vessels landed on either side to skirt them. Montreal also guards the confluence of the Ottawa and Saint Lawrence Rivers, forming a large and slow pool known as Lac des Deux Montagnes. Arcing over the northwestern section of the island, just north of the rapids, this gentle entrance into the Saint Lawrence acted like a bay, providing relatively safe harbor to vessels coming down the Ottawa from the continent's northern and western interior. The island provided access to New York and beyond via the Richelieu River, which lies just ten miles overland to the southeast and meets the Saint Lawrence thirty miles downstream. The island thus stood at an intersection of water routes that linked the western Great Lakes via the Ottawa River with Appalachia and the Atlantic Ocean.[6]

Montreal's first colonial settlement came in 1642 by the Societé Notre-Dame de Montréal pour la Conversion des Sauvages de la Nouvelle-France, a group of Catholic mystics who envisioned the island as a frontier mission, a dangerous but divine post that would draw Native families for spiritual and physical healing. Although the town was originally called Ville Marie to distinguish it from the larger island called Montreal, over time it came to be called Montreal. The society acknowledged the need for a town and farms on the island to provision the mission and to give a critical mass of settlers for the missionaries' security, but the settlement's purpose required that Indians be drawn to Montreal rather than be pushed aside. Merchant interests supporting the enterprise also saw the advantage of attracting Indians to the island, making it a key gathering point for dispersed sources of furs and a convenient location for plying Native customers with French goods. Recognizing both spiritual and secular advantages, the Jesuit priest Barthélemy Vimont declared that the island "gives access and an admirable approach to all the Nations of this vast country . . . so that, if peace prevailed among these peoples they would land thereon from all sides."[7]

6. Jacques Cartier, *The Voyages of Jacques Cartier*, ed. Ramsay Cook, trans. H. P. Biggar (Toronto, 1993), 65.

7. Quoted in W. J. Eccles, *The Canadian Frontier, 1534–1760*, rev. ed. (Albuquerque, N.Mex., 1983), 40.

But peace did not prevail, and Montreal's centrality became its greatest liability as well as its best asset. Drawing Native allies also attracted their Iroquois enemies, who needed little encouragement after several French attacks in the previous decades had grown out of France's alliance with the Iroquois's enemies. One early planner expressed the sense of foreboding felt by many potential French settlers of Montreal, who feared that at any moment "all the trees of that island would change into as many Iroquois." One measure of this fear was the fact that the society had obtained the island for free from the company that controlled New France, whose associates recognized the site's potential but thought no French settlement there could survive its perceived dangers.[8]

Following decades of French-Iroquois warfare, Montreal's small number of French settlers expanded the small collection of houses into a town in the final third of the seventeenth century. With a combined force of colonial militia, regular troops, and Native allies, the French bludgeoned the Iroquois to the negotiating table, concluding a peace that finally took hold in 1667. Over the next forty years Montreal's population—both French and Native—rose dramatically as the town of Montreal took shape alongside several Indian towns that relocated to the island at this time of relative calm. The simultaneous rise of French and Indian settlements was no coincidence. They relied upon and fed one another, each a walled enclave linked in a larger island community that could not have existed without both colonial and indigenous elements.

Several Indian towns grew around the island and on its surrounding shores. The largest and most vibrant was known as Sault Saint-Louis by the French and Kahnawake by its Mohawk settlers. Located on the south shore of the Saint Lawrence River just across from Montreal, this settlement began with little more than a dozen Iroquois who left their villages in 1667 to avoid factional conflict over their embrace of French trade and alliance. Over the next twenty years a growing number of Iroquois migrants joined them, choosing proximity to a colonial town that could provide European goods and solidify French alliances. The 1660s were a decade of chastening for the Iroquois, leaving many with little but charred farmland to sustain families torn by factional conflict. Montreal promised a new beginning. And for the pro-French factions within Iroquoia it offered a path to pursue their interests without the interference of their Anglophile kin. En-

8. "Tous les arbres de cet Isle se devraient changer en autant d'Iroquois": [François Dollier de Casson], *Histoire de Montréal, 1640–1672* (Montreal, 1871), 18.

couraged by the Jesuits and provided ample land to settle and plant crops, this small group slowly swelled to several hundred in the 1680s and reached more than one thousand by 1700.[9]

A handful of smaller Indian villages appeared around the island at about the same time. The most diverse village was La Montagne, just northwest of the French town, settled by fragments of Huron, Iroquois, and various Algonquian-speaking nations in the late-1670s. We know very little about the nature of this town in the seventeenth century, but by Joseph's time there were two to three hundred residents living in ethnic clusters near a fort that contained a church and a small garrison. Sault au Récollet, situated a few miles northwest of the French town, was meant as a refuge for Christian Indians but ended up attracting a group of mixed religious sentiments and a range of approaches to French cultural integration that created internal tension on issues like liquor consumption. Sometimes seen as a replacement for La Montagne, both villages persisted simultaneously long after they split. Along with a substantial Nipissing village on Isle aux Tourtres and several smaller, seasonal villages erected during the spring and summer months, the Native population rose dramatically during the final quarter of the seventeenth century, surpassing two thousand permanent or semipermanent residents by 1700.[10]

The colonial town of Montreal grew in tandem with neighboring Indian towns. As the Iroquois threat subsided during the 1670s, Montreal's advantageous location drew merchants, missionaries, and enterprising craftsmen to settle there. The island's total French population reached 1,400 by 1681 and about 3,000 by 1700. During these years the town of Montreal took shape, growing from a cluster of about thirty homes in 1665 into a respectable colonial town of about 1,600 just forty years later, with a large portion of the growth occurring in the short span between 1686 and 1693. Larger than any individual Native village around the island, the town's population

9. Gretchen Lynn Green, "A New People in an Age of War: The Kahnawake Iroquois, 1667–1760" (Ph.D. diss., College of William and Mary, 1991); Louis Lavallée, *La prairie en Nouvelle-France, 1647–1760* (Montreal, 1992), 51–61; Evan Haefeli and Kevin Sweeney, *Captors and Captives: The 1704 French and Indian Raid on Deerfield* (Amherst, Mass., 2003), 55–77; Allan Greer, *Mohawk Saint: Catherine Tekakwitha and the Jesuits* (New York, 2005), 89–110; Daniel K. Richter, "Iroquois versus Iroquois: Jesuit Missions and Christianity in Village Politics, 1642–1686," *Ethnohistory,* XXXII (1985), 1–16.

10. Jan Grabowski, "The Common Ground: Settled Natives and French in Montréal, 1667–1760" (Ph.D. diss., University of Montreal, 1993), 59–87, offers the best overview of the various towns, villages, and encampments around the island in the late-seventeenth and eighteenth centuries.

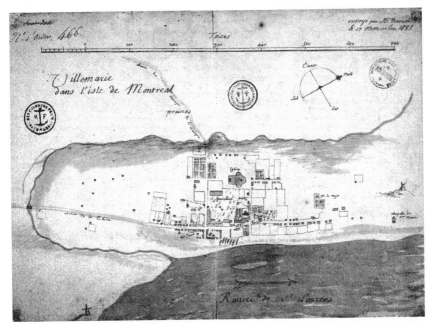

FIGURE 20. *Villemarie on the Island of Montreal. 1685. ANOM, Aix-en-Provence.*
FR COM 03DFC466C. Permission Archives Nationales d'Outre-Mer

was still outnumbered by the combined population of Native towns surrounding it. And this was just how colonial officials wanted it. Not only did
a close body of Native allies provide military security, but they also drew
pelts and goods to the French that otherwise would go to their English
rivals. As consumers of French goods and traders who reexported French
goods to other Native villages, Montreal's settled Indians proved as essential
to the town's commercial success as to its security.[11]

The physical form of Montreal drew upon the island's natural and Native
histories as it transformed from mystical dream to practical reality. Placed
at an inlet along the island's southern edge, the town took advantage of an
inward flow in the river's current ideal for loading and unloading cargoes.
The spot was, in fact, the site of a long-standing Indian portage road that
early French maps identify as "Chemin de Lachine," or the Lachine Trail,

11. Louise Dechêne, *Habitants and Merchants in Seventeenth-Century Montreal*, trans.
Liana Vardi (Montreal, 1992), table A; Mario Lalancette and Alan M. Stewart, "De la ville-
comptoir à la ville fortifiée: evolution de la forme urbaine de Montréal au XVIIe siècle," in
Sylvie Dépatie et al., eds., *"Habitants et Marchands" Twenty Years Later: Reading the History
of Seventeenth- and Eighteenth-Century Canada* (Montreal, 1998), 259.

which later developed into an important colonial road in the eighteenth century linking the city to the island's western settlements. The earliest buildings on the town site clustered along the Chemin de Lachine, which eventually became Rue Saint-Paul. Another Native path, quite possibly one noted by Cartier leading to the base of Mount Royal, connected Montreal to the Indian town at La Montagne. Within town the "chemin des sauvages de la montagne" became Rue Saint-François-Xavier, which ran alongside the Sulpician seminary to meet Rue Saint-Paul near the port. At the intersection of these Native paths, renamed for Catholic saints and squared by imperial surveyors, stood the market square, less than half a block from Lamoureux's house. Linking the island's northern interior to its western terminus, these paths also represented the joining of Native and colonial worlds that characterized Montreal's early history. As the last point to unload cargoes from the east and the first safe point to reenter the river after skirting the rapids from the west, the city's commercial advantages combined with its human geography to facilitate trade between the Atlantic and the North American interior.[12]

But Montreal did not urbanize spontaneously. During the 1680s French officials mandated urban density by prohibiting private ownership of large tracts of land within the town's boundaries, which were precisely defined between 1686 and 1693 with only minor modifications thereafter. French-Iroquois relations began to deteriorate again in 1684, raising alarm at the scattered and poorly defended condition of the town. With so much of the land claimed by so few proprietors, it was also impossible to develop a critical mass of residents and services for a functioning market town. In 1688 New France's intendant explained that building the city would provide the necessary amenities for a growing population and provide a place for it "to take cover from the attacks of the colony's enemies." One year later, a devastating attack on Montreal Island by fifteen hundred Iroquois warriors only heightened the urgency of developing Montreal and its defenses, and a mostly wooden palisade was completed by the mid-1690s. By 1701, when the Iroquois met in Montreal to establish a lasting peace with New France and its Native allies, the town they entered was substantially different from

12. "Villemarie dans l'isle de Montreal," Nov. 13, 1685, FR ANOM 03DFC466C, ANOM; "Plan de la Ville de Montreal levé en l'année 1704," Nov. 15, 1704, FR ANOM 03DFC468A, ANOM. These paths are shown on the earliest surviving maps of Montreal, as the town itself was just emerging, a fact suggesting that they preceded French settlement. The northward route is clearly labeled as an Indian trail.

the one they visited in the 1660s, having developed from a scattered mission village to an urban center on the rise. In its search for military protection and economic stability, Montreal's urbanization mirrored the town building of its Indian neighbors.[13]

By the 1710s, when Joseph came to Montreal as a slave, there were about four thousand French settlers in the Montreal district and about two thousand settled Indians: one thousand at Kahnawake and another thousand at other settlements around the island. When combined with the Native peoples who came to Montreal to visit relatives, trade with French and Indian settlers, or hold diplomatic meetings with French officials, Indian populations approached parity with their French neighbors. In the broader context of the upper Saint Lawrence Valley and Great Lakes, of course, Indians were far more numerous. Because most Natives visited the city more often than rural French villages, colonists living within the town interacted with Indians far more than those living in the countryside. Mohawk women came to Montreal to visit French chapels, Nipissing men brought deer meat to the market square, Oneida families visited their French friends, enslaved Apache girls carried water to the garden. Particularly in Joseph's neighborhood slaves from all over the central quadrant of North America converged in a relatively tight space, interacting daily. One could hear a dozen or more Amerindian languages spoken around the island, especially three Algonquian tongues (Anishinaabemowin, Nipissing, and Abenaki) and two Iroquoian languages (Mohawk and Oneida).[14]

Joseph's master, François Lamoureux dit Saint-Germain, was both a product and a proponent of the close relationship between Indian and French frontier towns in the Saint Lawrence Valley. According to most surviving records, including the trial transcript, Lamoureux fitted the standard profile of a petty merchant in eighteenth-century Montreal. Born and reared in Canada, Lamoureux married a slightly younger woman, fathered several children, and settled in a modest stone home on Rue Saint-Paul in the city's commercial district. The Lamoureux family was devoutly Catholic in every outward way. His wife, Marguerite Ménard, claimed to attend

---

13. Lalancette and Stewart, "De la ville-comptoir à la ville fortifiée," in Dépatie et al., eds., *"Habitants et Marchands" Twenty Years Later*, 274. For the 1689 attack, known as the "Lachine Massacre," see Eccles, *Canadian Frontier*, 120.

14. Grabowski, "The Common Ground," 59–87, and "French Criminal Justice and Indians in Montreal, 1670–1760," *Ethnohistory*, XLIII (1996), 405–429; Dechêne, *Habitants and Merchants*, trans. Vardi, table A.

mass several times a week, and the couple saw to the religious education of their children. Both Lamoureux and his wife acted as godparents for their friends' and neighbors' children. But Lamouruex was also something of a thorn in the side of local and French officials, facing a steady barrage of prosecutions for unlicensed and illegal trade during the 1710s and 1720s.[15]

Lamoureux had two residences. The first was within the walled *centre ville*, or downtown, of Montreal, on Rue Saint-Paul. According to witnesses in Lamoureux's various trials, an almost constant stream of Indian men and women flowed down Rue Saint-Paul into Lamoureux's home and ware-house. In one of his many smuggling trials, he acknowledged that "many Indians frequent his house" but protested that they were doing legitimate business there. It was a plausible defense, especially given Lamoureux's li-censed profession as a gunsmith, which attracted a steady clientele of Saint Lawrence Indians who used the weapons for hunting and defense. As a petty merchant, Lamoureux also ran a constant business of small, in-kind exchanges with individual Indian partners, a pattern several witnesses mentioned without ever suggesting it was out of the ordinary.[16]

French authorities had originally built a palisade around the city to repel Iroquois attacks, but, during the first half of the eighteenth century, the wall mostly functioned as a means of controlling traffic into and out of the city. Soldiers posted at each of the city's gates inspected goods, checked papers, and questioned anyone who seemed not to belong. But the soldiers knew that Indians did belong in the city, so they rarely interfered with their pas-sage into and out of town. Like many merchants on his street, Lamoureux probably boarded some of the soldiers who monitored the ports, placing him in a position to influence the degree of their scrutiny. He also lived in an especially advantageous position along the city's southern wall, with his backyard abutting the temporary Indian villages erected each summer for trade and diplomacy. One record indicates that he might have even owned some of the land used for the encampment. When he stayed with his master

---

15. "Procès contre Nicolas Sarrazin, avironnier, Pierre Sarrazin et Joseph, esclave panis de François Lamoureux, accusés d'avoir préparé un voyage de traite dans l'Outaouais, sans permis," Feb. 18, 1712, BANQ-M, TL4, S1, D1328. For more on Lamoureux, see Brett Rush-forth, "Insinuating Empire: Indians, Smugglers, and the Imperial Geography of Eighteenth-Century Montreal," in Adam Arenson, Barbara Berglund, and Jay Gitlin, eds., *Frontier Cities: Encounters at the Crossroads of Empire* (Philadelphia, forthcoming 2012).

16. "Procès contre François Lamoureux dit Saint-Germain, armurier, accusé de vente d'eau de vie à des sauvages," Sept. 7, 1713, BANQ-M, TL4, S1, D1483.

on Rue Saint-Paul, then, Joseph's daily routine involved close interactions with other Indians in a dense urban setting.[17]

Not unlike many of his neighbors, Lamoureux also had a home and a large tract of land in the more rural part of the island, which he inherited from this father: a fief called Bellevue. The name of the Catholic parish there, Sainte-Anne-du-Bout-de-l'Île (the end of the island), signaled the spot's remoteness. Lamoureux, his slaves, and his tenants grew wheat and other crops there for food and occasional sale or barter. But the land's most important contribution to Lamoureux's finances was in smuggling, made possible by the site's location along the route from the Pays d'en Haut to Montreal. Colonial officials found it impossible to curtail illegal trade on the western end of Montreal, in part because the Indians themselves bristled at any efforts to cut off this supply stream for cheaper French goods. Many, including the colony's governor during much of Lamoureux's life, not only turned a blind eye to smugglers but engaged in illegal trade themselves.[18]

Lamoureux's connection to the Indian community at the edge of the island went well beyond commerce. As a métis, he embodied the ties of kinship that were so central to his trade. His father, Pierre, was a fur trader, and his mother, Marguerite Pigarouiche, was an Algonquian-speaking Indian (of an unknown nation) born in the mission village of Sillery near Quebec. Lamoureux's learning to speak his mother's Algonquian dialect from his youth would explain his facility with the many Algonquian tongues he mastered as an adult trader. It is likely that Lamoureux's grandfather was Étienne Pigarouich, the famed Algonquian Christian who made several prominent appearances in the *Jesuit Relations* as a model convert turned apostate and then back again.[19]

---

17. Adhémar database, Centre Canadien d'Architecture, Montreal; Archives de la Province, *L'île de Montréal en 1731: aveu et dénombrement de messieurs de Saint-Sulpice* (Quebec, 1943), 7, 130.

18. For colonial officials and controversies over smuggling, see Rushforth, "Insinuating Empire," in Arenson, Berglund, and Gitlin, eds., *Frontier Cities;* Jean Lunn, "The Illegal Fur Trade out of New France, 1713–1760," Canadian Historical Association, *Annual Report*, 1939, 61–76; Yves F. Zoltvany, "Rigaud de Vaudreuil, Philippe de, Marquis de Vaudreuil," *DCB*, II.

19. For Lamoureux's mother, see marriage, Sept. 22, 1693, Notre-Dame-de-Montreal, FHL; marriage contract for François Lamoureux dit Saint-Germain and Marguerite Ménard, July 26, 1712, Montreal, *RAB du PRDH*, 95131; Cyprien Tanguay, *Dictionnaire généalogique des familles canadiennes depuis la fondation de la colonie jusqu'à nos jours* (Baltimore, 1967), I, 342. Étienne Pigarouich's wife was also named Marguerite and is known to have children near the age of Lamoureux's mother; see baptism of Mar. 3, 1643, Sillery,

For three generations by Lamoureux's time, Catholicism had also established ties between large numbers of Indians and French colonists. Catholic ideology and ritual produced a network of fictive kin relationships that
linked French and Native Catholics through godparenting. Lamoureux's
sister, Barbe, for example, was the godmother of Louis, son of Oukiakoua-
migou and Marie Nikens, both Algonquians most likely from La Montagne. Lamoureux's neighbor, a merchant named Louis Babis, acted as
godfather. Lamoureux's stepmother, Barbe Le Scel, acted as godmother to
the son of Michel Keskabikat and Marie-Madeleine, Algonquians (probably
Nipissings) from the west end of the island. These acts might have sometimes linked the Lamoureux family with their biological Algonquian relatives, but more often they created a new kind of kinship that bound them
by ritual rather than blood. At a minimum, such records demonstrate that
French, métis, and Native communities maintained close contact with one
another across a wide spectrum of settings never restricted to trade. And,
for some, these acts must have both reflected and reinforced those relationships through the culturally powerful symbols of Catholic ritual. Surviving
records do not provide a direct, one-to-one correlation between Lamoureux's kinship — real or fictive — and his smuggling, but, in places where such
records survive, these relationships produced commercial as well as familial
connections. And, whatever the particular reasons for the success of his
trading, Lamoureux highlights the familial, geographic, and commercial
dynamics that bound Indians and colonists in a web of interdependence
spun by colonial forces beyond their control.[20]

It is only in the context of Indians' pervasive influence on Montreal that
we can understand Joseph's experience as Lamoureux's slave or, indeed, the
broader dynamics of Indian slavery in the Saint Lawrence Valley. The events
surrounding Joseph's interrogation in a 1712 smuggling trial open a window
onto this world, allowing a glimpse of Joseph's daily activities and how they
were shaped by Montreal's free Indian and métis populations. Even in the
heart of this colonial settlement, Joseph, like all slaves on Rue Saint-Paul,

---

RAB du PRDH, 74130. For Pigarouich's life and confession, see Elsie McLeod Jury, "Pigarouich, Étienne," DCB, I; Jesuit Relations, XXV, 249–257 (quote, 257).

20. Baptism of Aug. 12, 1700, Notre-Dame-de-Montréal, FHL; baptism of Feb. 28, 1705,
of Apr. 26, 1705, of Aug. 15, 1713, Sainte-Anne-de-Bellevue, FHL. For Catholicism and kinship in a similar setting, see Susan Sleeper-Smith, "Women, Kin, and Catholicism: New Perspectives on the Fur Trade," Ethnohistory, XLVII (2000), 423–452. The parish had multiple
iterations, including one as Sainte-Anne-du-Bout-de-l'Ile and another as Sainte-Anne de
Bellevue.

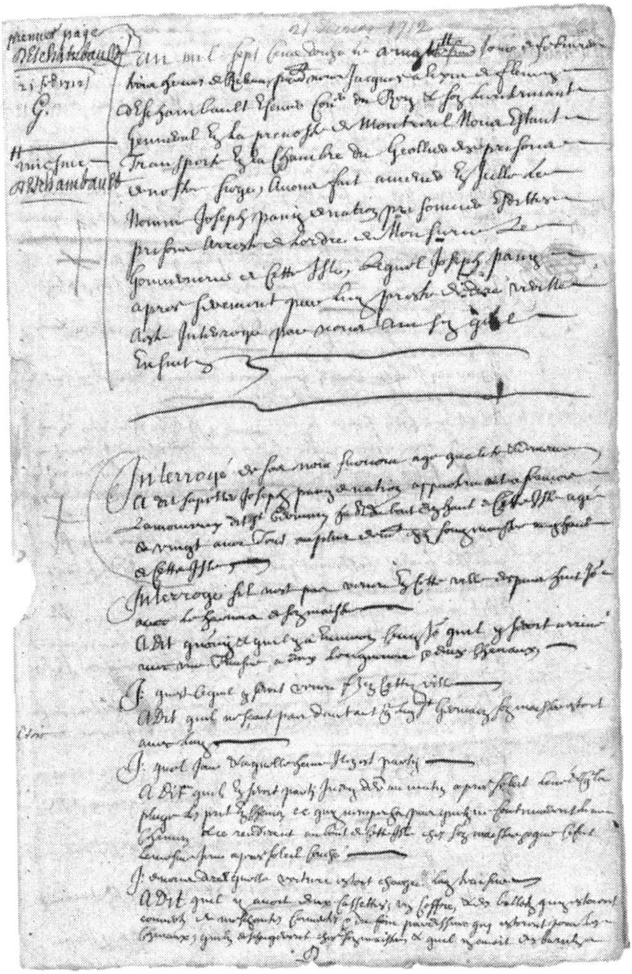

FIGURE 21.
Interrogation
of Joseph. *1712.*
BANQ-M, TL4,
S1, D1328.
*Permission
Bibliothèque
et Archives
Nationales du
Québec, Centre
d'Archives de
Montréal*

lived in a world nearly as influenced by Indians as by Europeans. He traded with them in his master's house; he rowed canoes with them on journeys to the Pays d'en Haut; he traveled with them and bartered with them around the island. And he belonged to a métis master with strong personal ties to independent Indian villages around the island. Within this context, slaveholders like Lamoureux found ways to use slaves profitably in an economic environment that differed fundamentally from the household economies of the Pays d'en Haut and the protoindustrial plantations of the Caribbean.

Joseph was arrested and taken to the royal prison in February 1712 as part of a wide-ranging investigation of his master, François Lamoureux, and two of Lamoureux's associates, the coureurs de bois Nicolas and Pierre

Sarrazin. The three had long been suspected of smuggling liquor and conducting unlicensed trade to the Ottawas in the Pays d'en Haut. But finding hard evidence had been difficult, as all of them also traded legally around the island. Joseph's arrest was ordered by Montreal's governor, Claude de Ramezay, who argued that smuggling hurt his city by diverting profits and weakened the crown's authority by diminishing its influence over trade. The governor rightly suspected that Joseph was key to the investigation, because he would have been involved in loading, unloading, and transporting the contraband for his master.[21]

During the trial, the court asked Joseph twenty-one questions, ranging from the basics of his identity to highly specific details of his journeys between Rue Saint-Paul and Lamoureux's home at the edge of the island. The one thing that was never in question was Joseph's legal standing as a slave. Clearly identified as "Joseph, panis slave of François Lamoureux dit St. Germain" and occasionally referred to as Lamoureux's "domestic," court officials and witnesses generally just called him "Lamoureux's pany." Almost no one used Joseph's name. Even Lamoureux, who had given Joseph his French name, simply called him "my pany." Only three years after Raudot's 1709 ordinance defining "Panis" Indians as legally enslavable, panis / pany had become a widely used synonym for slave. At least in the transcript of his court testimony, Joseph echoed this identification, describing himself as belonging to the "panis nation." He also had little choice but to acknowledge his enslaved status, noting that he "belonged" to Lamoureux, whom he called "his master" throughout the interrogation.[22]

When it came to the details of his activities, his answers became murkier. By all accounts, Joseph routinely carted goods to and from Lamoureux's

21. "Procès contre Nicolas Sarrazin, avironnier, Pierre Sarrazin et Joseph, esclave panis de François Lamoureux, accusés d'avoir préparé un voyage de traite dans l'Outaouais, sans permis," Feb. 18, 1712, BANQ-M, TL4, S1, D1328. For Claude de Ramezay's crusade against Montreal's smugglers, including his superior, the colony's governor, see Yves F. Zoltvany, "Ramezay, Claude de," *DCB*, II.

22. Discussion of Joseph's trial is based on the following sources: "Procès contre Nicolas Sarrazin, avironnier, Pierre Sarrazin et Joseph, esclave panis de François Lamoureux, accusés d'avoir préparé un voyage de traite dans l'Outaouais, sans permis," Feb. 18, 1712, BANQ-M, TL4, S1, D1328; "Procès contre Pierre Sarrazin, coureur des bois, et François Lamoureux dit Saint-Germain, seigneur du fief de Bellevue au bout d'en haut de la ville de Montréal, arquebusier de son métier, ainsi que contre Nicolas Sarrazin et le Panis nommé Joseph, domestique (esclave) et complice dudit Lamoureux," Feb. 18, 1712, BANQ-Q, TL5, D502. The second dossier was prepared by the clerks of the Superior Council in Quebec and contains both duplicate and additional testimony from Joseph, Lamoureux, and many other witnesses.

farm at Bellevue. On one of these journeys, Joseph transported a huge cargo of trade goods across the island in a sleigh pulled by two horses. Stacked full of barrels, satchels, wrapped bundles, and small casks, the load was covered to protect it from the weather, so the court questioned whether Joseph had been asked to leave during a storm to reduce the likelihood of being caught. Why else, they reasonably asked, would he choose to leave in such weather? Answering their leading question, he deftly explained that the storm began after he left, but the tone of their questions shows that they were not convinced. When pressed about what he was transporting, Joseph claimed, rather incredibly, to know nothing of his cargo's contents, including what was in several small casks that generally contained brandy. Joseph then introduced a long story about where the goods originated, insisting that Sarrazin had loaded the sleigh at a relative's house and that he only unloaded it into his master's barn at Bellevue. Becoming frustrated with the slave's obfuscation, court officials suspected that his testimony had been coached and asked whether his master had told him what to say when questioned. When he denied it, they pressed again, asking whether Sarrazin had promised him a reward for keeping their illegal activities secret and whether his master had coerced him into silence. He claimed that he had not even talked to them about it and that he had only taken the loaded sleigh from one point to another as they instructed.

The outlines of Joseph's duties emerge from even this cautious, scripted testimony. Lamoureux often relied upon his slave to move trade goods between his two residences. Joseph loaded sleighs and canoes, he traveled in bad weather, and he performed a range of maintenance and household chores at both of Lamoureux's homes, his warehouse, and his barn. Lamoureux also offered Joseph's services for hire, a common enough practice for the court to ask whether Sarrazin, Lamoureux's accomplice, had paid Joseph to cart goods across the island and how much he had paid. Joseph answered, "Yes, but that it was [paid] to his master and not to him and he did not know how much." In most cases, no one would know whose goods the slave was transporting around the island, a ruse providing deniability to the smuggler who paid Lamoureux for Joseph's labor.

Joseph was thus useful for his ability to obscure his master's or master's clients' involvement in smuggling. With the island continually crossed by free Indians who lived beyond the reach of French criminal justice, officials were cautious when interfering with the movements and trade activities of local Indians. Smuggling alcohol, firearms, or gunpowder to them was not especially complicated, particularly when Joseph could be the middleman to distance Lamoureux from the actual exchange of goods. On one trip, Lamoureux sent Joseph ahead with illegal trade goods, trailing far enough behind that no one would see them together. Within town, everyone would have known that Joseph was Lamoureux's slave, but that was not necessarily true in Montreal's rural parishes between the town and Bellevue. Joseph would have known the consequences of raising suspicions were he confronted, and he developed a habit of asking few questions and giving short answers. When answers were demanded, Joseph vaguely said he was moving a load "for the said St. Germain, his master." Unlike Lamoureux, Joseph could credibly claim to know nothing of the origin or destination of the goods he carried.

Lamoureux honed this system over two decades, using Joseph and other slaves to obscure his smuggling at Bellevue and in the heart of Montreal. Accused again in 1726 of selling brandy to Indians, the court reminded Lamoureux that, however successful he had been at evading prosecution, everyone knew of his crimes. But, with the help of Suzanne, another enslaved Indian, he again escaped responsibility. Like Joseph, Suzanne allowed Lamoureux to establish an alibi elsewhere while she acted as his agent with local Indian customers. Neighbors had seen some Indians enter the house with skins and leave with barrels. But such observations, in themselves, were not enough to demonstrate illegal trade. Lamoureux's business as a gunsmith and petty merchant routinely brought Natives to his home, and the timing of the visits was never clear. To shield her master from culpability, Suzanne not only denied witnessing any illegal trade but claimed never to have seen the other Indians enter the house that afternoon. She also established an alibi for Lamoureux and his wife, noting that she had been caring for the family's children because her master and mistress were away. Like Joseph, she apparently understood that one of her roles in this household was to provide cover for her master's criminal activity.[23]

Linking Rue Saint-Paul to the distant West, Lamoureux's smuggling activities often took him to the Pays d'en Haut. Court records suggest that Joseph accompanied him on multiple journeys between 1712 and the mid-1720s, rowing the canoe, carrying loads around portage points, preparing meals, and probably hunting and fishing along the way if supplies ran low. There were no illusions about who held the upper hand in the relationship between Lamoureux and his slaves, but the mobility of enslaved indi-

23. "Procès contre François Lamoureux dit St-Germain, arquebusier et marchand, accusé de vente de boisson aux sauvages," July 8, 1726, BANQ-M, TL4, S1, D3289.

viduals like Joseph did provide a measure of independence denied to those performing more easily supervised tasks. That Joseph had damning information about his master's illegal activities must also have required Lamoureux to offer incentives as well as threats. This may explain why Lamoureux worked to get Joseph released from prison after his testimony was complete. As other interrogations dragged on, royal court officials kept Joseph in prison, probably to irritate Lamoureux and possibly to erode Joseph's resolve to protect his master. After suffering in these uncomfortable and brutally cold conditions for more than a week, Joseph became ill. According to Lamoureux, who visited him in prison, Joseph's health was deteriorating so quickly that death seemed imminent. He demanded his slave's release, perhaps a bargain struck for Joseph's continued cooperation. Over the next several years, Joseph and Lamoureux would find themselves in a similar situation many times, including the following year when Lamoureux was accused of selling liquor to neighboring Nipissing Indians who nearly murdered a priest. Joseph's ability to travel to western posts, to work closely with Lamoureux's associates, and to engage in trade all attest to the influence of free Indians on slavery in Montreal. Those liberties did not allow him to flee to safety. As far as surviving records reveal, he died Lamoureux's slave. But such limited autonomy did shape how he experienced slavery and how the colony could (and could not) shape its practice.[24]

Joseph's mobility was not uncommon for enslaved Indians, especially for young men in Montreal and surrounding settlements. Between 1710 and 1760, dozens of slaveholders hired out their Indian slaves to merchants for journeys to Detroit, Michilimackinac, or other far western posts. Forty-four contracts hiring a "panis" survive in the colony's notarial records, although some involved former slaves long since freed by their masters. Joseph Laroze, for example, a freed slave described as a "frenchified Indian" ("sauvage francisé"), engaged himself in 1736 for three years for a fur trade expedition to the Pays d'en Haut. A year later Jean-Baptiste Lefort signed on as an engagé for a voyage to Ottawa country. The contract noted that he was a

24. "Procès contre Nicolas Sarrazin, avironnier, Pierre Sarrazin et Joseph, esclave panis de François Lamoureux, accusés d'avoir préparé un voyage de traite dans l'Outaouais, sans permis," Feb. 18, 1712, BANQ-M, TL4, S1, D1328. The best treatment of the illegal fur trade between Montreal and Albany is Jan Grabowski, "Les Amérindiens domiciliés et la 'contrebande' des fourrures en Nouvelle-France," *Recherches amérindiennes au Québec*, XXIV (1994), 45–52. The best treatment in English, although dated, remains Lunn, "The Illegal Fur Trade," Canadian Historical Association, *Annual Report*, 1939, 61–76.

"pany," but described him as a "naturalized Indian" ("sauvage naturalisé") and a voyageur.[25]

Contracts survive for about twenty enslaved Indians, who were either forced or given permission by their masters to travel west. Many voyages, like Joseph's, would have never generated a contract because the journey was illegal or because the slave accompanied his master and required no agreement. Only one of these contracts involved an enslaved Indian woman, hired as a personal servant to Louise Barrois on her journey from Montreal to Detroit. The rest involved adult male slaves, granted permission by their masters to travel with a merchant and his crew. Although some contracts specified that all wages would go to the slaveholder, others were silent on this matter, leaving open the possibility that the "panis" listed in the contracts had been allowed a season of freedom to pursue their own profit.[26]

In one contract, notarized in 1735, Jacques Godefroy de Vieuxpont, a seigneur near Trois-Rivières, hired his slave, Jean-Baptiste, to Louis Gatineau for a journey to the Saint Joseph River post. Although the notary wrote that the act occurred "with the consent of Godefroy de Vieuxpont, his master," it lists Jean-Baptiste as the recipient of the contract's three-hundred-livre payment. As Jean-Baptiste's master, Godefroy had legal claim over the slave's wages, so the contract stipulated that the payment must be made "in the presence of the said Sr. Godefroy." Godefroy might have promised his slave some of the wages, but no law obligated him to honor that agreement. If he pocketed the entire three hundred livres, this contract alone would have nearly repaid the slave's purchase price. André Marsil saw the potential for even greater profits, hiring out two of his slaves as engagés in two years: one for a voyage to Michilimackinac in 1736 and another in 1737 for Detroit.[27]

25. For Laroze, see "Engagement en qualité de voyageur de Joseph Laroze," Greffe Lepailleur de LaFerté (Montreal), FHL, film 1643384. For Lefort, see "Engagement en qualité de voyageur de Jean-Baptiste Lefort," May 17, 1737, Greffe Lepailleur de LaFerté (Montreal), FHL, film 1643384.

26. Based on a search in the *Parchemin* database, s.v. "panis," "esclave," and "engagement." *Parchemin* is a digitized catalog of extant notarial records for New France. Hélène Lafortune, Normand Robert, and Serge Goudreau, *Parchemin: banque de données notariales du Québec ancien, 1635–1885* (Montreal, 1986). For a detailed explanation of the database's content and function, see Hélène Lafortune, Normand Robert, and Serge Goudreau, *Parchemin s'explique: guide de dépouillement des actes notariés du Québec ancien* (Montreal, 1989). Accessed at BANQ-M and the Nahum Gelber Law Library, McGill University. For Barrois, see Trudel, *Dictionnaire des esclaves*, 227.

27. "Engagement en qualité de voyageur de Jean-Baptiste," June 7, 1735, Greffe Lepailleur de LaFerté (Montreal), FHL, film 1643384; "Engagement de Joseph, par André Mercil," June 3, 1736, Greffe Porlier (Montreal), FHL, film 1430237; "Engagement en qualité de voya-

Merchants, too, could profit from hiring slaves rather than French workers for trade voyages. In 1718, Montreal merchant François Poulin de Francheville hired an Indian slave named Jean for a journey to Michilimackinac. The contract required Jean to load trade goods at Montreal, assist in all aspects of the journey to the post (including the route's thirty portages), then load canoes with beaver pelts at Michilimackinac and return to Montreal with the merchant. Poulin de Francheville agreed to pay two hundred livres in trade goods and sixty livres in colonial currency. That year, the average French engagé hired for this journey cost about four hundred livres, making the slave one-third cheaper than the French worker, and much easier to coerce.[28]

The opportunities these journeys opened to slaves themselves are impossible to document but not difficult to imagine. Escape was feasible, but not likely. Traveling in small but cohesive groups that worked, ate, and camped together, enslaved Indians would have probably had less unsupervised time on a western voyage than they had in Montreal. And the same problems of distant travel through enemy territory would have faced anyone bold enough to run off alone. Reentering the territory of the nation who had captured, tortured, and sold them posed its own set of dangers and must have been a source of some anxiety. But there were some advantages. The work of a western voyage required a measure of cooperation that would have placed slaves on par with French contract laborers in terms of daily experience. All of them rowed, most carried at least something across portage points, and everyone had to be fed amply to remain strong. For some enslaved Indian men, western voyages were also among the few opportunities to earn money of their own. Although most masters took their contractual wages, some did not, and any extra labor performed along the way might have carried the possibility of private remuneration.[29]

It is also possible that some enslaved Indians traveling on voyages to the

geur de Joseph Marsil," June 16, 1737, Greffe Lepailleur de LaFerté (Montreal), FHL, film 1643385.

28. Engagement of May 13, 1718, Greffe Jean-Baptiste Adhémar (Montreal), BANQ-M; Trudel, *Dictionnaire des esclaves*, 63. For other examples, see "Engagement en qualité de voyageur de François," May 27, 1735, Greffe Lepailleur de LaFerté (Montreal), FHL, film 1643384; "Engagement en qualité de voyageur de Renaud," July 22, 1747, Greffe Simmonet (Montreal), FHL, film 1464530; "Engagement en qualité de voyageur de Régis," July 9, 1756, Greffe Danré de Blanzy (Montreal), FHL, film 1430178.

29. For the best treatment of voyageurs' work environment and social relations, see Carolyn Podruchny, *Making the Voyageur World: Travelers and Traders in the North American Fur Trade* (Lincoln, Nebr., 2006).

Pays d'en Haut were returning to Detroit, Michilimackinac, or other posts where they had spent substantial time before they were sold to the Saint Lawrence. If they renewed old relationships or started new ones, they left no traces in the historical record. It is quite possible that some of these men had lovers or children among the enslaved of the Pays d'en Haut. But, whatever the experience of individual slaves on western voyages, most returned to Montreal to live, like Joseph, in a fluid social world where thousands of free Indians circulated daily. They found space for movement, and a large proportion of their labors was structured by the merchant activities of French and métis slaveholders with deep connections to the Pays d'en Haut.

MARIE-JOACHIM

"She said . . . that it was only fear that caused her to confess . . .
because the Sieur Desrivières and his wife told her that if she confessed . . .
nothing bad would happen to her, and if she did not confess she would
be hanged."—Interrogation of Marie-Joachim, enslaved Fox Indian,
in her 1725 theft trial

If Joseph's experience reveals the influence of free Indians and western trade activities on slavery in Montreal, the case of Marie-Joachim, an Indian slave belonging to Lamoureux's neighbor, Julien Trottier dit Desrivières, provides an unusually rich example of the social relations that evolved around slavery in the Saint Lawrence Valley. Serving as a slave for nearly twenty years there, Marie-Joachim lived with at least two masters and several fellow slaves, always within walking distance of more than one hundred other enslaved Indians. In the close quarters of her neighborhood along Rue Saint-Paul, Marie-Joachim navigated complex currents of authority and affection with the enslaved and free people surrounding her. Although she had a great deal of mobility within this small world, developing a wide range of relationships that were often affectionate and supportive, her enslaved status ensured that she would remain profoundly vulnerable throughout her life.

Marie arrived in Montreal in 1714, with her first master, Pierre Biron. Captured in the early stages of the Fox Wars, she became Biron's slave at Detroit and then was taken to Montreal, where she served as Biron's domestic. Like Lamoureux, Biron was an enterprising merchant with strong ties to the Native and métis communities of the Pays d'en Haut that included the brandy trade. He was a witness to Daniel Villeneuve's 1709 marriage to an Ottawa woman, and his son married into the Cuillerier family. He and his family maintained close ties to the Illinois country. After Biron died in 1718, his widow hired out Marie-Joachim to Desrivières, moving her half a mile to Rue Saint-Paul, one block east of Lamoureux and Joseph, where Desrivières kept a home and an attic full of trade goods for his profession as a western merchant. In 1725 Desrivières accused Marie-Joachim of stealing hundreds of items from his inventory over the previous year. During the trial that followed, Montreal's royal court called twenty-three witnesses, whose testimony produced nearly two hundred pages of written documentation. As they provided details relevant to the crime, they also painted a portrait of slaves' daily activities that are visible in no other way.[30]

In her first two interrogations, Marie-Joachim admitted to the theft, offering a detailed narrative that explained her motives and the methods she used to avoid detection. When presented with a list of missing items, she testified "that it is true that she stole all of these things . . . and that she gave all of them to Guignolet (the younger), named Jean-Baptiste." According to Marie-Joachim, Guignolet "was in love with her and had told her that he needed the goods so he could provide for them." She explained that she and Guignolet had been having an affair for a year and that he had "promised to marry her." The level of detail she provided would have been difficult to fabricate. She had sometimes gone to the attic with Guignolet, sneaking her master's key or picking the lock with a knife and standing guard while he filled his pockets with Desrivières's merchandise. Other times, she had slipped in unnoticed to steal a few items herself. When this happened, the couple would meet at night in a nearby alley to exchange goods and spend

---

30. The central source of information about Marie-Joachim is the court record from her 1725 trial for theft, comprising 189 pages of transcribed testimony, court orders, etc. "Procès entre Julien Trottier DesRivières, marchand, plaignant, et Marie-Joachim, panise, esclave de la veuve Biron, et Jean-Baptiste Gouriou dit Guignolet, soldat de Blainville, fils du sergent Jean-Baptiste Gouriou dit Guignolet, accusés respectivement de vol et de recel," July 17, 1725, BANQ-M, TL4, S1, D3159. For Marie-Joachim's arrival, see baptism of May 19, 1714, Notre-Dame-de-Montreal, FHL. For brandy, see "Ordonnance de l'intendant Bégon qui condamne Pierre Plassan et Pierre Biron à payer à Joseph Furtade les vins qu'ils ont achetés à raison de 300 livres la barrique et les eau-de-vie (alcools) à raison de 600 livres la barrique," June 26, 1714, BANQ-Q, E1, S1, P984. For Biron's connection to Villeneuve, see baptism of Sept. 2, 1709, Notre-Dame-de-Montréal, FHL. For Biron's trade activities at Detroit, see Permis par M. de Ramezay à . . . Pierre Biron, Apr. 30, 1715, AC, MG8-C8, transcript, I, 106, National Archives of Canada, Ottawa. It is possible that this license was granted to his son of the same name. For Biron's Illinois country connections and his son's family ties to the region, see "Enregistrement d'une permission accordée par Jean Bouillet de La Chassaigne, lieutenant du roi et commandant de Montréal, au sieur Biron . . . pour aller chercher sa femme et deux de ses enfants aux Illinois," Sept. 26, 1725, BANQ-M, TL4, S34, P181.

some time alone. Throughout the year, Marie said that she had been assured that they were saving up enough to escape and establish a new life together.

Marie's reputed lover was Jean-Baptiste Gouriou dit Guignolet, an eighteen-year-old soldier stationed in Montreal who came from a poor family with a bad reputation. Not knowing the content of Marie's testimony, he opted for denial. When the court asked whether he knew Marie-Joachim, he admitted that he had seen her around town but said that he did not know her at all, that they had never been in love, and that he never solicited any stolen goods from her. It might have been the couple's plan all along to deny the theft if they were accused, because, as Marie-Joachim later admitted, no one ever caught them stealing or passing along the contraband and they had kept their relationship secret from all but their closest confidants. Guignolet might have hoped to escape unscathed and to avoid implicating his lover in a crime that, because it was committed by a slave against her master, could bring harsh punishment.

It is impossible to tell whether Guignolet really was "in love with her," as she claimed, but his actions suggest otherwise. Promising her marriage and freedom, he persuaded Marie-Joachim to risk everything to steal from her master. Despite his assurances that the stolen goods would allow the couple a fresh start, as soon as he had them, he sold them for his own profit. More than a dozen witnesses testified that Guignolet's younger sister, Marie-Anne, had sold them items stolen by Marie-Joachim: French-milled soap, ribbons, pins, sifting cloths, beads, knives, vermilion, and hatchets. When asked where the goods came from, Marie-Anne admitted that her brother had given them to her and promised to pay her for selling them. One witness testified that, as the trial approached, Guignolet confronted Marie-Joachim on the street, yelling loud enough for witnesses to hear: "Is it true that you said that you gave me some things? That is a lie, you never gave me anything." Visibly distressed, she yelled back, "Get out of here, you wretch," and crossed the street to avoid further conflict.

As court officials interrogated witnesses to determine whose version of the story was more credible, they uncovered the details of Marie-Joachim's daily routines as well as her relationships with her master, other slaves, and her French lover. From this testimony, it becomes clear that enslaved Indians were a prominent feature of Montreal's social landscape. They circulated relatively freely around the city's streets, making acquaintances, and even friends, among free and enslaved neighbors. For example, Marie-Joachim developed a long-term friendship with Marie Aumier, a French day laborer whose husband was a brickmaker and a tenant farmer. The religious who ran the Hôtel-Dieu, which stood across the street from Marie-Joachim's home, employed Aumier and owned the land where they lived and farmed. The two Maries crossed paths daily as they performed their labors, and over time they grew close. In a clear sign of trust, months before the trial Marie-Joachim had entrusted her friend with the secret of her affair and her continuing theft. Aumier did not betray her friend willingly, but under the pressure of interrogation she revealed the slave's confession.

Marie-Joachim developed her closest friendship with another Indian slave, Marie-Joseph, who belonged to Pierre Raimbault, the king's attorney overseeing the case who lived on the same block and who was Desrivières's father-in-law. Witnesses testified that they saw the slaves together often, so the court called Marie-Joseph to testify against her friend. With her master looming over her at the trial, Marie-Joseph must have feared the consequences of a misstep. She quickly admitted that Marie-Joachim had confided in her the previous year about stealing some beaver pelts and deerskins and giving them to Guignolet, but she also insisted that she had no firsthand knowledge of the crime. She had seen the two together from time to time and witnessed their public altercation but considered it possible that her friend was lying about stealing from her master.

Like Joseph and other male slaves who traveled around the island regularly, Montreal's female domestic slaves like Marie-Joachim spent many hours away from their masters' direct supervision. During typical days she found ample opportunity to steal her master's keys, take items from the attic, and transport the goods to Guignolet. She left many nights to meet her lover in an alley. She went on walks with her friend and fellow slave, Marie-Joseph, confiding in her at a time of crisis. She cared for animals and took goods to the public market. Yet the fact that these details came to light in neighbors' court testimony also indicates that someone was often watching when her master was not. When Montreal residents testified to slaves' whereabouts or activities, they confirmed that they knew exactly who the slaves were. Perhaps more important, they also knew *whose* they were. When masters and mistresses left their slaves alone, their neighbors testified that they noticed where these slaves went, to whom they spoke, and how they spent their time. When Charlotte Denis saw Marie-Joachim carrying her master's attic key, for example, she confronted her and "asked her why she had taken the said key." Marie-Joachim offered a plausible excuse. "The said *panise* told her," Denis informed the court, "that she had to get some linens out of the attic, and that she had carried away [the key] without thinking." Although Marie-Joachim initially sidestepped her neighbor's challenge, that watchful eye reminded Marie of the dangerous course she was taking. This informal system of shared surveillance evolved to meet the demands of an urban environment that fostered slaves' mobility.

Yet slaves also watched their French neighbors, and the courts occasionally compelled them to testify against them. It is not likely that a slave's testimony could, by itself, ever have led to the conviction of a French colonist, but slaves still occasionally provided essential information. While running an errand for Jacques Testard de Montigny, his master who lived on the eastern end of Rue Saint-Paul, Jacques-Charles witnessed an assault. His testimony provided key details, and the accused, the day laborer Étienne Brazeau, was found guilty. Slaves must have resisted giving such testimony, as it could put them in danger of retaliation. Like Lamoureux's slaves Joseph and Suzanne, who chose to cover for their master when under interrogation, many probably held their tongues when it came to testifying against French colonists. Jacques-Charles might have paid for his testimony with his life. Given Brazeau's documented penchant for violence, it is tempting to hold him responsible for Jacques-Charles's sudden and unexplained death less than three months later.[31]

The close association of Marie-Joachim with her neighbors generally occurred in the course of her normal labor as a domestic slave. Enslaved Indians tended gardens, took goods to market, ran errands, did laundry outside, and looked after a surprising number of domestic animals. The most common relationships forged among Indian slaves in New France developed through casual, daily contact at the market, in village streets, at mills or warehouses, or in their masters' homes. As in most societies with small enslaved populations, New France had neither the demographic density nor the separate living quarters that tended to form a distinct slave community: an independent sphere of cultural and social activity that supported slaves' efforts to forge bonds with family and friends. Nevertheless, many enslaved Natives lived in areas like Rue Saint-Paul that could be characterized as slave neighborhoods: localized pockets where slaves' prevalence afforded them unique opportunities for friendship and intimacy, albeit with restricted autonomy.[32]

31. "Procès entre Mathieu Larchevêque, journalier, époux de Catherine Achin, plaignant, et Anne Pinsonnault, épouse de Nicolas Brazeau, charron, son fils Étienne Brazeau, journalier, et son gendre Pierre Martineau, journalier, accusés de voies de fait," Dec. 7, 1731, BANQ-M, TL4, S1, D3888. Jacques-Charles gave his testimony in January and died in May. See burial of May 21, 1732, *RAB du PRDH*, 150862.

32. For the "slave community," see Lorena S. Walsh, *From Calabar to Carter's Grove: The*

Despite these supports, the limits of Marie-Joachim's independence quickly became clear as the trial progressed. She was not allowed to witness the proceedings, but gossip seems to have reached her, and by the time of her third interrogation a week into the trial she decided to change her testimony. Pleading that she did not understand how the legal system worked and what the consequences of her confession might be, Marie claimed that she had stolen nothing of any value and "that it was only fear that caused her to confess." When notice came of her arrest, her master and mistress had "told her that if she confessed . . . nothing bad would happen to her, and if she did not confess she would be hanged." She believed them, or felt she had no choice but to comply in any case. Marie's bewilderment is palpable in the trial record. In her final testimony she told the court three times how afraid she was, a fear that was reinforced when her master came to the prison and talked to her "through the bars" to be sure she confessed to the crimes. For all of her mobility and social connections, then, Marie-Joachim remained profoundly vulnerable. Taken advantage of by a French soldier who abandoned her at the first sign of danger, she confessed because her master threatened to have her killed, and it was her friends' testimony that ultimately confirmed her guilt.

Within similar limits, New France's enslaved Indians formed a wide range of relationships, from casual acquaintances to legally recognized marriages. Although the latter were rare, as many as forty entered into legally recognized unions between 1710 and 1760. Their experiences offer another angle from which to view the dynamics of slavery in Montreal and other Saint Lawrence towns. One of the greatest limitations on these marriages, as on slaves' lives in general, was their short duration. Especially when Indian slaves married each other, one partner almost always died within two or three years of the ceremony. As in most slaveholding societies, children from slave couples belonged to their mother's master, meaning that the father had no practical claim to the child, especially when the mother

History of a Virginia Slave Community (Charlottesville, Va., 1997); Allan Kulikoff, *Tobacco and Slaves: The Development of Southern Cultures in the Chesapeake* (Chapel Hill, N.C., 1986); Jean Butenhoff Lee, "The Problem of Slave Community in the Eighteenth-Century Chesapeake," *WMQ*, 3d Ser., XLIII (1986), 333–361; Peter Kolchin, "Reevaluating the Antebellum Slave Community: A Comparative Perspective," *Journal of American History*, LXX (1983–1984), 579–601; John W. Blassingame, *The Slave Community: Plantation Life in the Antebellum South* (New York, 1972). For "slave neighborhood," see Anthony E. Kaye, "Neighbourhoods and Solidarity in the Natchez District of Mississippi: Rethinking the Antebellum Slave Community," *Slavery and Abolition*, XXIII (2002), 1–24.

died or the marriage dissolved. With no property to bring to the marriage and no realistic hope for creating a long-term relationship or a family, slaves had little incentive to unite with other slaves.[33]

Indian slaves obviously stood to benefit much more by marrying French colonists. More than three times as many marriages fell into this category as those occurring between slaves, reflecting slaves' predictable desire to ally themselves with those of a higher status. In addition to gaining access to family support networks and a measure of economic independence, a slave's marriage to a French colonist could sometimes grant a female slave her freedom. Enslaved men could not count on such measures to free them, but marriage to a French woman would at least guarantee the legal freedom of their children, since free women bore free children. French incentives to marry slaves are more difficult to discriminate. Some, like the petty merchant Pierre Chauvet dit La Gerne, might have just fallen in love. Sometime after the death of his first wife, Marie-Madeleine Gaudin, the forty-year-old Chauvet struck up a relationship with his neighbor's slave, a much younger Fox woman named Marie-Madeleine. Unwilling to live apart from his lover, in 1726 Chauvet sneaked into the home of her master, Pierre-Thomas Tarieu de La Pérade, and helped her escape. Outraged at the loss of his slave and the insult of having a social inferior invade his home, La Pérade persuaded the intendant to send soldiers to retrieve Marie-Madeleine and, if Chauvet resisted, to conduct him to prison in irons. It is difficult to imagine how, but the persistent Chauvet found a way to evade the order, marrying Marie-Madeleine only four months later in a rural parish near Quebec. Perhaps they did so by stealth—Chauvet apparently provided the priest a different last name (Channel instead of Chauvet)—but it is more likely that he paid La Pérade for her freedom. The fact that their four children were never referred to as slaves indicates that Marie-Madeleine became legally free by 1729 at the latest.[34]

33. For marriages, see Trudel, *Dictionnaire des esclaves*, xxiv–xxv. Even in France's Caribbean slave colonies, marriage between slaves was quite limited. Bernard Moitt, *Women and Slavery in the French Antilles, 1635–1848* (Bloomington, Ind., 2001), 80–100.

34. "Ordonnance de l'intendant Bégon qui enjoint au capitaine de la côte de la Chevrotière, ou autre officier de milice sur ce requis, de retirer des mains du nommé Lagerne (Lajerne) une esclave Panis Renarde (Amérindienne) nommée Madeleine qu'il a enlevée furtivement la nuit de la maison du sieur de la Pérade (Tarieu)," July 17, 1726, BANQ-Q, E1, S1, P1749. For their family, see marriage of Nov. 11, 1726, *RAB du PRDH*, 77504; baptism of Oct. 12, 1729, Notre-Dame-de-Québec, FHL; baptism of Mar. 16, 1732, Saint-Jean-Baptiste-de-Nicolet, *RAB du PRDH*, 154291, and baptism of Feb. 13, 1735, 154312. The record of Chauvet's and Marie-Madeleine's marriage is a transcript, so "Channel" could be a transcription

Both church policy and colonial law demanded the public reading of banns, notifications that announced all upcoming marriages, for three successive Sundays. The banns functioned as a safeguard against someone's marrying when not legally or morally free to do so. In the case of slaves, banns would inform masters of any slave's seeking to marry without their permission, thus ensuring slaveholders' control over their slaves' marriage decisions. Despite the scrupulous adherence to this procedure in all cases of New France's slave marriages, no surviving record documents a master's ever filing a formal objection to a slave's marriage. More likely than not, slaveholders did not need to follow formal procedures to deny their slaves the right to marry but could merely assert their authority over the decision. The publication of banns would also discourage a slave from lying about his or her legal status to a potential marriage partner, a deception that would invalidate the marriage in any case. But, unlike France's tropical colonies, which minutely regulated slaves' marriages, the law in New France was never clear.[35]

Sometimes, French family members formally used this procedure to block a relative's marriage to a slave. When Jean Cardinal attempted to marry a neighbor's slave in 1721, his mother and her friend filed a formal complaint, "declar[ing] that they opposed . . . the future marriage between Jean Cardinal on the one hand, and a *panise* residing in the home of the Sieur de Collonge on the other hand." The Cardinals, a prominent fur trading family at Detroit, owned at least two Indian slaves themselves: symbols of an elite social status that would have been threatened by a son who married so far beneath his station. Jean might have merely been following the customs of the Pays d'en Haut, where he came of age, incorporating an enslaved woman into his household as a wife.[36]

In other cases, the French family either lacked the funds to file a notarized complaint, had strong reasons to allow the marriage, or both. Such was the case with Nicolas, an Indian slave living in Varennes just east of Montreal. When his French companion, Catherine Guertain, became pregnant with his child, her father allowed the couple's marriage. As a poor farming family, the Guertains had little social status to lose, but an illegiti-

---

error, and in any case the likelihood of keeping their whereabouts secret for the long term is slim.

35. Jean de La Croix de Saint Vallier, *Catechisme du Diocese de Québec* (Paris, 1702), 298.

36. "Opposition au mariage de Jean Cardinal et d'une panis demeurant chez le sieur de Coulonges," Feb. 8, 1721, BANQ-M, TL4, S1, D2607. For the cardinals' slaves, see Trudel, *Dictionnaire des esclaves*, 295.

mate birth could diminish what reputation they had among their neighbors. After the publication of two banns, Catherine's father and priest agreed to allow the marriage to proceed before publishing the third bann. Four months later, Catherine delivered a healthy son, the first of three children born to the couple, all of whom inherited their mother's free status.[37]

Nicolas enjoyed greater social privileges than most of his enslaved contemporaries, some of whom did not even survive to a marriageable age. Yet Nicolas would never enjoy the social and economic privileges of marriage afforded to even the poorest of French peasants. In New France, as in old, marriage consisted of two essential and complementary components: the religious ceremony performed by a Catholic priest and its civil counterpart, the marriage contract. Designed to regulate marital property relations, including dowries and inheritances, marriage contracts accompanied nearly every marriage in New France, even among the peasantry. In the mid-eighteenth century, fully 96 percent of all recorded marriages had corresponding civil contracts.[38]

Yet, predictably, not one slave marriage enjoyed the protection of a marriage contract. Because slaves were property themselves, they had no legal claim to the "marriage community": the money, goods, and land accumulated by the couple during the course of their marriage. For men like Nicolas, this meant that his wife, as the only autonomous partner, had sole legal control over all of the couple's goods. For enslaved women, it meant that they had no guarantee of inheritance. Rather than class, slave status determined the lack of marriage contracts. Among French widows and widowers who had married an Indian slave, always without a marriage contract, nearly all who later married French colonists enjoyed contractual protection. Typical of this phenomenon, a soldier named Raymond Calmet first married a Fox slave named Geneviève Quarris in 1752 without any accompanying marriage contract. Following her death, he remarried a young French woman,

---

37. Marriage of Nov. 18, 1720, *RAB du PRDH*, 90586; baptism of Mar. 12, 1721, Sainte-Anne-de-Varennes, FHL; Trudel, *Dictionnaire des esclaves*, 214–215. For another example, see Marriage of Apr. 4, 1731, *RAB du PRDH*, 149707. Peasant families rarely exercised control over the marriage decisions of their children, since threatening them with the loss of a meager inheritance held little persuasive power. In this case, however, the parents could have asserted their authority under the regulations to block the marriage. See Dechêne, *Habitants and Merchants*, trans. Vardi, 251.

38. Dechêne, *Habitants and Merchants*, trans. Vardi, 240, writes: "Whereas in France only the comparatively well off procured a notarized marriage contract, Canadian settlers of all classes went through the signing ritual as a matter of course. . . . The exceptional circumstances of colonial life . . . made these legal conventions a necessity."

Marie-Catherine Chaunierre, in 1756. The couple signed a marriage contract five days before their wedding. The lack of marriage contracts aptly symbolizes the limited control that slaves exercised over their personal relationships. Indian slaves were doubly acculturated to value family and kinship relations, first in their home villages and then in New France, where the common idiom of social, legal, and religious life was that of the family. Yet, at every turn, the colony's slaves faced a reality that denied them access to the relationships that French colonists placed at the core of their own social structure. By closing the pathways to kinship afforded by indigenous slavery, colonists exercised a form of coercion that might have been as disorienting as slaves' lack of freedom.[39]

In less formal ways, however, enslaved Indians in the Saint Lawrence Valley developed emotional and physical relationships with one another and with French colonists. These bonds are documented far more thoroughly for enslaved women than men. As in the posts of the Pays d'en Haut, the most reliable indicators of intimate relationships—birth and baptism records—identify the mother but not necessarily the father. Occasional court cases bring to light enslaved men's relationships, as when Constant broke into the home of the widow Saint Pierre to steal a pair of shoes in 1756. He admitted in court that, in addition to the shoes, he hoped he would get the chance to "caress" three enslaved women who slept in the kitchen. Accompanied by his friend Joseph, a neighboring Indian slave, he climbed through a window, took the shoes, then tried to break into the kitchen with the other slaves. The widow Saint Pierre discovered the intruders, but they frightened her so badly that she bolted, fell, and broke her arm.[40]

Women's relationships are easier to see. Marie-Angélique, a slave belonging to Pierre Larrivé, became pregnant in 1730. Questioned before a Montreal court, "she testified to being five months pregnant by Jean-Baptiste Maillot, inhabitant of Boucherville, who resides at the fort of the said Boucherville." But, rather than demanding anything of Maillot, the court ordered Larrivé's wife, Marie-Anne Payet, "to watch over the said Marie panise [and] to be sure to have the child baptized after its birth." Born to an enslaved mother, the infant would belong to the Larrivé family, dissolving Maillot's rights and responsibilities as the child's father. The record indi-

39. Trudel, *Dictionnaire des esclaves*, 16–17; contract of Sept. 26, 1756, Greffe Lalanne (Quebec), FHL.

40. "Procès contre Constant, esclave panis de Raimbault de Saint-Blain, fils, accusé d'entrée par effraction," Nov. 24, 1756, BANQ-M, TL4, S1, D6131.

cates that neither the slave nor her lover objected to the outcome. Maillot never appeared, likely hoping to avoid financial responsibility for the slave's medical expenses. For her part, Marie-Angélique showed little interest in either Maillot or their child, possibly harboring the concerns of many enslaved women about bringing a child into the world as a slave. Her despair led court officials to doubt the infant's safety, so, to prevent the slave from harming or abandoning the child, a judge "enjoined the said Marie, panise, to preserve her fruit."[41]

Compare this with the case of Charles, the Indian slave of Antoine Mesnard, who fathered a child with his neighbor's eighteen-year-old French servant, Charlotte Rondeau. Sometime in 1741, Charles and Charlotte began a secretive relationship. Not long after they began seeing each other, Charlotte became pregnant with his child. When she realized that she would be discovered, Charlotte confessed to her priest and informed her master, who quickly initiated legal proceedings to force Charles's master to pay for the child's expenses. In 1732, the intendant had declared that masters were liable for the actions of their servants, making Mesnard an easy target for litigation. In a harsh ruling, the court concluded:

> That the said Antoine Mesnard is sentenced, as the owner of Charles Mesnard . . . his slave, to provide a nurse to the child born of carnal relations had by the said Charles Mesnard with the said Charlotte Rondeau . . . to pay for the said nurse the first three months at the rate of fifteen livres per month, the next fifteen months at the rate of ten livres, and the remainder of the time that the said child will be nursing at the rate of seven livres per month . . . to feed him and rear him in the Catholic, Apostolic, and Roman religion until the age of eighteen . . . and also to pay to the said Charlotte Rondeau . . . the sum of two hundred livres.

To pay this fine, which came to about 450 livres, Mesnard hired out Charles later that year as a voyageur to Michilimackinac. This served the dual purpose of generating much-needed revenue and of separating Charles from his newly created family. In this case, because the father was a slave whose

41. "Procès entre Marie, panise, esclave de Pierre Larrivé de Boucherville, plaignante, et Jean-Baptiste Maillot, habitant le fort de Boucherville, accusé d'avoir mis enceinte la plaignante," July 14, 1730, BANQ-M, TL4, S1, D3734. For mother's death, see Trudel, *Dictionnaire des esclaves*, 12.

master could be compelled to pay, the father's paternity was central to the discussion.[42]

As they interacted with French colonists, slaves almost all learned to speak French well enough to communicate. Because New France's slave population depended on the slave trade rather than reproduction, most slaves likewise entered the colony speaking only their native tongue. Yet most of them learned French and eventually spoke it as their primary, if not their only, language. The colony's court records provide the most reliable evidence that nearly all of the colony's Indian slaves eventually learned to speak fluently in French. New France's legal officials consistently recorded the presence of translators in cases involving free Indians, mostly in trials that involved illegal French trade to the independent Indian settlements around Montreal. Although about thirty enslaved Indians appeared in the royal courts between 1700 and 1760, not one required a translator. Moreover, hundreds of witnesses testified to hearing or carrying on casual conversations with these slaves without ever suggesting a language barrier.[43]

Many factors encouraged slaves' rapid transition from their native languages to French, but none was more important than simple necessity. Most slaveholders owned only one or two Indian slaves, and these usually came from different regions. Slaves therefore had limited opportunity to speak their native tongues with fellow captives. Moreover, domestic slavery required constant communication about the varied needs and demands of a master or mistress. Thus, to avoid punishment for failing to follow instructions, slaves had to make a quick study of French. And, while many French colonists learned basic communication in the languages of allied Indian

42. "Procès entre Clément de Sabrevois de Bleury, demandeur, et Antoine Ménard, défendeur, pour le payement des frais d'entretien d'un enfant né d'un esclave appartenant au défendeur," Feb. 21, 1742, BANQ-M, TL4, S1, D4825. For the 1732 declaration, see "Ordonnance qui, attend que tout maître est responsable civilement des faits de son domestique, condamne le nommé Travers en l'amende de six livres parce que son domestique a coupé et charrié un voyage de bois pris sur la terre du sieur de Lespinay," Feb. 8, 1732, LAC, M68-A6, XI, 91.

43. For cases involving free Indians needing interpreters, see, for example, "Procès contre Louise Leblanc, épouse de Paul Bouchard, accusée d'avoir vendu de l'eau de vie à un sauvage," Aug. 7, 1710, BANQ-M, TL4, S1, D1248, "Comparution de René Robineau, sieur de Portneuf, pour servir d'interprète en langue abénaquis, dans une cause indéterminée impliquant un sauvage," Aug. 5, 1713, D1471, "Procès contre Barrois, accusé de traite illégale avec les sauvages," Aug. 6, 1716, D1991, "Procès contre Pierre Ozanne, de Lachine, et Simon Valois, aussi de Lachine, accusés de vente de boisson aux sauvages au Lac Saint-François," Apr. 27, 1723, D1991.

nations, only a handful could speak Fox or Sioux (much less Apache or Pawnee), and most of these men and women spent little time in Saint Lawrence settlements. Perhaps the most significant factor that facilitated slaves' rapid acquisition of French language skills was the fact that most slaves entered the colony when they were still very young. Because the ability to learn a new language declines with age, the relative youth of the Indian slave population also worked to foster linguistic assimilation. In time, the youngest slaves might have entirely forgotten their native languages.

Because of slaves' small numbers, their close supervision, and their suppression by a powerful Catholic elite unwilling to allow substantial cultural deviation, Native slaves were far less likely to enjoy religious and cultural independence than their peers in the planter colonies. Structural inducements to cultural assimilation were reinforced by the relative youth of most new Indian slaves. Because more than half were captured during their early childhood, they were more culturally malleable and therefore tended to assimilate more quickly than the older slave populations found in plantation societies, where some 86 percent of newly arrived Africans had passed their mid-teens. As a result, slaveholders were relatively successful in cultivating and enforcing French cultural and social norms in the lives of their slaves.[44]

Yet, even as slaveholders attempted to "frenchify" their slaves, they also erected barriers to their full assimilation to maintain social and cultural distance between themselves and their human property. The souls of the enslaved might have been precious to them, but not nearly so dear as the labor of their bodies. Slaveholders therefore found ways to limit slaves' access to key markers of French cultural identity in order to keep them from assuming parity with their French masters. Denied cultural independence, slaves could thus fashion their identity only from within a culture dedicated to enforcing their inferior status. Even under these difficult conditions, some slaves did retain a strong sense of identity, but even this identity could work against slaves whose origins were almost by definition among an enemy nation.

As the most potent force for assimilation available to New France's slaveholders, Catholicism dominated the cultural experience of the colony's Indian slaves. But the Christianization of New France's Indian slaves ultimately depended upon the actions of their masters and mistresses. While a large number of the colony's slaveholders baptized their charges, many did

44. See David Eltis, "The Age and Sex of Africans in the Transatlantic Slave Trade, 1663–1713," in Eltis, ed., *The Rise of African Slavery in the Americas* (New York, 2000), 285–292.

not do so until they were gravely ill. In 1737, for example, Jean-Baptiste-Nicolas-Roch de Ramezay, the son of Montreal's late governor, baptized his twelve-year-old male slave, Louis-Jean-Baptiste, "when," according to the parish priest, "he was in danger of death." The priest's assessment of the slave's health proved accurate, for he died two weeks later. Ramezay followed the same pattern with another slave a decade later. In November 1746, he presented for baptism a severely ill slave, twelve-year-old Louis-Joseph, who died the following January. Ramezay's slaves were not alone in their deathbed baptisms. Of all Indian slaves for whom both baptism and death dates are available, nearly half died within a year of their baptism, and two-thirds died within three years of receiving the rite. During years of epidemic disease, many of these slaves were baptized "conditionally," meaning that their baptism was performed by the unordained or that the recipient had not yet been sufficiently instructed to express an informed acceptance of Catholicism. Many were like an unnamed "Indian, about eleven years old, belonging to Pierre de Pelletier, [who] was baptized at home and then died."[45]

For all of their cultural indoctrination based on the notion of equal souls, New France's slaves remained vulnerable to abuse, sickness, and early death. They were often the target of taunting and derision, making such interactions a liability as much as a benefit. Sometime during the 1710s, for instance, a Sieur Cuillerier bought an adult male slave with only one eye, the other probably burned during the ritual tortures of indigenous slavery. As a cruel joke, Cuillerier and his neighbors called the slave Cyclope. In 1721, Cuillerier's ten-year-old neighbor, Alexandre Celle dit Duclos, paid the ultimate price for his taunting: Cyclope lived up to his monstrous name by shooting the child dead in the streets of Montreal. When the victim's father threatened to kill him, Cyclope wisely fled, never to return.[46]

In less dramatic ways, slaveholders also inflicted discomforts on their slaves by providing them with substandard food and clothing. Masters routinely set aside the less desirable food for servants and slaves. Fresh milk and butter, for example, went first to the master's family, with aging or tainted dairy products marked for slaves' and servants' consumption. In one case, a servant, tiring of her inferior fare, decided to dip into the but-

45. Baptism of Mar. 31, 1737, *RAB du PRDH*, 180541, burial of Apr. 15, 1737, 181144; baptism of Sept. 26, 1755, Lachine, FHL ("baptized at home"); Trudel, *Dictionnaire des esclaves*, 69.

46. "Procès contre Cyclope, panis du sieur Cuillerier, accusé de meurtre," July 7, 1721, BANQ-M, TL4, S1, D2641.

ter reserved for her master's children. Discovered by her master, she was beaten and sent to prison for several days. Eventually, the court ordered her release, not because imprisonment seemed too severe, but rather because the servant "was not formally imprisoned" by the proper authorities. Such protections were almost never extended to the enslaved. Never established by formal law, the extent of masters' right to punish their slaves remained a matter of varied interpretation throughout the eighteenth century in New France. But most punishments and deprivations remained entirely at slaveholders' discretion.[47]

Most Indian slaves had sufficient clothing for the warmer months, but evidence suggests that they suffered during New France's chilling winters. Enslaved women generally dressed like French servants, in plain dresses and shoes, and occasionally a hat. When Marie-Joachim was accused of stealing from her master's home, one witness testified that she carried the goods away "in her hat that was on her head." As a discretionary expense, slaves' shoes might have been withheld or kept in poor repair. At the onset of winter in 1756, Constant, a male Indian slave, became so desperate for some warm shoes that he broke into a neighbor's house to steal a pair.[48]

Slaves generally slept on the kitchen floor. Marie-Joseph Angélique, one of the colony's few African slaves before the late-1740s, testified in 1734 that she slept on a pallet in her master's kitchen. The three enslaved women belonging to the widow Saint Pierre were also described in a court proceeding as sleeping together "in the kitchen." Male slaves generally shared the same floor space, but occasionally they had to sleep outside, with no protection from the elements, even during the winter months. One Indian slave, Joseph, said that he preferred this arrangement to the confines of his master's home, because it allowed him the freedom to visit other slaves in the area at night. A few much luckier slaves enjoyed more comfortable accommodations, including Elisabeth, who not only slept in a bed but also possessed her own quilt.[49]

47. "Procès Catherine Menault dit Desbrandes, native de Rochefort, fille de Louis Menault, capitaine d'armes de la marine, servant, plaignante, et son patron, de Lacome, accuse d'ub-s de pouvoir," Feb. 25, 1722, BANQ-M, TL4, S1, D2701.

48. "Procès entre Julien Trottier DesRivières, marchand, plaignant, et Marie-Joachim, panise, esclave de la veuve Biron, et Jean-Baptiste Gouriou dit Guignolet, soldat de Blainville, fils du sergent Jean-Baptiste Gouriou dit Guignolet, accusés respectivement de vol et de recel," July 17, 1725, BANQ-M, TL4, S1, D3159, and "Procès contre Constant, esclave panis de Raimbault de Saint-Blain, fils, accusé d'entrée par effraction," Nov. 24, 1756, D6131.

49. Procès contre Marie-Josèphe-Angélique, née au Portugal, esclave noire de Thérèse

TABLE 3. Age at Death of Indian Slaves in New France's
Parish and Hospital Records, 1700–1760

Age at Death (N = 793)	Proportion
0–4	7 %
5–9	16
10–14	27
15–19	24
20–24	13
25–29	4
30–39	5
40–49	3
50+	1

When epidemics struck, there was little masters could do to save their slaves. But most seem to have tried, either out of concern for the slave's well-being or out of fear of losing their property. The records of the Hôtel-Dieu in both Montreal and Quebec list hundreds of slaves admitted for sickness. Taken at face value, records that indicate slaves' age at death present a grim picture of life expectancy, suggesting that fully half of enslaved Indians died by the age of fourteen, and three-fourths before turning twenty. These numbers stand out even more in a colony with high life expectancies by early modern standards. The most demographically comparable group — French children immigrating into New France with their parents — arrived in the colony at an average of eleven years old, just younger than the typical Indian slave. Yet these immigrants apparently lived four times as long, dying at about age sixty rather than fifteen.[50]

---

de Couagne, veuve de Poulin de Francheville, et Claude Thibault, faux-saunier, accusés d'incendie criminel," Apr. 11, 1734, BANQ-M, TL4, S1, D4136, "Procès contre Constant, esclave panis de Raimbault de Saint-Blain, fils, accusé d'entrée par effraction," Nov. 24, 1756, D6131; BANQ-M, inventory of Feb. 19, 1732, 068–3905. The court document suggests that the coverlet was "à l'usage d'Elisabeth," which excluded it from the general reckoning of the estate.

50. See, for example, "Liste de malades," Hôtel-Dieu de Québec, Nov. 14, 1689, RAB du PRDH, 412949. These lists, contained in the database for both the Montreal and Quebec hospitals, list Indian slaves among the patients throughout the French regime. The median age at death for all slaves in surviving records, averaged for all decades, was 14.1 years. The mean age at death for all slaves, averaged for all decades, was 15.6 years. For the data on French immigrants, see Hubert Charbonneau et al., The First French Canadians: Pioneers in the St. Lawrence Valley, trans. Paola Colozzo (Newark, Del., 1993), chap. 8, esp. 184, figure 27.

There are many reasons why these figures misrepresent slaves' overall experience. First, those who died young were the most likely to appear in parish records as they were under more constant supervision by French colonists who could take them to priests for a quick baptism or last rites. Those who lived longer were more likely to become free, to leave the colony by choice or sale, or to exercise their independence by remaining non-Christians. They were also less remarkable, and thus less likely to appear in non-Catholic records. What is more, many older slaves who appear in judicial, notarial, or financial records were in their twenties or thirties, and their death dates cannot be found. And some of them did not know their ages, like Marie-Joachim, who thought she was about twenty years old at trial when she was actually twenty-five. So, even as they indicate the harsh environment of slavery in New France, death statistics cannot demonstrate an accurate demographic picture.[51]

But living conditions were inhospitable, straining slaves' bodies and impairing their resistance to foreign and familiar microbes, and increased the likelihood of death. The violent tortures of capture, the rigors of transportation, the blows of corporal punishment, the deficiencies of food and clothing, and the exhaustion of retiring from hard labor to a hard floor without blankets or bedding all diminished slaves' ability to rebound from sickness or injury. The psychological stress of enslavement combined with these physical pressures to threaten slaves' health and longevity. Marie-Joachim died a slave in 1733, possibly from smallpox, but there is a good chance she was weakened by inadequate food or protection from the elements. Despite her baptism, after a few ceremonial words by the priest, her body was taken beyond Montreal's city wall and buried in an unmarked grave.[52]

Slaves also faced physical abuse. Aside from the routine violence perpetrated by their masters, Monteal's slaves faced their greatest threat from soldiers. In 1710, for instance, the freed slave Pierre Voisin of Laprairie "was attacked, beaten, and outrageously assaulted" by three soldiers. In self-defense, Pierre stabbed one of the soldiers, Étienne Metenier dit Larose, who survived the attack and demanded Pierre's criminal prosecution. Enough people had witnessed the original attack that the court re-

51. "Procès entre Julien Trottier DesRivières, marchand, plaignant, et Marie-Joachim, panise, esclave de la veuve Biron, et Jean-Baptiste Gouriou dit Guignolet, soldat de Blainville, fils du sergent Jean-Baptiste Gouriou dit Guignolet, accusés respectivement de vol et de recel," July 17, 1725, BANQ-M, TL4, S1, D3159.

52. Burial of Feb. 14, 1733, Notre-Dame-de-Montreal, FHL.

leased Pierre unpunished. Indeed, Montreal's royal court considered only three cases of antislave violence between 1700 and 1760, one assault and two murders, all of which were committed by soldiers. As commoners with limited social networks to support them, New France's soldiers often took out their own frustrations by lashing out to humiliate those less powerful than they. Yet perhaps the most important reason for their violence relates to the structure of the slave system itself. At least in theory, Indian slaves originated among enemy nations with whom New France was at war. Many of the colony's soldiers fought in western campaigns against these peoples, and they harbored deeply personal animosities towards them.[53]

Because the Fox Wars lasted so long and claimed so many lives, French colonists developed a deep hatred for the Fox people. Even before the wars, French opinion of the Foxes reflected the sentiments of their Indian allies, especially the Illinois, who considered them to be demons. Drawing on French cultural conceptions of foxes' qualities, colonists explained their belligerence by maligning their Fox adversaries as a "Cruel nation," characterized by the wily treachery of the animal whose name they bore. French dictionaries described the fox as a "smelly, nasty, sneaky animal" and used fox metaphors to describe acting in a sly or disingenuous manner. As the war progressed, these sentiments grew more pervasive among the French, leaving Fox slaves increasingly vulnerable to French mistreatment.[54]

In 1739, when the Fox-Chickasaw alliance threatened to engulf the Illinois country, Vicar-General Jean-Pierre de Miniac ordered New France's

---

53. "Procès contre Pierre Voisin, un panis habitant de Laprairie, accusé de coups et blessures au couteau sur un soldat lors d'une bagarre," Nov. 9, 1710, BANQ-M, TL4, S1, D1264, "Procès contre Lapalme, factionnaire, soldat de la compagnie Contrecoeur, accusé du meurtre de Jacob, panis, esclave de Julien Trottier, sieur DesRivières," June 13, 1728, D3433, "Procès contre les soldat Sanscartier, Langevin et Lajeunesse, accusé d'avoir assassiné Antoine, un nègre qui travaillait au moulin à scie de monsieur de Ramezay à Chambly," Feb. 4, 1719, D2323. For soldiers, see W. J. Eccles, "The Social, Economic, and Political Significance of the Military Establishment in New France," in Eccles, *Essays on New France* (Oxford, 2007), 110–124.

54. Antoine Denis Raudot, "Memoir concerning the Different Indian Nations of North America," in W. Vernon Kinietz, ed., *The Indians of the Western Great Lakes, 1615–1760* (Ann Arbor, Mich., 1940), 383. For "cruel nation," see Mesaiger to Du Tisné, Oct. 15, 1724, *Wis. Hist. Coll.*, XVI (1902), 450. Le Beau expressed the common animalization of Foxes in New France in his description of a French-Fox battle: "These Foxes, who have fine noses, no doubt sensed the approach of their hunters," the French. Claude Le Beau, *Aventure du Sr. C. Le Beau, avocat en parlement, ou voyage curieux et nouveau, parmi les sauvages de l'Amérique Septentrionale* ... (Amsterdam, 1738), 169; Académie française, *Dictionnaire* (Paris, 1694), s.v. "renard."

clergy to pray for a French victory over their enemies. The church "established particular prayers against those who use violence to arrest [French] progress," namely, the Foxes and the Chickasaws. For French soldiers this climate reinforced suspicions of the enemy at home. Especially for soldiers returning from the Mississippi campaigns, this environment would have made it very difficult to see Fox or Chickasaw slaves as anything other than internal enemies and thus legitimate targets of violence.[55]

JACOB

"My God, I am dead."—Last words of the Fox slave Jacob, Montreal, 1728

For Jacob, another Fox slave belonging to Desrivières, soldiers' anti-Fox sentiments might have proved fatal. In the early morning hours of June 12, 1728, Jacob carried a load of trade goods to Montreal's docks along the Saint Lawrence River, bearing papers authorizing him to load a canoe and travel a short distance for his master. As he placed the merchandise into his master's canoe, three armed soldiers approached him. One of them, a sentinel named Jean Gaboureau dit La Palme, exchanged insults with Jacob and during the argument that followed beat the slave with the butt of his musket. La Palme then shot him at point blank range. Jacob grabbed his chest, took two lurching steps, fell on his left side, and died. Jacob's master demanded that Montreal's criminal court try La Palme for killing his slave, so the following day court authorities arrested La Palme and charged him with murder. Over the next six weeks dozens of witnesses testified to various elements of the crime, making it clear that La Palme had overstepped his role as sentinel and killed the slave in anger.[56]

To understand Jacob's murder and the trial that followed, it helps to contrast it with a similar killing, which occurred in 1719 at the sawmill of Montreal's governor Claude de Ramezay. On a brisk February afternoon, a French soldier named Sanscartier entered the mill where Ramezay's black slave, Antoine, was working. The soldier insulted the slave and then attacked him with a stick and a short sword. Although some witnesses suggested that Antoine wielded an axe in the fight, the autopsy report clearly

---

55. Jean-Pierre de Miniac, "Mandement ordonnant des prières publique pour obtenir de Dieu de vaincre les ennemis," Sept. 7, 1739, *Mandements, lettres pastorales, et circulaires des évêques de Québec* (Quebec, 1887), I, 557–558.

56. "Procès contre Lapalme, factionnaire, soldat de la compagnie Contrecoeur, accusé du meurtre de Jacob, panis, esclave de Julien Trottier, sieur DesRivières," June 13, 1728, BANQ-M, TL4, S1, D3433.

indicates that the slave hunkered to the ground trying to shield himself from the assault. After sustaining defensive wounds to his hands and arms, Antoine received a fatal blow to the temple. The soldier and his two friends ran away, leaving Antoine's body, where it was discovered in a pool of his frozen blood.[57]

These cases shared many details, both involving unsupervised adult male slaves performing tasks for their masters, who were insulted and then killed by soldiers. But the cases took very different paths. The trial of Sanscartier, who murdered a black slave, proceeded predictably. Witnesses blamed the slave for provoking the soldier, but ultimately the court ordered Sanscartier imprisoned and his goods seized for the benefit of Claude de Ramezay, the slave's owner. Nearly all New World slave codes, including those for the French Caribbean, treated the unprovoked murder of a slave primarily as a property crime, requiring the perpetrator to pay a large fine to the slave owner to compensate for the loss.[58]

The trial for Jacob's murder began in much the same way as the earlier case. For the first four days of testimony, the court gathered evidence to support a conviction. But, on the fifth day of trial, New France's governor, Charles de Beauharnois, intervened. He told the court that the murdered slave belonged to the Fox nation, with whom the French were again at war. Thus, according to Beauharnois and several prominent officers who signed a petition to the court, the case was "purely a military matter and cannot be considered by ordinary judges."[59]

The governor's reasoning did not persuade the court, however, and it proceeded with little regard to his demands, ultimately convicting La Palme of murdering the slave. Although the court followed the law, which confirmed the enslaved status of captured Fox Indians in a 1726 runaway case, the governor pardoned La Palme, explaining that as the colony's chief military officer he controlled decisions relating to soldiers and enemy Indians. La Palme lost neither his property nor his freedom, and Jacob's owner re-

57. "Procès contre les soldat Sanscartier, Langevin et Lajeunesse, accusé d'avoir assassiné Antoine, un nègre qui travaillait au moulin à scie de monsieur de Ramezay à Chambly," Feb. 4, 1719, BANQ-M, TL4, S1, D2323.

58. Ibid. For laws regarding the homicides of slaves, see Thomas D. Morris, *Southern Slavery and the Law, 1619–1860* (Chapel Hill, N.C., 1996), 161–181.

59. "Procès contre Lapalme, factionnaire, soldat de la compagnie Contrecoeur," June 13, 1728, BANQ-M, TL4, S1, D3433; "Copie de la délibération des officiers de la garnison de Montréal sur l'affaire du soldat La Palme," June 19, 1728, ANOM, Colonies, C11A, L, 213–213v.

ceived no compensation for his slave's death. Showing that French-Native diplomacy shaped slave law in unpredictable ways, eleven of the twelve officers who signed a petition supporting the governor's actions owned at least one Indian slave. Over the following decade Governor Beauharnois would acquire at least seven slaves from the Fox nation, whom he held, not as prisoners of war, but as domestic slaves. And François de Gannes, another of the petition's signatories, had appealed to the court less than one year before to enforce the terms of sale for one of his own Indian slaves.[60]

Even with the support of the colony's military establishment, Beauharnois's authority was not enough to resolve the dispute. Equally insistent, the intendant pressed the court to proceed with La Palme's prosecution, arguing that the slave's murder was a simple matter of civil justice. To override the intendant's decision, Beauharnois turned to the crown, and, after hearing the governor's account, "his majesty was kind enough to pardon the soldier." Although the king did so on the grounds that La Palme had acted in self-defense, he made a point to remind the intendant that the case did, indeed, fall under military jurisdiction.[61]

The controversy surrounding Jacob's murder could be read as a straightforward example of the early modern power struggle between civil and military legal authority. Yet, because the same courts responded so differently to the murders of an African and an Indian slave, it is clear that something more was at work. Enslaved Indians' direct connection to colonial wars shaped their standing in colonial law as soldiers interacted with them in colonial towns. What is more, in the absence of clear and universal legal standards, most French officials offered situational explanations for the status of individual Indian slaves. This, too, distinguished Indian and African slaveries in the colony. In the late-1740s, while France was at war with the English, many black slaves from New England and New York arrived in New France, as either captives or runaways. To clarify the legal status of these new arrivals, the governor of New France declared that they were slaves rather than prisoners of war, "every Negro being a slave wherever he is." Although this was not the law in France or in French colonies with large free black populations, the governor's statement became the law of New France, instantly and universally categorizing all black people as slaves. The

60. For pardon, see Beauharnois et Hocquart au ministre, Oct. 22, 1730, ANOM, Colonies, C11A, LII, 105–109v.

61. "Lettre du Ministre à M. Hocquart," Apr. 19, 1729, Collections Moreau de Saint-Méry, ANOM, F3, XCV.

French obviously could not create a comparably uniform standard for Indians. Not only did New France have a substantial free Indian population, but the colony's very survival during wars with the English also depended upon allied Indian warriors who demanded French gifts, feasts, and deference. In Montreal, especially, where the majority of Indian slaves resided, the French routinely displayed (if only for show) great respect for Indian diplomats and fur traders. Definitions of Indian slavery would remain more contextual and thus more contestable.[62]

Jacob's story reveals the complex and often contradictory ways that indigenous and Atlantic slaveries melded and clashed in the eighteenth-century Saint Lawrence Valley. Like Jacob, nearly all of the colony's Indian slaves arrived as war captives taken by allied Indians. But, in French settlements along the Saint Lawrence River, these captives also became slaves, defined as legal commodities of their masters. These two forms of slavery sometimes complemented each other, strengthening alliances through symbolic acts of diplomacy and providing a steady supply of Indian laborers to French settlers. French traders and Indian warriors both supported the system because its violence brought the two peoples together in a common interest.

But Jacob's murder also points to tensions between the diplomatic system of indigenous slavery and the institutionalized structures of Atlantic slavery. Neither the court nor the governor viewed the murder as a straightforward property crime, as they had with Antoine's killing. Montreal's legal authorities, although pressured by a slaveholder seeking justice, treated the killing as a standard crime, as they had considered Marie-Joachim's theft or Joseph's smuggling. To Governor Beauharnois, on the other hand, because a soldier on duty had killed an enemy with whom the French were actively at war, the killing was a matter of military justice. Although he clearly did not intend his intervention as a way of shaping slave law, the implication was that as enemy combatants in an active military campaign Fox captives did not have the same status as other chattel slaves. By pardoning Jacob's killer,

62. "Tout negre etant Esclave dans quelque pays qu'il Soit": June 16, 1750, ANOM, Colonies, C11A, XCV, 159–159v. For Montreal and Quebec's negligible free black population, see Robin W. Winks, *The Blacks in Canada: A History*, 2d ed. (Montreal, 2000), chap. 1; Trudel, *Dictionnaire des esclaves*. On the position of freed slaves under the Code Noir, see Léo Elisabeth, "The French Antilles," in David W. Cohen and Jack P. Greene, eds., *Neither Slave nor Free: The Freedmen of African Descent in the Slave Societies of the New World* (Baltimore, 1972), esp. 153–154. For changing French views of free blacks, see Pierre H. Boulle, *Race et esclavage dans la France de l'Ancien Régime* (Paris, 2007), 21–46, 168–198.

the governor muddled the legal standing of Indian slaves as property, explicitly linking their legal standards to the vagaries of French-Indian diplomacy and warfare.

This uncertainty registered in the insecurity of slaves as legal property. Some slaveholders speculated that the king would eventually abolish Indian slavery altogether. One early slave sale, notarized in 1714, expressed this concern by stating that the seller, Joseph Fleury d'Eschambault de Lagorgendière, offered the buyer "no guaranty . . . in the event that his majesty frees the *panis* slaves that are in this country." Lagorgendière's future slave purchases further indicate his doubts about the status of Indian slavery. Of the fourteen additional slaves he purchased before his death in 1755, only two were Indians; the other twelve were Africans acquired through his position as an agent of the Company of the Indies.[63]

These concerns circulated widely. In a notarized slave sale from 1731, Louis Chappeau sold to Pierre Guy a slave he claimed to be a Plains Apache. But he added a caveat to the contract. "In case the said Indian is taken from the said Pierre Guy, whether by order of Monseigneur the Governor General or by another, as being a Fox, in that case the said Chappeau promises and obliges himself to reimburse to the said Pierre Guy the said sum of two hundred livres." Diplomatic uncertainty created a strong incentive to identify slaves as "panis," the only group unambiguously enslavable under the 1709 ordinance protecting slaves as property. As far away as Isle Royale notaries felt obligated to certify Indian slaves' identity as "panis," as in a 1727 contract recording the sale of Louise, a twenty-five-year-old Indian woman who had been "raised as a slave in Canada." The document identified her as a "Panis . . . that nation being subject to slavery."[64]

At least one enslaved Fox woman, named Marguerite, absorbed enough of this information to believe that she should be free. In 1724 when she initiated her freedom suit, French officials were at peace with her people and conducting negotiations in Montreal, where she lived and worked. She

63. Sale of Apr. 27, 1714, Greffe Chambalon (Quebec), BANQ-M.

64. "Et au cas que ledit Sauvage fust retiré des mains dudit Pierre Guy soit par l'ordre de Mgr le Gouverneur Général ou par autre, comme Renard en ce cas ledit Chappeau promet et s'oblige rembourcer audit Pierre Guy ladite somme de deux cent livres": Chicago Historical Society, French America Collection, box 2, I, 162. The author thanks Alexandre Dubé for sending this reference and Scott Heerman for sending photographs. "Elevée en qualité d'esclave en Canada": "Panis . . . cette nation etante sujete a lesclavage," Sale Contract, Aug. 20, 1727, LAC, Fonds des Colonies, Notariat de I'lle Royale (Louisbourg), G3, MMLVIII.

argued that the governor's assurances to return Fox captives constituted a legal proclamation that all Fox slaves should be released. Although the one surviving summary of this case offers no explanation of its outcome, she must have failed to persuade the court. Fox slaves continued to flow into New France after 1724 with no mention of any court ruling that would have determined their enslavement to be illegal.[65]

During the 1720s and 1730s, New France's legal officials struggled to define the boundaries of legitimate enslavement, settling finally on vague criteria that allowed the enslavement of "Indians with whom we have no commerce . . . and all other Indians with whom we or our allies are at war." This law formally linked the status of Indian slaves in New France to their status in the French-Indian alliance system. In other words, as the alliance changed—as New France expanded westward, made new friends, or reconciled with old enemies—the legal status of a slave could change overnight. The insecurity of Indian slaves as property made African slaves more valuable in New France's labor markets. The average enslaved African sold for twice the value of his Indian counterpart, at an average of about seven hundred livres.[66]

Yet African slaves remained rare in New France because of the colony's place in transatlantic shipping patterns. The occasional black slave to arrive in the colony was much more likely to come from New York or New England than Africa, the Caribbean, or Louisiana. This scarcity likely contributed to their greater value as objects of conspicuous consumption. Transatlantic and intercolonial slave traders could never justify bringing black slaves to Canada for a price that, despite being much higher than Indian slave prices, never reached the nine-hundred-to-one-thousand-livre average in Martinique and Saint-Domingue. Until a few dozen enslaved African Americans from the English colonies arrived as captives in the colonial wars of the late-1740s, well more than nine of every ten enumerable slaves in Montreal were American Indian rather than African. During the 1750s this infusion of captives constituted 15 percent of all new slaves, a number that, although higher than the 5 percent of the 1720s, remained modest.[67]

65. Registre des procès-verbaux d'audiences, 1722–1725, BANQ-M, TL4, S11, D8.

66. Marcel Trudel, *L'esclavage au Canada français: histoire et conditions de l'esclavage* (Quebec, 1960), 99–125.

67. For sources of black slaves, see Winks, *The Blacks in Canada*, 1–23; Trudel, *Dictionnaire des esclaves*, 7–263. For slave prices in the French Caribbean, see Robert Louis Stein, *The French Slave Trade in the Eighteenth Century: An Old Regime Business* (Madison, Wis., 1979), 141.

To reiterate the government's claim that Indian slavery stood on the same legal footing as African slavery, however, in 1730 the intendant reprinted and circulated Raudot's 1709 ordinance protecting Indian slave property, but to little avail. Because the ambiguities of the 1720s had arisen in spite of the 1709 law, it was unlikely that circulating the original ordinance would resolve the problem. In 1733, Philippe You d'Youville de La Découverte sought to capitalize on this uncertainty by contesting the court's right to seize and sell one of his slaves. That year, to satisfy one of La Découverte's impatient creditors, a Montreal court ordered Pierre, a twenty-six-year-old Plains Apache slave, confiscated and sold at auction. The slave, who had served La Découverte for at least ten years, commanded a standard price of 351 livres, nearly enough to cover the debt. But La Découverte, incensed at the action, appealed to the Superior Council for the return of his slave. Rather than arguing the terms of his debt, however, La Découverte declared "null and injurious to religion the sale of the Indian in question" and demanded redress from the council for "ordering the sale of a Christian at auction, where he was sold like an animal."[68]

La Découverte's dramatic critique of Indian slavery fooled no one. His father had been one of New France's earliest Indian slave traders, and his mother had initiated the colony's first legally recognized slave sale. Together, he and his siblings owned at least five Indian slaves in 1733 and as a family would purchase and sell three more within the decade. His sister-in-law was the niece of Pierre Gaultier de Varennes de La Vérendrye, who was just coming into his own as the most influential Indian slave trader of the 1730s and 1740s. The Superior Council thus affirmed the lower court's decision, granting to La Découverte the right to buy back his slave for the full sale price, plus food and medical expenses. To make a point, the council fined La Découverte thirty-two livres to cover court costs.[69]

Despite his failure to recover his slave, La Découverte touched a nerve with the colony's leadership, who felt that the case highlighted the need to establish clear legal standards for Indian slavery. In a letter to Versailles in the fall of 1733, Governor Beauharnois and intendant Hocquart explained the significance of the case, requesting in the strongest possible terms a

68. Pierre-Georges Roy, ed., *Inventaire des ordonnances des intendants de la Nouvelle-France conservées aux archives provinciales de Québec* (Beauceville, Que., 1919), II, 146–147; baptism of Sept. 11, 1723, *RAB du PRDH*, 45968; Trudel, *Dictionnaire des esclaves*, 86.

69. Roy, ed., *Inventaire des ordonnances*, II, 146–147; Trudel, *Dictionnaire des esclaves*, 86, 429–430.

clear statement from the crown regulating Indian slavery. Beauharnois and Hocquart suggested that all "Panis and Padoucas" could be considered slaves "as well as all other Indians who are not allies with France and who are sold, traded, or given to the French by allied Indians." In a failed attempt to clarify, they suggested a list of legitimate targets: "the Panis, Padoucas, and other Indians with whom we have no commerce, as well as the Fox, Chickasaw, Eskimo, and all other Indians with whom we or our allies are at war." Conveniently, this list was a precise enumeration of the nations from which Beauharnois's slaves originated.[70]

In addition to the ambiguities of language (alliance and commerce were imprecise terms then as now), Beauharnois and Hocquart guaranteed persistent instability by attaching the legal status of Indian slaves directly to the shifting realities of French-Indian relations. The "Padoucas," or Plains Apaches, are a case in point. During the 1720s, Louisiana's governor formed an alliance with this nation, exchanging guns for skins in a bold effort to edge out Spanish competition in the region. Beauharnois did not recognize this alliance, however, and continued to treat Apaches as enemies and thus potential slaves of New France. Not everyone agreed with his position. Diron d'Artaguiette, who commanded the Illinois post for a time, refused to allow the trade to continue in Illinois, arguing that "this is an unjust war made against two nations who have never insulted the French." He therefore ordered all such slaves to be confiscated and freed.[71]

Unsatisfied with their own efforts to shore up the legal foundations of Indian slavery, the governor and intendant requested an official declaration of policy from Versailles. In 1735, they received the disappointing answer. "The king . . . does not approve of their proposal to decide the status of the *Panis* Indians or others by explicit law," wrote their French superiors. But "the colony's judges may . . . conform themselves to the custom of considering these Indians as slaves, and masters who shall wish to grant them freedom shall do so by notarial deed." Beauharnois and Hocquart might have preferred silence. The crown's decision reduced the standing of Indian slavery to that of "custom," multiplying the ambiguities they sought to eliminate. Yet the response from Versailles was consistent with the previous half century of slave law in the French Atlantic, allowing local conditions and

70. Beauharnois et Hocquart à Maurepas, Oct. 4, 1733, ANOM, Colonies, C11A, LIX, 108–112.

71. "Extrait d'une lettre du gouverneur Beauharnois à d'Artaguiette, commandant aux Illinois [1735]," ANOM, Colonies, C11A, LXIII, 259.

the evolution of local customs to dictate slave law in France's various colonies. The French crown also worried, as it would express a few years later, about the ethical and geopolitical implications of sanctioning the enslavement of Indians. In Louisiana and the Caribbean, French fears of combined African-Indian resistance made officials wary of authorizing the widespread enslavement of Indians. The recent Natchez revolt and growing collusion between Caribs and African slaves in Martinique yielded French policies that sought to separate and antagonize Indians and Africans rather than place them on equal footing.[72]

Realizing that his only option was to regulate Indian slavery locally, in 1736 the intendant issued an ordinance to make manumissions more uniform and verifiable. "We have learned that several persons in this colony have freed their slaves by merely telling them that they were at liberty to leave," the decree began. "We order hereafter that all persons in this country, regardless of their status, who desire to free their slaves must have a notary prepare and certify a deed." Hocquart concluded with the warning that he and the courts would consider "null and void all cases of emancipation in which the said process is not observed." Hocquart's pronouncement proved insufficient to overcome the many mixed messages about Indian slavery in the colony. Among the thousands of preserved notarial deeds produced between 1736 and the end of the French regime, not one certified the release of an Indian slave. Yet, even if the decree had changed the practice of manumission, the fundamental insecurity of Indian slave property would have remained a concern for potential investors. The modest scope of the ordinance might have reflected Hocquart's resignation that efforts to introduce elements of Caribbean slave law into New France had little chance of success.[73]

The cases surrounding Jacob's murder and Marie-Joachim's thefts and all the legal rulings after them underscore the particularity of slave law

72. "Memorandum of the King to MM. de Beauharnois and Hocquart," Apr. 11, 1735, ANOM, série B, LXIII, in Public Archives of Canada, *Report concerning the Archives of Canada* (1904), part 2, 211. For the Natchez rebellion, see Daniel H. Usner, Jr., *Indians, Settlers, and Slaves in a Frontier Exchange Economy: The Lower Mississippi Valley before 1783* (Chapel Hill, N.C., 1992), 65–76; Gwendolyn Midlo Hall, *Africans in Colonial Louisiana: The Development of Afro-Creole Culture in the Eighteenth Century* (Baton Rouge, La., 1995), 100–104.

73. "Ordonnance de l'intendant Hocquart qui porte qu'à l'avenir tous les particuliers de ce pays qui voudront affranchir leurs esclaves seront tenus de le faire par un acte passé devant notaire don't il sera gardé minute et qui sera en outre enregistré au greffe de la juridiction royale la plus prochaine," Sept. 1, 1736, BANQ-Q, E1, S1, P2855.

in New France. Not governed by the legal codes developed in and for the Caribbean, slavery in New France became at once less perilous and less predictable. This uncertainty could work to slaves' advantage, occasionally allowing them access to a colonial judicial system denied their Caribbean counterparts. But for the vast majority who never had recourse to these options—and for those whose safety was undervalued in the absence of clear legal standards—the colony's ad hoc approach often made it more difficult to anticipate the system's limits and opportunities.

MARIE-MARGUERITE

"That is the law in the Caribbean, the same law must exist in this country
for Indian slaves."—Marc-Antoine Huard de Dormicourt, Quebec, 1740

Marie-Marguerite spent thirteen years as a slave on Rue Saint-Paul and would have known Joseph, Marie-Joachim, and Jacob well, all living within a few blocks of one another. She must have experienced similar challenges and opportunities, but there is no record of her time in Montreal. Her story opens a window onto another set of experiences that are equally important to understanding the contours of slavery in Montreal but more difficult to document. Like slaves in the Pays d'en Haut who often faced transport to the Saint Lawrence, from the 1730s through the 1750s many Saint Lawrence slaves also faced export to the distant Caribbean. Having passed through the hands of at least three different masters between 1726 and 1740, Marguerite reached her limits when she was sold to a French naval officer, Marc-Antoine Huard de Dormicourt, who wanted to ship her to Martinique. Beginning in the 1730s, many French planters with ties to Canada supplemented their supply of African slaves on the island by importing Indians from New France. Marguerite had heard of the horrors of life on a sugar plantation, and she looked for a way out. While in Quebec awaiting passage to the Caribbean, she managed to gain the sympathy of an amateur legal advocate, Jacques Nouette, a newcomer from Paris probably motivated by the need to make a name for himself in the colony. With the support of sympathetic clergy, they gained an audience with the Superior Council and sued for her freedom.[74]

74. "Procès opposant Marc-Antoine Huard de Dormicourt, à Marguerite Duplessis Radisson, se disant la fille naturelle de feu sieur Duplessis Faber (Lefebvre), frère du sieur Duplessis Faber, résidant à Montréal, capitaine d'une compagnie dans les troupes de la Marine, qui conteste le fait qu'elle soit une esclave, et plus particulièrement celle du sieur

Rumors recently circulating around the Atlantic of two French legal rulings had renewed the question of whether any territory under French rule could allow slavery, particularly of American Indians. In 1738, at the conclusion of a highly public trial, a Paris court freed a slave by the name of Jean Boucaux, awarded his freedom on the grounds that "there are no slaves in France." Those opposing the ruling feared the consequences if *"the commotion from the news of this bogus victory, that of a slave over his master,* would reach the very heart of our colonies." The second was the 1739 case of a runaway Indian slave in Martinique, whose appeal for freedom elicited a decree from Versailles ordering that Indians could not be enslaved in France's Caribbean colonies. As ships, people, and letters circulated these ideas throughout the French Atlantic, Marguerite and Nouette (who had still been in Paris in 1738) used the moment of uncertainty to launch her case.[75]

Appearing before the Superior Council, the colony's highest court, Nouette presented a complex argument—really several distinct arguments—for her freedom. Recalling the founding charters of the private companies that settled New France, he argued that because the Indians of North America were "obedient to his majesty [the king of France]" and because Marguerite "professed the Catholic, apostolic, and Roman religion, her slavery should cease because she became a subject of the king." Nouette also asserted that the ambiguous status of Indian slaves could be determined only with "a [notarized] bill of sale," which her new master had not obtained.

Hedging his bets, Nouette then claimed that Marguerite was never a slave, but rather the freeborn métis child of a French father and a local Indian woman. Calling her "Marguerite Duplessis, the illegitimate daughter of the late Sieur Duplessis-Fabert," Nouette castigated her present master, who inexplicably "imagined that the plaintiff was his slave [and] held her

Dormicourt," Oct. 1, 1740, BANQ-Q, TL5, D1230. All material on Marguerite is from this trial record unless otherwise noted. For Nouette, see Pontbriand au ministre, Oct. 30, 1742, ANOM, Colonies, C11A, LXXVIII, 429–430; Hocquart au ministre, Nov. 3, 1743, ANOM, Colonies, C11A, LXXX, 274–275v.

75. For the best treatment of the Boucaux case, see Sue Peabody, *"There Are No Slaves in France": The Political Culture of Race and Slavery in the Ancien Régime* (Oxford, 1996), 23–56. For the quote, see Ilona Vernez Johnson, "The Reinvention of Slavery in France: From the Jean Boucaux Affair to the Eve of the Haitian Revolution" (Ph.D. diss., Pennsylvania State University, 1998), 86. Case of 1739: Edit du Roy, Mar. 9, 1739, ANOM, Colonies, série B, LXVIII, 15–15v.

in irons without cause." Despite her low social status, Nouette insisted on her liberty: "Although she does not have the advantage of being the fruit of a legitimate marriage, she was not born of a slave and as a result she was born free." Initially, the court seemed to believe him, or at least to give him the benefit of the doubt, for it released Marguerite into his custody and recorded her name in the trial record as "Marie-Marguerite Duplessis-Fabert," with no mention of her slave status. Freed from bondage, assisted by a strong advocate, and seemingly supported by the court, Marguerite must have felt hopeful that her long ordeal would soon be over.

But her hopes did not last for long. Her new master, Dormicourt, stormed to the council's chambers and demanded the return of his slave. Calling her "a wench and a libertine, a thief, [and] a drunk," he expressed his outrage that such a person would "animate the charity of the clergy . . . making them partisans of wenches and sluts." Keeping a more even tone, the court asked him to present evidence of her slave status. He first produced the record of her baptism, performed in Montreal in 1730, which indicated that she was not the daughter of Duplessis-Fabert: she "belonged" to him. Then there was testimony from a number of men who had either bought, sold, or known Marguerite over the previous several years (including Joseph's smuggling partner, Nicolas Sarrazin). Finally, Dormicourt called upon her first French master, René Bourassa, who testified that he received Marguerite at Green Bay in 1726 "as a gift" from a Winnebago warrior named Ouenigueri. After hearing this testimony the intendant issued the decision of the Superior Council, declaring Marguerite to be Dormicourt's legal chattel, whom he could ship to Martinique at will. As Dormicourt had hoped, she seems to have departed within days, never to see North American soil again.[76]

Dormicourt framed the controversy in simple terms, insisting that slavery was legal in the French colonies, he had bought her according to French law, and he thus had a right to take her where he pleased. He argued, as Michel Bégon had a generation before, that to create distinct legalities would undermine the legal and economic basis of slavery in all the colonies and threaten the foundations of French colonialism. "No one but the king could declare on this subject to make it different," he said. "If a change were

76. For the intendant, see "Ordonnance de l'intendant Hocquart qui déclare Marguerite Radisson dite Duplessis esclave de Marc-Antoine Huart (Huard), chevalier Dormicourt, lieutenant dans les troupes du détachment de la Marine," Oct. 20, 1740, BANQ-Q, E1, S1, P3281; baptism of July 8, 1730, Notre-Dame-de-Montréal, FHL.

made, it would cause great confusion and disorder in this country." Dormicourt's plantation on Martinique was one of many that had arisen since the late seventeenth century, designed around the extraction of labor from the enslaved. The logic of Caribbean slavery emphasized its perpetuity, its inheritability, and, above all, its profitability. To the extent that it acknowledged the act of enslavement at all, it was kept at a distance and justified with the legal fictions of the law of nations.

But, on her body, Marguerite carried the history of another kind of slavery. A broad scar enveloped one of her eyes, a wound her Native captors gave her to express a very different understanding of slavery. Where French slaveholders focused on the perpetuation of a slave's subordinate status as a laborer, distancing themselves from enslavement, indigenous slavery valued the act of enslavement and the immediate process of domestication that followed above all else. She came into French possession, not by purchase, but by a ceremonial gift ratifying an alliance between her master, Ouenigueri, and a representative of the French king. By highlighting both the connections and tensions between New France and the Caribbean, Marie-Marguerite's story suggests how and why these slaveries came to be differentiated in French practice and, eventually, in French memory.

Marie-Marguerite first became a slave in the late-1710s or early 1720s as part of an indigenous slave system that operated in the North American interior. Born in western Iowa or Nebraska, Marguerite would have only just begun to help her mother with domestic and horticultural work when, at the age of six or seven, a group of Iowa warriors raided her village. Iowa raids against their enemies became especially significant around 1720, as they faced the most disruptive population shift in recent memory. Pushed by the westward movements of other Siouan peoples and pulled by the lure of the distant Spanish trade, the Iowas moved into the region that would bear their name sometime between 1717 and 1725. Marguerite's capture at about the same time suggests that her people were among those whose villages the Iowas sought to displace from their newfound territorial home.[77]

Enslaving Marguerite therefore became a symbolic act of conquest, a bodily expression of Iowa dominance. During the 1720s, in addition to vanquishing enemies, the Iowas sought to widen their circle of allies and to strengthen existing friendships. Marguerite became an important element

77. Mildred Mott Wedel, "Iowa," in *Handbook*, XIII, *Plains*, part 1, 432–435. For the best overview of the Plains movements and warfare during this period, see Pekka Hämäläinen, "The Rise and Fall of Plains Indian Horse Cultures," *JAH*, XC (2003–2004), 833–862.

in their efforts to shore up an alliance with their linguistic and cultural cousins, the Winnebagos. Sometime between 1721 and 1726, her Iowa captors removed her from their village, offering her as a gift to the Winnebagos as a token of their loyalty. In the Winnebago village not far from Green Bay, Marguerite came under the control of Ouenigueri, a respected warrior who acted as an intermediary between the Iowas and the French. Originally a symbol of enmity, Marguerite was now an emblem of friendship. In these two roles, she fulfilled the two central purposes of indigenous slavery. The Iowas weakened their enemies by raiding and capturing her people, and they strengthened a strategic alliance with the Winnebagos by giving her as a symbolic present to a warrior named Ouenigueri.[78]

Following the logic of indigenous slavery, Ouenigueri presented Marguerite as a gift to the French at a pivotal period in his own people's history. As the French and their allies grew more threatening during the second phase of the Fox Wars, the Fox-allied Winnebagos sued for peace. Insisting on their desire to maintain friendly trade relations with the French, several Winnebago warriors traveled to Green Bay in 1726 to offer presents to the French at that post. One of them, possibly Ouenigueri, assured the French delegation, "I have always done the will of my father," the French governor. And with a rich offering of gifts he assured, "I give you my word [that I will remain at peace]." One of these presents was Marie-Marguerite, offered to René Bourassa, the post commander's business partner and one of the most skilled traders and diplomats in the region.[79]

Shortly after receiving Marguerite from Ouenigueri, Bourassa gave or sold her to his business partner's wife, who took her to Montreal the following year, where they lived on Rue Saint-Paul in the heart of the slave neighborhood. There, Marguerite entered a legal and social system designed to keep her and her fellow slaves in perpetual bondage as productive laborers. Like her enslaved neighbors, Marguerite worked within the confines to negotiate spaces for herself within the colony, taking advantage of the fluid social relations and relative mobility that characterized Montreal's urban slave life. She also exploited the legal ambiguities created by the demands and dynamics of Indian alliances, using questions over Indi-

78. Wedel, "Iowa," in *Handbook*, XIII, *Plains*, part 1, 432–435; Gilles Havard, *Empire et métissages: Indiens et Français dans le Pays d'en Haut* (Paris, 2003), 126.

79. "Procès opposant Marc-Antoine Huard de Dormicourt, à Marguerite Duplessis Radisson," Oct. 1, 1740, BANQ-Q, TL5, D1230; Cass manuscripts, *Wis. Hist. Coll.*, III (1904), 153 ("I give you my word"); Lignery to Liette, Jun. 15, 1726, ANOM, Colonies, C11A, XLVIII, 415–418v.

ans' place in French colonial society to suggest that she, like so many others, should be free.

The idea of trading American Indians to the Caribbean as slaves took hold shortly after Raudot's 1709 ordinance. In the spring of 1710, for example, a Huguenot merchant named Mounier launched his ship, *La Hollande*, for the French islands of the Caribbean. Only a few miles downriver, the vessel encountered rough waters, struck rock, and broke into pieces. Mounier swam to safety, but much of his cargo washed away. Village residents along the south shore of the Saint Lawrence salvaged what they could from the wreckage: some candles, a few containers of butter, and some wood. But Mounier personally saved his most valuable possession. Among the merchandise intended for sale to the islands, Mounier held an Indian slave who could earn him as much as nine hundred livres in Martinique, three times his purchase price. Following the accident, Mounier dragged his slave ashore and brought him to Quebec to await another voyage. But the slave, possibly having discovered that Mounier intended to sell him to a sugar plantation, ran away. Mounier immediately sought the assistance of the intendant, Jacques Raudot, to recover his lost property, explaining that he had legitimately purchased the slave from Montreal's highest-ranking judge, François-Marie Boüat.[80]

Mounier probably expected more support from the intendant than he received. Raudot had issued the ordinance protecting Indian slavery less than one year earlier, insisting that Indian and African slaves would belong as unrestricted property to their purchasers. Consistent with the earlier ordinance, Raudot granted to Mounier the right to "recover his panis wherever he finds him" and reminded anyone who might harbor the slave that he

80. For recovered goods from shipwreck, see ordinance, Aug. 24, 1710, MG8-A6, Fonds des Ordonnances des intendants de la Nouvelle-France, LAC, transcript, III, 487–489, ordinance of Mar. 18, 1710, MG8-A6, III, 335–336, ordinance of Aug. 4, 1710, III, 407–408. For Mounier and Raudot, see "Ordonnance qui permet au sieur Mounier de reprendre son Panis," Mar. 23, 1710, III, 319–321. Mounier is the name of a prominent Huguenot merchant family mostly from La Rochelle, with several family members engaged in business in New France. Although the 1710 document gives few details about Mounier, he likely came from this family. His Huguenot background, intriguingly implied by the name of his ship, is supported by his absence from the Catholic Church records of the period. See J. F. Bosher, *The Canada Merchants, 1713–1763* (Oxford, 1987), especially chaps. 6–7; Bosher, "Mounier, Jean-Mathieu," *DCB*, IV; Jean-Marie Leblanc, "Mounier, François," *DCB*, III. For slave prices in the French Caribbean, see Stein, *French Slave Trade*, 141, which gives an average price of 923 livres for a slave sold to the French islands. Although this average is given for the late 1730s, Stein posits a relatively stable price structure for the first half of the eighteenth century.

or she would face a fifty-livre fine for doing so. Yet Raudot also took pains to explain to Mounier that the 1709 ordinance did not permit the sale of Indian slaves outside New France. French Atlantic slavery depended upon the legal pluralism that both guaranteed local administrative control over slavery and restricted the application of local law in other French settings. Raudot therefore declared that Indian slaves, unlike African slaves, could not leave the colony. "Our authority in matters of law does not extend beyond this colony," the intendant reasoned, "thus the panis cannot be considered slaves unless they remain here, and it is therefore not permissible to transport them for trade elsewhere." To compensate Mounier, Raudot ordered that the original owner would have to buy back the slave were he recovered, since Mounier had bought him for the sole purpose of export. This decision must have offered little comfort to Mounier, who hoped to launch a lucrative trade in Indian slaves with the sugar islands. Raudot's ruling, combined with the dangers of intercolonial shipping during the War of the Spanish Succession, meant that no Indian slaves are known to have gone from New France to the Caribbean for nearly twenty years.[81]

During these decades of relative isolation, New France and the Caribbean developed in radically different directions despite all the efforts of Raudot, Bégon (fils), and other colonial leaders to follow Caribbean models of colonial development. The most striking changes were demographic. In the Caribbean, the enslaved population exploded to serve a growing number of plantations in Martinique, Guadeloupe, and, increasingly, Saint Domingue, which officially became a French possession only in 1697. The total African population of the French Caribbean grew from just more than 33,000 in 1700 to more than 160,000 in 1730, and the production of staples kept pace with this spectacular surge in labor.[82]

Subtler changes are harder to measure, but the conversations about the relationship between Africans and enslavement began to shift in tone during these years as well. These discussions did not initially develop as a way to justify the enslavement of Africans, which by the 1710s was reaching a point beyond serious discussion. Instead, the growing tendency to create racialized labels stemmed from colonists' concerns over policing slaves' behavior and in controlling pathways out of slavery through flight, resistance,

81. "Ordonnance qui permet au sieur Mounier de reprendre son Panis," MG8-A6, III, 319–321.
82. James Pritchard, *In Search of Empire: The French in the Americas, 1670–1730* (Cambridge, 2004), 425.

or manumission. Witness the case of Babet Binture, an African slave in Martinique who in 1705 challenged her slave status by claiming to have been born free on the island. Colonial officials took Babet's claim seriously, hearing witnesses for both sides, interviewing the slave and her mistress to ascertain the justice of the woman's claim. Having "diligently examined" the evidence, they determined that "the said Babet Binture not having been able to produce any ticket nor justifying evidence for the claimed freedom, which she has never enjoyed until now, we have dismissed and do dismiss the pretensions of the said liberty, [and] declare her a slave." The ruling and others like it strengthened the legal presumption that a person of African descent was a slave in the absence of contrary evidence. As a punishment for the slave's frivolous suit, Mithon sentenced her to a month in chains in the local prison.[83]

Unwilling to yield, Babet and her two sisters (who also sought freedom) turned their sexual charms on colonial leadership, "pay[ing] frequent and long visits to the Intendant, who gives them peaceful and private audiences, such that it often occurs that judges, individual parties, or others having business with the Intendant must wait three or four hours outside the locked door to his office." Satisfied with their appeals, the intendant ordered Babet's case to be reheard in 1708 by the Superior Council. Under the intendant's leadership, the council ordered all three women freed, declaring "the said Babet, Negress, and all her children free and emancipated from birth, to enjoy their freedom like the other freedmen." For the next few years, Babet and her sisters ran a nightclub that catered to free blacks, urban slaves, runaways, and pirates. Martinique's new governor, who took his post a year after Babet's emancipation, heard reports of her activities and the intendant's indiscretions, leading him to appeal to the crown for Babet's reenslavement. Worried that "such conduct by the Intendant could incite the Negroes' insolence," the governor also berated Babet—and by implication free blacks in general—as "madams, whores, fences of stolen property and runaway slaves." The governor's complaints echoed a growing concern in Martinique over the destabilizing influence of free blacks, particularly their supposed assistance to runaway slaves, a concern that led his predecessor to request a royal law ordering that any free black who har-

83. The case and its implications for manumission law are documented in Sue Peabody and Keila Grinberg, eds., *Slavery, Freedom, and the Law in the Atlantic World: A Brief History with Documents* (Boston, 2007), 36–42, 37 (quote).

bored a runaway "will be deprived of their freedom and that they and their entire family residing with them will be sold to the King's profit." Although such a harsh punishment was never enacted, the crown responded to these concerns by placing new restrictions on emancipation, requiring that masters gain permission from colonial authorities before freeing their slaves.[84]

Although the movement against free people of color in the French Caribbean did not peak until the second half of the eighteenth century, laws and customs regulating people's activities based on skin color stood at the heart of the slave system's repressive and brutal success. Rather than evolving as a justification of enslavement, then, racializing discourses in the French Caribbean centered on limiting pathways out of slavery and maintaining control of those who navigated those paths successfully. Over time, a greater equation of slavery with blackness in the Caribbean and in France linked the two concepts in ways that would have been inconceivable in the seventeenth century. Census records that once recorded "mulatto, Negro, and Indian slaves" by 1719 collapsed those categories into a single group, sometimes labeled "negro" or "negress," other times merely "slaves."[85]

During these years, too, legal language regarding slaves changed, eliminating discussion of Indians as legitimate slaves and deemphasizing "nègre," with its more complex historical connotations, in favor of "noir," or black. In the early eighteenth century, Caribbean colonists developed a shorthand for the 1685 ordinance governing slave law, calling it the "Code Noir," or Black Code, for the first time in the early 1700s. As Jacques Savary des Brûlons explained in his *Dictionnaire universel de commerce* (1726), "Code Noir is the name given in France's American Islands to Louis XIV's ordinance of March 1685 concerning the regulation of those islands, and which must be observed there primarily in relation to the Negroes." The informal title used in the Caribbean eventually took hold in France, and the ordinance was labeled Code Noir for the first time in print in a 1718 Paris edition. When the crown released a revised edition of the ordinance for Louisiana in 1724, the title became official. Thereafter, every published edition labeled the ordinance the Code Noir. Individual laws that amended or expanded on the ordinance's provisions began referring slaves merely as "blacks" with growing frequency in the first quarter of the eighteenth century. "Nègre,"

84. Ibid.
85. Guadeloupe, Recensements, 1644–1722, FHL; Martinique, Recensements, 1700–1788, FHL.

when it was used, became a synonym for slave, as "panis" had become in North America.[86]

As notions of just-war slavery strengthened in New France, Caribbean discussions of African slavery began to rely much less on notions of African sovereignty and international law than they had in the seventeenth century. By the 1730s it became increasingly common in France and the Caribbean to abandon notions of great African kingdoms in favor of a more backward reading of the continent's peoples. Joseph-François Lafitau, for example, more famous for his writings about Indians, also wrote a history of Portuguese exploration. When discussing the slave trade, he characterized "les Nègres" as "miserable people, nearly nude, inhabiting a sterile and sandy country, living without clear laws, having nothing to live in but some tents." A far cry from Bouton's and Pelleprat's prosperous, law-bound kingdoms, this version of Africa drew closer to Aristotelian natural slavery. But one of the appeals of this rhetoric was that it also justified the control of free people of color, who shared physical traits with the enslaved majority.[87]

In the Caribbean, Indian slaves were technically illegal after about 1700, but until 1719 census takers still enumerated their populations. Despite Indian slaving's being a capital crime in Martinique, sporadic French slave raids against South American Indians continued for the next thirty years, although it is impossible to tell how many Indians blended into the massive population of enslaved Africans. But there were some, and, when, in 1737,

86. "Code Noir. C'est le nom que l'on donne dans les Isles Françoises de l'Amérique, à l'Ordonnance de Louïs XIV. Du mois de Mars 1685, touchant la police de ces Isles, et ce qui doit s'y observer, principalement par raport aux Négres." Jacques Savary Brûlons, *Dictionnaire universel du commerce* (Amsterdam, 1726), I, 798. For Caribbean references, Moreau de Saint-Méry transcribed a letter from 1706 that referred to the 1685 ordinance as the "Code Noir," publishing it in *Loix et constitutions des colonies françoises de l'Amérique sous le vent* (Paris, 1785–1790), II, 73. See also Collection Moreau de Saint-Méry, ANOM, F3, XC, 1713. For printed editions that adopted the title "Code Noir," see *Le code noir, ou Édit du Roy servant de règlement pour le gouvernement et l'administration de justice et la police des isles françoises de l'Amérique, et pour la discipline et la commerce des nègres et esclaves dans ledit pays* (Paris, 1718); *Le code noir, ou edit du roy, servant de règlement pour le gouvernement et l'administration . . . de la Loüisiane* (Paris, 1727). Census records from Guadeloupe (1699) and Martinique (1701, 1708, 1715, 1719) were consulted at the Archives Départementales de la Martinique, Fort-de-France, Martinique and at the FHL.

87. Joseph-François Lafitau, *Histoire des découvertes et conquestes des Portugais . . .* (Paris, 1733–1734), I, 30–31 ("miserable people"); Boulle, *Race et esclavage*, 17–46; Jeffer B. Daykin, "'They Themselves Contribute to Their Misery by Their Sloth': The Justification for Slavery in Eighteenth-Century French Travel Narratives," *European Legacy*, XI (2006), 623–632.

one of these Indian slaves ran away, his master appealed for help in recovering him. Unsure how to proceed, the governor made an appeal of his own to the French crown. Finally, in March 1739, the king issued the ordinance prohibiting the enslavement of "Caribs and Indians" in Martinique and the other French Caribbean settlements. The logic of the king's 1739 decree reveals the central concerns of French authorities both in Martinique and in the broader French geopolitical universe. According to the letter from Versailles:

> The trade in Caribs and Indians creates two great problems. The first is that frequently the traders, who have little conscience, make slaves of free people whom they find defenseless and with whom the French are not at war; and the second is that, when they buy from one Carib nation prisoners taken in war with another nation, those of the conquered nation pursue their revenge against the French whom they find in their land for the slavery of their compatriots: sometimes also the nations make peace among themselves, and, unable to return the prisoners [they have] sold, pursue their vengeance against the French who are in their land and massacre them.[88]

The king's "two great problems" can be summarized as morality and mortality. On the side of morality, the king expressed concern that venal traders would victimize innocent Indians rather than capture slaves according to European laws of war. This objection could have applied equally to the African slave trade, which by 1739 brought thousands of souls every year to the French Caribbean, many of whom were captured in just this way. But since the seventeenth century the French had adopted the elaborate fiction of Nigritie to explain the origins of their African slaves.

Such a fiction could never withstand the daily scrutiny that came from living among both the enslavers and their potential victims, which was the situation the French faced in the Caribbean basin. They saw greedy traders grabbing women and children and burning villages. And, of course, in addition to French morality, this meant mortality. In the Caribbean and Guiana, French missionaries and traders witnessed firsthand the spiraling violence that came from a single raid to gather fewer than twenty slaves. They saw trade routes cut off and potential converts turned into enemies. They saw the effects of slave exports on an indigenous political economy that depended on the circulation, rather than the extraction, of captives for the

88. Mar. 9, 1739, ANOM, Colonies, série B, LXVIII, 15–15v.

resolution of warfare. All of this reinforced the notion that, at least in South America and the Caribbean, just-war doctrine and the law of nations were insurmountable barriers to the Indian slave trade.

Despite the united opposition of crown and colonial administration, however, a small-scale Indian slave trade persisted in the Caribbean through the late-1730s and into the early 1740s. The allure of profits, combined with a recent decline in slave shipments due to growth of Saint Domingue, made slaves—any slaves—highly valuable. With demand high despite potential legal troubles, Canadian exporters and ship captains began to invest in slaves for export. Joseph Chavigny de Lachevrotière de Latesserie, a ship's captain and wealthy Atlantic merchant, bought Plains Apache and Fox slaves in 1737 to take with him to Martinique, paying in molasses, pepper, and cheap liquor, along with cash.[89]

The story of Joseph-Gabriel, Chavigny's young Plains Apache slave, illustrates the complex connections between voyageurs, western merchants, military personnel, and French négociants at Quebec that yielded slaves for the Caribbean trade. Probably in 1736, Joseph-Gabriel became the slave of Jean-Baptiste Normandin dit Beausoleil, a former voyageur turned western merchant. Normandin used his connections in the Mississippi Valley trade to buy the slave for an unknown price, reselling him in 1737 for 300 livres to François-Augustan Bailly de Messein, a cadet in the colonial troops near Montreal. Five months later, Joseph-Gabriel changed hands again when Bailly de Messein sold him to the Atlantic merchant Joseph Chavigny de Lachevrotière. For rights to the slave, Chavigny paid 250 livres cash and two barrels of molasses.[90]

A month before purchasing the Apache boy, Chavigny bought a thirteen-year-old Fox girl for 350 livres from Hugues Jacques Péan de Livaudière. As part of the contract, Péan agreed to care for the slave "until the departure of the said sieur de la Chevrotière, which will be at the end of the following month." At that time, Chavigny would claim the slave and take her with him. Bought only three weeks before Chavigny left for the Caribbean, Joseph-Gabriel almost certainly joined his new master on the journey. Whether he merely served as a ship's slave or was sold again in the Caribbean, we do not know. But, in 1749, Chavigny repeated the same pattern, buying a teenaged

89. Sale of May 9, 1737, Greffe Loiseau (Montreal), BANQ-M; sale of Oct. 1, 1737, Greffe Boisseau (Québec), BANQ-M, and sale of Sept. 14, 1737.

90. Sale of May 9, 1737, Greffe Loiseau (Montreal), BANQ-M; sale of Oct. 1, 1737, Greffe Boisseau (Québec), BANQ-M.

female slave in late September before an October departure for Martinique. For 400 livres worth of pepper and coffee, he gained a slave that would sell on that island for well more than twice her purchase price.[91]

At first glance, Chavigny's Atlantic connections seem to place him outside the norm of New France's locally dominated slave trade. Yet his family history tied him directly to the trade networks of the western Great Lakes. His relatives, third-generation Canadians by the 1740s, had traded furs and possibly slaves with the Ottawas at Michilimackinac as early as the 1670s. In any case, Chavigny stood at the end of a long line of traders who first acquired slaves from the Mississippi Valley and western Great Lakes and transferred them to merchants or military officers, who then sold them at least once again to their final destination along the Saint Lawrence. Only slaves destined for Detroit or Michilimackinac avoided the distant and often dangerous trek to Montreal.[92]

Following Chavigny's lead, in the winter of 1741–1742, Philippe-Marie d'Ailleboust de Cerry guided his small ship, the *Saint Joseph*, into the harbor at Saint Pierre, Martinique. After paying the necessary port taxes, he met with several merchants who wished to buy his cargo. In addition to the usual wheat, peas, butter, and timber he carried from Quebec for other merchants, Ailleboust offered a far more profitable commodity to be sold on his own account: an enslaved Indian. He found a ready buyer in a broker who purchased slaves at the port and sold them around the island to French planters. The buyer promised to give Ailleboust his money once he sold the slave, presumably with the assurance of a higher payoff. But, shortly after the second sale, before any money changed hands, the slave ran away, boarding a trade vessel for a one-way trip to an unspecified Spanish territory.[93]

The slave's motives for leaving the island were surely complex, but the reason he left his master is clear: he was told that he was free. During the second transaction, someone raised an objection, asserting, "The Indian must be considered free in recognition of the ordinance that prohibits the

91. Sale of Sept. 14, 1737, Greffe Boisseau (Québec), BANQ-M; sale of Sept. 14, 1749, Greffe Panet (Québec), BANQ-M, quoted in "La vente des esclaves par actes notariés sous les régimes français et anglais," *Rapport de l'archiviste de la province de Québec*, 1921–1922 (Quebec, 1922), 116.

92. Jean-Jacques Lefebvre, "Chavigny Lachevrotière, François de," *DCB*, II. François de Chavigny was with Tonty in the West, possibly observing some of the slave exchanges that brought him his first slaves from the Ottawas.

93. Oct. 15, 1741, ANOM, Colonies, C11A, CXXI, 102v–103.

enslavement of Carib Indians on the islands." The case went before a local judge, who reviewed the decree issued three years earlier banning Indian slavery. "His majesty has determined to prohibit the inhabitants of the islands to trade Carib or Indian slaves," the ordinance read, declaring that all such slaves "shall be and remain free." Predictably, the judge ruled the slave released, forbidding anyone to profit from his sale. Ailleboust thus lost the money he had paid when he bought the slave from a Montreal merchant, probably for about three hundred livres.[94]

But Ailleboust did not make an unreasonable gamble when he bought a slave in Montreal for resale in the Caribbean. Instead, he followed a pattern of commerce that had yielded substantial profits for many of his contemporaries. A slave bought in Montreal or Quebec for three hundred to four hundred livres could yield a thousand livres or more in Martinique, making the slave trade by far the most promising moneymaker for Canadian merchants involved in Caribbean commerce. Export records are sparse, so we may never know how frequently Indian slaves traveled between the two colonies (still an open question), but by 1740 it was common enough that Marie-Marguerite's master, Dormicourt, declared before a Quebec court that his fellow planters "often take them to the islands to serve as slaves." To be sure, this was a self-interested proclamation. The planter was trying to persuade the judge to allow him to take his slave out of the colony. But many other sources—notarized deeds, court records, merchants' and governors' correspondence, and sacramental records—confirm that Ailleboust was far from alone in wishing to supply Indian slaves to Martinique.[95]

A man of some influence, Ailleboust appealed to Martinique's highest authorities to recuperate his losses. Intervening on his behalf, the governor and intendant wrote to France explaining the case and seeking guidance. They were unsure, given the reasoning behind the 1739 ban on Indian slavery, whether it should apply to Indian slaves from Canada. They acknowledged that local Indians, especially the Caribs, could not be enslaved, "as the French are not at war with them." But they believed that Ailleboust's slave had been legitimately captured. "In Canada the Panis Indians are regarded and traded as slaves, and if the Indian in question is truly of that

94. Oct. 9, 1742, ANOM, Colonies, série B, LXXIV, 138, and Mar. 10, 1739, LXVIII, 15v.

95. "Procès opposant Marc-Antoine Huard de Dormicourt, à Marguerite Duplessis Radisson, se disant la fille naturelle de feu sieur Duplessis Faber (Lefebvre), frère du sieur Duplessis Faber, résidant à Montréal, capitaine d'une compagnie dans les troupes de la Marine, qui conteste le fait qu'elle soit une esclave, et plus particulièrement celle du sieur Dormicourt," Oct. 1, 1740, BANQ-Q, TL5, D1230.

nation," they speculated, "the sieur de Cery had the right to sell him as he did." A few months later, the crown replied in total agreement:

> We have received the letter that you honored us by writing on 9 October 1742 on the subject of the Panis Indian that the Sieur Daillebout de Cery bought from a merchant of Montreal. The judge was mistaken in applying to this Indian the king's ordinance of 9 March 1739 which declared all Caribs and Indians of free birth. This ordinance only concerned those nations against whom the French are not at war, as they are with the Panis, but when the Indian in question saw that he was declared free, he left on a boat for Spanish territory. . . . We need to render to Sieur Daillebout the justice that he is due.[96]

Knowing little of the actual relationship between the "Panis" and the colonists of New France, the crown offered a plausible fiction drawn from the one created by Raudot and his successors in the early eighteenth century. The Panis were presumed to be legitimately enslaved, at least in part because the system of compartmentalized slavery required the crown to respect local legal customs regulating the institution in exchange for a widespread recognition of France's free soil policy. Yet the reasoning that supported their enslavement reinforced the imperative that only a distant and poorly understood people could be presumed to have been legitimately enslaved.

News of Caribbean acceptance of Panis enslavement made its way to Canada, and exports slowly increased in the 1740s. Only a few years after Canadian Indians became clearly legitimate slaves in Martinique, New France officials proposed a vast expansion of the Indian slave trade between the two colonies. Hoping to capitalize on the growing availability of Indian slaves in Montreal and Quebec, in 1747 Governor La Galissonière wrote to Paris and Martinique requesting permission to begin exporting hundreds of Indian slaves to the Caribbean. The governor had been born in Rochefort and spent more than a decade in the shadow of his grandfather, Michel Bégon (père), the primary author of the 1685 ordinance and a promoter of slavery. Martinique's governor, Charles de Caylus, described the La Galissonière proposal in 1748: "He tells me that he has quite a large quantity of Panis Indians" who could be shipped to the island as slaves. Caylus approved of the plan, complaining less than five months after learning of it, "I have still not seen the arrival of any of these Panis. I hope they will come soon."[97]

96. Oct. 9, 1742, ANOM, Colonies, série B, LXXIV, 138.
97. "Me marque qu'il avoit une assés bonne quantité de sauvages Panis" and "Je n'ay pas

La Galissonière also presented the plan to his superiors in France, who responded with enthusiasm in 1749. Addressing La Galissonière's successor, Governor Jacques-Pierre de Taffanel de La Jonquière, as well as intendant François Bigot, the naval council urged the Canadians to give the plan prompt consideration. Governor La Jonquière and intendant Bigot responded quickly, writing only two months later that, although they recognized the proposal's many advantages for New France, they could not understand the appeal for Martinique's slaveholders, as Indians would make bad slaves. "The Indian, although a slave, does not work," they claimed. "He is not like the Negro. He is lazy and cannot be kept indoors however well or badly treated. . . . They cannot breathe unless they are returned to the woods, and it is nearly impossible for them to learn a trade." Because both men were new to the colony, they had only a passing knowledge of how slavery functioned there. Conflating the behavior of free and enslaved Indians, they echoed what was becoming a transatlantic understanding of Indians' racial inferiority.[98]

Over the previous half century, free Natives' refusal to bow to French demands shaped a new racial discourse about Indians that developed in tension with, if not explicit opposition to, Indian slavery. Although colonists began the settlement of New France with an attempt to become "one blood and one people" with Indians through a policy of assimilation, later generations came to believe that their dream of changing Indians would never be realized. By then there was ample evidence to suggest that Indians would not yield easily to French influence. Independent Native allies, including Indians living in the Saint Lawrence villages, refused to submit to French authority, reinforcing notions of Indians' inclination to savage (literally, wild or untamed) behavior. These practical frustrations, combined with emerging scientific and natural history discourses about blood and

jusqu'a present vû arriver aucun de ces panis. Je souhaite qu'il en vienne bientot," Nov. 7, 1748, Collection Moreau de Saint-Méry, ANOM, F3, XCV. Caylus noted in the beginning of the letter that La Galissonière's original letter was dated June 18, 1748.

98. "Le sauvage quoyque Esclave, ne travaille point, Il ne ressemble pas au Nègre, Il est paresseux et on n'a Jamais pû en Conserver dans Les maisons quelque bon ou mauvais tratement qu'on leur ait fait. . . . Ils ne Respirent qu'à s'en Retourner dans Les bois et Il seroit presque Impossible de leur faire apren[dre] Un métier": Bigot et La Jonquière au Ministre, Sept. 26, 1749, Collection Moreau de Saint-Méry, ANOM, F3, XCV. Thanks to Pierre Boulle, who provided me with a transcript of this letter, which I have since consulted in the original. See also Council de la Marine à Jonquière et Bigot, May 4, 1749, série B, XCIX, 70–71; Public Archives of Canada, *Report* (1905), part 1, 117, which offers a thorough summary and partial translation.

inheritance, suggested that Indians' innate characteristics, including their basic intellectual and moral capacities, were more deeply rooted in birth and genealogy than assimilationists had hoped. This reasoning inspired a string of declarations about Indians' inherent inferiority, beginning with the infamous words of Governor Philippe de Rigaud de Vaudreuil, who insisted that Indians' "bad blood" should never be mixed with "good" French blood. Speaking out against intermarriage, Vaudreuil warned that children of French-Native unions would embrace independence rather than subjection: "All the French men who have married savage women have been licentious and lazy and have become intolerably independent; and the children they have are even lazier than the savages themselves." For all its negativity about Indians, this was never an ideology tied to slavery. Indeed, by insisting on Indians' independence and laziness, French racial discourse argued that Indians' basic characteristics ensured that they would fail as slaves. Embracing this logic, Bigot and La Jonquière rejected their predecessors' export plan, preventing what would have become a significant expansion of the Indian slave trade in New France.[99]

Ironically, those most committed to Indian slavery found themselves arguing against prevailing French racial attitudes, claiming instead that Indians were hard-working, intelligent, and capable of submission to authority. Those who supported La Galissonière's Atlantic export proposal, for example, believed that Indian slaves could be purchased as children, immersed in French culture and religion, and taught to master a trade. To persuade others that his proposal would work, La Galissonière praised Indians' capacity for work: "The Indians of Canada are without comparison stronger and more vigorous than those" who lived in the Caribbean. Whether he really believed this assessment, he understood that French attitudes regarding Indians' weakness, laziness, and independence could dissuade others from supporting the Indian slave trade.[100]

Then, too, the legal structures of Indian slavery in New France rested on a foundation of ethnic specificity rather than racial generality. Because

99. Aubert, "'The Blood of France,'" *WMQ*, 3d Ser., LXI (2004), 439–478; Masarah Van Eyck, "'We Shall Be One People': Early Modern French Perceptions of the Amerindian Body" (Ph.D. diss., McGill University, 2001), 95–148; Saliha Belmessous, "Assimilation and Racialism in Seventeenth- and Eighteenth-Century French Colonial Policy," *American Historical Review*, LX (2005), 322–349; Jennifer M. Spear, "Colonial Intimacies: Legislating Sex in French Louisiana," *WMQ*, 3d Ser., LX (2003), 75–98.

100. Bigot et La Jonquière au Ministre, July 26, 1749, Collection Moreau de Saint-Méry, ANOM, F/3/95.

French colonists relied so heavily upon their Indian allies for trade and military protection, they never intended to enslave all of America's native peoples. Instead, slave law in New France specifically distinguished between those Indians who could be enslaved and those who could not. The law demanded that only specific Indian nations, rather than all members of a supposed Indian race, were subject to enslavement. Because allied Indians supplied New France with its Indian slaves, the system could function only to the extent that French colonists maintained careful distinctions among the various Indian nations with whom they interacted. As a result, the practice of Indian slavery made it more difficult to characterize all Indian peoples as belonging to a single race.

The alliance system therefore prevented the social and institutional dimensions of slavery from relying on the idea of racial inferiority. Bigot's and La Jonquière's insistence that Indian slaves were fundamentally different from African slaves accurately identified what subsequent observers of slavery in New France have overlooked: that Indian and African slaveries in the colony operated as parallel, and often competing, slave systems. Yet it was not Indians' racial characteristics, or even cultural ideas about work or social hierarchies, that set them apart from black slaves. Indian slaves were different from African slaves because of structural differences between the two slave systems—differences that were created by the demands of alliance building. Linked independently to the French-Indian alliance system, racial thinking and slavery both grew in importance during the 1740s and 1750s as colonial wars once again threatened the survival of New France. As French colonists depended more heavily on Indian allies, their inability to coerce them grew ever more frustrating, prompting a new wave of statements regarding Indians' supposedly inherent incapacity for submission and obedience. At the same time, however, allied warriors seized a growing number of captives from enemy nations. These prisoners became slaves, passing into French towns through long-established networks of diplomacy and commerce. Frustrated by their allies' unwillingness to submit to their commands, French colonists could enact their dreams of control and order on the bodies of their Indian slaves.

It is impossible to tell how many enslaved Indians traveled from Quebec to Martinique. Records are sparse. There are some clues that the idea, at least, became very attractive to French merchants. In January 1755, six Indian slaves arrived in Martinique from Quebec on the ship *La Legere*. The shipping record specifically notes that the vessel's captain had permission from the governor of New France to bring the slaves to the island, where they sold for one thousand livres apiece. The following year, French merchant Pierre Fesquet wrote to his agent at Quebec asking him to load, in addition to the standard cargo of timbers and fish, "twenty or thirty savages or even more if they can be suitably lodged without their numbers causing illness." "These Indians should not cost more than 150–200 livres or at most 300 livres." Even his least optimistic scenario—twenty Indian slaves bought at 300 livres each—would have yielded Fesquet nearly 14,000 livres in gross profits if all the slaves survived. It is unclear just how pervasive this practice became, but Fesquet's tone indicates that his request was not entirely out of the ordinary. Still, we only know of Fesquet's request because his letters were seized by British ships during the Seven Years' War, meaning that neither the letters nor the slaves were ever delivered.[101]

Whatever the numbers, they could not have made a substantial difference in the overall volume of slaves reaching the French Caribbean in the mid-eighteenth century. But the process of trade and the restrictions placed upon it suggest how fundamentally the African slave trade differed from the trade in captive Indians during the eighteenth century. Indian slavery in New France was inseparable from the strategic violence that produced slaves in the first place. Canadian governors issued lists of specific Native peoples who could and could not be enslaved, and these lists shifted with the changing demands of French-Indian alliances in New France. To legitimize permanent property rights in slaves—to make Indian slavery more like African slavery—required a willing ignorance of the process of enslavement. This had profound implications for the relationship between race and slavery in New France and the Caribbean. When only specific Indian nations could be enslaved but others were honored, it was impossible to erect a racially defined slave system in New France.

With an ocean between them and their slaves' former homes, on the other hand, Caribbean masters did not have to face the dangers of slave raids and counterraids. They did not honor African delegations in their settlements; they did not rely on independent African nations for their military defense. Nor did they have to ask sticky moral questions about the process of enslavement. They could thus erect a social system designed to coerce and control people, not by specific village, culture, or language group, but by race. Indeed, French Caribbean planters so thoroughly wedded the ideas of

101. AN, Archives des Colonies, F2-C, article 4, fol. 228 (La Legere). I would like to thank Ken Donovan for providing me with this citation. Fesquet to Derit, Mar. 18, 1756, quoted in Bosher, *The Canada Merchants*, 17 ("twenty or thirty savages").

race and slavery that even Indian slaves entering their society were called Negroes or mulattoes in census records, laws, and church records. But for Ailleboust and his Indian slave, the distinctions between Indian slavery in the Saint Lawrence Valley and African slavery in the Caribbean could not have been more clear. These differences cost Ailleboust several hundred livres and opened new possibilities for his slave, whose life had begun in western North America, passed through the Pays d'en Haut and into the Saint Lawrence Valley, only to be transformed again by his sale and then escape in the Caribbean.

❖ Indian slavery in Montreal developed as part of France's Atlantic strategy of creating locally governed slave societies within a legally pluralistic kingdom. Rather than following the logic of Caribbean slavery, which French colonists originally set out to mimic, in New France slavery remained closely tied to the alliances and relationships the colony forged with its Indian allies. This new logic made slaves' legal standing uncertain, which could have contradictory effects. For many, as French colonists repeatedly complained, it opened avenues for leaving the system of slavery. This uncertainty made slaves as property an uncertain and therefore undervalued investment. But slaves' shaky legal status could also have dangerous consequences for slaves, as when Jacob's murder went unpunished.

Montreal's slaves suffered the bodily afflictions of physical abuse, substandard food and clothing, uncomfortable and degrading sleeping quarters, and a strong possibility of early death. Moreover, although slaveholders encouraged, if they did not force, their slaves to adopt many elements of French culture, they nevertheless denied them access to the most important markers of French cultural identity, including family formation, full participation in Catholicism, and a respectable means of making a living. Within these constraints, however, New France's Indian slaves developed friendships and alliances that punctuated their daily routines with as much community as coercion. But these relationships, cut short by high death rates, rarely developed into stable, long-term unions. Instead, despite some legal uncertainty, nearly all Indian slaves remained minors in others' households for the duration of their lives, even when they lived well into adulthood.

Those whose journey continued to the Caribbean, like Marie-Marguerite, found themselves enmeshed in a social world fundamentally different from the one they had negotiated in the Pays d'en Haut or the Saint Lawrence Valley. Not only was the labor regime far more brutal, but the legal practices that defined their status also structured their experiences in new and startling ways, bringing into sharp relief the degree to which their enslavement within an indigenous political economy in North America had shaped their lives as slaves there. Marie-Marguerite's journey reminds us that, however much Dormicourt, her new master, wished to draw parallels between the life she had lived in Montreal and the one that awaited her in Martinique, they were worlds apart.

epilogue

OF THE INDIAN RACE

The alliances that allowed French expansion into the Pays d'en Haut in the 1660s brought indigenous and Atlantic slaveries into a dialogue that would shape Native and French colonial societies for a century. French losses in the Seven Years' War drew them apart. Forced to cede Quebec in 1759 and Montreal and the western posts in 1760, France yielded all of its North American colonies to Britain and Spain in 1763. Although French population, culture, and language remain important in Canada and the Pays d'en Haut to this day, French colonial realignment so thoroughly severed connections between Canada and the French Caribbean that the historical memory of their earlier ties all but disappeared. If silently, the legacies of the previous century continued to influence the way Native and French communities thought about and practiced slavery.

In North America, the complexities of alliance politics that drove the slave trade throughout the French period faltered temporarily with the assumption of British control but continued to guide colonial-Native relations in the territories formerly claimed by France. As British traders and colonial leaders arrived at Detroit and Michilimackinac in the 1760s, the Indians of the Pays d'en Haut greeted them with caution, unsure of how the newcomers would behave. Both sides seemed prepared to make new accommodations and create new norms, but negotiating the terms of the relationship—from material questions like the price of goods to cultural questions like what language to speak—proved difficult. As it did with the French, slavery became both a source of tension and a site of creative adaptation in British-Indian relations. Over the previous hundred years, Native responses to French colonialism, especially strategic slave raids targeting potential French allies, had only deepened the connections between indigenous slavery and alliance. These raids also served to reinforce ethnic distinctions among the Indians of the Pays d'en Haut, countering early French efforts to cluster all of the region's Indians into a single category. The significance of Natives' regional and linguistic divisions, as well as the ways that slavery both revealed and reinforced them, was lost on most British officials, who carried to the Pays d'en Haut a set of ideas about Indians that emphasized their supposed racial similarities over their cultural and historical particularities. By misreading this essential aspect of slavery's history in French North America, British officers blundered their way into a conflict that grew to terrifying proportions in 1763, when an Ottawa warrior named Pontiac struck back after the execution of an enslaved Indian woman at Detroit. Although the violence of Pontiac's War intensified anti-Indian racial thinking in Britain's eastern colonies, a grudging accommodation returned to the former French settlements, restoring the Indian slave trade to Detroit and Michilimackinac. Following patterns of kin making and forced assimilation that emerged in French, Native, and métis households during the first half of the eighteenth century, Indian slavery continued in the Pays d'en Haut well into the 1790s.[1]

A very different dynamic emerged in the Caribbean. During the final three decades before New France fell to the British, the Indian slave trade from Canada to Martinique created commercial interests that countered the persistent pressure to ban Indian slavery in the Caribbean. Because there was money to be made from Canadian slaves—in the slave trade and by the labor they provided—Caribbean planters resorted to elaborate arguments to make legal and moral space for Indian slavery. New France supplied the narratives of justification that allowed Caribbean officials to declare Panis Indians legitimate slaves, injecting just-war rhetoric into discussions of Caribbean slavery long after the islands had shifted toward more racially charged rationales. The end of New France's slave trade in the 1760s thus silenced a counternarrative to the resurgent story of natural slavery, which equated African ancestry with an unfitness for freedom and civic equality. Inverting this racial logic, Caribbean colonists and royal officials crafted a new set of laws guaranteeing freedom to members of the "Indian race," suggesting that they had never been meant for slavery. They also reimagined the history of Indian slavery in the French Atlantic in ways that simultaneously denied its importance and explained its failures in racial terms. Far from a straightforward description of the colonial past, the idea that

1. Gregory Evans Dowd, *War under Heaven: Pontiac, the Indian Nations, and the British Empire* (Baltimore, 2002); Peter Silver, *Our Savage Neighbors: How Indian War Transformed Early America* (New York, 2008).

Indians were naturally unfit for slavery originated as a slaveholder's tale inseparable from its logical counterpart: that Africans were born to be slaves.

WE ARE NOT YOUR SLAVES

*"Although you have conquered the French, you have not yet conquered us.
We are not your slaves."*—Minweweh, Ojibwa warrior, 1761

In the summer of 1762, drawn by the new commercial prospects opened by the British takeover of the western Great Lakes, John Clapham left Boston to engage in the Indian trade at Detroit. Upon his arrival there, Clapham bought two adult Indian slaves, a man and a woman, to assist him in his travels by carrying his trade goods and rowing his canoe. Under the terms of France's capitulation of the Saint Lawrence and the Pays d'en Haut, colonists were allowed to "retain their Negroes and Pawnee Indian slaves," a guarantee that allowed the Indian slave trade to continue well into the British period. Clapham's trip began well, but on his return home his fortunes ran out. Once beyond the protection of English forts, Clapham's Indian slaves bludgeoned him to death, cut off his head, threw his body overboard, and paddled ashore with all of his goods.[2]

News of the murder spread quickly through the British colonies, and within weeks papers in Boston, Providence, and Philadelphia had printed accounts of the crime. The flow of information had been rapid, but the details were murky. The fullest account appeared in the *Boston Gazette* on November 22:

> We hear that Mr. William Clapham, a young Gentleman belonging to this Town, having been a Trading among the Western Tribes of Indians at Detroit, was murdered by one of his Negro Servants as he was crossing Lake Erie in a Battoe on his Return, the Negro who was in the Stern taking an Opportunity struck him in his Back with a Tomahawk, and then threw him over board; as soon as he had done this horrid Deed, and got ashore with the Battoe, he went to the Indians, and informed them of the Affair, imagining they would be pleased with it;

2. *Wis. Hist. Coll.*, VII (1876; 1908), 147. Article 47 of the capitulation of the Saint Lawrence reads, in full: "The Negroes and panis of both sexes shall remain, in their quality of slaves, in the possession of the French and Canadians to whom they belong; they [the French] shall be at liberty to keep them in their service in the colony, or to sell them; and they may also continue to bring them up in the Roman Religion." Adam Short and Arthur G. Doughty, eds., *Documents Relating to the Constitutional History of Canada, 1759–1791* (Ottawa, 1907), 28.

instead of which he with the other Servant were secured and sent to the Commanding-Officer at Pittsburg, on the Ohio.[3]

Even to a casual reader the account must have seemed muddled. Why would African slaves have had a tomahawk? Why would they immediately inform the Indians, imagining they would be pleased? As more details emerged, it became clear that early reports got nearly everything wrong. Clapham's name was John, not William; the slaves were Indians rather than African Americans; and the prisoners were taken to Detroit instead of Pittsburgh. "It has been reported to me," Johnson wrote to Gladwin at Detroit, "that a Cruel and Inhuman Murder was lately committed on the Body of Mr. John Clapham, on the route from the Detroit to Presqu'Isle, Supposed to be Done by Two Panis Slaves, now in custody at your Post." A host of Indian informants, and indeed the prisoners themselves, corroborated Johnson's description of events.[4]

If Britain's Indian agents eventually gathered more complete details about the case, their handling of the episode showed that they misunderstood its significance. Sending instructions to Detroit, Jeffery Amherst noted that, because this was the first intercultural murder since the British takeover, it offered an ideal opportunity to display British power. By meting out "the most Exemplary Punishment" to the prisoners, he hoped that the British could assert their authority and demonstrate that they would not stand for Indians' killing British subjects. To that end, Amherst demanded that the prisoners be hanged and their corpses be displayed in the public square. A few days later, in a separate letter to Gladwin, William Johnson offered the same advice, granting the commander at Detroit "full power for putting the Sentence into Execution in the most Publick Manner, as a Terror to others from being Guilty of Such Crimes for the future."[5]

Before Gladwin could hold a trial, the male slave escaped from British custody and fled to the Illinois country. Unable to find him, Gladwin tried the woman alone. In late April 1763, Gladwin reported to Amherst that the

3. *Providence Gazette; and Country Journal,* Nov. 20, 1762; *Boston Gazette,* Nov. 22, 1762; *Pennsylvania Gazette,* Dec. 2, 1762.

4. William Johnson to Henry Gladwin, Sept. 15, 1762, in Charles Moore, ed., *The Gladwin Manuscripts: With an Introduction and an Historical Sketch of the Conspiracy of Pontiac* (East Lansing, Mich., 1897), 674–675.

5. Jeffrey Amherst to Henry Gladwin, Sept. 15, 1762, Amherst Papers, PRO, WO 34/49, fol. 313. I thank Ian Steele for sharing this citation with me. William Johnson to Gladwin, Sept. 19, 1762, *WJP,* X, 519–521.

female slave "was Sentenced to be Hanged, for being an Accomplice in the Murder of the Late Mr. Clapham, which I had put in Execution in the most Publick manner." Amherst responded with approval:

> Altho' I am always Sorry to Consent to the Sending of any Unhappy Wretch out of this World, yet the Execution of the Panis Woman, who was an Accomplice in the Murder of the Late Mr. Clapham, has my Approbation, the Crime for which She Suffered being so very Heinous that Nothing Less than her Life could Atone, and Indeed I Sincerely Wish the Chief Perpetrator of that Murder had not Escaped, but that he might have Shared the same Fate, that the Example might have been the Stronger.[6]

Rather than terrifying Detroit's Indians, the execution enraged them. Only days after the hanging, the Ottawa war chief Pontiac invited leaders from nearby Ottawa, Ojibwa, and Potawatomi villages to discuss an attack on the British in reprisal. Growing concerned, Gladwin sent sober warnings to his counterparts commanding at Forts Pitt, Sandusky, and Presque Isle. The Indians "are Ill Disposed," he warned. "They say We mean to make Slaves of them . . . and that they had better Attempt Something now, to Recover their Liberty, than Wait till We were better Established." Within two weeks, on May 7, 1763, Indians attacked at Detroit in what would become the opening campaign of Pontiac's War, a conflict that claimed hundreds of British and Indian lives, bringing the British presence in the West to the brink of destruction.[7]

It is possible to explain Indians' anger over the slave's execution as a straightforward rejection of colonial legal authority. To be sure, Detroit's Natives demanded that crimes, especially murders, resolve according to their own codes of justice. When they did not wish to cooperate, Indians refused to turn over prisoners or, when they did release them, demanded their pardon. In this case, Pontiac and his allies did neither. To begin with, British officials never demanded that the Indians turn over the slaves. Indeed, Gladwin learned of the crime only when Indians brought the slaves to Detroit and released them into his custody. Nor is there evidence that any-

---

6. Henry Gladwin to Jeffrey Amherst, Apr. 20, 1763, *WJP*, IV, 95–96; Amherst to Gladwin, May 29, 1763, *WJP*, IV, 98.

7. Gladwin to Amherst, Apr. 20, 1763, *WJP*, IV, 95–96. The best overall treatment of the war is Dowd, *War under Heaven*.

one objected to the slave's execution. Indians in the Pays d'en Haut found nothing unusual in dispatching a treacherous slave; their own customs demanded it. According to William Johnson, the murder "is held in such Detestation by all the Indians in that Quarter who only have as earnestly entreated the offenders might be burnt for the same at Detroit, and offered themselves to put the murderers to that Death if they might be permitted as a proof of their wrath against the perpetrators of so great a Crime." Had Gladwin allowed the Natives to carry out the sentence as they requested, the incident could have generated trust rather than suspicion.[8]

Instead, Gladwin and his counterparts squandered the opportunity by failing to distinguish between Detroit's free and enslaved Indians. Reflecting the growing tendency to imagine Indians as a single race of people (Amherst often spoke of "the whole race of Indians"), British officials viewed Clapham's murder as a simple case of an Indian's killing a British subject. Should such a crime go unpunished, they feared, all Indians might follow the slaves' example, threatening the security of British traders and officers in the West. When Gladwin wrote, "I think it would have a good effect if an example were made" of the murderers, he meant for Detroit's free Indians to be the students of his violent object lesson.[9]

Gladwin's logic betrayed a poor understanding of the local cultures of slavery created by a century of French-Native interactions in the Pays d'en Haut. What affinity should Detroit's Indians feel for these slaves, who were their enemies and, as manifest by their enslavement, their inferiors? Indian warriors from the region had, in the recent past, raided the slaves' villages, bound, beaten, and humiliated them, and then sold them to their allies. To equate free Ottawas, Ojibwas, or Potawatomis with these slaves was among the worst insults Gladwin could have given. Detroit's free Indians feared that the British "meant to make slaves of them," because Gladwin and his colleagues had already drawn the equation in their speeches surrounding the slave's execution. This affront explains Pontiac's rallying cry during the councils immediately before his attack on Detroit, in which he condemned

8. Richard White, *The Middle Ground: Indians, Empires, and Republics in the Great Lakes Region, 1650–1815* (Cambridge, 1991), 343–351; Johnson to Amherst, Oct. 1, 1762, *WJP*, III, 887. Gladwin reported that the slaves "were Delivered up by a Party of Indians," without specifying the nation that turned them over. Gladwin to Amherst, Apr. 20, 1763, *WJP*, IV, 95.

9. Jeffery Amherst to William Johnson, Aug. 27, 1763, in John Romeyn Brodhead, *Documents relative to the Colonial History of the State of New-York*, VII, ed. E. B. O'Callaghan (Albany, N.Y., 1856), 545; Henry Gladwin to Jeffrey Amherst, Amherst Papers, PRO, WO 34/39, fols. 126–127.

the "insults which he and his nation had received from the Commandant and the English officers."[10]

Central to the immediate tensions that drove Pontiac and his allies to fight, slavery became the most pervasive theme in the rhetoric used to justify Pontiac's War. In 1761, when the British arrived to take possession of Michilimackinac, the Ojibwa war chief Minweweh reminded the newcomers that, although they now commanded the fort, they could not dictate their will to the region's Natives. "Although you have conquered the French," Minweweh told Alexander Henry, "you have not yet conquered us. We are not your slaves." Two years later, in 1763, Minweweh led his band of Ojibwas in the attack on Michilimackinac that inaugurated Pontiac's War in that region. Throughout the West, Indians would invoke similar words to claim that they joined the war to frustrate British attempts to enslave them.[11]

The Ojibwas, Ottawas, and Potawatomis expressed their anger through the idiom of slavery for complex linguistic and historical reasons that are clear only within the context of the region's history of indigenous slavery. When French translators conveyed British demands to Detroit's Indians, they would have struggled to find appropriate terminology to express anything but the worst reading of British intent. Algonquian dialects had no adequate term to express the European political status of "subject." This absence did not mean, as Thomas Gage claimed, that "no Nation of Indians have any word which can express, or convey, the Idea of Subjection."[12]

On the contrary, two sets of words indicated subjection and mastery in the Ottawa and Ojibwa languages. Those most commonly used by French translators derived from *awakaan*, meaning both domesticated animal and slave. This word might have been the closest French translators could come when rendering British demands that Indians demonstrate due subjection. The second set of terms, arising from the root verb *dibenim*, meant to control, master, or own. When applied to a person, the verb suggests enslavement. Even in the absence of real British threats to Indians' independence, the language of British political authority alienated Detroit's Natives, especially when rendered by French intermediaries interested in casting the British in a bad light. Henry Gladwin's comparing his ostensible allies to

10. Pontiac quoted in Dowd, *War under Heaven*, 118.

11. David Armour, "Minweweh," *DCB*, III; Dowd, *War under Heaven*, esp. 63–70.

12. Quoted in Dowd, *War under Heaven*, 181. Johnson, who might have been Gage's source for this assertion, concurred: "Neither have they any word which can convey the most distant idea of subjection," quoted in White, *Middle Ground*, 294.

a murderous slave therefore only confirmed fears of British domination. When he called Detroit's Indians "dogs" and "hogs"—which he reportedly did with some frequency—Gladwin unwittingly evoked the same powerful image of slavery. Ottawa- and Ojibwa-speakers would have quickly associated their two most common domesticated animals, or *awakaanag*, with their own domestication and slavery.[13]

But slavery had more than conceptual meaning to Indians surrounding Detroit and Michilimackinac in 1763. For nearly a century, these Natives had supplied New France with Indian captives, and they had interacted regularly with French-owned Indian slaves. Algonquian and French cultures both defined nonallied Indians as legitimate victims of slavery. Indeed, beginning in the 1730s French legal codes expressly allowed the enslavement of nonallied nations while forbidding allies' victimization, structuring the Indian slave trade according to the contours of French-Indian alliances.[14]

Over the course of that century, generations of Indians had used slavery to shape the colonial encounter with their French allies. Whether offering slaves as ceremonial gifts or strategically enslaving enemies to avoid their alliance with the French, Indians seized the initiative of French diplomacy by seizing the bodies of enemies whom they considered dogs. Although the incentives of this trade would shift the priorities of indigenous slavery, favoring trade over incorporation, Indians' understanding of slaves as domesticated, subordinate members of their host community remained central to their relations with enemies and their trust of those who would like to be their friends. For their part, the French learned that, however different their own conceptions of slavery might have been, the demands of alliance required them to consider their slaves' people to be enemies. Whether in the spectacular violence of the Fox Wars or the more subtle manipulations of Sioux diplomacy, New France's allies counted on the French to recognize distinctions between their slaves and those who had captured them. Over time, the French reluctantly obliged, trading their dream of a universal alliance in the Pays d'en Haut for a steady supply of enslaved Indians from that region and beyond.

Pontiac and his Ottawa kin had participated in this slave trade, forming

13. John D. Nichols and Earl Nyholm, *A Concise Dictionary of Minnesota Ojibwe* (Minneapolis, Minn., 1995), 14, 45. For more on *awakaan*, see Chapter 1, above. Gladwin in Dowd, *War under Heaven*, 65.

14. Beauharnois and Hocquart to Maurepas, Oct. 4, 1733, ANOM, Colonies, C11A, LIX, 108–112.

ties with Detroit's principal French slaveholders. From the earliest stages of the conflict, Pontiac relied on these friendships, especially with Pierre Labutte and Antoine Cuillerier, representatives of Detroit's two largest slaveholding families. Both had marital ties to the Ottawa community. From Pontiac's first formal message to the British commander to the final peace negotiations in late 1764, the Ottawa leader relied on "M. La Bute the Interpretor and a Frenchman that could speake English." Because Labutte also spoke Ojibwa and Potawatomi, he played the most prominent diplomatic role of any non-Native at Detroit. Antoine Cuillerier's influence in both French and Native circles made him the centerpiece of Pontiac's plan to reclaim the old order at Detroit. On May 10, 1763, the day after the first British death in the war, Pontiac invited two British officers to Cuillerier's home to discuss a truce. "The purport of Pondiac's first speech," one of the officers reported, "was to inform the French and Indians that he turned out the Commandant (meaning Major Gladwin) and desired them to look upon and regard Monsieur Cuillerie as their Father and Commander." According to Robert Rogers, "Mr. Cuellierry accepted of their Offer of being made Commandant, if this Place [Detroit] was taken."[15]

Cuillerier never got the chance. Despite a series of dramatic Native victories over British garrisons throughout the West, by late summer 1764 Pontiac's War had all but ended. A massive British counteroffensive, although not nearly as successful as the British had hoped, diminished resistance and persuaded many Natives to negotiate a truce. At Detroit and Michilimackinac, a new order emerged that linked French and British merchants with Indian villages in a sustained, if occasionally tense, relationship. Britain's improved diplomatic position among the Indians after 1764 allowed British traders, for the first time, to play a substantial role in the Indian slave trade. This arrangement thrived for another two decades, becoming so successful that William Savery could write in 1793, "The Chippeway [Ojibwa] Indians being at continual war with the Pawnee nation, of whom they take many prisoners, men, women, and children, they bring them into this settlement, and sell them at from ten to one hundred pounds each; and it is computed, that at present there are here about three hundred of these poor creatures in slavery."[16]

15. Franklin B. Hough, ed., *Diary of the Siege of Detroit in the War with Pontiac . . .* (Albany, N.Y., 1860), 15–16, 86; Louis Chevrette, "Pontiac," *DCB*, III, 528; Moore, ed., *Gladwin Manuscripts*, 643, 656; Dowd, *War under Heaven*, 123.

16. Jonathan Evans, comp., *A Journal of the Life, Travels, and Religious Labours, of*

"The case comes down to a question of status, indeed, the court must decide whether Marianne is of the Indian or African race."
—Court dossier, Saint Domingue, 1784

When colonial newspaper reports mistook the two murderous "Panis Slaves" for "Negro servants," they evoked another legacy of slavery and the slave trade in French North America: French colonists' desire to make Indian slavery function like the African slavery of France's island colonies. The equation of "the Panis" with the people called les Nègres by the French provided a reliable fiction that allowed Indian slavery to remain legal even when the vagaries of Indian alliances weakened the legal standing and property value of Indian slaves. Given France's legally pluralistic approach to slavery, the pressures of alliance politics could shape slavery in French North America in conversation with rather than opposition to other forms of slavery in the French empire.

These local adaptations produced the creative new fictions that made racialized views of Indians work against their enslavement. Slaves' legal status depended on their particular ethnic, rather than broadly racial, identity, mirroring Detroit Indians' frustration with British attempts to label them slaves and dogs alongside their enemies. The kind of independence that led Pontiac and his allies to resist the British fueled French suspicions that Indians were untamable. Frustrated with their inability to exercise more coercive authority over Indians in their North American colonies, French colonial and metropolitan thinkers developed a racialist discourse that characterized Indians as too free for slavery. As the dominant population and the driving force of the colonial economy, free Indians, far more than the enslaved, shaped French racial attitudes toward North America's Native peoples.

After France's withdrawal from North America, French writers and legal authorities used the fiction of Indians' natural unfitness for slavery to

---

William Savery (London, 1844), 34. For Indian slavery and the economies of Detroit and Michilimackinac after the British takeover, see E. A. S. Demers, "John Askin and Indian Slavery at Michilimackinac," in Alan Gallay, ed., *Indian Slavery in Colonial America* (Lincoln, Nebr., 2009), 391–416; Elizabeth Sherburn Demers, "Keeping a Store: The Social and Commercial Worlds of John Askin in the Eighteenth Century Great Lakes, 1763–1796" (Ph.D. diss., Michigan State University, 2010); Catherine S. Cangany, "Frontier Seaport: Detroit's Transformation into an Atlantic Entrepôt, 1701–1837" (Ph.D. diss., University of Michigan, 2009).

overwrite a century of history in New France and the Caribbean. Although both colonial and royal officials approved trading enslaved Indians from North America to the Caribbean as late as 1749, shortly after the end of the Seven Years' War the law—and the narrative crafted to justify it—evolved to reflect the myth of the indomitable savage. During a 1767 investigation into the legal status of a mixed-race family in Saint Domingue, colonial officials sought the king's advice on the standing of people with Indian versus African descent. The response from Versailles was unequivocal. "The king has always admitted . . . an essential difference between Indians and Negroes," wrote the minister of the Marine. "The reason for this difference is that Indians are born free, and have always maintained the advantage of their liberty in the colonies, whereas Negroes were only introduced there to live in slavery, an original stain that extends to all of their descendants, which the gift of liberty cannot efface." Unsullied by slavery, those who descended from "the Indian race should be assimilated with the king's subjects from Europe . . . [and] they may, as a result, claim every responsibility and honor available in the colonies, but . . . his majesty intends that they first prove their genealogy in a manner that there remains no doubt about their origin."[17]

As the French state placed new constraints on free people of color in its island colonies, scores of people were called upon to give proofs of their ancestry to determine their legal standing. Well aware of the legal distinctions articulated in 1767, many free people of color responded by claiming to be of Indian, rather than African, descent, particularly "mulattos," according to one contemporary, "whose skin color classes them with Indians and Savages." One who made this claim was Marianne, a laborer in the southern Saint Domingue province of Les Cayes. Marianne claimed to be an Indian

17. "Sa Majesté a toujours admis . . . une différence essentielle entre les Indiens et les Negres; la raison de cette différence est prise de ce que les Indiens sont nés libres, et ont toujours conservé l'avantage de la liberté dans les Colonies, tandis que les Negres n'y ont été introduits que pour y demeurer dans l'état d'esclavage; premiere tache qui s'étend sur tous leurs descendans, et que le don de la liberté ne peut effacer . . . ceux qui proviennent d'une Race Indienne, doivent être assimilés aux Sujets du Roi originaires d'Europe, et qu'ils peuvent, en conséquence, prétendre à toutes les Charges et Dignités dans les Colonies; mais . . . Sa Majesté entend qu'il prouveront préalablement leur généalogie, de maniere qu'il ne reste aucun doute sur leur origine": "Lettre du Ministre aux Administrateurs, contenant un décision sur trois points relatifs aux Races Noires et Indiennes," Jan. 7, 1767, in M. Moreau de Saint-Méry, *Loix et constitutions des colonies françoises de l'Amérique sous le vent* . . . (Paris, 1785–1790), V, 80–81. John Garrigus discusses this case and its context more fully in *Before Haiti: Race and Citizenship in French Saint-Domingue* (New York, 2006), 148–149.

whose family had worked as free laborers for generations. She argued that as a free woman she was owed decades of back wages by the family she had been working for, who had treated her as a slave and refused to pay her. Rather than focusing on Marianne's personal history of enslavement or freedom, the court centered its deliberations on the issue of race. "The case comes down to a question of status," wrote one court official. "Indeed the court must decide whether Marianne is of the Indian or African race; whether she is free or not; whether she and her children should be assimilated among the whites or regarded as slaves." The echo from the 1767 royal declaration is clear. Irrespective of an individual's personal history, the state considered Indians to be legally free and entitled to full assimilation. But the burden of proof rested on Marianne, and she could not produce enough documentation (what the court called "titres," or proofs of status) to demonstrate that she was an Indian rather than mixed-race with African ancestry. In the absence of clear evidence, Marianne's attorney embraced the court's racialist logic, arguing that she had all the proofs she needed: "1. in her color; 2. in her hair; 3. in the proportions of her nose." Because there were "so many proofs written on her face," he said, there could be no question that she was "of the Indian race" and therefore free.[18]

Instead of arguing that an Indian could be a slave—a position that became untenable after 1767—the opposing attorney decided to dispute the concept of race itself. Reminding the court that only documentation could establish civil status, he argued that bodily appearance was "insufficient to prove that she is an Indian; and indeed smooth hair, a thin, straight nose, and a tawny complexion are not traits belonging only to Indians." Far from a reliable guide to a person's ancestry, physical appearance could be deceptive and was thus a dangerous rule for courts to follow. "Nature," he concluded, "always likes to confuse physical features and color." He was correct from a legal standpoint. The law, in fact, required unambiguous documentation of ancestry. But, because the evidence was so strong that Marianne was an Indian, she made a convincing case for her freedom. No record survives of the case's final outcome, but the process itself is revealing. Marianne embraced her own phenotypic racialization as a pathway to freedom while her

18. Trial summary, 1784, ANOM, Collection Moreau de Saint-Méry, F3, XCV, 19–36. For "mulattos," see M. L. E. Moreau de Saint-Méry, *Description topographique, physique, civile, politique, et historique de la parti française de l'isle Saint-Domingue* (Philadelphia, 1797–1798), I, 68.

master deconstructed the relationship between physical features and legal status to keep her enslaved.[19]

In ways both clarifying and disorienting, Marianne's case illustrates how ideas about race and slavery diverged for American Indians as they converged for Africans in the eighteenth century. By Marianne's time, being racialized an African brought the presumption of slavery. Being racialized an Indian meant freedom. Notions of Indians' natural liberty also influenced narratives of their historical enslavement. Among other things, the 1767 order declaring Indians' freedom was a historical argument about Indian slavery: they were born free and always preserved that liberty in French colonies. The minister's reasoning elided a century of experience in New France, where thousands of enslaved Indians labored under French colonial control, sought by a wide swath of colonial society from merchants to government ministers.

Expressed most forcefully in the French Caribbean, the notion that Indians were naturally untamable, and thus made poor slaves, became a widely accepted maxim, persisting even in modern explanations of why Africans were enslaved in far greater numbers than Indians. In North America, this idea confronted the reality of Indian slavery by imagining the enslavable "Panis" as the lone exception to the rule of Indians' unfitness for bondage. In the 1790s, with Indian slavery persisting at Detroit and Montreal, observers read the history of Indian slavery in this light. "The Panis, or, as the English pronounce it, the Pawnees, are a people considerably civilized, cultivated the ground, and built Houses," wrote the English historian John Williams in 1792. Because they were "brought up in habits of Industry," he explained, they "will work, but no other Indians will; and for that reason, when taken Prisoners of War, they are not put to death as other Indians are, but are sold to the English, French, etc. for Slaves . . . they are frequently to be met with in Canada, and in other parts of America, in the condition of Slaves." As Jacques Raudot had done in 1709, Williams drew comparisons between Indian and African enslavement, claiming that even Indians equated the terms "Panis" and slave so completely "that they call the Negroes in the English Colonies, English Pawnees, and Black Pawnees." Williams knew noth-

19. Trial summary, 1784, ANOM, Collection Moreau de Saint-Méry, F3, XCV, 19–36. Looking at many similar cases involving free people of color, Garrigus demonstrates that the burden of proof was on the person claiming Indian ancestry: "In other words, society would consider self-proclaimed Indians to be African until proven otherwise" (*Before Haiti*, 149).

ing about the actual Pawnees, speculating that they were the famed white Indians descended from a twelfth-century Welsh explorer named Prince Madog. But in his formulation of their history he reiterated the French fiction of a distant and sovereign people enslaved in just wars, the only recognized exception to Indians' racial unfitness for slavery. By noting the persistence of the Indian slave trade in former French territories a full thirty years after the British takeover, Williams also revealed the long shadow cast by a system of slavery that stretched across half a continent for more than a century. For tens of thousands involved as slavers, war casualties, traders, slaveholders, or the enslaved, the bonds of alliance that brought French and Native societies together in the seventeenth and eighteenth centuries were inseparable from the bonds of slavery.[20]

20. John Williams, *Farther Observations on the Discovery of America, by Prince Madog ab Owen Gwynedd, about the Year, 1170* (London, 1792), 15, 17. Modern historians have often reiterated these fictions, uncritically accepting the racially charged logic behind them. Repeating the explanations of colonial-era slaveholders, Richard S. Dunn wrote that because they "were far too savage to catch and tame.... Indians made poor slaves. The men in particular would only hunt and fish 'and if forced to any labor, eyther hang themselves or Runne away.'...What really mattered was that Indians could not be turned into acceptable agricultural laborers and Negroes could.... Captive Africans fell into lockstep as menial laborers. The most tragic thing about Afro-American slavery is that all of the black man's admirable human qualities—his sociability, adaptability, endurance, loving kindness, and domesticated, disciplined culture—earned him nothing but debasement in the New World." *Sugar and Slaves: The Rise of the Planter Class in the English West Indies, 1624–1713* (Chapel Hill, N.C., 1972), 74.

APPENDIX A

Algonquian Language Sources: Summary and Sample Word List

The argument developed in Chapter 1 about Algonquian understandings of captivity and slavery grew out of a close reading of all known sources on seventeenth-century captivity in the Pays d'en Haut. Many of these sources—missionary letters, merchant journals, official reports, and travel narratives, for example—have been widely cited and discussed for decades. Others, like the archaeological reports indicating frequent, low-level violence and skeletal markers suggestive of slavery, have been debated in the secondary literature; and, where I was aware of a disagreement with my interpretation, I have cited alternative views.

The least familiar but most illuminating material was drawn from four unpublished dictionaries and phrase books created by Jesuit missionaries in the seventeenth and early eighteenth centuries. Totaling nearly two thousand manuscript pages, these guides minutely detail several dialects within the Algonquian language family, particularly within Miami-Illinois and Anishinaabemowin (Ojibwa and Ottawa). The dictionaries vary in their quality, legibility, and comprehensiveness, but each of them exhibits a deep familiarity with the Algonquian dialect in question.[1]

The most complete, reliable, and accessible of these manuscripts is an Illinois-to-French dictionary and phrase book, compiled between 1689 and 1696 by the Jesuit Jacques Gravier and the former coureur de bois and Jesuit layworker Jacques Largil-

---

1. Louis André, "Preceptes, phrases, et mots de la langue algonquine outaouaise pour un missionnaire nouveau," ca. 1688, MS, photocopy, John Wesley Powell Library of Anthropology, Smithsonian Institution, Washington, D.C.; Jacques Gravier and Jacques Largillier, "Dictionnaire illinois-français," ca. 1690s, MS, Watkinson Library Special Collections, Trinity College, Hartford, Conn.; Antoine-Robert Le Boullenger, "Dictionnaire français-illinois," ca. 1720s, MS, John Carter Brown Library, Brown University, Providence, R.I.; Pierre Du Jaunay, "Dictionarium gallico-outaouakum," 1748, MS, photocopy, John Wesley Powell Library of Anthropology, Smithsonian Institution, Washington, D.C. A fifth major dictionary, also of Miami-Illinois, was discovered in 1999 but is not yet accessible for public research. Michael McCafferty, who has a copy of the manuscript as a consultant for the Miami Tribe of Oklahoma, generously checked it for several keywords relating to slavery / captivity. My analysis of those words appears in the text of Chapter 1. For details about this source, see Michael McCafferty, "The Latest Miami-Illinois Dictionary and Its Author," *Papers of the Thirty-sixth Algonquian Conference* (2005), 271–286, and David Costa, "The St-Jérôme Dictionary of Miami-Illinois," (2005), 107–133. Michael McCafferty identified Jacques Largillier as the scribe and possible contributor to the Gravier manuscript. He also demonstrated that Carl Masthay's identification of this manuscript as "Kaskaskia" is incorrect. The Watkinson Library includes McCafferty's findings, which are forthcoming in print, with the dictionary's provenance information.

lier. First a student and teacher of linguistics in France, Gravier studied the Ottawa language (in the same Algonquian subgroup as Miami-Illinois) for several years, both in Quebec and in an Ottawa village, before arriving in the Illinois country in 1689. An assiduous student, occasionally criticized by colleagues for spending too much time on linguistic studies, Gravier learned to speak the Illinois language with near-native fluency by the early 1690s after working for several years with Native tutors and informants from the Kaskaskia, Peoria, and Wea villages to master the differences between Illinois and Ottawa. In the end, his Jesuit colleagues credited him with systematizing "the principles of their language, and . . . the rules of grammar" that allowed them to work successfully among the Illinois in the early eighteenth century. So thorough was his and his companions' understanding of the language by the 1690s that Pierre Deliette—himself a fluent Illinois-speaker, trader, translator, and diplomat—asserted, "The reverend Jesuit fathers . . . speak their language perfectly."[2]

Gravier's French collaborator, Jacques Largillier, supplemented Gravier's academic approach with a more practical and contextual understanding of the language, hard-won through more than two decades of living among and trading with the Illinois. Because he accompanied Jacques Marquette on his 1674 travels through the Illinois country, Largillier was in the first French party to meet the Illinois and among the first to learn their languages and customs. Embedded in Illinois culture more fully than Gravier because he accompanied Illinois men on hunting and trading journeys, Largillier would have mastered colloquial Algonquian in a way that might initially have eluded the missionary. Working together, their expertise complemented each other's, even as both men continued to rely heavily on Illinois assistance to correct their misunderstandings and to supply subtle connotations.[3]

Containing several thousand phrases and more than twenty-two thousand individual Algonquian words, the Gravier-Largillier dictionary exhibits a contextualized and nuanced understanding of Illinois idioms and a linguist's command of grammar and syntax. According to David Costa, the foremost authority on the Miami-Illinois language, "The data found in the French sources is especially valuable in that, since it is from such an early time period, it is highly unlikely that the system had yet been influenced by the European systems of French or English." The Miami-Illinois dictionaries, for example, were comprehensive enough to allow Costa to reconstruct a complete grammar of that language in the 1990s, when no native speaker survived.[4]

2. Tracy Neal Leavelle, "'Bad Things' and 'Good Hearts': Mediation, Meaning, and the Language of Illinois Christianity," *Church History*, LXXVI (2007), 368; Charles E. O'Neill, "Gravier, Jacques," *DCB*, II; Pierre Deliette, "Memoir of De Gannes [Deliette] concerning the Illinois Country," in Theodore Calvin Pease and Raymond C. Werner, eds. and trans., *The French Foundations, 1680–1693*, Collections of the Illinois State Historical Library, XXIII (Springfield, Ill., 1934), 362 ("speak their language perfectly").

3. Raymond Douville, "Largillier, Jacques," *DCB*, II; Leavelle, "The Language of Illinois Christianity," *Church History*, LXXVI (2007), 363–394.

4. David J. Costa, "The Kinship Terminology of the Miami-Illinois Language," *Anthropological Linguistics*, XLI (1999), 29 ("especially valuable"); Costa, *The Miami-Illinois Language* (Lincoln, Nebr., 2003).

Because it was designed to help Jesuits communicate with the Illinois and never meant for publication, the Gravier-Largillier manuscript (like its Anishinaabe counterparts) provides a much more candid and detailed cultural portrait than the Jesuits published in their much more widely cited *Relations*. Alphabetized by Algonquian rather than French words, the Gravier-Largillier dictionary reveals relationships among words and concepts that are not visible in dictionaries organized around French translations, many of which may not have been apparent to the French authors themselves. It also contains many phrases that have no easy French equivalent and were thus omitted from other guides.[5]

5. Costa, *Miami-Illinois Language,* 11; Costa, "The St-Jérôme Dictionary of Miami-Illinois," 107–133, *Papers of the Thirty-sixth Algonquian Conference* (2005): "In addition to the fact that the Gravier dictionary simply has more data than either of the other two, the understanding of the Miami-Illinois language demonstrated in Gravier is often superior" (131).

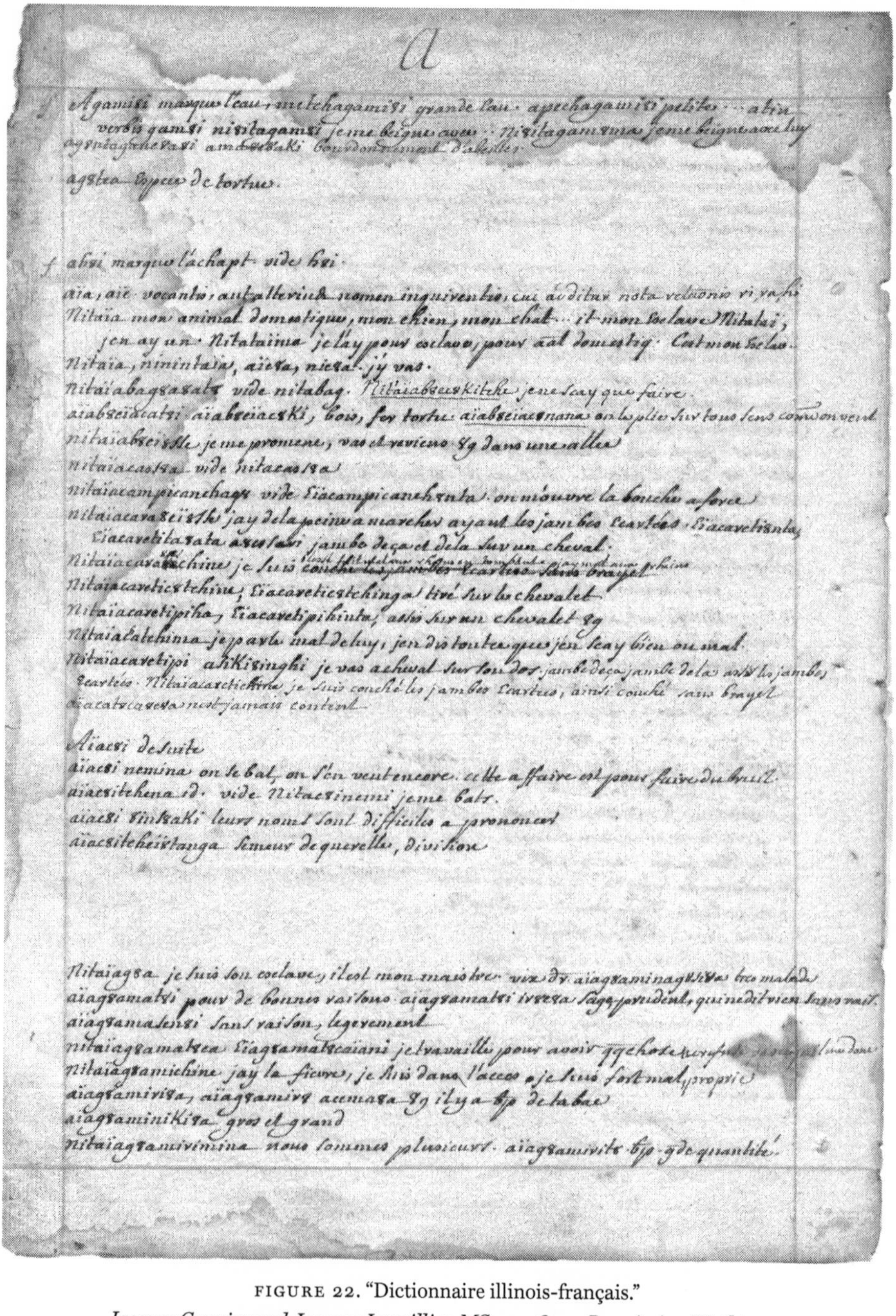

a

FIGURE 22. "Dictionnaire illinois-français."
Jacques Gravier and Jacques Largillier. MS, ca. 1690s. Permission Watkinson
Library Special Collections, Trinity College, Hartford, Conn.

ALGONQUIAN WORDS AND PHRASES RELATING TO SLAVERY / CAPTIVITY: THE GRAVIER-LARGILLIER ILLINOIS DICTIONARY (CA. 1690S)

Illinois Word/Phrase [MS Page]	Gravier's French/ Latin Gloss	Author's Translation of Gravier [and notes]
acha8e nitaïa [1]	[none provided]	[my dog/slave/domestic animal runs around][6]
nitachitahan [4]	j attache avec un clou, une epingle. it[em] je colle avec instrument	I attach [it] with a nail, a pin. Also, I bind with an instrument
nitachitah8ra [4]	je le lie entroitement, attache a.	I tie it together, attached to
achitampirinta [4]	attaché au poteau pour estre brulé.	tied to the post to be burned
ac8essem8a [10]	genisse, chienne, femelle de beste	heifer, bitch, female animal
nitaïa [14]	mon animal domestique, mon chien, mon chat. it[em] mon esclave	my domestic animal, my dog, my cat, also my slave [literally, "my possession"]
nitataïma [14]	je l'ay pour esclave, pour a[nim]al domestiq. Cest mon esclav[e]	I have him/her as a slave, as a domestic animal. That is my slave
nitaïag8a [14, 19]	je suis son esclave, il est mon maistre vix d[icitu]r. il ma mis au jeu, dit un esclave. ce mot est rare.	I am his slave, he is my master, it is scarcely said. he gambled me, said by a slave. this word is rare.
nitanessacanti a8ihia8i [28]	celuy que jay fait esclave, que jay amené. je bats toujours. vide ninessa	the one that I enslaved, that I brought. I always beat. see ninessa
nita8embima [36]	cest mon parent, dit le boureau a qui conque amene un esclave	that is my relative, said by the executioner to the one who brings a slave
arem8a [55]	chien, tte beste domestique et par mepris esclave	dog, all domestic animals, and as a term of contempt, slave
nitata8im8tara nic8issa [75]	je luy confie mon fils pour qq temps en esclave qu jay fait pendant que je retourne a la charge. it[em] je dis a mon fils, a l'esclave de m'attendre la qq temps	I give him my son for a time as a slave, which I do until I return to take charge of him. also I say to my son, to the slave to wait there for me for a while

6. Carl Masthay, *Kaskaskia Illinois-to-French Dictionary* (Saint Louis, Mo., 2002), 47, translates the phrase as "my dog, animal, servant runs here and there."

Illinois Word/Phrase [MS Page]	Gravier's French/ Latin Gloss	Author's Translation of Gravier [and notes]
atchicaneȣa [76]	blessé brulé marqué de cicatrices restées a la jambe	wounded, burned, marked with scars on the leg
iscȣchita [111]	qui a l'oreille coupée	someone who has a cropped ear
eheȣa, eheȣita piȣa [147]	celuy qui fait le cry quand on arrive au village apres avoir fait coup sur l'ennemy qui est ordinairement le chef de la bande	the one who cries out when arriving at the village after having struck the enemy who is usually the chief of the band
nitintara. tareȣa entarata [168]	je lay pour esclave	he/she is my slave
entachita [168]	luy qui ma pour escl[ave]	he/she who has me as a slave [master/mistress]
nitintarehigȣa [169]	il m'a donné	he gave [him to] me
nitintaremihagȣa [169]		[Miami-Illnois linguist Carl Masthay translates as "he gave him to me, or he made him my property"][7]
nitintarerima kikiȣnaȣa [169]	jen suis le maitre	I am the master of it/him/ her
nitintaretaȣa [169]	je luy donne cela, je l'en fais le maistre	I give him that, I make him the master of it
iscȣ, iscȣi *saepe* icȣ [176]	marque du deffaut	mark of imperfection/defect
isȣchichȣnta [176]	a qui on a coupé une ou deux Oreilles	[said] to someone who had one or two ears cropped
iscȣchipagȣta [176]	mordu a l'oreille, oreille emportee avec les dents	bitten on the ear, ear removed with the teeth
iscȣicȣrechȣnta [176]	qui a le nés coupé	someone who has a cropped nose
nitiscȣicȣrepȣa [176]	je luy coupe le nés avec les dents	I crop his nose with my teeth
iscȣicȣreta [176]	a qui le nés manqué	[said] to someone who is missing his/her nose

7. Ibid., 122.

Illinois Word/Phrase [MS Page]	Gravier's French/ Latin Gloss	Author's Translation of Gravier [and notes]
isc8inekich8nta [76]	main coupee	hand cut/cropped
kiki8i mikintangha [198]	qui commende aux autres travaillant; maistre ouvrier	someone who commands others to work; master worker [overseer]
kiki8na8a [199]	esclave	slave
kiki8na8arakiagana [199]	vile membrum servae de viris sensu metaphor	slave woman's vile/cheap vagina, said metaphorically about men
nikikipenara [199]	je marque 8e mon esclave pour le cognoistre	I mark for example my slave to know him
kikit8inaki8a [202]	il chante sa chanson de mort avant que de se battre ou avant que de mourir, un vieillard, une vieille, un malade	he sings his death song before being beaten or before being killed, an old man, an old woman, a sick person
niki8inakiha [209]	je le fais eslcave, le prend en guerre. luy fait chanter sa chanson de mort.	I make him a slave, I capture him in war. I make him sing his death song
niki8inakiha areni [209]	je luy oste son brayet la traite en esclave	I lift remove her breechcloth, treat her like a slave
kitachi8eta [223]	premiere femme. it[em] la plus aimée, qui est maitresse de tout	first wife. also the most loved, who is mistress of all
matchirini8a [259]	gueux, esclave. cest une injure. it[em] mechant homme	low-life/villain, slave. it is an insult. also, bad/wicked man
matchirinisse [259]	vocat injurieux gueux, mechant	vocative [case] insult: low-life, bad man [a diminutive vocative case of the previous entry, meaning pathetic/sorry little bad man ... emphatic direct address to a low-life or a slave][8]

8. The author thanks Michael McCafferty, who clarified the connotation of the diminutive vocative case in this word.

Illinois Word/Phrase [MS Page]	Gravier's French/ Latin Gloss	Author's Translation of Gravier [and notes]
ninessacanta [340]	mon esclave celuy qui jay amené, it[em] que jay tüé *raro hoc sensu*	my slave, the one whom I brought, *also* whom I killed *rarely in this sense* [derives from the root word to beat, batter, bludgeon, sometimes connoting beating to death]
atchipemahi ninintira [349]	je luy ramene ses gens pris en guerre	I return to him those captured in war
nipahi8acanti [350]	enfarge de nuit pr le prisonier	nighttime fetters for the prisoner [halter]
8chit8a kic8. 8chihe8a atinta8aganari, niarinta a8ira [377]	elle porte qq chose, mene une esclave a son mary. d'une jeune mariée a qui on a doné une esclave quon mene chez le mary	she carries something, brings a slave to her husband. of a young bride to whom has been given a slave that she brings to her husband's home
8echihe8a, 8echihata atintaraganari [388]	on luy a donné pour dote un esclave	he gave him a slave for a dowry
8iss8erim8e8a, 8iss8erim8eta [400]	qui a plusieures chiens, bestes privees	someone who has several dogs, privately owned animals
ni8itchir8ntama8a [404]	j'ayde son esclave	I help his slave
nipacachima [409]	je lave l'esclave pour luy donner la vie	I wash the slave to give him life
pacamaganeki8a [409]	le chef du party de guerre ppose un prix a celuy qui tura le 1r enemy	the chief of the war party offers a prize to whoever kills the first enemy
nipagic8arintan [417]	je vomit, laisse tomber de ma bouche	I vomit, let it fall from my mouth [c.f. nisicarintama8a ac8i8ssemahi]
pichi8eta [465]	qui amene des esclaves, qui a fait coup sur l'ennemy	someone who brings slaves, who struck the enemy
nipitchikiatta8a [479]	je luy apporte des chevelures, des esclaves que je luy donne	I bring him scalps/slaves that I give him

Illinois Word/Phrase [MS Page]	Gravier's French/ Latin Gloss	Author's Translation of Gravier [and notes]
pitchikimeȣa [479]	un esclave s'enfuit. il accourt icy. il est arrivé icy ayant esté deliver	a slave flees. he runs here. he arrived here after being freed
nipitchikiȣinakiha [479]	j'amene icy de loing un esclave	I bring a slave here from far away
nipitchinakiha [479]	idem et frequentius	the same [as above] and more frequently
rapahȣteȣi [493]	attaché a la place avec un lien	bound/tied to a place
nirapakerima [493]	je l'adopte a la place du mort	I adopt him/her in place of the dead
nisicarintamaȣa acȣiȣssemahi [527]	je done la vie a cinq prisoniers	I give life to five prisoners [verb = to vomit]
sȣpikipacaminta [533]	bien battu en esclave	badly beaten like a slave
tetepacahȣaȣaki [572]	on leur a donné un baston blanc a porter aux esclaves	they were given a white stick to take to the slaves
atetipacahȣmari [573]	le baton de l'esclave ou sont entortillés des plumes tout autour	the slave's stick with feathers wrapped all around it
tetipacahȣaȣa [573]	on luy a donné un tel baston a porter, scil a l'esclave	one gave him such a stick to carry, that is, to a slave

APPENDIX B

"Ordinance Rendered on the Subject of the Negroes and the Indians Called Panis"

This ordinance was issued by New France's intendant, Jacques Raudot, on April 13, 1709. A report to Paris summarized its contents as an order declaring "that the panis and Negroes who have been, and who will be bought shall be owned by those who have bought them." Although many (myself included) have written that this ordinance "legalized" Indian slavery in New France, that is not strictly accurate. Raudot's ordinance only clarified the legal standing of slavery, which in New France had never been declared or determined to be illegal. Louis XIV authorized African, but not Indian, slavery in New France in 1689, and his silence on the issue of Indian slavery undermined its legal standing without rendering it illegal. So the 1709 ordinance functioned more like a clarifying court ruling than an entirely new law. For the next half century, however, New France's officials repeatedly cited Raudot's ordinance as the basis of slavery's legality in the colony. Chapter 3 provides a full analysis of this ordinance, its origins, and its legal context. Chapter 6 treats the evolution of slave law in the colony, including a discussion of how the text of this law shaped subsequent policies and court rulings. There are two surviving versions of Raudot's ordinance. The copy transcribed and translated here was the original kept by Raudot in the papers of the intendancy, now held by the Bibliothèque et Archives Nationales de Québec (BANQ) in Quebec City. The other was a copy sent from Quebec to Paris in 1709 as part of an annual report on the affairs of the colony. It now resides in the Archives Nationales d'Outre Mer (ANOM) in Aix-en-Provence, France.[1]

Aside from a few minor spelling and punctuation discrepancies, the text of the ordinance is identical in both documents. Raudot's original has two brief marginal notes missing in the copy, and the copy has a one-sentence heading summarizing the ordinance that is not in Raudot's original. The signatures are also different. Raudot, of course, signed the copy in Quebec. The copy in France notes Raudot's signature in the same hand as the text but is signed separately by "Bigot," although it is unclear who this

---

1. "Ordonnance de Mr Raudot Intendant de Canada—qui ordonne que les panis et Negres achaptez et qui Le seront par la suitte appartiendront a ceux qui les auroient acheptez—en datte du 13 avril 1709," Apr. 13, 1709, ANOM, Colonies, C11A, XXX, 334–335; Jacques Raudot, "Ord[onan]ce rendüe au sujet des neigres et des Sauvages nommez Panis," Apr. 13, 1709, BANQ-Q, E1, S1, P509. For a published, though not entirely accurate, transcription, see "Ordonnance Rendue au sujet des Negres et des Sauvages appellés Panis," in *Ordonnances des intendants et arrêts portant reglements du Conseil Superior de Quebec* (Quebec, 1806), II, 67–68. I have given some phrases a slightly different English gloss from my earlier published works, but in no case did the essential meaning of the translation change.

could be. Of the four best-known Bigots in the colony, two were Jesuits (Jacques and Vincent), one died in 1708 (François), and the last (François, the future intendant) was six years old.

I have attempted to retain the original rambling feel of Raudot's text (which is essentially a very long run-on sentence), but I have introduced some commas where they seemed absolutely necessary for clarity in English. My hope is that by providing a full transcription along with my translation, those who work in French can come to their own sense of the document's original tone and subtler meanings, which are difficult to convey in a comprehensible translation.

TRANSCRIPTION

Ayant une Connoissance parfaite de lavantage que cette Colonie retireroit si on pouvoit seurement y mettre par des achapts que les habitans en feroient, des Sauvages quon nommee panis dont la nation est tres Eloignée de ce païs, et quon ne peut avoir que par les Sauvages qui les vont prendre chez Eux et les traffiquent le plus souvent avec les anglois de la Caroline et qui en ont quelques fois vendu aux gens de ces païs, lesquels se trouvent souvent frustrez des sommes considerables quils en donnent par une idée de liberté que leur inspirent ceux qui ne les ont pas achetez, ce qui fait quils quittent quasi toujours leurs maitres, et ce soub pretexte quen france il ny a point desclaves, ce qui ne se trouve pas toujours vray par raport aux Colonies qui en dependent, puisque dans les Isles de ce Continent tous les negres que les habitans achettent, sont toujours regardez comme tels, et comme toutes les colonies doivent etre regardées sur le meme pied et que les peuples de la nation Panis sont aussy necessaires aux habitans de ce pais pour la Culture des terres et autres ouvrages qu'on pouroit entreprendre, comme les Negres le sont aux isles et que mesme ces sortes dengagements sont tres utille a cette Colonie etant necessaire den assurer la proprieté a ceux qui en ont acheté et qui en acheteront a lavenir;

Nous soub le bon plaisir de Sa Majesté ordonnons que tous les Panis et Negres qui ont eté achetez et qui le seront dans la suite appartiendront en plaine proprieté a Ceux qui les ont achetez, comme etant leurs esclaves, faisons deffenses aux d. Panis et Negres de quitter leurs maitres et a qui que ce soit de les debaucher sous peine de 50# damende ordonnons que la presente ordonnance sera luë et publiée aux endroits accoutumez en villes de Quebec, Trois Rivieres et Montréal, et quelle sera enregistrée aux greffes des prevotez dicelles a la diligence de Nos Subdeleguez fait et donné en Notre hotel a Quebec le 13 avril 1709 Signé Raudot

[Marginal Notes in Raudot MS]
13 avril
ord.ce renduë au sujet de neigres et des sauvages nommez Panis

Leu et publié a leglise de la basse ville issuë de la messe de sept heures et a la porte de leglise parroissialle de cette ville de quebec issuë de grande messe le 21e avril 1709 par moy huissier audiancier en la prevoté de quebec y resident Ruë St. Pierre Signé Congnet

It is well known the advantage this colony would gain were its inhabitants able to securely purchase the Indians called Panis, whose country is far distant from this one, and who can only be obtained from Indians who capture them in their territory and sell them to the English of Carolina, and who have sometimes sold them to the people of this country, who find themselves cheated out of the considerable sums paid for them because of the notions of liberty inspired in them by those who have not bought them, which means that they almost always desert their masters under the pretext that there are no slaves in France, which is not necessarily true for the colonies attached to it, since in the islands of this continent all the Negroes bought by the inhabitants are always regarded as such, and as all colonies ought to be considered on the same footing, and as the people of the Panis nation are needed by the inhabitants of this country for agriculture and other enterprises that might be undertaken, like Negroes in the Islands, and as these bonds are very important to this colony, it is necessary to guarantee ownership to those who have bought or will buy them;

We, according to His Majesty's good pleasure, order that all the Panis and Negroes who have been bought, and who shall be bought hereafter, shall be fully owned as property by those who have purchased them as their slaves, we forbid the said Panis and Negroes to abandon their masters and order a 50 livre fine against anyone who corrupts them[.] we order that the present ordinance be read and published in the customary places in the towns of Quebec, Three Rivers, and Montreal, and that it be registered by the notaries of those jurisdictions by the diligence of our sub-delegates, done and given at our residence at Quebec the 13th of April 1709, Signed Raudot

[Marginal Notes in Raudot MS]
April 13, 1709
ordinance rendered on the subject of the negroes and the indians called Panis

Read and published at the church in lower town after seven o'clock mass and at the door of the parish church of quebec after high mass the 21st of April 1709 by me, court bailiff in the jurisdiction of quebec and resident of Rue St. Pierre signed Congnet

APPENDIX C

Notes on the Demography of Enslaved Indians

It is impossible to know the exact number of enslaved Indians traded by the French and their Native allies in the seventeenth and eighteenth centuries. Unlike the African slave trade, which provided multiple opportunities to count the enslaved, especially at ports of embarkation and sale, Indian slaves filtered into New France and circulated among its settlements in multiple directions, one or two at a time, with no clear loading or unloading point, similar to how enslaved Africans arrived at the Atlantic coast. What is more, Native, métis, and French slave traders had many reasons to mask their involvement. Often a companion to illegal or unlicensed trade, and thus not an activity traders broadcast, slave trading could also implicate traders in the violence of enslavement if they were seen to encourage war to obtain captives. Military officers benefited from the slave trade as part of colonial diplomacy, but, because they could be reimbursed by the crown for the costs of diplomatic gifts given to Indians, they did not want to reduce those payments by offsetting their expenses with the value of Native slaves given to them as diplomatic gifts.

Colonists' obfuscation also makes it difficult to discover slaves' ethnic origins. Most appear in the historical record for the first time long after their enslavement, already bearing French names and often living with their second or third French master. As I argue in Chapters 3, 4, and 6, traders and slaveholders had many incentives to obscure the ethnic identity or regional origin of their slaves, and the term *panis/pany*—often misunderstood as a straightforward ethnonym for the Pawnees—enjoyed wide usage as a synonym for the word *esclave*, or slave. When specific ethnic identifiers do appear, they sometimes refer to the enslaver rather than the enslaved, which is especially striking when the enslaved is identified as being from an allied nation. Taken together, these factors ensure that any demographic profile of the enslaved Indian population in New France can only be a rough estimate, albeit with demonstrable lower limits.

Certain biases in surviving sources are also significant. Catholic baptismal and burial records, for example, tend to record younger people more often in part because the priest's burden of proof was lower for their "sufficient instruction" (see Chapter 5) and because older slaves were more able to resist priests' overtures. Court records, on the other hand, tend to favor adults, as they were the most likely to be involved in or witness to activities that interested the court. But only a few dozen enslaved people appear in court records, so when paired with about seventeen hundred in Catholic records the overall picture of average age and life expectancy is artificially low.

Recognizing the limits of surviving sources, I have used available information to reconstruct a composite portrait of the enslaved population. I built a database that contains up to eight points of information (name, master/mistress, ethnic origin, sex, the year of first appearance in the records, age at first appearance, age at death, and location) about 1,814 individually identifiable enslaved Indians who appear in New France's records between 1660 and 1760. I began with the data in Marcel Trudel's monumental *Dictoinnaire des esclaves et de leurs propriétaires au Canada français,* a biographical dictionary Trudel constructed over the course of four decades that includes brief entries on both slaves and slaveholders in French Canada. Using Trudel's book as a bibliography I then confirmed the information on nearly all entries in primary sources (a few dozen were from sources I could not gain access to), finding his record to be extremely reliable but adjusting when necessary. I then added to the database as I found new enslaved individuals in the course of my research.

The richest source of information on individuals was the Catholic parish records of the Saint Lawrence Valley and the Pays d'en Haut. Identifying these records was greatly aided by the *RAB du PRDH,* an electronic database produced by the Programme de Recherche en Démographie Historique at the Université de Montréal. It is an updated, digitized, and searchable version of their forty-seven-volume *Répertoire des actes de baptême, mariage, sépulture, et des recensements du Québec ancien, 1621–1799.* I viewed the records themselves at the Family History Library in Salt Lake City, Utah. The records of notaries and royal courts in Montreal and Quebec also had valuable information on individual slaves. The *Parchemin* database, produced by the Société de Recherche Historique Archiv-Histo, was invaluable in identifying nearly two hundred notarial documents recording sales, hiring contracts, and estate inventories. Available at only a handful of institutions, I consulted it at the Library and Archives of Canada, the Nahum Gelber Law Library at McGill University, and the Bibliothèque et Archives Nationales du Québec in Montreal, where I also consulted the original manuscripts of the court cases discussed throughout the book. Notes for Chapters 3–6 provide full citations for all sources consulted for the database.

INDEX

Abenaki (Wabanaki) Indians, 161, 309

Adoption of captives: Sioux Indians and, 17–18; meaning of, in the Pays d'en Haut, 47–51, 58–59, 66–67, 391; and ethnic identity, 63; French practice of, 181, 268–269

African kingdoms: and justifications of slavery, 95, 98–109, 112–114, 356; French treaties with, 101; comparisons of, to Indian polities, 113–114, 116–117, 165

Ailleboust d'Argenteuil, Pierre d', 162

Ailleboust de Cerry, Philippe-Marie d', 359–361

Alcohol: as motive for enslavement in African cultures, 109; and masking hunger, 126; smuggling of, 183, 303, 315–316, 320

Algonquian languages: early records of, 18–19, 383–391; and ethnic boundaries, 23; words in, relating to slavery, 19, 35–40, 62, 67, 268, 375–376, 378, 383–391; insults in, 35–36, 58, 66–68, 374–376, 387–391

Allouez, Claude, 20, 62, 67, 222

André, Louis, 36–37, 43, 56, 67

Anishinaabe Indians. See Ojibwa Indians; Ottawa Indians; Potawatomi Indians

Antoine (black slave), 338–341

Apache / Plains Apache Indians, 166, 186, 221, 237–243, 251, 280, 309, 342, 344–345, 358

Arikara Indians, 168, 170

Aristotle, 88–91

Artaguiette, Diron d', 345

Assiniboine Indians: ties of, to Crees and Monsonis, 23; settlement patterns of, 28; French efforts to befriend, 143; anti-Sioux slave raids by, 193, 229, 234, 245, 251; as opponents of French-Sioux alliance, 196, 222, 227, 230, 237; slave trade with, outlawed, 232; as source of French slaves, 259; French intermarriage with, 285

Aulneau, Jean-Pierre, 231–232

Baptism: and slavery metaphors, 67; and free soil doctrine, 85; and slaves and Code Noir, 131; and not freeing slaves, 131–132; and Iroquois galley slaves, 148; of enslaved Indians, 154–155, 162, 168, 171, 182, 185–186, 190, 194, 198, 205, 208–211, 213, 217, 235–236, 253, 255, 258–274, 282, 285, 292, 311–312, 321, 326, 328, 329, 333, 336, 344, 349; and Catholic indoctrination, 271–274

Barbary corsairs, 78–79, 82–85, 147

Barbe (slave), 261–263

Barrois, Louise, 279, 281, 318

Barrois, Marie-Anne, 281

Batiscan: hemp growing in, 188–189; as destination for Fox slaves, 208, 211

Beauharnois, Charles de: as slaveholder, 186, 215; and Sioux delegation, 193–196, 247, 250–251; and Fox slaves, 212, 215, 218, 269; and Fox Wars, 216, 218; and support of Sioux trade, 228–229, 235; and stopping Sioux slave trade, 232; and abandonment of Sioux post, 234; and Plains Apache slaves, 241; and trial for murdered Fox slave, 339–341; and slave law, 344–346

Bégon, Michel (father): opposition of, to free soil, 74–77; as drafter of Code Noir, 122–123, 125–128; and legal pluralism, 133, 349; and Iroquois galley slaves, 148, 151–152; influence of, on New France officials, 176, 361

Bégon, Michel (son): on Caribbean model in New France, 138–139, 353; on expanding slavery, 176–177; on slavery and agricultural production, 189, 191, 211

Bienville, Jean-Baptiste Le Moyne de, 164, 238–239

Bigot, François, 362–364

Binture, Babet, 354

Biron, Pierre, 209, 320–321

Bisaillon, Michel, 168, 209

Blondeau, Maurice, 178–179, 295

Bodin, Jean: on slaves as family, 50n; antislavery sentiments of, 78–82, 86, 93; and rejection of natural slavery, 89–90; on slavery and just war, 90–92; on African kingdoms, 98; on Spain's enslavement of Indians, 111; on interests of states and slaveholders, 130

Bordeaux, 81–82, 86–87, 89

Bouat, François-Marie, 209–210, 352

Boucaux, Jean, 348

Boucher, Pierre, 3, 4n, 40–41, 141

Bougainville, Louis-Antoine de, 276, 283, 299–300

Bourassa, Charlotte, 258, 289

Bourassa dit La Ronde, René, 209, 231–232, 234–235, 259, 261, 266, 284–287, 289, 349, 351

Bourgmont, Étienne de Véniard, sieur de, 54, 167–168, 238–239, 243

Bouton, Jacques, 95, 104–106, 108–109, 113, 117, 356

Brazil, 9, 82, 86, 96, 110–111, 120–122

Cadillac, Antoine Laumet de Lamothe, 29, 52, 221, 226

Cahokia, 20–21, 44

Callière, Louis-Hector de, 155–158, 249–250

Calumet, 30–34, 51, 56–57, 63–64, 169, 193–194, 197, 199, 221, 223–224, 244, 247–252

Carver, Jonathan, 24, 245–246, 248

Caylus, Charles de, 361–362

Census records: for Detroit, 261, 276, 278–280; racial labels in, 355–356

Chappeau, Louis, 342

Charlevoix, Pierre-François-Xavier de, 32, 38, 44, 53, 220, 249

Chartier, René, 180

Chaussegros de Léry, Gaspard, 243, 275

Chauvin, Charles, 261

Chavigny de Lachevrotière, Joseph, 358–359

Chiasson, Jean, 189–190

Clapham, John, 371–374

Code Noir: origins and authorship of, 122–124; naming of, as "Code Noir," 124, 355; provisions of, 125–132; application of, in New France, 265

Comanche Indians, 242–243

Coulipa (Fox slave), 217–219

Cree Indians: ties of, to Assiniboines and Monsonis, 23; settlement patterns of, 28–29; anti-Sioux slave raids by, 193, 227, 229–234, 236–237, 245, 251, 259; and French alliance, 196, 222, 224; French intermarriage with, 285

Cuillerier dit Beaubien, Antoine, 281–284, 377

Cuillerier dit Beaubien, Jean-Baptiste, 281–283

Cyclope (slave), 333

Dagneau Douville de Lamothe, Guillaume, 261–262

Dan, Pierre, 83–85

Deliette, Pierre, 38, 46, 69, 167–168, 170, 216, 384

Denonville, Jacques-René de Brisay, marquis de, 146–148, 150–151

Desrivières, Julien Trottier dit, 211, 320–321, 323, 338

Detroit: slave trade in, 168, 207, 209, 290; as site of conflict among Native peoples, 200–205; slaveholding in, 253–255; slavery and sexuality in,

255, 259–263; and religion, 265–267, 269–270, 273; slaves' agricultural production in, 274–278, 281–283; British takeover of, 369–378, 381

Disease: demographic recovery from, through slavery, 46, 197; and ritual tasks of indigenous slaves, 60; and Indian slaves, 113, 217, 333, 335–336; provisions of, 125–132; among Sioux Indians, 227; and Indian slave trade, 245–246, 269

Dogs: slaves as, 19, 35–40, 67, 268, 375–376, 378, 387; and rituals of war, 37–38; eating of, in war feasts, 37–38; in Native societies, 51–55; ritual sacrifice of, 52–53; as hunters, 53–55; as pack animals, 54, 60; as term of contempt, 62, 67, 387

Domitilde (Oukabe), 258, 266, 287

Dormicourt, Marc-Antoine Huard de, 347, 349–350, 360, 367

Dubuisson, Jacques-Charles Renaud, 201

Du Jaunay, Pierre, 55, 253, 259, 268, 272–273

Dulhut, Daniel Greysolon, 139, 143–145, 224

Du Tertre, Jean-Baptiste, 108–110, 113, 117–118

English: as enemies of New France, 138, 140, 142, 151, 155, 160, 164, 196, 205, 275–276, 278, 282, 287–288, 307, 341; as prisoners, 161, 180, 296–297; Indian slave trade and, 163–164, 395; colonies of, as models for slavery, 176–177; and smuggling, 209; as source of African and African-American slaves, 340, 343; takeover of Pays d'en Haut by, 371–377; use by, of term "panis," 381–382

Enslavement: and ethnic identity, 12; centrality of, to indigenous slavery, 19, 29; as domestication, 36–38; and masculine honor, 39–40, 44; as distinct from slavery, 78, 89–93

Férolles, Pierre Eléonore de, 121–122

Fesquet, Pierre, 365

Fézeret, René-Claude, 154

Fictive kinship. See Kinship

Fleury d'Eschambault de Lagorgendière, Joseph, 342

Food: as means of controlling slaves, 17, 40, 47, 126, 333–334; in diplomatic rituals, 34, 51, 60, 143, 221, 248–249, 282, 286, 341; production of, by slaves, 59, 113, 137, 176–177, 184, 254, 274, 276, 278–279, 281, 283–284, 286, 298, 311; stealing of, 125–126; slave preparation and serving of, 254

Forestier, Marguerite, 295

Fort Saint Joseph, 253, 256–257, 261, 265–266, 268, 273–274, 280, 285, 297, 318

Fox Indians: settlement patterns of, 21, 27; anti-Missouri slave raids by, 22; linguistic and cultural ties of, to Sauk and Kickapoo Indians, 23; slave metaphors among, 39; and Sioux Indians, 62; and Illinois Indians, 63, 199; and Iroquois Indians, 151, 199; as slaves, 173, 185–186, 197–198, 206–221, 252, 269, 281, 284, 289, 291, 294, 320, 326, 328, 337–340, 342–343, 358; at Great Peace of Montreal, 156, 200; and Ottawa Indians, 199; and Ojibwa Indians, 200; alliance of, with French, 197–199; and Fox Wars, 197–221, 247, 251; anti-Sioux sentiments of, 222; as barrier to Sioux trade, 227–229; efforts by, to ally with Sioux, 235; French demonization of, 337

Fox Wars, 197–221, 247, 251

Free soil doctrine in France, 73–95, 97, 110, 133, 135, 137

Froger, François, 121–122, 129

Fur trade: eighteenth-century collapse of, 136, 138, 156, 175; in early New France, 139–140; and French-Native alliances, 142–143, 145, 201, 341; and Indian slave trade, 153–154, 162–163,

167–168, 181, 192, 327, 359; New France's shift from, 176, 178, 192; slave labor in, 179, 181–182, 184, 191, 317–320; interruption of, during Fox Wars, 208; among Sioux, 228, 233; Native and métis women's role in, 266–267; at Detroit, 275, 280, 282; at Michilimackinac, 284, 289; in Montreal, 303–304, 311

Gaillard, Guillaume, 186–187, 210
Galley slaves, 6, 73, 75, 77–78, 86, 88, 95–96, 145–152
Gamelin, Ignace, 209, 229, 295
Gannes, François de, 294, 340
Gastineau, Jean-Baptiste, 209
Gastineau, Louis, 209
Gauntlet, 42–43
Gladwin, Henry, 280, 374–377
Godefroy de Vieuxpont, Jacques, 318
Godparents, 171, 209, 265–267
Gosselin, Cécile, 295
Gravier, Jacques, 4, 36–37, 39, 48, 55, 58, 67, 383–391
Great Peace of Montreal (1701), 138, 155–158, 200, 226, 237, 248–250, 308
Green Bay, 25, 27, 64, 67, 168, 202, 214, 231, 243, 349, 351
Grotius, Hugo, 79, 90–95, 122, 125, 137
Guiana, 112, 116, 121–122, 357
Guignolet, Jean-Baptiste Gouriou dit, 321–323
Guy, Pierre, 342
Guyart, Marie, dite Marie de l'Incarnation, 140

Halters, 3–5, 8–10, 40–41, 79
Hamelin, Charles, 253–254
Hemp: for Native halters, 3; produced by enslaved Indians, 177, 188–189, 211
Hennepin, Louis: as Sioux captive, 15–18, 42, 224; on the calumet, 30, 32; and Sioux slaving raids, 37, 40, 44–45; and mapping the Mississippi, 42; on fictive kinship, 47; on gendered labor, 57,

60–61; on assimilation of indigenous slaves, 65–66
Hervieux, Jean-Baptiste, 194
Hervieux, Louis, 194
Hocquart, Gilles, 189, 344–346
Hubert dit Lacroix, Jacques, 269
Hubert dit Lacroix, Pierre, 179–180
Huron Indians, 24–25, 139–141, 156, 160, 199, 202, 215, 221, 278–280, 282, 306

Illinois Indians: settlement patterns of, 21, 26; ties of, to Miami Indians, 23; and Iroquois warfare, 26
Iron collars, 7–8, 131
Iroquois Indians: and ethnic "shattering," 12, 24–26; and captive marking, 43; as threat to New France, 139–140, 144–145, 180, 305–306, 308; absence of slave trade with, 141–142; as galley slaves, 145–153; and Great Peace of Montreal, 155–156, 248–249; demands by, for slaves, 156–161, 226–227; as motivation for French-Fox alliance, 199–201; settlements of, in Saint Lawrence Valley, 305–307, 309
Isle-aux-Tourtres, 183, 306
Isle Royale, 342

Jacob (Fox slave): identity of, as Fox Indian, 173; tasks assigned to, 212; murder of, and resulting trial, 338–341, 346–347, 366
Jean-René (slave), 154
Jesuits: and Algonquian languages, 4, 18, 35–37, 48–49, 55–56, 58, 226, 383–391; and Caribbean slavery, 104, 106–108; and South American slave raiding, 122; as supporters of Indian slavery, 270; slaves' indoctrination and baptism by, 270–272; as traders, 282
Jolliet, Louis, 50, 154, 179
Joseph (slave in Montreal), 302–303, 309–317
Joseph (slave, husband of Marie-Anne dit L'Anglais), 180–181

Joseph-Gabriel (Plains Apache slave), 358

Kahnawake (Sault Saint-Louis), 161, 248, 305, 309
Kansa Indians, 54, 239, 242
Kickapoo Indians: settlement patterns of, 21, 27; linguistic and cultural ties of, to Fox and Sauk Indians, 23; in Fox Wars, 198, 201
Kinship: fictive nature of, for slaves, 17, 47–51, 63, 66, 68, 70, 143, 203–205, 254–256, 264–265, 268–269, 329; and French-Native alliances, 50, 224, 279–281, 287–288, 311, 312

La Boétie, Étienne de, 82
Labutte, Pierre Chesne dit, 278–281
Lac des Deux Montagnes, 303–304
Lachine, 168, 171, 180–182, 290, 295, 304, 307–308
La Colle (Monsoni war chief), 234, 245, 259
Lafitau, Joseph-François, 232, 356
La Galissonière, Roland Michel Berrin, comte de, 296–297, 361–363
Lagorgendière, Joseph Fleury d'Eschambault de, 342
Lahontan, Louis-Armand de Lom d'Arce, baron de, 34–35, 45, 55, 59–60, 66
La Jonquière, Jacques-Pierre de Taffanel de, 236, 274, 362–364
Lake of the Woods, 231, 233, 236
Lambert, François, 294
La Montagne, 302, 306, 308, 312
Lamothe Cadillac, Antoine Laumet de, 29, 52, 221, 226
Lamoureux dit Saint Germain, François, 178, 295, 309–317, 320–321, 324
Langlade, Augustin, 266, 272, 287
Langlade, Charles-Michel Mouet de, 269, 284–285, 287–290
L'Anglais, Marie-Anne dit, 180–181
La Palme, Jean Gaboureau dit, 338–340

La Pérade, Pierre-Thomas Tarieu de, 182–183, 187–188, 293, 326
La Plante, Clément Lérigé de, 234–235, 284–285
La Plante, Marie-Catherine Lérigé de, 289
La Potherie, Claude-Charles Le Roy, Bacqueville de, 30, 32, 170
La Prairie, 207, 284, 294
Largillier, Jacques, 383–391
Las Casas, Bartolomé de, 111, 114
La Vérendrye, Jean-Baptiste Gautier de, 231–232
La Vérendrye, Pierre Gaultier de Varennes et de, 229–236, 245, 258, 284, 344
Leduc dit Persil, François, 262
Lefebvre, Joseph-Laurent, 211, 294
Legal pluralism, 77, 133–134, 192, 265, 353, 366, 378
Legardeur de Repentigny, Agathe, 190
Legardeur de Repentigny, Louis, 284
Legardeur de Repentigny, Pierre, 208
Legardeur de Saint-Pierre, Jacques, 233–234, 296
Legardeur de Saint-Pierre, Jean-Paul, 161
Lemoyne, Augustin, 210
Lemoyne, Catherine, 294
Lemoyne de Longueuil, Charles, 210
Le Roy, Louis, 88–90
Lestage, Pierre, 185, 209
Le Sueur, Pierre, 30, 143, 226
Lignery, Constant Marchand de, 208, 213
Loisel, Antoine, 85–86
Louis (African slave), 73–78
Louisiana, 163–164, 167, 238–241, 274, 343, 345–346, 355

Mallet, Pierre, 259
Marguerite (Fox slave), 342–343
Marguerite-Caroline (Sioux slave), 263
Marguerite-Geneviève (Fox slave), 198, 252
Marianne (slave at Michilimackinac), 260

Marianne (slave in Saint Domingue), 378–381
Marie-Angélique (slave), 239
Marie Anne (slave), 259
Marie-Athanase (slave), 253–254
Marie de l'Incarnation, 140
Marie Françoise (slave), 259
Marie-Joachim (slave), 209, 320–326, 334, 336, 341, 346–347
Marie-Louise (Fox slave), 198
Marie-Madeleine (La Gerne), 326
Marie-Marguerite (Marguerite Duplessis-Fabert), 347–366
Marin, Paul, 193–194, 217
Marquette, Jacques, 30, 32–33, 50–51, 61, 68, 142–143, 384
Marriage: and Native alliances, 20, 23, 25–26, 70, 280, 285, 289, 320; of slaves, 131, 181–182, 255–274, 325–329
Martinique, 12–13, 16, 73–74, 95–97, 107, 110, 112, 114, 117–121, 123, 127, 130, 132–133, 137–139, 165, 343, 346–350, 352–354, 356–362, 364, 370
Mercier, Hiérome, 85
Miami Indians: settlement patterns of, 21, 26; and ties to Illinois Indians, 23; use of slaves by, 58, 64; relations of, with Iroquois, 151; as slave traders, 154, 162–164; intermarriage by, with French, 183, 266, 279–281; as enemies of Fox Indians, 199–200, 202, 217; at Great Peace of Montreal, 249; at Pickawillany, 288
Michilimackinac: as multiethnic trading center, 25; slaves traded at, 61, 65, 154, 159–160, 168, 178–180, 207, 231–232, 295–296; diplomatic negotiations at, 144–145, 151; Indians as slaves at, 169, 252–273, 284–292; trade voyages to, by enslaved Indians, 317–320; and Pontiac's War, 369–370, 375–377
Mikinak, 288
Minweweh, 371, 375
Missouri Indians, 26, 41, 46, 167–170, 239, 242

Monsoni Indians: ties of, to Crees and Assiniboines, 23; anti-Sioux slave raids by, 193, 229–230, 232–234, 245, 247, 259
Montagnais Indians, 139–140, 261
Montaigne, Michel de, 82

Naming of slaves, 45, 253–254, 258, 267–268
Natchez revolt, 346
Natchitoches, 241
Nicolas, Louis, 35, 54, 223, 225
Nigritie: and French justifications of slavery, 102–105; comparisons of, with North America, 112, 165, 171
Nissowaquet, 287–288
Nolan Lamarque, Charles, 181, 295
Nose cropping, 43–44, 68–69, 388
Nouette, Jacques, 347–348
Noyelles de Fleurimont, Nicolas-Joseph, 235–236

Ojibwa Indians: linguistic and cultural ties of, to Potawatomi and Ottawa Indians, 23; settlement patterns of, 28–29; slavery metaphors among, 66; giving of slaves by, in diplomacy, 154; at Great Peace of Montreal, 156; as enemies of Fox Indians, 199–202; and Fox Wars, 207, 215, 221; Sioux alliance with, 222; opposition by, to French-Sioux alliance, 237; as slaveholders in French villages, 253–254; at Detroit, 278; and René Bourassa, 284; and Pontiac's War, 371, 373–377
Ononguicé, 155, 157
Osage Indians, 169–170, 238, 242, 289
Ottawa Indians: linguistic and cultural ties of, to Potawatomi and Ojibwa Indians, 23; settlement patterns of, 28–29; and calumet ceremony, 30; and Jesuit linguists, 36; and Sioux slave raids, 39, 64, 158–161; captive adoption among, 47; as allies of Illinois Indians, 50; ritual sacrifice of dogs by,

52; slave metaphors among, 55–56, 67; as source of French slaves, 61, 64–65, 154, 168, 180, 278, 289–290, 302; and French alliance, 143–145, 151; at Great Peace of Montreal, 156–158, 248–249; as enemies of Fox Indians, 199–202, 205; and Fox Wars, 207, 214–215, 221–222; as enemies of Sioux Indians, 224, 226, 237; intermarriage of, with French, 258, 266, 280–281, 285, 287–288, 320; and Pickawillany, 288–289; trade by, with French smugglers, 314; voyages among, by enslaved Indians, 317; and Pontiac's War, 370, 373–377; and Jesuit linguists, 383–384

Ottawa River, 304
Ouabankikoué, Marguerite, 266–267, 279
Ouenigueri, 215, 349–351
Outachia, 248–249

Panis(e): as legal slaves, 136–137, 344–346, 393–395; meaning of, 165–173, 314, 397; comparisons of, to "Negroes," 174, 192, 196, 355–356, 378, 381–382; as term to obscure slaves' origins, 173, 211, 342–343; and Caribbean slave trade, 352–353, 360–361, 370
Pascal (slave), 162–163, 182–183
Pawnee Indians: and origins of calumet ceremony, 30; as distinct from "panis," 165–173, 381–382, 397; and French-Spanish conflict, 237–238; anti-Apache raids by, 242–243
Pelleprat, Pierre, 107–110, 112, 116–118, 356
Pemoussa, 202–205, 251
Périer, Étienne, 240
Pickawillany, 288–289
Polygamy, 58–59, 68–69, 254, 389
Pontiac's War, 370–377
Potawatomi Indians: linguistic and cultural ties of, to Ojibwa and Ottawa Indians, 23; as Sioux allies, 27; slaves among, 60; release of slaves by, 62;

giving of slaves by, in diplomacy, 64, 249, 289; at Great Peace of Montreal, 156–157; and Fox Wars, 202; and calumet ceremony, 249; French alliances with, 278–281, 287; and Pontiac's War, 373–375, 377

Radisson, Pierre-Esprit, 223
Raimbault, Pierre, 323
Rale, Sébastien, 35, 39–40, 42, 47
Ramezay, Catherine de, 210
Ramezay, Claude de, 184–186, 200, 210, 314, 338–339
Raudot, Antoine-Denis, 52–53, 63, 136–137, 168–169, 175–176
Raudot, Jacques, 135–139, 161, 164–165, 173–176, 182, 191–192, 196, 207, 210, 292, 294, 314, 344, 352–353, 361, 381, 393–395
Réaume, Marie Madeleine, 266
Renards. See Fox Indians
Richelieu River, 304
Rivard-Loranger, Marie Catherine, 208
Ruette d'Auteuil, François, 152–153

Saint-Lo, Alexis de, 83
Sans Crainte, Jean-Baptiste, 258
Sauk Indians: linguistic and cultural ties of, to Fox and Kickapoo Indians, 23; settlement patterns of, 21, 27; slaves among, 60; at Great Peace of Montreal, 157; and Fox Wars, 198, 201, 214
Schoelcher, Victor, 6–7
Seven Years' War, 236, 269, 297, 299, 365, 369, 379
Sexual violence: by Indians, 19, 68–70; by French colonists, 255–256, 258–264, 274
Shackles: French irons as, 5–10; wampum configured as, 203
Sign language, 16, 41
Sinagos, 39, 64
Sioux Indians: name of, 15n–16n; and Louis Hennepin, 15–18; settlement patterns of, 21, 27–28; as enemies of

the Illinois, 26, 50, 222; as enemies of Foxes, 27, 216, 222; use of the calumet by, 30, 223, 250–251; and rituals of war, 37–38, 53; and use of sign language, 41; and captive sorting, 44–45; humiliation of slaves by, 60; release of captives by, 62, 64; giving of slaves by, to form alliances, 143, 233; as targets of slaving raids, 158–160, 193, 226–227, 230–235; winter counts of, 159, 227–228; as slaves, 173; delegations of, in Montreal, 193–196, 226, 250–251; as enemies of Crees and Assiniboines, 222; French trade with, 223–224, 226–229, 233–234; desire by, for French alliance, 224, 226–227; temporary French ban on slaves from, 232; collapse of French alliance with, 232–237; as slaves, 259, 263, 284, 286, 291, 294

Skaianis (freed slave), 181–182

Slaves, French as, 76, 82–85

Slaves, Indian: population of, 10, 291–292, 397–398; as gifts, 11, 58, 61, 63–65, 142–144; tasks of, in Native villages, 17, 19, 57, 59–70; naming of, 45, 253–254, 258, 267–268; as personal property, 46–47, 51, 55–58, 74–75, 93, 124–125, 136, 139, 165, 173, 182–183, 192, 195, 207, 210, 237, 241, 247, 258, 274, 292, 294, 328, 332, 339, 341–344, 346, 352, 365–366, 378, 388, 394–395; as cultural translators, 61, 65, 246; tasks of, in French villages, 113, 138, 179–180, 183–191, 211–212, 276, 278, 283–284, 286, 298, 300, 315–319, 324; ability of, to speak French, 331–332; clothing of, 334

Slave trade, African: nature of, 6–8; and free soil, 73–77; during fifteenth and sixteenth centuries, 81–82, 86–88; and treaties with African kings, 101; Iberian precedents for, 110; French

reliance on foreign sources for, 119–120; failed support for, in New France, 152–153, 176–177, 343

Slave trade, Indian: from New France to the Caribbean, 12–13, 347–353, 356–367; as anticolonial strategy, 196–197, 206, 221, 236–237; from Pays d'en Haut to Montreal, 290–297

Songs and singing: of war, 17, 37–38; of death (chansons de mort), 44–46, 389; of slaves, 56; to honor African kings, 101

South Carolina, 9, 163–164, 394–395

Sugar, 7, 9, 13, 96, 110, 112, 120, 127–128, 176, 347, 352

Surveillance: of slaves by Indians, 17; of slaves by French, 125–126; as "shared surveillance," 324

Suzanne (slave), 316, 324

Toulouse: and French free soil, 79–80, 82, 88

Vaudreuil, Philippe de Rigaud de, 158–162, 175, 191, 197–198, 200–202, 205–206, 210–215, 249, 363

Villeneuve, Constant, 255, 258, 260

Villeneuve, Daniel (father), 256, 258, 266, 320

Villeneuve, Daniel (son), 258

Vinsenne (Vincennes), Jean-Baptiste Bissot de, 154, 207–208, 295

Wampum, 64, 203, 249–250, 282

Wichita Indians, 168, 170, 242

Winnebago (Ho Chunk) Indians, 46, 168, 198, 214–215, 296, 349, 351

You de La Découverte, Pierre, 162–163, 182–183

You d'Youville de La Découverte, Philippe, 344